Globalizations from Below

Globalizations from Below uses a Constructivist International Relations approach that emphasizes the centrality of normative power to analyze and compare the four globalizations 'from below.'

These are: (1) the counter-hegemonic globalization represented by the 'movement of movements' of alter-globalization transnational social activists, who try to put an end to the Neoliberal nature of the Western-centered globalization 'from above'; (2) the non-hegemonic globalization enacted by 'ant traders' that are part of the transnational informal economy; (3) the partially similar Chinese-centered globalization, whose entrepreneurial migrants are strongly influenced and instrumentalized by the Chinese state; and (4) the first wave globalization 'from below' that paralleled (and outlived) the 1870–1914 globalization 'from above.' This book identifies their common features and uses them to define the concept of globalization 'from below' as a set of socio-economic or socio-political processes that involve large transnational flows of people, goods, and/or ideas characterized at least in part by informality. They are enacted by entrepreneurial or activistic individuals who either take advantage of the normative power of the hegemon at the origin of an international order and an associated globalization 'from above,' or – explicitly or implicitly – transgress, contest, and try to redefine dominant economic, legal, political, and socio-cultural norms, thus challenging the existing international order and globalization 'from above.' By constructing a unified theoretical framework, this book attempts to open a new field of interdisciplinary research that should take globalizations 'from below' out of their current scholarly marginality.

This is one of the first scholarly works to collectively present more than one globalization 'from below,' and will be of great interest to students, scholars, and researchers of International Relations, International Political Economy, Development Studies, Economic History, Anthropology, Diaspora Studies, and Chinese Studies.

Theodor Tudoroiu is a Senior Lecturer in the Department of Political Science of the University of the West Indies, St. Augustine Campus, Trinidad and Tobago.

Rethinking Globalizations
Edited by Barry K. Gills, University of Helsinki, Finland and Kevin Gray, University of Sussex, UK.

This series is designed to break new ground in the literature on globalization and its academic and popular understanding. Rather than perpetuating or simply reacting to the economic understanding of globalization, this series seeks to capture the term and broaden its meaning to encompass a wide range of issues and disciplines and convey a sense of alternative possibilities for the future.

Re-Globalization
New Frontiers of Political, Economic and Social Globalization
Edited by Roland Benedikter, Mirjam Gruber and Ingrid Kofler

Labour Conflicts in the Global South
Edited by Andreas Bieler and Jörg Nowak

Time, Climate Change, Global Racial Capitalism and Decolonial Planetary Ecologies
Edited by Anna M. Agathangelou and Kyle D. Killian

Globalizations from Below
The Normative Power of the World Social Forum, Ant Traders, Chinese Migrants, and Levantine Cosmopolitanism
Theodor Tudoroiu

Economics and Climate Emergency
Edited by Barry K. Gills and Jamie Morgan

Global Political Leadership
In Search of Synergy
Małgorzata Zachara-Szymańska

For more information about this series, please visit: https://www.routledge.com/Rethinking-Globalizations/book-series/RG

Globalizations from Below
The Normative Power of the World Social Forum, Ant Traders, Chinese Migrants, and Levantine Cosmopolitanism

Theodor Tudoroiu

LONDON AND NEW YORK

First published 2023
by Routledge
4 Park Square, Milton Park, Abingdon, Oxon OX14 4RN

and by Routledge
605 Third Avenue, New York, NY 10158

Routledge is an imprint of the Taylor & Francis Group, an informa business

© 2023 Theodor Tudoroiu

The right of Theodor Tudoroiu to be identified as author of this work has been asserted in accordance with sections 77 and 78 of the Copyright, Designs and Patents Act 1988.

All rights reserved. No part of this book may be reprinted or reproduced or utilised in any form or by any electronic, mechanical, or other means, now known or hereafter invented, including photocopying and recording, or in any information storage or retrieval system, without permission in writing from the publishers.

Trademark notice: Product or corporate names may be trademarks or registered trademarks, and are used only for identification and explanation without intent to infringe.

British Library Cataloguing-in-Publication Data
A catalogue record for this book is available from the British Library

Library of Congress Cataloging-in-Publication Data
A catalog record has been requested for this book

ISBN: 978-1-032-32371-8 (hbk)
ISBN: 978-1-032-32375-6 (pbk)
ISBN: 978-1-003-31471-4 (ebk)

DOI: 10.4324/9781003314714

Typeset in Times New Roman
by codeMantra

Aux Alexandrins des quatre coins du monde

Contents

Acknowledgments xi
Preface xiii

1 Introduction 1

2 Globalizations and Normative Power: Theoretical Aspects 11
  2.1 *The Western-Centered Globalization 'from Above' and the American-Led International Order 12*
  2.2 *Normative Power 16*
     The United States as a Normative Power 18
     Normative Power and Globalizations 'from Above' and 'from Below' 20
  2.3 *The Emerging Chinese-Led International Order and the Chinese-Centered Globalization 'from Above' 23*
     China as a Normative Power 26
     China's Norms 29
     The Belt and Road Initiative 30
     Socialization of Elites and the Chinese-Centered Globalization 'from Above' 33
  2.4 *The First Wave Globalization 'from Above' 39*
     Hegemony, Liberalism, and Paradoxes 46
  2.5 *The Globalizations' Triangle 51*
  2.6 *Transnationalism 53*

3 The Counter-Hegemonic Globalization 'from Below' 71
  3.1 *A 'Movement of Movements' 71*
     The Global Justice Movement 76
     The Programmatic Dimension 82
  3.2 *Political Resistance: The 'Battle of Seattle' and the World Social Forum 89*

viii Contents

        The World Social Forum 91
        Yellow Vests at a Tea Party 94
   3.3 Legal Resistance: Challenging Intellectual Property Rights 98

4 The Non-Hegemonic Globalization 'from Below'   106
   4.1 Informal Economy and 'Ant Trade' 107
        The Rise of the 'Ant Traders' 109
   4.2 Defining the Non-Hegemonic Globalization 'from Below' 115
        Structure, Agency, and International Relations Theories 117
        Informality, Power, and Resistance 120
        Interacting Globalizations and Ambiguity 124
   4.3 Practical Resistance: Challenging Intellectual Property Rights 126
        Counterfeit, Resistance, and Fake Modernity 131
   4.4 Social Networks and Diasporas 132
   4.5 Production Centers, Flows, and Nodes 139
   4.6 Guangzhou's 'Chocolate City' 142
        Sino-African Tensions 150
        Understanding the African Presence 155
   4.7 La Salada's Baroque Economies 158
        The 'Informal State' 163
        Plebeian Democracy, Proletarian Microeconomies, and
          Neoliberalism 'from Below' 166
   4.8 Normative Clashes, Ambiguities, and Agency 171

5 The Chinese-Centered Globalization 'from Below'   187
   5.1 From 'Ant Traders' to Entrepreneurial Migrants 188
        A Highly Mobile Middleman Minority 191
   5.2 The Influence of the Chinese State 196
        'Upgrading' – and Instrumentalizing – the Migrant 200
        The Overseas Chinese State 203
        'Working' the Overseas Chinese 207
        Incentives 212
        Co-Opting the 'Old' Migrants 214
   5.3 The Chinese Entrepreneurial Migrants in Ghana 215
        The Chinese 'Ant Traders' in Ghana 220
        Vulnerability 222
        Beijing's Influence 225
        Galamsey and Social Conditionality 226
   5.4 Defining a Complex Globalization 231
        Interacting Globalizations and Normative Power 235

6 The First Wave Globalization 'from Below'   245
   6.1 Cosmopolitanism and Extraterritoriality in Semi-Colonial
       Port Cities 246

  Semi-Colonialism 248
  Extraterritoriality 254
  Cosmopolitanism 257
  Levantine Cosmopolitanism 262
  Treaty Port Cosmopolitanism in China 266
 6.2 *The First Wave Globalization 'from Below' in Alexandria* 270
  Khedives and Great Powers 271
  Alexandria and Its Foreigners 273
  A City Run by Non-Egyptians 277
  Alexandria's Ethnic Minorities and the Globalization
   'from Below' 280
 6.3 *The First Wave Globalization 'from Below' in Shanghai* 288
  Concessions-based Semi-Colonialism 288
  A City Run by the Non-Chinese 291
  Shanghai's National Minorities and the Globalization
   'from Below' 299
 6.4 *Of Globalizations and Modernities* 307

7 A Constructivist Theory of Globalizations 'from Below'   318
 7.1 *Theoretical Considerations* 319
  Normative Power, Agency, and Constructivism 320
 7.2 *Globalizations 'from Below' – Characteristics and Definition* 331
  Enemies and In-Group Clashes 331
  Features 335
  Definition 344
 7.3 *The Future of the Globalizations 'from Below'* 345

Index   357

Acknowledgments

I would like to thank Routledge and Emily Ross, the Senior Editor for Politics and International Relations, for supporting this project.

I would also like to thank three anonymous reviewers for their useful suggestions.

Finally, I am grateful to Dr. Anna Kuteleva and Dr. Mingyuan Zhang for the very useful conversations on topics relevant to this book.

Preface

As a child, I had a passion for history maps. Because some of them marked Egypt as a British possession, I saw no difference between the status of that Mediterranean land and Saint Helena or the Gold Coast. This is why I was surprised to find an anthology of *French*-language poetry from the Nile valley. Even more puzzling, most of those poets did not have French family names. They did not seem Arab either. Instead, there was a *macédoine*[1] of Mediterranean and Levantine individuals that history had strangely placed in Egyptian – and, more specifically, Alexandrian – settings. I had the impression of discovering a hidden, disappeared world inhabited by fascinating migrants. Differently from their numerous contemporaries who reached Montreal, New York, or Buenos Aires, they were not assimilated. They lived for generations among a much larger Arab population in an Ottoman province that was militarily occupied by the British but formally ruled by an Albanian dynasty, which presented itself as Turkish. They chose to speak mainly French – while being proficient in two or three more languages such as Italian, Greek, Ladino, or English, but not necessarily Arabic – and to construct themselves as citizens of the universe. To me, this early discovery was the beginning of an unfinished love story with the cosmopolitan world of Alexandria. Of course, mine is hardly an isolated case. As Professor Jane Pinchin once wrote, 'few places have had as passionate a character. Few have shaped as many sensibilities.'[2]

At that time, I did not realize that this was also my first, bookish encounter with the only globalization 'from below' that had ever existed. The following decades, however, witnessed the birth and growth of three new members of this exotic, 'from below' family. Like Alexandria, these social phenomena are powerful but discreet. They fight hegemons, reshape world trade, and construct alternative modernities. But their informal nature often compels their actors to keep a low profile. Critically, they have been studied separately by specialists of narrow fields that have never made the effort of bringing them under the common analytical roof of one Social Sciences concept. Consequently, they remain understudied and largely unknown to the general public. This is the scholarly gap this book tries to fill. Hopefully, a new interdisciplinary field of research will emerge able to do justice to millions of 'ant traders' and transnational social activists. These small and apparently weak actors are reshaping the world and its 'conceptions of normal.' The time has come for academia to reshape its own approach and fully acknowledge their existence, efforts, and impact.

Notes

1 A mixture of fruits or vegetables; a confused mixture. The term was inspired by the ethnic diversity of the Balkan region of Macedonia (Merriam-Webster online).
2 Pinchin, Jane Lagoudis (1977) *Alexandria Still: Forster, Durrell, and Cavafy*, Princeton, NJ: Princeton University Press, p. 4.

1 Introduction

This book is the first scholarly work that establishes globalizations 'from below' as a concept in Social Sciences. This is done by setting up a Constructivist theoretical framework that takes into consideration both structural factors and agency, emphasizes cognitive factors, and is centered on the concept of normative power. Despite its reliance on an International Relations approach, this work attempts to open a new field of interdisciplinary research. It represents an invitation to specialists of all relevant fields to engage 'from below' topics within a unified and coherent analytical framework. The following pages bring together all four past and present globalizations 'from below,' which have previously been studied as completely separate social phenomena. Until now, the scholars interested in these discreet but massive global processes have come from very different fields and have never paid attention to their common traits. Parochialism has contributed to the low profile of their research, which is dwarfed by the interest in the Western-centered globalization 'from above' and largely unknown to the general public. In fact, it would be interesting to find out how many of the readers of these lines – who are likely to be familiar with at least some scholarly aspects of globalizations – have even heard of counter-hegemonic, non-hegemonic, Chinese-centered, and first wave globalizations 'from below.' Despite their lack of popularity, these highly interesting social processes are vast and significantly affect the world we live in. Still, I am not proposing a work of vulgarization that comparatively presents four globalizations 'from below' for the mere information of readers. I analyze these globalizations in order to construct a theory, define a new concept, and – hopefully – initiate a shift in scholarly practices.

The case selection is easy to justify. I scrutinize all the globalizations 'from below' that have ever existed. Three are contemporary and represent, entirely or in part, reactions to the dominant Western-centered globalization 'from above.' This is why the counter-hegemonic, non-hegemonic, and Chinese-centered globalizations 'from below' share a large number of features. The fourth is the first wave globalization 'from below,' which accompanied – and considerably outlived – the 1870–1914 first wave globalization 'from above.' Some of its characteristics are significantly different

DOI: 10.4324/9781003314714-1

2 Introduction

as they reflect the structural conditions of another historical period. Yet, many features are surprisingly similar and confirm the fact that all four globalizations 'from below' pertain to the same conceptual category. To give just an example, both the first wave and Chinese-centered ones rely on the normative power of their respective hegemon; analytically, this places them into a highly homogeneous sub-group as opposed to that of the counter-hegemonic and non-hegemonic globalizations 'from below,' which explicitly or implicitly challenge the hegemon, as well as its international order and globalization 'from above.'

Given that some of these terms – non-hegemonic? Chinese-centered? – are certainly not familiar to all readers, I will continue with the brief presentation of the concerned 'from below' social phenomena. To start with, the counter-hegemonic globalization 'from below' has been studied by specialists of transnational social movements, who define it as

> the vast set of networks, initiatives, organizations, and movements that fight against the economic, social, and political outcomes of hegemonic globalization, challenge the conceptions of world development underlying the latter, and propose alternative conceptions.
>
> (Santos 2005: 29)

Its transnational social activists reject the Neoliberal Western-centered globalization 'from above' under the famous banner of 'another world is possible' (Halbert 2005). This ambitious and complex effort has led to the development of the global justice movement as a 'movement of movements' characterized by heterogeneity, diversity, flexibility, horizontality, and bottom-up participatory politics. It represents a radical experiment in participatory democracy that seeks global social justice and is marked by a redistributive ethos. As interactions are based on the cultural logic of networking, participants form a very loose and fluid system; accordingly, the globalization they enact is necessarily complex, contradictory, and ambiguous. But there is also a sense of solidarity and an emerging common identity. They allow small and weak actors to project normative power in ways conducive to 'benevolent forms of world order' (Falk 1997: 19). It is in Chapter 3 that I examine the political dimension of this transnational process and its most impactful forms of manifestation: the huge protest demonstrations held in Seattle (1999), Washington (2000), Quebec City (2001), and Genoa (2001), as well as the even more influential and still active World Social Forum. The same chapter also explores the much less known law-related dimension of the counter-hegemonic globalization 'from below,' which represents a bottom-up challenge of the Neoliberal international legal regimes. The case of the legal struggle against the intellectual property international regime is analyzed in detail in Subchapter 3.3 because it is comparable to the day-to-day *de facto* challenging of the same regime by the numerous actors of the non-hegemonic globalization 'from below' involved in the informal international trade in counterfeit goods. Despite appearances, the counter-hegemonic and non-hegemonic globalizations 'from below' are much closer than a superficial observer may think.

The latter, non-hegemonic globalization 'from below' has been explored by scholars from Anthropology, Sociology, Development Studies, Entrepreneurship, Diaspora Studies, and Diaspora Business Studies. They define it as

> the transnational flow of people and goods involving relatively small amounts of capital and informal, often semi-legal or illegal transactions, often associated with 'the developing world' but in fact apparent across the globe.
>
> (Mathews and Alba Vega 2012: 1)

Its discreet but vast flows pertain to the transnational informal economy and are enacted by 'ant traders,' a concept that brings together the overlapping categories of transnational shuttle traders, local vendors of imported goods, and entrepreneurial migrants. Similar to the transnational social activists of the 'movement of movements,' these small and apparently weak actors are in fact 'powerful actors who develop strategies and mobilise resources to overcome geographical, political or cultural boundaries' (Gilles 2015: 19). Diasporic and migrant communities and networks play a critical role in the working of this globalization due to the comparative advantage provided by the social capital on which they rely. Chapter 4 also examines the 'informal notaries' and 'middleman minorities' critical to the non-hegemonic globalization 'from below,' as well as its geography consisting of production centers, flows, and nodes. Critically, it identifies resistance to Neoliberalism as a prominent feature of this globalization and analyzes the major normative power clash that opposes the latter to the Western-centered globalization 'from above.' In much of the Global South, the latter's flows of goods are clearly outcompeted by those of the 'ant traders.' In fact, the non-hegemonic globalization 'from below' is 'the only globalization that many inhabitants of the extreme periphery may ever experience' (Mathews 2011: 236). Without its foreign goods, they 'would be excluded from globalisation' (Zack 2015: 135): '"globalization from below" is globalization as experienced by most of the world's people' (Mathews and Alba Vega 2012: 1). Accordingly, this impactful process has aptly been described as a '*globalización popular*' (people's globalization) (Ribeiro 2012) that connects the 'poor, but hungry for modernity' citizens of peripheral regions with the rest of the world (Peralva 2003: 191; Tarrius 2002). It 'provides access to flows of global wealth that otherwise would not reach the more vulnerable ranks of any society' (Ribeiro 2006: 233). In the words of an African trader in Guangzhou, 'what I do is good for Africa' (Yang 2011: 115). A street peddler from Mexico City similarly argued that the transnational trade he was involved in 'is not a problem, it is a solution. The problem was created elsewhere; we are solving it' (Mathews and Alba Vega 2012: 2). At the same

4   *Introduction*

time, this is a very complex globalization. The case study of the significant African presence in the Chinese city of Guangzhou presented in Subchapter 4.6 shows the negative social reactions and political responses that the 'from below' globalization can trigger even in its most important node. Subchapter 4.7 presents a second case study, which uses the largest illegal market in Latin America, Argentina's La Salada, to illustrate the alternative practices and 'proletarian microeconomies' that bring together emancipatory processes and new regimes of submission as part of the 'counterfeit' modernity proposed by the non-hegemonic globalization 'from below.'

The Chinese-centered globalization 'from below' is studied by scholars pertaining to the same fields mentioned in the case of the non-hegemonic one but represents a separate global process. It is defined as

> the massive transnational flow of people and goods that is enacted by Chinese entrepreneurial migrants, targets mainly Belt and Road Initiative partner states, relies on business and social ethnic networks, and is based in part on informal transactions. Critically, this process is in large measure entangled with China's policies and projection of normative power intended to construct a Chinese-centered international order.
>
> (Tudoroiu 2022: 2)

Chapter 5 analyzes it as a Constructivist international regime, which successfully associates China's 'from above' hegemony within the Belt and Road Initiative with the 'from below' actorness of the Chinese entrepreneurial migrants. The latter are autonomous, but their actions are strongly influenced by the Chinese state. China's government is at the origin of domestic socio-economic conditions, discourse, and policies that explain massive outmigration. Moreover, as expressions of state transnationalism, the highly effective overseas Chinese work and united front work of the overseas Chinese state have succeeded in constructing a deterritorial Chinese identity for most 'new' entrepreneurial migrants. It is the instrumentalization of this cultural identity that keeps them in Beijing's orbit and compels them to respect hundreds of Chinese laws that regulate their duties. At the same time, as shown in the case study of the Chinese entrepreneurial migrants' presence in Ghana (see Subchapter 5.3), much of their economic success is due to their protection by the political elites of the Belt and Road Initiative partner states that have accepted China's social norm, which often represents a strong form of conditionality. This is part of a larger plan: the Chinese-centered globalizations 'from below' and 'from above' form a virtuous circle used by the leadership in Beijing to construct a new, Chinese-led international order. It may be useful to preempt any confusion related to the use of 'hegemon' and 'hegemony' in the Chinese context. At present, within the larger international system, China is just a counter-hegemon that challenges America's hegemony. However, within the new international order, globalization 'from above,' globalization 'from below,' and associated international regimes that Beijing is constructing, China plays the role of a fully fledged hegemon.

Finally, the first wave globalization 'from below' interests mainly researchers in Social History, Cultural History, History of Entrepreneurship, Diaspora Studies, and Diaspora Business Studies. It can be defined as the flows of migrants, goods, and ideas associated with semi-colonial cosmopolitan port cities, made possible by the changes brought by the 1870–1914 first wave globalization 'from above,' and enacted by 'subaltern cosmopolitans' that imperialist great powers used to weaken non-European states. By exploiting extraterritoriality and the semi-colonial balance of power, these small and apparently weak actors became highly autonomous from all states. Their agency led to 'from below' globalized processes that no great power had planned, expected, or could control. The independent nature of these processes allowed the first wave globalization 'from below' to significantly outlive the 'from above' one. This very interesting social phenomenon has seldom been studied as a globalization in its own right. It developed in states such as the Ottoman Empire, Egypt, China, Persia, and Siam. Chapter 6 analyzes it using the highly relevant case studies of Alexandria and Shanghai. An autonomous Alexandrian municipality was established that 'let non-Egyptians run the city' (Mansel 2011: 131) while the Shanghai Municipal Council in control of the International Settlement became 'a semi-independent governing structure' that showed 'substantial independence' from Chinese but also consular authorities (Goodman 2000: 893). In these port cities, 'subaltern cosmopolitans' such as the Maltese, Algerian, and Tunisian colonial subjects of Britain and France, unaffluent Italian and Greek petty traders, and the numerous White Russians and Jewish refugees contributed to the establishment of a cosmopolitanism that was 'tolerant and progressive' (Mansel 2011: 142–143). As a social and cultural praxis based on inter-communal fluidity and social porosity, this cosmopolitanism was at the origin of the important ideational component of the first wave globalization 'from below.' This included a political discourse and practice that turned the concepts of 'free city' and 'cosmopolitan republic' into reality; and the libertarian crusade launched by progressive activists against the ultranationalism and fascism that took over their countries of origin. Importantly, the social praxis of 'everyday cosmopolitanism' made this 'from below' globalization contribute to the 'appropriation, integration, and hybridisation of various cultural influences,' which, in turn, 'produce[d] new visions of modernity' (Lewis 2016: 10).

These four globalizations 'from below' share numerous features that are extensively discussed in Subchapter 7.2. They include common forms of manifestation, the importance of informal activities, the 'from below' nature of actors, the exploitation of interstices and niches ignored by the globalizations 'from above,' the mobility of actors, transnationalism that may evolve into cosmopolitanism, an impact in terms of social emancipation and progress, the proposition of alternative modernities, and the trend toward heterogeneity, contradictions, and tensions. Here, I will only emphasize their informal and 'from below' dimensions. For the former, the flows of people, goods, and ideas, as well as the business, social, and activistic transnational networks that make them possible, have a pronounced tendency to take advantage of the lower costs, lack of constraints, and flexibility associated with informality. At the same time, they cannot completely elude the rules imposed by globalizations 'from above' and states. Hence the frequent mix of formal, informal, semi-legal, and illegal features specific to all globalizations of this type. The 'from below' nature of their actors is well captured by the 'subaltern' dimension analyzed by scholars of the first wave globalization 'from below' (Hanley 2017: 13, 175–177; see Subchapter 6.1), as well as those who explore the 'subaltern cosmopolitan' politics and legality of the counter-hegemonic globalization 'from below' (Santos 2005: 29; see Subchapter 3.1). Gustavo Ribeiro's aforementioned analysis of the non-hegemonic globalization 'from below' as a *'globalización popular'* (people's globalization) (Ribeiro 2012) is relevant for the same aspect in the case of the latter globalization, as is the actorness of petty traders and galamsey miners for the Chinese-centered one (see Chapter 5). On the one hand, 'from below' simply makes reference to the fact that actors are small and weak. They cannot be compared to the powerful hegemons, multilateral institutions, multinational corporations, and states of the globalizations 'from above.' On the other hand and more importantly, 'from below' characterizes the very working of these globalizations. As shown in Subchapter 4.2, the term 'low-end globalization' is sometimes inappropriately used instead of non-hegemonic globalization 'from below.' 'Low-end' correctly points to the tendency of this globalization's discreet actors to stay 'under the radar of the law' (Mathews and Yang 2012: 95). Yet, it hides their challenge of the dominant globalization 'from above.' To make a comparison with the realm of revolutionary movements, it would be a bit difficult to speak about 'low-end' regime change. 'From below,' on the contrary, is indicative of a bottom-up effort that challenges the *status quo* (Tudoroiu 2022: 14). Indeed, the three present globalizations 'from below' fight the Western-centered globalization 'from above.' There were very serious tensions between the first wave globalizations 'from below' and 'from above,' too. Accordingly, 'from below' defines the fundamental positioning of such globalizations as challengers of 'from above' structures and actors.

In many regards, their challenge is very effective. Globalizations 'from below' represent powerful phenomena that change social relations globally and locally. This is done through various projections of normative power, which brings the discussion to the theoretical framework proposed by this book. Here, I will only sketch its basic features that are developed in Chapters 2 and, especially, 7. The concept of normative power was first introduced by Ian Manners, who defined it as the 'ability to shape conceptions of normal' in world politics. As such, it 'is, ultimately, the greatest power of all' (Manners 2002: 240, 253). As shown by empirical evidence, globalizations 'from below' cannot emerge in isolation. They always rely on the triangular relationship between an actual or emerging hegemonic international order, a globalization 'from above' that both supports and is reinforced by this order, and one or more globalizations 'from below' that either join this virtuous circle or challenge it. Normative power represents the cement that ties together the international order and the globalization 'from above.' Globalizations 'from below' may develop as a complementary result of the same hegemonic projection of normative power: first wave cosmopolitan migrants or present Chinese entrepreneurial migrants are used as pawns by the hegemon and, in the process, launch and enact a globalization 'from below.' In other situations, the globalization 'from below' is due to an anti-hegemonic projection of normative power associated with the effort of 'from below' normative actors to challenge, explicitly or implicitly, the dominant international order and globalization 'from above.' Critically, the small actors are able to legitimize themselves by shaping 'conceptions of normal' because they propose solutions to the inbuilt injustices and detrimental effects of the globalization 'from above' they challenge. I argue that this complex relationship is best analyzed by the International Relations Constructivist approach that I introduce in Subchapter 7.1. It takes advantage of Constructivism's strong cognitivist dimension, which allows normative power to be used as a central concept; and of its ability to take into account, first, the structural factors related to the international order and globalization 'from above' and, second, agency, which is decisive in understanding the success of 'from below' actors.

Based on this theoretical framework and using the findings of Chapters 3–6, I define globalizations 'from below' as heterogeneous and often contradictory socio-economic or socio-political processes that involve large transnational flows of people, goods, and/or ideas characterized, at least in part, by informality. They are enacted by entrepreneurial or activistic individuals who either take advantage of the normative power of the hegemon of an international order and an associated globalization 'from above,' or – explicitly or implicitly – oppose it by transgressing, contesting, and trying to redefine dominant economic, legal, political, and socio-cultural norms in ways that challenge the existing international order and globalization 'from above.' In all cases, they exploit the interstices and niches unoccupied by the globalizations 'from above'; and propose nothing less than alternative versions of modernity. While representing the result of a mainly International Relations analysis, this definition can be used as the basis of an interdisciplinary research effort able to take globalizations 'from below' out of their current scholarly marginality and general public indifference.

Turning to the organization of the book, the readers have to be aware of the atypical split of the theory between Chapters 2 and 7. It is in the latter chapter that the in-depth theoretical analysis of the globalizations 'from below' is placed. This decision was dictated by the need to make full use of the findings of Chapters 3–6. As made clear at the very beginning of this Introduction, this book uses the analysis of the four globalizations 'from below' to construct a theoretical framework and define a new concept. Chapter 2 introduces key theoretical elements and places the globalizations 'from below' in the context of the international order and globalization 'from above' that are essential to their emergence. But it cannot contain an analysis that relies heavily on findings not yet presented and is full of references to sections that the reader has not yet seen. This analysis is more appropriately located in the book's final, analytical chapter where both the theoretical approach and the concept of globalizations 'from below' are discussed in full. Another issue that I have to mention stems from the fact that this is a book narrowly interested in globalizations 'from below.' Accordingly, I limited the discussion of 'from above' ones to what is strictly necessary to my analysis. Specialists of the Neoliberal globalization may be frustrated by the absence of familiar elements or authors they encounter in their daily readings. But their inclusion would have increased the length of the text without adding any contribution to its 'from below'-centered analysis. Finally, as already mentioned, the three present globalizations 'from below' are in certain regards different from the much older 'first wave' one. This made me order Chapters 3–6 non-chronologically. The reader should become familiar with the more homogenous and, I would say, relevant features of the first group before seeing the predictably different post-1870 situation. Starting with the latter would uselessly have created expectations or even convictions infirmed by more recent globalizations.

In terms of methodology, the book relies on the huge volume of available secondary sources. As already mentioned, the counter-hegemonic globalization 'from below' has extensively been studied by specialists of transnational social movements. Scholars from Anthropology, Sociology, Development Studies, Entrepreneurship, Diaspora Studies, and Diaspora Business Studies have similarly explored the non-hegemonic and Chinese-centered globalizations 'from below.' The first wave globalization 'from below' has been analyzed by researchers in Social History, Cultural History, History of Entrepreneurship, Diaspora Studies, and Diaspora Business Studies. As a result, there are thousands of relevant books, peer-reviewed articles, and conference papers, to which numerous reports, newspaper articles, website pages, and other sources available on the Internet have to be added. I have tried to use the most reputable and, when possible, the most recent ones. I should also mention that I made use of a number of case studies that are relevant to my analysis. They include Guangzhou's 'Chocolate City' and Argentina's La Salada for the non-hegemonic globalization 'from below'; the case of the Chinese entrepreneurial migrants in Ghana for the Chinese-centered globalization 'from below'; as well as Alexandria and Shanghai for the first wave globalization 'from below.'

The book is structured as follows. Chapter 2 introduces and, in part, develops the book's theoretical framework. Chapters 3–6 analyze the counter-hegemonic, non-hegemonic, Chinese-centered, and first wave globalizations 'from below.' Finally, Chapter 7 uses their findings to continue, complement, and complete the theoretical discussion in Chapter 2. It sets up the aforementioned Constructivist theoretical approach and uses it to define and analyze the concept of globalizations 'from below.' The possible future evolution of these globalizations is scrutinized in the last subchapter.

References

Falk, Richard (1997) 'Resisting "Globalisation-from-Above" through "Globalisation-from-Below",' *New Political Economy*, 2(1), pp. 17–24.

Gilles, Angelo (2015) 'The Social Construction of Guangzhou as a Translocal Trading Place,' *Journal of Current Chinese Affairs*, 44(4), pp. 17–47.

Goodman, Bryna (2000) 'Improvisations on a Semicolonial Theme, or, How to Read a Celebration of Transnational Urban Community,' *The Journal of Asian Studies*, 59(4), pp. 889–926.

Halbert, Debora (2005) 'Globalized Resistance to Intellectual Property,' *Globalization*, 5(2), https://globalization.icaap.org/content/v5.2/halbert.html

Hanley, Will (2017) *Identifying with Nationality: Europeans, Ottomans, and Egyptians in Alexandria*, New York: Columbia University Press.

Lewis, Su Lin (2016) *Cities in Motion: Urban Life and Cosmopolitanism in Southeast Asia, 1920–1940*, Cambridge: Cambridge University Press.

Manners, Ian (2002) 'Normative Power Europe: A Contradiction in Terms?,' *Journal of Common Market Studies*, 40(2), pp. 235–258.

Mansel, Philip (2011) *Levant: Splendour and Catastrophe on the Mediterranean*, New Heaven and London: Yale University Press.

Mathews, Gordon (2011) *Ghetto at the Center of the World: Chungking Mansions, Hong Kong*, Chicago; London: The University of Chicago Press, epub edition.

Mathews, Gordon, and Carlos Alba Vega (2012) 'Introduction. What Is Globalization from Below?,' in Gordon Mathews, Gustavo Lins Ribeiro, and Carlos Alba Vega (eds.) *Globalization from Below: The World's Other Economy*, London and New York: Roudledge, pp. 1–15.

Mathews, Gordon, and Yang Yang (2012) 'How Africans Pursue Low-End Globalization in Hong Kong and Mainland China,' *Journal of Current Chinese Affairs*, 41(2), pp. 95–120.

Peralva, Angelina (2003) 'Alain Tarrius, La mondialisation par le bas. Les nouveaux nomades de l'économie souterraine, Paris, Balland, 2002,' Book review, *Cahiers Internationaux de Sociologie*, Nouvelle série, 114, pp. 191–193.

Ribeiro, Gustavo Lins (2006) 'Economic Globalization from Below,' *Etnográfica*, X(2), pp. 233–249.

Ribeiro, Gustavo Lins (2012) 'La globalización popular y el sistema mundial no hegemónico,' *Nueva Sociedad* (Buenos Aires), No. 241, September-October, https://nuso.org/articulo/la-globalizacion-popular-y-el-sistema-mundial-no-hegemonico/

Santos, Boaventura de Sousa (2005) 'Beyond Neoliberal Governance: The World Social Forum as Subaltern Cosmopolitan Politics and Legality,' in Boaventura de Sousa Santos and César A. Rodríguez-Garavito (eds.) *Law and Globalization from Below. Towards a Cosmopolitan Legality*, New York: Cambridge University Press, pp. 29–63.

Tarrius, Alain (2002) *La mondialisation par le bas. Les nouveaux nomades de l'économie souterraine*, Paris: Balland.
Tudoroiu, Theodor (2022) *China's Globalization from Below: Chinese Entrepreneurial Migrants and the Belt and Road Initiative*, Abingdon, Oxon: Routledge.
Yang, Jian (2011) *The Pacific Islands in China's Grand Strategy: Small States, Big Games*, New York: Palgrave Macmillan.
Zack, Tanya (2015) '"Jeppe" – Where Low-End Globalisation, Ethnic Entrepreneurialism and the Arrival City Meet,' *Urban Forum*, 26(2), pp. 131–150.

2 Globalizations and Normative Power
Theoretical Aspects

This chapter introduces and, in part, develops the book's theoretical framework by emphasizing the close relationship – based on normative power – that brings together international orders, globalizations 'from above,' and globalizations 'from below.' From the very beginning, it is important to make clear that, as explained in more detail in Subchapter 2.5, the in-depth theoretical analysis of the globalizations 'from below' is placed in Chapter 7. This decision was dictated by the need to make full use of the findings of Chapters 3–6. This is not a book that uses a pre-existing theory to study the four globalizations 'from below.' It is a book that uses the analysis of these globalizations to construct a theoretical framework and define a new concept. Placing in this chapter an analysis that relies heavily on elements not yet presented – and is full of references to sections that the reader has not yet seen – makes little sense. This analysis is more appropriately located in the book's final, analytical chapter, which is large and highly theoretical. Another decision I took is to limit the discussion of globalizations 'from above' to aspects that are relevant to globalizations 'from below.' It would be counterproductive to overload this chapter with 'from above' elements that might comfort readers familiar with the Neoliberal globalization but are irrelevant to the topic of this book.

Subchapter 2.1 presents the evolution and features of the present American-led international order and explains why the structural power associated with this order and conducive to the Western-centered globalization 'from above' cannot provide a theoretical basis for this book. Subchapter 2.2 provides a detailed analysis of the concept of normative power and shows its importance in explaining the intimate relationship that exists between international orders and globalizations 'from above' and 'from below.' Subchapter 2.3 examines China's current efforts to use its specific type of normative power to construct a Chinese-led international order and two associated Chinese-centered globalizations 'from above' and 'from below.' This is done in the framework of the Belt and Road Initiative (BRI), whose key contribution consists of the socialization of the political elites of partner states. Subchapter 2.4 presents the 1870–1914 first wave of globalization, emphasizing specific features that are surprisingly different from those of

DOI: 10.4324/9781003314714-2

the present similar process. This leads to the discussion in Subchapter 2.5 of the diversity that, unknown to many, characterizes the globalizations 'from above,' and their relationship with the globalizations 'from below.' Finally, Subchapter 2.6 examines the concept of transnationalism and the key role played by transnational actors in the construction and working of globalizations 'from below.'

2.1 The Western-Centered Globalization 'from Above' and the American-Led International Order

It is difficult to imagine a reader of these lines unfamiliar with the Neoliberal globalization 'from above' that shapes innumerable aspects of our lives. The first three results of a simple Google search provide almost identical definitions: globalization 'means the speedup of movements and exchanges' of 'human beings, goods, and services, capital, technologies or cultural practices'; the 'trade in goods and services, technology, and flows of investment, people, and information'; or the 'spread of products, technology, information, and jobs.' These 'increased interactions' have led to 'growing interdependence of nations around the globe' or 'between different regions and populations around the globe' (Peterson Institute for International Economics 2019; Youmatter 2020; Fernando 2020). The three sources discuss various aspects of globalization. None of them mentions the globalist, skeptic, and transformationalist schools, for which readers need to use more scholarly works (Martell 2007 would be a good starting point). But they do insist on the fact that 'the wide-ranging effects of globalization are complex and politically charged'; they benefit 'society as a whole' – there is 'unprecedented economic wealth' – but also 'harm certain groups.' The uneven distribution of positive effects, the 'concentration of wealth and power in the hands of a small corporate elite,' and the difficulties encountered by 'smaller competitors' are mentioned. Finally, a critical question is asked: 'how do we make globalization more just?' (Peterson Institute for International Economics 2019; Youmatter 2020; Fernando 2020). While the three texts predictably ignore the existence of 'from below' globalizations, this final question implicitly points to the counter-hegemonic globalization 'from below' and resonates with the reasons at the origin of the non-hegemonic one. Another key aspect is implicitly suggested. The three definitions of globalization take for granted the existence of a unifying worldwide framework; and the only in-text quote comes from a former President of the International Monetary Fund (IMF). While not explicitly mentioned, there clearly is a background that has made the Western-centered globalization possible: a favorable international order.

To a Realist, such an order is 'an organized group of international institutions that help govern the interactions among the member states.' Unsurprisingly, orders are created and managed by great powers (Mearsheimer 2019: 9). Yet, other International Relations schools insist on the fact that 'international order is not simply an artifact of concentrations of power,' a 'political formation imposed by the leading state' (Ikenberry 2018: 20). Instead, it represents 'a regular, lasting pattern of state behaviors (foreign policies and transaction flows)' based on 'an underlying structure of institutions, rules, norms, and discourses that structure and shape state practices.' From states to civil-society groups, all associations that shape state behavior through their actions carry and reproduce this underlying structure. The international order can be understood as a 'configuration of different practices across domains' that range from war and diplomacy to trade and humanitarian action. The unifying factor that ties these practices together is represented by overlapping values and norms (Allan *et al.* 2018: 845). In practical terms, an international order is a complex, multilayered, and multifaceted 'aggregation of various sorts of ordering rules and institutions.' It includes the norms of sovereignty and 'a sprawling array of international institutions, regimes, treaties, agreements, [and] protocols' (Ikenberry 2018: 20). One type of international order is particularly relevant for the present period: the hegemonic order, within which 'a leading state or coalition can establish and impose rules on other great and secondary powers' (Allan *et al.* 2018: 845). Again, there is a fundamental difference between the Realist followers of Kindleberger, who emphasize the role of power, and the more numerous Cox (and, implicitly, Gramsci)-inspired scholars who acknowledge the importance of consent. The latter is secured 'through the production and reproduction of a legitimating ideology [that] serves to promote and protect the taken-for-granted rules and ideas that structure international order' (*Ibid.*). While, in certain fields, international rules and institutions do narrowly reflect the hegemon's interests, in many others they are the expression of 'negotiated outcomes based on a much broader set of interests' (Ikenberry 2018: 20).

The present liberal international order follows this pattern as it is closely associated with American hegemony. Indeed, at the end of World War II, the United States and its allies created 'a multifaceted and sprawling international order, organized around economic openness, multilateral institutions, security cooperation and democratic solidarity' (*Ibid.*, 7). It was the United States that anchored alliances, stabilized the world economy, fostered cooperation, and championed 'free world' values. Western Europe and Japan were fully incorporated into the new order, which – in the geopolitical context of the Cold War – also allowed for the development of the Western security community. Until 1989, this was not a truly global order because it did not include communist countries and their Third World clients. But the end of bipolarity led to democratic transitions and the integration into the Neoliberal world-economy of all states except North Korea and Cuba. NATO expanded and GATT was transformed into the World Trade Organization (WTO). The complex interdependence studied by scholars in the 1970s (see Keohane and Nye 1977) developed into fully fledged globalization. By the mid-1990s, the pre-1914 level of integration of the first wave of globalization was finally reached. The liberal order centered on America and the other Western liberal democracies during the Cold War was characterized by five key features: co-binding security arrangements mitigating dynamics of anarchy; penetrated reciprocal hegemony that enhanced legitimacy through access and shared decision-making; the integration of semi-sovereign and partial great powers as a mechanism to incorporate problem states; economic openness that helped exploit comparative advantage and create interdependence; and civic identity, which moderated conflict and facilitated integration (Deudney and Ikenberry 1999: 181; Jahn 2018: 46; Ikenberry 2018: 7, 18). These features fit perfectly an international order – or, rather, a liberal international subsystem (Jahn 2018: 46) – that was 'small and thick' (Ikenberry 2018: 10). They were much less effective, however, in managing the truly global system that emerged after the end of the Cold War. This has significantly contributed to the present crisis of the liberal international order, which helps explain China's assertiveness and the ensuing Chinese-centered globalization 'from below' (see Subchapter 2.3).

Another inflection point in the evolution of the American international order was represented by the Neoliberal turn operated during the Thatcher-Reagan era. The Washington Consensus upgrading of the order's core norms and values greatly contributed to the aforementioned development of the Western-centered globalization 'from above.' At the same time, it has allowed many activists and scholars to confidently depict the US-led international order as a 'class-based, elitist hegemony strongly imbued with explicit and implicit racial and colonial/imperial assumptions' (Parmar 2018: 152). In their view, this order is based on 'fundamentalist capitalism' that has generated 'maldistribution of wealth, income, and opportunity'; has 'increased inequality, divided populations, undermined support for free trade'; and, overall, has affected the 'bottom billion' in a deeply negative way (Jahn 2018: 46). Most Liberals resolutely reject such views, but it is difficult to deny that the counter-hegemonic and non-hegemonic globalizations 'from below' have developed precisely in response to these problems. To numerous 'from below' actors, the intertwining and mutual reinforcement of the American-led international order and Western-centered globalization 'from above' represent a vicious circle that has to be stopped or bypassed.

To many scholars, the ability of the United States to impose Neoliberalism as the dominant ideology of global capitalism and dramatically accelerate the development of the globalization 'from above' is closely related to America's structural power. Of course, this is not the only possible approach. Kindleberger-inspired Realists give preference to relational power, which in this case represents the ability of the hegemon to impose (through coercion or inducement) the alignment with its interests on each of the members of the international regime represented by the global economic system. Joseph Nye's interpretation of soft, hard, and smart power, as well as the concept of symbolic power first introduced by Pierre Bourdieu, can also be used. Still, such approaches lack the sophistication of – and, in terms of popularity, remain marginal with respect to – the one based on structural power. This concept 'describes the balance of advantage built into systems of states' interaction.' It represents 'a pervasive systematic bias in favour of a particular actor underlying any power relationships that may be specified' (Kitchen and Cox 2019: 735, 741). Structural power was defined as structural constitution, i.e., 'the production and reproduction of internally related positions of super- and subordination, or domination, that actors occupy' (Barnett and Duvall 2005: 55). Two different dimensions have been identified. The 'purely structural' one concerns 'a structure that implicitly empowers certain forces or entities independent of contemporary agency.' For its part, the 'agent-based' structural power represents 'the capacity of an actor to change the underlying structures of socio-economic and political life in line with its interests' (Holden 2009: 13). The United States did change these underlying structures to its advantage, but the structure it constructed also works in ways compatible with the 'purely structural' perspective. Overall, historical path dependencies, institutions, norms, laws, and mechanisms of interaction create opportunities and constraints that allow the hegemon to exercise power in an indirect and diffuse way that has been described as institutional, impersonal, and unintentional (Kitchen and Cox 2019: 742). The concept of structural power was introduced by the British School of International Political Economy and, more specifically, by Robert Cox, whose Gramscian views it reflects. However, within that same school, it is Susan Strange who turned structural power into a versatile theoretical instrument she used to explore various aspects of American hegemony. In particular, she identified the four planes that constitute the four-sided pyramid of structural power: the security, production, finance, and knowledge structures, which give 'the power to decide how things shall be done' (Strange 1988: 25; Kitchen and Cox 2019: 741; Holden 2009: 13). More recently, constructivist understandings of structural power have emerged, which emphasize the role of '"justification narratives" that socialise actors and limit what can be imagined as possible within networks of collective norms' (Kitchen and Cox 2019: 743). This approach explains the Western-centered globalization 'from above' as a result of American structural power that, in turn, it helped reinforce.

However, the use of structural power as this book's main theoretical instrument encounters two major obstacles. On the one hand, this type of power is not very useful when globalizations 'from below' are analyzed that challenge, explicitly or implicitly, US hegemony and the associated globalization 'from above.' The activists and 'ant traders' that enact these globalizations simply are not in the position to exercise structural power, even if some of them might have such an objective. On the other hand, this is not 'the highest power of all.' Even in the case of international orders and related globalizations 'from above,' a different form of power exists whose explicative power is superior. This is normative power, which can be used to analyze all past and present globalizations. This is why I chose it as the basis for this book's theoretical framework.

2.2 Normative Power

The concept of normative power was first introduced by Ian Manners in a paper presented at the *European Community Studies Association Biennial Conference* in 2001 (Manners 2001). However, it was the seminal article published one year later by the same author in the *Journal of Common Market Studies* (Manners 2002) that made the concept widely known and placed it at the origin of nothing less than 'a neo-normative turn in theorising the EU's international presence' (Whitman 2013: 171). Normative power is defined as the 'ability to shape conceptions of normal' in world politics. As such, it 'is, ultimately, the greatest power of all' (Manners 2002: 240, 253). Manners' emphasis, however, was not on normative power itself, but on 'Normative Power Europe.' In French, the terms *pouvoir* and *puissance* are used to indicate the difference between the two concepts. The former is related to the capacity to influence the behavior of others while the latter designates a great power (in this case, the European Union). Manners and his numerous followers have explored various aspects of the EU as a normative power, i.e., 'as a foreign policy actor intent on shaping, instilling, diffusing – and thus "normalising" – rules and values in international affairs through noncoercive means' (Tocci 2007: 1). This continues an older tradition in theorizing the European construct as it combines François Duchêne's 'civilian power' with Johan Galtung's 'ideological power' (Whitman 2013: 172). In the early 1970s, Duchêne argued that West Europeans had largely adopted 'amilitary' values; and this was turning the European Economic Community into a major international actor exerting essentially civilian forms of power (Diez 2005: 617). In addition to pursuing its interests by non-military means, it 'aim[ed] to "civilize" international politics in the sense of making war a non-acceptable instrument' (Diez 2013: 197). Manners further developed this idea by arguing that a normative power also 'binds itself to international norms, whether they are in its interest or not'; the main influence of such a power 'is not merely through non-military (mostly economic) means, but through the force of ideas' (*Ibid.*). This is how the European Union – and, more generally, any normative power – can ultimately 'define what passes as "normal" in world politics' (Persson 2018: 194). This 'setting of standards' based 'on ideas and conscience' obviously makes normative power different from relational or structural power (Diez and Manners 2007: 175). Furthermore, it is not exaggerated to establish a hierarchy. As already mentioned, Manners aptly noted that normative power is 'the greatest power of all' (Manners 2002: 253).

Because it emphasizes 'the independent power of norms to influence actors' behaviour,' the 'normative power argument has a distinctly social constructivist ring to it' (Diez 2005: 616). Indeed, typical Constructivist processes represent an important part of the international actions of normative powers. 'Palpable constitutive effects' are involved: perceptions, attitudes, and identities of partner states are altered through the internalization of norms promoted by a normative power; this happens while such states 'do not perceive to be following somebody else's goals, but their own' (Kavalski 2014: 305). This obviously represents a key factor in the construction of an international order. In this context, the normative core – which confers to a normative power 'a unique identity featured by a group of norms that it is committed to both domestically and internationally' (He 2016: 94) – is particularly important. Critically, it provides the legitimacy that allows normative powers to be recognized as such (Kavalski 2014: 303, 305, 308–309, 322). One would therefore expect the influence of a normative power to be exclusively 'exerted by norms themselves rather than military arsenals or economic incentives' (Diez and Manners 2007: 175). Indeed, 'in its ideal or purest form,' normative power is an ideational concept based on normative justification; it should be completely alien to the use of physical force or material incentives (Manners 2009: 2). However, normative power can in fact go alongside other forms of power; economic incentives and military capabilities may – and frequently do – underpin it (Diez 2005: 616; Diez and Manners 2007: 176). Unlike civilian power, normative power is not incompatible with the use of military force to back up the spread of normative values (Diez and Manners 2007: 180). This is why this concept can explain the construction of an international order by great powers such as the United States, which is hardly an example of civilian power. In fact, the European Union itself is sometimes perceived as a rather ambiguous case. It should be reminded that Manners' work made normative power 'immensely popular in EU studies' (Forsberg 2011: 1186). Today, it is 'nearly impossible to discuss any aspect of the EU's foreign policy without at least a token reference' to this concept (Kavalski 2017: 152). The abundant associated literature notes that it is in the post-Cold War era that the European Union developed from civilian to normative power (Diez and Manners 2007: 175). By pursuing normative aims through predominantly normative means (Diez 2013: 195), it 'has been conceptualised as a different type of actor in world politics' (Diez 2005: 619). In particular, it employs its normative power to 'construct a normative hegemon in the European periphery' (He 2016: 92). However, it is only within this periphery and in a few other individual countries that the EU is actually perceived as a normative power. Elsewhere, this perception is absent. This is the case in the United States, Brazil, China, India, Russia, South Africa, and the Pacific. In Canada, Australia, New Zealand, Africa, and South East Asia, the normative dimension is only 'somewhat visible' (Larsen 2014: 904). Yet, this does not prevent the European Union from representing a useful case study that allows for the identification of features shared by other normative powers.

The EU normative basis consists of five 'core' and four 'minor' norms. The first group includes peace, liberty, democracy, the rule of law, and respect for human rights and fundamental freedoms. The 'far more contested' norms in the second group are social solidarity, anti-discrimination, sustainable development, and good governance (Manners 2002: 242). Various mechanisms have been identified that contribute to the international diffusion of these norms. Ian Manners mentioned contagion, informational diffusion, procedural diffusion, transference, overt diffusion, and cultural filter (*Ibid.*, 244–245; Manners 2013: 40–47). Other authors argue that the European Union has influenced its normative targets in its own image (He 2016: 92) using persuasion, activation of international norms, shaping the discourse (changing mainstream perceptions of what is 'normal'), and setting an example for others to follow (Forsberg 2011: 1184). International socialization is equally important: the change in the behavior of other actors 'relies primarily on socialisation processes' (Diez and Manners 2007: 180). Like any other normative power, the EU '"socialize[s]" others and influence[s] their self-identification by the norms it believes in' (He 2016: 93). Manners placed this change within a more complex process. His understanding of the 'use and analysis' of normative power is based on three elements: principles that need to be seen as legitimate; actions that 'must involve persuasion, argumentation, and the conferral of prestige or shame'; and impact, which involves socialization, partnership, and ownership: 'socialisation as an impact of the promotion of principles in world politics should be seen as being part of an open-ended process of engagement, debate and understanding' (Manners 2009: 2–4). It should be noted that 'the positioning of an actor as a normative power' 'can have a significant bearing on that actor's socializing capacities and ability to influence the international identities of its counterparts' (Kavalski 2014: 305). This is particularly important in the case of China, whose rise as a normative power has considerably increased its ability to socialize the political elites of BRI partners. In turn, this has considerably enhanced the Chinese-centered globalizations 'from above' and 'from below' (see Subchapter 2.3).

The cases of both the European Union and China show that the first stage in becoming a normative power is represented by the transformation into a normative actor. This type of actorness includes action trigger, policy processes/structures, and performance structures. But this is not sufficient. The second, decisive stage is represented by the actual shaping of the international environment by the actor's normative foreign policy (He 2016: 93). The problem is that, in analytical terms, the assessment of both stages is rather difficult. The instruments used by various normative actors, as well as their objectives, are diverse and in continuous change. Actors (and observers) frequently diverge in their normative understandings and interpretations. Consequently, in many cases, 'the issue is really less *whether* a nation is a 'normative power,' but *the degree* to which it is one' (Hamilton 2008: 77–78; emphasis in the original). This aspect is relevant to many of the contemporary states that, as explained in Subchapter 2.3, try to become normative powers. Critically, it has also marked the debate on the normative character of the hegemon of the present international order: the United States.

The United States as a Normative Power

Indeed, it was noted that America represents 'a particularly interesting case' as 'much of the writing within the normative power discourse develops the concept *in contrast* to the US' (Diez 2005: 621; emphasis in the original). The 'perplexing case' of the United States combines vocal advocacy of multilateral rules and institutions, democracy, human rights, and the rule of law with a certain degree of resistance against entanglement in institutional commitments and obligations, and reluctance to being tightly tied to normative standards and principles. The frequent use of military force has to be added (Hamilton 2008: 82–83). More generally, there is also the fundamental issue of the compatibility between normative power and hegemony. Manners saw a clear opposition between these two concepts, but this was mainly due to his understanding of hegemony in realist terms. Other scholars have convincingly argued that a Gramscian view of hegemony, which 'shifts the focus from the power of brute force to the power of ideas and consensus,' thus ensuring legitimacy, 'brings hegemony close to Manners's definition of normative power' (Diez 2013: 195, 200; see also Hyde-Price 2006; Diez and Manners 2007: 174). Accordingly, the hegemonic status cannot prevent the United States from representing a normative power. On the contrary, it is through the use of normative power that its hegemony has in large measure been constructed and maintained. At least since President Woodrow Wilson and his Fourteen Points, the American 'international engagement has had strong normative under-, if not over-tones' (Diez 2005: 621). They were particularly visible in the post-World War II creation of multilateral institutions intended to 'civilise international politics' (*Ibid*.; Diez and Manners 2007: 180) that have played a key role in the setting up of the US-led international order and, eventually, in the development of the Western-centered globalization 'from above.' These institutions were a projection of American norms. They '(intentionally or not) safeguarded US interests' because they 'would spread a conception of life that would match that of the US.' This is to say that the new hegemonic international order was constructed on the basis of American ideals, interests, and purposes (Diez 2005: 622) as part of a process where 'the US has advanced normative goals through normative means with largely normative results' (Hamilton 2008: 102). Even the unilateral use of military power as exemplified by the Middle Eastern wars launched by President Bush included a major normative component. Indeed, it was underpinned 'by a secure belief in the universal validity of [America's] own norms and a missionary zeal to spread these norms to places marked as "evil"' (Diez 2005: 623). It is therefore legitimate to argue that 'the US serves regularly as a major "norm entrepreneur" – at times with failure, but at other times with considerable success' (Hamilton 2008: 106). Yet, unlike the European Union, the United States paradoxically refuses at times to bind itself to international treaties based on the very norms it promotes (Diez 2005: 622). This is to say that the United States is not always a normative international actor. Its behavior is characterized by a varying blend of approaches. It may simultaneously act as a guardian of established norms; a norm entrepreneur that promotes stronger human rights and democratic norms that may challenge the normative status quo; a norm externalizer that advances norms for others but does not adopt them; and a norm blocker when its own interests are directly threatened. In different regions, policy areas, and points in time, the United States has displayed a fluid mix of hegemonic, imperialist, *realpolitik*, and status quo foreign policy. Accordingly, as in the case of newer normative powers mentioned in the previous paragraph, 'the more appropriate question is not *whether* the US is a normative actor but *the degree to which* it is one' (Hamilton 2008: 77, 139–142; emphasis in the original). When the issue of the creation and maintenance of the American-led international order and the associated globalization 'from above' is taken into consideration, that degree is undoubtedly high. As both phenomena are based on American norms that the United States has actively and effectively promoted, they cannot be dissociated from a successful projection of US normative power. This illuminates the close relationship between this type of power, international orders, and globalizations 'from above.'

Before concluding this section, it may be useful to emphasize the fact that, as shown in the previous paragraph, only a Gramscian understanding of hegemony is compatible with normative power (Diez 2013: 195, 200; Hyde-Price 2006; Diez and Manners 2007: 174). Accordingly, this book adopts a legitimacy-based, Gramscian view of hegemony, which I further discuss in Subchapter 7.1.

Normative Power and Globalizations 'from Above' and 'from Below'

As shown in the following subchapters, the close relationship between normative power, international orders, and globalizations 'from above' revealed by the American example also exists in the case of the two other globalizations 'from above.' As part of its increasingly visible efforts to challenge US hegemony, China is using normative power to enhance its own globalization 'from above' that is conducive to the creation of a new international order. More specifically, the Chinese projection of normative power targets the socialization of the political elites of BRI partner states, which internalize Beijing's norms and align their states' policies with Chinese interests (see Subchapter 2.3). Similarly, the first wave of globalization 'from above' was associated with a specific multipolar order that allowed a number of Western powers to exercise a type of collective hegemony. Their projection of normative power 'Europeanized' the world in ways comparable with today's 'Americanization' (see Subchapter 2.4).

The forms taken by the relationship between normative power and globalizations 'from below' are less homogenous. This is the direct consequence of the fact that some of these globalizations resist or overtly challenge globalizations 'from above' while others are associated with and supported by them. The second group is much easier to analyze. It includes the Chinese globalization 'from below' and the first wave globalization 'from below.' Both are enacted by entrepreneurial migrants who take advantage of the opening of target countries by the projection of Chinese and Western normative power in the framework of the respective globalizations 'from above' (see Subchapters 5.2 and 6.1). Accordingly, the relationship between normative power and globalization 'from below' is direct. The latter develops as an effect of the former. The overall picture is that of an emerging (Chinese) or actual (Western) international order associated with mutually reinforcing globalizations 'from above' and 'from below.' The elements of each such triangle are bound together by the normative power projected by the hegemon. Obviously, different mechanisms are at work in the case of the counter-hegemonic and non-hegemonic globalizations 'from below.' Both are directly linked to the present Western-centered globalization 'from above' and the American-led international order that supports it; but the relationship is antagonistic in nature. Yet, normative power continues to play a key role. It is just that, instead of relying on the same projection of normative power as the globalization 'from above,' these two globalizations 'from below' try to produce their own normative power. Indeed, the activists of the counter-hegemonic globalization 'from below' work overtly and explicitly toward the creation of an alternative set of norms that should replace the Neoliberal ones, thus reshaping the Western-centered globalization 'from above' and putting an end to the hegemonic international order. It would be very difficult to argue that this does not represent a process intended to construct a non-state normative actor with the 'ability to shape conceptions of normal' (Manners 2002: 240; see Subchapter 3.1). In a more discreet way, the non-hegemonic globalization 'from below' has a similar objective. Its 'ant traders' are hardly vocal because the informal, semi-legal, or illegal nature of their activities compels them to keep a low profile. But they are *de facto* challenging the Neoliberal globalization 'from above,' as well as the authority of states, multinational corporations, and multilateral institutions whose rules they infringe on a daily basis. The simple fact that, despite this obvious challenge, their massive presence is tolerated all over the Global South – and, on a more modest scale, in the Global North – shows that they have succeeded in shaping 'conceptions of normal.' Accordingly, 'ant traders' represent a normative actor that actually exerts normative power. Moreover, this is a fundamental aspect related to their very existence. Such traders cannot survive if their normative efforts are unsuccessful. When they fail to shape local understandings of 'normal' – that is, to ensure that their activities are tolerated despite their non-conformity with laws and regulations – repression ensues and they are put out of business. This seldom happens; despite their lack of an explicit ideology, the actors of the non-hegemonic globalization 'from below' are much more effective in projecting normative power than their counter-hegemonic counterparts.

This leads to the conclusion – that I further substantiate in Subchapter 7.1 – that all globalizations 'from below' are closely associated with normative power. The latter represents the cement that ties together an international order and a globalization 'from above.' Globalizations 'from below' may develop as a complementary result of the same hegemonic projection of normative power; or as an antagonistic projection of the same type of power originating in the effort of 'from below' normative actors to challenge, explicitly or implicitly, the dominant international order and globalization 'from above.' Therefore, it is reasonable to argue that globalizations 'from below' and their complex relationship with international orders and globalizations 'from above' cannot be understood outside an analytical framework that fully takes into consideration the importance of normative power.

Before addressing the very interesting case of China's normative power and its role in Beijing's efforts to construct a new international order accompanied by Chinese-centered globalizations 'from above' and 'from below,' it may be useful to discuss a particular aspect of the 'from below' globalizations that oppose the hegemon. As shown in the next two chapters, both the counter-hegemonic and non-hegemonic globalizations 'from below' represent 'response[s] from below to the dispossessive effects of neoliberalism' (Gago 2014/2017: 68; Gago 2012: 77); they reflect 'the need to control the forces of global capital' (Brecher *et al.* 2000: 17). The question may be formulated, are they specific reactions to the Western-centered globalization 'from above' or mere responses to the more general consequences of capitalism? The answer starts from the basic fact that no globalization 'from below' can emerge in response to non-globalized forms of capitalism. We could imagine a counterfactual post-World War II international system dominated by the Axis and based on corporatist, deeply anti-liberal economic principles. Heavy protectionist barriers would have prevented the development of a globalization 'from above.' It is obvious that even the harshest domestic conditions within these protectionist, non-globalized states could have not resulted in a globalization 'from below.' Hard borders and very limited transnational interactions would have compelled small actors to act domestically. Present 'ant traders' and social activists can act transnationally and construct globalizations 'from below' only due to the structural conditions created by the Western-centered globalization 'from above.' In this context, they fight Neoliberalism rather than capitalism in general. Only a limited part of the 'movement of movements' and almost nobody among the 'ant traders' want to put an end to capitalism itself. Richard Falk explicitly mentioned the social-democrat but unquestionably capitalist model of 'the compassionate state, as typified by the humane achievements of the Scandinavian countries up through the 1980s' (Falk 1997: 19–20) as an objective for the counter-hegemonic globalization 'from below.' Therefore, it can be confidently stated that the globalizations 'from below' that oppose the hegemon are reactions to specific features of the globalization 'from above,' not capitalism in general. Accordingly, they do not question the normative power-cemented triangle formed by an international order, a globalization 'from above,' and one or more globalizations 'from below.' The next subchapter examines the Chinese version of this relationship.

2.3 The Emerging Chinese-Led International Order and the Chinese-Centered Globalization 'from Above'

It is difficult to find an analysis of China's foreign policy that does not mention the cautious approach adopted by Deng Xiaoping in the late 1970s and preserved by successive leaderships during the following four decades: 'coldly observe, secure our positions, cope calmly, conceal our capabilities and bide our time, keep a low profile, never take the lead and make a contribution' (Ferdinand 2016: 941). China joined the American-led international order and has taken part in the working of its multilateral institutions. To varying degrees, it was even socialized by these institutions and other international regimes (Kent 2002; Johnston 2008; Tao 2015; Hao 2015; He and Feng 2015: 401; Yang 2017). However, Beijing's attitude was not passive. It tried to launch a process of reciprocal socialization, through which rising powers hope to reshape the order they are socialized into by renegotiating some of the norms that define it (Terhalle 2011: 341, 351; Tudoroiu 2021: 14). The creation and working of the BRICS group, for example, can be understood as an effort to achieve increased voting power in multilateral financial organizations intended to allow China to shape financial global governance. But observers in Beijing 'see only a rather discouraging picture on this front' (Tang 2018: 38). Significant progress in reforming global governance could not be achieved due to American hegemony and the existence of 'so many (veto) players' (*Ibid.*). This contributed to President Xi's adoption of the 'periphery policy' also known as 'peripheral diplomacy.' At the 2013 Work Forum on Peripheral Diplomacy and the 2014 Central Conference on Foreign Affairs, the then-new leader brought to an end the previous foreign policy focus on the West. Instead of concentrating on powerful international players such as the United States or the Franco-German axis, external efforts would target 'contact zones with less powerful actors' (Vangeli 2019: 82). Analysts identified either a preference for immediate neighbors in Asia or a more general rebalancing of relations with Asia, Europe, and Africa (Callahan 2016: 1–2, 6, 13). Indeed, these two directions of Chinese external action have been most prominent. The promotion of regionalism in East and Central Asia is closely associated with President Xi's strategy of 'realizing the China dream of the great rejuvenation of the Chinese nation.' Through the development of 'shared beliefs and norms that will build the "community of shared destiny" of the Sino-centric regional order,' Asian states will be socialized. This will 'make China a normative power that sets the rules of the game' for regional – or even global – governance (Callahan 2016: 1–2, 5, 6, 13). The ultimate goal is to create a regional order reminiscent of the tributary system historically centered on the Chinese Empire. Its implicit hierarchy will place benevolent China at the center and other, clientelary states at the margins, thus constructing 'a new regional order alternative to the Pax Americana' in Asia (Li 2017: 24). In fact, a Chinese international order could emerge 'over Eurasia and beyond' (Acharya 2018:

5). A scholarly effort to provide theoretical support for this strategy is worth mentioning, even if – for the time being – it has had little impact on politicians in Beijing. The *Tianxia* Approach was developed by Zhao Tingyang based on the teachings of Confucius and other traditional Chinese philosophers. It rejects Western ontology and epistemology and criticizes the West, as well as the anarchical international system (that it describes as a non- or failed world). The ancient concept of 'all under heaven' (*Tianxia*) is used as the ideational basis for reaching a sort of Chinese-supervised international harmony. There will be the 'Oneness' of the world, as well as the acceptance of its diversity; and a new international order mirroring the traditional East Asian tributary or suzerain system. Tribute paying-style client states will willingly follow China's benevolent and wise guidance in a unified world clearly superior to the present Westphalian anarchy (Kim 2016; Demir 2017; Zhang and Chang 2016). It goes without saying that Beijing hardly has the potential for implementing such a grandiose plan in the near future, which explains policymakers' lack of interest (Tang 2018: 36). But in a cognitive environment dominated by the 'China dream,' President Xi's 'community of shared destiny' and Zhao Tingyang's post-anarchical model may one day converge in ideational and perhaps geopolitical terms.

The other focus of Chinese external action is on promoting interregional cooperation and coordination. The aforementioned failure to significantly increase Beijing's influence within American-created and led multilateral institutions did not bring the end of such efforts. On the contrary, they have continued as suggested, among others, by successful lobbying resulting in the election of Chinese nationals as heads of the Food and Agriculture Organization, International Telecommunication Union, International Civil Aviation Organization, the United Nations Industrial Development Organization, and various United Nations programs (U.S.-China Economic and Security Review Commission 2020). However, the Chinese discourse in multilateral institutions unveils an interesting aspect. Terms are used that 'suggest disapproval of the notion of the [international] order being US-led or based on a democratic community' (Nieuwenhuizen 2019: 185). Beijing's diplomats never speak of a 'liberal' order and reject the concept of 'democratic community.' Instead, they try to introduce Chinese concepts such as 'win-win cooperation' or the aforementioned 'community of shared destiny.' Existing rules are presented as 'unfair' while a 'democratic and equitable' international order is promoted in opposition to the 'rules-based' one (*Ibid.*, 189, 193). This veiled rejection of the *status quo* is accompanied by the much more visible setting up of alternative international institutions. These include the BRI, the Asian Infrastructure Investment Bank, the BRICS New Development Bank, the Shanghai Cooperation Organization, and a large number of regional fora such as the Forum on China-Africa Cooperation, the China-Community of Latin American and Caribbean States Forum, the China-Central and Eastern European Countries Cooperation Forum, the China-Pacific Island Countries Economic Development and Cooperation Forum, the China-Caribbean Economic and Trade Cooperation Forum, and the Lancang-Mekong Cooperation Framework. The scale of this enterprise has convinced many scholars that China is actually constructing 'parallel, or "shadow" institutions, that may challenge, but also supplement or even supplant the existing international order' (Vangeli 2018: 64). 'They challenge the Pax Americana' in terms of geopolitics, international economic leadership, and international institutions (Layne 2018: 100).

Indeed, in recent years a shift has taken place in many analysts' perception of Chinese intentions with respect to the US-created and led international order. When, in September 2015, President Xi called for the reform of 'unjust and improper arrangements in the global governance system,' observers agreed that 'Beijing realizes that a propitious moment has arrived to push for the reform of the international order, and that such a moment should be seized' (Wu 2018: 1003). However, the old understanding of such calls as referring to limited change still prevailed. Leaving aside the Maoist views of a marginal group that still see China as a revolutionary state, two main positions were identified among policymakers in Beijing. One is based on the idea that adjustments in favor of developing countries should be made under Chinese lead to improve the current international order, but the latter is mostly acceptable. The other one is even less ambitious, as it does not call for China to lead such reforms. Instead, they should result from its cooperation with both Western and Global South states. President Xi was believed to vacillate between these two positions, leaning slightly toward the first one 'as he matures as a leader and as world events may necessitate' (Tang 2018: 34–35). Overall, observers still argued that the elites in Beijing agree that the current international order is not entirely just and change is needed; but they are in disagreement on how far-reaching this change should be and how it should be made. The resulting approach represents 'a mixture of preservation and reformation' (Wu 2018: 1006). President Xi wants 'a leading role' for his country (Goldstein 2020: 182). He nevertheless 'does not seek fundamental transformation, but only piecemeal modification of the existing order' (Tang 2018: 40). China has 'adopted a reformist rather than revisionist agenda' (Goldstein 2020: 185). Half a decade ago, such views were predominant. In recent years, however, a different perception developed and is on the point of taking preeminence. Scrutiny of China's actions in East Asia and its construction of a comprehensive set of international institutions has made many analysts argue that its 'engagement with the international order is contradictory' (Bandaranayake 2020: 121; Mazarr *et al.* 2018: 103). Beijing 'is playing a double game.' It operates both in the framework of the current international order and outside of it, 'sponsoring a new China-centric international system which will exist alongside the present system and probably slowly begin to usurp it' (Jacques 2009: 362; Layne 2018: 109). While they continue to 'follow a path of progressive engagement with the liberal international order, Beijing's leaders are also leading a formidable assault on this order' (Halper 2010: 2; Layne 2018: 109).

26 *Globalizations and Normative Power*

The fading out of the 'limited change' thesis is part of a larger debate concerning the decline of the American hegemon and the associated end of the liberal international order. Power transition theorists bluntly state that 'the Pax Americana's days are numbered' (Layne 2018: 111). 'The liberal order is facing an existential challenge'; it has already 'begun to fray and fragment' (Acharya 2018: 4). For their part, adepts of the lock-in thesis that include John Ikenberry, Stephen Brooks, and William Wohlforth believe that the declining United States can nevertheless '"lock in" the Pax Americana's essential features, including its rules, norms and institutions,' thus ensuring the survival of the present international order (Layne 2018: 104). This debate falls outside the scope of this chapter, which is limited to the theoretical analysis of the relationship between international order, globalizations, and normative power. Consequently, I will only mention the fact that, out of the numerous scenarios proposed by various scholars, the most likely seems to be John Mearsheimer's vision of a future international system based on three different orders: a thin realist international order and two thick bounded orders led by the United States and China. The former will rely on global institutions that will continue to facilitate international cooperation in fields such as economic exchanges and climate change. But an antagonistic relationship will develop between the two bounded orders that will represent a hybrid between the Cold War and the pre-1914 situations. The intense security and economic competition opposing them 'will be the central feature of international politics over the course of the twenty-first century' (Mearsheimer 2019: 44). Under such conditions, it is logical to expect the development of two geographically separate globalizations 'from above,' each of them limited to one of the two camps (for more details see Tudoroiu 2022: 314–317). The predictable impact on the current globalizations 'from below' is discussed in Subchapter 7.3. At this point, I will return to the present stage of China's rise and, more specifically, to its key instrument: normative power.

China as a Normative Power

As shown earlier in this chapter, the European Union is a normative power *par excellence* while the very construction of the current international order is the result of a projection of American normative power. But the category of normative actors is hardly limited in these two cases. In recent decades, a surprisingly large number of rising normative powers have emerged. They include India, Japan, Brazil, Russia, Turkey, the ASEAN (Hall 2017; Kavalski 2016; Kumar 2008; Zupančič and Hribernik 2013; Dauvergne and Farias 2012; Makarychev 2008; Oktav and Çelikaksoy 2015; He 2016) and, most prominently, China. While all of them try to exercise normative power, the patterns they follow differ considerably. The EU model is based on rules. That of India relies on its millennia-old civilization. Japan emphasizes responsiveness to its partners' needs. The only common aspect is that, for all normative actors, 'the expression of what is "normal" invokes certain agenda and entails power relations' (Kavalski 2014: 306, 324). China is no exception: it has adopted an original, relationship-based model, and uses it to challenge America's normative power.

The 'Confucian cosmos' (Qin 2016: 36) and, perhaps more importantly, historical recollection of imperial glory and decline have led to introspective reflexivity (Kavalski 2014: 313) that, in turn, has made China 'prioritize sociality, personalization, and reciprocity' (Kavalski 2017: 155) in its external relations. The associated type of normative power focuses on dialogue, as China 'understand[s] that a position of leadership cannot be inflicted upon others (by force or through domination), but needs to be earned (in the process of interaction)' (Kavalski 2014: 313). The resulting 'harmonious respect for the other' (Kavalski 2018: 94) represents 'a cardinal virtue' of Beijing's interactions with foreign partners that typically take the form of 'an intense and skilful diplomacy of respect' (Womack 2008: 21). Even the tiniest Pacific or Caribbean island-states are entitled to a 'flattering diplomatic demarche' (Bernal 2016: 3162). Starting with President Xi, the Chinese leadership 'lavishes attention on the[ir] leadership' (Womack 2008: 21). This includes high ranking visits to their remote capitals and red carpet treatment of their officials in Beijing (French 2014: 10). Far from representing a simple protocol detail, this unusual approach has significantly contributed to China's triumphant reception in the Global South and its successful socialization of the political elites of BRI partner states (see below). Because it is rule-based, the European Union's normative model follows the logic of appropriateness. For its part, normative power China is characterized by practices of interaction and the logic of relationships. Instead of optimizing transactions, it tries to optimize relationships. Instead of using the preponderance of power to maximize benefits, it prefers to stabilize beneficial relations. Instead of bargaining, it accommodates unilaterally the partner's perceived needs. Its norms are not defined in terms of rights and obligations. As illustrated by the BRI, they emerge and develop as behavioral standards that the other side accepts in the process of interaction (Womack 2008: 20–21; Kavalski 2014: 313–314). The highly theoretical work of Yaqing Qin, a major Chinese Constructivist scholar, is most relevant to this approach. Using the Confucian concept of relationality (*guanxi*), Qin defines power as the ability to manage relations, which he views as the basic unit of analysis in International Relations theory. Rationality and relationality are perceived as complementary. International cooperation is not due to self-interest calculations but to the level of intimacy and importance of the relationship (Qin 2016; Qin 2018; Summers 2019: 210; Demir 2017: 98). By reframing normative power as relational practice, China is 'altering the suspicion and bias from past interactions and opening up opportunities for new relationships,' which rely 'on the affective feeling produced by the process of repeated interactions' (Kavalski 2017: 154). This makes actors exercise self-restraint and commit to the interaction. Ethical obligations and commitments shape and mediate action and agency both cognitively and affectively: 'the relational normativity of China's global outreach is embedded in the very practices through which ideas of sociality are shared' (*Ibid.*, 155). Consequently, an international order based on the Chinese type of normative power would be fundamentally different from the American one; and the Chinese-centered globalization 'from above' presented later in this subchapter is not a mere copy of the Neoliberal, Western-centered one.

Beyond International Relations, China's *guanxi* applies to many other domains. In fact, it is a Confucian-inspired 'tradition of nuanced balancing of relationships within the family, society, the state, and the international community' (*Ibid.*, 151). Even '"Chinese capitalism" is "guanxi capitalism"' (Nyíri 2005: 170). Under the influence of relationality, actors of all social interactions are committed to respond appropriately to social demands and expectations. Intricate relational networks emerge due to 'the practice of unlimited exchange of favours and underpinned by reciprocal obligations, assurances, and mutuality' (Kavalski 2017: 151). Domestically and internationally, the importance of reciprocity tends to transform relations into ends rather than means. However, *guanxi* is not perfect. Critically, it 'implies both a propensity and a capacity for living *with* and *in* ambiguity.' On the one hand, a very 'negative flavour of *guanxi* comes from its association with graft' (Kavalski 2018: 91, 95). The absence of EU-type rules allows Chinese projections of normative power to be unconstrained by cumbersome rules and regulations. But they also tend to be indifferent to the rule of law, openness, transparency, and financial responsibility. In the framework of the BRI, Chinese-socialized political elites have been convinced to accept Beijing's practice of secretively negotiating large infrastructure agreements that are not disclosed to the public. This seriously damages good governance in partner states where corrupt leaders warmly welcome the absence of any governance-related conditionality. On the other hand, for almost a century, social scientists such as Bronislaw Malinowski and Marcel Mauss, as well as some of their numerous followers in the fields of Anthropology, Psychology, and Sociology, have studied relationality outside the Chinese context. Their similar concept of 'social exchange' or 'diffuse reciprocity' emerged based on the study of native peoples in the South Pacific and the Pacific Northwest. Eventually, it was extended to the analysis of the exchange of gifts and favors, as well as other similar universal social practices. One of the key findings, first identified by Raymond Firth in his study of the Kula exchange among native people in the South Pacific, is that social exchange is vulnerable to exploitation. 'Indebtedness engineering' is a practice which participants in relationality-based processes can easily fall victim to (Vuving 2019: 224). Returning to the BRI, the highly criticized Chinese 'debt-trap diplomacy' illustrated by the well-known case of the Hambantota port in Sri Lanka represents a clear exploitation of partner states' vulnerabilities. It can be concluded that China's relationality-based normative power has been most useful in supporting its successful actions in the Global South conducive to the creation of a new, Chinese international order (and, as shown in the following sections, of an associated globalization 'from above'). 'On the recipients' side, however, *guanxi* may not always result in harmonious outcomes' (Tudoroiu 2022: 30).

China's Norms

Normative power is obviously based on norms, and those defining China's actions are as original as the nature of its normative power. Two aspects have to be mentioned. First, this book deals exclusively with Chinese norms related to the construction of a new international order through a globalization 'from above' that mainly targets the Global South. Accordingly, these norms are not – or not entirely – present in interactions with Western actors such as the US or the Franco-German axis. They have been tailored for the specific conditions and audiences of the Global South, and it is in this geographical area that they are mainly employed. Second, norms are essential to China's normative power, but relationality makes them somewhat different from the case of European Union's rule-based normativity, for example. They are only instruments of order, not its embodiment (Paltiel 2007: 236). An important consequence is that some of them are not explicitly formulated by the government in Beijing. Rather, 'they are implicitly present in its *guanxi* practice and have to be deduced from actual policies and actions' (Tudoroiu 2022: 31). The publicly acknowledged norms – on which the discourse on China's 'win-win' cooperation is based – are the famous Five Principles of Peaceful Coexistence included in the Sino-Indian treaty signed in 1954 by Zhou Enlai and Jawaharlal Nehru: mutual respect for each other's territorial integrity and sovereignty; mutual non-aggression; mutual non-interference in each other's internal affairs; equality and cooperation for mutual benefit; and peaceful coexistence. They became so popular that, in 1955, they were included in a modified form among the ten principles of the non-aligned movement adopted at the Bandung conference (Panda 2014). But in addition to these much publicized Kantian norms, China's interactions with the Global South are also based on a more pragmatic – and discreet – normative set composed of one general norm, as well as political, economic, and social normative subsets. The general norm states that 'cooperation with China needs to be established and developed as it is genuinely beneficial to the target country in general and to its elites in particular' (Tudoroiu 2021: 41). Its cognitive dimension is perhaps more important than the normative one. It is intended to convince target audiences that 'China's rise is inevitable; there are rich rewards for those who co-operate with it; resistance is futile' (*The Economist*, April 17, 2019). The political subset is much more specific as it requires: (1) the diplomatic non-recognition of Taiwan; (2) the rejection of any contact with (including not issuing entry visas to) the Dalai Lama; (3) the non-criticism of China's lack of democracy and infringement of human rights; (4) the non-criticism of its repressive policies and practices in Tibet, Xinjiang, and Hong Kong; (5) support for China's position in international fora that debate these issues; and (6) a Chinese-friendly attitude in international and multilateral institutions, conferences, and public debates (Tudoroiu 2021: 41). Except for the last one, the political norms are well encapsulated in the 'no Taiwan, no Tibet, no Tiananmen Square' formula used by a Trinidadian respondent (Tudoroiu 2020: 5). The economic normative subset was conceived to support the Chinese-centered globalization 'from above' through the expansion of Chinese firms' activities in partner countries. Its norms state that (1) the activity of Chinese firms should encounter no obstacle; (2) a political, economic, legal, and informal framework of interaction as favorable as possible to these firms should be set up with the assistance of the target country's government; and (3) whenever possible, a business pattern should be adopted that circumvents traditional bidding processes, which are to be replaced with government-to-government agreements (Tudoroiu 2021: 42). The latter are the aforementioned secretively negotiated, undisclosed agreements that damage the partner states' good governance. Finally, the social normative subset supports the Chinese-centered globalization 'from below.' It contains only one norm, which prevents the governments of partner states from regulating the inflow or economic activities of Chinese entrepreneurial migrants (*Ibid.*, 43). As explained by a former Zambian finance minister, Fred Mutesa,

> whenever his government sent delegations to Beijing for talks, in at least one session they would be leaned upon to maintain relaxed immigration policies toward Chinese. The language, he said, wasn't particularly subtle either; something along the lines of: We are making so many friendly gestures to your country, building roads and stadiums, etc. We would consider it a friendly gesture if you did not enforce such strict immigration controls on our citizens.
>
> (French 2014: 83)

Examples ranging from Jamaica to Ghana show that this is a general Chinese practice in the BRI partner states that – despite relationality – can lead to harsh retaliation when the social norm is infringed (Tudoroiu 2022: 36; see Subchapter 5.3).

This complex set of norms is employed by China in its projection of normative power in the Global South intended to lead to the construction of a new international order. This ambitious enterprise relies on the development of a Chinese globalization 'from above' supported by the BRI.

The Belt and Road Initiative

Widely seen as a 'signature foreign polic[y] of President Xi Jinping' (Summers 2018: 33), the BRI is a 'kind of operating system for Xi's vision of an interconnected, China-centric order positioned as an alternative to the existing rules-based international system' (Kalathil 2018: 55). Its inception is associated with the beginning of President Xi's tenure. The land-based 'Silk Road Economic Belt' and the 'twenty-first century maritime Silk Road' were announced in September and October 2013, respectively, even if the official launching took place only in March 2015, when China's State Council published the 'Vision and Actions on Jointly Building Silk Road Economic Belt and Twenty-First Century Maritime Silk Road' (Summers 2018: 25; National Development and Reform Commission *et al.* 2015). Such documents emphasize 'national rejuvenation' and the achievement of a 'community of common destiny' across 'the Indo-Pacific and beyond' (Kliman *et al.* 2019: 4). Analysts have spoken more explicitly about 'pushing' present global political economy shifts 'further or faster in the direction of China, while incorporating more rapidly into the global economy areas which had previously been peripheral' (Summers 2018: 34). The Initiative was defined as a 'state-led infrastructure-heavy spatial fix to facilitate the development of networks of capital' (*Ibid.*). In part, its creation tried to find a solution to China's industrial materials excess capacity and surplus of capital (Lairson 2018: 40; Sun and Payette 2018: 789). But the resulting massive construction of a 'system of roads, railways, oil and natural gas pipelines, fiber-optic and communication systems, ports, and airports' creates new forms of connectedness conducive to interdependence and economic growth for all participants (Lairson 2018: 40). This is intended to show that 'connection, interaction, and cooperation with China can lead to development in areas where Western countries and international financial institutions have failed to deliver' (Kalathil 2017: 171; Rolland 2017). Success would be highly beneficial to the prestige of the Chinese economic model (Sun and Payette 2018: 788–789). Another connection between domestic and external aspects is represented by the regional dimension. Initially, the initiative aimed 'to reintegrate Africa and the Middle East into a system of accumulation "with Chinese characteristics"' (Merwe 2019: 197) through six major economic corridors (see Cau 2018: 43–44). Their starting points were located in underdeveloped Chinese borderlands; this is 'a way to broaden China's strategic hinterland while stabilizing its periphery' (Kalathil 2017: 172; Rolland 2017). Both neighboring states and the 'chronically underperforming western regions' will benefit (Rippa 2017: 2). But already in 2018, observers could note that the initial Initiative was 'not the same as the BRI that exists today' (Hillman 2018b). From the six corridors, it had extended to remote regions such as the South Pacific and Latin America. It incorporated a 'Silk Road on Ice' over the Arctic Ocean and a cyberspace 'Digital Silk Road' (*The Economist*, July 26, 2018a). That same year, half of the Chinese investment related to 173 BRI infrastructure projects was directed outside the initial corridors (Hillman 2018a: 1). The Belt and Road Initiative is today 'essentially a new global architecture' whose reach ranges from infrastructure construction and trade to policy dialog and people-to-people exchange (Alon *et al.* 2018: 2). It should be mentioned that many of the associated ideas, policies, projects, and platforms for cooperation existed before the Initiative and were simply placed under the 'new umbrella term' (Vangeli 2018: 63). Critics pointed to 'a marketing exercise, rebranding everything that China does abroad under slogans that flatter Mr. Xi's global pretensions' (*The Economist*, July 26, 2018b). Yet, there is novelty: 'not in the content, but in the strategic emphasis' (Summers 2018: 33). Disparate pre-existing elements were synthesized and streamlined into one comprehensive and global vision (Vangeli 2018: 63). Accordingly, the impact of the BRI 'will be much greater (...) than that of the sub-national policy practices which preceded it' (Summers 2018: 34).

Institutionally, the Belt and Road Initiative consists of a complex set of formal and informal institutional arrangements. While at first view economic aspects are concerned, these arrangements are mainly political in nature and are entirely subordinated to President Xi Jinping and the Communist Party of China. Indeed, it is the President who provides critical guidance through speeches given at various events and regular study sessions (Rolland 2019: 227). The 'Leading Small Group on Advancing the Construction of the Belt and Road' supervises all activities, takes major decisions, and finds solutions to disagreements. Created in late 2014 and based at the State Council, it brings together representatives of the most important Chinese governing entities. It is assisted by the 'Office of the Leading Small Group on Advancing the Construction of the Belt and Road' located within the National Development and Reform Commission; and by the 'Belt and Road Promotion Center,' which is responsible for strategic planning. BRI leading small groups were also created in all relevant ministries and provinces (*Ibid.*, 226; Yu 2018: 228). The projects formally associated with the Initiative benefit from the participation of 19 ministries and agencies and 32 provinces (Yu 2018: 229). Importantly, the China International Development Cooperation Agency was created in 2018 as a vice ministry-level entity able to respond to the increasing complexity of BRI-related policies and activities. Its main objective is to enhance the use of development assistance as a component of BRI diplomacy (Kalathil 2018: 54; Sun 2019; Development Aid 2019; Rudyak 2019; Tudoroiu 2021: 64–65). The 'BRI financial ecosystem' is responsible for investment and construction contracts amounting to no less than US $573.31 and 577.92 billion, respectively, during the 2014–2018 period (He 2019: 9). It includes the two policy banks, China Development Bank and China ExIm Bank; four state-owned Chinese commercial banks, the Industrial and Commercial Bank of China, the Bank of China, the China Construction Bank, and the Agricultural Bank of China; the Silk Road Fund; funding from several Chinese local governments; the BRICS New Development Bank; and the Asian Infrastructure Investment Bank (for a detailed presentation of all these institutions, see Tudoroiu 2021: 56–66; Tudoroiu 2022: 41–47). The BRI arbitration and dispute settlement mechanism is represented by the two Chinese International Commercial Courts established in 2018 in Xi'an for overland trade cases and in Shenzhen for maritime ones. Yet, both have been criticized for not being genuinely international courts. Like all courts in China, they are ultimately subordinated to the political control of the Communist Party, which raises serious doubts with regard to their legitimacy and impartiality (Selga 2019; *The Economist*, June 6, 2019; *The Economist*, June 13, 2019; Ferdinand 2016: 945; Tudoroiu 2021: 63–64). Another key group of BRI actors is represented by the Chinese 'state-owned enterprises' (SOEs), a term that hides the fact that some of them are hybrid or private-owned. Their worldwide expansion is the direct consequence of the 'Go out' or 'Going Global' national strategy adopted back in 1999. By 2014, their number amounted to 180 (Mohan *et al.* 2014: 59). Much of their success is due to the close collaboration with the Chinese state and the Chinese policy banks. Critically, China's economic normative subset was specially conceived to help them benefit from economic opportunities in the BRI partner states. For their part, executives of these enterprises frequently develop close relationships with local political leaders that significantly contribute to the Chinese socialization of political elites in Belt and Road Initiative states (see below). Finally, the numerous regional cooperation fora mentioned earlier in this subchapter – which include the well-known FOCAC, the Forum on China-Africa Cooperation – open channels for bilateral interaction that are most beneficial to the expansion of the BRI in the numerous concerned regions.

Overall, the Belt and Road Initiative represents a huge enterprise that, in many regards, is reminiscent of the American construction of multilateral institutions that helped establish the US-led international order and, eventually, led to the development of the Western-centered globalization 'from above.' Similarly, China greatly increases its 'gravitational pull on other states and firms' (Lairson 2018: 41). What is different is the absence of a Chinese 'top-down masterplan with specific orders emanating from above' (Manuel 2019: 5). 'Bureaucratic opaqueness and overarching policy-related uncertainty' have been mentioned as serious consequences (Yu 2018: 229); lower echelons desperately try 'to flesh out the vague intentions from the top' (Manuel 2019: 5–6). This is explained by the difference between the rule-based nature of America's normative power and China's relationship-based normative model. Relying on the *guanxi* dimension, the BRI is 'developed inductively, it is informed by the various practices on the ground, while remaining flexible to the changing circumstances' (Vangeli 2018: 60). Instead of creating rigid structures, Beijing has set up a '"structuring structure" that silently creates a dominant code of communication and practices' (*Ibid.*, 79). This is most visible in the ability of the Initiative to bring about the socialization of BRI political elites on which the Chinese-centered globalization 'from above' is based.

Socialization of Elites and the Chinese-Centered Globalization 'from Above'

The Chinese socialization of these elites is a vast topic that I analyzed in a previous work (Tudoroiu 2021). Perhaps the most important aspect revealed by the effectiveness of this huge enterprise is related to the fundamental nature of the Belt and Road Initiative: despite its unquestionable geopolitical and geoeconomic importance, the BRI is primarily a projection of Chinese normative power. The remarkable success of China's 'state-led infrastructure-heavy spatial fix' in facilitating 'the development of networks of capital' (Summers 2018: 34) is dwarfed by the generalized acceptance of Beijing's norms all over the Initiative. The 'conceptions of normal' of political elites are reshaped to fit Chinese interests, which enhances the Chinese-centered globalizations and is conducive to the emergence of a Chinese-led international order.

International socialization is defined as a 'process by which principled ideas held by individuals [or agents] become norms in the sense of collective understandings about appropriate behaviour which then lead to changes in identities, interests and behaviour' (Park 2014: 337; see Risse *et al.* 1999: 11; Checkel 1999: 548; Johnston 2001: 494). Normative understandings are internalized through social interaction. New definitions of interest emerge that are independent of exogenous material constraints (Johnston 2003: 108). Identity – relatively stable, role-specific understandings and expectations about self that represent 'a property of international actors that generates motivational and behavioral dispositions' (Wendt 1999/2003: 224; Flockhart 2006: 94–97) – also changes. In turn, the interaction of actors with modified identities can even lead to a different Wendtian 'culture' of international anarchy. Socialization by the European Union and other international organizations has been scrutinized by numerous scholars. International socialization by hegemons has also been studied, most notably by John Ikenberry and Charles Kupchan (Ikenberry and Kupchan 1990). Even the Soviet Union – followed by Russia – socialized its client states (Tudoroiu 2015). Lack of space prevents me from discussing the differences between the socialization processes involving the elites and the society of the target country (see Tudoroiu 2022: 47–50). The political elites – 'individuals and small, relatively cohesive and stable groups with disproportionate decisional power to affect (…) national outcomes' (Körösényi 2018: 41; Higley 2018: 27; Best and Higley 2018) – are easier to socialize and have a key advantage: being in control of state institutions, they swiftly align state policies with newly internalized norms. 'Socializing the elites also means socializing the state,' even if the socialization of the entire state-society complex remains incomplete (Tudoroiu 2021: 8). This is why the preferred target of socializers in general and of China in particular is represented by politicians and high-level bureaucrats in control of or able to influence relevant state institutions and political parties. An important theoretical aspect is represented by the degree of socialization. Certain authors have identified three or four such degrees or stages (Park 2014: 340; Wendt 1999/2003; Risse *et al.* 1999), but I prefer the older and clearer two-stage model proposed by Jeffrey Checkel. This scholar defined Type I socialization as being based on material rewards that incentivize actors to learn a role. They might not agree with that role, but do act in accordance with expectations associated with it to get material benefits. The more advanced Type II socialization makes material incentives irrelevant. Actors go beyond role playing and accept new norms as the right thing to do. The 'taken for granted' logic of appropriateness replaces instrumental calculation (Checkel 2005: 804). It is obvious that Type II is more difficult to reach and requires considerable more efforts on the socializer's side. This is why China mainly tries to achieve the Type I socialization of the BRI political elites. There are cases where Type II socialization is envisaged in the longer term – one example being the Commonwealth Caribbean (Tudoroiu and Ramlogan 2019; Tudoroiu 2020) – but in most of the Belt and Road Initiative there is little need for such ambitious results. China's leaders are fully satisfied if political elites in partner states 'play well their role of friendly junior partners as long as the Chinese norms are respected and result in economic and political benefits for China' (Tudoroiu 2022: 51).

Two mechanisms of international socialization are employed. The first is the micro-process of persuasion. This is part of the process of normative suasion, which 'involves changing attitudes without use of either material or mental coercion' (Flockhart 2006: 97). The target has to identify positively with the socializer's social group and have a desire for inclusion in it (*Ibid.*); in the Chinese case, the group is of course represented by the Belt and Road Initiative. Successful normative suasion has a constitutive effect – it can change an actor's interests and reconstitute its identity (Acharya 2011: 2). The micro-process of persuasion encourages norm-consistent behavior through ongoing, iterative interactions. They modify attitudes without overt material or mental coercion (Johnston 2001: 499; Flockhart 2006: 97; Park 2014: 338). The BRI political elites are to be convinced that Chinese norms, values, and causal understandings are right and ought to be operative in their own behavior. Successful internalization leads to a situation where 'new courses of action [will be] viewed as entirely reasonable and appropriate' (Johnston 2003: 113–115; Johnston 2008: 25). The typical framework for persuasion is represented by interpersonal interactions among target political elites and various representatives of the Chinese state and state-owned enterprises, which explains the flurry of meetings and visits organized by Beijing. Secret diplomacy is particularly effective (Terhalle 2011: 353); the Chinese use it especially under the form of abovementioned secretive negotiations of large infrastructure agreements. The 'variable of vanity' is also important. It is exploited through 'China's flattering diplomatic demarche' that allows leaders of small or poor states 'for a fleeting moment to live the illusion of respect' (Bernal 2016: 3162, 3230–3241). This is part of the 'logic of relationships' specific to the Chinese relationality. Indeed, the strategy toward the BRI political elites gives priority to optimizing relationships rather than transactions, which greatly contributes to legitimizing the harmony-seeking, benevolent socializer (Womack 2008: 20–21; Kavalski 2014: 313–314).

However, it is the second mechanism that is more effective. This is the micro-process of role playing or mimicking (Johnston 2008: 24), which is part of the process of cognitive role playing associated with Jeffrey Checkel's Type I socialization. As already shown, what is internalized in this process is the obligation to pretend that norms are followed rather than the norms themselves. Mimicking most frequently stems 'from social incentives to accept another actor as a behavioral exemplar' (*Ibid.*; Simmons 2013: 371). Within the BRI, Beijing uses a wide range of instruments that fall into this category: 'corruption, support for authoritarian regimes, military cooperation, exploitation of ideological affinities, party-to-party relations, taking advantage of the liberalization imposed by Western creditors, trade dependency, and political influence activities' (Tudoroiu 2021: 252). These are customized to fit specific local conditions. But there is a general instrument that is always – and most successfully – employed: the Chinese loan-financed and constructed prestige infrastructure projects. They are typically presented as development assistance, despite the fact that interest rates usually are only marginally preferential while contractors, labor, and materials have to be entirely or mainly Chinese. Furthermore, overindebtedness may ensue. But these projects are enormously popular among the BRI political elites because of their undeniable effectiveness in increasing those elites' political legitimacy and electoral support. Whenever possible, inaugurations are calculated to take place shortly before elections and figure prominently in electoral campaigns. By exploiting the 'power-centered, interest-driven, and often corruptible nature of policymaking processes' (Vangeli 2019: 79), the Chinese incentives convince the BRI political elites to adopt a strongly utilitarian way of reasoning that brings benefits to this group instead of the rational-instrumentalist logic meant to benefit the public (*Ibid.*, 80). Empirical data suggest that the 'socialization of the BRI political elites has relied more on material incentives resulting in cognitive role playing than on normative suasion' (Tudoroiu 2021: 251). As an effect, these 'elites could be rather complacent' in their attitude toward China and tend to show an 'uncritical understanding of the matters at stake' (Vangeli 2019: 80). Overall, persuasion and mimicking result in the enthusiastic acceptance of the Chinese norms by targeted elites. Once socialized, their members sincerely believe that, as stated by Beijing's general norm, the cooperation with China is genuinely beneficial to their country and to themselves, individually and as a group. They willingly implement the economic normative subset, which opens the economies of BRI countries to Chinese firms and allows them to benefit from a clearly preferential treatment. The replacement of traditional bidding processes with government-to-government agreements is particularly advantageous, as it eliminates both local and Western competitors. In turn, executives of large Chinese companies frequently if not always establish close relationships with members of the local political elites and contribute to their further socialization (Tudoroiu 2021: 62).

    The result is the significant enhancement of the Chinese-centered globalization 'from above' sometimes mentioned in the literature as 'globalization with Chinese characteristics.' Its target is nothing less than a 'significant spatial reorganization of global capitalism' (Ayers 2013: 13; Mohan *et al.* 2014: 13). China 'has gone from being a vessel to becoming an increasingly transformative actor in its own right [that] reinvent[s] globalization in its own image' (French 2014: 3–4). The accommodation to a global order largely defined by Western actors and interests (Tull 2008: 7; Ziso 2018: 2) is coming to an end; the attitude toward the Western-centered globalization follows a similar trajectory. Globalizations 'from above' can be understood, at least in part, as 'the externalization of particular national forms of capitalism in particular historical periods' (Henderson *et al.* 2013: 1221). Today, a shift from America to China is taking place. The associated reproduction of the structures of global political economy is based on the 'more dominant role' of the Chinese capital (Summers 2018: 28), which uses the multilateral institutional framework of the BRI exactly as the United States used in the past the Bretton Woods institutions and the GATT/WTO to develop its own globalization 'from above.' The Chinese projection of normative power that supports this globalization challenges the 'West's near-monopoly in setting standards' (*The Economist*, July 26, 2018b). China 'is pushing to change global norms' (Office of the Director of National Intelligence 2021: 4). It is 'gradually jettisoning many of the norms and conventions used by the United States and Europe throughout their long and hitherto largely unchallenged tutelage of the Third World' (French 2014: 4). This obviously enhances Beijing's ability to influence the global political economy through the self-interested redefinition of what is 'normal.'

In many regards, the development of the Chinese globalization 'from above' mirrors the process that led to the development of the Western-centered globalization. Both are hegemonic constructs associated with an international order, set up through projections of normative power, supported by multilateral institutions, and enacted by large companies (Chinese state-owned enterprises and Western multilateral corporations, respectively). However, there are two important differences. First, America's globalization developed on virgin land. The Chinese one faces a mature rival globalization supported by an aggressive and still powerful incumbent hegemon. There was no other choice than the 'periphery policy' that has pushed the BRI toward the Global South and the eastern and southern peripheries of the European Union. This delays and diminishes the direct confrontation with powerful adversaries such as the US and the Franco-German axis, but also limits the reach of the Chinese globalization 'from above' to developing countries that show a discouraging record of payment defaults and economic crises. It is not certain that such an environment is conducive to successful economic cooperation in the long run; and, even if it does, it could result in a Chinese globalization with features very different from the Western one. Furthermore, a peripheral strategy may delay and diminish the conflict with America, but cannot completely prevent it. President Trump's poorly managed Indo-Pacific strategy failed to provide an effective response, but the Biden administration seems able and willing to launch a much better organized counteroffensive. The decades-long 'diplomatic duel' between China and Taiwan shows the considerable difficulties encountered by Beijing in a race for the allegiance of developing countries. Similarly fighting against the United States will be much more difficult.

The other major difference comes from China's specific features. Both the totalitarian recent past and the Confucian emphasis on authority have contributed to the key role played by the state within the Chinese economy in general and BRI-related activities in particular. The Initiative has been framed as a call for collective rather than unilateral action (Vangeli 2018: 66). President Xi stated explicitly that the BRI would 'not become a "Chinese Club," a Sino-centric political grouping' (Hillman 2018b). However, it is China that issued – and finances – this call (Summers 2018: 34). Features such as the subordination of the two BRI commercial courts to the Chinese judicial system clearly show that, unlike the IMF or the WTO, the institutional framework of China's globalization 'from above' – with the exception of the Asian Infrastructure Investment Bank – is not only controlled but actually owned by the Chinese state. This explains why Beijing's diplomats systematically avoid the 'liberal order' term in their discourse. The anti-liberal dimension is further enhanced by the Chinese relationality-based normative model. Its emphasis on optimizing relationships rather than transactions has an unexpected consequence: it gives preference to bilateral as opposed to multilateral interactions. The BRI does represent a multilateral framework, as do the numerous regional fora set up by Beijing. But China typically insists on conducting actual interactions on a bilateral basis, and within these bilateral interactions it favors government-to-government agreements implemented by Chinese state-owned enterprises with loans from Chinese state-owned banks. In the process, good governance, financial responsibility, transparency, and anti-corruption are always ignored and frequently damaged. Needless to say, this is the opposite of Neoliberal – and, more generally, liberal – norms and practices promoted by the multilateral institutions associated with the Western-centered globalization. The Chinese globalization 'from above' has not yet reached maturity and its features may evolve in unpredictable ways in the coming years, especially under the effect of the coming American counteroffensive. But it is clear that, in terms of norms and practices, it will continue to be very different from the Western one.

One such difference that is most relevant for this book concerns the relationship between the two Chinese-centered globalizations. The Western-centered globalization 'from above' has antagonistic relationships with the counter-hegemonic and non-hegemonic globalizations 'from below,' which have developed precisely as forms of resistance to its domination. In the Chinese case, the 'from above' and 'from below' globalizations form, on the contrary, a virtuous circle. Both are expressions of China's projection of normative power: the economic normative subset opens the BRI partner states to the Chinese globalization 'from above' while the social normative subset does the same thing for the 'from below' globalization. Once established, the globalization 'from above' constantly provides new material incentives that enhance the Chinese socialization of local political elites. This further stimulates the respect of the social norm, which improves the situation of the Chinese entrepreneurial migrants and their globalization 'from below.' In turn, prominent Chinese entrepreneurial migrants frequently become preferred intermediaries between local decision-makers and Chinese firms, which use them to 'open doors' in the target country. This is just the most visible of the various ways in which actors of China's globalization 'from below' contribute to the development of the 'from above' one (see Chapter 5). It can be concluded that an harmonious triangular relationship is developing that is based on China's normative power and brings together its emerging international order and the intertwined, mutually reinforcing Chinese globalizations 'from above' and 'from below.'

2.4 The First Wave Globalization 'from Above'

The first, 'golden' age of globalization (Zinkina *et al.* 2019: 195) is seldom entitled to more than one or two general statements placed at the beginning of the numerous works that deal with the more fashionable contemporary globalization 'from above.' Uninformed audiences tend to show indifference, or even contempt, when comparisons are made. And yet, the study of the first wave of globalization is essential to the understanding of globalizing processes. First, it illuminates a key aspect: how (and why) globalizations emerge and die. Second, similarities between the first and present waves are accompanied by analytically useful key differences: 'the checklist by 1900 is hardly identical to what it would become by the year 2000' (Stearns 2010: 122). More than one century ago, there were 'constraints and regional hesitations' followed by 'substantial pushback.' 'The movement was "nascent and incomplete," and it was "interrupted by events of the twentieth century"' (*Ibid.*, 91). Some believe that we are experiencing a superior phenomenon. To the so-called globalists, the triumphant march that started at Bretton Woods led to Keohane's and Nye's complex interdependence of the 1970s (Keohane and Nye 1977) and to the more recent 'unstoppable' hyperglobalization. But crises, populism, the decline of the liberal international order, and associated Chinese counter-hegemonic moves suggest that globalization-unfriendly 'events of the twentieth century' may, at least in part, reproduce themselves in the near future. Accordingly, when globalization theoretical schools are considered, I find it difficult to share the globalists' enthusiasm. I do not go, however, as far as to accept the skeptics' dark views. I prefer a transformationalist perspective (Martell 2007) that acknowledges the role of evolving ideas and the fallacy of brute determinism. This post-positivist approach allows for the analysis of the first wave of globalization as a useful case study that can complement and enrich the theoretical conclusions drawn from the scrutiny of the present globalization 'from above.'

To begin with, it is important to stress the fact that globalizations represent a narrow category. Many journalists and some scholars expand it to include the Great Discoveries or historical processes as remote as the Neolithic Revolution. To elucidate this issue, the world history literature has to be engaged. World history is a subfield of history defined as the study of 'interaction among peoples of diverse cultures.' It emphasizes the fact that long-distance trade, the spread of plagues and religions, and numerous other trans-civilizational contacts have existed long before our time (Mazlish 1998: 386). World history developed considerably after World War II, mainly in reaction to the perceived Eurocentric bias of historical approaches centered on Western nation-states. This aspect is closely connected to the trend of identifying pre-1870 globalizations located in non-European geographies. Both can ultimately be understood as ways to avoid 'imposing Western metanarratives upon other peoples' histories' (Making History 2008). While world history became highly popular after 1945, it was exactly one hundred years ago that one of its major authors, Arnold Toynbee (1889–1975), began to work on his monumental *A Study of History*, whose 12 volumes were published between 1934 and 1961. Toynbee's 'attempt at world history' was strongly influenced by the first wave globalization he had experienced in his youth. In fact, he was an advocate of the return to the universalism of that globalization both between the two World Wars, when he strongly supported the League of Nations, and after 1945 (Lang 2011: 749–750). His work has been described as trying to explain the complex relationship between 'universalization and fragmentation' (*Ibid.*, 782). The British historian was one of the early critics of the 'egocentric illusion [of] the misconception of the unity of history – involving the assumption that there is only one river of civilization, our own' (Toynbee 1946: 37). His response was to initiate what would become a key feature of world history, its focus on civilizations (Mazlish 1998: 393). Instead of relying on the Western one, his *magnum opus* analyzed no less than 21 present, past, 'arrested,' and 'abortive' civilizations as diverse as the Andean, Sinic, Mayan, Indic, Far Eastern, Arabic, Hindu, Mexic, Yucatec, Polynesian, and Eskimo ones (Toynbee 1934–1961). While the emphasis was on the common features and trajectories of these civilizations, their various interactions were also scrutinized. These interactions became the specific object of analysis of another major world historian, Fernand Braudel (1902–1985), who led the French *Annales* School during its second period and turned it into a very influential center of scientific research. In line with Toynbee, Braudel wrote *A History of Civilizations* as a textbook for French schools. However, he became famous due to two highly original works: *The Mediterranean and the Mediterranean World in the Age of Philip II* (Braudel 1949) and the three-volume *Civilization and Capitalism, 15th–18th Century* (Braudel 1967; Braudel 1979). Relevant to this subchapter, these books moved the emphasis of world history from civilizations to what Braudel called *économie-monde* (world-economy). The French scholar rejected the theses of Marx and Weber on the beginning of capitalism.

Instead of the decline of feudalism or the Protestant reformation, he associated its origin with the development of commercial capitalism in the 11th and 12th centuries, which only much later developed into industrial capitalism. From that period, world-economies emerged that were not global and could coexist; each of them, however, represented a 'world.' At first, they were centered on a dominant core capitalist city whose commercial and financial influence spread far beyond its borders. This was the case of Venice in the 14th and 15th centuries, Anvers from the end of the 15th century to the middle of the 16th century, Genoa from the middle of the 16th century to the first quarter of the 17th century, and Amsterdam from the second quarter of the 17th century to the beginning of the 18th century. In the 18th and early 19th centuries, two nation-states, England and France, imposed their own world-economies. Maritime expansion led to the incorporation of newly discovered regions, especially during the 14th and the 15th centuries under the leadership of Venice and in the 17th century under that of Amsterdam (Braudel 1979; Heston 2002; Van der Wee 1981: 34–35; Parker 1987: 479). Moreover, Braudel identified some capitalist features – which led to extended commercial relations with the outer world – in the case of the Roman, Ottoman, Mughal, and other empires. The Romans traded in the Indian Ocean, the Chinese in the East Indies, Indian Banyans in Moscow, and Armenian merchants from Persia all over the world. Accordingly, there was an Indian world-economy extending from Calicut and Cambay to Malacca and an Islamic world-economy that covered Africa's Eastern Coast, Egypt, the Arabian Peninsula, Turkey, and Persia (Braudel 1979; Heston 2002).

The next step in the theoretical development of world history was represented by the upgrading of Braudel's world-economy to world-system. This was done by Immanuel Wallerstein (1930–2019), who acknowledged his intellectual debt to the French scholar by co-founding the Fernand Braudel Center for the Study of Economies, Historical Systems, and Civilizations at the State University of New York at Binghamton. Similar to a world-economy, a world-system is not necessarily global; but it represents a closed, integrated area that is bound together by common rules and flows of goods, capital, and labor. Unlike world-empires, world-systems incorporate multiple political entities. They form an interstate system that does in no way hamper the interactions between its various regions. Wallerstein concentrated much of his efforts on studying the development of the modern capitalist world-system, which emerged in the 16th century due to the mercantile competition among West European states and eventually expanded to the entire planet. A core-semi-periphery-periphery structure was created, which is well illustrated by the strikingly similar subordination of Iberian America and Eastern Europe to the Western core and by the intermediate position of Mediterranean Europe (Wallerstein 1980; Franke 2014: 5–6, 8; Mazlish 1998: 387). As World System Theory is included in the curriculum of any undergraduate International Relations program, there is little need to provide further details on this approach. However, Wallerstein believed that the coming into being of the first global world-system was triggered by the so-called great geographical discoveries. Other world-systems historians disagreed. Janet Abu-Lughod (1928–2013) argued that the rise of the Western system studied by Wallerstein was possible only due to the collapse of a previous long-standing global world-system that existed between the 12th and the 15th centuries and reached its peak at the end of the 13th century. It was based on four cores: the Middle East, China and the northern steppe of Central Asia, the Indian Ocean, and the towns of developing Western Europe located mainly in Flanders, France, and Italy. Its fall was due to the closing of China under the Ming dynasty that, at least in part, was an indirect consequence of the Black Death (Abu-Lughod 1990: 275–278). Another scholar was even more ambitious in identifying pre-modern world-systems. André Gunder Frank (1929–2005) is well-known as a theorist of the Dependency School, but he was a marking member of Wallerstein's Fernand Braudel Center and brought his own contribution to the development of the world-systems theory. Most notably, he argued that the Asian-African-European landmass, as well as its outlying islands, was part of a world-system by 600 BC. A smaller world-system existed by 1500 BC that included Mesopotamia and Egypt. But the first one emerged in or before 2500 BC when Mesopotamian Sumer established relations with Anatolia and the Indus civilization. Overall, 'all sedentary "civilized" and most nomad "barbarian" peoples on the Afro-Eurasian ecumene land mass have jointly participated in a single – even if multicentric – world system for several millennia' (Frank 1990: 228; 231).

Some of the details of the findings of world history and world-systems scholars may be debatable, but nobody can deny the existence of various economically interconnected areas long before 1870. It is very tempting to see these early world-economies or world-systems as globalizations. The problem is that interconnectedness does not necessarily mean globalization. For this advanced stage to be reached, a high level of integration has to exist among the regions that form a world-economy or world-system. A fully fledged globalization mirrors the vivid picture of the world in 1914 provided by Kevin O'Rourke and Jeffrey Williamson. Worldwide, there were few villages or towns uninfluenced by distant foreign markets, without foreign-financed infrastructure, with no imported engineering, manufacturing, or business skills, or with labor not affected by international migration. Intimate economic connections erased part of the gap between poor and rich regions. There was a global trade boom resulting in flourishing export sectors and associated prosperity. There were also outcompeted industries and farmers that voiced populist complaints and demanded protection from cheap foreign products and compensation for the losses they suffered. Financial panics reached speedily distant corners of the globe. Policymakers were losing the ability to control national economies (O'Rourke and Williamson 1999: 2). Today's readers will have no problem in recognizing these familiar settings. Christopher Columbus' contemporaries, on the contrary, would certainly have expressed some surprise. Long-distance trade in luxury goods – illustrated, for example, by the original Silk Road – has existed since Antiquity; but a globalization 'from above' requires a ratio of commodity trade to GDP that camels or galleons cannot provide. This changed only when technological progress brought in steamers and trains. It is interesting to note that, in her aforementioned analysis of world-systems, Janet Abu-Lughod identified and compared three global ones: the 4-core world-system of the 12th–15th centuries presented in the previous paragraph; the 16th–20th-century Western world-system, which reached its peak at the end of the 19th century (i.e., during the first wave globalization); and the present one. These three world-systems are characterized by different degrees of integration: 'modest but increasing,' 'high but uneven,' and 'high and increasingly even,' respectively. This mirrors their degree of technological development. The level, diffusion, and ability to 'eradicate space' of the technology specific to the three world-systems are low, moderate, and high, respectively (Abu-Lughod 1990: 284). The existence of a world-system that is only 'modestly' integrated is not sufficient to ensure the development of a globalization. For the latter to emerge, the world-system needs a high degree of integration, which, in turn, can be provided only by advanced technological development. This is why Abu-Lughod's 12th–15th-century world-system failed to produce a globalization and the 16th–20th-century system experienced one only close to its peak at the end of the 19th century. It should be added that, while in common parlance world history and global history are used indiscriminately, there is an important difference between them. As shown earlier in this subchapter, world history is the more general study of 'interaction among peoples of diverse cultures.' Global history is narrowly 'concerned with the history of globalization, and the study of processes of globalization in the past' (Mazlish 1998: 386; Making History 2008). World historians such as Toynbee, Braudel, and Wallerstein worked outside the subfield of global history. Their research illuminated interesting aspects of interconnectedness that can be considered to represent prerequisites of genuine processes of globalization. But their findings do not support the claim that globalizations existed before 1870.

In quantitative terms, the difference between mere interconnectedness and fully fledged globalization is shown by the aforementioned ratio of commodity trade to GDP. Between 1870 and 1913, in Europe, this indicator increased from 29.9 to 36.9 percent. Even if the large intra-European trade is set aside, there was an increase from 9.2 to 13.5 percent. The 1913 value for the United States was 12 percent. Nobody can believe that such levels could have been reached within world-systems in the 13th or 16th centuries, not to mention Antiquity. The first wave of globalization was also marked by impressive international integration. From 1870 to 1913, the difference in wheat prices between Liverpool and Chicago fell from 57.6 to 15.6 percent. That for bacon between London and Cincinnati diminished from 92.5

to 17.9 percent. For iron bars, the American-British price gap was reduced from 75 to 20.6 percent. The London-Rangoon price difference for rice diminished from 93 to 26 percent; the Liverpool-Bombay cotton one from 57 to 20 percent. Much of this was due to cheaper land and sea transportation. The cost of shipping wheat from Chicago to New York shrank from 17.2 to 5.5 percent of the Chicago price; the New York to Liverpool shipping cost similarly fell from 11.6 to 4.7 percent (Daudin *et al.* 2010: 6–7). Steam was, of course, the key factor. Paddle wheels steamships first appeared early in the 19th century, but they were very vulnerable to rough seas. This limited their use to coastal and river travel, which could hardly trigger a globalization. But in the 1840s, screw propellers started to be used, and, during the 1870s, triple expansion engines were introduced that allowed ships to travel far longer distances before refueling. The duration of a transatlantic crossing diminished from one month to almost one week by 1900. Unprecedentedly dense contacts were established over oceans, as well as rivers in Africa or China. Refrigerated containers introduced in the 1870s turned Argentina and New Zealand into meat suppliers of the entire world (Stearns 2010: 93–94). The Suez Canal, completed in 1869, significantly diminished navigation time and cost. It reduced the distance between India and Europe to half and that between China and Europe by more than a quarter. The Panama Canal had a similar effect: it shortened sea travel between the US Atlantic and Pacific coasts with 18,000 miles and ten days (Daudin *et al.* 2010: 7; Stearns 2010: 96). However, being completed in 1913, it influenced only the last year of the first wave globalization. Trains, on the contrary, played a key role from the very beginning. By the 1860s, they started to connect America's two shores. The construction of the trans-Siberian railway was initiated in 1891. Large parts of it were in use long before the completion of the entire project in 1916. Communications were also concerned. The telegraph, invented in 1837, was transformed from a regional to a global device when undersea cables started to be installed. The first transatlantic line opened in 1866. In 1868, the Indo-European Telegraph Company was chartered that would connect India to Persia, Russia, Germany, and Britain. Australia was also connected to Europe in 1871. International phone lines began to be built in the 1890s. Guglielmo Marconi set up transatlantic radio connections in 1901 (Stearns 2010: 95–96).

This spectacular technological progress and the associated increase in global connectivity led to and were, in turn, further enhanced by the similarly spectacular expansion of capital, trade, and migration (Zinkina *et al.* 2019: 196). International capital markets in 1900 are frequently described as 'surprisingly well integrated' (D'Onofrio and Rousseau 2018: 106) or as having reached a level of integration that 'was extremely impressive' (Daudin *et al.* 2010: 9). Indeed, in response to the variation of rates of return, 'capital flow[ed] flexibly across countries' (D'Onofrio and Rousseau 2018: 106). Europe acted as the world's banker and dominated foreign direct investment. Countries rich in resources and benefitting from good access to its capital – the United States and Canada, but also Australia and Argentina – reached prosperity between 1870 and 1913. Transfer of capital was also important from Western to less developed economies in Southern, Central, and Eastern Europe. In 1914, 42 percent of the global foreign investment came from Britain, 20 percent from France, and 13 from Germany. If Belgium, the Netherlands, and Switzerland are added, the total represents no less than 87 percent of global investment (Daudin *et al.* 2010: 11). At only 2.5 billion, the American capital placed abroad (in current US dollars) was vastly inferior to British, French, and German levels (19.5, 8.6, and 6.7 billion, respectively) (Zinkina *et al.* 2019: 199). No less than 32 percent of Britain's wealth was held overseas. In fact, the size of total foreign assets provides a useful illustration of the rise and fall of the first globalization. From only 7 percent of the global GDP in 1870, it reached almost 20 percent from 1900 to 1914. During the Great Depression, in 1930, it was 8 percent. Protectionist policies and World War II further diminished it to 5 percent in 1945. Eventual growth was almost imperceptible, with only 6 percent being reached in 1960. The 1914 level of integration was paralleled only in the 1970s. It was from that time that the present globalization 'from above' became visible: total foreign assets reached 25, 49, and 92 percent of the global GDP in 1980, 1990, and 2000, respectively (Daudin *et al.* 2010: 11). The similar 1870–1913 development of commerce has already been presented. It should be added that, in addition to the aforementioned progress in transportation, this expansion was stimulated by the gradual spread of the gold standard. The latter limited exchange rate fluctuations, which, in turn, led to the reduction of uncertainty in trade. Furthermore, trade in goods was accompanied by the increasingly important trade in services. In 1913, Europe's total exports amounted to $11 billion. Britain's 1911–1913 annual surplus in business services trade averaged more than $800 million (*Ibid.*, 8–9). At the same time, economic and, more specifically, industrial development triggered major labor-related changes that had a key consequence: 'levels of migration exploded in the later 19th century' (Stearns 2010: 103). After 1900, more than one million people emigrated every year. The decadal emigration rate per thousand in the 1880s was 141.7 for Ireland and 95.2 for Norway. As Italians and East Europeans joined the process, the same indicator reached 107.7 for Italy in 1901–1910. The Western European annual outmigration average rate increased from 2.2 per thousand in the 1870s to 5.4 in the 1900s. Not everybody moved to America. Many Italians emigrated to France and many Irish chose to live in Britain. For certain countries, there were also important return rates. Overall, the migratory phenomenon was 'most impressively globalized, even compared with today' (Daudin *et al.* 2010: 15). These huge flows were accompanied by a process of cultural globalization: 'suggestions of a new, global popular culture also emerged' (Stearns 2010: 98). There was a diffusion of foods, organized international tourism emerged, and formal student exchanges reached important levels. Diseases were also diffused, but this was countered by the global adoption of a new medical approach

46 *Globalizations and Normative Power*

initially developed in Western Europe (*Ibid.*, 98, 103, 104, 113). New forms of international exchanges included World Fairs, the 1876 Philadelphia one being the first to take place outside of Europe. The Venice Biennale was launched in 1895, the modern Olympics in 1896, and the awarding of Nobel prizes in 1901 (Daudin *et al.* 2010: 19).

It is beyond a shadow of a doubt that most of these developments would have been impossible without major advances in transportation and communications and, more generally, in the absence of substantial scientific and technological progress. The first wave of globalization witnessed the 'first technology-induced compression of time and space' (Gekas 2009: 101). However, technology did not suddenly disappear in 1914; globalization did. Scientific and technological factors were necessary, but not sufficient for the first globalization to emerge and survive. This depended on both 'the technologies and *policies* that simply made moving around the world easier than ever before' (Stearns 2010: 98; emphasis added).

Hegemony, Liberalism, and Paradoxes

It was noted that 'most of the Victorian-era globalisation occurred under Pax Britannica' (Baldwin and Martin 1999: 29). Accordingly, while the importance of other variables is acknowledged, many scholars tend to rely on the Hegemonic Stability Theory in their explanation of the first globalization 'from above': 'the rise and fall of Great Britain in the nineteenth century corresponds nicely with the first wave' (Chase-Dunn *et al.* 2000: 92). A superficial observer might draw the *déjà vu*-scented conclusion that a liberal hegemon simply used its position to impose a liberal international order and an associated globalization 'from above;' hence the policies mentioned in the previous paragraph. The similarity between such a scenario and the post-1945 American enterprise is so strong that the analysis of the 1870–1914 episode would bear little interest. In fact, two important differences need to be taken into consideration. Despite Britain's hegemony in a number of important fields, the 1870–1914 international order was essentially multipolar; and, after 1879, all other major economic actors put an end to their liberal policies, which were replaced with protectionist ones. Far from being a perfect mirror of the present situation, the international context of the first wave of globalization is very useful in showing that quite different conditions can nevertheless lead to rather similar globalizing processes.

A detailed examination of Britain's international position in the last part of the 19th century and at the beginning of the 20th falls outside the scope of this chapter. I will only remind the fact that its hegemonic status was very real in key fields such as trade and finance, as well as in naval and – in a certain measure – colonial matters. But, in a Eurocentric world, the Franco-Prussian War of 1870–1871 put an end to Britain's role of a balancer in Europe. Since the Congress of Vienna, the government in London had been the arbiter of continental great powers in their continuous struggle for preeminence. The rise of Germany – and the eventual replacement of Bismark's *Realpolitik* with the much more ambitious *Weltpolitik* of Wilhem II – turned the United Kingdom in a 'normal' actor compelled to join the anti-German camp in a geopolitical landscape increasingly dominated by two antagonistic blocs. Moreover, for a large part of the 19th century, Britain had also been the dominant industrial power of the world. It supplied huge amounts of manufactured goods even to industrialized – or, at that time, industrializing – countries such as France or the German states. Yet, during the first wave of globalization, the American and German competitors succeeded in reaching a higher industrial output. It should be added that, while Britannia ruled the seas, France was by far the largest exporter of cultural goods. These critically included the French language as both an instrument of international communication and a social status indicator. Overall, the British hegemony was very different from the United States' more recent one. It only covered some fields; it did not include military supremacy; and, in certain domains, it severely declined during the 1870–1914 period. Accordingly, London was unable to impose a unipolar international order. The first wave of globalization was associated with multipolarity. Major decisions had to be negotiated among interested great powers. The partition of Africa, for example, was significantly marked by the 1884–1885 Berlin Conference where Britain had no means to simply impose its interests over those of other European states. The international order of this period can be described as hegemonic only if the Western great powers are perceived as exercising a collective hegemony. In many regards, this is a valid approach even if concerned powers varied in time. Initially, Britain and France were the best positioned players. In 1870, the still developing United States was only half a decade away from a terrible civil war while Germany and Italy were still completing their national unification processes. Yet, the first two would soon become key members of the club. Rome also joined in, even if its position remained rather marginal. The situation of two other states was similarly ambiguous. Russia was an uncontested great power but had a semi-peripheral status in terms of socio-economic development. Moreover, its international interests and actions were limited to areas close to its borders. Austria-Hungary was even less relevant: its key extra-European enterprises included the participation of 300 marines to the repression of the Boxer Rebellion in China and the exploration of the uninhabited Franz Josef archipelago in the Arctic Ocean. Finally, Japan's rise was limited to the Far East and became visible only toward the end of the concerned period. This was spectacular if compared to the semi-colonial status of the Ottoman Empire or China, but insufficient to shape a globalization. Overall, Russia, Austria-Hungary, and Italy did play important political roles in regional affairs but had a much more modest impact on the overall international order and the associated globalization – even if nobody ignores the merits of the Italian opera, Viennese operetta, and Russian ballet that charmed audiences worldwide. The first globalization 'from above' was therefore mainly the construct of a small group of Western great powers, out of which only the United States was extra-European. They had few rules and no multinational institutions; they exercised a fluid collective hegemony which did not prevent major in-group rivalries; and, with the exception of Britain, they adopted liberal policies only for a brief period of time.

Indeed, the situation of liberalism during this period is most paradoxical. Even the anti-liberal supporters of the counter-hegemonic globalization 'from below' will agree that it would be quite difficult to construct a protectionism-based globalization 'from above.' If Nazi Germany or the Soviet Union had reached a hegemonic status, there would be no globalization today. The first wave of globalization did emerge in the context of a general move toward the adoption of liberal policies; but that move soon came to an end. It all started with the 1815–1846 rise of British liberalism. By the 1830s, the world's 'first industrializer' had good self-interested reasons to advocate free trade (Stearns 2010: 97). Between 1846 and 1860, it made constant and ultimately successful efforts to convert European states to its liberal creed. New policies were adopted all over the continent – and, more hesitantly, in the United States – leading to the 1860–1879 liberal period that gave birth to the first globalization 'from above.' Tariff barriers to imports decreased significantly and free trade became the norm. But this lasted only two decades. After 1879, all states except Britain progressively slid back toward protectionism (Baldwin and Martin 1999: 14; Chase-Dunn *et al.* 2000: 90–92; Stearns 2010: 97; Daudin *et al.* 2010: 8–9). Yet, the globalization process continued to develop until 1914. Contributing factors include colonialism and imperialism. Huge formal and informal empires emerged during this period whose economies were extensions of European ones (Baldwin and Martin 1999: 14; Daudin *et al.* 2010: 8). Besides actual conquest, the Opium Wars and the arrival of America's 'black ships' in the Bay of Tokyo illustrate the pattern of opening up remote lands to the global economy: 'it was literally impossible now for any large region to isolate itself from international trade and international visitors' (Stearns 2010: 97). The fact that there was no war between the main powers between 1871 and 1914 also favored trade (Daudin *et al.* 2010: 8; Baldwin and Martin 1999: 29).

In addition to the early decline of liberalism, the first globalization surprises present observers because it emerged and developed 'without any effective international institutions or formal rules' (Baldwin and Martin 1999: 29). Differently from the Bretton Woods multilateral institutions or GATT, international organizations were consequences, not causes of this globalization. The International Telegraph Union (1865), the Universal Postal Union (1874), and the Paris Convention on Industrial Property (1883) were some of the scientific and technical organizations created and expanded in response to the need for coordination associated with the new globalized context. Some international political organizations followed, such as the Hague Permanent Court of Arbitration at the origin of the International Court of Justice. They were accompanied by the adoption of humanitarian standards.

The Red Cross, established in 1863, greatly expanded its reach. The first and second Geneva Conventions of 1864 and 1907 and the Hague Conventions of 1899 and 1907 codified the modern-day law of war. International non-governmental organizations, which first emerged in the 1860s, developed significantly during the 1880s (Daudin *et al.* 2010: 18–19; Stearns 2010: 98, 107–110). Such institutional structures and ideational changes reinforced the globalization 'from above,' but certainly did not represent its main engines.

Scholars have also identified economic differences between the first and the current globalizations 'from above' that are important enough to justify titles such as 'Two Waves of Globalisation: Superficial Similarities, Fundamental Differences' (Baldwin and Martin 1999). First, initial conditions were very different. In the 19th century, 'all the world was poor and agrarian.' The present globalization, on the contrary, found a world where colonialism had contributed to the sharp division between the rich North and the poor South (*Ibid.*, ii, 29). The overall effects in terms of economic development were similarly different. Stimulated by the very large initial income gap, the present wave of globalization has deindustrialized the North – which has experienced rapid income convergence – and brought the very fast industrialization of a part of the South. The first one, on the contrary, industrialized the North – where income convergence was nevertheless slow – and deindustrialized the South, thus creating wide income divergence between the two regions. For transportation and communication, costs fell equally fast in the first globalization. During the present one – and especially since 1980 – communication costs diminished much faster than transport ones. This is part of a wider difference: 'trade in ideas is more important in the second wave' (*Ibid.*, 6, 29). The first globalization was characterized by long-term capital flows mainly consisting of investment from the North in primary product sectors and railroads in the South. The present one is based on huge intra-industry short-term flows 'driven by a frenetic pace of information exchange and advances in information technology' that focus on manufacturing, services, and outsourcing. Finally, the nature of trade is different. More than one century ago, commerce was mainly inter-industry and was driven by differences in factor endowments and technology. Today, it is intra-industry and driven by scale economies and product differentiation (*Ibid.*, 29).

An even bigger difference is related to a concept that, today, we tend to perceive as the quintessential enemy of globalization: nationalism. It is quite difficult to associate nationalists with a predisposition for intense international cooperation. We would hardly expect somebody with President Trump's ideas to construct or expand a globalization. And yet, this is exactly what happened from 1870 to 1914. This period simultaneously witnessed the progress of international integration and the expansion of triumphant nationalism from the West and Latin America to India, Turkey, the Arab lands, and some African leaders. The Ottoman and Habsburg multinational empires faced increasing difficulties in preserving their control on ethnic groups animated by the new nationalist pathos. Colonial empires started to be challenged by the nationalist movements that would eventually bring their downfall. Nevertheless, until 'the violent explosion of national rivalries that constituted World War I' (Stearns 2010: 117–118) brought it to an end, the first globalization emerged and expanded in parallel with the rise of its archenemy. This is a fascinating phenomenon that, as explained in Subchapter 6.1, led to the simultaneous development of nationalism and a specific form of cosmopolitanism. In turn, the latter provided the basis for the first globalization 'from below.' A final difference between the two waves of globalization concerns the degree of commitment of their respective participants. Today, there can be little doubt that, with the exception of North Korea and perhaps Cuba, the entire planet is fully globalized. During the first wave, significant divisions existed among levels of commitment in Western Europe, at one extreme, and regions such as the Middle East or China, at the other. Even there, reformers and businessmen hailed new ideas and opportunities brought by the contact with remote lands. But Western domination of trade, as well as imperialism, did generate serious resistance. Accordingly, the 'basic decision to commit to globalization had yet to come' (*Ibid.*, 118).

Ultimately, all these differences make many contemporary observers claim that the first globalization was 'nascent and incomplete' (*Ibid.*, 91); that is, inferior to the one we are experiencing. Still, few deny that it was a genuine globalization 'from above' whose overall trajectory was similar to that followed by the present globalization at least until the mid-1990s, when the pre-1914 level of integration was finally reached and the post-Cold War world was resolutely moving toward 'hyperglobalization.' It can be argued that both similarities and differences come mainly from the specific type of hegemony and the associated projection of normative power that characterize the two waves. After 1945, the liberal hegemon used its normative power to impose a liberal international order based on clear norms and rules, supported by formal multilateral institutions, and conducive to a globalization 'from above.' This pattern has the obvious advantage of ensuring unity, coherence, and effectiveness. From 1870 to 1914, there was no unity: hegemony was exercised collectively by an evolving group of rival Western powers. There was little coherence: these powers shared common liberal values only for one decade and then split between liberalism (Britain) and protectionism (everybody else). And there was limited effectiveness: the international organizations that could significantly have enhanced globalization emerged belatedly and remained modest. A conclusion could be drawn about the *quality* of the normative power projection that constructs a globalization. In the last part of the 19th century, Western powers did shape what is 'normal' in global politics and were able to associate this new normal with globalization. But they represented a less-than-perfect hegemon whose inbuilt problems predictably translated into imperfections of its normative power and the ensuing globalizing construct. Still, all this is less important than the fact that even such problems were unable to prevent the first globalization from surviving and developing for almost half a century. Despite its dramatic 1914 end, the first wave shows that globalizations 'from above' are resilient phenomena.

The same can be said about the first wave globalization 'from below,' parts of which outlived the 'from above' one for decades. Similar to the present Chinese case, the two post-1870 globalizations relied on the same projection of normative power. From Alexandria to Shanghai, migrants to semi-colonial port cities benefited from the favorable framework created by the normative power of the Western hegemonic powers, which had established a specific international order and an associated globalization 'from above.' However, China's present entrepreneurial migrants have adopted its deterritorialized nationalism, which allows the Chinese-centered globalizations 'from above' and 'from below' to form a virtuous circle that serves Beijing's geoeconomic and geopolitical interests (see Chapter 5). The migrants of the first wave globalization 'from below' were cosmopolitan, acquired a significant degree of autonomy, and, at times, tried to project their own normative power in ways detrimental to the interests of the great powers that were protecting them (see Chapter 6). As its 'from above' counterpart, the first wave globalization 'from below' reveals interesting aspects that usefully complement the findings of more recent case studies.

2.5 The Globalizations' Triangle

The strange coexistence of nationalism and first wave cosmopolitanism is a good example of empirical elements associated with globalizations 'from below' that include a significant theoretical dimension, which could have been presented in this chapter. This is not an exception. The equally paradoxical deterritorialized nationalism successfully promoted by the overseas Chinese state among China's entrepreneurial migrants in the BRI states, or the specific features of the transnational social movements involved in the counter-hegemonic globalization 'from below' fall in the same category. However, I believe that separating the analysis of such topics into a theoretical section inserted here and an empirical one placed in a different chapter would be detrimental to the coherence and quality of this book. Returning to the example of cosmopolitanism, such a separation would be rather frustrating. This is a phenomenon characterized by closely interwoven theoretical and empirical aspects anchored in a specific political, economic, and social context. The theory cannot be understood by somebody unaware of that context; and the depiction of factual elements needs to be accompanied by a theoretical analysis. Scrutinizing this topic in two different chapters would be analytically counterproductive with no benefit other than the respect for a rigid scholarly convention. Consequently, I decided to place the entire study of each globalization 'from below' in a separate chapter.

Even more importantly, I have to remind that, as mentioned in the Introduction and at the very beginning of this chapter, it is in Chapter 7 that I

52 Globalizations and Normative Power

decided to place the in-depth theoretical analysis of the globalizations 'from below' as a Social Sciences concept. I made this decision after thoroughly considering all relevant factors and implications. Critically, I am not using a pre-existing theory to study these four globalizations. On the contrary: I am using the findings of chapters that explore each of them to construct a common theoretical framework and define a new concept. It does not make much sense to present here the detailed theory and definition of globalizations 'from below' based on elements that the reader will see later on. This line of reasoning is reinforced by an aspect related to the academic background of this book's potential audience. It is highly unlikely that a majority of its readers may be familiar with more than one globalization 'from below.' Much of what they are going to read pertains to unfamiliar fields or subfields of the Social Sciences. It would be quite frustrating to first see the conclusions drawn from the analysis of unknown phenomena and, one hundred pages later, to finally find out their details and understand the logic of those conclusions. This, I believe, fully justifies my atypical choice of complementing the present chapter with the analysis placed in the highly theoretical Chapter 7. However, the inquisitive readers interested in understanding *hic et nunc*[1] all the details of the theoretical approach I propose can do it without delay: they should simply jump to the beginning of Chapter 7 and read it before the chapters dealing with each globalization 'from below.' Personally, I think that following the normal order of chapters will lead to a better understanding of the book's overall contribution.

Returning to the present chapter, its main goal is to discuss the more general but critical aspects of the relationship between international order, globalization 'from above,' and globalization 'from below.' The latter cannot exist in the absence of 'from above' globalizing processes. Previous subchapters show that, in turn, globalizations 'from above' rely – in addition to technological progress – on favorable policies and conditions that cannot exist outside of a hegemonic international order. They are always the result of a projection of normative power, which reinforces the order previously or simultaneously constructed by the hegemon. It is at this point that significant divergences emerge between the findings of this chapter and common expectations due to the unconscious extrapolation of the present globalization's features. When speaking about globalizations 'from above,' present-day people spontaneously think of a pattern based on a liberal hegemonic great power, clear norms and rules, formal multilateral institutions, and a resulting liberal international order. Moreover, 'liberal' means in fact Neo-liberal, which implicitly involves negative socio-economic consequences. The victims are smaller and weaker actors that need to defend themselves. Accordingly, ensuing globalizations 'from below' can only be hostile to the dominant one. However, the first wave of globalization shows that the hegemon does not need to be one great power. There can be collective hegemony, and the composition of the hegemonic group may even change in time. More importantly, the hegemon does not need to be genuinely liberal. In many regards, China is not; and, except for Britain, the hegemonic powers of the first globalization adopted protectionism after only one decade. Norms and rules do not need to be clear. More than one century ago they were not, and China's relationality makes their formal content irrelevant. Its unacknowledged norms are at least as important as the much-vaunted Five Principles. Similarly, the first globalization shows that the existence of multilateral institutions is not absolutely necessary. Even the international order that supports globalizations may not need to be genuinely liberal. Within the BRI, China speaks of multilateralism but exclusively promotes bilateral relationships between itself and each partner state. It only opens their economies for its own state-owned enterprises through government-to-government agreements that eliminate competition from any other country. If a fully fledged Chinese global or bounded order is constructed, all its member states will be closely connected with the hegemon's economy; but there will be no framework to stimulate horizontal cooperation among them. Liberalism-as-we-know-it will be greatly distorted if not completely missing. Finally, the first wave of globalization shows that, when it is present, liberalism does not need to be Neoliberalism. Even then there are winners and losers of a globalization, but socio-economic polarization may be less dramatic. Among the smaller and weaker actors, this could result in globalizations 'from below' that, far from resisting or even challenging the globalization 'from above,' combine with it in a virtuous circle similar to the Chinese one.

All this shows that globalizations actually come in many shapes and forms. Their features are much more diverse than one might expect. Still, there is always a triangular relationship between an actual or emerging hegemonic international order, a globalization 'from above' that both supports and is reinforced by this order, and one or more globalizations 'from below' that either join this virtuous circle or challenge it. The cement that binds together the elements of this triangle is the hegemon's normative power. Its projection directly constructs the order and the globalization 'from above.' The case of the globalizations 'from below' is more interesting. Its actors can simply take advantage of the same power projection; or, despite their Lilliputian condition, they can try to transform themselves into sources of normative power and impose their own 'conceptions of normal.'

2.6 Transnationalism

As repeatedly stated, the most important goal of this chapter is to analyze the triangular relationship mentioned in the previous paragraph. However, before proceeding to the study of the four globalizations 'from below,' a key concept related to all globalizations has to be discussed. The term 'transnational' and its derivatives are mentioned 25 times in the chapter on the counter-hegemonic globalization 'from below'; 74 times in the chapter that analyzes the non-hegemonic globalization 'form below'; 45 times in the chapter on the Chinese-centered globalization 'from below'; and 10 times in the chapter that explores the first wave globalization 'from below' (which, due to the specific features of that historical period, gives preference to the concept of cosmopolitanism as discussed in Subchapter 6.1). Transnationalism and transnational actors cannot be ignored by any scholar involved in the study of globalizations. In fact, two decades ago, the entire field of International Relations experienced the so-called 'transnational turn,' which 'attributed a considerable degree of importance to transnational activities beyond the state' (Terhalle 2016: 290). The resulting theoretical apparatus is most relevant to this book as it reveals the central role played by transnational actors in the creation and development of globalizations 'from below.'

The term 'trans-national' was first used by Randolph S. Bourne in an article he published back in 1916 in the *Atlantic Monthly*. During World War I, Americans of Anglo-Saxon descent distrusted immigrants they associated with certain European powers. Bourne argued that 'trans-nationality' limited such attitudes in the United States by creating a strong cosmopolitan state, which transcended nationalism and its negative consequences. This interpretation of transnationalism as a form of cosmopolitanism was, in fact, mirroring widely shared understandings specific to the first wave globalization (see Chapter 6). However, the eventual evolution of the term brought it closer to the realm of 'border-crossing actors or networks' (Malet and Anderson 2017: 4). Scholars seem to have a preference for the exploration of its 'conceptual' or 'intellectual' history (see 'Capturing the Transnational: A Conceptual History,' Jönsson 2010; 'International Relations and Transnational Actors: a Short Intellectual History,' Risse 2013: 428–430). They place the first manifestations of transnationalism in the Middle Ages and identify the Renaissance Medici and Fugger 'family businesses' as examples of fully fledged transnational actors that were active in Western Europe, India, and China. In the scholarly realm, Immanuel Kant's cosmopolitanism (see Subchapter 6.1) and the ideas about free trade and peace shared by Adam Smith and John Stuart Mill were the first contributions to the emergence of the new concept. Those of David Mitrany, Ernest Haas, and Karl Deutsch were added during the 1940s and the 1950s (Risse 2013: 428–429; Thiel and Maslanik 2010: 11). But it was Raymond Aron's conception of 'transnational society,' set up in his *Paix et guerre entre les nations* (Aron 1962), that directly influenced Robert Keohane and Joseph Nye in making a major contribution to the field. The special issue of *International Organization* on 'Transnational Relations and World Politics' they co-edited in 1971 (which was also published that same year as a book) (Keohane and Nye 1971; Jönsson 2010: 23) introduced the current understanding of transnationalism as part of their Complex Interdependence theoretical approach. It was at this time that scholarly works finally started to be published that turned transnational actors and relations into their main topic instead of just mentioning them as secondary aspects of other socio-political phenomena (Risse 2013: 429). However, a strong Realist reaction followed, with Robert

Gilpin arguing that transnational actors such as multinational corporations are nothing more than agents of states (Gilpin 1971; Gilpin 1975). Kenneth Waltz's Neorealism and the Hegemonic Stability Theory soon emerged that similarly rejected the autonomy of all sub-state actors. Even Keohane's Neoliberalism discouraged the study of transnationalism because it emphasized interstate cooperation under international anarchy (Risse 2013: 429–430). But this negative trend was stopped by the end of the Cold War, which represents the 'central transformative event in the historical development' of transnational actors (Tallberg *et al.* 2013: 4). As it 'opened up considerably more structural space for nonstate actors to maneuver,' the latter's activities 'mushroomed' (Terhalle 2016: 290; Thiel and Maslanik 2010: 12). Four causal factors were identified. First, the democratization of previously communist and authoritarian states revived the civil society domestically, which increased the potential for transnational linkages. The fall of communism also liberalized economic activities and opened borders, which led to the dramatic expansion of trade and investment relations. Second, certain civil society groups experienced growing formalization, which increased their ability to engage in cross-border activities. Third, the spectacular development of the Western-centered globalization 'from above' greatly stimulated economic, political, social, and cultural transnational interactions. Fourth, states and international organizations engaged certain categories of transnational actors in processes of norms creation and development, as well as standard-setting; accepted them as compliance watchdogs and reviewers of implementation processes; and incorporated their expertise into the operation of international organizations (Terhalle 2016: 290). Unsurprisingly, these changes were reflected in a surge of scholarly research on transnational actors and processes in International Relations, Sociology, Anthropology, Geography, Economics, and other Social Sciences. Transnationalism became an instrument used to study migration, diasporas, citizenship, and identities. The 9/11 attacks added fields such as terrorism and organized crime (Jönsson 2010: 28). This expansion of the concept's domains of applicability was the first component of the aforementioned 'transnational turn' in global politics (Terhalle 2016: 290). The second one was the rise of postpositivist approaches in general and of Constructivism in particular, which led to a 'normative turn' in the research on transnational actors. Principled ideas began to be studied as the engine of transnational activism. Epistemic communities and advocacy networks became the object of analyses that targeted the transnational promotion and diffusion of causal knowledge and norms, respectively (Thiel and Maslanik 2010: 12–13). During the 1990s, research concentrated on the influence of transnational actors on interstate relations, which concerned both intergovernmental organizations and individual states. This trend continues, as illustrated by the study of transnational social movements involved in the counter-hegemonic globalization 'from below.' But in the 2000s, a new direction of research was added that focuses on the contribution of transnational actors to rule-making and the provision of collective goods, i.e., to transnational governance. This concept includes 'governance with governments,' which may be based on public-private partnerships, and 'governance without governments,' such as private self-regulation (Risse 2013: 426). It should nevertheless be mentioned that, despite the remarkable progress of this field of research, not all International Relations scholars perceive it as a useful development. Realists continue to reject the idea that non-state actors can act autonomously. Marxists also believe that entities such as the multinational corporations are nothing more than agents of capitalist states. The only genuine transnational actors they acknowledge are those involved in class struggles. Only Neoliberals and Constructivists share favorable views. The former believe that the bargaining and monitoring of trade or the protection of the environment are processes best understood in a transnational perspective. Constructivists go much further. Their emphasis on values, norms, and ideas makes them perceive the international environment as a 'globally diverse world' whose various 'actors, interests, and identities (...) aim at the advancement of pluralistic values in an increasingly transnational political space' (Thiel and Maslanik 2010: 4). This is why it is not exaggerated to argue that, in the realm of International Relations, Constructivism is best endowed to study transnationalism, as well as closely related phenomena such as globalizations.

Given the diversity of the Social Sciences fields that make use of transnationalism, a widely accepted definition is still missing. Almost all studies of related phenomena start by quoting the 1971 seminal work of Keohane and Nye. In its Introduction, they defined transnational interactions as 'the movement of tangible or intangible items across state boundaries when at least one actor is not an agent of a government or an intergovernmental organization' (Nye and Keohane 1971a: 332). However, they understood transnational relations as the sum of transnational and transgovernmental interactions; the latter involve 'governmental subunits across state boundaries' (*Ibid.*). Accordingly, the two scholars defined transnational relations as 'contacts, coalitions, and interactions across state boundaries that are not controlled by the central foreign policy organs of governments' (Nye and Keohane 1971b: 331). Other authors have coined definitions that diverge considerably due to their focus on aspects specific to their respective fields of research. For example, Gralf-Peter Calliess and Jens Steffek identified three distinct 'definitional strategies' related to the use of transnationalism in Political Science and Law. Transnationalism can be an umbrella concept that covers all cross-border regulatory arrangements; it can be limited to arrangements in the private sector; or it can focus on public-private regulatory arrangements (Calliess and Steffek quoted by Jönsson 2010: 29–30). In migration studies, the same concept was defined as 'the ways in which immigrants develop intensely networked social fields that span geographic, cultural and political borders and connect home and host societies through multifarious linkages' (Zack 2015: 135). Some of these narrower definitions are useful to the understanding of certain globalizations 'from below' and are therefore discussed in their specific context (see Subchapter 4.4 for the migration studies one). However, as this book needs a unifying theoretical framework, I chose to use a general definition inspired by but different from those proposed by Keohane and Nye for transnational interactions and relations. I define transnational relations as contacts, coalitions, and interactions across state boundaries where at least one actor is not an agent of a government or an intergovernmental organization. Keohane and Nye excluded the involvement of 'the central foreign policy organs of governments.' Such an approach is too narrow to allow for the study of globalizations 'from below' enacted by small actors that take advantage of the support provided by the hegemon of a globalization 'from above.' To give a clear example, the Chinese globalization 'from below' cannot be understood without taking into consideration the overseas Chinese state, which is a central foreign policy organ of China's government deeply involved in the transnational relations of the Chinese entrepreneurial migrants (the Chinese 'state transnationalism' is discussed in detail in Subchapter 5.2). 'From below' actors are autonomous and always play the main role within the transnationalism associated with globalizations 'from below.' Yet, the latter are complex and diversified social phenomena that, in two cases out of four, actually rely on state – and, more specifically, hegemonic – support.

This brings the discussion to the definition of transnational actors, which is as disputed as that of transnational relations. For example, David Malet and Miriam Anderson provided a typically Constructivist understanding of this concept, which comprises 'entities that work through non-state mobilizing structures, entities that are perceived to be beyond the state, and those who self-identify as transnational' (Malet and Anderson 2017: 5). I prefer to use the perhaps more consensual definition proposed by Markus Thiel and Jeffrey Maslanik. It depicts transnational actors as 'political, social, cultural, and economic agents or groups that have transsocietal relations across borders. They pursue their goals somewhat independently of governmental considerations' (Thiel and Maslanik 2010: 1). The 'somewhat independently' aspect eliminates any incompatibility with the globalizations 'from below' supported by a hegemon mentioned in the previous paragraph. Lists of transnational actors often mention multinational corporations, international non-governmental organizations (including religious ones), transnational social movements, epistemic communities, advocacy networks, diasporas, migrant networks, international terrorist groups, transnational criminal organizations, and individuals. One way or another, all of them take advantage of the interconnectedness created by the Western-centered globalization 'from above.' Not all, however, are relevant to the case of globalizations 'from below.' The latter obviously exclude multinational corporations, which are 'from above' actors *par excellence*. Out of the international non-governmental organizations, transnational social movements, epistemic communities, advocacy networks, and individuals, only those that adopt, explicitly or implicitly, an alter-globalist agenda pertain to the counter-hegemonic globalization 'from below.' Parts of diasporas, migrant networks, and transnational 'criminal' organizations (for example, those involved in the informal international trade in counterfeit goods), as well as many individuals (such as the 'ant traders'), enact the non-hegemonic and Chinese-centered globalizations 'from below.' The first wave globalization 'from below' also included a large number of political refugees. These are very different actors involved in very different activities. But they all have in common the fact that 'they organize across national borders in transnational arrangements or coalitions to realize their objectives' either independently or autonomously from 'governmental oversight and control' (Thiel and Maslanik 2010: 3). The cumulative effect of their transnational 'arrangements or coalitions' was powerful enough to lead to the emergence of four fully fledged globalizations.

Given the number and variety of these transnational actors, no definitive typology has been established. However, Thomas Risse proposed a classification based on two dimensions. On the one hand, with respect to their internal structure, actors above the level of individuals can be either formal organizations or more loose and non-hierarchical networks. On the other hand, based on their constitutive purposes, transnational actors can be associated with either instrumental – that is, mainly economic – gains (they struggle for 'the well-being of the organization' and its members, to put it more elegantly) or the promotion of ideas and knowledge (and, more precisely, of 'principled beliefs or what they see as a (global) common good') (Risse 2013: 427–428; Jönsson 2010: 31; Thiel and Maslanik 2010: 3–4). But the distinction between for-profit and non-profit activities is not always clear-cut. The global justice movement and the Chinese entrepreneurial migrants find easily their place in one of these categories. Yet, some of the cosmopolitan actors of the first wave globalization 'from below' were, at the same time, traders and political activists. The 'ant traders' of the non-hegemonic globalization 'from below' are obviously interested in money, but they – sometimes, knowingly – also fight Neoliberalism and, in places such as Argentina's La Salada, construct alternative modernities. This is why 'it is useful to think of this distinction as a continuum rather than sharply divided classes of actors' (Risse 2013: 428). Other criteria were also used to classify transnational actors. Based on their relations with states or intergovernmental organizations, Gralf-Peter Calliess and Jens Steffek divided such actors into lobbyists, partners, adversaries, and functional substitutes for states, which perform regulatory functions (Calliess and Steffek quoted by Jönsson 2010: 36). In their analysis of 'contentious politics,' Charles Tilly and Sidney Tarrow took into consideration a more sensitive dimension. They noted that, during the 1990s, the study of transnationalism focused on movements related to human rights, environmental concerns, and women's movements. As they fight oppression, torture, land mines, or pollution, these are 'good' movements. After 9/11, a 'different family of transnational movements developed' that is based on religious fundamentalism and the 'terrorism industry.' Al Qaeda and the Islamic State pertain to this category of 'bad' movements (Tilly and Tarrow 2015: 201). At first view, such a classification relies on moral values. However, any follower of Antonio Gramsci and Robert Cox will argue that this is, in fact, about power and its ability to legitimize a highly politicized perception of a reality that is understood very differently in Washington and Raqqa. The implications of this line of reasoning go far beyond the issue of Islamist terrorism. In the words of Markus Thiel and Jeffrey Maslanik, 'transnational does not simply signify international; it refers to the organization of power beyond the state' (Thiel and Maslanik 2010: 3). The powerful actors of the American-led international order and Western-centered globalization 'from above' discussed in Subchapter 2.1 have been rather successful in imposing their views on what is 'good' and 'bad' in economic, political, social, and cultural terms. Obviously, this is a projection of normative power that has reshaped 'conceptions of normal' worldwide. The small and weak actors dissatisfied with this situation are unable to change it by acting alone or as part of alliances limited to the frameworks of nation-states. It is in this respect that transnationalism reveals itself as a fundamental dimension of globalizations 'from below.' By adding a cross-border dimension, it hugely expands the repertoire and capabilities of small actors up to the point where the effects of their 'contacts, coalitions, and interactions' become comparable with those of hegemons, multilateral institutions, and multinational corporations. This allows them to contribute 'to the normative creation of international order' (*Ibid.*) by constructing their own globalizations.

Of course, not all transnational actors choose to fight hegemons. A classification can be made based on their positioning with respect to the hegemonic projection of normative power and, implicitly, the related 'from above' globalization. Arguably, such a classification is more useful to the understanding of the global role played by transnational actors than many of the typologies presented in the previous paragraph. Its first category is that of transnational actors associated with the globalizations 'from above.' It includes multinational corporations, as well as many international non-governmental organizations, epistemic communities, and individuals that, directly or indirectly, contribute to the 'from above' projection of normative power of the Neoliberal globalization and/or fully accept its effects. The second category is that of 'from below' transnational actors that, while producing and projecting their own normative power, create a globalization 'from below' by relying mainly on the projection of normative power of the hegemon of a globalization 'from above.' This is the case of Chinese entrepreneurial migrants that enact the Chinese-centered globalization 'from below' and the cosmopolitan actors of the first wave globalization 'from below.' The final category includes all actors that, explicitly or implicitly, challenge the Neoliberal globalization 'from above.' As already mentioned earlier in this subchapter, it comprises various international non-governmental organizations, transnational social movements, epistemic communities, and advocacy networks, as well as many individuals and parts of diasporas, migrant networks, and transnational economic organizations involved in informal/illegal trade. It is due to their efforts that the counter-hegemonic and non-hegemonic globalizations 'from below' emerged and developed. A legitimate question concerns the possible existence of a fourth category, that of transnational actors that do not take part in any globalization. I strongly believe that no such entity can exist today. Even transnational associations of cat lovers or poetry readers take advantage of the interconnectedness associated with the Western-centered globalization 'from above.' Their functioning either fits 'conceptions of normal' shaped by this globalization, implicitly supporting it, or – if an André Breton is in command – tries to revolutionize them, which brings it within the counter-hegemonic globalization 'from below.' In a globalized era, all transnational actors are part of a globalization; and all globalizations 'from below' are the direct product of the 'contacts, coalitions, and interactions' of such actors.

The following chapters analyze the role played by transnational actors in the creation and working of the four globalizations 'from below' against the backdrop of the international order-globalization 'from above'-globalization 'from below' triangular relationship discussed in the previous subchapters. The specific features of each globalization 'from below' are also scrutinized. Their common elements are identified in order to construct a general theoretical framework and provide a definition of the concept of globalizations 'from below,' which is done in Chapter 7.

Note

1 Here and now (Latin).

References

Abu-Lughod, Janet (1990) 'Restructuring the Premodern World-System,' *Review* (Fernand Braudel Center), 13(2), pp. 273–286.

Acharya, Amitav (2011) *Asian Regional Institutions and the Possibilities for Socializing the Behavior of States*, ADB Working Paper Series on Regional Economic Integration No. 82, Asian Development Bank, https://www.adb.org/publications/asian-regional-institutions-and-possibilities-socializing-behavior-states

Acharya, Amitav (2018) *Constructing Global Order: Agency and Change in World Politics*, Cambridge, United Kingdom; New York: Cambridge University Press.

Allan, Bentley B., Srdjan Vucetic, and Ted Hopf (2018) 'The Distribution of Identity and the Future of International Order: China's Hegemonic Prospects,' *International Organization*, 72(4), pp. 839–869.

Alon, Ilan, Wenxian Zhang, and Christoph Lattemann (2018) 'Introduction,' in Wenxian Zhang, Ilan Alon, and Christoph Lattemann (eds.) *China's Belt and Road Initiative. Changing the Rules of Globalization*, Cham, Switzerland: Palgrave Macmillan, pp. 1–14.

Aron, Raymond (1962) *Paix et guerre entre les nations*, Paris: Calmann-Lévy.

Ayers, Alison J. (2013) 'Beyond Myths, Lies and Stereotypes: The Political Economy of a "New Scramble for Africa",' *New Political Economy*, 18(2), pp. 227–257.

Baldwin, Richard E., and Philippe Martin (1999) 'Two Waves of Globalisation: Superficial Similarities, Fundamental Differences,' *NBER Working Papers* 6904, National Bureau of Economic Research, https://www.nber.org/papers/w6904

Bandaranayake, Sukitha (2020) 'China and the International Order. By Michael J. Mazarr, Timothy R. Heath, and Astrid Stuth Cevallos,' Book review, *Journal of East Asian Studies*, 20(1), pp. 121–123.

Barnett, Michael, and Raymond Duvall (2005) 'Power in International Politics,' *International Organization* 59(1), pp. 39–75.

Bernal, Richard L. (2016) *Dragon in the Caribbean: China's Global Re-Dimensioning - Challenges and Opportunities for the Caribbean* (Revised and Updated Edition), Kindle Edition, Kingston, Jamaica: Ian Randle Publishers.

Best, Heinrich, and John Higley (eds.) (2018) *The Palgrave Handbook of Political Elites*, London: Palgrave Macmillan.

Braudel, Fernand (1949) *La Méditerranée et le monde méditerranéen à l'époque de Philippe II*, Paris: A. Colin.

Braudel, Fernand (1967) *Civilisation matérielle et capitalisme, XVe-XVIIIe siècle*, Tome I, *Les Structures du quotidien : le possible et l'impossible*, Paris: A. Collin.

Braudel, Fernand (1979) *Civilisation matérielle et capitalisme, XVe-XVIIIe siècle*, Tome I, *Les Structures du quotidien : le possible et l'impossible*, Tome II *Les Jeux de l'échange*, Tome III *Le Temps du monde*, Paris: A. Collin.

Brecher, Jeremy, Tim Costello, and Brendan Smith (2000) *Globalization from Below: The Power of Solidarity*, Cambridge, MA: South End Press.

Callahan, William A. (2016) 'Chinas "Asia Dream": The Belt Road Initiative and the New Regional Order,' *Asian Journal of Comparative Politics*, 1(3), pp. 226–243.

Cau, Enrico (2018) 'Geopolitical Implications of the Belt and Road Initiative: The Backbone for a New World Order?,' *Contemporary Chinese Political Economy and Strategic Relations: An International Journal*, 4(1), pp. 39–105.

Chase-Dunn, Christopher, Yukio Kawano, and Benjamin D. Brewer (2000) 'Trade Globalization since 1795: Waves of Integration in the World-System,' *American Sociological Review*, 65(1), pp. 77–95.

Checkel, Jeffrey T. (1999) 'Social Construction and Integration,' *Journal of European Public Policy*, 6(4), pp. 545–560.

Checkel, Jeffrey T. (2005) 'International Institutions and Socialization in Europe: Introduction and Framework,' *International Organization*, 59(4), pp. 801–826.

D'Onofrio, Alexandra, and Peter L. Rousseau (2018) 'Financial Development, Trade Openness and Growth in the First Wave of Globalization,' *Comparative Economic Studies*, 60, pp. 105–114.

Daudin, Guillaume, Matthias Morys, and Kevin H. O'Rourke (2010) 'Globalization, 1870–1914,' in Stephen Broadberry and Kevin H.O'Rourke (eds.) *The Cambridge Economic History of Modern Europe Volume 2. 1870 to the Present*, Cambridge: Cambridge University Press, pp. 5–29.

Dauvergne, Peter, and Déborah B. L. Farias (2012) 'The Rise of Brazil as a Global Developmental Power,' *Third World Quarterly*, 33(5), pp. 903–917.

Demir, Emre (2017) 'The Chinese School of International Relations: Myth or Reality?,' *All Azimuth*, 6(2), pp. 95–104.

Deudney, Daniel, and G. John Ikenberry (1999) 'The Nature and Sources of Liberal International Order,' *Review of International Studies*, 25(2), pp. 179–196.

Development Aid (2019) 'Introducing China's New Development Agency CIDCA - Big Expectations to Change the Country's Foreign Aid Sector and Make a Difference to the World,' September 24, https://www.developmentaid.org/#!/news-stream/post/50469/introducing-chinas-new-development-agency-cidca-big-expectations-to-change-the-countrys-foreign-aid-sector-and-make-a-difference-to-the-world

Diez, Thomas (2005) 'Constructing the Self and Changing Others: Reconsidering "Normative Power Europe",' *Millennium: Journal of International Studies*, 33(3), pp. 613–636.

Diez, Thomas (2013) 'Normative Power as Hegemony,' *Cooperation and Conflict*, 48(2), pp. 194–210.

Diez, Thomas and Ian Manners (2007) 'Reflecting on Normative Power Europe,' in Felix Berenskoetter and Michael J. Williams (eds.) *Power in World Politics*, New York: Routledge, pp. 173–188.

Falk, Richard (1997) 'Resisting "Globalisation-from-Above" through "Globalisation-from-Below",' *New Political Economy*, 2(1), pp. 17–24.

Ferdinand, Peter (2016) 'Westward Ho-the China Dream and "One Belt, One Road": Chinese Foreign Policy under Xi Jinping,' *International Affairs*, 92(4), pp. 941–957.

Fernando, Jason (2020) 'Globalization,' *Investopedia*, December 12, https://www.investopedia.com/terms/g/globalization.asp

Flockhart, Trine (2006) '"Complex Socialization': A Framework for the Study of State Socialization,' *European Journal of International Relations*, 12(1), pp. 89–118.

Forsberg, Tuomas (2011) 'Normative Power Europe, Once Again: A Conceptual Analysis of an Ideal Type,' *Journal of Common Market Studies*, 49(6), pp. 1183–1204.

Frank, Andre Gunder (1990) 'A Theoretical Introduction to 5,000 Years of World System,' *Review* (Fernand Braudel Center), 13(2), pp. 155–248.

Franke, Maria (2014) 'When One Country's Land Gain Is Another Country's Land Loss...: The Social, Ecological and Economic Dimensions of Sand Extraction in the Context of World-Systems Analysis Exemplified by Singapore's Sand Imports,' Working Paper, No. 36/2014, Hochschule für Wirtschaft und Recht Berlin, Institute for International Political Economy (IPE), Berlin, https://www.econstor.eu/bitstream/10419/97163/1/784933251.pdf

French, Howard W. (2014) *China's Second Continent. How a Million Migrants Are Building a New Empire in Africa*, New York: Alfred A. Knopf.

Gago, Verónica (2012) 'La Salada: ¿un caso de globalización «desde abajo»? Territorio de una nueva economía política transnacional,' *Nueva Sociedad*, Sep/Oct, 241, pp.63-78, https://nuso.org/articulo/la-salada-un-caso-de-globalizacion-desde-abajo-territorio-de-una-nueva-economia-politica-transnacional/

Gago, Verónica (2014/2017) *Neoliberalism from Below: Popular Pragmatics and Baroque Economies*, Durham: Duke University Press, revized edition of *La razón neoliberal: economías barrocas y pragmática popular*, Buenos Aires: Tinta Limón, 2014.

Gekas, Athanasios (Sakis) (2009) 'Class and Cosmopolitanism: the Historiographical Fortunes of Merchants in Eastern Mediterranean Ports,' *Mediterranean Historical Review*, 24(2), pp. 95–114.

Gilpin, Robert (1971) 'The Politics of Transnational Economic Relations,' in Robert O. Keohane and Joseph S. Nye Jr. (eds.) *Transnational Relations and World Politics*, Cambridge, MA: Harvard University Press, pp. 48–69.

Gilpin, Robert (1975) *U.S. Power and the Multinational Corporation: The Political Economy of Foreign Direct Investment*, New York: Basic Books.

Goldstein, Avery (2020) 'China's Grand Strategy under Xi Jinping: Reassurance, Reform, and Resistance,' *International Security*, 45(1), pp. 164–201.

Hall, Ian (2017) 'Narendra Modi and India's Normative Power,' *International Affairs*, 93(1), pp. 113–131.

Halper, Stefan (2010) *The Beijing Consensus: How China's Authoritarian Model Will Dominate the Twenty-First Century*, New York: Basic Books.

Hamilton, Daniel S. (2008) 'The United States: A Normative Power?,' in Nathalie Tocci (ed.) *Who Is a Normative Foreign Policy Actor? The European Union and its Global Partners*, Brussels: Center for European Policy Studies, pp. 76–155.

Hao, Shinan (2015) 'China's Socialization in East Asian International Society. An Assessment from the English School Perspective 1,' *Quarterly Journal of Chinese Studies*, 3(4), pp. 82–104.

He, Alex (2019) 'The Belt and Road Initiative: Motivations, Financing, Expansion and Challenges of Xi's Ever-expanding Strategy,' *CIGI Papers* No. 225, September, Centre for International Governance Innovation, Waterloo, ON, https://www.cigionline.org/sites/default/files/documents/no.225.pdf

He, Jiajie (2016) 'Normative Power in the EU and ASEAN: Why They Diverge,' *International Studies Review*, 18(1), pp. 92–105.

He, Kai, and Huiyun Feng (2015) 'Transcending Rationalism and Constructivism: Chinese Leaders' Operational Codes, Socialization Processes, and Multilateralism after the Cold War,' *European Political Science Review*, 7(3), pp. 401–426.

Henderson, Jeffrey, Richard P. Appelbaum, and Suet Ying Ho (2013) 'Globalization with Chinese Characteristics: Externalization, Dynamics and Transformations,' *Development and Change* 44(6), pp. 1221–1253.

Heston, Alan (2002) 'Review of Fernand Braudel, Civilization and Capitalism, 15th-18th Century,' *Economic History Services*, August 1, https://eh.net/book_reviews/civilization-and-capitalism-15th-18th-century/

Higley, John (2018) 'Continuities and Discontinuities in Elite Theory,' in Heinrich Best and John Higley (eds.) *The Palgrave Handbook of Political Elites*, London: Palgrave Macmillan, pp. 25–39.

Hillman, Jonathan (2018a) 'Game of Loans. How China Bought Hambantota,' in Nicholas Szechenyi (ed.) *China's Maritime Silk Road Strategic and Economic Implications for the Indo-Pacific Region*, Washington, DC: Center for Strategic and International Studies, pp. 7–10, https://www.csis.org/analysis/chinas-maritime-silk-road

Hillman, Jonathan (2018b) 'China's Belt and Roller Coaster,' *Nikkei Asian Review*, September 14, https://asia.nikkei.com/Opinion/China-s-Belt-and-Roller-Coaster

Holden, Patrick (2009) *In Search of Structural Power: EU Aid Policy as a Global Political Instrument*, Farnham, Surrey, England; Burlington, VT: Ashgate.

Hyde-Price, Adrian (2006) '"Normative" Power Europe: A Realist Critique,' *Journal of European Public Policy*, 13(2), pp. 217–234.

Ikenberry, G. John (2018) 'The End of Liberal International Order?,' *International Affairs*, 94(1), pp. 7–23.

Ikenberry, G. John, and Charles A. Kupchan (1990) 'Socialization and Hegemonic Power,' *International Organization*, 44(3), pp. 283–315.

Jacques, Martin (2009) *When China Rules the World: The Rise of the Middle Kingdom and the End of the Western World*, London: Allen Lane.

Jahn, Beate (2018) 'Liberal Internationalism: Historical Trajectory and Current Prospects,' *International Affairs*, 94(1), pp. 43–61.

Johnston, Alastair Iain (2001) 'Treating International Institutions as Social Environments,' *International Studies Quarterly*, 45(4), pp. 487–515.

Johnston, Alastair Iain (2003) 'Socialization in International Institutions: The ASEAN Way and International Relations Theory,' in G. John Ikenberry and Michael Mastanduno (eds.), *International Relations Theory and the Asia-Pacific*, New York; Chichester, West Sussex: Columbia University Press, pp. 107–162.

Johnston, Alastair Iain (2008) *Social States: China in International Institutions, 1980–2000*. Princeton, NJ: Princeton University Press.

Jönsson, Christer (2010) 'Capturing the Transnational: A Conceptual History,' in Christer Jönsson and Jonas Tallberg (eds.) *Transnational Actors in Global Governance Patterns, Explanations, and Implications*, Houndmills, Basingstoke, Hampshire: Palgrave Macmillan, pp. 22–44.

Kalathil, Shanthi (2017) 'Globalization Chinese-Style,' review of *China's Eurasian Century? Political and Strategic Implications of the Belt and Road Initiative* by Nadège Rolland, *Journal of Democracy*, 28(4), pp. 170–174.

Kalathil, Shanthi (2018) 'Redefining Development,' *Journal of Democracy*, 29(2), pp. 52–58.

Kavalski, Emilian (2014) 'The Shadows of Normative Power in Asia: Framing the International Agency of China, India, and Japan,' *Pacific Focus*, 29(3), pp. 303–328.

Kavalski, Emilian (2016) 'The EU-India Strategic Partnership: Neither Very Strategic, Nor Much of a Partnership,' *Cambridge Review of International Affairs*, 29(1), pp. 192–208.

Kavalski, Emilian (2017) 'Normative Power Europe and Normative Power China Compared: Towards a Relational Knowledge-Production in International Relations,' *Korean Political Science Review*, 51(6), pp. 147–170.

Kavalski, Emilian (2018) 'Chinese Concepts and Relational International Politics,' *All Azimuth*, 7(1), pp. 87–102, 155–156.

Kent, Ann (2002) 'China's International Socialization: The Role of International Organizations,' *Global Governance*, 8(3), pp. 343–364.

Keohane, Robert O., and Joseph S. Nye (1977) *Power and Interdependence: World Politics in Transition*, Little, Brown.

Keohane, Robert O., and Joseph S. Nye Jr. (eds.) (1971) *Transnational Relations and World Politics*. Cambridge, MA: Harvard University Press.

Kim, Hun Joon (2016) 'Will IR Theory with Chinese Characteristics Be a Powerful Alternative?,' *The Chinese Journal of International Politics*, 9(1), pp. 59–79.

Kitchen, Nicholas, and Michael Cox (2019) 'Power, Structural Power, and American Decline,' *Cambridge Review of International Affairs*, 32(6), pp. 734–752.

Kliman, Daniel, Rush Doshi, Kristine Lee, and Zack Cooper (2019) *Grading China's Belt and Road_Report*, Center for a New American Security, April 8, https://www.cnas.org/publications/reports/beltandroad

Körösényi, András (2018) 'Political Elites and Democracy,' in Heinrich Best and John Higley (eds.) *The Palgrave Handbook of Political Elites*, London: Palgrave Macmillan, pp. 41–52.

Kumar, Radha (2008) 'India as a Foreign Policy Actor - Normative Redux,' in Nathalie Tocci (ed.) *Who Is a Normative Foreign Policy Actor? The European Union and its Global Partners*, Brussels: Center for European Policy Studies, pp. 211–264.

Lairson, Thomas D. (2018) 'The Global Strategic Environment of the BRI: Deep Interdependence and Structural Power,' in Wenxian Zhang, Ilan Alon, and Christoph Lattemann (eds.) *China's Belt and Road Initiative. Changing the Rules of Globalization*, Cham, Switzerland: Palgrave Macmillan, pp. 35–53.

Lang, Michael (2011) 'Globalization and Global History in Toynbee,' *Journal of World History*, 22(4), pp. 747–783.

Larsen, Henrik (2014) 'The EU as a Normative Power and the Research on External Perceptions: The Missing Link,' *Journal of Common Market Studies*, 52(4), pp. 896–910.

Layne, Christopher (2018) 'The US-Chinese Power Shift and the End of the Pax Americana,' *International Affairs*, 94(1), pp. 89–111.

Li, Shubo (2017) *Mediatized China-Africa Relations. How Media Discourses Negotiate the Shifting of Global Order*, Singapore: Palgrave Macmillan.

Makarychev, Andrey S. (2008) 'Rebranding Russia: Norms, Politics and Power,' in Nathalie Tocci (ed.) *Who Is a Normative Foreign Policy Actor? The European Union and Its Global Partners*, Brussels: Center for European Policy Studies, pp. 156–210.

Making History (2008) 'Global History,' https://archives.history.ac.uk/makinghistory/themes/global_history.html

Malet, David, and Miriam J. Anderson (2017) 'Introduction: The Transnational Century,' in David Malet and Miriam J. Anderson (eds.) *Transnational Actors in War and Peace: Militants, Activists, and Corporations in World Politics*, Washington, DC: Georgetown University Press, pp. 1–23.

Manners, Ian (2001) 'Normative Power Europe: The International Role of the EU,' paper presented at the *European Community Studies Association Biennial Conference*, Madison, May 31–June 2.

Manners, Ian (2002) 'Normative Power Europe: A Contradiction in Terms?,' *Journal of Common Market Studies*, 40(2), pp. 235–258.

Manners, Ian (2009) 'The Concept of Normative Power in World Politics," *DIIS BRIEF*, May, Danish Institute for International Studies, https://pure.diis.dk/ws/files/68745/B09_maj_Concept_Normative_Power_World_Politics.pdf

Manners, Ian (2013) 'The European Union's Normative Power in a more Global Era,' *EU Studies in Japan*, 33, pp. 33–55.

Manuel, Ryan (2019) 'Twists in the Belt and Road,' *China Leadership Monitor*, September 1, https://www.prcleader.org/manuel-belt-road

Martell, Luke (2007) 'The Third Wave in Globalization Theory,' *International Studies Review*, 9(2), pp. 173–196.

Mazarr, Michael J., Timothy R. Heath, and Astrid Stuth Cevallos (2018) *China and the International Order*, Santa Monica: RAND Corporation.

Mazlish, Bruce (1998) 'Comparing Global History to World History,' *The Journal of Interdisciplinary History*, 28(3), pp. 385–395.

Mearsheimer, John (2019) 'Bound to Fail: The Rise and Fall of the Liberal International Order,' *International Security*, 43(4), pp. 7–50.

Merwe, Justin van der (2019) 'The One Belt One Road Initiative: Reintegrating Africa and the Middle East into China's System of Accumulation,' in Li Xing (ed.) *Mapping China's 'One Belt One Road' Initiative*, Cham, Switzerland: Palgrave Macmillan, pp. 197–218.

Mohan, Giles, Ben Lampert, May Tan-Mullins, and Daphne Chang (2014) *Chinese Migrants and Africa's Development. New Imperialists or Agents of Change?*, London: Zed Books.

National Development and Reform Commission, Ministry of Foreign Affairs, and Ministry of Commerce of the People's Republic of China, with State Council authorization (2015) 'Vision and Actions on Jointly Building Silk Road Economic Belt and 21st-Century Maritime Silk Road,' March 18, http://en.ndrc.gov.cn/newsrelease/201503/t20150330_669367.html

Nieuwenhuizen, Simone van (2019) 'Australian and People's Republic of China Government Conceptions of the International Order,' *Australian Journal of International Affairs*, 73(2), pp. 181–197.

Nye, Joseph S., and Robert O. Keohane (1971a) 'Transnational Relations and World Politics: An Introduction,' *International Organization*, 25(3), pp. 329–349.

Nye, Joseph S., and Robert O. Keohane (1971b) 'Transnational Relations and World Politics: A Conclusion,' *International Organization*, 25(3), pp. 371–398.

Nyíri, Pál (2005) 'The "New Migrant": State and Market Constructions of Modernity and Patriotism,' in Pál Nyíri and Joana Breidenbach (eds.) *China Inside Out: Contemporary Chinese Nationalism and Transnationalism, Budapest*, New York: Central European University Press, pp. 141–175.

O'Rourke, Kevin H., and Jeffrey G. Williamson (1999) *Globalization and History: The Evolution of a Nineteenth-Century Atlantic Economy*, Cambridge, MA; London: The MIT Press.

Office of the Director of National Intelligence (2021) *Annual Threat Assessment of the U.S. Intelligence Community*, April 9, 2021, https://www.dni.gov/index.php/newsroom/reports-publications/reports-publications-2021/item/2204-2021-annual-threat-assessment-of-the-u-s-intelligence-community

Oktav, Özden Zeynep, and Aycan Çelikaksoy (2015) 'The Syrian Refugee Challenge and Turkey's Quest for Normative Power in the Middle East,' *International Journal*, 70(3), pp. 408–420.

Paltiel, Jeremy T. 2007. *The Empire's New Clothes: Cultural Particularism and Universal Value in China's Quest for Global Status.* New York: Palgrave Macmillan.

Panda, Ankit (2014) 'Reflecting on China's Five Principles, 60 Years Later,' *The Diplomat*, June 26, https://thediplomat.com/2014/06/reflecting-on-chinas-five-principles-60-years-later/

Park, Susan (2014) 'Socialisation and the Liberal Order,' *International Politics*, 51(3), pp. 334–349.

Parker, William N. (1987) 'Civilization and Capitalism, 15th–18th Century. Volume 3: The Perspective of the World. By Fernand Braudel. Translated by Sîan Reynolds. New York: Harper & Row, 1984,' *Business History Review*, 61(3), 478–480.

Parmar, Inderjeet (2018) 'The US-Led Liberal Order: Imperialism by Another Name?,' *International Affairs*, 94(1), pp. 151–172.

Persson, Anders (2018) '"EU Differentiation" as a Case of "Normative Power Europe" (NPE) in the Israeli-Palestinian Conflict,' *Journal of European Integration*, 40(2), pp. 193–208.

Peterson Institute for International Economics (2019) 'What Is Globalization?,' https://www.piie.com/microsites/globalization/what-is-globalization

Qin, Yaqing (2016) 'A Relational Theory of World Politics,' *International Studies Review* 18(1), pp. 33–47.

Qin, Yaqing (2018) *A Relational Theory of World Politics*, Cambridge: Cambridge University Press.

Rippa, Alessandro (2017) 'Centralizing Peripheries: The Belt and Road Initiative and Its Role in the Development of the Chinese Borderlands,' *International Journal of Business Anthropology*, 7(1), pp. 1–21.

Risse, Thomas (2013) 'Transnational Actors and World Politics,' in Walter Carlsnaes, Thomas Risse, and Beth A. Simmons (eds.) *Handbook of International Relations*, Second Edition, London: SAGE Publications, pp. 426–452.

Risse, Thomas, Stephen C. Ropp, and Kathryn Sikkink (eds.) (1999) *The Power of Human Rights: International Norms and Domestic Change*, Cambridge: Cambridge University Press.

Rolland, Nadège (2017) *China's Eurasian Century? Political and Strategic Implications of the Belt and Road Initiative*, Seattle, WA, and Washington, DC: National Bureau of Asian Research.

Rolland, Nadège (2019) 'Beijing's Response to the Belt and Road Initiative's "Pushback": A Story of Assessment and Adaptation,' *Asian Affairs*, 50(2), pp. 216-235.

Rudyak, Marina (2019) 'The Ins and Outs of China's International Development Agency,' the Carnegie Endowment for International Peace, September 2, https://carnegieendowment.org/2019/09/02/ins-and-outs-of-china-s-international-development-agency-pub-79739

Selga, Eriks K. (2019) 'China's New International Commercial Courts: Threat or Opportunity?,' Foreign Policy Research Institute, Asia Program, May 29, https://www.fpri.org/article/2019/05/chinas-new-international-commercial-courts-threat-or-opportunity/

Simmons, Beth A. (2013) 'International Law,' in Walter Carlsnaes, Thomas Risse, and Beth A. Simmons (eds.) *Handbook of International Relations*, Second Edition, London: SAGE Publications, pp. 352–378.

Stearns, Peter N. (2010) *Globalization in World History*, Abingdon, Oxon: Routledge.

Strange, Susan (1988) *States and Markets*, London: Pinter Publishers.

Summers, Tim (2018) 'Rocking the Boat? China's "Belt and Road" and Global Order,' in Anoushiravan Ehteshami and Niv Horesh (eds.), *China's Presence in the Middle East. The Implications of the One Belt, One Road Initiative*, Abingdon, Oxon: Routledge, pp. 24–37.

Summers, Tim (2019) 'A Relational Theory of World Politics. By Yaqing Qin,' Book review, *International Affairs* 95(1), pp. 210–211.

Sun, Guorui, and Alex Payette (2018) 'The Sino-US Trade War: Survival, Domestic Reforms and the Belt and Road Initiative,' *Contemporary Chinese Political Economy and Strategic Relations: An International Journal*, 4(3), pp. 781–819.

Sun, Yun (2019) 'One Year on, the Role of the China International Development Cooperation Administration Remains Cloudy,' April 30, https://www.brookings.edu/blog/africa-in-focus/2019/04/30/one-year-on-the-role-of-the-china-international-development-cooperation-administration-remains-cloudy/

Tallberg, Jonas, Thomas Sommerer, Theresa Squatrito, and Christer Jönsson (2013) 'Explaining the Transnational Design of International Organizations,' http://papers.ssrn.com/sol3/papers.cfm?abstract_id=2106660

Tang, Shiping (2018) 'China and the Future International Order(s),' *Ethics & International Affairs*, 32(1), pp. 31–43.

Tao, Jing (2015) 'China's Socialization in the International Human Rights Regime: Why Did China Reject the Rome Statute of the International Criminal Court?,' *Journal of Contemporary China*, 24(96), pp. 1–19.

Terhalle, Maximilian (2011) 'Reciprocal Socialization: Rising Powers and the West,' *International Studies Perspectives*, 12(4), pp. 341–361.

Terhalle, Maximilian (2016) 'Transnational Actors and Great Powers during Order Transition,' *International Studies Perspectives*, 17(3), pp. 287–306.

The Economist, April 17, 2019, 'Hope Remains for Western Solidarity. Look at Embassies in Beijing,' https://www.economist.com/china/2019/04/20/hope-remains-for-western-solidarity-look-at-embassies-in-beijing

The Economist, July 26, 2018a, 'China's Belt-and-Road Plans Are To Be Welcomed—and Worried About,' https://www.economist.com/leaders/2018/07/26/chinas-belt-and-road-plans-are-to-be-welcomed-and-worried-about

The Economist, July 26, 2018b, 'China Has a Vastly Ambitious Plan to Connect the World,' https://www.economist.com/briefing/2018/07/26/china-has-a-vastly-ambitious-plan-to-connect-the-world

The Economist, June 13, 2019, 'The Rule of Law in Hong Kong,' https://www.economist.com/leaders/2019/06/13/the-rule-of-law-in-hong-kong

The Economist, June 6, 2019, 'A Belt-and-Road Court Dreams of Rivalling the West's Tribunals,' https://www.economist.com/china/2019/06/06/a-belt-and-road-court-dreams-of-rivalling-the-wests-tribunals

Thiel, Markus, and Jeffrey Maslanik (2010) 'Transnational Actors,' *Oxford Research Encyclopedias*, International Studies, https://oxfordre.com/internationalstudies/view/10.1093/acrefore/9780190846626.001.0001/acrefore-9780190846626-e-105

Tilly, Charles, and Sidney Tarrow (2015) *Contentious Politics*, Second Revised Edition, New York: Oxford University Press.

Tocci, Nathalie (2007) 'Profiling Normative Foreign Policy: The European Union and Its Global Partners,' CEPS Working Document No. 279, December, Centre for European Policy Studies, Brussels, https://www.ceps.eu/ceps-publications/profiling-normative-foreign-policy-european-union-and-its-global-partners/

Toynbee, Arnold (1934–1961) *A Study of History*, Vol. I–XII, Oxford: Oxford University Press.

Toynbee, Arnold (1946) *A Study of History* (Somervell Abridgedment), Oxford: Oxford University Press.

Tudoroiu, Theodor (2015) 'The Reciprocal Constitutive Features of a Middle Eastern Partnership: the Russian-Syrian Relation,' *Journal of Eurasian Studies*, 6(2), pp. 143–152.

Tudoroiu, Theodor (2022) *China's Globalization from Below: Chinese Entrepreneurial Migrants and the Belt and Road Initiative*, Abingdon, Oxon: Routledge.

Tudoroiu, Theodor, and Amanda Reshma Ramlogan (2019) 'China's International Socialization of Caribbean State-Society Complexes: Trinidad and Tobago as a Case Study,' *Asian Journal of Political Science*, 27(2), pp. 157–176.

Tudoroiu, Theodor, with Amanda R. Ramlogan (2020) *The Myth of China's No Strings Attached Development Assistance: A Caribbean Case Study*, Lanham, MD: Lexington Books.

Tudoroiu, Theodor, with Amanda R. Ramlogan (2021) *China's International Socialization of Political Elites in the Belt and Road Initiative*, Abingdon, Oxon: Routledge.

Tull, Denis M. (2008) 'China in Africa: European Perceptions and Responses to the Chinese Challenge,' SAIS Working Papers in African Studies, https://www.

swp-berlin.org/fileadmin/contents/products/fachpublikationen/Tull_China_Africa_SAIS_WP.ks.pdf
U.S.-China Economic and Security Review Commission (2020) 'PRC Representation in International Organizations,' April, https://www.uscc.gov/sites/default/files/2020-04/PRC_Representation_in_International_Organizations_April2020.pdf
Van der Wee, Herman (1981) 'The Global World View of Fernand Braudel,' *Itinerario*, 5(2), pp. 30–36.
Vangeli, Anastas (2018) 'The Normative Foundations of the Belt and Road Initiative,' in Wenhua Shan, Kimmo Nuotio, and Kangle Zhang (eds.) *Normative Readings of the Belt and Road Initiative: Road to New Paradigms*, Cham, Switzerland: Springer, pp. 59–83.
Vangeli, Anastas (2019) 'A Framework for the Study of the One Belt One Road Initiative as a Medium of Principle Diffusion,' in Li Xing (ed.) *Mapping China's 'One Belt One Road' Initiative*, Cham, Switzerland: Palgrave Macmillan, pp. 57–89.
Vuving, Alexander L. (2019) 'Emilian Kavalski. (2018). The Guanxi of Relational International Theory. London: Routledge. 129 pp. ISBN: 978-1-138-08878-8,' Book review, *Journal of Asian Security and International Affairs*, 6(2), pp. 221–224.
Wallerstein, Immanuel (1980) *The Modern World-System II: Mercantilism and the Consolidation of the European World Economy, 1600–1750* (New York: Academic Press).
Wendt, Alexander (1999/2003) *Social Theory of International Politics*, New York: Cambridge University Press.
Whitman, Richard G. (2013) 'The Neo-Normative Turn in Theorising the EU's International Presence,' *Cooperation and Conflict*, 48(2), pp. 171–193.
Womack, Brantly (2008) 'China as a Normative Foreign Policy Actor,' Working Document No. 282, Brussels: Centre for European Policy Studies, https://papers.ssrn.com/sol3/papers.cfm?abstract_id=1337618
Wu, Xinbo (2018) 'China in Search of a Liberal Partnership International Order,' *International Affairs*, 94(5), pp. 995–1018.
Yang, Xiangfeng (2017) 'The Anachronism of a China Socialized: Why Engagement Is Not All It's Cracked Up to Be,' *The Chinese Journal of International Politics*, 10(1), pp. 67–94.
Youmatter (2020) 'Globalization: Definition, Benefits, Effects, Examples - What Is Globalization?,' October 6, https://youmatter.world/en/definition/definitions-globalization-definition-benefits-effects-examples/
Yu, Jie (2018) 'The Belt and Road Initiative: Domestic Interests, Bureaucratic Politics and the EU-China Relations,' *Asia Europe Journal*, 16(3), pp. 223–236.
Zack, Tanya (2015) '"Jeppe" - Where Low-End Globalisation, Ethnic Entrepreneurialism and the Arrival City Meet,' *Urban Forum*, 26(2), pp. 131–150.
Zhang, Yongjin, and Teng-Chi Chang (eds.) (2016) *Constructing a Chinese School of International Relations. Ongoing Debates and Sociological Realities*, Oxon and New York: Routledge.
Zinkina, Julia, David Christian, Leonid Grinin, Ilya Ilyin, Alexey Andreev, Ivan Aleshkovski, Sergey Shulgin, and Andrey Korotayev (2019) *A Big History of Globalization: The Emergence of a Global World System*, Cham, Switzerland: Springer.

Ziso, Edson (2018) *A Post State-Centric Analysis of China-Africa Relations. Internationalisation of Chinese Capital and State-Society Relations in Ethiopia*, Cham, Switzerland: Palgrave Macmillan.

Zupančič, Rok, and Miha Hribernik (2013) 'Normative Power Japan: The European Union's Ideational Successor or Another "Contradiction in Terms"?,' *Romanian Journal of Political Science*, 13(2), pp. 106–136.

3 The Counter-Hegemonic Globalization 'from Below'

This chapter examines the counter-hegemonic globalization 'from below' understood as a 'movement of movements' that intends to put an end to the Neoliberal characteristics of the Western-centered globalization 'from above.' Subchapter 3.1 presents and analyzes its evolution, features, weaknesses, and merits. This huge effort for change enacted by highly heterogeneous groups and individuals shows that small and weak non-state actors can produce normative power. The political culture they have created – which is characterized by a grassroots paradigm, diversity and horizontality, and redistributive ethos – is conducive to and, one day, might result in 'benevolent forms of world order.' Subchapter 3.2 scrutinizes the political dimension of this struggle and its most impactful forms of manifestation: the 1999–2001 protest demonstrations initiated by the 'Battle of Seattle' and the World Social Forum (WSF). The rather atypical cases of the Gilets Jaunes and the Tea Party movement are also briefly discussed. Subchapter 3.3 explores the much less known law-related dimension of the counter-hegemonic globalization 'from below,' which represents a bottom-up challenge of the Neoliberal international legal regimes. The case of the struggle against the intellectual property international regime is analyzed in detail because it is comparable to the *de facto* challenging of the same regime by the numerous actors of the non-hegemonic globalization 'from below' involved in the informal international trade in counterfeit goods. Ultimately, the counter-hegemonic and non-hegemonic globalizations 'from below' are much closer than a superficial observer may think.

3.1 A 'Movement of Movements'

The three definitions of globalization presented in Subchapter 2.1 do not ignore the fact that the 'wide-ranging,' 'complex,' and 'politically charged' effects of globalization do 'harm certain groups' while wealth and power are concentrated in the hands of a small corporate elite. Accordingly, they ask a critical question: 'how do we make globalization more just?' (Peterson Institute for International Economics 2019; Youmatter 2020; Fernando 2020). Yet, they do not provide a clear answer. This can be generalized to all liberal analyses that bother to deal with the shortcomings of the Western-centered globalization 'from above': the latter may not be perfect as its positive effects are unevenly distributed; but in the long run, everybody will benefit from the emergence of a prosperous global economy. At the same time, a different approach exists that formulates the 'more just' question in terms closer to Lenin's 1902 'What Is to Be Done?' – that is, by proposing a critical view and a radical solution. Supporters of this approach tend to reformulate the very definition of the current 'hegemonic' globalization. They acknowledge that its understanding as a 'more generic process' related to 'the shrinking of space and increased permeability of borders' does 'sometimes' exist. But normally, 'when people invoke "globalization," they usually mean the prevailing system of transnational domination.' This process 'is more accurately called "neoliberal globalization," "corporate globalization," or perhaps "neoliberal, corporate-dominated globalization"' (Evans 2019: 736). It is 'from above' not simply because associated structures are located at the systemic level; rather, this label is justified by the fact that all involved efforts are top-down: they 'emanate from powerful entities and are imposed on those with less or little power' (Ritzer and Dean 2019: 487). What globalization has created is nothing less than a 'neoliberal regime of hegemonic despotism.' Through unprecedented mobility, capital has acquired 'decisive structural power at the level of communities and states' (Carroll and Ratner 2010: 17). The ongoing dynamic of global economic restructuring is characterized by its 'negative essence': 'economistic' policy-making 'subjugates' governments, political parties, leaders, and elites while 'often accentuating distress to vulnerable and disadvantaged regions and peoples' (Falk 1997: 17). The Neoliberal globalization 'is creating more poverty, misery, and environmental destruction than the world has ever known' (Brecher *et al.* 2000: 121). There is a sort of 'market mysticism' that disregards adverse social effects without paying attention to 'the realities of human suffering.' All this 'presages a generally grim future for human society (...) [and] induces a climate of resignation and despair' (Falk 1997: 17). This very critical view is accompanied by a radical – or even revolutionary – program: globalization does not refer only to the powerful capital-related forces of integration. It also concerns 'the internationalization of resistance to those forces,' i.e., the actions of the transnational civil society and networks of lobby groups that intend 'to change the relationships between these societies and the states and industries that dominate them' (Niezen 2004: 57–58). This is what Richard Falk, an international law scholar, called 'globalization-from-below' back in 1993. The current name, *counter-hegemonic* globalization 'from below,' further emphasizes the militant, anti-Neoliberal dimension.

Normative power is closely associated with this globalization's discourse and practice. Falk explicitly mentioned the 'normative potential' of the globalization 'from below,' which relies on 'widely shared world order values: minimising violence, maximising economic well-being, realising social and political justice, and upholding environmental quality.' These are conducive to 'benevolent forms of world order' (Falk 1997: 19). The present situation is due to a specific historical setting. The globalization 'from above' would be very different in a prevailing ideological climate conditioned by social democracy instead of Neoliberalism; or if states were under stronger countervailing societal or transnational pressures. A recurring reference is 'the compassionate state, as typified by the humane achievements of the Scandinavian countries up through the 1980s' (*Ibid.*, 19–20). The emergence of the counter-hegemonic globalization 'from below' is a fundamental point of inflexion that 'defines an epoch in human history' (Brecher *et al.* 2000: 121). While their respective norms and goals are very different, it is easy to note the similarity between this project and China's global enterprise presented in Subchapter 2.3. In both cases, a projection of normative power is used to replace the present international order and the associated globalization 'from above.'

In practical terms, there is a consensus among anti-Neoliberal activists that the Western-centered globalization has created problems that can be addressed only through global politics (della Porta *et al.* 2006: 235). Actual reactions to such problems fall into two categories. There is local, grassroots resistance 'based on the concreteness of the specifics of time and place,' i.e., against actions such as the destruction of a forest; and transnational resistance that brings together knowledge and political action from hundreds of civic initiatives. It is the aggregation of all these forms of protest and resistance that represents the essence of the counter-hegemonic globalization 'from below' (Falk 1997: 19). Its actors translate 'the need to control the forces of global capital' (Brecher *et al.* 2000: 17) into mainly 'anti-debt, anti-sweat (referring to sweatshops in developing countries) and anti-war' concerns. Cultural homogenization under the pressure of Western – and mainly American – culture, media, and consumerism is also rejected (Martell 2017: 325). At a conceptual level, the reaction to the detrimental impact of Neoliberalism is framed as a struggle for global justice. The central problem is identified as the lack of legitimacy of the current globalization 'from above' due to its inability 'to distribute the gains of economic growth among the peoples of the world on an equitable basis and in greater accordance with human needs' (Khlif and Pousset 2014: 39). While, as shown later in this chapter, large-scale mobilization has been used as a protest tactic, 'the battle against neoliberalism plays out primarily in the realm of ideas'; sustainable social transformation is to be reached through ideological change (Pleyers 2019: 747). In this context, the emphasis of the global justice economics discourse has moved from suffering and poverty to social conflict and social agency. The goal is to replace Neoliberalism's maximization of efficiency with an approach that focuses on social and political issues: global justice 'is a matter of re-conquering the spaces lost by democracy to the financial sector.' Activists try to create spaces of democratic debate in as many as possible spheres while attacking the International Monetary Fund (IMF), the World Bank, G7, G20, and the World Trade Organization (WTO), which they aptly identify as the key structures that support the

Neoliberal globalization 'from above' (*Ibid.*, 748–749). An interesting aspect is the attention paid to the 'important silences' of the present global governance matrix, which are acknowledged to be as important – and dangerous – as Neoliberalism's overtly stated principles. These silences include social transformation, popular participation, social contract, social justice, power relations, and social conflict. The Western-centered globalization 'from above' replaces them with alternatives that are 'negative in the sense that they define themselves by opposition to the legitimacy concepts' (Santos 2005: 35). Problem solving replaces social transformation; the participation of selected stakeholders has taken the place of popular participation; self-regulation is used instead of social contract; positive sum games and compensatory policies replace social justice; there is stability of flows instead of social conflict. Some of these alternatives could be positive if taken separately, but their use to silence legitimate concepts makes them tools of social exclusion and economic polarization. The counter-hegemonic globalization 'from below,' on the contrary, has a project of social inclusion and social redistribution that tries to put an end to this silencing (*Ibid.*, 35–36): its objective is to bring about 'a worldwide economic and political democratization' that 'transfer[s] wealth and power to ordinary people' and 'restores those elements of democracy, diversity, and ecological balance that globalization from above has destroyed' (Brecher *et al.* 2000: xi).

As explained in more detail in the next subchapter, this huge effort for change is enacted by highly heterogeneous groups and individuals. This is a 'movement of movements' that brings together environmentalists, poor people's movements in the South and their supporters in the North, advocates for small farmers, as well as labor, women's, and consumer movements (Brecher 2000). Despite this extreme diversity, there is a general perception of a common movement being constructed. Convergence has become possible due to the common interests that were created by the globalization 'from above' and now transcend national and interest-group boundaries. Much of this convergence is negative as it represents the rejection of Neoliberal influence and actions. But there is also a positive dimension based on the common values of democracy, environmental protection, community, economic justice, equality, and human solidarity (Brecher *et al.* 2000: 15). The path followed by the global justice movement has little to do with the use of conventional electoral politics. It is obvious that such an effort would be futile given the fact that the main political parties 'have subscribed to a programme and orientation that accepts the essential features of the discipline of global capital' (Falk 1997: 20). Instead, the counter-hegemonic globalization 'from below' changes the conditions of human action through the use of a 'Lilliput Strategy': worldwide, movements emerge in socially marginal locations, form networks that cross national borders, and develop a sense of solidarity, common beliefs, and a common program. These are used 'to impose new norms on corporations, governments, and international institutions' (Brecher *et al.* 2000: xi, 26).

The Counter-Hegemonic Globalization 'from Below' 75

Accordingly, definitions of the counter-hegemonic globalization 'from below' have been constructed that present the huge process of resistance to Neoliberal exploitation and oppression through the empowerment of marginalized people and struggle against global structures of domination and exploitation (Kimura-Walsh and Allen 2008: 202) 'with the goal of building an Earthwide collectively rational and democratic commonwealth' (Chase-Dunn 2002: 55). Perhaps the most popular is that formulated by Boaventura de Sousa Santos, who defined this globalization as

> the vast set of networks, initiatives, organizations, and movements that fight against the economic, social, and political outcomes of hegemonic globalization, challenge the conceptions of world development underlying the latter, and propose alternative conceptions.
> (Santos 2005: 29)

The focus of this complex process is on the struggles against social exclusion. There is a clear 'redistributive ethos in its broadest sense,' which targets the redistribution of resources that are material, social, political, cultural, and symbolic in nature. These struggles are political but also legal. 'Subaltern cosmopolitan' politics and legality propose radical alternatives to established principles, which are challenged in 'a vast social field of confrontational politics and law' characterized by two main processes: global collective action based on the transnational networking of linkages that are local, national, and global; and 'local or national struggles, whose success prompts reproduction in other locales or networking with parallel struggles elsewhere' (*Ibid.*, 29–30). It should be mentioned that 'subaltern cosmopolitanism' is an important element of the first wave globalization 'from below' discussed in Subchapter 6.1. Another important feature of this globalization 'from below' is related to the concept of hegemony mentioned – negatively – in its very name. One may tend to associate the idea of redistribution with mainly material aspects. This is not the case. As already mentioned, sustainable social transformation is to be reached through ideological change (Pleyers 2019: 747). The overall effort is 'ideological as much as material, aiming to displace dominant ideas of capitalism, and global relations' (Martell 2017: 331). The counter-hegemonic dimension is based on 'transformative politics articulated through a neo-Gramscian approach' (Carroll and Ratner 2010: 7), i.e., on an understanding of hegemony as a combination of force and legitimacy. This is where normative power becomes most visible. In terms of legitimacy, the present Neoliberal globalization originates in the reshaping of 'conceptions of normal' by the American hegemon through a projection of normative power (see Subchapter 2.2). As stated in its definition, the counter-hegemonic globalization 'from below' challenges the *conceptions* of world development underlying the hegemonic globalization (Santos 2005: 29): it tries to 'shape conceptions of normal' using its own projection of normative power. This is why 'Gramscian ideas have been used to explain the anti-globalization movement' (Martell 2017: 332) and to define the nature of its counter-hegemonic enterprise.

The use – or, rather, misuse – of 'anti-globalization' in this context points to a frequent confusion. The social justice movement and its globalization 'from below' want to put an end to Neoliberalism, not to the globalization 'from above' *per se*. Their struggle is not against globalization, but for its replacement with a more humane one. This is why the correct term, first used in French as *altermondialisation*, is alter-globalization, not anti-globalization. It is important to remind that genuine advocates of anti-globalization do exist, and this is why the confusion of terms should be avoided. The antiglobalizers seek to restore local and/or state control (Halbert 2005) and put an end to the present global flows of goods, people, and ideas. They are as heterogeneous as the alter-globalizers, but three main categories can be identified. The first shares a 'frontier' mentality that emphasizes self-determination; the Scottish National Party is given as an example. The second is composed of isolationists who want to protect their national borders and stop any involvement in global processes; they include the supporters of Western populist leaders. Finally, religious fundamentalists argue that global processes prevent the return to a pure version of their religion. Ultranationalist and neofascist groups share a similar type of reasoning (Ritzer and Dean 2019: 488). Some green and anarchist groups also advocate anti-globalization (Martell 2017: 331), but in general those who try to bring the globalization 'from above' to an end tend to be politically more conservative. For their part, most – but not all – alter-globalists tend to be closer to the political left. In a way, they are also more moderate: while their counter-hegemonic project is undoubtedly radical, they do not perceive their struggle as a zero-sum game. They believe that it is possible 'to reconcile global market operations with the well-being of peoples and with the carrying capacity of the earth' (Falk 1997: 24). In their view, a non-liberal globalization is clearly superior to a world dominated by protectionism and nationalism.

The Global Justice Movement

In order to understand the actual working of the counter-hegemonic globalization 'from below,' its 'movement of movements' dimension needs to be scrutinized in more detail. In large measure, the resistance to Neoliberal globalization relies on social movements. These are networks of groups and activists that share an emerging identity, are involved in conflictual issues, and use forms of participation that are mainly unconventional. Such networks are informal and the plurality of groups and individuals they bring together does not tend to be well structured from an organizational point of view. Social movements are not organizations. Moreover, at least in part, they function outside normal political institutions. But members of these loosely linked networks do feel that they are part of a collective effort (della Porta *et al.* 2006: 20, 234; Ritzer and Dean 2019: 493). Global social movements mirror these features at the transnational level. They are 'supranational networks of actors that define their causes as global and organize protest campaigns that involve more than one state' (della Porta *et al.* 2006: 18). They are quite diverse and cover a variety of fields. But those that target the Neoliberal globalization 'from above' represent a special case characterized, on the one hand, by frequent overlaps among groups and individuals engaged in various alter-globalization campaigns; and, on the other, by the progressive intensification of the interactions among them. As a result, a truly organized global form of resistance has emerged whose actors identify themselves with the movement, 'define themselves as global citizens, know about global developments, and express a sense of solidarity with the deprived in the world.' They engage in unconventional action, have succeeded in setting up a global organizational structure, and understand the conflict as global in scope (Ritzer and Dean 2019: 493–494; della Porta *et al.* 2006). This movement has become very visible because its members actively and vocally 'refuse, resist, rebel, denounce, petition, campaign, and create alternative practices opposed to neoliberal globalization and capitalism' (Reitan 2013: 338; Ritzer and Dean 2019: 495). The expansion of the areas it targets has had a similar effect. Issues of identity, autonomy, environmental sustainability, gender, anti-colonialism, and indigenous rights have been added to the traditional left focus on class struggle and economic redistribution (Ritzer and Dean 2019: 495). All this has brought a significant contribution to the emergence of a global civil society (della Porta *et al.* 2006: 20) intended to impact global governance in a way directly inspired from the positive influence of national civil societies on their respective governments. Two patterns of action have been identified that characterize the interactions between the components of the movement. The local-global-local pattern is specific to states – mostly located in the Global South – where governments are not responsive to the needs of their citizens and ignore the demands of domestic social movements and non-governmental organizations. The latter bypass their governments and get support from non-governmental organizations in the North and/or transnational non-governmental organizations. These pressure Northern states, which, in turn, may convince the faulty governments to act appropriately. This approach has been used to protect human and indigenous rights or the environment, but also in global justice movement actions targeting multinational corporations. Another pattern is based on the use by transnational non-governmental organizations of local partners in the Global South as proof of global support or democratic legitimacy, which helps them advance their global agendas (Ritzer and Dean 2019: 495–497).

The actors involved in the counter-hegemonic globalization 'from below' and the numerous movements it brings together have already been briefly mentioned. In the Global South, they include groups pertaining to 'the most marginalized classes – landless peasants, subsistence farmers, and indigenous peoples;' in the Global North, there are 'members of marginalized communities (...) – the "inner Third World" of laid-off industrial workers, migrants, and informal laborers,' but also progressive people of faith and activist-researchers (Santos and Rodríguez-Garavito 2005: 2). The latter are illustrated by writers such as Naomi Klein or the group around the French monthly *Le Monde Diplomatique*, which was behind the ATTAC (Association for a Tobin Tax to Aid Citizens) initiative (Martell 2017: 325). It is interesting to note that many such activists come from the same social classes as those involved in the Neoliberal globalization 'from above,' which is also the case of many supporters of transnational non-governmental organizations such as Greenpeace or the Rainforest Alliance (Ritzer and Dean 2019: 487). A basic classification of these diverse actors can be made that starts precisely with individuals. They can be prominent activists such as José Bové, the famous French farmer, trade unionist, and – more recently – politician, or anonymous people who refuse to buy global products or boycott global chains of coffee shops such as Starbucks. A second level is represented by the numberless small grassroots groups that are locally active in their opposition to some or all aspects of globalization. Most remain wholly local phenomena, but some develop into transnationally active groups that are part of the third, genuinely global level (*Ibid.*, 488). A different three-tier categorization is based on the levels of governance targeted by these actors. Some of them focus on the local level by promoting 'participatory, convivial, and sustainable values in daily practices, personal life and local spaces.' For example, Latin American indigenous movements that include the Zapatistas have adopted an inclusive approach that focuses 'on community development through local autonomy, participatory self-government, alternative education systems, and improvements in the quality of life' (Pleyers 2019: 750). Other groups choose to target national or global level institutions in an effort to modify their Neoliberal orientation. There was even a dispute triggered by the idea that 'more power at one level of governance is necessarily disempowering to people at others' (Brecher *et al.* 2000: 40). However, different from the anti-globalization groups, most alter-globalists tend to agree that global regulation and governance are actually required to empower local and national communities and polities: actions at the global level play a critical role in establishing greater control over global capital. Accordingly, the three levels of action can and should be mutually supportive, reinforcing each other's policies and structures (*Ibid.*).

Finally, the actors of the counter-hegemonic globalization 'from below' can be classified based on their ideological features. A first group comes from the traditional left and predictably emphasizes labor, anti-corporate, socialist, and/or global reformist aspects. A second one is 'more postmodern expressive': it perceives alter-globalization less as a political cause with specific political goals and more as a framework letting plural identities be discovered, flourish, and develop. Symbolic and representational politics are more important than political ends or material goals. Such democratic and open-ended movements are more interested in the process – meetings, demonstrations, street performances – than in its end, which is in no way predetermined. The third category is represented by more formally organized transnational non-governmental organizations that act as pressure groups on politicians. They address issues such as the environment, global poverty, sweatshops, and fair trade that they intend to solve through means other than free trade. Examples include Oxfam, Save the Children, and Care International. Most of them have salaried staff and hierarchical structures. Ironically, sometimes they begin to resemble the corporate structures they target in their daily activities (Martell 2017: 327). The fourth category is at the other extreme. More anarchist elements reject not only capitalism but also formal institutional politics. They are more localist, call for radical democracy, and use direct action and anti-politics: instead of trying to seize state power, their efforts are intended to delegitimize it. They want to dismantle the mechanisms of rule in order to gain greater space or autonomy. As mentioned earlier in this subchapter, their radicalism takes some anarchist groups beyond the rejection of Neoliberalism; they are fully fledged anti-globalizers, who want to put an end to any form of globalization 'from above.' Certain environmentalist groups are in the same situation, as their preference for self-sufficiency and rejection of trade and transport that lead to carbon emissions are incompatible with globalization. However, the most numerous supporters of anti-globalization – who therefore do not qualify as actors of the counter-hegemonic globalization 'from below' – are the protectionists and nationalists of both left and right. The former try to protect workers in the North from losing their jobs or receiving lower wages due to industries relocating abroad and competition from newly industrialized developing countries (*Ibid.*, 327–328). Their increasingly visible right-wing counterparts oppose immigration, as well as Westernization in the Global South and Americanization in Western Europe (Ritzer and Dean 2019: 488; Martell 2017: 328). The recent populist wave visible from the United States and Britain to India and Brazil obviously represents the best illustration of this final category. Returning to the genuine alter-globalizers, it is clear that they are 'quite globalist and globalized' (Martell 2017: 329). This is why their common enterprise is aptly depicted as a globalization 'from below.'

As shown by its highly heterogeneous membership, the 'movement of movements' is characterized by a 'political culture based on diversity and horizontality' (Massiah 2019: 756). Its grassroots paradigm, the absence of a clearly identified leadership, and the weight of flexible organizational formats are the opposite of the top-down model specific to the Western-centered globalization 'from above' (Halbert 2005; della Porta *et al.* 2006: 235). Multiple allegiances that cross state boundaries and the variety of globalization-related issues it addresses make it unique (Halbert 2005). In terms of repertoires, older nonviolent forms of protest are combined with certain innovations such as consumerist protests and new tactics of civil disobedience. In terms of objectives, there is the 'blend of Old Left attention to issues of social justice with new social movements' focus on differential rights and positive freedoms, which are more and more integrated in common visions' (della Porta *et al.* 2006: 235). In fact, the genealogy of the counter-hegemonic globalization 'from below' goes farther than the Old Left. What we see today is a 'historical movement of emancipation that is an extension and renewal of the historical movements of earlier periods.' They include historical movements for decolonization, freedom, social emancipation, and protection of environment (Massiah 2019: 754). The transition from these movements to the present counter-hegemonic globalization 'from below' did of course take time. The relatively recent 'movement of movements' has its own history. It started in the 1990s, with local and national anti-Neoliberal mobilizations such as the now famous Zapatista rebellion in Mexico, Bolivian 'water and gas wars,' the struggle of Indian farmers against the WTO, and South Korean workers' movements. By 1999, huge mobilizations in the Global North that started with the 'Battle of Seattle' (-see the next subchapter) were accompanied by the development of numerous civil society networks, which included ATTAC, the Transnational Institute, Global Trade Watch, and Focus on the Global South. Global coalitions such as Vía Campesina, the World March of Women, and Jubilee South were also established. In January 2001, the first WSF brought together many of these very different actors in Porto Alegre, Brazil (see the next subchapter). The 9/11 attacks and the ensuing securitization of international terrorism by the United States and its allies led to the end of mass demonstrations in the Global North, but the ascending trajectory of the overall global movement did not stop there. On the contrary, a second phase began that was marked by the development of local, national, continental, and global Social Forums. As explained in the next subchapter, its 'three high points' were the 2002 Florence European Social Forum, the 2004 Mumbai WSF, and the 2005 Porto Alegre one. It was only after 2005 that a series of less successful events marked the beginning of a third, more 'hesitant phase' (Pleyers 2019: 745–746). The 2006 World Social Forum held simultaneously in Bamako, Caracas, and Karachi and the 2007 one in Nairobi were less attended and showed a more limited social and economic diversity. Activists and non-governmental organizations supporting formal political actors and regimes became more prominent while the weight of grassroots activists diminished. Some major organizations such as ATTAC, the Wombles, and many social centers in Italy became less active while others – such as Barcelona's Movimiento de Resistencia Global – simply disappeared. At present, the main actors are loosely knit networks of groups, small organizations, individual activists, and media sources (*Ibid.*, 746–747). Yet, this is far from representing the end of the counter-hegemonic globalization 'from below.' This issue is discussed in Subchapter 3.3.

One of the many paradoxical aspects of the 'movement of movements' is its relationship with governments that support some of its goals. Theoretically, this is an important topic because some scholars argue that the 'dichotomising distinction between above and below is only a first approximation' when globalizations come under close scrutiny. Indeed, there are 'numerous cross-cutting diagonal alignments' between grassroots forces and governmental policies. 'Coalition possibilities' vary from one field to another. Certain governments may be supportive of initiatives concerning economic and social rights. Other governments may prefer to assist groups advocating environmental protection or disarmament (Falk 1997: 20). Anarchists would of course reject any such alliance, but alter-globalization activists with different ideological orientations try to strengthen social, economic, and environmental state agency that goes against the Neoliberal discourse and practice. They believe that it is precisely through progressive policies adopted and implemented by national policy makers, governments, and institutions that broad social change can occur (Pleyers 2019: 751). Some of the 'pink,' leftist governments in Latin America have figured prominently in interactions of this type. In Brazil, the Workers' Party of President Lula was very supportive of radical social movements; it is not by chance that the first WSF was held in Porto Alegre (see the next subchapter). However, some alter-globalizers considered the 2003–2011 Brazilian President too moderate and 'too subservient to neoliberalism' (Martell 2017: 326). They preferred the radicalism of Presidents Hugo Chávez in Venezuela and Evo Morales in Bolivia. The latter was even a leading activist of social and indigenous people's rights movements in his country. For his part, President Chávez tried to use the global justice movement in his wider effort to construct a coalition directed against American imperialism and Neoliberalism based on partners as diverse as the ALBA alliance (which included Cuba and Bolivia), Iran, Russia, and China (Pleyers 2019: 751; Martell 2017: 326). Results were mixed and, eventually, Venezuela's deepening socio-economic crisis made the support of the government in Caracas totally irrelevant to the global justice movement. This suggests that tactical alliances may be formed with certain governments at certain times, but the counter-hegemonic globalization is fundamentally a 'from below' one that – as any globalization of this kind – can ultimately rely only on small and weak non-state actors.

Overall, elements presented in this subchapter fully justify Richard Falk's contrasting of the Western globalization 'from above,' which is conducive to homogeneity and unity, with the counter-hegemonic globalization 'from below' that 'tends towards heterogeneity and diversity, even tension and contradiction' (Falk 1997: 24). This leads to very weak ties between its '- from below' actors – 'a mix of very different bedfellows,' many of whom 'will not get on well together' (Martell 2017: 329). They form a very loose and highly fluid system, which 'is continually changing its style, messages, and constituencies.' As a result, the counter-hegemonic globalization is 'highly complex, contradictory, and ambiguous' (Ritzer and Dean 2019: 486, 488). It confronts difficult dilemmas, such as reinforcing the power of local movements through transnational networks but without redefining local interests; leveraging global structures of power without becoming complicit in them; and transcending the North-South divide (Evans 2019: 737).

Its participants – which range from wildly unstructured to rigidly institutionalized elements – have many conflicting interests, and sometimes even 'previously defined themselves in part via negative reference to each other' (Brecher *et al.* 2000: 16). They have been criticized for being too diverse to form a genuine movement; for being mainly oppositional instead of relying on a positive framework; and because of their limited effectiveness associated with operating outside spheres where decisions are really made (Martell 2017: 333). And yet, the counter-hegemonic globalization 'from below' has developed in ways that have turned diversity into one of its central values. Its advocates argue that cooperation does not need uniformity. Instead of a centralized organization, a network of networks has emerged that facilitates cooperation. Actors are extremely diverse, but there is a new recognition of common interests stemming from the effects of the Neoliberal globalization 'from above.' These interests and mutuality have led to a solidarity that 'increasingly forms the basis for the relationships among different parts of the movement' (Brecher *et al.* 2000: 16). Moreover, intense processes of frame bridging lead to the development of tolerant identities (della Porta *et al.* 2006: 235). Despite inbuilt problems and temporary setbacks, the 'movement of movements' and the counter-hegemonic globalization 'from below' are in no way an endangered species. Critically, their small and weak actors have succeeded in projecting normative power in a way that is actually influencing world politics.

The Programmatic Dimension

While there can be little doubt about the general goals of the counter-hegemonic globalization 'from below' and the 'movement of movements' on which it relies, the high degree of heterogeneity and the loose nature of their activistic structures have prevented the adoption of a common program. However, normative and programmatic enterprises have been at the core of the intellectual production of a number of scholars that, in addition to analyzing the features of the counter-hegemonic globalization 'from below,' involved themselves in the advancement of its ideational dimension. This is why the contribution of two of the most important such scholars, Richard Falk and Jeremy Brecher, needs to be briefly examined. Many of their ideas have already been mentioned in the previous sections and do not need to be repeated. What I scrutinize here concerns the programs they have proposed, which are most relevant for the normative power dimension of the counter-hegemonic globalization 'from below.'

As already mentioned, Richard Falk was the first to use the term 'globalization-from-below' in 1993. He wrote a large number of articles and books on this topic. One of them, *Predatory Globalization: A Critique* (Falk 1999), was entirely constructed on the opposition between the Neoliberal globalization 'from above' and the various forms of resistance of the counter-hegemonic globalization 'from below.' Falk clearly anchored the development of these two globalizations in a specific historical context. By the mid-1990s, nearly 90 percent of the world's population lived under Neoliberalism. This situation was the result of rapid change. Two decades earlier, this type of capitalism was experienced by only 20 percent of humanity, as the rest was 'subjected either to command socialist economies or to clumsy Third World efforts to combine capitalism and socialism' (Falk 1998: 102; Sachs 1997: 11). The end of the Cold War completely discredited Marxist-inspired economic models in what used to be called the Second and Third Worlds. In the West, it led to an ideological atmosphere conducive to the total replacement of Keynesian economic policies with strongly Neoliberal approaches that relied on the autonomy of the private sector. Critically, an 'economistic' view of social policies was adopted based on privatization, fiscal austerity, efficient allocation of resources, and international competitiveness. This led to the erosion of previous social compromises between labor and business. At the same time, societal attitudes turned against the welfare state. Generalized distrust developed of approaches to problem-solving centered on government and public sector intervention. The political leverage of trade unions declined steadily. Ameliorative rhetoric and proposals were perceived with increasing skepticism. Importantly, there was the waning of industrialism, as well as pressure to face the competitive advantages of the Asia-Pacific region and other parts of the Global South such as cheap skilled labor and minimal regulation (Falk 1998: 101). The Neoliberal consensus among political elites worldwide depoliticized the state. Governments, political parties, and leaders accepted the discipline of global capital. They 'indulge[d] a kind of market mysticism' obsessed with the promotion of economic growth. Their ideological certitudes shaped economic policies in ways that disregarded adverse social effects and the realities of human suffering. The ensuing reduction of public expenditure on education, health care, welfare, job creation, and protection of the environment 'often accentuat[ed] distress to vulnerable and disadvantaged regions and peoples' (Falk 1999: 127; Falk 2001: 46; Falk 1998: 101).

In response to this dramatic development, the 'globalization-from-below' emerged that Falk defined as

> an overall effort to moderate market logic by reference to the following values embodied in "normative democracy", a view of democracy that takes account of the emergence of global village realities: consent of affected peoples; rule of law in all arenas of decision; human rights; effective modes of participation; accountability; support for public goods to address basic needs; transparency; and non-violence as a principle of public order.
>
> (Falk 1998: 99)

Before addressing the critical issue of normative democracy, it is important to emphasize the fact that this scholar associates the movement for change

84 The Counter-Hegemonic Globalization 'from Below'

with the *global* civil society, a concept that he prefers to *transnational* civil society. The latter term, he argues, 'root[s] the identity of the actors in the subsoil of national consciousness.' This is inappropriate because what we are witnessing is a process of constructing a global polity, which goes far beyond 'crossing borders.' For the time being, such a polity 'remains mostly emergent'; yet, it 'is already partly extant' (*Ibid.*). More specifically, the counter-hegemonic globalization 'from below' plays the historic role of challenging and transforming the deeply detrimental features of the Western-centered globalization 'from above' in two ways. On the one hand, there is the negative response: it resists the excesses and distortions of Neoliberalism. On the other hand and more positively, it constructs alternative ideological and political spaces that are part of the aforementioned emerging global polity. In fact, even the negative response is not 'dogmatically opposed to globalization-from-above' (*Ibid.*, 100). The point is not to dismantle it; rather, the promotion of a strong social agenda is accompanied by the explicit intention of retaining most of the benefits of the Western-centered globalization 'from above' (Falk 1997: 24; Falk 1998: 102). Falk unconditionally rejects anti-globalization agendas, which rely on 'dangerous chauvinistic and extremist societal energies' that threaten the very 'achievements of the modern secular world' (Falk 1998: 100).

His views take a radical normative turn when he discusses the two interrelated developments on which, in his opinion, the success of the counter-hegemonic globalization 'from below' depends: consensus needs to be achieved on the abovementioned concept of normative democracy; and the struggle has to be won on the positioning of institutions of governance that frame the Western-centered globalization 'from above.' As shown in the previous paragraph, Falk centers the very definition of the counter-hegemonic globalization 'from below' on the concept of normative democracy, which he presents as the foundation of this globalization in both theoretical and practical terms. He argues that this is the only concept that can ensure its coherence. First, normative democracy provides a unifying ideology able to mobilize and bring together the disparate social forces of the global civil society. Second, it provides the political energy needed to accomplish their huge tasks. Moreover, its normative dimension highlights the importance of ethical and legal norms, implicitly 'reconnecting politics with moral purpose and values' (*Ibid.*, 106). As mentioned earlier in this subchapter, Falk analyzed the normative potential of the counter-hegemonic globalization 'from below,' which relies on 'widely shared world order values: minimising violence, maximising economic well-being, realising social and political justice, and upholding environmental quality' (Falk 1997: 19; 1999: 130; 2001: 49). By introducing the concept of normative democracy and using it to define the counter-hegemonic globalization, he took one step further toward understanding this globalization as a projection of normative power (see below). Falk presented the eight elements of normative democracy enumerated in his definition of the counter-hegemonic globalization 'from below' not as a 'wishlist,' but as 'explanatory of an embedded consensus.' They include the consent of citizenry expressed through elections but also referenda, rights of petition and recall, and direct democracy, which may be more appropriate for specific political communities; the rule of law, which should include the normative claims of civil initiatives such as codes of conduct, conference declarations, and societal institutions; human rights, which should incorporate economic, social, and cultural rights and should have both individual and collective dimensions; participation, which should extend to all forms of social governance (thus including workplace and home); accountability, which should also concern the working of the market and international institutions; public goods, which should include aspects related to education, health, housing, protection of the environment, culture, and regulation of economic globalization (an example being the introduction of the Tobin tax); transparency, which should put an end to public sector secrecy and covert operations; and non-violence, which includes demilitarization and the end of weapons of mass destruction, but also ensuring security at city and neighborhood levels (Falk 1998: 107–108). These elements make normative democracy a very ambitious call for change that can indeed serve as a unified political program to be adopted by the various groups and individuals associated with the 'movement of movements.' Its full implementation would certainly lead to a 'politics of reconciliation' that, while preserving much of the dynamism of the present globalization 'from above,' would create a genuine global democracy based on social equilibrium (*Ibid.*, 108). Importantly, the implementation of the eight elements of Falk's normative democracy clearly represents a way of 'shaping conceptions of normal.' Their turning into reality by the small actors of the counter-hegemonic globalization 'from below' constitutes a clear projection of normative power. Such a process is by no means close to completion; but there can be little doubt about the reliance of this globalization on normative power.

The other precondition of success identified by Richard Falk in his analysis of the counter-hegemonic globalization concerns the institutions of governance. They include multilateral institutions and other international organizations but also – and perhaps more importantly – the state. Previous sections have mentioned various cross-cutting alignments between grassroots forces and governmental policies in fields such as the protection of the environment or disarmament, as well as the case of anti-Neoliberal leftist governments in Latin America. However, Falk optimistically sees the possibility for much deeper convergence. In both the Global North and the Global South, the state has been captured by Neoliberal elites and interests associated with the Western-centered globalization 'from above.' Therefore, a key goal of activistic 'from below' actors has to be 'to reinstrumentalize the state to the extent that it redefines its role as mediating between the logic of capital and the priorities of its peoples' (*Ibid.*, 109). The Neoliberalism of political elites of all orientations has made alter-globalizers believe that the use of electoral politics is futile. Still, Falk argues that social forces can succeed in forcing a change of mind among social-democratic leaderships, which would lead to 'the establishment of a compassionate state' (Falk 1999: 132; 2001: 51). Moreover, coalitions between social movements and states might even be joined by transnational corporations and banks. A longer-term view of their own interests could make them understand the advantages of a better world free from Neoliberalism's tensions and social polarization. To contemporary audiences, all this may sound unlikely. But Falk reminds that, in the past, social democracy and the welfare state were created through similar – and similarly unlikely – convergencies (Falk 1998: 109–110). This is a valid line of reasoning. Relevant to this book, it should be noted that such a change of mind among statesmen and business elites will not come by itself. If it does happen, it will be the result of the normative effort of small and weak actors 'from below' resulting in new understandings of normal.

Another major scholar interested in the development of the normative and programmatic dimension of the counter-hegemonic globalization 'from below' is Jeremy Brecher. His numerous works – which he often produced in co-authorship with activists such as Tim Costello and Brendan Smith – pay special attention to labor aspects and especially to the Neoliberal 'race to the bottom,' 'in which workers, communities, and whole countries are forced to compete by lowering wages, working conditions, environmental protections, and social spending' (Brecher and Costello 1998: xvii). This orientation is visible in Brecher's very definition of

> 'globalization from below' – a common interest in resisting the race to the bottom, which is reflected in developing alliances among workers, farmers, environmentalists, consumers, poor people, and people of conscience that cross national borders and the global division of North and South.
>
> (*Ibid.*)

This view is associated with a wider effort to redefine the rights and duties of international institutions, states, and citizens, as well as the very concept of sovereignty (Brecher *et al.* 2000: 43). Brecher argues that the latter is increasingly understood as a right of peoples at multiple levels, including the subnational one. Depending on specific situations, the classical, 'absolutist' interpretation of national sovereignty may be either threatened or enhanced due to the preeminence in a decision-making process of transnational or domestic factors, respectively (Brecher and Costello 1998: 78–79). Similarly, human rights are broadened to include the right to participate in decision-making processes. This leads to the emergence of a 'transborder participatory democracy' based on the right of all people to control every decision that affects them. Accordingly, the concept of political legitimacy is modified in a way that creates an obligation for both governments and international institutions to protect human rights and the environment at all levels, which 'reinforces the concept of a multilevel world order' (Brecher *et al.* 2000: 44). Like Falk, Brecher is aware of the fact that this fundamental transformation is still 'fragmented and ineffective.' To stimulate it, the counter-hegemonic globalization 'from below' needs to use the 'Lilliput Strategy' briefly described earlier in this chapter. Similar to the actions of civil society that put pressure on the national government, transnational citizen action represents the instrument that allows the victims of the Neoliberal globalization 'from above' to 'start affecting the global players and eventually change the rules of the game' (Brecher and Costello 1998: 105–106). The Lilliput Strategy relies on local grassroots organizations that construct global strategic alliances and networks of mutual aid. In turn, these structures set up and implement rules protecting the interests of Neoliberalism's victims. This is a rather difficult task because the highly heterogeneous actors of the counter-hegemonic globalization 'from below' have both common and conflicting interests. The latter include historical tensions between countries and regions; divergence among constituencies; and gaps between the economic and political spheres. Moreover, there is a mix of conflicts inherited from the pre-globalization period, those created by the Western-centered globalization 'from above,' and those generated by the social movements themselves. As a solution, Brecher proposed a set of 'guidelines for Lilliputian linking' that includes the linking of self-interest with common interests; the global to the local; North and South; constituencies across borders; particular identities with wider commonalities; issues and constituencies; the threatened with the marginalized; different power sources; struggles against targeted institutions; resistance with institutional change; and economic issues and democratization (*Ibid.*, 106–116; Brecher *et al.* 2000: 47). These elements delineate a 'vision' that opposes the Neoliberal globalization 'from above.' Brecher is fully aware of the fact that such a vision is in fact a complex process that brings together many converging elements. This makes it different from a 'universal faith,' a conventional political ideology, or a shared utopia. Importantly, it differs from more common proposals intended to reshape the architecture of the global economy in two ways: it requires a 'profound shift of wealth and power,' and associates this change with the actorness of 'from below' actors (Brecher *et al.* 2000: 61–63). The specific movements that participate in the counter-hegemonic globalization 'from below' remain rooted in their specific concerns. But the common vision reframes their actions in a way that connects them with the broader issues experienced by other components of the global movement. Particular movements become integral parts of a common struggle (*Ibid.*, 63). Moreover, as part of the process of 'moving from resistance to transformation,' Brecher and his colleagues proposed an actual draft program for the counter-hegemonic globalization 'from below,' which articulates the vision's positive objectives and intends to impose a fully democratic control on globalizing processes. The draft program is organized around seven principles whose reach ranges from bringing the 'race to the bottom' to an end to curbing international financial speculation. First, labor, environmental, social, and human rights conditions have to be leveled upward. Relevant standards should be forced on corporations and incorporated into national law. International trade agreements should establish floors instead of ceilings. Second, local, national, and global institutions should be fully democratized. In particular, global corporations should be made legally accountable and compelled to follow a democratically established code of conduct. Third, decisions should be made as close as possible to those they affect. This goes far beyond subsidiarity. The economic sector should be community-controlled and corporations locally accountable. States and regions should not compete to provide economic advantages that attract companies. Fourth, global wealth and power should be equalized. Proposed changes range from ethical shopping and investment to the revival of the North-South dialogue. Developing countries should have access to technical knowledge and global markets while sustainable development should become a key priority. Fifth, the global economy should be converted to environmental sustainability. Environmental agreements should be enforceable. Trade ones should incorporate environmental protections. Sixth, prosperity should be created by meeting human and environmental needs. Development should be encouraged instead of austerity. Food production should respond to local needs instead of being export-oriented. Long-term investment and national full employment policies should be promoted. Finally, there should be protection against global boom and bust. Capital controls and the Tobin tax should be imposed. Demand in the major economies should be coordinated, exchange rates should be stabilized, and international monetary regulation should be developed. A permanent insolvency mechanism should be established for indebted countries (Brecher *et al.* 2000: 66–67, 69–79). Obviously, such far-reaching objectives would not be easily accepted by the Neoliberal establishment. Therefore, Brecher and his colleagues also proposed a set of steps for the 'organizational development' of the counter-hegemonic globalization 'from below.' They include the creation of venues allowing for the discussion of long-range objectives independently from the debates on immediate tactical decisions; the establishment of vehicles for self-critical reflection on the movement and its actions; the linking of organizations that would enhance the unity of the movement; increasing the legitimacy of representatives of the movement; allowing new groups to join the movement under conditions that are acceptable to them; improving direct connections between grassroots groups around the world; linking large protest movements that take place in different countries; and establishing a symbolically important annual day and week for coordinated events worldwide (*Ibid.*, 90).

It is not difficult to note that, while they are differently presented, the eight elements of Falk's normative democracy and the seven principles of Brecher's draft program, as well as his proposed steps for organizational development, closely overlap. Together, they provide both a basis for the analytical understanding of the counter-hegemonic globalization 'from below' and an explicit plan for future action. Critically for this book, such action clearly represents a projection of normative power intended to dramatically reshape the Neoliberal 'normal' of the Western-centered globalization 'from above' in line with the humane view advocated by 'from below' actors. For the time being, the proposals of Falk and Brecher have not been turned into an explicit, widely accepted program. But their content is highly representative for the claims of the 'movement of movements' made visible by the political struggles presented in the next subchapter.

3.2 Political Resistance: The 'Battle of Seattle' and the World Social Forum

The numerous actions associated with the counter-hegemonic globalization 'from below' are highly diversified. Taken individually, many may seem of minor importance; but this does not prevent them from having a significant long-term cumulative effect. However, I chose to present here only those actions of political resistance that have been the most impactful in revealing the power of the 'movement of movements,' contributing to the emergence of a global public sphere, and helping to reframe the debate on the Neoliberal, Western-centered globalization 'from above'; in other words, those that are the most representative for the political (as opposed to the legal) dimension of the counter-hegemonic globalization 'from below.' They include the 1999–2001 massive protests held mainly – but not exclusively – in the Global North and the WSF that, despite its somewhat different nature, played a comparable role worldwide. This choice is, of course, subjective and leaves aside key episodes such as the Zapatista movement. Indeed, it is the 1996 First Intercontinental Encounter for Humanity and against Neo-Liberalism – organized in opposition to NAFTA by the Zapatista Army of National Liberation in the Mexican state of Chiapas – that is recognized as the 'first step in building the international movement against neo-liberal globalization.' It was described as nothing less than 'the first major social movement since the fall of the Berlin Wall' and directly inspired the next 'intergalactic encounters' in Barcelona, Spain (1997), and Belém, Brazil (1999) (Slater 2004: 215). However, reasons of space compel me to limit the number of case studies. Moreover, I believe that – in terms of both participation and impact – Seattle or the WSF is even more representative of the key interactions associated with the counter-hegemonic globalization 'from below.' I do briefly discuss the cases of the French Gilet Jaunes and the Tea Party movement in the United States precisely because of their dissimilarities with the WSF, which suggest a possible extension of the repertoire of the movements pertaining to the counter-hegemonic globalization 'from below.'

Between 1999 and 2001, the most visible form of manifestation of the global justice movement in the Global North was represented by mass protests at WTO, World Bank, IMF, and G8 meetings (Martell 2017: 325). The best known – but, as shown below, hardly the only ones – were held in Seattle (1999), Washington (2000), Quebec City (2001), and Genoa (2001) (Kimura-Walsh and Allen 2008: 202). It was the WTO that, in 1999, became the 'focal point for the emergence of the contemporary resistance to neo-liberal globalization' (Halbert 2005). While the IMF and the World Bank had been criticized for two decades as champions of Neoliberalism, the relatively new WTO – created in 1995 through the upgrading of the General Agreement on Tariffs and Trade (GATT) – was experiencing its most dynamic stage of development. Its free trade-related activity was particularly important for the opening up of national economies, which greatly contributed to the spectacular acceleration of the Neoliberal globalization 'from above.' The conference that started on November 30, 1999, was expected to continue the pre-1995 series of major GATT negotiations by launching the Millennium Round. Its objective was to further develop market liberalization, especially in investment and public services. Seattle was chosen because, due to Microsoft, it had become 'emblematic of the New Economy' (della Porta et al. 2006: 1). In fact, the 1999 'battle' would turn this city into a symbol of the global justice movement. The protest of 50,000 anti-Neoliberal demonstrators who sought to articulate a discourse of social justice and equity moved the focus of mass media and the attention of worldwide audiences from the international negotiations to the streets. 'The 1999 "battle in Seattle" became a watershed event for global resistance to the WTO' (Halbert 2005). Unlike less publicized previous marches in India or Mexico, this was 'a turning point and the high point of an aggregation process' that involved social movements from all over the world (della Porta et al. 2006: 7). Participants came mainly from the Global North, but their objectives were most relevant to both the North and the South. Importantly, protests were successful: they contributed to the premature end of the conference, which blocked the proposed WTO Millennium Round (Brecher et al. 2000: 26). More importantly, the 'battle' made even *Newsweek* acknowledge that 'there are now two visions of globalization on offer, one led by commerce, one by social activism' (Brecher 2000). Nobody could ignore the counter-hegemonic globalization 'from below' anymore. A global public sphere had emerged that was centered on the criticism of Neoliberalism and demands for 'another globalization' and a new politics (della Porta et al. 2006: 9, 232). During the following two years, all major international summits faced protest demonstrations and counter-summits that, frequently, got wider press coverage than the summits that triggered them. This was the case of the January 2000 Davos World Economic Forum, the February 2000 Bangkok UNCTAD meeting, the April 2000 Washington meetings of the IMF and the World Bank, the June 2000 Geneva UN summit on poverty, the June 2000 OECD meeting in Bologna, the July 2000 G8 Okinawa meeting, the September 2000 Prague meetings of the IMF and the World Bank, the December 2000 Nice EU summit, the February 2001 Davos World Economic Forum, the April 2001 Quebec City Free Trade Area of the Americas summit, the June 2001 Gothenburg EU summit, and the July 2001 Genoa G8 summit. To give an example illustrative of the scale of these protests, the 2001 G8 summit provided the occasion for eight hundred organizations to participate in the Genoa Social Forum counter-summit, which mirrored the previous year's Porto Alegre WSF. No less than 300,000 people marched against the G8, a figure largely superior to Seattle's 50,000. Many Genoa-inspired demonstrations followed in Italy and the rest of Europe. The next European Social Forum, held in Florence in November 2002, brought together one million demonstrators (*Ibid.*, 3, 6, 9; Slater 2004: 215; Pleyers 2019: 746). However, by then an important shift in international politics had taken place. The 9/11 terrorist attacks and the ensuing decision of the Bush administration to center its foreign policy on fighting Islamist terrorism had a strong and lasting impact on Global North audiences. Accordingly, attention to and participation in counter-globalization demonstrations started to diminish in both North America and Western Europe. Furthermore, many summits of multilateral institutions were organized in relatively remote and well-guarded locations. It is not by accident that the Doha Round of the WTO was launched in November 2001 in the capital of Qatar, where social protest was much easier to control. Yet, 'resistance to neo-liberal globalization ha[d] become part of the international landscape' (Halbert 2005). Despite their short lifespan, the huge protests of 1999–2001 did achieve important results: they 'reframed the debate on globalization, put its advocates on the defensive and forced change in the rhetoric if not the actions of world leaders and global institutions' (Brecher 2000). During the Seattle 'battle,' President Clinton decided to endorse the use of sanctions to enforce international labor rights. Protests blocked negotiations for the Multilateral Agreement on Investment, as well as the WTO proposed Millennium Round; and forced the adoption of a treaty on genetically engineered products (Brecher et al. 2000: 26). More generally, their cultural and ideological impact rivaled that of their corporate adversaries (Evans 2019: 737) and significantly helped diffuse the vision of another, more humane globalization. Finally, as mentioned in the previous subchapter, the end of summit-related mass demonstrations did in no way bring the global justice movement to an end. On the contrary, it simply led to a new phase based on the development of local, national, continental, and global Social Forums – a phase that certain scholars did not hesitate to describe as 'a golden age for the global justice movement' (Pleyers 2019: 746).

The World Social Forum

The Social Forums in general and the WSF in particular have operated as a unifying space for the transnational actors of the counter-hegemonic globalization 'from below' under the famous banner of 'another world is possible' (Halbert 2005). The WSF, whose activists first met in January 2001 in Porto Alegre, Brazil, emerged, on the one hand, from the Seattle-style summit-related protests. On the other, it was influenced by Latin American movements such as the Zapatista one and, especially, by the Hemispheric Social Alliance constituted in 1999 as a network of coalitions of citizens and labor organizations representing no less than 45 million people (Slater 2004: 215). In practical terms, it was in 1998 that a group of social movements and organizations in Brazil – that critically included the Brazilian Workers' Party – used the support of the French monthly *Le Monde Diplomatique* and the associated ATTAC group to explore a new strategy: establishing an alternative to the World Economic Forum held in Davos, Switzerland (Slater 2004: 214; Evans 2019: 737). This annual meeting of the international business elite was aptly perceived as one of the most powerful symbols of the Western-centered globalization 'from above.' It is there that the advances of the Neoliberal world economic policy are discussed and shaped (Halbert 2005). Replacing the 'Economic' with 'Social' in the new forum's name showed the fundamentally different emphasis of the nascent strategy. The latter was created by the coordinator of the Brazilian Entrepreneurs Association for Citizenship, the director of *Le Monde Diplomatique*, and the chair of ATTAC, who met in 2000 in Brazil. The new 'social' forum would be held in Porto Alegre at the same time as the 'economic' one in Davos. It soon received the support of Brazilian civil society organizations, the mayor of Porto Alegre, and the governor of the Rio Grande do Sul state, where the city is located (Slater 2004: 214–215). Both politicians were members of the Brazilian Workers' Party, which was established as a 'classic Marxist socialist mobilizational party.' Its struggle 'for dignity and economic security in the workplace and classic agendas of social protection' combined with the more global agenda of ATTAC in shaping the new forum as a champion of the counter-hegemonic globalization 'from below.' The Workers' Party's control of the municipal administration in Porto Alegre enabled the infrastructural investments required for a meeting of such proportions; but it also contributed to the important role played by local and transnational trade unions in the WSF (Evans 2019: 737–738). From January 25 to 30, 2001, 5,000 participants from no less than 117 countries, as well as thousands of Brazilian activists, representing 'diverse social movements, labour unions, peasant organizations, indigenous people's organizations, women's movements, NGOs, [and] youth organizations' discussed the negative impact of Neoliberalism and the need for a new global solidarity in the Catholic University of Rio Grande do Sul and Porto Alegre's streets, parks, and cultural centers (Slater 2004: 214). Perhaps more than the 'battle of Seattle,' the WSF became a widely known symbol of the counter-hegemonic globalization 'from below.' In the following years, similar meetings attracted increasingly large audiences: 50,000 and 100,000 in Porto Alegre in 2002 and 2003; 120,000 in Mumbai, India, in 2004; and 170,000 in 2005, again in Porto Alegre. The 2002 European Social Forum in Florence should also be mentioned; this continental forum and the 2004 and 2005 WSFs represented the climax of this phase of the global justice movement (Pleyers 2019: 745–746).

The Counter-Hegemonic Globalization 'from Below' 93

The WSF is not a political movement or actor. It only represents an arena where ideas on global issues are exchanged. But it has the undeniable merit of representing a clear progress with respect to the Seattle-type initiatives, which simply staged protests. The WSF is based on the idea that more needs to be done; that positive proposals have to be elaborated, and a forum must be created to generate them. Its powerful 'another world is possible' slogan encapsulates the key principle of this coordinated rejection of Neoliberalism (Ritzer and Dean 2019: 497–498). In more practical terms, five main political objectives have been identified. First, there is the defense of democracy and social justice. Second, the struggle for a more just and equal new economic, financial, and trade international order. Third, the struggle for peace and the opposition to war and militarism (Slater 2004: 217). It should be noted that global justice activists strongly opposed the war in Iraq; a global day of action on February 15, 2003 was attended by no less than 12 million people worldwide (Pleyers 2019: 746). Fourth, the defense of the sovereignty and the right to self-determination of all peoples, especially indigenous ones, with special attention being paid to social rights. And fifth, the protection of biodiversity, perceived in relation to the idea that food security is a basic human right that requires democratic land reforms and peasant access to land (Slater 2004: 217). In its effort to reach these objectives, the WSF has turned itself into a new public space where transnational actors meet to deal with issues of globalization (Halbert 2005). Much of this has been based on cyberactivism. The WSF is based on the cultural logic of networking, which includes the construction of horizontal ties among members that are diverse and autonomous; free and open communication of information; decentralized coordination and directly democratic decision-making; and networking that is self-directed. Accordingly, the Forum is 'a radical experiment in participatory democracy,' which eventually developed links with a variety of similar movements that include Occupy, the Arab Spring, and global feminism (Ritzer and Dean 2019: 498). Activists have constantly emphasized the fundamental opposition between the 'predatory and homogenizing' Neoliberal globalization 'from above' that 'promotes competitiveness, hierarchy, conformity and the primacy of the cash nexus' and the counter-hegemonic globalization 'from below.' The latter is characterized by 'heterogeneity, diversity and bottom-up participatory politics'; moreover, in terms of spatiality, the ethic of its participatory democracy expanded to global, supra-national, national, regional, local, and community levels (Slater 2004: 219–220). Critically, the global justice movement's 'articulation of a different way to globalize' has succeeded in associating the emergence of the global civil society with issues of democracy, social justice, and 'resistance to a tightly controlled international regime that benefits the few at the expense of the many' (Halbert 2005). The formidable impact of this movement is illustrated by the fact that even World Bank representatives and some right-wing politicians asked to participate in the Porto Alegre WSF (Pleyers 2019: 746).

However, as mentioned in the previous subchapter, the 'movement of movements' started to decline after 2005. Meetings continued, and expanded geographically: the 2006 'polycentric' WSF was held in Bamako, Caracas, and Karachi; the 2007 one in Nairobi. More recent meetings were located in Tunis (2015), Montreal (2016), and Salvador de Bahia, in Brazil (2018) (Ritzer and Dean 2019: 498). In fact, the geography of the movement has changed, with new poles emerging in North America, the Maghreb, sub-Saharan Africa, and South Korea, while Western Europe became less visible. For a time, Latin America remained very active: the January 2009 WSF – that was held at Belem, in Brazil's Amazon region, and prominently addressed environmental concerns – was attended by no less than 130,000 activists. The 2010 People Summit against Global Warming held in Cochabamba, Bolivia at the initiative of President Evo Morales brought together 25,000 participants from 147 countries, including many indigenous people (Pleyers 2019: 747). But setbacks experienced by leftist forces, which lost power in many Latin American countries, diminished political support for such initiatives, which ultimately followed the same downward trend visible in Europe. Worldwide, WSF meetings were less attended and less socially and economically diverse. The balance of membership changed in favor of groups that supported formal political actors and regimes, while the number of grassroots activists diminished (*Ibid.*). More importantly, the absence of practical results began to become a handicap. The 'another world is possible' discourse has deeply impacted the world of globalization-related ideas. But the movement's extreme diversity makes the adoption of concrete political proposals difficult. Consequently, its intentions to bring about a new, more just and humane world have failed 'to produce actions that actually help make that world a reality' (Ritzer and Dean 2019: 497–498). Still, the counter-hegemonic globalization 'from below' is far from coming to an end.

Yellow Vests at a Tea Party

It should be reminded that the WSF does in no way represent the only form of manifestation of this globalization. In fact, one of the reasons for the Forum's relative decline may well be the emergence of narrower similarly minded movements. The best known is, of course, the Occupy wave that, one decade ago, began by 'taking over' Wall Street and rapidly extended to no less than 951 cities in 82 countries (Rogers 2011). As mentioned in a previous paragraph, this transnational movement established links with the WSF (Ritzer and Dean 2019: 498), which is indicative of the convergence of their goals. However, two dissimilar cases are more interesting as they illustrate the unexpected widening of the repertoire of movements pertaining to the counter-hegemonic globalization 'from below.' One is that of the French Gilets Jaunes (Yellow Vests), an extremely loosely organized movement of protest triggered in November 2018 by opposition to a fuel tax that soon developed into 'an important example of progressive populism calling for social and economic justice' (Wilkin 2020). The 'populist' label is often used by critics in a derogatory way and alludes to the absence of a unified ideology, which represents an important difference between this movement and the WSF. Yet, the French protests have two clear causes: the long-term negative consequences of the 2008 financial crisis, which were aggravated by President Macron's Neoliberal policies; and deep dissatisfaction with the political establishment. Accordingly, the Gilets Jaunes ask for anti-Neoliberal socio-economic measures and, critically, strongly advocate some form of direct or participatory democracy. The Sixth French Republic should replace the current one, with a political system based on popular assemblies that should be responsible for policy-making and nominating 'delegates rather than representatives' (*Ibid.*). This agenda immediately brings to mind the radical programs proposed by Richard Falk and Jeremy Brecher (see Subchapter 3.1). Despite the absence of organization and ideology, the Gilets enact a popular protest for social and economic justice that fits the profile of counter-hegemonic movements analyzed by the two scholars in all but one regards. French mass media emphasized the simultaneous launching of similar protests in Chile, Lebanon, Sudan, Ecuador, Algeria, and Haiti. *Le Monde* titled one of its 2019 articles 'From Local Trigger to Global Revolt: the Worldwide Convergence of Struggles' (Thibault *et al.* 2019). However, the Gilets Jaunes remains a nation-scale alter-globalization movement that has shown little interest in forging close links with like-minded protesters abroad. For the counter-hegemonic globalization 'from below' to be successful, Brecher and his colleagues explicitly mentioned the linking of large protest movements that take place in different countries as one of the key steps of the 'organizational development' they proposed (Brecher *et al.* 2000: 90; see Subchapter 3.1). The fact that the Gilets prefer to ignore this obvious aspect may simply represent an atypical exception; but it could also be a specific feature of a new type of movement characterized by indifference to ideology and organization. Indeed, it is not illogical to see a direct connection between internal and transnational 'disorganization.' If this trend develops worldwide, the functioning and effectiveness of the counter-hegemonic globalization 'from below' could be negatively affected.

An even more surprising example is that of the Tea Party movement in the United States. As mentioned in Subchapter 3.1, most alter-globalists tend to be closer to the political left. Atypically, the Gilets Jaunes have no ideology. For its part, the Tea Party is strongly ideologized, but it clearly pertains to the political right. Moreover, many of its critics perceive the movement as an incarnation of the extreme right: 'the Tea Party followers are a bunch of racist, homophobic, know-nothing, white, lower-class, gun-toting hicks' (Etzioni 2011: 197). Even less radical assessments claim that its members are mainly white, male, conservative, and – despite their frequent appeals to freedom – share 'a strong authoritarian pulse.' While racial resentment is not the primary cause of their actions and political program, 'racial resentment colors members' judgments about government aid to the poor' (Arceneaux and Nicholson 2012: 700, 709). The group is not homogeneous. Some members take less extreme positions, even if they are relatively conservative. However, this concerns only less than 20 percent of the membership (*Ibid.*, 702, 709). While right-wing, the Tea Party lacks a clear unifying ideology and represents 'an odd fusion of libertarianism and social conservatism' (Havercroft and Murphy 2018: 1021–1022). The movement emerged in early 2009 in reaction to the 2008 financial crisis – which it associated with the Neoliberal globalization 'from above' – and the US government's response to it. Unfriendly observers add, as a causal factor, hostility toward 'the policies and the person of the country's first African American President' (Tilly and Tarrow 2015: xiii). In organizational terms, it is composed of three different and rather divergent structures. The Tea Party Patriots represent the movement's neo-conservative grassroots base. The Tea Party Express and Tea Party Nation, on the contrary, are mainly controlled and funded by Neoliberal elites from the Republican Party and large US corporations. This support has significantly contributed to the development of the movement but has also led to a struggle between its popular membership and corporate elites over the priority to be given to social or economic issues (Cao 2017: 106–107). Given their strong right-wing leaning and dissatisfaction with globalization, one would expect the grassroots Tea Party Patriots to have adopted an anti-globalization agenda relying, in Richard Falk's words, on 'dangerous chauvinistic and extremist societal energies' (Falk 1998: 100; see Subchapter 3.1). However, this is not the case. Tea Party members are alter-, not anti-globalists. Similar to the 'mainstream' components of the counter-hegemonic globalization 'from below,' they believe that the Neoliberal globalization 'from above' is responsible for domestic socio-economic difficulties and loss of control over politics. To correct these issues, they propose a different globalization, not a retreat into protectionism. Differences emerge only when their recipe for another globalization is scrutinized.

Tea Party criticism of the Western-centered globalization 'from above' keeps Neoliberal economic, political, and cultural elites responsible for 'economic doldrums, the loss of control over politics and the collapse of the national community' (Cao 2017: 111). Economically, free trade and the elites' 'imperative of money' are identified as causing unemployment, higher taxes, and capital outflows. The cheap labor of undocumented immigrants is perceived as particularly damaging. Politically, republican ideals are threatened by multilateral institutions and international conventions. The formalization and bureaucratization of global decision-making prevent citizens from having their opinions taken into consideration. Culturally, undocumented immigrants and multiculturalism threaten the nation, which is understood as a pre-constituted community composed of patriots such as the Tea Party members. There is moral collapse: the national moral order is disrupted by the rising crimes perpetrated by undocumented immigrants. Moreover, new economic immigrants refuse to be assimilated into the American culture (Cao 2017: 112–115). Except for the socio-cultural dimension, most of this criticism is similar to that formulated by the 'regular' actors of the counter-hegemonic globalization 'from below.' However, the Tea Party's solution to all problems is not based on the idea of creating a humane globalization that should benefit all victims of Neoliberalism. On the contrary, measures are proposed that would restore American supremacy within the US-led international order to the exclusive advantage of US citizens. Economically, major tax reform should ensure the US expansion on the global market. Undocumented immigrants should be registered, heavily taxed, and excluded from social welfare. Taxation should also be used to discourage capital flights. A general tax cut for businesses should enhance the global competitiveness of US firms. Internationally, Washington should withdraw from organizations and treaties that are detrimental to its interests and restore US global dominance. Finally, immigrants should be assimilated, mainly through education reform and, critically, by fighting leftist Liberals who promote immigration and multiculturalism (*Ibid.*, 113–118). Unlike the Gilets Jaunes' goals, the Tea Party agenda has nothing in common with the programs put forward by Richard Falk and Jeremy Brecher. This explains the support received by this movement from Neoliberal elites in the Republican Party and some US corporations. Such elites may actually benefit from the implementation of Tea Party plans. More importantly, this is a disturbing example of a movement that gives a frustratingly narrow interpretation to its stated libertarian goals and, in fact, is not counter-hegemonic (at least when the US hegemony is concerned, be it Neoliberal or not). The small actors' projection of normative power is intended to reinforce the hegemon, not to weaken it. Like the Gilets Jaunes, the Tea Party proposes an unexpected extension of the repertoire of 'from below' movements. But its features are so remote from those discussed earlier in this chapter that one can wonder if the Tea Party should not be seen as representative for an alternative, *pro*-hegemonic type of globalization 'from below.' For obvious reasons, this trend is less likely to develop outside the United States. But if it does, a future edition of this book may need a separate chapter to deal with it.

However, despite the emergence of atypical movements such as the Gilets Jaunes and the Tea Party and the relative decline of the WSF, the 'genuine' counter-hegemonic globalization 'from below' discussed in this chapter is far from disappearing. At present, it may not be able to generate radical change. But the global justice movement continues to put constant pressure on actors at all levels involved in the Neoliberal globalization 'from above.' 'While it may never be the case that we can create another world, the past ten years can teach us that we can still try to make the world we live in a better one' (Halbert 2005).

3.3 Legal Resistance: Challenging Intellectual Property Rights

The previous subchapters have analyzed the most visible dimension of the counter-hegemonic globalization 'from below': the protest actions and Social Forums that try to put an end to the Neoliberal features of the Western-centered globalization 'from above' through transnational activism. This is an essentially political approach that, at first view, has nothing in common with the discreet actions of the other globalizations 'from below.' The situation is in fact more complex. On the one hand, the 'ant traders' of the non-hegemonic globalization 'from below' similarly challenge the Neoliberal international order (see Chapter 4). On the other, in addition to its very visible political dimension, the counter-hegemonic globalization 'from below' includes a key law-related component intended to dismantle Neoliberal international legal regimes. One of its most important targets is the protection of intellectual property rights, which it perceives as an unjust hegemonic set of laws, norms, and enforcement mechanisms that perpetuate structural inequalities between the Global North and Global South. While using different instruments, this struggle against the 'increasingly severe legal regime [that] criminalizes copyright infringement' (Schweidler and Costanza-Chock 2009: 1, 4; Halbert 2005) has very much in common with the day-to-day *de facto* challenging of the same regime by the numerous small traders involved in massive transnational flows of counterfeit goods (see Subchapter 4.3). In order to illuminate this seldom noted connection between the counter-hegemonic and non-hegemonic globalizations 'from below,' the present subchapter analyzes the legal struggle of social justice activists against the WTO Agreement on Trade-Related Aspects of Intellectual Property Rights (TRIPS).

The counter-hegemonic globalization 'from below' is compelled to fight legal battles against existing hegemonic structures and practices simply because, as mentioned in Subchapter 3.1, the unequal exchanges and power relations of the Neoliberal globalization 'from above' are crystallized in both politics and law. Consequently, 'subaltern cosmopolitan' politics and legality propose radical alternatives to established principles, which are challenged in 'a vast social field of confrontational politics and law' (Santos 2005: 29–30). Numerous initiatives launched by the global justice movement 'have spurred an unprecedented effervescence of debate and experimentation in bottom-up legal reform and new international legal regimes' (Santos and Rodríguez-Garavito 2005: 2). This alternative, bottom-up perspective on law and globalization perceives legal orders as including, in addition to the official law of legislatures and courts, 'the myriad legal rules created and enforced by such disparate social actors as civil society organizations, corporations, and marginalized communities.' At the same time, law-centered strategies created to fight the Neoliberal globalization amplify the voice of its victims – 'indigenous peoples, landless peasants, impoverished women, squatter settlers, sweatshop workers, or undocumented immigrants' (*Ibid.*, 4). The bottom-up approach is therefore close to longstanding Global South initiatives such as the 'alternative law' movement in Latin America or 'social action litigation' in India (*Ibid.*). As law is normative by definition, this is perhaps the best illustration of the counter-hegemonic globalization 'from below' as a projection of normative power coming from small and weak actors that nevertheless try to redefine the meaning of 'normal' globally.

Counter-hegemonic legal efforts are most visible in the field of intellectual property. The latter is a generic term that describes a series of legal regimes concerning copyright, trademark, and patent law, as well as *sui generis* regimes protecting specific kinds of innovations. The protection concerns intangible aspects of products (Halbert 2005). Historically, related issues were managed by the World Intellectual Property Organization, a United Nations agency established in 1967 (World Intellectual Property Organization 2021). But due to decolonization, the delegates of developing states soon outnumbered those from the North and prevented them from advancing their agenda. During the 1980s and especially the 1990s, the development of the digital environment led to the massive growth of what corporations called global piracy. As intellectual property was turned into an important business tool, concerned firms intensified efforts to protect internationally their intangible products through stricter laws (Halbert 2005). Unsurprisingly, the United States became their champion. It has used the US Trade Representative's Special 301 status to put pressure bilaterally on other states to adopt and enforce intellectual property laws. There is a watch list of countries that do not comply; they can become the object of trade sanctions. It was during the 1986–1994 Uruguay Round of GATT – which resulted in the creation of the WTO – that the opportunity arose to add to this bilateral approach a multilateral one. The American intellectual property position at these negotiations was greatly influenced by multinational corporations such as Pfizer, IBM, and Monsanto. Their intense and ultimately effective lobbying was due to the reliance of their exports on various forms of intellectual property such as patents, trademarks, or copyrights that were easy to copy and needed to be protected internationally. The approach they chose was to conceptualize intellectual property as a trade issue. The argument was that the absence of intellectual property laws was equivalent to a barrier against free trade. Developed countries turned this idea into an important principle of the future trade architecture. They were able to impose it mainly because the issue drew little public interest. Only the Northern business elites active in fields such as entertainment, software, agriculture, and pharmaceutics were really interested in issues such as copyright and patent law. Consequently, Washington's considerable pressure on states resisting this agenda succeeded in imposing the signing of the WTO Agreement on TRIPS in 1996. It basically imposed on all WTO members compliance with the intellectual property regime of developed states. All countries had to harmonize their laws with the minimum standards elaborated in the agreement, which were based on the legal systems of the United States, Western Europe, Japan, and Australia. While these states had to make only minor adjustments, substantial changes were imposed on developing countries. In many cases, considerable efforts were required to construct the legal and enforcement infrastructure, and to educate citizens and businesses in line with TRIPS provisions. New members of the WTO were required to sign the agreement. A dispute resolution mechanism was set up leading to sanctions against states that violate the TRIPS agreement. As a result, an international regime was created as part of the Western-centered globalization 'from above' that protects intellectual property through a hegemonic set of laws, norms, and enforcement mechanisms (Schweidler and Costanza-Chock 2009: 3; Halbert 2005). In order to legitimate, preserve, and further expand it, both developed states and concerned multinational corporations are actively involved in lobbying, propaganda campaigns, diffusion of educational materials, and other tactics. They argue that intellectual property rights serve the public interest, contribute to the development of poor countries, and protect creativity and innovation. They also engineer new technologies that are turned into enforcement mechanisms and try to block technologies used to challenge their control. This is most visible in the realm of music and film distribution, which witnesses a 'legal, technical, and discursive war against filesharing, remix culture, fair use, and the public domain.' Copyright infringement is criminalized by an increasingly severe legal regime that also erodes fair use and constantly extends the length and the scope of copyright (Schweidler and Costanza-Chock 2009: 1, 5, 7).

Developing countries were compelled to accept the TRIPS agreement and join the intellectual property international regime, but many of their citizens were alarmed by what they perceive as a way to perpetuate North-South structural inequalities. They argue that the protection of the interests of multinational corporations disregards those of Global South countries and prevents access to new technologies (Halbert 2005). Similarly, vocal protests took form within the civil society. As they incarnate the interests of Neoliberal states and multilateral corporations, the TRIPS has become the target of harsh criticism coming from a multitude of actors. They include groups fighting for access to AIDS medication in South Africa, access to seeds in India, and control of traditional knowledge in Hawaii or Australia. Strategic alliances were put in place that bring together indigenous, as well as environmental non-governmental organizations, North-South alliances of groups of farmers and peasants, associations of traditional healers, religious organizations opposed to the patenting of lifeforms, and development institutions and activists concerned with food security threats. The coalition of these highly diverse groups led to the emergence of a vibrant political movement opposed to intellectual property laws. Its members have developed a global language of resistance intended to unite all those who participate in this struggle for greater equity and social justice. Most importantly, this resistance is radical. It does not seek limited change within the existing legal regime. Instead, similar to the largest 'movement of movements' of which it is part, it wants to put an end to the Neoliberal protection of intellectual property imposed by the WTO. The social rights of people are to be given preference over the economic interests of multinationals. One key direction of action has been to translate abstract legal language into words accessible to the general public. Instead of technicalities about copyright and patents, activists speak about real-life harms such as lack of medicine, the biopiracy of materials, or the appropriation of traditional knowledge. This has made vast audiences understand the actual impact on their lives of issues that initially seemed technical and remote, thus allowing the movement to 'literally take the abstract world of TRIPS to the streets' (Halbert 2005). By mobilizing millions around intellectual property issues, interconnected groups in the Global North and Global South develop pressure from below intended to put an end to the allegiance of their respective governments to the TRIPS international regime. While, for the time being, such an in-depth change is hardly visible, 'the concept of intellectual property rights has come to be seen as a central problem with neo-liberal globalization' (*Ibid.*). The discourse on equitable access to knowledge, culture, health care, seeds, and technology has turned the rejection of intellectual property rights into a key concern of many transnational social movements that focus on environmental, human rights, indigenous peoples, and North-South disparity issues. They have joined the anti-TRIPS movement in an effort 'to limit, subvert, ignore, or abolish IP in different sectors' (Schweidler and Costanza-Chock 2009: 2; Halbert 2005).

Actual forms of resistance range from everyday practice to counter-projects that challenge private ownership and commodity logic in an effort to develop an ethic of collaborative post-scarcity production. They are enacted by activists, non-governmental organizations, grassroots social movements, and scientists, but also by some governments and businesses at local, national, and international levels, both inside and outside the world of policy. The intellectual property international regime is contested through many basic daily practices that people often do not even associate with a political stance. They include the use of generic drugs; the planting and purchasing of non-patented foods; the use of Creative Commons materials (such as Wikipedia); the use of free and open-source software; and the free sharing of audiovisual material and software that abundant antipiracy propaganda, severe legal penalties, digital rights management (DRM) technological control, and lawsuits have failed to curb (Schweidler and Costanza-Chock 2009: 4–5). No less than 70 percent of the software used in India is illegal; in many parts of the Global South, piracy is 'a culture of the copy that exists alongside livelihood and labor' (Liang 2011: 172–173). Technologies of resistance have been developed that include popular software tools, which break digital media and software encryption; but also ways to avoid genetic use restriction technologies (GURTs). The so-called 'Terminator seeds' produced by agribusiness firms cannot be replanted or adapted to local environments;

their large-scale adoption would devastate small farmers, which explains the massive mobilization against their use. There are of course more traditional forms of protest and direct action such as marches, sit-ins, disruptions of meetings, and the like; and policy battles on issues that range from copyright duration to public funding for medical research. It is important to note that the activistic framing of intellectual property issues is remarkably diversified. The related Neoliberal discourse has been challenged from various perspectives that include human rights, with an emphasis on food security and access to medicines; consumer rights, referring mainly to digital rights management and file sharing; civil liberties, associated with free speech arguments against intellectual property; the right to development, where numerous Global South-related issues are discussed; access to knowledge, that brings together development, human rights, and consumer rights aspects; cultural, political, and economic sovereignty, which includes issues such as indigenous and traditional knowledge, cultural theft, and biopiracy; and the commons that apply to most sets of shared resources. These frames, which frequently overlap, influence the way actors 'analyze the problem, develop strategies, imagine solutions, and distribute resources' (Schweidler and Costanza-Chock 2009: 7, 9, 11, 35).

The bottom-up legal reform efforts parallel and complement the political actions of the global justice movement. Both represent 'from below' initiatives that try to put an end to the Neoliberal features of the Western-centered globalization 'from above.' Due to their much higher visibility, the protest demonstrations and Social Forums are generally perceived as more impactful while the legal struggle continues to be commonly considered as much narrower and rather abstract. In fact, such views fail to acknowledge the magnitude and importance of the various forms of resistance against the intellectual property international regime. In practical terms, the numerous anti-copyright actions that infringe the Neoliberal intellectual property legal regime on a daily basis can be considered more effective than two decades of meetings and counter-summits. Critically, they follow the same logic as the informal international trade in counterfeit goods. Despite appearances, there is a fundamental convergence between the counter-hegemonic and non-hegemonic globalizations 'from below' that I further discuss in Subchapter 4.3.

To summarize, the counter-hegemonic globalization 'from below' represents a vast and complex anti-Neoliberal effort that takes the form of a 'movement of movements' characterized by heterogeneity, diversity, flexibility, horizontality, and bottom-up participatory politics. Subaltern cosmopolitan political but also legal initiatives propose radical alternatives to the established principles of the Western-centered globalization 'from above.' This radical experiment in participatory democracy is a struggle for global social justice that seeks social inclusion and is marked by a redistributive ethos. As interactions are based on the cultural logic of networking, participants form a very loose and fluid system; accordingly, the globalization they enact is necessarily complex, contradictory, and ambiguous. But there is also a sense of solidarity and an emerging common identity. They allow small and weak actors to project normative power in ways conducive to 'benevolent forms of world order' (Falk 1997: 19). Despite the overwhelming influence of Neoliberal multilateral institutions, states, and multinational corporations, these 'from below' actors believe that 'another world is possible'; and the counter-hegemonic globalization 'from below' that intends to construct it represents a fundamental point of inflexion that 'defines an epoch in human history' (Brecher et al. 2000: 121). For the time being, actual results are hardly spectacular. But the 'movement of movements' did contribute to the emergence of a global public sphere that has reframed the debate on the Neoliberal globalization, putting its advocates on the defensive and forcing a change in their rhetoric (Brecher 2000). At less visible levels, actions such as breaking digital media encryption or rejecting GURT seeds challenge the Neoliberal legal international regimes on a large scale and in very effective ways. Protest movements and Social Forums may have ups and downs, but the counter-hegemonic globalization 'from below' is not going to disappear: 'even if its current expression were to fail, the movement would rise again, because it is rooted in a deep social reality: the need to control the forces of global capital' (Brecher et al. 2000: 17).

References

Arceneaux, Kevin, and Stephen P. Nicholson (2012) 'Who Wants to Have a Tea Party? The Who, What, and Why of the Tea Party Movement,' *PS, Political Science & Politics*, 45(4), pp. 700–710.
Brecher, Jeremy (2000) 'Globalization from Below,' *The Nation*, November 16, https://www.thenation.com/article/archive/globalization-below/
Brecher, Jeremy, and Tim Costello (1998) *Global Village or Global Pillage: Economic Reconstruction from the Bottom Up*, Second Edition, Cambridge, MA: South End Press.
Brecher, Jeremy, Tim Costello, and Brendan Smith (2000) *Globalization from Below: The Power of Solidarity*, Cambridge, MA: South End Press.
Cao, Hao (2017) 'Diagnosis and Prognosis of Neo-Liberal Globalization: From the Tea Party Movement's Perspective,' *Global Media and Communication*, 13(2), pp. 105–122.
Carroll, William K., and R. S. Ratner (2010) 'Social Movements and Counter-Hegemony: Lessons from the Field,' *New Proposals: Journal of Marxism and Interdisciplinary Inquiry*, 4(1), pp. 7–22.
Chase-Dunn, Christopher (2002) 'Globalization from below: Toward a Collectively Rational and Democratic Global Commonwealth,' *The Annals of the American Academy of Political and Social Science*, 581, pp. 48–61.
della Porta, Donatella, Massimiliano Andretta, Lorenzo Mosca, and Herbert Reiter (2006) *Globalization from Below. Transnational Activists and Protest Networks*, Minneapolis; London: University of Minnesota Press.
Etzioni, Amitai (2011) 'The Tea Party Is Half Right,' *Society*, 48(3), pp. 197–202.

104   The Counter-Hegemonic Globalization 'from Below'

Evans, Peter (2019) 'Counterhegemonic Globalization: Transnational Social Movements in the Contemporary Political Economy,' in Frank J. Lechner and John Boli (eds.) *The Globalization Reader*, Sixth Edition, Hoboken, NJ; Chichester, West Sussex: John Wiley & Sons, epub edition, pp. 736–744.

Falk, Richard (1997) 'Resisting "Globalisation-from-Above" through "Globalisation-from-Below",' *New Political Economy*, 2(1), pp. 17–24.

Falk, Richard (1998) 'Global Civil Society: Perspectives, Initiatives, Movements,' *Oxford Development Studies*, 26(1), pp. 99–110.

Falk, Richard (1999) *Predatory Globalization: A Critique*, Cambridge: Polity Press.

Falk, Richard (2001) 'Resisting "Globalization-from-Above" through "Globalization-from-Below",' in Barry K. Gills (ed.) *Globalization and the Politics of Resistance*, Houndmills, Basingstoke, Hampshire: Palgrave, pp. 46–56.

Fernando, Jason (2020) 'Globalization,' *Investopedia*, December 12, https://www.investopedia.com/terms/g/globalization.asp

Halbert, Debora (2005) 'Globalized Resistance to Intellectual Property,' *Globalization*, 5(2), https://globalization.icaap.org/content/v5.2/halbert.html

Havercroft, Jonathan, and Justin Murphy (2018) 'Is the Tea Party Libertarian, Authoritarian, or Something Else?,' *Social Science Quarterly*, 99(3), pp. 1021–1037.

Khlif, Wafa, and Joanna Pousset (2014) 'It Takes (More Than) Two to Tango: Informal Tango Market Dynamics in Barcelona,' *Society and Business Review*, 9(1), pp. 36–50.

Kimura-Walsh, Erin, and Walter R. Allen (2008) 'Globalization from above, Globalization from below: Mechanisms for Social Disparity and Social Justice in Higher Education,' in Rodney K. Hopson, Carol Camp Yeakey, and Francis Musa Boakari (eds.) *Power, Voice and the Public Good: Schooling and Education in Global Societies*, Bingley: Emerald Group Publishing Limited, pp. 201–230.

Liang, Lawrence (2011) 'Beyond Representation: The Figure of the Pirate,' in Mario Biagioli, Peter Jaszi, and Martha Woodmansee (eds.) *Making and Unmaking Intellectual Property: Creative Production in Legal and Cultural Perspective*, Chicago: University of Chicago Press, pp. 167–180.

Martell, Luke (2017) *The Sociology of Globalization*, Second Edition, Cambridge; Malden, MA: Polity Press, epub edition.

Massiah, Gustave (2019) 'The Twelve Assumptions of an Alter-Globalisation Strategy,' in Frank J. Lechner and John Boli (eds.) *The Globalization Reader*, Sixth Edition, Hoboken, NJ; Chichester, West Sussex: John Wiley & Sons, epub edition, pp. 753–759.

Niezen, Ronald (2004) *A World Beyond Difference: Cultural Identity in the Age of Globalization*, Malden, MA; Oxford; Victoria, Australia: Blackwell Publishing.

Peterson Institute for International Economics (2019) 'What Is Globalization?,' https://www.piie.com/microsites/globalization/what-is-globalization

Pleyers, Geoffrey (2019) 'The Global Justice Movement,' in Frank J. Lechner and John Boli (eds.) *The Globalization Reader*, Sixth Edition, Hoboken, NJ; Chichester, West Sussex: John Wiley & Sons, epub edition, pp. 745–752.

Reitan, Ruth (ed.) (2013) *Global Movement*, New York: Routledge.

Ritzer, George, and Paul Dean (2019) *Globalization: The Essentials*, Second Edition, Hoboken, NJ; Chichester, West Sussex: John Wiley & Sons.

Rogers, Simon (2011) 'Occupy Protests around the World: Full List Visualised,' *The Guardian*, November 14, https://www.theguardian.com/news/datablog/2011/oct/-17/occupy-protests-world-list-map

Sachs, Jeffrey (1997) 'New Members Please Apply,' *Time,* July 7, pp. 11–12.
Santos, Boaventura de Sousa (2005) 'Beyond Neoliberal Governance: The World Social Forum as Subaltern Cosmopolitan Politics and Legality,' in Boaventura de Sousa Santos and César A. Rodríguez-Garavito (eds.) *Law and Globalization from Below. Towards a Cosmopolitan Legality,* New York: Cambridge University Press, pp. 29–63.
Santos, Boaventura de Sousa, and César A. Rodríguez-Garavito (2005) 'Law, Politics, and the Subaltern in Counter-Hegemonic Globalization,' in Boaventura de Sousa Santos and César A. Rodríguez-Garavito (eds.) *Law and Globalization from Below. Towards a Cosmopolitan Legality,* New York: Cambridge University Press, pp. 1–26.
Schweidler, Christine, and Sasha Costanza-Chock (2009) 'Common Cause: Global Resistance to Intellectual Property Rights,' in Dorothy Kidd, Clemencia Rodriguez, and Laura Stein (eds.) *Making Our Media: Mapping Global Initiatives Toward a Democratic Public Sphere,* Volume II, Cresskill, NJ: Hampton Press, http://web.mit.edu/schock/www/docs/cs_scc_common_cause.pdf
Slater, David (2004) '"Another World is Possible": On Social Movements, the Zapatistas and the Dynamics of "Globalization from Below",' in David Slater (ed.) *Geopolitics and the Post-colonial: Rethinking North-South Relations,* Malden, MA; Oxford; Carlton, Victoria, Australia: Blackwell Publishing, pp. 197–222.
Thibault, Harold, Gary Dagorn, Service international, Nicolas Bourcier, and Aline Leclerc (2019) 'Du déclencheur local à la révolte globale : la convergence des luttes dans le monde,' *Le Monde,* November 8, updated December 3, 2020, https://www.lemonde.fr/les-decodeurs/article/2019/11/08/du-declencheur-local-a-la-revolte-globale-la-convergence-des-luttes-dans-le-monde_6018514_4355770.html
Tilly, Charles, and Sidney Tarrow (2015) *Contentious Politics,* Second Revised Edition, New York: Oxford University Press.
Wilkin, Peter (2020) 'Fear of a Yellow Planet: The Gilets Jaunes and the End of the Modern World-System,' *Journal of World-Systems Research,* 26(1), pp. 71–102.
World Intellectual Property Organization (2021) 'Inside WIPO,' Geneva, https://www.wipo.int/about-wipo/en/
Youmatter (2020) 'Globalization: Definition, Benefits, Effects, Examples - What is Globalization?,' October 6, https://youmatter.world/en/definition/definitions-globalization-definition-benefits-effects-examples/

4 The Non-Hegemonic Globalization 'from Below'

This chapter analyzes the non-hegemonic globalization 'form below,' a discreet but vast flow of people and goods enacted by huge numbers of 'ant traders.' Subchapter 4.1 discusses the general features of the transnational informal economy, briefly presents its expansion in recent decades in various regions of the Global South, and uses the example of monuments to the 'shuttle trader' in the Commonwealth of Independent States to illustrate the tremendous impact of this phenomenon in economic, social, and cultural terms. Subchapter 4.2 provides a definition of the non-hegemonic globalization 'from below' and discusses its theoretical dimension from an International Relations perspective. Resistance to Neoliberalism is identified as the source of a major normative power clash that opposes this globalization 'from below' to the Western-centered globalization 'from above.' The ambiguous relationship is also analyzed that exists, at times, between the non-hegemonic and counter-hegemonic globalizations 'from below.' Subchapter 4.3 scrutinizes one of the most successful components of the non-hegemonic globalization 'from below': large-scale counterfeiting, which is analyzed as a form of resistance against the Western-centered globalization 'from above.' This practice contributes to multifaceted, in-depth changes in the economic, social, and cultural conditions of large disadvantaged social groups. A fundamental redefinition of what is 'normal' takes place that constructs a way of life based on informality and associated with an anti-Neoliberal, 'fake' – or, rather, 'counterfeit' – modernity. Subchapter 4.4 analyzes the importance of diasporic and migrant communities and networks for the development of the non-hegemonic globalization 'from below.' In the context of transnationalism, migrants' social capital allows them to shape the global and local business environment. The related concepts of 'informal notaries' and 'middleman minorities' are also discussed. Subchapter 4.5 examines the production centers, flows, and nodes of the non-hegemonic globalization 'from below.' Particular attention is paid to two key nodes, Dubai and Yiwu – the world's re-exportation platform of the 1990s and the largest present wholesale market of small commodities in the world, respectively. Peripheral nodes such as Bangkok and Istanbul are also briefly analyzed. Subchapter 4.6 consists of a detailed case study of

DOI: 10.4324/9781003314714-4

the Chinese city of Guangzhou. Its transformation into the most important node of the non-hegemonic globalization 'from below' led to a significant African presence. However, serious Sino-African tensions have emerged as a result of Chinese efforts to supplant African intermediaries; heavy repressive measures adopted since 2008 by the authoritarian Chinese state, which perceives the presence of a large alien group as challenging its control of the society; and racial tensions enhanced by the rejection of Africans as a 'middleman minority.' The downgrading of the 'bridge' between Africa and China to ethnic enclave to trading post is illustrative of the negative social reactions and political responses that the massive development of the non-hegemonic globalization 'from below' can trigger even in places that are among this globalization's greatest beneficiaries. A second case study is presented in Subchapter 4.7. It concerns the largest illegal market in Latin America, Argentina's La Salada. Created as a 'from below' response to the dispossessive effects of Neoliberalism, it is part of a 'migrant economy' that includes large numbers of illegal family workshops and clandestine sweatshops. The projection of normative power associated with La Salada's participation in the non-hegemonic globalization 'from below' has been so effective that political actors and the state itself feel legitimate to disrespect the law and extract profits from illegal activities such as the sale of counterfeit goods, which is informally taxed. The 'counterfeit' modernity of La Salada's 'hodgepodge' of alternative practices and 'proletarian microeconomies' includes a puzzling combination of emancipatory processes conducive to a 'plebeian democracy' and new regimes of submission characterized by 'a certain monstrosity.' Finally, Subchapter 4.8 uses the findings of the case studies to discuss some of the key features of the non-hegemonic globalization 'from below,' the at times unexpected normative clashes and ambiguities associated with its working, and the issue of its actors' agency.

4.1 Informal Economy and 'Ant Trade'

As shown in the previous chapter, it is difficult to deny the remarkable impact of events such as the 'Battle of Seattle' or the World Social Forum on the global public. The various consequences of this activistic success include an unexpected confusion: the media and many scholars tend to understand the globalization 'from below' exclusively as *counter-hegemonic* globalization 'from below.' In turn, 'this bias hinders researchers from seeing other forms of non-hegemonic globalization' (Ribeiro 2006: 234). This chapter analyzes one such form that, despite its discreet nature, is certainly larger and arguably more influential than the 'movement of movements.' This is the non-hegemonic globalization 'from below,' an important component of the global political economy 'in which nation states' normative and repressive roles are heavily bypassed on the economic sphere' (*Ibid.*). The informal transnational economy enacted by millions of small traders mainly – but not exclusively – from the Global South represents a globalization 'from below' that is in no way inferior to the counter-hegemonic one. Moreover, despite the 'non-hegemonic' label, it challenges the Neoliberal globalization 'from above' perhaps more effectively than the activists of Porto Alegre.

This transnational phenomenon cannot be understood outside the more general informal economy, which certain scholars define as 'all licit economic activities that are not regulated by the state and that are taken for economic gain, either in money or in kind' (Yükseker 2003: 137). The problem with such definitions is the 'licit' nature of concerned activities: 'illegal economic activities (...) are not included in this definition' (*Ibid.*). In fact, ambiguity toward normative and legal frameworks is an essential feature of both the informal economy and the non-hegemonic globalization 'from below.' As shown in more detail in the next subchapter, 'informal' frequently means semi-legal and illegal. Limiting the definition to 'licit' activities simply not regulated by the state would leave aside an important part of this economy. To give a basic example, shuttle traders typically undervalue goods they import and bribe customs officials to close their eyes to the lower value and smaller customs duties. This is fully illegal but widely spread in many Global South countries. It would be absurd to argue that the numberless small merchants involved in such illicit activities do not pertain to the informal economy. It is precisely by having their, at times, illegal acts tolerated by authorities and perceived as legitimate by the society that the actors of the non-hegemonic globalization 'from below' redefine 'conceptions of normal' and, therefore, succeed in projecting normative power (see Subchapter 4.8). In this context, it is difficult – or, rather, impossible – to establish clear borders between informal, semi-legal, illegal, and criminal activities. While this is far from representing a generally shared opinion, this book is based on the idea that both the 'moderately' informal transnational economy and that associated with the darker world of transnational organized crime belong to the non-hegemonic globalization 'from below.' Returning to more consensual aspects, the analysis of the informal economy was initially a part of development studies and interested a rather limited number of anthropologists, economists, and sociologists. During the 1980s, there was a significant increase in scholarly interest due to changes brought by the Western-centered globalization 'from above.' On the one hand, there was a global reorganization of production that included subcontracting, flexible specialization, the 'global factory,' as well as the expansion of non-waged forms of work and off-the-books labor. On the other hand, economic crises in the Third World stimulated informal wage labor and subsistence activities (*Ibid.*, 129). Overall, the informal economy developed considerably, a process that continued in the following decades. While, in many societies, it is difficult to distinguish between formal and informal economic sectors (Mathews and Alba Vega 2012: 2), a number of specific features of the informal economy have been identified that are valid in both developing and developed countries. First of all, the formal and informal sectors are systemically connected; the border separating them fluctuates based on the balance of economic and social forces. The status of informal labor is not homogenous: informal workers such as immigrants, homeworkers, women, and children pertain to the category of downgraded labor; but there is also the category of informal entrepreneurs, which includes members of ethnic minorities and, most relevant for the non-hegemonic globalization 'from below,' resourceful immigrants. Finally, the development of the informal economy depends on the tolerance of the state, which implicitly acknowledges the disenfranchisement of a part of the working class (Yükseker 2003: 129–130). The informal economy does exist in the Global North, but it is in the Global South that it is most developed. Sub-Saharan Africa is constantly presented as 'the most informalized region in the world': as much as 73 percent of the labor force employed in non-agricultural sectors works informally; in certain parts of West Africa, this reaches 90 percent (Lee 2014: 15–16; Mathews and Yang 2012: 98). Even more developed Global South countries have surprisingly large informal sectors. In Argentina, the underground economy represents 35 percent of the total (Khlif and Pousset 2014: 37); in the apparel industry, the figure is 78 percent. Accordingly, the informal economy 'can no longer be considered marginal from any point of view' (Gago 2014/2017: 37, 108). Moreover, in many cases, the borders between the formal and informal are blurred. The latter is no more limited to the small-scale activities of the poor; as shown later in this chapter, other social categories are equally involved (Lee 2014: 15). But the poor do represent the majority, and Neoliberal socio-economic polarization has compelled many of them to work and even live in a perpetual state of informality. In the major cities of the Global South, no less than 40 percent of the population lives in illegal conditions; in certain cases, this reaches 70 percent. Between 70 and 95 percent of all new housing is constructed illegally. In such places, stealing electricity and water is a common practice (Liang 2011: 171–172). To depict this strange reality, scholars have even coined the concept of 'fake' modernity (see Subchapter 4.3).

The Rise of the 'Ant Traders'

A part of the informal economy is domestic and concerns exclusively the production of and trade in goods and services that take place on a local or national scale. But the Neoliberal globalization 'from above' has opened borders, increased global awareness and interconnectedness, reduced communication and transportation costs, and created new international business opportunities. Differentials in prices, exchange rates, and customs duties are easier to identify and exploit. This is valid for all merchants, but informal ones are at an advantage in the case of developing countries where the 'normal' cross-border trade – which is controlled by local or multinational companies that are part of the globalization 'from above' – is hampered by red tape, more costly, or simply missing due to discouraging market conditions. Accordingly, people that have already been drawn into informal local trade due to unemployment, poor wages, or landlessness have an incentive to expand their activities internationally (Yükseker 2003: 136). The term 'ant traders' is used in various regions of the world to designate the millions of individuals engaged in this type of cross-border trade. At the El Paso–Ciudad Juarez border crossing and elsewhere on the American–Mexican border, *'comercio hormiga'* ('ant trade') designates an impressive system of smuggling (*'fayuca'*) of small amounts of goods from the United States to be sold in Mexico. This is the only source of revenue for large numbers of Mexican petty traders (Gauthier 2012: 138; Mathews and Alba Vega 2012: 4). Southern France is connected with the Maghreb through Spain or even Italy by the complex networks of numberless 'ant traders' that carry forgeries and smuggled goods or simply import normal merchandise outside official EU quotas. These 'new nomads of the underground economy' are frequently immigrants who have to navigate the complex world of national authorities, local merchants, middlemen from the Maghreb or Senegal, and various mafias. As shown in Subchapter 4.4, their 'migrant societies (...) generate "new cosmopolitanisms" which are now invisible or hidden or displayed in mixity. New forms of identities then occur, founded on the capacity of multiple belonging' (Bruneau 2010: 45–46; Tarrius 2001; Tarrius 2002). The Russian exclave of Kaliningrad, located between Poland and Lithuania, has less than one million inhabitants. Yet, before the Eastern enlargement of the European Union, there were eight to nine million people who crossed its borders every year. This was – and, on a smaller scale, still is – 'ant trade' once more: petty merchants repeatedly go on the other side of the border to sell small amounts of goods (Cichocki *et al.* 2001: 56); to avoid paying full customs duties, they systematically bribe customs officers. At the fall of communism, this phenomenon took mass proportions in the former Soviet republics, where at times it influenced the very structure of the society (see below). In Turkey, which represents one of the key destinations of traders from the Commonwealth of Independent States (CIS), it is called *valiz ticareti* (suitcase trading) (Keyder 1999: 178) because it is literally by suitcase that goods are transported. As such, they are considered 'accompanying baggage' and are not taxed as imports or exports (Yükseker 2003: 134). In Russian, the petty cross-border merchants are called челноки (*chelnoki*), i.e., shuttle traders: indeed, they continuously commute between the country of origin and neighboring ones. The magnitude of this phenomenon is illustrated by the fact that the OECD has even established a definition of shuttle traders as 'individual entrepreneurs [who] buy goods abroad and import them for resale in street markets or small shops.' This is, of course, part of the informal economy: 'often the goods are imported without full declaration in order to avoid import duties' (OECD 2004). 'Trade tourism' is another term employed in the formerly communist area (Sasunkevich 2015: 4).

The impressive development of the 'ant trade' in this region has contributed significantly to the overall expansion of the transnational informal economy that led to the present non-hegemonic globalization 'from below.'

This type of commerce, however, existed in many parts of the Global South long before this globalization emerged. To give two examples from my region, mostly female Jamaican 'higglers' have commuted for more than a century between rural and urban areas to trade staples and necessities. During the 1970s, they turned their previously modest journeys into transnational ones by traveling on a regular basis to Haiti, Panama, and Miami. In Barbados, even 'fashion-conscious female office-workers at multinational data-processing firms' get their cloth from female traders who have similarly shuttled for a long time to the rest of the Caribbean, Miami, and Venezuela (Yükseker 2003: 133–134). Similar practices are even older in Africa. At independence, arbitrarily drawn borders severed preexisting commercial routes. Trade continued – frequently, in the form of smuggling – because the bureaucratic apparatuses of the new states were weak and unable to reinforce effective border controls. Eventually, lack of industrial development and economic crises further stimulated the need for foreign goods, the availability of 'ant traders,' and the state's inability to limit the informal transnational flows of merchandise. For example, in Mobutu's Zaire, participants in such flows included poorly paid urban dwellers, landless and unemployed people from the countryside, and corrupt customs and government officials (*Ibid.*, 133). Yet, it was in the late 1980s and the 1990s that the 'ant trade' expanded tremendously on the scale of the entire Global South. Contributing factors start with the shrinking of the world brought by the Western-centered globalization 'from above.' The aforementioned opening of borders, increased global awareness and interconnectedness, and reduced communication and transportation costs created new business opportunities for small traders. On a darker note, the debt crisis of the 1980s in Latin America and elsewhere in the developing world led to an increase in poverty that multiplied the number of people dependent on the cheaper goods of the informal market. Crisis-related unemployment turned numerous individuals into informal traders; where possible, they soon extended their business journeys to neighboring countries. The decade-long debt crisis was finally brought to an end through the Neoliberal measures adopted under the guidance of the Bretton Woods institutions. These measures – which critically included the highly unpopular Structural Adjustment Programs – brought most of the developing world within the Western-centered globalization 'from above.' They also had dramatic social consequences: at least in the short- and medium-term, strong socio-economic polarization ensued, which further increased poverty and, consequently, the reliance on the informal economy.

Another factor is represented by the end of the Cold War, the fall of communism, and the dismantlement of the Soviet Union. The Moscow-controlled area in Eurasia, as well as many Soviet client states in the Third World, joined the American-led international order and the Western-centered globalization 'from above.' The transition from centrally planned to market economy was long and difficult; it required the support of the IMF and the acceptance of its Neoliberal policies, which replicated the Third World nexus between social polarization, poverty, and informal economy. The associated rise of the 'ant trade' was most impressive in the Commonwealth of Independent States where, before President Gorbachev's Perestroika, the Soviet totalitarian regime strictly controlled the centrally planned economy. Shops were state-owned; the only officially accepted form of private trade was represented by the small and well-regulated peasants' fruit and vegetable markets. At the same time, 'the Soviet economy of deficit created substantial ground for informal economic activities' (Sasunkevich 2015: 4). Concepts such as the 'economics of shortage' were coined to explain the situation of communist states. In the Soviet Union, a parallel 'second economy' developed in response to the prohibition of most private activities, the serious problems of the production and distribution of goods, and large-scale corruption (Yükseker 2003: 130). But very few of its actors were able to cross the rigid borders of the Soviet Union. When Mikhail Gorbachev came to power in 1985, the transnational informal trade was barely existent. Some years later, it had become one of the main forms of commerce in many regions of the new Commonwealth of Independent States. This phenomenon has allowed scholars to draw a conclusion that applies to the non-hegemonic globalization 'from below' as a whole: the significant development of the 'ant trade' on which this globalization is based 'not only describes a particular economic practice but also refers to certain historical, economic and social contexts in which this activity emerged and has been operated' (Sasunkevich 2015: 4). In Hungary and Poland, the beginning of shuttle trade was associated with the open-air markets that the more liberal regimes in those countries started to partially tolerate during the 1970s and the 1980s in response to the economic insufficiency of communism. In the Soviet Union, the informal cross-border trade could develop only in the particular historical context of the Perestroika, and reached maturity during the transition to capitalism in the early 1990s. Three factors contributed to this major change. First, there was the collapse of state-owned production and distribution systems, which led to serious shortages of common consumer goods. Second, the relaxation of border restrictions made travel to neighboring countries possible. Third, 'ant trade' was one of the very few strategies of economic survival available to the numerous post-Soviet losers of the transition from communism to savage capitalism (*Ibid.*, 4–6; Yükseker 2003: 134, 136). Different from the Visegrad countries or the Baltic states, in most of the Commonwealth of Independent States the fall of communism led to authoritarianism, the theft of state property by oligarchs grouped around the dictator, rampant corruption, deindustrialization, and large-scale poverty. There was pervasive *déclassement*: many former clerks, engineers, or teachers set up street stalls or became 'ant traders.' Impoverished pensioner-traders (female ones being known as '*babushka*,' i.e., grandma) could be seen everywhere desperately trying to resell all sorts of things. Moreover, an association of informal trade with illegal and immoral speculation was inherited from the Soviet era. This negative perception was further enhanced by the morally doubtful economic success of businessmen who owed their prosperity to corruption-based relationships with public officials. Accordingly, 'ant trade' was perceived as a low-status and contemptible activity; but it also brought enviable economic advantages. It was 'experienced as humiliation and professional denigration by some and as promising and exciting opportunities by others' (Skvirskaja 2018: S48–S49; Sasunkevich 2015: 4).

Despite status-related issues, hundreds of thousands of 'ant traders' progressively set up flows of consumer goods that connected the various countries of the Commonwealth of Independent States, Asia, Europe, and North Africa. As already mentioned, Turkey was one of the main elements of this vast market. By the mid-1990s, its annual official trade with Russia amounted to $3.3 billion and its overall official exports to $20–25 billion. The 'ant trade' with the former Soviet republics reached no less than $10 billion per year. Customs duties were underpaid while retailing in the CIS evaded taxation as it was carried out in marketplaces (Yükseker 2003: 134–135). Even larger flows have connected the post-Soviet area with China. They were triggered by the normalization of political relations between Moscow and Beijing and, in particular, by the 1992 Sino-Russian treaty, which waived visa requirements for overland group tourism in bordering provinces. Large numbers of petty traders started to commute between Russia's Far East and Siberia, on the one side, and the Chinese Heilongjiang and Inner Mongolia regions, on the other (Nyíri 2002: 24; Xiang 2003: 25). For a time, there was the impression that this is a transitory phenomenon that would come to an end when the 'sharks of capitalism' would replace the 'ant trader.' This change has never arrived; on the contrary, even today newcomers join the Russian-Chinese cross-border trade (Skvirskaja 2018: S51). In the former Soviet republics of Central Asia, a similar development led to the setting up and impressive expansion of huge bazaars that serve as nodal points for the 'ant trade.' In countries such as Kyrgyzstan, the 'poverty shock' triggered by the fall of the Soviet Union was dramatic: in the first five years after independence, the industrial output fell from 28 to 12 percent of GDP, taking 64 percent of the Kyrgyz below the poverty line (Spector 2017: 30; Abazov 2003: 546, 552). Informal trade became a means of survival. A tenth of the entire population engaged in commerce by 1996. There were regions where one family in three relied entirely or mainly on trade-related income (Spector 2017: 27; 29–30). Many of them commuted to neighboring China or traveled to more remote Turkey. The goods they imported were – and still are – sold in the huge Dordoi and Karasuu bazaars located in Bishkek and Osh. Transactions are highly informal: no less than 70 percent of the 'ant traders' make oral agreements and do not use bank accounts (Rudaz 2020: 17). These traders are mainly 'women of all ages and backgrounds' (Spector 2017: 31). By 2006, at Dordoi, 70 percent of them were Kyrgyz and 25 percent Russian; at Karasuu, in the southern Uzbek-inhabited region, 70 percent were Uzbek and 30 percent Kyrgyz (Karrar 2017: 646). Similar to but on a larger scale than the Barakholka and Bolashak bazaars in Kazakhstan's Almaty, Dordoi and Karasuu became huge retail and also wholesale markets serving as key regional logistics hubs (Rudaz 2020: 12; *Akipress.com*, December 6, 2018; Sadovskaya 2016: 62). 'A new market economy of transnational linkages' emerged (Rudaz 2020: 16). 'Ant traders' from other Central Asian republics and Southern Russia arrive every early morning at Dordoi in hundreds of buses to buy and take away Chinese-made goods that are cheaper there than in China or Dubai (Spector 2017: 29). These informal re-exports reached 75 percent of the Kyrgyz imports from China in the 2000s. At US $8.1 billion, in 2008, their value was higher than the country's GDP (Alff 2016: 440).

The rise of informal cross-border trade has been so impressive in the Commonwealth of Independent States that it led to the development of an unexpected symbolic dimension. It was Veronika Cherkasova – a Belarusian investigation journalist murdered in 2004 in her own apartment, likely on orders from the dictator in Minsk – who, the first, wrote about the imaginary erection of a 'monument to the shuttler.' In an article about the massive 'ant trade' at the Belarus-Polish border, she imagined the dark stone statue of a mature, solidly built woman carrying huge bags. 'Hungry children and not a very sober husband' hamper her movements; a stern border guard stands in front of her. The inscription states 'She has struggled...' (Cherkasova 2006; Sasunkevich 2015: 3). The idea did not stay in the realm of literature. The Soviet-inherited appeal of monuments remains surprisingly high in the Commonwealth of Independent States. In a matter of years, such statues were actually constructed all over the region. The first one was inaugurated in 2003 in the town of Bagrationovsk, on the border between the Russian exclave of Kaliningrad and Poland (and not far from the border crossing depicted in Cherkasova's article). By then, a visa regime had been introduced in preparation for the Polish accession to the European Union that, at least temporarily, put the 'ant traders' out of business. The statue was the first to be constructed, but it was nicknamed 'the monument to the last shuttle' (*Polsergmich*, September 8, 2016). This danger was absent elsewhere, even if at times threats of a different nature replaced it. In 2006, a similar statue was erected in Slavyansk, in the Donetsk. This Ukrainian town eventually made the news as the first to be seized by Russian-supported rebels during the 2014 war; it was retaken by the Ukrainians later that year. The 2006 monument shows a man with a suitcase and a carry-on stepping over a symbolic groove: the border (*Ibid.*). Following a logic very different from that of the future war, the crossing of the groove/border suggests that efforts of the 'from below' traders bring together countries that politics 'from above' separate. This message is shared by the symmetrical Russian monument in Belgorod, located only 25 miles north of the border with Ukraine. Two men – likely father and son – energetically struggle with the same combination of suitcases and carry-on bags that connect markets and countries (*Dreamstime.com*, October 05, 2015). Other 'ant trader' statues were aptly placed at the entrance of large markets or bazaars. One, showing two robust women – a former teacher and a former engineer – overloaded with huge bags, was unveiled in July 2009 in front of the main entrance of Tagansky Ryad, the Ural's largest merchandise market located in Yekaterinburg, Russia. The pedestal, in the shape of the globe, suggests the huge distances covered by the region's traders (*Russia-IC*, July 21, 2009). Another monument – husband and wife accompanied by two enormous crates – is located next to the new covered market in Berdsk, close to Russia's Novosibirsk (*Novos.mk.ru*, September 3, 2015). The abovementioned huge Dordoi Bazaar has its own gold-colored monument placed at the main entrance, which similarly shows a man and two women with their respective bags (*Akipress.com*, December 6, 2018). At the other end of the Commonwealth of Independent States, the Slavyansk-Belgorod Ukrainian-Russian dialogue of monuments is mirrored by that between statues erected on the Russian-Chinese border. One is located in Blagoveshchensk, on the Russian bank of the Amur River, in front of China's Heihe. It shows a highly dynamic young man carrying two huge suitcases. An inscription echoes the monument's positive message: 'for the hard work and optimism of the entrepreneurs of the Amur' (Kucera 2009). The other one is the only monument of this type located outside the Commonwealth of Independent States. It is situated in the border city of Manzhouli, in China's Inner Mongolia, which was one of the first Chinese land border cities opened up back in 1992 for trade with neighboring Russia. The importance of the 'ant trade' for Manzhouli's prosperity is well illustrated by the statues of two men and a woman – all of them Caucasian – on the point of packing goods presumably bought in China for sale on a Russian market (Reynolds 2014). In a general conclusion, the 'ant trade' is hardly specific to the Commonwealth of Independent States. But this unparalleled abundance of monuments is illustrative of the tremendous regional impact of this phenomenon in economic, social, and cultural terms. It started suddenly and unexpectedly; it was triggered by a dramatic economic decline that led to humiliating large scale poverty and *déclassement*; it became a permanent feature of the CIS societies, as shown by its persistence three decades after the fall of communism; it has led to a culture of mobility and exchange that was unimaginable under the rigid control of the totalitarian Soviet Union; and, despite the harsh conditions that ensure its survival, it is permeated by the surprising optimism mentioned in the Blagoveshchensk inscription. It can be concluded that the post-Soviet 'ant trade' provides a remarkable example of how the non-hegemonic globalization 'from below' has emerged in specific historical, economic, and social contexts (Sasunkevich 2015: 4) and has actually 'changed the world as we know it' in a large region of the Global South.

4.2 Defining the Non-Hegemonic Globalization 'from Below'

It is clear that the flows of people and goods presented in the previous subchapter are not part of the Western-centered globalization 'from above.'

Shuttle traders from the Commonwealth of Independent States, as well as the Istanbul shopkeepers and small-scale manufacturers who provide goods that fill their suitcases certainly form a transnational trade network. But this is part of an informal economy that has very little to do with the multinational corporate sector or with the multilateral institutions that govern the Neoliberal globalization (Yükseker 2003: 135). The relentless efforts of numberless 'ant traders' have constructed the very different non-hegemonic globalization 'from below,' which develops spontaneously in all the economic niches and interstices neglected by the Western-centered globalization 'from above' (Tudoroiu 2022: 2) and is defined as

> the transnational flow of people and goods involving relatively small amounts of capital and informal, often semi-legal or illegal transactions, often associated with 'the developing world' but in fact apparent across the globe.
> (Mathews and Alba Vega 2012: 1)

Unknown to many, petty and apparently insignificant actors have succeeded in setting up *'des processus économiques lourds,'* powerful economic processes that escape the framework of public action and states' control (Peralva 2003: 191; Tarrius 2002) but do shape the international political economy of a large part of the planet. It is remarkable that such a major impact has been achieved by mere 'business without lawyers and copyrights, run through skeins of personal connections and wads of cash' (Mathews and Alba Vega 2012: 1). Operations typically involve small amounts of capital, but actors become upwardly mobile through the use of infrastructural advancements provided by the Western-centered globalization 'from above' (Yang 2011a: 3). Frequently, their activity includes 'semilegal or illegal transactions under the radar of the law' (Mathews and Yang 2012: 95; see the following sections) such as smuggling, counterfeiting, or underground banking (Yang 2011a: 3). In this globalization, 'the line between formal and informal activities is a fluid one' (Yükseker 2003: 132). As shown in Subchapter 4.4, networks – including ethnic ones – play an important role. 'Ant traders' act based on a logic of deterritorialization: they are 'actors between worlds with the ability to be here and there at the same time.' They define 'circulatory territories' (Khlif and Pousset 2014: 39), directly and – at least in much of the Global South – successfully competing with the flows of people and goods of the Neoliberal globalization 'from above.' In fact, this globalization 'from below' is 'the only globalization that many inhabitants of the extreme periphery may ever experience' (Mathews 2011: 236). Indeed, most of sub-Saharan Africa and other similar regions are affected by the severe underdevelopment of formal retail activities. Many buyers rely on petty trading, street vending, and hawking. Without the foreign goods brought by the non-hegemonic globalization 'from below,' they 'would be excluded from globalisation' (Zack 2015: 135): '"globalization from below" is globalization as experienced by most of the world's people' (Mathews and Alba Vega 2012: 1). Accordingly, this impactful process has aptly been described as a *'globalización popular'* (people's globalization) (Ribeiro 2012b) that connects the 'poor, but hungry for modernity' citizens of peripheral regions with the rest of the world (Peralva 2003: 191; Tarrius 2002). It 'provides access to flows of global wealth that otherwise would not reach the more vulnerable ranks of any society' (Ribeiro 2006: 233). In the words of an African trader in Guangzhou, 'what I do is good for Africa' (Yang 2011a: 115). A street peddler from Mexico City similarly stated that the transnational trade he was involved in 'is not a problem, it is a solution. The problem was created elsewhere; we are solving it' (Mathews and Alba Vega 2012: 2). In fact, the 'ant traders' solve two problems: that of the large social groups of impoverished consumers who get access to desired goods; and that related to their own precarious socio-economic situation. As mentioned in Subchapter 4.1, people engage in informal transnational trade due to 'joblessness, barriers to entry into the formal labor market (especially in the case of women), below-subsistence wages, and landlessness' (Yükseker 2003: 136). They are excluded from participating in and benefiting from the Neoliberal globalization 'from above.' Ultimately, it is 'social exclusion [that] is the *raison d'être* for globalization from below' (Khlif and Pousset 2014: 39). The latter 'open[s] an avenue for upward mobility or the possibility of survival in national and global economies that are not capable to provide full employment for all citizens' (Ribeiro 2006: 235). This is to say that the non-hegemonic globalization 'from below' restores to the poor their 'capacity for initiative' (Peralva 2003: 192; Tarrius 2002). This important agency-related aspect has a direct impact on the theoretical understanding of the globalization under scrutiny.

Structure, Agency, and International Relations Theories

It is easy to note that the 'ant trade' and its actors are more frequently studied by specialists in Anthropology, Sociology, Development Studies, Entrepreneurship (Rui 2018: S14), Diaspora Studies, and Diaspora Business Studies than by economists specialized in trade. However, in addition to aspects specific to all these fields, there is a connection with the theory of International Relations that is most relevant; in fact, it has influenced the very name of this globalization. When the informal transnational economy began to be studied as a form of globalization, the 'from below' term had already been associated with the counter-hegemonic globalization presented in the previous chapter. The 'non-hegemonic' label was chosen to differentiate these two globalizations 'from below' using the key criterion of their relationship with the hegemony on which the Western-centered globalization 'from above' is based. Gustavo Lins Ribeiro has introduced the term 'non-hegemonic world-system' to designate 'the markets, flows, and trade networks that are part of globalization from below.' He called it non-hegemonic 'simply because it is not the dominant form of globalization seeking to mold us in its image, but rather an alternative to this, following different pattern and rules' (Ribeiro 2012a: 221). As a concept, the 'non-hegemonic world-system' combines Immanuel Wallerstein's World System Theory with a Gramscian understanding of hegemony, which represents 'the naturalized and silent exercise of power, the naturalization by different social groups and classes of the sanctioned modes of the reproduction of social life' (*Ibid.*, 233). Both Gustavo Ribeiro and Gordon Mathews went into more detail to explain that Wallerstein's approach – based on a core-semiperiphery-periphery hierarchical structure – does provide a useful analytical framework, but 'can be rightfully criticized for its emphasis on states as the locus of globalization, leaving aside subnational and supranational processes of globalization that bypass states' (Mathews 2011: 235). In fact, the interactions of the non-hegemonic globalization 'from below' 'take place against this world economic backdrop.' They do 'not fit much contemporary theorizing concerning global capitalism' because, instead of a movement of producers and capital from the core to the periphery, there is a movement of traders 'from the extreme periphery to the semiperiphery to buy cast-off, knockoff, or copy goods from the core.' It is only these goods that move 'from core to semiperiphery to extreme periphery' or simply from semiperipheries such as China to periphery (*Ibid.*, 235–237). This view based on the World System Theory represents the only effort to place the non-hegemonic globalization 'from below' in the framework of International Relations theories. In fact, in most of the literature, this is a marginal aspect whose treatment is limited to a quick reference to Ribeiro or Mathews. Frequently, 'core' and 'periphery' are employed as mere synonyms for Global North and Global South. Essentially, the International Relations dimension is not perceived as important by scholars interested in anthropological, sociological, development, or entrepreneurship issues; and the easy-to-understand World System view seems to provide a reasonable theoretical framework. Furthermore, it is part of the wider and highly appreciated contribution of the aforementioned scholars to the study of the non-hegemonic globalization 'from below,' which implicitly provides a high degree of legitimacy.

This book proposes an International Relations view of globalizations 'from below.' The associated International Relations theoretical framework is therefore essential. The problem with the use of the World System Theory (Wallerstein 1974, 1980) is that it represents a positivist structural approach. As all positivist theories, it claims that objective knowledge is possible and absolute truth can be scientifically proved. It can identify laws of the social world in general and the International Relations in particular, which dictate the course of human history. Wallerstein combined two neo-Marxist approaches – Dependency Theory and Johan Galtung's Structural Imperialism – with Fernand Braudel's *long durée* vision to explain what he sees as the present core-periphery structure of the international system. This hierarchical structure is analyzed as the effect of economic factors that emerged in the early modern era and critically led to the industrialization and ensuing international supremacy of what eventually became the core of the international system. In constructing his theory, the American scholar followed the Marxist economic determinism of Dependency and Structural Imperialism. The purely materialist chain of causality he identified looks very much like Marx's Economics-based iron law of history that humans cannot escape. It is important to mention that more sophisticated forms of post-positivist neo-Marxism exist, which are inspired by the Frankfurt School and Antonio Gramsci. The best known is Robert Cox's Critical Theory (Cox 1981/1986) which adds to material (i.e., economic) factors the power of ideas and institutions. As all post-positivist theories, this approach denies the existence of 'objective,' inescapable laws of history: ideas can and do change the course of historical events. Importantly, Critical Theory is explicitly based on a Gramscian understanding of hegemony similar to that of Ribeiro. Such an understanding, however, is incompatible with the determinism of Wallerstein's view, where ideas have no place: the core dominates the periphery due to a historical process based on the early transition to capitalism that led to economic, political, and military superiority; legitimacy is a mere side effect. Gustavo Ribeiro's aforementioned combination of World System Theory and legitimacy-based, Gramscian hegemony is therefore inherently flawed. An even more important issue is that, unlike Cox, Immanuel Wallerstein constructed a theory that is structural in nature: similar to Galtung's Structural Imperialism or Waltz's Neorealism, it explains all international interactions as direct and inevitable consequences of the way the international system is structured. In this view, any political or economic international development is due to the basic fact that the core dominates and exploits the periphery. This is an extreme position within the structure-agency debate that has represented a key aspect in the development of the International Relations theory that I prefer, Constructivism. Because World System is a structural (or systemic) theory, it leaves no place for the agency of actors. This is to say that, within the non-hegemonic globalization 'from below,' the 'ant traders' are prisoners of higher forces and act as mere puppets of systemic factors they cannot challenge. Implicitly, the non-hegemonic globalization 'from below' is an expression of impersonal, overwhelming factors very similar to those taken into consideration by the globalist view of the Western-centered globalization 'from above': they lead to an unstoppable process that human decisions and actions cannot influence or control. My impression is that neither Ribeiro nor Mathews were fully aware of this dimension of the World System Theory. They have never mentioned it while their studies suggest that 'ant traders' do play a highly autonomous role. Gustavo Ribeiro even states, 'I am seriously taking into account one of anthropology's most powerful assets: the consideration of the agent's points-of-view' (Ribeiro 2006: 234). Unfortunately, acknowledging the role of actors is incompatible with the use of Wallerstein's theory. This book argues that the non-hegemonic globalization 'from below' is in large part the result of agency. The Constructivist analysis I propose does not deny the importance of structural factors. I acknowledge the fact that both the counter-hegemonic and non-hegemonic globalizations 'from below' are consequences of and responses to the dominant Western-centered globalization 'from above.' In part, the economic activities of the 'ant traders' are simple rational choice reactions to the constraints and opportunities created by this globalization. But they are not entirely due to these structural causes. Ideas of a different nature also are at work. The 'ant traders' may not have a clearly defined ideology such as that of the alter-globalist activists. But, as shown at the end of the previous section, they are part of a globalization that restores the 'capacity for initiative' of victims of Neoliberalism (Peralva 2003: 192; Tarrius 2002). Such agency is influenced by individual aspirations of upward social mobility, subjective personal plans and ambitions, and even adventurous entrepreneurial decisions. Through their aggregation, 'trading cultures of circulation' (Castillo 2014: 240; Lee and LiPuma 2002) emerge and develop that are translocal in nature (Ribeiro 2006: 247). As shown by the post-Soviet example presented in the previous subchapter, they can transform entire societies up to the point of being reflected in monumental art. All this can be explained with relative ease by a theoretical approach such as Constructivism, which gives a prominent role to the intersubjective dimension and acknowledges the importance of agency. The reliance on World System Theory, on the contrary, has limited the International Relations analysis to a very basic use of the concepts of core, semiperiphery, and periphery; and has brought to light little more than the differences between the directions of flows associated with the Western-centered globalization 'from above' and the non-hegemonic globalization 'from below,' respectively. To an anthropologist or a specialist in entrepreneurship, this may seem sufficient; to them, International Relations aspects are of marginal importance. But anthropology or entrepreneurship cannot provide a theoretical framework able to fully analyze *all* globalizations 'from below.' As explained in Chapter 7, it is only using an International Relations approach that this becomes possible. This approach, however, cannot be the World System Theory. It is in the last part of the section 'Normative Power, Agency, and Constructivism' of Subchapter 7.1 that I discuss the features of the Constructivist framework I propose.

Informality, Power, and Resistance

As part of the informal economy, the non-hegemonic globalization 'from below' consists, as already shown, of 'business without lawyers and copyrights, run through skeins of personal connections and wads of cash' (Mathews and Alba Vega 2012: 1). It 'typically involves self-employment, small-scale operation, labour intensiveness, skills obtained outside the formal educational system, and unregulated markets' (Mathews and Yang 2012: 98). Its typical actors are the shuttle traders that travel periodically to neighboring countries, Dubai, or China to buy or sell goods that tend to escape the normal regime of taxes and customs duties. Due to the importance of ethnic networks (see Subchapter 4.4), many such traders are entrepreneurial migrants or members of local ethnic or religious minorities. Street vendors of global gadgets enact the same globalization even if they only resell locally goods informally imported from the same countries. However, even these numerous vendors 'are but the tip of the iceberg, in a huge parallel global economy' (Ribeiro 2006: 234). Gustavo Lins Ribeiro described it as a pyramid composed of 'diverse types of segments and networks.' The upper levels are shared by various forms of corruption, money laundering, and Mafia-style activities. The much larger bottom of the pyramid relies on the massive involvement of poor people. The entire structure is cemented by networking and brokerage among transnational, national, regional, and local agents. The activities in the lower segments of this pyramid represent the non-hegemonic globalization 'from below' (*Ibid.*; Ribeiro 2012a: 225). It goes without saying that, given its informal character, this globalization cannot be measured: 'there are no reliable statistics, only rough estimates' (Mathews and Yang 2012: 98). Such estimates, as well as qualitative studies, do nevertheless allow for a credible assessment of this phenomenon's geographical distribution. The latter 'is most readily apparent in the developing world' (*Ibid.*), even if 'it is present today in every society on the globe: "globalization from below" is by no means synonymous with "developing-world globalization"' (Mathews and Alba Vega 2012: 10). As shown in Subchapter 4.1, this mirrors the distribution of domestic informal economy, which in countries such as the Democratic Republic of Congo reaches no less than 90 percent (Mathews and Yang 2012: 98), but also exists in developed states. On the one hand, this has led scholars to argue that 'everywhere in the world, globalization from below is impossible to stop; it is inevitable' (Mathews and Alba Vega 2012: 10). On the other, the North-South contrast is due not to the fact that 'developing-world economies do not seek to regulate, but rather because they lack the means to do so, compared to their more regulated and policed developed-world counterparts' (*Ibid.*). This brings the discussion to the critical issue of efforts made to repress the non-hegemonic globalization 'from below,' which are part of a major normative power clash.

When they can act more or less freely, the 'ant traders' are very effective competitors of the 'normal' actors of the Western-centered globalization 'from above.' At the same time, because of their informal nature, their 'activities defy the economic establishment everywhere on the local, regional, national, international and transnational levels' (Ribeiro 2006: 234). It is hardly surprising that the economic and political elites whose interests are affected portray their rivals as a threat to the establishment. They 'create a transgressive image of the workers and entrepreneurs of the non-hegemonic system' and use 'the control of state apparatuses and wider political structures' (Ribeiro 2012a: 230) to redefine international and national laws and regulations in ways that make the informal economy illegal. 'Most of the time such activities are treated as police matters, as the focus of elaborate repressive action' (Ribeiro 2006: 234). Governments typically try to repress the non-hegemonic globalization 'from below' and turn it into Neoliberal globalization 'from above' through the use of three instruments: banking, formalization, and fiscalization. 'Ant traders' are pressed to open and use bank accounts, formally register their businesses, and pay taxes (Mathews and Alba Vega 2012: 10). Similar to the more general informal economy discussed at the beginning of this chapter, the non-hegemonic globalization 'from below' includes formal, informal, semi-legal, illegal, and criminal activities that tend to be perceived as fully legitimate by the traders themselves and are socially accepted by the general population (Ribeiro 2013: 34). Technically, selling fake and/or illegally imported smartphones in the streets of a Global South city is 100 percent illegal. And yet, involved peddlers hardly look like enemies of the society. Many such 'ant traders' 'either do not know or do not want to know' the criminal ramifications of their commercial activities: such ignorance 'is important to reinforce these social actors' self-perception as workers and as citizens (as opposed to criminals) struggling for the survival and hope of prosperity of their families' (Ribeiro 2012a: 226). Neither their customers nor the society at large sees them as criminals. On the contrary, they are appreciated as useful providers of otherwise unavailable cheap goods. Moving to a more radical example, drug trafficking is almost universally associated with the sinister category of transnational organized crime. But its sudden disappearance would bring despair to millions all over the planet (and this might be a severe understatement). Moreover, the selective decriminalization of drugs adopted in recent years by various governments in the Global North is a good illustration of the relative and arbitrary legal boundaries that fragment the formal to criminal continuum. The same act may be legally acceptable or a crime after and before a certain date, or on the two sides of the same border. This can be generalized to many other fields: 'the line between formal and informal activities is a fluid one' (Yükseker 2003: 132). In addition, processes pertaining to different legal categories 'may intertwine, feed on each other, and keep hierarchical relations' (Ribeiro 2012a: 225). This is why I believe that it is impossible to clearly separate the informal transnational economy from the criminal transnational economy. Consequently, I consider the latter to be part of the non-hegemonic globalization 'from below.'

Returning to the efforts of the establishment to suppress the informal economic activities enacted by large numbers of poor 'ant traders' by demonizing and declaring them illegal, it is clear that 'there is no moral monopoly of honesty by any social segments'; this is simply done on the basis of power differences (*Ibid.*, 221–222). Two approaches can be adopted to analyze this phenomenon. One is ultimately based on class struggle: 'definitions of what is legal and illegal often reflect the history of power relationships among differentiated social segments and classes' (Ribeiro 2006: 234). The other one is closer to the scope of this book: it relies on 'the structuring power of the globalization from above' (Ribeiro 2012a: 223). It is the overwhelming power of the Western-centered globalization 'from above' that, internationally and nationally, translates into the use of political, legal, economic, and fiscal instruments to repress the rival globalization 'from below.' The (re)definition of legal and illegal 'reflects the institutional logics of power holders operating within state apparatuses and private firms' in ways that harm, on purpose, the interests of actors placed in 'subaltern positions in social and political systems' (*Ibid.*, 223–225). This is clearly a projection of normative power conceived by key actors of the Neoliberal globalization as a systematic effort to suppress the non-hegemonic globalization 'from below.' If the informal international trade is nevertheless flourishing in the Global South, this is due mainly to the limited capacities of states (Yükseker 2003: 135): 'globalization from below can prosper where the state has less capacity or will to regulate' (Mathews and Alba Vega 2012: 8). In Africa, for example, the declining capacities of states related to corruption, poor border controls, lack of industrial development, endemic foreign currency problems, and inadequate roads prevent the effective repression of the informal transnational trade. For their part, extremely difficult socio-economic conditions limit the will of concerned states to suppress activities that are ultimately useful to their national economies and citizens. Informal exports bring in much-needed foreign currency. Informal imports do involve outflows of foreign currency and a loss in tariff revenues, but provide essential goods that are otherwise unavailable: 'this may be the main lifeline of the population' (Yükseker 2003: 135–136). Consequently, the numerous developing states that find themselves in this situation are far less able and willing to repress the non-hegemonic globalization 'from below' than Global North states. However, they are hardly free to make their own choices. Examples such as the piracy of Western brand names in Turkey show how global regulation is strongly supported by local corporate actors, as well as multinational corporations that put pressure on the government as they want to be the only ones in control of the brand trade (*Ibid.*, 135; the issue of pirated goods is presented in Subchapter 4.3). While results are uneven in the Global South and the Global North, the Western-centered globalization 'from above' is using its tremendous power in a global war against the non-hegemonic globalization 'from below.'

The latter, however, is not a passive victim. Systematically, its '"alternative" transnational agents disregard or bypass the normative and regulating power of nation-states.' In many parts of the developing world, they are most successful: 'nation states' normative and repressive roles are heavily bypassed on the economic sphere' (Ribeiro 2006: 234, 247). From the perspective of its actors, 'informal trade constitutes a resistance to the nation–states and to the logic of capital' that 'serves the purpose of economic survival' (Yükseker 2003: 136); it is 'a response from below to the dispossessive effects of neoliberalism' (Gago 2014/2017: 68; Gago 2012: 77). In both normative and practical terms, the Western-centered globalization 'from above' pictures its rival as 'an evil that must be suppressed' (Mathews and Alba Vega 2012: 10). The non-hegemonic globalization 'from below,' however, was successful in reshaping 'conceptions of normal' among large audiences in ways that lead to its perception as beneficial and make its suppression impossible (*Ibid.*). This significant production of normative power is at the core of the non-hegemonic globalization 'from below,' which represents a strong form of resistance against the normative, political, and economic dominance of the Neoliberal globalization 'from above.' Consequently, the 'non-hegemonic' label is rather inappropriate. The globalization of the 'ant traders' is not less anti-hegemonic than the counter-hegemonic one. While it does not proclaim an explicit anti-Neoliberal ideology, *de facto* it acts in ways that diminish the reach of the Western-centered globalization 'from above' on a much larger scale and more effectively than the 'movement of movements' presented in the previous chapter.

One of the consequences of this situation is related to the terms employed in the literature: it shows the inappropriateness of the term 'low-end globalization' that is sometimes used instead of globalization 'from below.' 'Low-end' correctly points to the tendency of this globalization's discreet actors to stay 'under the radar of the law' (Mathews and Yang 2012: 95). Yet, it also hides their challenge of the dominant globalization 'from above.' To make a comparison with the realm of revolutionary movements, it would be a bit difficult to speak about 'low-end' regime change. 'From below,' on the contrary, is indicative of a bottom-up effort that can – and, in this case, does – challenge the *status quo* (Tudoroiu 2022: 14). The non-hegemonic and counter-hegemonic globalizations 'from below' are therefore much more similar than a superficial observer might think. However, a general conclusion cannot be drawn on the opposition between globalizations 'from below' and 'from above.' The Chinese globalization 'from below' is opposed to the Western-centered globalization 'from above,' but forms a virtuous circle with the Chinese globalization 'from above' (see the next chapter). Globalizations are complex phenomena that interact in various and at times unexpected ways. This aspect is further analyzed in the following section.

Interacting Globalizations and Ambiguity

Previous pages have shown the antagonistic character of the relationship between the Western-centered globalization 'from above' and the non-hegemonic globalization 'from below.' It is beyond a shadow of a doubt that the former wages a global crusade against the latter, which it appropriately identifies as a dangerous challenger. However, the non-hegemonic globalization does more than simply waging its own, more discreet anti-Neoliberal crusade. Its relations with the globalization 'from above' are in fact 'complementary and contradictory' (Mathews and Alba Vega 2012: 6). Moreover, between the two rival globalizations, 'borderlines are multifarious and imprecise' (Ribeiro 2012a: 225). First of all, the non-hegemonic globalization 'from below' could have not emerged without the major changes brought by the Western-centered globalization 'from above.' The latter's remarkable results in terms of global interconnectedness and mutual awareness 'have also opened the door to the development of international interaction among weaker actors.' Concerned factors include technological progress but also the global diffusion of certain social values and 'the development of a conscience of transnationally-shared elements' (Fonseca and Malheiros 2004: 132). More unexpectedly, processes have emerged through which agents of the two globalizations communicate and interact. 'Politics is shown to be the channel most capable of creating flows' of this type. Economic ones include money laundering, the use of formal transnational financial instruments in informal activities, and corruption. Differences between the two globalizations 'are blurred in the liminal situations where connecting mechanisms allow for the articulation of common political and economic interests of agents and brokers from both' (Ribeiro 2012a: 229–230). The fundamental element that makes such cooperation possible is the fact that 'ant traders' do not seek to destroy capitalism. Their globalization is 'from below,' but it is nevertheless based on free-market principles. Far from being radicals or revolutionaries, the actors of the non-hegemonic globalization 'from below' 'simply [want] to make their livings within their societies.' Various limitations and constraints force them to take the path of informal activities, but they 'have the same desires as the secretaries, analysts, executives, bankers, and lawyers' of the rival globalization: 'that of becoming affluent.' While more brutal interactions also exist (see Subchapter 4.7), in general these actors tend to construct 'a warmer, more human' globalization that, different from the Neoliberal one, 'does not necessarily sever human social bonds' (Mathews and Alba Vega 2012: 7–8, 11; Ribeiro 2012a: 225).

In this, the similarity with the counter-hegemonic globalization 'from below' is once more apparent. Given their common points, one would expect certain forms of cooperation to develop between the two globalizations 'from below.' However, paradoxical situations were noted where alter-globalization movements have served as instruments of the Neoliberal globalization 'from above' in countering the informal activities of the 'ant traders.' One such case was studied by Robert Shepherd at Washington's Eastern Market, a historic public market in a major city of the Global North where the non-hegemonic globalization 'from below' takes the form of a diverse array of immigrant vendors selling imported goods. In recent decades, such public markets have experienced increased internationalization as immigrants benefit from a number of comparative advantages with respect to local traders in the specific context of micro-market import settings. But, far from celebrating marketplace diversity, an unexpected alliance of city officials, community leaders, and local vendors sought to restrict the activities of the immigrants on the basis of a discourse of localism and authenticity that rejects the 'cheap' and 'foreign,' i.e., the defining features of the non-hegemonic globalization 'from below.' This is illustrative of a wider American urban phenomenon that is increasingly visible at the local level of public life. A 'coalition of anti-globalization critics, organic and natural food proponents, and urban planners' – that is, a surprising mixture of actors of the counter-hegemonic globalization 'from below' and the Western-centered globalization 'from above' – 'advocate for a public market space protected from the standardization of global capitalism.' This discourse claims to protect and promote market diversity and the interests of 'an ambiguously defined "community".' In fact, it 'leads to a "cleaning up" of market diversity' (Shepherd 2012: 187) by putting immigrant vendors out of business. Ultimately, the Neoliberal globalization fights 'ant traders' that try to exploit a niche in the Global North 'through an ideological smokescreen proclaiming "you don't belong here"' (Mathews and Alba Vega 2012: 54), and affluent neighborhood activists support it. These activists are members of movements pertaining to the counter-hegemonic globalization 'from below,' but also represent 'an urban, highly cosmopolitan and privileged group of elites.' There is an underlying tension between these 'privileged people located at the center of the global trade system' and the actors of the non-hegemonic globalization 'from below' who are poor and come from more marginal areas. This tension – that cannot be dissociated from class and status differences – has helped to turn the 'ant traders' into targets of alter-globalization activists who believe that 'resisting global forces means protecting and privileging an abstract "local"' (Shepherd 2012: 200). Ironically, this makes them objective allies of the Neoliberal globalization 'from above' and adversaries of the non-hegemonic globalization 'from below' that challenges it.

However, such paradoxical situations represent the exception rather than the rule. In the huge majority of cases, both globalizations 'from below' oppose the 'from above' one. One of the fields where their actions show a remarkable degree of convergence is presented in the next subchapter.

4.3 Practical Resistance: Challenging Intellectual Property Rights

Subchapter 3.3 Legal Resistance: Challenging Intellectual Property Rights has presented the important law-related component of the counter-hegemonic globalization 'from below' intended to dismantle Neoliberal international legal regimes. One of its key targets is the protection of intellectual property rights, which alter-globalists perceive as an unjust hegemonic set of laws, norms, and enforcement mechanisms that perpetuate structural inequalities between the Global North and Global South. The struggle of the social justice movement against the 1996 Agreement on Trade-Related Aspects of Intellectual Property Rights (TRIPS) of the World Trade Organization includes forms of resistance that range from everyday practice to counter-projects that challenge private ownership and commodity logic in an effort to develop an ethic of collaborative post-scarcity production. The unsophisticated but vast level of daily practices – which many people may not even associate with a political stance – includes, among others, the large-scale distribution and use of audiovisual material, software, and various other goods generally labeled as pirated (Schweidler and Costanza-Chock 2009: 4–5, 23). It is on this point that the convergence of the counter-hegemonic and non-hegemonic globalizations 'from below' is most visible. Indeed, counterfeiting goods and smuggling them to countries whose citizens are too poor to buy the original represent a key activity of the non-hegemonic globalization 'from below' (Yang 2011a: 3). Cheap counterfeit goods mostly made in China contribute to 'enabl[ing] Africa and other developing-world regions to experience globalization' (Mathews and Yang 2012: 95). From a moral point of view, there are important differences between making inferior copies of pharmaceutical products, which may kill patients, and copying, cheaply and poorly, a DVD or a Louis Vuitton bag that nobody could otherwise afford in a poor community (Mathews and Alba Vega 2012: 9). But the Neoliberal globalization 'from above' makes no such subtle differences. The TRIPS international legal regime places all pirated goods in the same category and national governments, as well as international agencies, accordingly make considerable efforts to repress their production and trade. Results, however, seem disproportionately modest. Due to advancements in communications and the deregulation of commodity flows, counterfeiting has become 'a global-extensive mode of operation' and 'a sophisticated global business specializing in wideranging goods.' In 2007, the value of these goods reached US $250 billion (Yang 2016: 18). The 2013 figure was US $461 billion, equal to 2.5 percent of world trade or the GDP of Austria (OECD and EUIPO 2016: 11). In 2015 and 2016, the international trade in goods fell by 13 percent and 3 percent, respectively. But the international trade in counterfeit and pirated products increased to US $509 billion in 2016. For the European Union, imports of such goods expanded from 5 percent of all imports in 2013 to 6.8 percent in 2016, representing no less than Euro 121 billion or US $134 billion (OECD and EUIPO 2019: 11, 17). It can be argued that counterfeiting is one of the most successful components of the non-hegemonic globalization 'from below' and one that has developed on a significant scale even in the Global North.

Technically, there is a clear difference between counterfeiting and piracy. In the literature on intellectual property rights, the former term is used for goods that usurp the brand or trademark of another product. Piracy refers to the infringement of copyright through the reproduction of artistic creations or technology-based works. Yet, in common language, this distinction is frequently blurred. Both terms are taken as synonyms of fake, knock-off, pirate copy, or bootleg (Yang 2016: 16). Etymologically, 'piracy' hardly needs any explanation. But 'counterfeit' comes from the late 13th century Anglo-French '*countrefet*,' a form of the Old French '*contrefait*' (which continues to exist in Modern French). In turn, French inherited it from Latin:

'*contra*' means 'against,' 'in opposition to,' while 'facere' stands for 'to make' (Online Etymology Dictionary 2021). Counterfeit goods are therefore 'counter-made,' which 'implies an oppositional relation to what is simply "made" – that is, produced under normal, if not normalized, conditions.' Their value is not intrinsic; it 'depends on the recognition of counterfeit as relational to the IPR-protected, authorized branded commodity.' Ultimately, 'the counterfeit matches the brand in emblematizing an "intensive economy" predicated upon information' (Yang 2016: 17). It should be noted that, while they are trade-related *par excellence*, both the brand and the associated counterfeit are cultural objects. They 'emerge from a meaning-generative process. They are produced in circulation, not just transmitted by it' (*Ibid., 16*). A brand such as Apple – and the 'cult' created around it – is 'created by the interactions between specific types of circulating forms and the interpretive communities built around them' (Lee and LiPuma 2002: 192; Yang 2016: 16). Similarly, the objecthood of the counterfeit cannot emerge outside the process of circulation and without 'a community of meaning makers who are cognizant of the institutional arrangement that authorizes the brand's "original" status' (Yang 2016: 16–17). Economically, brands and especially superlogos – i.e., brands, such as Apple, that are recognized globally as symbols of privileged status – 'generate an exceptional surplus based on [their] symbolic value, on what [they] mean as a status symbol for consumers' (Ribeiro 2012a: 231–232). But this exceptional surplus exists only in the context of a monopoly. The development of counterfeiting and piracy has triggered competition for the control of the surplus. These activities have 'a subversive potential that puts in danger a major force underneath capitalist reproduction' (*Ibid.*, 233) and the associated Neoliberal globalization 'from above.' This is why, for this globalization, the repression of counterfeiting and piracy represents a critical issue. As these activities are essential components of the non-hegemonic globalization 'from below,' major tensions between the two globalizations ensue.

The demand for counterfeit and pirated goods is influenced by factors that include features of the product such as price or perceived quality; characteristics of the individual consumer such as their economic situation but also their attitude toward piracy; and the consumer's institutional environment, which may refer to the availability of pirated products but also the risk of penalties. The supply is driven by market opportunities; technological and distribution challenges; and risks. It should be noted that there are two types of markets for counterfeit and pirated goods. On the so-called secondary one, buyers are aware of the illicit nature of the merchandise. On the primary market, on the contrary, they ignore it. Because they believe that products are original, one cannot speak of demand for pirated goods in this case (OECD and EUIPO 2016: 21, 23). The overall trade in counterfeit and pirated products is strongly influenced by gaps in governance. High levels of corruption, as well as poor enforcement of intellectual property rights, are particularly impactful. Other contributing factors include the existence of free trade zones, where counterfeiters benefit from good infrastructure and limited oversight; production and logistic facilities; and trade facilitation policies (OECD and EUIPO 2018: 2–3; 2019: 15, 17). Many industries are affected: fake products include common consumer goods, business-to-business products, IT goods, and luxury items. Ten main sectors are particularly vulnerable: foodstuff; pharmaceutical products; perfumery and cosmetics; leather articles and handbags; clothing and fabrics; footwear; jewelry; electronics and electrical equipment; optical, photographic, and medical equipment; and toys, games, and sports equipment. Statistics based on the number of seizures in 2011–2013 and 2014–2016 show that the same eight categories of products were most pirated: footwear; clothing; leather articles; electrical machinery and equipment; watches; sunglasses; perfumes and cosmetics; and toys and games. However, new counterfeit products were also identified: fur skins and artificial fur salt; sulfur; earth and stone; lime and cement; and ores, slag, and ash. There was also an important quantitative increase in the trade of counterfeit guitars and construction materials. This dynamic 'proves that counterfeiters apply very aggressive strategies, dynamically looking for all kinds of profit opportunities' (OECD and EUIPO 2019: 11, 30, 32; 2017).

Most of the companies that fall victim to counterfeiting and piracy are located in Western Europe and the United States. Yet, a growing number of manufacturers from Singapore and Hong Kong, as well as emerging economies such as Brazil and China, are also affected by this type of activity (OECD and EUIPO 2019: 12). In terms of place of production, the fake goods 'originate from virtually all economies on all continents'; however, some countries are massively involved while others are much less active (OECD and EUIPO 2018: 2). By far, China and Hong Kong are the most important producers of such goods (OECD and EUIPO 2019: 12). China – 'since at least the 1990s, the "faking" nation' – has been the uncontested champion. In both the United States and the European Union, seized Chinese counterfeit goods 'far exceed those of other countries' (Yang 2016: 18). Yet, the quality of these copies is often less than perfect. It is South Korea that produces fine imitations of luxury goods, which have turned it into 'the world capital of supercopies'; and Italy that specializes in counterfeits that incorporate high-quality craftsmanship and materials (*Ibid.*, 18–19). Closer to the Chinese pattern but much more modest in terms of volume, India, Malaysia, Pakistan, Thailand, and Vietnam also are important producers. In sectors such as leather goods, foodstuffs, and cosmetics, Turkey is a key producer of pirated goods that are exported to the European Union (OECD and EUIPO 2019: 15; 2017: 13). To reach customers worldwide, counterfeit goods 'follow complex trading routes, misusing a set of intermediary transit points' (OECD and EUIPO 2019: 11). The most important such transit points are Hong Kong, Singapore, and the United Arab Emirates (mainly Dubai). They receive large amounts of pirated products in containers and re-export them in small parcels by post or courier services. Regionally, the same process takes place in Saudi Arabia and Yemen, which add to the United Arab Emirates as key transit points for exports to Africa; in Albania, Egypt, Morocco, and Ukraine for counterfeit goods sent to the European Union; and in Panama for pirated products re-exported to the United States. Small shipments make the work of enforcement authorities more difficult and accordingly diminish the chance of detection. This is why 43 percent of all shipments had less than ten items by 2016 (OECD and EUIPO 2019: 11, 15; 2017: 13–14). All these transactions are very discreet. This changes considerably in the country of destination, where huge counterfeit goods markets have developed. Internet sales increase constantly, but physical markets continue to play a key role (Office of the USTR 2020: 33). They exist everywhere: the K Street corridor in Washington and Canal Street in New York are perhaps the best examples of the Global North (Yang 2016: 17). They are, however, dwarfed by the enormous similar markets located all over the Global South. The Office of the United States Trade Representative constantly updates – for repressive purposes – the Notorious Markets List, which presents prominent 'markets that reportedly engage in or facilitate substantial piracy or counterfeiting' (Office of the USTR 2020: 1). They include Yiwu International Merchandise City located in Yiwu, in China's Zhejiang Province. With 50,000 vendors, this is the largest small commodities market worldwide that provides all sorts of goods, mainly in bulk, to 'ant traders' from all continents. Despite some measures taken by local authorities, pirated goods – especially handbags, shoes, and apparel – are sold openly. The same is true for other huge markets located in Asia: the Dordoi Bazaar in Bishkek presented in Subchapter 4.1; the Patpong Market, a popular night market in Bangkok where counterfeit sports apparel, watches, handbags, pharmaceuticals, and DVDs can be easily found; and the Grand Bazaar in Istanbul, where some of the 4,000 shops located on 61 covered streets sell counterfeit jewelry, watches, perfumes, cosmetics, wallets, handbags, and leather goods. To limit further examples to one region, the Argentinean police arrested in September 2019 about 100 mobile street vendors ('*manteros*') involved in trademark counterfeiting in association with Senegalese organized crime. But they were much less effective in dealing with the enormous La Salada (three markets covering 50 acres) whose impressive counterfeiting activities are presented in Subchapter 4.7. In neighboring Paraguay, Ciudad del Este – located on the triple border between Paraguay, Argentina, and Brazil – is a well-known hub for the production of and trade in pirated goods sold mainly to Brazilian customers. In Brazil itself, a series of raids ('*Operação Comércio Legal*') led to the seizure of no less than 400 tons of pirated products in 2019 alone. They included ten tons of toys and cosmetics, as well as half a million counterfeit watches from São Paulo's Rua 25 de Março market and other surrounding locations (Office of the USTR 2020: 5–6, 34, 37–39, 41, 43). Such operations certainly are impressive; but the fact that they only marginally affect the overall flow of pirated goods illustrates the formidable scale of this process and the magnitude of the challenge it represents to the Western-centered globalization 'from above.'

Counterfeit, Resistance, and Fake Modernity

Because counterfeit and piracy defy the legal logic of intellectual property rights, they represent a 'mode of subversion of market rules' (Gago 2014/2017: 41) that challenges the Neoliberal globalization 'from above' and is repressed by its agents: 'the pirate as a criminal figure invites the legal attention of the state and of private enforcers' (Liang 2011: 168). The nature and consequences of this antagonism, however, go much further. It was noted that, in addition to the legal dimension, practices such as counterfeit and piracy bring forth alternative visions that stem from a defiance of the cultural logic of intellectual property rights (Yang 2016: 23). Counterfeiting leads to 'parody and devaluation' (Gago 2014/2017: 41), which, in turn, have important social consequences. Access to brands is normally restricted to more affluent social classes. Counterfeit products expand consumption to disadvantaged social segments; this is why, as shown in Subchapter 4.2, the non-hegemonic globalization 'from below' is a *'globalización popular'* (Ribeiro 2012b). Instead of a simple subversion of market rules, piracy can be perceived as 'the popular affirmation of these rules.' It 'disrupts the trademark's prestige as a sign of exclusivity'; popular classes use and display the brand, thus devaluating the original. Ultimately, this is about nothing less than 'the construction of a way of life' (Gago 2014/2017: 41, 2012: 76). Indeed, this is a large-scale, long-term process that has considerable socio-economic consequences. What counterfeiting leads to is a fundamental redefinition of what is normal. The beginning of this chapter has briefly mentioned the huge number of people who live in a perpetual state of informality. Forty percent of the population of major Global South cities – and no less than 70 percent in certain cases – live in illegal conditions and steal electricity and water. Predictably, 'the people who live in this perpetual state of illegality also engage in other networks of illegality.' Counterfeiting simply adds another layer to the preexisting 'illegal city': from gray market mobile phones to pirated DVDs or Mp3s, counterfeit goods have become part of the day-to-day informal urban landscape. In such environments, piracy is a normal 'culture of the copy that exists alongside livelihood and labor, profit and pornography' (Liang 2011: 171–173). In a global world dominated by mobility and by the 'growing market of forgeries that allow access to that movement,' such as fake passports or marriage licenses, counterfeiting ultimately defines a *'modernidad falsa'*: a fake – or, rather, counterfeit – modernity 'where everything happens as a copy, under the guise of a false object or apocryphal document.' The Neoliberal globalization 'from above' relies on and tries to reinforce the reign of the original, understood as a space dominated by legality. Yet, this space of homogeneous and regulated modernity is in crisis. The culture of the counterfeit associated with the non-hegemonic globalization 'from below' has brought a heterogeneity that is infiltrating vast areas where, despite various forms of repression, 'a type of production that is defined by its clandestine nature is publicized and expanded.' In this other, counterfeit modernity, 'the *original* is produced underground, and the counterfeit *copy* is openly distributed' (Gago 2014/2017: 37–38, emphasis in the original, 2012: 68; Comaroff and Comaroff 2009: 22).

It can be concluded that counterfeit and piracy are far from representing a mainly commercial issue. Due to their massive scale, these practices have significantly contributed to multifaceted, in-depth changes in the economic, social, and cultural conditions of large disadvantaged social groups located mainly but not exclusively in the Global South. Critically, a way of life based on informality is constructed that diverges from that prescribed by the Neoliberal view of modernity. In part, this overlaps with the practices of resistance of the counter-hegemonic globalization 'from below.' As explained in Chapter 3, the latter also uses other related instruments as part of its much better coordinated, ideology-based challenge of the Western-centered globalization 'from above.' Yet, if results are compared, the counterfeit and piracy dimension of the discreet non-hegemonic globalization 'from below' can be assessed as more impactful: it has already redefined understandings of 'normal' in ways and on a scale inaccessible to the much more vocal 'movement of movements.'

4.4 Social Networks and Diasporas

All globalizations rely on some form of capital, which 'may be understood as the basic set of resources that an economy and a society need for their development and dynamics' (Fonseca and Malheiros 2004: 133). Various such forms can be identified that include economic and business, social, human, and ecological capital. The Western-centered globalization 'from above' relies on the economic and business one. In the case of the non-hegemonic globalization 'from below,' on the contrary, the 'organizing principle' is represented by social capital, which is defined as 'social networks and reciprocity norms associated to them that, such as physical capital (tools) and human capital (knowledge), are able to create individual and collective value and may be object of investment' (*Ibid.*, 134). Very different from the economic and business capital, the social one consists of non-tangible elements such as trust and mutual obligations. Because it focuses on the relationship between individuals and institutions, it can be approached from a Putnam-inspired, more institutionalized perspective; or from a more informal one, which emphasizes 'links, ties and trust relations associated to groups of individuals, eventually organised in some form of community' (*Ibid.*). It is this latter view that has been used in the study of the non-hegemonic globalization 'from below' by associating it with social networks. Networks are essential to analyses of transnational social formations inspired by the work of Manuel Castells (Castells 1996/2009). The nodes and hubs of a network connect its component parts, which are dependent upon but also autonomous from the network's complex system of relationships. Today, 'dense and highly active networks spanning vast spaces are transforming many kinds of social, cultural, economic and political relationships' (Vertovec 2009: 4–5). Within the non-hegemonic globalization 'from below,' 'social networks engender trust that facilitates contractual arrangements that promote trade' (Rauch 2001). In the world of 'ant trade,' most contracts are oral, laws and regulations are infringed on a regular basis, and legal mechanisms of dispute settlement are seldom taken into consideration. Accordingly, cheating is always possible and trust plays an essential role. Social networks provide solutions by 'developing a stock of mutual obligations. [They] engineer trust through mutuality' (Casson 2010: 18). This is why there are 'thousands of social networks that are in pendular movements of variable scale among different nodes' of the non-hegemonic globalization (Ribeiro 2012a: 226). These trade-related social networks characterized by connectivity, flexibility, reciprocity, and transnationality (Liu and van Dongen 2016: 808) are very different from the networks of the Neoliberal globalization 'from above.' An important difference concerns the fact that they 'engage in practices within informal systems previously constructed by diasporas and migratory networks or typical grassroots economic forms' (Ribeiro 2012a: 226). The grassroots aspect needs little comment as it is associated with the very visible universe of street and market vendors who represent the majority of 'ant traders.' It is the migratory and diasporic dimension that is most interesting as 'some of the largest diasporas (...) are greatly involved in the flows of people, commodities and information within the non-hegemonic world-system' (*Ibid.*). Migration studies have shown that 'within the so-called ethnic economy niches, social capital seems to be a key condition of settlement and success' (Fonseca and Malheiros 2004: 134). The same type of capital is also present in the case of non-ethnic businesses, but it is much less relevant. Migrants have to rely on social capital because their insertion procedures are typically based on social networks of acquaintances or relatives. Accordingly, migration in general and the creation of small ethnic businesses in particular 'strongly rely upon the extent and density of the networks and on the principles of trust and mutual obligations among acquaintances' (*Ibid.*). It is through the use of social capital that 'ethnic entrepreneurs make and keep connections between home and host countries' and, at the same time, are successful in 'provid[ing] services to maintain their culture, such as groceries, restaurants, hair and nail shops, and travel agencies' (Koh and Malecki 2016: 61). This significantly contributes to the close relationship between the non-hegemonic globalization 'from below,' which includes migrants' trade connections between homelands and countries of settlement, and the development of diasporic communities enhanced by activities that maintain their specific culture.

The term diaspora 'denote[s] religious or national groups living outside an (imagined) homeland' (Faist 2010: 9). As a social form, diasporas are defined by the relationship between ethnic groups that are globally dispersed but collectively self-identified; the 'territorial states and contexts' where they have settled; and the 'homeland states and contexts' of origin (Vertovec 2009: 4). Importantly, diasporas are marked by 'a founding fact of transstate shift of location' that explains their socio-cultural distinctiveness, and a certain degree of loyalty to an origin or homeland that can be real, symbolic, or mythic. They are always 'anchor[ed] in allegiances that imply a reference to a common narrative and plight'; the 'dispersal is granted a special ideological significance' (Ben-Rafael and Sternberg 2009: 2). The utopian idealization of the land of origin and the work of an elite group of cultural and political brokers combine to 'give the homeland ultimate salience within diasporic consciousness' (Quayson and Daswani 2013: 3). In turn, this creates a specific type of solidarity that helps diasporic communities to avoid assimilation. Criteria such as religion, a combination of race and culture, enterprise, and politics have been used to identify four types of diasporas. The first, illustrated by the Chinese, East Indian, and Lebanese examples, is 'structured around an entrepreneurial pole.' The origin is often associated with 'a colonial context in which the ruler assigned their various commercial and enterprise activities (Indians and the Lebanese in Africa, the Chinese in South-East Asia)' (Bruneau 2010: 39). The second type is that comprising Jews, Greeks, Armenians, and Assyro-Chaldeans; it is based on religion, frequently associated with a specific language. The third type relies on a political pole, especially when the homeland is occupied by a foreign power. Finally, in the case of the fourth type, it is a racial and cultural pole that defines a shared identity, as exemplified by the African diaspora (*Ibid.*, 40). It should be noted that a diaspora does not need to be 'structured around an entrepreneurial pole' in order to be very active within the non-hegemonic globalization 'from below.' In all cases, a diaspora does not represent a homogenous community. It 'must not be perceived as a discrete entity but rather as being formed out of a series of contradictory convergences of peoples, ideas, and even cultural orientations' (Quayson and Daswani 2013: 4). Numerous social sciences that include Anthropology, Political Science, Migration Studies, Media Studies, Religion, and Postcolonialism have analyzed diasporas in association with a 'paired term': transnationalism (*Ibid.*, 4, 20). A more general understanding of this concept and its importance for the study of all globalizations 'from below' were presented in Subchapter 2.6. With respect to migratory phenomena, two interpretation of transnationalism exist. The narrow one simply concerns the 'migrants' durable ties across countries.' The wider understanding associates it not only with 'communities, but all sorts of social formations, such as transnationally active networks, groups and organisations' (Faist 2010: 9). It is this latter view that is relevant to migrants' involvement in the non-hegemonic globalization 'from below.' In this context, transnationalism was defined as 'the ways in which immigrants develop intensely networked social fields that span geographic, cultural and political borders and connect home and host societies through multifarious linkages' (Zack 2015: 135). Migration-related transnationalism is a complex concept that concerns the 'various flows and counterflows and the multi-striated connections they give rise to'; they include the movement of people, as well as 'notions of citizenship, technology, forms of multinational governance, and the mechanisms of global markets' (Quayson and Daswani 2013: 4). In the 1990s, the related concept of transnational community emerged (Bruneau 2010: 44), of which the diaspora represents a subset. Transnational communities are more general because their modes of identification can be ethnic or cultural, but also elective – based, for example, on class, sexuality, or professional interest; environmentalist transnational communities also exist. In the context of demography, the transnational community takes the form of migrant community, which sometimes is used as a synonym for diaspora. However, transnationalism insists on the fact that 'migrants do not easily substitute old homes for new ones in a straightforward way.' Their lives are 'simultaneously connected between two or more nation-states' by processes variously referred to as 'circuits,' 'networks,' 'social fields,' 'social spaces,' or 'chain migration.' Transnationalism is the result of 'a multiplicity of historical trajectories or pathways' and therefore there are 'multiple ways of being transnational' (Quayson and Daswani 2013: 4–5). However, all transnational migrant communities are based on specific mobility know-how. They 'link the global to the whole range of greatly different local, networking places' (Bruneau 2010: 43). These migrants return periodically to the place of origin, where they invest part of their income; at least some members of their family intend to stay or to return there. While they seek to obtain the nationality of the host country, they also retain their initial citizenship. In fact, these migrants do not completely leave their place of origin; accordingly, 'there is no uprooting from the territory and society of origin, nor trauma, as in the case of diasporas' (*Ibid.*, 43–44). At times, specific forms of transnational nationalism develop within these communities. An example is that of immigrants from Turkey to the European Union, which shows that transnational networks of migrant associations are able to bypass states. A dense interaction of actors has led to the emergence of a transnational space where Islamist and secular Turks, Alevis, Kurds, and Lazes participate in a common process of political socialization (*Ibid.*, 44). While this example is not necessarily relevant to the working of the non-hegemonic globalization 'from below,' it does show the high degree of autonomy of transnational communities with respect to both homeland and country of settlement, as well as the original connections they construct between these territories. To explore the latter, scholars have developed various approaches and concepts. For example, 'mobile societies' have been defined as representing 'small, mobile, and less integrated social formations' forged by networks that operate in and connect various nation-states and geographical regions (Marsden 2018: 85–86). In his analysis of 'ant traders' in the Western Mediterranean, Alain Tarrius focuses on 'migrant societies that generate 'new cosmopolitanisms'": due to encounters between mobile groups, 'new forms of identities then occur, founded on the capacity of multiple belonging.' 'Territories of movement' develop, where 'cross-border entrepreneurs and nomads move with goods they loaded up on in their place of origin to sell in different cities of the host country that they are familiar with' (Bruneau 2010: 45–46; Tarrius 2001, 2002). A critical role is played by a special category of migrants: the 'informal notaries,' intermediaries specialized in moving goods over borders and circumventing taxation mechanisms. They return regularly to their place of origin in the Maghreb or West Africa, where they have family and community ties and invest their earnings; this is their essential geographical reference. Yet, it is in the country of (temporary) settlement – France, Spain, or Italy – that they are both essential helpers of the 'ant traders' and 'interlocutors who are very much valorised by regional and local, political and police authorities.' Accordingly, 'their identity is not a diasporic one: it is a "nomadic identity" based on partial and short-lived hybridisation ("*métissage*")' (Bruneau 2010: 46–47; Tarrius 2001). New 'nomadic' networks combine with older diasporic ones and sedentary market places to create a 'bazaar economy' in the Mediterranean Basin that circulates licit and illicit goods (Gobe 2004: 422; Peralva 2003: 192; Tarrius 2002), thus expanding the reach of the non-hegemonic globalization 'from below.'

Tarrius' 'informal notaries' are somewhat reminiscent of a much larger and better-studied category: that of 'middleman minorities,' a concept developed by Hubert Blalock in the 1960s and Edna Bonacich in the early 1970s. It was widely used by sociologists in the United States during the 1980s, but in the following decade it 'fell out of favour with the rise of literature on diaspora and transnationalism.' It was Pál Nyíri who, more recently, made it once more popular in the migration-related literature (Nyíri 2011: 147; Blalock 1967; Bonacich 1973). Middleman minorities emerged in various colonial and imperial economies as 'groups that functioned as economic and political intermediaries between the rulers and the populace but were regarded as outsiders by both' (Nyíri 2011: 147). Historical examples include Jews in Europe, Armenians in Turkey, Lebanese in West Africa, Asians in East Africa, Parsis in India, Chinese in Southeast Asia, as well as Japanese and Greeks in the United States (Bonacich 1973: 583). All these minorities used transnational ethnic networks to obtain capital, labor, and business information, which allowed them to provide to both imperial or colonial rulers and subjects goods and services that were otherwise expensive or unavailable (Nyíri 2011: 147). Within the host societies, members of these minorities occupied an intermediate position and concentrated in 'middleman' occupations such as trader, money lender, rent collector, agent, labor contractor, and broker. Different from the past, today they obviously do not collect taxes on behalf of the colonial rulers and are not connected to the latter's commercial networks, which had a monopoly on foreign trade. But they do preserve the 'role of middleman between producer and consumer, employer and employee, owner and renter, elite and masses' (Bonacich 1973:

583; Nyíri 2011: 147). The main reason for this specialization is the absence of other paths of upward mobility due to the hostility these migrants face as a consequence of their cultural, religious, or racial features and to their legal vulnerability to expulsion. This pushes them toward marginal economic roles that are often perceived as deviant (e.g., usury). In turn, the local society begins to identify the group with a specific type of business and sees it as an economic, moral, and even sanitary threat. While middlemen merchants are often recognized as useful, they are always perceived as alien. Further reasons for hostility pertain to two categories. The first is economic: there are conflicts of interest with the clientele (buyers, renters, and clients), with competing local businesses, and with local labor. The second category concerns the perceived solidarity of the middleman community, whose members are seen as clannish and inassimilable while considering themselves superior to the locals. They are accused of being disloyal to the host country and draining it of its resources: they send money back home, do not engage in productive activities, import necessities from their country of origin instead of contributing to local industries, and so on. 'In a word, middleman groups are seen as parasites.' The 'country is being "taken over" by an alien group' (Bonacich 1973: 584, 590–592; Nyíri 2011: 147). Negative perceptions are further enhanced by 'predatory clientelism': to protect themselves from xenophobic attacks and possible legal discrimination, members of middleman minorities seek the patronage of local political elites, whom they assist as brokers and intermediaries in various fields. To the local society, this is synonymous with high-level corruption (Nyíri 2011: 147–148). The ensuing acute hostility can lead to riots, pogroms, exclusion movements, and large-scale expulsion. Due to these very real threats, such migrants do not plan to settle permanently in the host country. Consequently, they choose occupations based on short-term engagement, as well as 'portable or easily liquidated livelihood[s],' and have a pronounced tendency toward thrift (Bonacich 1973: 584, 589). Unsurprisingly, a high degree of internal solidarity develops based on trust, mutual assistance, and strong ethnic associations. Out-marriage is infrequent, there is residential self-segregation, language and cultural schools are established for children, and there are few lasting relationships with the local society. Involvement in politics is limited to issues that directly interest the minority. Love of the homeland, on the contrary, is well preserved due to surrounding hostility and to the activity of ethnic associations and schools. Links with members of the same ethnic group in other countries are also kept alive 'for these relationships will persist in the future towards which the sojourner points' (*Ibid.*, 585–586, 592). An interesting aspect of middleman minorities concerns the organization of their companies. To outcompete local rivals, they have to cut costs and this has led to an emphasis on family firms where a clear distinction between the interests of employer and employee is absent. Low-paid employees accept to work long hours for paternalistic employers and – to the despair of local workers – refuse to create or join trade unions. Basically, they feel closer to employers of the same migrant community than to the working class of the host country. Furthermore, they do not perceive themselves as permanent workers; rather, they are preparing to launch a business of their own. This is a phenomenon described by Weber as a pre-modern form of capitalism. Differently from the modern one – where employers treat free labor impartially as an economic instrument – it relies on 'primordial ties of family, region, sect, and ethnicity [that] unite people against the surrounding, often individualistic economy' (Bonacich 1973: 589). The effectiveness of this and other features specific to 'middleman communities' is illustrated by the historical economic success of migrants originating in Lebanon or South Asia. The first group is perhaps the most interesting because, despite its tiny homeland, it represents one of the most globally spread migrant minorities. This is the result of the highest emigration rate in the world recorded between 1890 and 1930, and of other migratory waves after World War II and during the 1970s. In Ecuador, '*Libanés*' is a synonym for rich. The 4,000 Lebanese in Liberia are believed to control two-thirds of the national economy (Moya 2018: xiii–xiv, xvii–xviii). The South Asian group, consisting of no less than 30 million people, is similarly impressive. Before World War II, its main target regions were Southeast Asia, South and East Africa, the Caribbean, Mauritius, and Fiji. In the post-war period, the United States, Britain, Canada, Australia, and the Middle East were added to the list. More importantly, the older diaspora associated with the colonial era is contrasted in the literature with the new one 'formed by people intimately connected to the monumental changes that have taken place in the ongoing "age of globalisation".' The so-called 'Non-Resident Indians' have 'changed the nature of the diaspora very fundamentally – and brought high levels of skill and entrepreneurial flair to their new "hostlands"' (Rai and Reeves 2009: 2–4). These Indian newcomers who preserve key features of the middleman minority are typical actors of the present non-hegemonic globalization 'from below.' In fact, the same features – ranging from family firms to the lack of will to settle permanently in the host country – are shared by many of this globalization's transnational networks, which rely on the social capital associated with their ethnic nature.

To summarize, social capital diminishes the perceived risk of opportunistic behavior, which turns social networks into important resources for entrepreneurship and business development. In particular, entrepreneurship develops amongst minority groups as their social capital reinforces shared social and informal institutional norms. This is most visible in the case of diasporas, where social capital is embedded in both local and international contexts, thus 'creat[ing] preconditions for entrepreneurship that are at least equal to those enjoyed by the majority population' (Dana *et al.* 2019: 205, 216). Within new migrant communities, transnational networks are therefore able to construct a 'space that is freer and more fluid than that within either the homeland' or the host society (Rai and Reeves 2009: 4). As an effect, 'diasporas and migrants are increasingly influencing the everyday conduct of international business, economy and society as a whole.' Through their dense interactions, they 'act and shape the global and local business environment that become more glocal, more transnational and interconnected' (Elo and Minto-Coy 2019: 1). This is to say that diasporic and migrant networks are key actors of the non-hegemonic globalization 'from below' that bring a major contribution to the huge circulation of people and goods whose geography is presented in the next subchapter.

4.5 Production Centers, Flows, and Nodes

The non-hegemonic globalization 'from below' is based on production centers where mainly cheap and often counterfeit goods are manufactured; flows typically supported by 'migratory networks and diasporas'; and nodes, which are the 'markets where global gadgets and copies of superlogos are sold' (Ribeiro 2013: 34). In large part, this geography overlaps with that specific to counterfeiting and piracy presented in Subchapter 4.3. The main production centers are located in Asia. They do include Malaysia, Singapore, South Korea, and Taiwan, but China – and especially the province of Guangdong – is by far the most important such center (*Ibid.*). This is due to the key factor of comparatively low prices. Chinese goods are critical to the non-hegemonic globalization 'from below' 'not because of their flashiness or fashion, but because they are relatively inexpensive and of acceptable quality.' A second cause is 'the fact that the rule of law remains quite flexible in China today, particularly in terms of knock-offs' (Mathews and Yang 2012: 98). By 2011, as much as 80 percent of the phones manufactured there were pirated. It is perhaps exaggerated to claim that 'if it were not for China, globalization from below would not be happening, at least certainly not on its current scale' (*Ibid.*): manufacturing would simply move to countries offering similar conditions, of which there are many in South East Asia and elsewhere. One should not underestimate the flexibility and adaptability of the transnational informal economy. In fact, given the continuous rise of wages in China, sooner or later much of the production of cheap goods will inevitably migrate to other locations. This trend is already visible in the textile industry, where 'China is not remaining competitive.' As an effect of high labor costs, many 'African traders (...) are now bypassing Guangzhou and moving to Turkey, Vietnam, and Bangladesh to do business' (Lee 2014: 59). But, for the time being, it is still in Guangdong that most goods originate. From there and other production centers, they 'are often smuggled, transported through all the various means available in the informal economy' (Mathews and Yang 2012: 98). Routes are seldom direct because – different from the case of the Neoliberal globalization 'from above' – 'ant traders' have to take into consideration not only transport infrastructure and costs but also smuggling and tax evasion opportunities. 'The final destination of the goods often remains a mystery': instead of being shipped directly to the destination market, they follow complicated routes as they are 'transshipped across borders illegally, evading customs officials' (Lee 2014: 20) or, more often, taking advantage of their self-interested leniency. By definition, 'corruption is endemic in the nodes and routes of the non-hegemonic world-system' (Ribeiro 2012a: 229). State policies are also very important: informal flows obviously avoid countries with strict and well-enforced customs regimes while highly tolerant import-export policies have turned places such as Dubai into regional or global hubs of the 'ant trade.' To give an example of the resulting zigzagged routes, African small merchants buy cheap goods in China's Guangzhou or Yiwu, textiles in Bangkok, and other merchandise in Dubai (see below). These goods are sent – possibly, by sharing one container among two or more traders – 'from Guangzhou to Hong Kong (very often), to Dubai, to Middle Eastern and African ports, where they are trucked to inland cities' (Mathews 2017: 105). 'African ports' may refer to previously anonymous places such as Kenya's Eastleigh, a Somali neighborhood of Nairobi that, until recently, did not even have sewage or water amenities. This, however, has not prevented it from becoming a node of the non-hegemonic globalization 'from below' that enormous amounts of goods and money transit every day (*Ibid.*, 109). The map of such nodes, therefore, contains both well-known Global South cities and previously marginal ports or inland towns between which impressive numbers of 'ant traders' 'are in pendular movements of variable scale' (Ribeiro 2012a: 226).

Dubai is one of the oldest and most important nodes. Starting in 1985, its government-created Free Zones eliminated trade barriers and minimized red tape. Today, there are 34 such zones that have contributed to the transformation of the city into a major regional trade, business, and financial center (EME Outlook 2021). In the 1990s, it became 'the world's re-exportation platform' (Bredeloup 2012: 30). The first 'ant traders' came mainly from the Middle East and the eastern coast of Africa. Progressively, other areas became connected to the new trade hub such as various African regions or the former Soviet republics of Central Asia. Initially, the rise of China as a production center represented a useful development: it was during their frequent trips to Dubai that small merchants bought Chinese merchandise from intermediaries. They began to go directly to Guangzhou only after 2000 (Verne 2017: 138); but, even today, many still buy Chinese goods in Dubai. Some even travel to both places. At first view, it may seem strange that 'ant traders' who typically get small margins of profit choose to buy Chinese merchandise in a market where prices are higher and the variety of goods on offer much more limited. In fact, the situation is more complex. Some cannot get a visa to enter China. Some prefer the more familiar environment of a Muslim city. Furthermore, English is widely spoken in Dubai and cheating is infrequent. Goods are already manufactured and can be bought on the spot, instead of waiting for them to be produced at a quality that may be inferior to that of samples. It takes only 15 days to ship a container from Dubai to a central African city as compared with 60 in the case of Guangzhou, which significantly shortens the business cycle. And there are goods – such as used cars – that are difficult to find in China. This is why the small wholesale shops on the narrow alleys of Dubai's Deira, often owned by Indian merchants, continue to be filled with 'ant traders' from the Middle East, Africa, and other regions. There has been a certain decline due to direct trips to Guangzhou or Yiwu, 'but Deira remains an alternative to China for many traders and a central node of low-end globalization' (Mathews 2017: 108–109).

If Dubai is the oldest of the key nodes of the non-hegemonic globalization 'from below,' Yiwu is the most recent. In the 1970s, it was one of the poorest rural counties in China's Zhejiang Province. Today, it is the country's 14th richest county. Over 80 percent of its population gave up farming for trade. It harbors the largest wholesale market of small commodities in the world. Inexpensive, nontechnical goods are produced, sold, and exported to 200 countries (Rui 2018: S14). An officially designated 'international trade city' (Marsden and Skvirskaja 2018: S2), Yiwu vocally welcomes all foreigners. The municipal government gave almost half the 50 seats of the mediating committee of the trading market to foreigners, holds annual meetings with members of the foreign community, grants 'unusual freedom of worship,' publishes an English language weekly, opened an international school, and even considers teaching Arabic in public schools (Roxburgh 2017). It was back in 1992 that the same government adopted a massive reform of the Futian Market. At present, it has five districts with 70,000 booths that sell in bulk no less than 1.7 million varieties of small commodities. Moreover, Huangyuan Market hosts 5,700 booths specialized in garments, to which ten other specialized markets and 30 streets have to be added. Overall, Yiwu hosts 'a breathtaking emporium covering 5.5 million sq metres' (Roxburgh 2017; Rui 2018: S20; Marsden and Skvirskaja 2018: S2). The customers are 'ant traders' from countries such as Afghanistan, Iraq, Syria, Yemen, Colombia, and the Commonwealth of Independent States (Marsden and Skvirskaja 2018: S2). In 2002, the first two importers of Yiwu goods were the United Arab Emirates (i.e., Dubai) and Russia; the latter, however, declined to fifth place in 2009 (Skvirskaja 2018: S51), mainly because of the growing number of African small traders: every year, 80,000 of them visit the city. In 2015, they bought no less than US $7.24 billion of commodities. Three thousand have officially settled in Yiwu, but the real number is believed to be close to 30,000 (Zhang 2016; Bodomo and Ma 2010: 288). This is the second-largest African presence in China after that in Guangzhou and certain scholars argue that 'the more efficient and civil treatment of Africans in Yiwu is one reason why Yiwu is eclipsing Guangzhou' as a node of the 'ant trade' (*Ibid.*, 283; for the situation in Guangzhou, see the next subchapter). However, certain African small merchants do complain of growing racial tensions, especially in the case of Muslims (Roxburgh 2017). A more general concern is related to the decline of the trading business in Yiwu's markets since 2014. This has been explained as a consequence of the turn of 'China's economy from rapid to slow growth' (Rui 2018: S20), but other factors threaten to enforce this trend. The government in Beijing tries to readjust the economy away from an export-led model and shift the basis of Chinese exports from the Yiwu-type cheap commodities to higher quality goods. It also critically scrutinizes the informality of the city's transactions with the rest of the world; such trading practices are increasingly seen as outdated and unsustainable, and a shift toward E-commerce is contemplated (Marsden and Skvirskaja 2018: S3; Roxburgh 2017). It is too early to anticipate if and how Yiwu will be able to adapt to such changes. For the time being, however, the magnitude of its 'ant trade' is so impressive that, despite years of decline, the city continues to be a major node of the non-hegemonic globalization 'from below.'

Other nodes, already mentioned in Subchapter 4.3 in relation to the trade in counterfeit and pirated goods, illustrate what was called 'the periphery of low-end globalization' (Mathews 2017: 108). Bangkok – and especially its Pratunam neighborhood – is the place where 'ant traders' buy textiles of better quality (and 30–40 percent more expensive) than the Chinese ones. They represent between 20 and 30 percent of the fabrics sold in East Africa. This involves considerable amounts of trade, but they do not compare to those of Yiwu or Guangzhou. Similarly, men's suits and shoes or baby products are produced in Istanbul, Turkey, at a better quality and more expensively than in China. Besides counterfeits sent to the European Union, such products are preferred by people in the Middle East 'who may disdain Chinese goods [and] desire Turkish goods, signifying, for them, Europe.' But, in the words of an Istanbul-based African logistics agent, 'most East African traders won't come here. They always go for the cheapest goods, buying in bulk – they'll be in China' (Mathews 2017: 106–107). Even more marginal nodes exist, such as the abovementioned Eastleigh in Kenya. All these places contribute to the continuous flows of people and goods on which the non-hegemonic globalization 'from below' is based. But, in addition to trade, they are the loci of complex socio-economic processes related to the uneasy interaction between states and 'ant traders' and/or to the 'fake modernity' discussed in Subchapter 4.3. To elucidate this important aspect, the following two subchapters analyze two of the most complex and interesting nodes of the non-hegemonic globalization 'from below': China's Guangzhou and Argentina's La Salada.

4.6 Guangzhou's 'Chocolate City'

Located less than two hours by train from Hong Kong, Guangzhou – then known as Canton – was first visited by Portuguese traders in 1517, followed by the Spaniards in 1575 and the English in 1636. After 1715, the latter became the dominant trading partner. Through the 1842 Treaty of Nanking, they opened the city to foreign trade (Lee 2014: 21). The 1949 communist taking over was followed by the closing of the country to Westerners.

Canton became Guangzhou while its foreign inhabitants were expelled in 1950–1951; like elsewhere in China, cosmopolitanism completely vanished (see Subchapter 6.3). It was only toward the end of the century that 'with the Pearl River Delta's emergence as the world's factory, (...) many foreigners began actively coming into Guangzhou' (Mathews 2017: 8). Today, the 13-million city (Liang and Le Billon 2020: 604) represents the most important node of the non-hegemonic globalization 'from below.' Its vast 'economic underworld' (Lee 2014: 27; Yang 2012: 155) is much larger than that of smaller nodes located close to it – Foshan, specialized in ceramics, Dongguan, which provides mainly shoes, and Shenzhen, famous for its electronics – or even Yiwu. Guangzhou is the main provider of garments, but 'ant traders' can find 'virtually every product imaginable, from solar lighting to heavy equipment to furniture to electronics to shoes to school bags' on its markets (Mathews 2017: 9). They come from all over the Global South to buy often counterfeit and always cheap goods desired by a clientele that cannot afford original products (Lee 2014: 27). In Guangzhou as elsewhere in China, most of these traders tend to come alone or in small groups for several days that are sufficient for their commercial activities. They seldom develop 'human social bonds' with the locals; some of them explicitly state that 'the Chinese [a]re not capable of being friends with foreigners' (Skvirskaja 2018: S52). Importantly, most of them do not intend to settle in Chinese cities. African traders represent a special category because of their numbers and especially because they have established a significant permanent presence in China.

They first arrived in Hong Kong in 1979 (Koh and Malecki 2016: 61), but numbers were very low. By the middle of the 1980s, mainly Malian and Guinean traders in precious stones settled in Bangkok (Bredeloup 2012: 29–30). Progressively, African merchants interested in other categories of goods set foot in Thailand, Malaysia, and Singapore. The Asian financial crisis of 1998 forced them to look for new markets; many of them moved to China. More than a quarter of the African 'ant traders' active in Guangzhou around 2016 had previously traded in cities such as Kuala Lumpur or Singapore (Zhou *et al.* 2016: 1574; Lee 2014: 26; Elochukwu 2019: 185). Another group followed a different path. During the 1990s, they began to commute between their African countries and Dubai, which at that time had become the main Middle Eastern and African hub of the non-hegemonic globalization 'from below.' Eventually, these shuttle traders started to travel to the Special Economic Zones in Southern China that produced most of the goods they bought in Dubai. Malian and Nigerian traders were the first to adopt this strategy. When the Ethiopian and Kenyan airlines launched flights to China, Addis Ababa and Nairobi became hubs of the 'ant trade.' Due to its modern transport infrastructure, Guangzhou represented the gateway for Africans interested in the output of factories in the Shenzhen special zone. After China's accession to the World Trade Organization in 2001, more than 900 wholesale markets emerged in Guangzhou. By 2006, the surrounding Guangdong Province provided more than 30 percent of the Chinese exports. The African presence intensified accordingly. When, as explained later in this subchapter, conditions significantly worsened in Guangzhou, a part of the African traders moved to Yiwu, thus contributing to its aforementioned transformation into the largest small commodities market worldwide (Bredeloup 2012: 31). As Yang Yang noted, 'the African traders are today's Arabs on the new "silk road", with cotton or synthetic clothes in the stead of silk, and freight services in the place of camels' (Yang 2011b: 4). In principle, 'they only want to make money in China and very few would like to live in China'; this is an idea they 'often shared freely and openly' (Yang 2011a: 8). It is clear that they come 'initially as sojourners with no intention to stay' (Zhou et al. 2016: 1574). Yet, African communities have developed in six Chinese cities: Guangzhou, Yiwu, Shanghai, Beijing, Hong Kong, and Macau. Estimates vary widely: various authors have placed the number of Africans in China at 20,000–60,000, 100,000, or even 250,000. Some are illegal residents while others are in fact African-based shuttle traders; it is, therefore, impossible to find accurate data. In terms of general features, most of them are merchants engaged in China's distributive sector; some were previously students or teachers; they are mainly self-made entrepreneurs; and they come mostly from West Africa and the Maghreb (Elochukwu 2019: 186). The majority are well educated: 60 percent have some college education, as compared to only 20 percent of the Chinese traders (Zhou et al. 2016: 1573). Some Africans arrive as English teachers, but they are progressively replaced by African students who have a better education and reputation. Once out of job, the former teachers reinvent themselves as traders. Many African students do the same after graduation or when they fail their academic careers; their experience in China makes adaptation easier (Elochukwu 2019: 186; Bredeloup 2012: 39). There are also Africans who get Chinese student visas because they cannot obtain normal ones; but, from the very beginning, trade is their only goal (Zhou et al. 2016: 1573). An unexpected category is related to transit migration: some Africans choose China as a stopover in their journey to Western Europe. Many fail and have to stay in China where they use trickery and fraud to make a living. While they tend to perceive themselves as heroic adventurers, both Chinese and African merchants 'consider these adventurers to be immoral figures who damage the African trade' (Bredeloup 2012: 39–40).

Overall, 87 percent of Africans present themselves as businessmen and 9 percent as traders (Huynh 2016: 507). Within these categories, a special group needs to be mentioned: reminiscent of the 'informal notaries' identified by Alain Tarrius in the West Mediterranean Basin, certain African traders serve as useful intermediaries to other merchants. Typically, they are well-established businessmen who came to Guangzhou in the early 2000s. They have long-term residence permits and own companies recognized by the Chinese authorities. In addition to a stable economic base in China, they have extended networks – that normally are family-based – in the country of origin. Such traders are active in the wholesale of manufactured goods, but also work as intermediaries: they offer services such as bargaining, warehousing, transit, customs clearance, and interpretation to short-term visiting small merchants. They make arrangements for letters of invitation from local firms or organizations, which allow Africans to apply for a Chinese business visa; help with the registration process for Chinese universities that give access to student visas; or simply buy fake visas for their customers. When the latter arrive, the intermediaries assist them in finding accommodation and provide business contacts. After the traders place their orders and return to Africa, intermediaries solve all issues related to production, packaging, and shipment (and get paid by both the African customers and their Chinese partners) (Bredeloup 2012: 33; Gilles 2015: 31–32). Critically, they help with informal money transfers. Chinese companies prefer payments in cash, which allow them to keep transactions informal and untaxed. However, without official contracts and customs declarations, Western Union or bank transfers, as well as amounts brought from abroad are limited to US $5,000 per day. The African intermediaries help by receiving their customers' money in an account they have in Hong Kong, going there by train to withdraw the money, and smuggling it into China. Without this key assistance, African traders' operations would be seriously hampered. More generally, the intermediaries' extensive and in-depth knowledge of Guangzhou's markets, supply and production chains, logistical infrastructure, official regulations, and informal practices are most helpful to their customers (Gilles 2015: 32, 38–39). About 200 such intermediaries also work as logistics agents. They deal only with the Chinese side of shipping, not with the African one. Known as trustworthy, they send goods by sea or air from Guangzhou to major African ports or airports such as Mombasa, Lagos, Eldoret, Matadi, Abidjan, Beira, Cape Town, or Lomé (Mathews 2015: 126; Yang 2011b: 6). Some intermediaries even open branches in various African countries to assist merchants who cannot travel to China. They receive the money and handle the customers' business for a commission (Bredeloup 2012: 33; Mathews 2015: 132). The most important role of the African intermediaries, however, is not logistic in nature. They essentially serve as very effective cultural brokers between Africans and Chinese. Indeed, they are persons that facilitate the 'border crossing of another person or group of people from one culture to another culture.' They 'help their customers in practically adjusting to Chinese life' and show them how to 'grease the wheels of commerce' in Guangzhou (*Ibid.*, 117, 119). 'Experiential knowledge and specific cultural competencies' help them to greatly facilitate exchanges. This ranges from the ability to speak Mandarin – or, less often, even Cantonese – to the knowledge of both African and Chinese norms, conventions, and business practices (Gilles 2015: 32–33). In an informal market where business agreements are mostly oral, African newcomers who deal directly with Chinese businessmen are often cheated. Contracts may not be respected at all; the quantity or quality of goods arriving in Africa might be inappropriate. In such situations, 'the chance of regaining money from Chinese salespeople is virtually nonexistent.' This seldom happens when African intermediaries supervise operations. They successfully 'perform the function of a guarantor, organising and mediating business deals between African customers and Chinese counterparts' (*Ibid.*, 33).

Intermediaries play a key role, but numerically they are just a tiny part of the huge flow of 'ant traders' who travel from Africa to Guangzhou. As already mentioned, this phenomenon began to take mass proportions after the Asian financial crisis of 1998, with African merchants and business brokers arriving initially from Hong Kong (Haugen 2018: 54), and intensified after 2001 (Koh and Malecki 2016: 61). Due to intense trade and its sizeable African community, 'Guangzhou is arguably the best-known Chinese city in Africa' (Elochukwu 2019: 187). Its numerous African visitors arrive – in principle, with no intention to stay – 'to pursue the "Chinese Dream" or to make "big" money' (Zhou *et al.* 2016: 1574). They can be divided into three groups. First, there are the expatriate employees of African import and export firms, who may also have side businesses. They interact with local manufacturers on a large scale but mainly through Chinese intermediaries. Second, there are independent merchants who operate their own small or medium firms and also use Chinese intermediaries. They have offices and live in Guangzhou, but may overstay their visas and/or shuttle to Hong Kong to circumvent visa restrictions. Finally, there are numerous and very diverse petty entrepreneurs who live among the locals and trade directly with the Chinese. They 'are often seen holding a calculator, large suitcases, and plastic garbage bags, so locals refer to them as "calculator merchants", "suitcase merchants", or "garbage bag merchants".' Successful ones upgrade their activity by setting up small or medium export firms and move into the second group (*Ibid.*, 1575). Some members of the third group actually shuttle between their country of origin and Guangzhou, where they only spend one week to order goods or up to three weeks if they decide to supervise the shipping (Li *et al.* 2012: 60–61). All categories trade a wide range of goods that include but are not limited to textiles, clothing, footwear, toys, cosmetics, perfume, leather products, handbags, backpacks, electronics, batteries, motorcycles, car parts, furniture, and construction materials (Li *et al.* 2012: 62; Zhou *et al.* 2016: 1574; Koh and Malecki 2016: 61). A very small number of these traders live in Guangzhou's Zhujiang New Town, a very expensive neighborhood that is home to many foreigners from Europe, Japan, and Latin America (Mathews 2017: 9–10). The huge majority of Africans, however, have chosen the districts of Xiaobei and Sanyuanli. Initially, they occupied the area surrounding Xiaobei Road and the Tianxiu Building. Eventually, the neighborhood north of the Guangzhou train station, as well as around Guangyuan West Road was added (Liang and Le Billon 2020: 610). This part of Guangzhou stretching 10 kilometers (Lee 2014: 22) became 'a functional and bustling area whose identity is itself tied to African presence' (Liang and Le Billon 2020: 611). Accordingly, it is known as 'Chocolate City,' 'Little Africa,' or 'Guangzhou's Harlem' (Yang

2011a: 2). Middle Eastern merchants and a much smaller number of Latin Americans also live in the area, but African traders are dominant (Liang and Le Billon 2020: 610). Chinese respondents often state 'I feel like I'm a foreigner here!' (Mathews 2017: 5). As 'ant trade' hubs, Xiaobei and Sanyuanli have huge wholesale markets, export logistics offices, and banks. There are also supermarkets, hair salons, private clinics, English-language kindergartens, mosques, and churches serving an African clientele (Liang and Le Billon 2020: 610–611). As elsewhere in China, the number of Africans is impossible to establish. In 2007, a rare official report mentioned 15,000 foreign residents in Guangzhou and 500,000 short-term foreign visitors. More recent official data indicated that 63,000 of the latter were African. Journalists spoke of 120,000 African permanent residents in 2008 and 100,000 in 2020. Western researchers believed that there were 15–20,000 of them both in 2007–2009 and 2017. The most conservative estimates come from Chinese researchers, who identified only 1,000 African traders and 32,000 visitors in 2007 (Bredeloup 2012: 29; Liang and Le Billon 2020: 610; Mathews 2017: 56–57). A cadre at the Guangzhou Social Science Institute bluntly explained the lack of published official statistics: the presence of African migrants is a 'sensitive subject' as 'China is supposed to be a non-immigrant country' (Yang 2011a: 1).

In terms of national origin, the largest two groups are the Nigerians and the Malians, followed by Ghanaians and Guineans. West Africans represent the majority, but traders come from all over the continent (Yang 2011a: 13; Zhou *et al.* 2016: 1573; Lee 2014: 22). In principle, their lingua franca is English. Native speakers of English seldom learn Chinese; on the contrary, non-native speakers do try to learn Mandarin (Mathews 2017: 57). Language combines with geographical origin and religion to create important differences between Xiaobei and Sanyuanli. In the former district, there are mainly Muslims from Africa, the Middle East, and China. The non-Chinese speak African languages, Arabic, and French (Huynh 2016: 516). A 'polyglot close-knit francophone community, mainly from West Africa' has emerged due to the fact that its members do not speak English and the Chinese do not speak French, which results in the group's relative isolation. It is concentrated around the 36-floor Tian Xiu Building on Xiaobei Road, near the Huaisheng Mosque, whose first four floors of wholesale shops are complemented by apartments, offices, and restaurants used by African migrants. 'The general feeling of bonhomie' has also attracted some English speakers in the neighborhood (Li *et al.* 2012: 57). Other trade centers in Xiaobei include Taoci, China-Africa Tradegate, Xiushanlou, Jinshan Xiangmao, and New Donfrac. Most shop owners are Chinese who have established African and Middle Eastern connections (Yang 2011a: 29). Customers are mostly short-term Muslim visitors from Africa and the Middle East. The market is most active in the evening, is more expensive, and has fewer shops than Sanyuanli. It is also more strictly controlled by the police (*Ibid.*, 18, 29; Mathews 2017: 11). More than two miles to the North,

Sanyuanli – known by local African merchants as Guangyuanxi – is located near the Guangzhou Train Station, on Guangyuan West Road. It contains over ten trading centers that include Canaan, Tian'en, and No: 88, and is home to a loose-knit Anglophone community made of mainly Christians from West Africa, with the Nigerians as the largest group (Li et al. 2012: 58; Mathews 2017: 11; Huynh 2016: 516). The Nigerians – who are mostly Igbo and Pentecostal Christian coming from southeastern Nigeria – are known to be 'very good at business.' They are so numerous that some respondents argued that Sanyuanli is more 'Nigerian' than 'African' (Liang and Le Billon 2020: 611; Yang 2011a: 13–14). The market, most active during the day, is Nigerian- and Ghanaian-based. Africans own around 20 percent of the shops. Many of them are long-term middlemen that sell goods to short-term visiting merchants from West Africa (Yang 2011a: 18, 27; Mathews 2017: 11). For years, reasons that include 'the romantic interest between young Chinese women and Nigerian men' made Sanyuanli 'the potential birth of a multicultural China' (Mathews 2017: 24). But intensive police raids against overstayers that began in August 2013 put an end to such prospects. Nigerians disappeared from stalls, where their Chinese employees or girlfriends replaced them. Since 2014, the previously bustlingly African Sanyuanli has been 'largely dormant' (*Ibid.*, 23–24; the issue of repression is discussed later in this subchapter). Finally, smaller numbers of Africans live in a third area. This is Foshan, a neighboring city of Guangzhou that cheap rent and good transportation turned into a major residential area for African traders who cannot afford Guangzhou hotels or do not have valid visas (Yang 2011a: 18–19).

In terms of gender, males are clearly predominant (Elochukwu 2019: 191; Bredeloup 2012: 37). This is somewhat surprising, as women represent 60 to 70 percent of cross-border traders globally (Desai 2009: 377). Among the Africans in Guangzhou, the female to male ratio is only 25/75 or 30/70 (Huynh 2016: 502). Moreover, some of the women came to China as spouses of male migrants. Most of the unmarried ones are single mothers who work as prostitutes or hawk African foods such as *moi-moi* and *jollof* (Elochukwu 2019: 191). However, this gendered division started to change after 2008, when the number of female traders began to grow (Huynh 2016: 503, 515). Their presence is more difficult to note simply because their stay in Guangzhou is normally limited to ten to fourteen days, which they use to order goods. A part of the male merchants tend to stay longer for sourcing and purchasing, and some of them become business handlers and middlemen; this gives them higher visibility (Mathews 2017: 57). The female traders are in their late 30s or 40s and tend to be married. They have better economic backgrounds than their male counterparts. To do business, they rely on family networks and friends while avoiding any other people. For their part, African prostitutes in Xiaobei are Muslim and work as individuals (Yang 2011a: 62). In Sanyuanli, most of them come from East Africa. However, numbers are not large because of local competitors (Elochukwu 2019: 192).

'Chocolate City' is marked by important cleavages: 'business secrets, ethnic backgrounds, and national reputation have shaped a culture with a high degree of mistrust within the community' (Niu 2017: 252). While there are no fights, antipathy exists between Arabs and Africans, as well as Indians and Africans, respectively (Mathews 2017: 12). Among the Africans, language, ethnic, and religious clusters have developed. As already shown, Xiaobei is mainly French-speaking and Muslim while Sanyuanli is English-speaking and Christian. There is no 'Pan-Africanist camaraderie.' English speakers, especially those from Nigeria, deride French speakers whom they call *zabarama.* The importance of nationalism and ethnicity is illustrated by the absence of any common African association, despite the existence of national, ethnic, and hometown ones. There is also inter-church rivalry, with churches defined by their national origins. Tensions have even resulted in the instigation to expel members of rival churches from China (Elochukwu 2019: 189). These rivalries overlap with marked inequalities between Africans with respect to important issues such as access to health care, and are hardly beneficial to people who basically live at the margins of the Chinese society (Bodomo 2020: 526). In compensation, 'there exists a tremendous sense of loyalty (...) among fellow countrymen and women.' Short-term visiting traders 'make efforts to buy from them and thus ensure their economic survival' (Lee 2014: 57). National, ethnic, and hometown associations have been established that 'function as social capital platforms for members' (Elochukwu 2019: 189). These members have created 'social networks to carve a suitable social status for themselves amidst precarity' (Amoah *et al.* 2020: 459). Associations provide counseling, pay hospital bills, give 'condolence envelopes,' and buy plane tickets for deported or sick members (Elochukwu 2019: 189). In fact, two types of networks exist: kin- and community-related 'networks of survival' that allow African newcomers – who may arrive in China with virtually no contacts – to advance in their career; and 'networks of accumulation' where resources circulate between more advantaged members to their mutual benefit (Marfaing and Thiel 2015: 65–67, 70–72, 77–79).

Of course, African traders go to Guangzhou to trade, and they bring a significant contribution to the development of the non-hegemonic globalization 'from below.' No less than 90 percent of the goods in African markets are imported from China, Thailand, and Indonesia (Lee 2014: 22), and a considerable part of this huge flow originates in 'Chocolate City.' African traders and middlemen play a 'vital middle link' between the world's largest center of production and 'a continent desirous of the flood of Chinese goods that these traders and middlemen abet and make a profit from' (Mathews 2017: 214). Analyses of the associated value chain have identified three stages. First, there is wholesale export and shipping either directly from Guangzhou or through Dubai. Second, there is wholesale and retail distribution in African points of entry that prominently include ports. Third, there are wholesale and retail activities in various African regions that are not close to major ports and airports (Lyons *et al.* 2012: 877). These activities are undertaken by two categories of traders: the African ones and the Chinese entrepreneurial migrants scrutinized in the next chapter. African 'ant traders' pertain to two categories. Some are Guangzhou residents who use their social capital locally and in their countries of origin to export goods both to their own retail or wholesale business in Africa and to their contacts there; they also provide assistance, counseling, shipping, and other services to the members of the second category. These are short-term visitors from Africa who only stay in Guangzhou the time needed to source goods. A small part of them have emigrated to the United States or Western Europe, but still have an import business in the African country of origin. They may also take goods to the United States or Europe, where they use relatives as distributors. Visitors buy goods from either factories or wholesalers for themselves but also other traders at home. Besides Guangzhou, they may extend their voyage to other places in Guangdong, the rest of China, or other countries – especially Dubai – to buy higher-quality products. Members of both categories tend to act both as retailers and wholesalers and center their distribution strategies on the use of family, village, or ethnic networks (*Ibid.*, 877, 879).

Obviously, none of these activities would be possible if they did not benefit both African and Chinese actors. Given the scale of their operations, one might believe that mutually beneficial cooperation is associated with more or less harmonious Sino-African relationships. In fact, day-to-day interactions reveal a situation that is increasingly characterized by a lack of harmony.

Sino-African Tensions

While both the Africans and the Chinese active in Guangzhou's markets are very diverse, each group perceives the other as highly homogeneous (Zhou *et al.* 2016: 1576). Much of their trade interactions are 'humorously refer[red] to as "calculator communication"': they are based on a very limited number of English or French words ('how much?' / 'combien?'), basic body gestures, and the typing of prices on a pocket calculator (Bodomo 2015: 148–151). In principle, relations are 'mutually beneficial, routine, and orderly.' Long-term business dealings sometimes lead to friendships. Trade processes are based on economic interdependence, but they tend to be 'socioculturally contentious.' (Zhou *et al.* 2016: 1576, 1581). Three main business patterns exist. African traders and Chinese manufacturers make deals either directly or through Chinese middlemen; and there is the 'one hand with cash and the other hand with goods' direct, face-to-face retail approach. Only the latter is less conflict-prone. The first two patterns are often affected by breach of contract. Africans bypass the middleman, who adopts a conflictive attitude; Chinese manufacturers delay delivery or ship goods of poor quality; or fake representatives of manufacturers steal the initial deposit money. Various frauds are possible because 'regulations are lax and uncertainty high' (*Ibid.*, 1576–1577). In the words of a merchant from West Africa who had settled in Britain, 'China was like the world turned upside down. The laws aren't followed in China. Contracts are like toilet tissue' (Mathews 2017: 6). Due to such obstacles, Sino-African business relations in Guangzhou follow a 'cycle through cooperation, conflict, and cooperation' (Zhou *et al.* 2016: 1577). As an effect, no less than 'half of the African traders who come to China lose the[ir] money' (Yang 2011a: 16). Some deeply antagonistic relationships have also been identified. African traders who own a shop cannot be rivaled by Chinese ones due to language and cultural affinities with clients from their countries of origin and their much better understanding of African market demands (Yang 2011b: 6). Consequently, the Chinese perceive them as threatening their control of transactions between Chinese manufacturers and African short-term visiting merchants. To prevent this, they block Africans' attempts to rent shops in malls and directly antagonize them (Elochukwu 2019: 192). African logistics agents and intermediaries find themselves in similarly difficult situations. The former may discover that their Chinese employees 'siphon off customers for their own side business' (Mathews 2015: 130). Due to their high rates of profit, African middlemen became targets of a well-organized offensive intended to supplant them. Chinese companies have placed their own agents locally but also in Africa and Dubai. To quote one Chinese middleman, 'Chinese should sell to Africans in Guangzhou. Africans shouldn't sell to Africans in Guangzhou' (*Ibid.*, 142, 216–217). Consequently, by 2012, 'Chinese nationals ha[d] begun to take over the African business places and to stand out as middlemen, representing the Chinese factories directly to the visiting businessmen.' The market was 'progressively controlled by Chinese intermediaries,' which raised serious questions about the future of the permanent African presence in Guangzhou (Bredeloup 2012: 46–48).

Similar questions are associated with the 'economic underworld' in which some of the Africans are involved (Yang 2011a: 4). Certain authors argue that 'Guangzhou's African migrant economy is three-quarters legitimate trade and one-quarter drug trafficking, Internet fraud and prostitution' (Elochukwu 2016: 1204). In fact, there is more: 'tax evasion, operating shops without a license, trading counterfeit goods, unauthorized money exchange, using forged documents, and so on' (Huynh 2016: 503). But it is true that drug trafficking is the most visible of these activities: 95 percent of imprisoned Africans in Guangzhou serve drug-related sentences. Most of them work with Chinese gangs and only distribute drugs (Elochukwu 2016: 1204–1206). Out of the Africans involved in drug smuggling and gang crimes, the majority are Igbo Nigerians (Niu 2017: 251). However, despite their visibility, serious crimes represent just a tiny part of the African 'underworld.' Most of it is associated with the semi-legal and illegal activities that always represent an integral part of the transnational informal economy. A good example is represented by the 'triple illegal person' label that correctly describes many

152   *The Non-Hegemonic Globalization 'from Below'*

long-term sojourners in Guangzhou: 'an illegal entrant, an illegal resident, and working illegally' (Lee 2014: 40). Such people are typical actors of the non-hegemonic globalization 'from below.' They perceive themselves as legitimate traders. The local society shares similar views or at least tolerates them. But to the Chinese state, they are criminals: in the words of an Igbo Nigerian who had a shop in a large Guangyuanxi mall, 'my life in China is like a gazelle (...) drinking from a water hole with crocodiles waiting to grab it' (Mathews 2017: 31). A similar example is represented by the widely spread 'underground banks.' These are illegal money exchange stores operated by Chinese under the disguise of cloth shops or restaurants. The exchange rate is higher than that of normal banks, but African traders do not have to show passports with expired visas. Without this illegal activity, much of the trade in Guangzhou would be seriously hampered. Ultimately, various types of 'informal finance provide opportunities for small and medium-sized enterprises' (Yang 2011a: 32–35, 115–116) that manufacture the huge amount of merchandise bought by African petty traders. More generally, the transnational informal economy has considerably contributed to the transformation of Guangzhou into a booming international economic center. The non-hegemonic globalization 'from below' benefits Guangdong and China as much as Africa and its 'large populations (...) who are now able to catch up with the world' (*Ibid.*, 115).

However, the Chinese authorities have progressively come to a different conclusion. Ensuing actions have triggered the beginning of the present phase of the permanent African presence in Guangzhou: after the 1990–2003 rise and 2004–2007 heyday, since 2008 we have been witnessing the 'fall of the "Chocolate City"' (Li *et al.* 2012: 62). In fact, it is in 2006 that Chinese media – which cannot be suspected of acting without orders from above – began to 'overwhelmingly portray African migration in a negative light.' All of a sudden, there was illegal migration, drugs, AIDs, counterfeit goods, scamming, and so on. The 'African population [was presented] as a source of danger and social ills, and migration as a source of alienation for the "local" population' (Liang and Le Billon 2020: 611; Li *et al.* 2012: 65). In 2007, in response to what it perceived as an exaggerated migratory inflow, the government in Beijing stated that 'China is not a migration-targeted country.' Progressive restrictions were imposed that considerably limited the chances of African traders to obtain or renew visas (Lee 2014: 26–27). Actual repression started in 2008 when preparations for the Beijing Olympic Games were accompanied by 'increased police violence against internal and external migrants' (Bredeloup 2012: 46). That year, local authorities in Guangzhou were criticized at the Chinese People's Consultative Conference for being weak and ineffective in controlling the African population. In response, a 'Triple Illegal' Management Team, various Foreign Management offices, a Foreign Management Center, and a new system of visa inspections were set up. As many as 2,175 local hotels were compelled to install registration software collecting information on foreigners (Li *et al.* 2012:

66–67). Police showed particular 'prejudice and hostile attitudes towards Guangzhou's African community' (Roxburgh 2017). This went so far that, in July 2009, more than one hundred Nigerians demonstrated against the local police (Li *et al.* 2012: 67). Repression, however, continued to intensify. In 2012, the 'Golden Dragon mall was definitely purged of its African tenants' (Elochukwu 2019: 187). That same year, the city security personnel started to 'prevent Africans from buying and selling goods on pedestrian footbridges or even just from congregating in public places' (Bodomo 2018: 64). Unable to face the new situation, many African traders moved to Yiwu, relocated to Bangkok, Jakarta, or Dubai, or returned to their countries of origin. In all, the impact 'was devastating': by 2012, almost half of the Sub-Saharan African traders had left Guangzhou (Bredeloup 2012: 46; Lee 2014: 41–43). A new wave of repression started in 2016. Locals newspapers reported that 'the African presence in Guangzhou (...) is fast diminishing and that Africans were leaving China "in droves"' (Bodomo 2018: 63). Chinese official estimates of the number of Africans legally residing in the city are particularly conservative. But they indicate a dramatic decrease from 16,000 in 2014 to 4,500 in mid-April 2020, which may well be relevant for the overall trend. However, the climax took the form of the 'maltreatment meted out on Africans in Chinese cities, such as Guangzhou, as part of measures to control the COVID-19 pandemic' (Castillo and Amoah 2020: 560–561). Even fully documented ones were evicted without prior notice from rented houses or hotel rooms and prevented from entering commercial venues. Moreover, it is increasingly difficult to overstay visas or otherwise circumvent the system given China's large-scale implementation of facial recognition and other mass surveillance and mobility control technologies. Accordingly, the pandemic episode 'may well be the last nail in the coffin of an already declining African population in Guangzhou' (*Ibid.*, 560, 562).

It is important to note that this trend is not exclusively due to the cold calculations of the leaders in Beijing. It is clear that they have taken the decision to sacrifice a part of the economic benefits of the non-hegemonic globalization 'from below' in exchange for a tighter grip on Guangzhou, which threatened to reach an undesired degree of diversity and cosmopolitanism. But tensions between Africans and the local population also exist that are mainly racial in nature. Observers have noted that Guangzhou is 'an acutely racially conscious city' (Mathews 2017: 29) where 'racialization influences most everyday Sino-African engagements' (Liang and Le Billon 2020: 604). Some scholars argue that Sino-African *trade*-related interactions may lead to conflictive situations, but these 'even when in the case of high intensity, have rarely manifested on racial terms' (Zhou *et al.* 2016: 1577). However, in general, there is a clear negative racialization of African migrants by the Chinese population of Guangzhou. To the locals, they may be entrepreneurially savvy, but remain a 'culturally "backward" lot from the poor, "uncivilized" "Third World"' (*Ibid.*, 1574). The Chinese believe that they 'negatively impact the neighbourhood' (90 percent), are 'innately unintelligent' (82.5 percent), 'lazy' (65 percent), and 'violent' (56 percent) (Liang and Le Billon 2020: 610). They are also 'impolite,' 'haggle over every ounce,' are 'dishonest,' and 'annoying' (Li *et al.* 2012: 66). Chinese traders doing business with Africans report 'unfair bargaining, fights between merchants and customers, and rudeness' (Lee 2014: 37). Locals interviewed by CCTV may state that Africans 'smelled bad' (Roxburgh 2017). Such insulting remarks and attitudes create a considerable degree of frustration among the African traders. As much as 65 percent of them state that they were only occasionally treated with respect; for 9.6 percent, this has never happened (Li *et al.* 2012: 66). One of them bluntly asked Yang Yang, 'are you even aware of how badly your people and your government treat us?' She was repeatedly told, 'we make money from our own people. We make African money. We never steal jobs from the Chinese. In fact, we create jobs for the Chinese. So why don't you Chinese leave us alone?' (Yang 2011a: 21, 26). Margaret Lee, an Afro-American scholar, was shocked by the racism she met during her fieldwork: 'the issue of Africans being called "black devils" or "monkeys" followed me wherever I went in Guangzhou. The racial tension was so overwhelming that I imagined being back in the United States during the Civil Rights era' (Lee 2014: 51). African traders typically note the awkward combination between the despising behavior of the Chinese and their interest in African trade-related profit. To quote a Nigerian petty merchant, 'I am from Lagos and the Chinese don't like Africans. They only need money' (Lee 2014: 33). Gordon Mathews was also repeatedly told that 'Chinese don't think about friendship but only about money!' 'The Chinese believe not in God but in gold!' (Mathews 2017: 214). Africans facing these various problems may state that 'it is really dangerous to do business here' (Lee 2014: 37).

Racial tensions were exacerbated during the Covid crisis when Africans were strangely scapegoated for a problem originating in Wuhan that had much to do with local bats, pangolins, or perhaps research laboratories, and nothing with Sub-Saharan people. The hostility of the authorities 'inadvertently created a space for suspicion and enmity between Africans and Chinese in places such as Guangzhou.' Even traders who have lived in the city for many years may 'begin to revaluate their racial identity.' Indeed, constant doubt and 'limited social support can be a recipe for poor mental wellbeing, and particularly among migrants' (Castillo and Amoah 2020: 563). This psychological dimension adds to the very real difficulty of overcoming bureaucratic obstacles to obtain or renew visas and to Chinese efforts to eliminate African middlemen and logistics agents. Africans in Guangzhou strongly resent 'the absence of policies and mechanisms to ensure decent living conditions [and an] enhanced sense of belonging and social equity' (Amoah *et al.* 2020: 462). Accordingly, pessimistic scenarios have been proposed that suggest that 'there will be little or no room for the irregular forms of migration, mobility and abode that have made possible the existence of thriving African communities in the Pearl River Delta region' (Castillo and Amoah 2020: 560). This is to say that the future of the non-hegemonic globalization 'from below' is rather dark in the city that became famous as its most important node.

Understanding the African Presence

Students of the African presence in Guangzhou have proposed three competing understandings of this socio-economic phenomenon: as a Sino-African socio-cultural bridge; an African trading post; and a transnational space resulting in an African enclave. These very different interpretations are due to the fact that the traders' 'trajectories, paces, and paths (...) subvert, confuse, and blur the notions of movement and settlement that are pervasive in traditional/structural/economistic approaches to migration' (Castillo 2014: 241). In terms of mobility, there are three categories of Africans in Guangzhou. The first includes the older, more established traders who have spent there more than a decade. They speak Chinese; some have Chinese or African families in the city. They are well connected, own offices and shops, and often act as intermediaries. They also 'influenc[e] and negotiat[e] the movement and temporary settlement of their fellow conationals.' Yet, even they are only temporary residents because 'there are no working "immigration" frameworks that would ensure their permanent stay or citizenship in the country' (*Ibid.*, 239). The second, massive category is represented by 'transients': the itinerant and semi-settled Africans who move frequently between their countries of origin and China. Ultimately, they have simply extended to the Asian country 'longstanding traditions of movement and trade – evidence of how certain African trading cultures of circulation, in their transnational mode, have finally reached China' (*Ibid.*, 240). Finally, there are the younger 'newly-arrived' Africans who, with different degrees of success, 'seek their fortunes in China.' Many fail and 'end up stranded or "immobile," (...) with difficult migratory statuses and a reliance on community networks to survive' (*Ibid.*). In all cases, the absence of a Chinese legal framework for permanent settlement makes 'normal' immigration impossible. Most African traders accordingly plan to leave China in the future and 'go through unpatterned cycles of rest and movement (never settling, always departing)' (*Ibid.*, 241). This is why it is difficult to find an agreement on one approach able to explain their situation.

Consensus, however, is emerging *against* one of the three aforementioned approaches. More than a decade ago, Adams Bodomo argued that the members of the 'emerging African trading community in Guangzhou' represent 'linguistic, cultural and business links and connections between their Chinese hosts and Africans in their home countries.' The future of this 'bridge' is highly promising: 'it is not far-fetched to foresee that in 100 years' time an African-Chinese Minority Ethnic Group could be demanding self-identity and full citizenship rights in the heart of Guangzhou' (Bodomo 2010: 693). By the time these lines were first written, the opposite trend was already visible. Since then, Bodomo himself has provided abundant evidence of the decline of the African presence as he depicted the increasingly hostile measures systematically adopted by the Chinese authorities (see, for example, Bodomo 2018: 63–64). Moreover, other scholars have noted a number of factors that are not indicative of African social integration such as 'residential clustering, a dislike of Chinese food, a reluctance to learn Chinese, [and] a strong orientation towards Africa for long-term investment, child-rearing and home-building,' to which they add 'the resentment of African practices by Chinese market managers and traders' (Lyons *et al.* 2012: 871). Furthermore, 'the deep-seated level of Chinese racism against blacks seems to work against Bodomo's theory' (Lee 2014: 56). Today, most authors reject the 'bridge,' sometimes speaking instead of a 'collapsing enclave' (Li *et al.* 2012: 51; Castillo 2014: 254; Lyons *et al.* 2012: 886; Lee 2014: 56; Liang and Le Billon 2020: 602–603, 622). Totally opposed to Bodomo's overoptimistic views, the minimalist 'African trading post' approach proposed by Brigitte Bertoncello and Sylvie Bredeloup (Bertoncello and Bredeloup 2007) analyzes the Africans' presence in Guangzhou as 'focused more on links to Africa and less on their Chinese environment' (Lyons *et al.* 2012: 871). The Chinese city is not perceived as fundamentally different from other similar trading posts established by Africans elsewhere in Asia. Such posts are described as a combination of the ancient Greek colony, the *emporion* – which 'is structured around a port and works as a foreign enclave working in close collaboration with the hinterland' – and the *Zongo* that, in countries such as Togo, Benin, Ghana, or Nigeria, expanded from the initial rest area for itinerant traders to a place 'reserved for foreigners, gradually allowing craftsmen, workmen, and merchants.' Because it is visited by and closely interacts with numerous locals, the trading post is different from an enclave (Bredeloup 2012: 29; see also Lee 2014: 19–20; Lyons *et al.* 2012: 886). Still, what other scholars see is precisely an African enclave in China. They present Xiaobei and Sanyuanli as places where, in addition to trade, 'African migrants try to make a living, even though there is not much local integration or assimilation.' Cultural and social differences maintain an 'invisible wall' between Africans and Chinese that strongly marks this transnational space (Lee 2014: 24), turning it into 'an ethnic enclave constantly responding to the changing demands of globalization' (Li *et al.* 2012: 55). Its socio-economic and spatial patterns coincide with those of ethnic enclaves as defined in the literature – urban 'highly visible geographically or spatially bounded ethnic centres' (Ong quoted in Li *et al.* 2012: 55) – as there is no 'integration socially or spatially of the local Xiaobei Chinese community and the transnational African community' (Lee 2014: 25).

The three approaches are mutually incompatible, but the evolution of the situation in Guangzhou ultimately allows for each of them to be considered valid during a specific period of time. Until 2007, there were good reasons to accept Bodomo's almost romantic view of a cosmopolitan Sino-African ethnic minority in the making. Unfortunately, due to the increasingly harsh measures adopted by the Chinese authorities and unfavorable attitudes among the local population, during the following years, 'the African trading diaspora in Guangzhou has become less of a "cultural bridge" and more of an enclave.' Moreover, the decline did not stop there: 'as pressures have worsened, it has also become more of an "outpost", with traders' ambitions for return "home" increasingly present in their plans' (Lyons *et al.* 2012: 886). The predictable future of Guangzhou is indeed one of short-term business visits that are not accompanied by a significant long-term African presence. Ultimately, what the city missed is nothing less than 'the potential birth of a multicultural China' (Mathews 2017: 24).

The dramatic reduction of the more or less permanent African population will not put an end to Guangzhou as a key node of the non-hegemonic globalization 'from below,' even if its importance will continue to diminish. But this phenomenon is illustrative of the structural tensions that emerge due to the negative perception by both state and society of a massive rise of the transnational informal economy that results in huge inflows of foreign 'ant traders.' It is important to identify the actual target of this hostility: is it the informal economy, the Chinese traders, or both? The Chinese authorities have repeatedly expressed concerns with regard to the semi-legal and illegal components of the transnational informal economy. But China is not the average Neoliberal state that wants to turn the non-hegemonic globalization 'from below' into the Western-centered globalization 'from above' as shown in Subchapter 4.2. Instead, it has an interest in – and a strategy of – replacing it with its own globalization 'from below,' an issue that I analyze in Subchapter 5.4. Eliminating African middlemen in Guangzhou so that Chinese nationals become intermediaries between Chinese manufacturers and African visiting traders – or, even better, having Chinese middlemen and petty traders taking Chinese goods directly to consumers in Africa – is part of this strategy. However, the Chinese globalization 'from below' pertains to the transnational informal economy as much as the non-hegemonic globalization 'from below.' The Chinese middlemen and petty traders are in no way alien to semi-legal and illegal economic activities. Moreover, while the Chinese authorities repressed the African traders in Guangzhou in a clear effort to significantly diminish their presence, they encouraged the same presence in places such as Yiwu as explained in the previous subchapter. In fact, the latter city has attracted many African traders previously located in Guangzhou. Accordingly, it can be argued that the Chinese state is not fighting the transnational informal economy. Its actual target mirrors that of the society: the 'problem' is represented by African long-term sojourners who are accused in Guangzhou of all the sins described by Edna Bonacich and Pál Nyíri in the general case of 'middleman minorities' (see Subchapter 4.4). These Africans are subject to hostility as a consequence of their racial and cultural features. Hostility combines with precarious legal status in limiting their path of upward mobility to the roles of middleman or logistics agent. The local society begins to identify the group with this specific type of business. Its members may be recognized as useful, but continue to be perceived as alien. Further hostility is due to economic factors such as rivalry with Chinese intermediaries and conflicts with local employees. As a result, African residents in Guangzhou are seen as inassimilable and illegitimate: 'Chinese should sell to Africans in Guangzhou. Africans shouldn't sell to Africans in Guangzhou' (Mathews 2015: 216). They find themselves in the typical situation of 'middleman minorities': 'in a word, middleman groups are seen as parasites.' The city 'is being "taken over" by an alien group' (Bonacich 1973: 583–584, 590–592; Nyíri 2011: 147). From the point of view of the authoritarian Chinese state, ensuing tensions endanger social stability in Guangzhou; the mere presence of a large alien group challenges its control of the society; and the economic prosperity of foreigners who transfer much of the profit to their countries of origin is not beneficial to China's economy. Unsurprisingly, the heavy-handed leadership in Beijing imposed the adoption of repressive policies that downgraded the African presence from potential cultural 'bridge' to ethnic enclave to trading post. Overall, the case of 'Chocolate City' in Guangzhou is illustrative of the negative social reactions and political responses that the massive development of the non-hegemonic globalization 'from below' can trigger even in regions and countries that are among this globalization's greatest beneficiaries.

4.7 La Salada's Baroque Economies

A very different but equally interesting case study is represented by the largest illegal market in Latin America, Argentina's La Salada. Its vast informal economy was even turned into the subject of a 2010 documentary, *Hacerme feriante* (Become a Stallholder) (IMDB 2021; YouTube 2021). A major node of the non-hegemonic globalization 'from below,' La Salada has developed as 'the poor people's shopping mall' (Forment 2015: S116) but also as 'a sort of laboratory for new forms of producing, consuming, and constructing networks of distribution and commercialization, structuring itself as a quarry of new types of employment' (Gago 2014/2017: 32). It is also an extreme example of the state's ambiguous relationship with and benefit from the informal economy. Located between the capital city of Buenos Aires and the Lomas de Zamora and La Matanza districts at its periphery, the market occupies no less than 18 hectares in a crime-ridden neighborhood located on the bank of Matanza (locally known as 'Riachuelo'), 'one of the most polluted rivers in the world' (Dewey 2014: 9; Savini 2011: 24). La Salada is associated with a large number of small illegal workshops (including 12,000 specialized in clothing) that assemble and finish goods, which 'are resold throughout the city, country, and region' (Office of the USTR 2020: 34). Its economic importance is illustrated by the fact that, in 2009, the market sold goods amounting to 15 billion pesos; that same year, the sales of all shopping malls in the country reached only 8.5 billion (Gago 2014/2017: 34; 2012: 66). Concerned goods include 'food, clothing, technology, leather goods, shoes, music, and movies,' even if textiles and footwear are predominant (Gago 2014/2017: 29). Trade is most successful because – as elsewhere in the nodes of the non-hegemonic globalization 'from below' – prices are very low. A cotton T-shirt sold for €17 in the rest of the country only costs €4. Women's shoes may be ten times cheaper than elsewhere (Peregil 2015). This is due to the informal nature of La Salada's economy, which includes large-scale counterfeiting. Low prices attract less affluent local customers but also traders from Argentinean provinces and neighboring countries such as Uruguay, Bolivia, Paraguay, and sometimes Chile. They arrive in long-distance buses to buy goods they resell back home (*Ibid.*).

La Salada was created by immigrants. In 1991, a group of Bolivian families specialized in the production of clothing – and 'sick of being exploited by factory bosses who paid them poorly and late' – settled on the site of long-abandoned thermal baths (*The Economist*, January 25, 2014). They created the 'Urkupiña' cooperative to sell their textile production. The initiative was so successful that the model was soon replicated by the 'Ocean' cooperative, set up by local people with political connections at the municipality level; and by the 'Punta Mogote' Center established by another group as a joint-stock company (Savini 2011: 25). Today, Punta Mogote has the best infrastructure, which even includes a radio station. Its *'La Salada está de moda'* ('La Salada is fashionable') program is broadcast on middle waves all over Argentina by Radio Splendid (Peregil 2015). La Salada is composed of the three initial fairs of Urkupiña, Ocean, and Punta Mogote; the one-mile long La Ribera where poorer stalls were installed up to the river bank (hence the name); and the '"intermediate fairs", set by neighbourhood residents who created improvised shopping malls adjacent to the main fairs' (Savini 2011: 24). La Ribera has been repeatedly described as 'totally illegal' (Schiavo *et al.* 2016: 401), 'a grey zone,' 'an irregular labyrinth,' 'the margin of the margin, the extreme of La Salada's informality' (Wilkis and Hacher 2012). Its 'most parlous stalls located along the riverbank' were in fact forcefully relocated in 2015 (d'Angiolillo 2015; Schiavo *et al.* 2016: 401). *The resulting market is impressive. There are* 30,000 stalls that, three days per week, are visited by 250,000 customers who arrive in 500–1,000 long-distance buses, as well as thousands of cars (*The Economist*, January 25, 2014; Richards 2017; Peregil 2015). This flow reminiscent of the Dordoi Bazaar in Kyrgyzstan (see Subchapter 4.1) provides stable employment to almost 110,000 people. No less than '40.000 families are living directly and indirectly from the complex' (Savini 2011: 30; Forment 2015: S118). Importantly, within a 30-km radius, there are as many as 12,000 textile workshops and sweatshops that own or rent stalls to sell their products. They provide employment for 50,000 more people, most of whom are undocumented immigrants. In fact, 60 percent of the market vendors are also undocumented Bolivians. Ten percent come from Peru or Paraguay; only the remaining 30 percent are Argentineans (Forment 2015: S118). Somewhat surprisingly, there are also much smaller numbers of Senegalese who sell cheap jewelry (Gago 2014/2017: 30). Stalls are not cheap. Four square meters may cost as much as US $100,000, which is more than on Buenos Aires' main shopping street, Avenida Alvear (*The Economist*, January 25, 2014). In addition, in Urkupiña, vendors have to pay US $200 of monthly expenses. Stalls in the streets outside the main three fairs are run by '*armadores*' who charge US $50 per day per seat. This is why some vendors prefer to work as peddlers without their own space (Savini 2011: 27). Costs are so high because of the significant profits stalls bring: every day, La Salada sells goods worth US $22 to US $44 million (*The Economist*, January 25, 2014). In fact, 'day' is a bit inappropriate: timetables frequently vary and the market – which used to operate on Tuesday, Thursday, and Sunday – can open at 3 pm or 11 pm; but, in most cases, sales take place from 2 am to 8 am (Peregil 2015; Wilkis and Hacher 2012). Due to the Covid crisis, La Salada was closed from March to October 2020, when it was reopened under the condition of operating at 50 percent of normal capacity on Monday, Wednesday, Saturday, and – from December 2020 – Sunday, from 7 am to 1 pm. However, large-scale disrespect of protective measures was soon noticed (*La Nación*, December 21, 2020).

Activities are not limited to trade and related production. Community services are provided that are financed and coordinated by the administrators of the three main fairs and the vendor's Association of Merchants, Professionals, and Industrialists. At different times, they have included assisting schools in the neighborhood, funding a technical school, opening community dining halls and children dining rooms, offering health insurance, supplying free medicines, donating clothing, and supporting neighborhood clubs in addition to paying for garbage removal, street maintenance, and public security (Savini 2011: 30; Forment 2015: S119). The fact that a market has to provide such social services reveals the root cause that led to the spectacular success of La Salada as an expression of the transnational informal economy. This huge market 'can be read as a response from below to the dispossessive effects of neoliberalism' (Gago 2014/2017: 7). Indeed, La Salada developed tremendously during the 2001 crisis in Argentina when, under the impact of demonetization, the informal economy took mass proportions (*Ibid.*, 6). In turn, the financial crisis was 'a product of the brutal neoliberal policies implemented in Argentina by former President Carlos Menem in the 1990s.' These policies and the crisis 'sharpened inequality (...) [and] generated a spread of basic survival modes among the impoverished working classes and modest middle classes.' New for Argentina, 'several food riots by middle class people' ignited while many poorer citizens had to become garbage pickers (Sassen 2011). Unsurprisingly, from 2002, 'an overall sustained increase in labor informality was observed' (Dewey 2014: 9). Politically, the dramatic socio-economic situation led to the electoral success of the Left, with Peronist Presidents Néstor Kirchner (2003–2007) and Cristina Fernández de Kirchner, his wife (2007–2015), controlling Argentina for more than a decade. In 2002, unemployment reached more than 20 percent and the poverty rate over 50 percent. The Peronists introduced social programs – prominently including the *'Plan Jefas y Jefes de Hogar'* ('Heads of Household Program') – that transferred cash to 20 percent of Argentina's households. However, 'contrary to its intention, the [Heads of Household] programme also provided incentives for its beneficiaries to engage in informal activities and collect both incomes' (Savini 2011: 21, 24). Informality was associated with no less than 50 percent of the total workforce in 2003. It then stabilized at 45 percent for the rest of the decade despite the end of the crisis (*Ibid.*, 22). By 2014, it was assessed at 35 percent (Khlif and Pousset 2014: 37). This general trend was even more pronounced in the textile industry, which is most relevant for La Salada. President Menem's liberalization of the Argentinean economy by the mid-1990s 'sent[t] the textile sector into a downward spiral' (Forment 2015: S120). The opening up of the country to cheaper imports led to 'the devastation of the national textile and clothing industry' (Sassen 2011). From 1993 to 2001, its added value diminished by 37 percent, demand by 36 percent, employment by 51 percent, worked hours by 45 percent, and real wages by 20 percent. Between 1996 and 2002, production diminished by 57 percent (Dewey 2014: 8). To survive, companies had to downsize, hire informal workers, and outsource production to clandestine sweatshops and family workshops (Forment 2015: S120). The percentage of informal textile workers increased from 59.15 percent in 2002 to 77.6 percent in 2010 (Dewey 2014: 17). Many of them were – and still are – Bolivian immigrants. They first came to Argentina during the economic boom of the 1990s as 'experienced workers and small entrepreneurs. Thus they brought with them knowledge and experience' (Sassen 2011). Eventually, they became the core of the no less than '31,000 small home-sweatshops spread throughout Buenos Aires province' (Dewey *et al.* 2017), which also hire Paraguayans, Peruvians, and Argentineans; 12,000 of these workshops are relatively close to La Salada where they sell most of their output (Forment 2015: S118). Interestingly, the quality of products can be very high because major brands outsource production to such workshops. The output is 'sold both in the city's fancy shops *and* in La Salada often for the lower-income households' (Sassen 2011; emphasis in the original). Important for the market's 'proletarian microeconomies' (see the following sections), there is a huge difference between family workshops and clandestine sweatshops. The former – which are as illegal as the latter – normally work for eight hours a day, even if at times this increases to ten hours or more. The family owns the workshop and a stall at La Salada where it sells most of its products (Forment 2015: S120). One can easily identify the pattern of migrant family firms discussed in Subchapter 4.4. In the sweatshops, on the contrary, 'entire families live in the same facility, and monthly earnings are about a third of the minimum wage.' They work 16–17 hours per day (Savini 2011: 29) and are kept in unhygienic conditions. There is large-scale human trafficking and 'slave labor.' Passports are typically confiscated by employers. Immigrants accept exploitation because in about one year they acquire technical skills, familiarize themselves with the local economic ecosystem, and save some money. This allows them to start their own family workshops (Forment 2015: S120), which significantly improves their socio-economic situation.

The illegal workshops are illustrative of La Salada's massive participation in the informal economy. Widespread semi-legal and illegal practices include 'trademarks infringement, smuggling, police corruption and intimidation, and political clientelism, (...) [as well as] slave and child labour' (Savini 2011: 29). As mentioned in Subchapter 4.3, a series of police raids were organized in September 2019 to put an end to a mobile street vendor network tied, rather surprisingly, to Senegalese organized crime involved in counterfeiting and human trafficking (Office of the USTR 2020: 5). Under normal conditions, however, 'the police are reckoned to be more complicit, demanding bribes in exchange for ignoring contraband goods' (*The Economist*, January 25, 2014). Tax evasion is as widespread as 'the systematic avoidance or circumvention of established and codified fiscal, labor, and security regulations' (Dewey 2014: 11). In early 2007, an official inquiry revealed that 90 percent of all vendors did not have a tax number (Forment 2015: S119). Typical for a phenomenon pertaining to the non-hegemonic globalization 'from below,' 'all shopping is done in cash, leaving ample room for fudging the accounts.' The difficulty to enforce 'normal' taxation practices is illustrated by a hilarious episode: 'in one 2009 tax raid vendors from Punta Mogote lobbed thousands of eggs at agents until they fled' (*The Economist*, January 25, 2014). Even more puzzling, a system of informal taxation exists that I describe in the next section. Informality covers all sectors, from production to commercialization to reselling in the outer provinces (Dewey 2014: 11). Moreover, there are active Mafia groups. By 2017, there had been at least five murders related to organized crime (Girón 2017b). 'Overall, the economy centered in La Salada shows that legality, and even more so, informality and illegality co-exist' (Dewey 2014: 12).

Informality is not limited to the national framework: the market 'is part of formal and informal international trading circuits that extend to other countries in Latin America' (Sassen 2011). La Salada has started as and continues to be part of a 'migrant economy.' Illegal immigrants provide an important part of the labor. In particular, undocumented Bolivians represent 60 percent of those who work in the market and most of the 50,000 textile workers active within a 30-km radius (Forment 2015: S118). They, as well as the vendors and buyers from other neighboring countries, turn the market into 'migrant territory.' These 'ant traders' 'open routes of distribution and commercialization toward their countries, while many of the goods arrive from various parts of the planet' (Gago 2014/2017: 30). As much as 20 percent of what is sold at La Salada is smuggled to Argentina (Wilkis and Hacher 2012), mainly from Bolivia; this includes merchandise made in China. Symmetrically, its goods – including counterfeit ones – are exported illegally to neighboring countries. La Salada is the center of a network of regional markets such as Los Altos in Bolivia's capital La Paz, thus sharing a 'border epistemology,' and operates in synchronism with key nodes of the transnational informal economy such as Guangzhou. This makes it a 'powerful place of popular consumption and commerce, with a transnational scope': 'a node in [the] expanding transnational network' (Gago 2014/2017: 16, 30, 54) of the non-hegemonic globalization 'from below.'

The 'Informal State'

It is obvious that the aforementioned coexistence of 'legality, (...) informality and illegality' (Dewey 2014: 12) would not be possible without at least the tacit support of political actors. In fact, observers have identified three different 'emerging logics' based on which La Salada operates: the corporatist mercantile one, associated with owners of stalls and workshops; the subsistence or 'necessity' logic of the numerous workers who find themselves in precarious labor situations; and 'a predominantly political logic, which includes those who have connections with the dominant political and economic power and articulate the concert of involved interests' (Schiavo et al. 2016: 394). These influential individuals play a key role: 'each fair has leaders/administrators that have formal and informal ties with state officials, community leaders and criminal groups' (Savini 2011: 26). Urkupiña was created as a cooperative, but by 2010 it was led by an administrator from the governing Peronist party. The board of Ocean, also a cooperative at first, came under the control of ex-military Argentinean nationalists. Punta Mogote, set up as a joint-stock company, was for a long time administered by Jorge Castillo of the Radical Party, the Peronists' traditional adversary. Only La Ribera remained 'an amorphous group with basic organisation "coordinated" by a Bolivian and Peruvian-based loose association that regulate almost 5,000 stalls through soft pacts and intimidation' (Ibid., 26, 28). The fact that the two largest fairs were led by representatives of the country's main political forces is illustrative of La Salada's importance for Argentina's political actors (Dewey 2014: 10). This should not be a surprise: the market is located on the border between Lomas de Zamora and La Matanza, the most populous districts of the province of Buenos Aires that are also home to most of its voters (Savini 2011: 28). What is surprising is the ambiguous relationship between the market and the state. During the 1990s, the latter was completely absent. City inspectors and police officers received bribes and ensured the complicity of state agencies. The success of the market, however, made them increase their demands. Unexpectedly, vendors and workers held a meeting where they rejected higher bribes. In protest, they organized demonstrations and marches while using newspapers, as well as TV and radio stations, to win public support (Forment 2015: S119). A particularly acute conflict developed 'between security forces, who unofficially tried to establish protection rackets, and the Bolivian community, which refused to accept any state regulation.' The Bolivian leader of the largest fair was imprisoned in 2001 for illegal trade and counterfeiting. He was soon found dead in his cell. Strangely, this event marked the beginning of a generally accepted informal tax system (Dewey 2014: 12). It should be mentioned that a formal system also exists; by 2011, the market administrations were paying annually US $8 million in taxes plus US $60.000 as Health and Safety tax (more than the French Carrefour supermarket chain, the largest in the country), US $26.000 as VAT, and US $4.700 for water and garbage collection (Savini 2011: 29). In addition, vendors in the three main fairs are registered as self-employed 'monotributistas' expected to pay a fixed monthly tax. This, however, is 'an obligation that, in practice, is no more than a recommendation'; there are many ways to avoid it (Dewey 2014: 11; Savini 2011: 29). What is paid is mainly due to the large-scale repressive measures taken in 2007 by the revenue service of the Buenos Aires province on orders from President Kirchner himself. In six raids, 250 agents investigated 9,000 vendors; as an effect, the number of registered ones increased from 10 percent to 77 percent. Yet, it took two more years until an 'information regime' was put in place to monitor each vendor (Forment 2015: S119–S120); and this was hardly sufficient to eliminate tax evasion and, more generally, the informal economy. However, as mentioned, since 2001 'a well-established informal taxation system' exists that is regulated by 'a robust institutional framework' (Dewey 2014: iii). On the one hand, there is a tax imposed on buyers arriving by long-distance bus. It is collected at random by a federal security force that does not register the amounts charged, which are not fixed. On the other hand, stalls that sell goods with brand logos have to pay a *'marca'* (brand) tax. It has to be paid to tax collectors inside the fairs and the police in the case of street vendors. Officially, this tax is presented as a compensation to be paid 'to the authorities or even to [concerned] companies' for copyright infringement. The amount of US $771,955 collected monthly (as of 2014) is distributed across eight national and provincial state agencies and the municipality of Montañitas. No company has ever received a penny. Paradoxically, the illegal 'economic activity is not abolished but taxed' (*Ibid.*, 13, 14, 16).

La Salada provides a good example of acceptance and exploitation by political actors of clearly illegal practices related to the transnational informal economy. Central, provincial, and local state agencies make informal institutional arrangements and adopt 'shadow policies' allowing them to extract financial benefits at the price of 'a dualization of a specific economic sector.' This is possible because concerned illegal activities are not morally contested by the society. On the contrary, they are 'mostly seen as harmless and are considered to have wealth-generating potential' because they represent 'sources of regular income and thus of consumption for poverty-stricken populations' (*Ibid.*, iii, 2). This is a typical example of a successful projection of normative power associated with the non-hegemonic globalization 'from below.' La Salada's 'ant traders' have been able to reshape the society's understandings of 'normal' so deeply that political actors and the state itself feel legitimate to disrespect the law and extract profits from illegal activities. Certain observers have even argued that the 'formal' authority of the state is replaced with 'a different aspect of governmental authority that regulates and manages the interstices between the formal, the informal, and the criminal: the "informal state"' (Savini 2011: 33). This other face of the 'divided' state tolerates important legal transgressions and protects involved groups 'in exchange for other type [of] contributions beyond taxing, that can be purely criminal, such as bribes, or not, for instance, popularity or votes' (*Ibid.*, 34). Indeed, the complex economic web connected to La Salada ultimately resulted in new political-economic articulations (Gago 2014/2017: 32). President Néstor Kirchner fully understood the political importance of the popularity of the market among the country's poor (*The Economist*, January 25, 2014; Girón 2017a). Accordingly, his government set up special programs that provided state credit lines to La Salada's small entrepreneurs (Dewey 2014: 19). His wife and successor, President Cristina Fernández de Kirchner, even took a group of representatives of the market to Angola in a 2012 visit intended to promote bilateral commercial relations. This was generally perceived as official recognition of and support for La Salada's informal economic model (Schiavo *et al.* 2016: 401; Dewey 2014: 13; Peregil 2015). It should be added that this trend was in no way limited to Argentina. The more radical leftist regimes in Venezuela, Bolivia, and Ecuador even adopted constitutional reforms that supported various forms of informal 'social and communitarian economy' and 'promoted their articulation with the rest of the economy as part of [their] drive toward development' (Gago 2014/2017: 7). Yet, a certain degree of ambiguity did exist during the Peronist administrations. As already mentioned, it was President Kirchner who ordered the massive 2007 campaign intended to put an end to tax evasion in La Salada. Symmetrically, the fall of Peronism did not trigger a return to Neoliberal orthodoxy. President Mauricio Macri came to power in 2015 on a resolutely Neoliberal platform. That very year, the Argentinean Chamber of Commerce protested formally against the 'abuse committed by many owners of [La Salada] who do not pay taxes or rents,' a situation mirrored in 'more than one hundred small illegal markets or "saladitas" in the city of Buenos Aires' (Peregil 2015); by 2013, all over Argentina there were no less than 500 such 'saladitas' (Forment 2015: S122). Officially, 'incorporating informal sectors into the formal tax paying economy [became] a priority for the government' (Richards 2017). In 2017, Jorge Castillo, administrator of Punta Mogote and self-proclaimed king of La Salada, and Enrique 'Quique' Antequera, administrator of Urkupiña, were arrested for various illegal activities that included tax evasion and copyright infringement (Klipphan 2021). The event was hailed by the Confederation of Small Businesses, whose head emphatically invoked the 'need to formalize the economy': the state 'is losing over $1 billion a year in lost taxes' (Richards 2017). However, it progressively became clear that the arrests were in large measure associated with a struggle for power within La Salada; the fight against informal activities was little more than a pretext (Girón 2017b; Richards 2017; Klipphan 2021). Furthermore, the 2018 monetary crisis initiated a new recession eventually aggravated by the Covid crisis. The Peronists returned to power in 2019. It was obvious to all political forces that fighting La Salada's informal economy 'would be politically risky' (*The Economist*, January 25, 2014).

Plebeian Democracy, Proletarian Microeconomies, and Neoliberalism 'from Below'

The ambiguous relationship between state and informal economy is only one of La Salada's features that turn it into a fascinating case study of the non-hegemonic globalization 'from below.' Verónica Gago, an Argentinean scholar, explored the details of a complementary dimension: the 'baroque economies' that have emerged within this large market as a 'plurality of forms in an uneven meshwork,' a *'hodgepodge'* of 'alternative economic practices' that 'resist neoliberalism while simultaneously succumbing to its models of exploitative labor and production' (Duke University Press 2017; Gago 2014/2017: 69). Unsurprisingly, the 'reign of the copy' is a prominent such practice: 'La Salada is part of the social representation of Buenos Aires as a synonym for copy or forgery, which is not necessarily associated with incorrectness' (Schiavo *et al.* 2016: 390). To the anti-crime agencies of the European Union and the United States, the market is 'the emblem of piracy, of the "trucho"' (Peregil 2015). Indeed, no less than 78 percent of Argentinean-made apparel is produced through illegal circuits. 'Made in India' or 'made in Thailand' tags are placed on much of the clothing manufactured by Bolivian migrants in illegal workshops located in Buenos Aires and sold at La Salada (Gago 2014/2017: 108). At the market, 40 to 60 percent of the stalls sell Adidas-, Puma-, Nike-, or Disney-branded counterfeit – and, therefore, cheap – garments (Dewey 2014: 9, 13). There are 'copies of Tommy Hilfiger shirts for 110 pesos (...) and flimsy "Ray-Ban" sunglasses' (*The Economist*, January 25, 2014). Videogames, CDs, and DVDs are sold both inside the fairs and on the streets; all are pirated (Peregil 2015). The extreme example of fake merchandise, however, is not transnational: a poodle puppy sold in June 2012 for US $150 proved to be a 'Brazilian rat,' i.e., a fluffy angora ferret given steroids at birth (which increased its size) and then groomed (Campbell 2013; *The Economist*, January 25, 2014). Like the ferret, La Salada's counterfeited cloth or footwear is 'an imperfect imitation of the original, a hybrid that [is] neither an accurate copy (...) nor something completely different.' It imitates brands and uses their logos to legitimate itself, but represents 'an invention: a product halfway between Andean culture, TV fashion, and the trial and error of the seamstresses.' The pirated brand 'becomes something with its own life and senses. Something new, different' (Wilkis and Hacher 2012). In 2008, *La Nación* published a strongly Neoliberal front-page analysis of La Salada titled 'A Trip to Argentina's Last Century.' It argued that the market represents nothing less than the 'reversal of progress,' a failed modernity (Forment 2015: S116). A more productive perspective, however, is centered on the concept of *'modernidad falsa,'* fake – or, rather, counterfeit – modernity (Gago 2012: 68) discussed in Subchapter 4.3. It perceives the Argentinean market – and its counterparts elsewhere in the Global South – as representative not of a failed/reversed/absent modernity, but rather as the product of an alternative modernity. Places such as La Salada – and the wider social environment they both represent and shape – accept and legitimate piracy as 'a culture of the copy that exists alongside livelihood and labor, profit and pornography' (Liang 2011: 173). As shown in the abovementioned *Hacerme feriante* documentary (IMDB 2021; YouTube 2021), 'La Salada is a space in which a type of production that is defined by its clandestine nature is publicized and expanded. (...) the *original* is produced underground, and the counterfeit *copy* is openly distributed' (Gago 2014/2017: 38; emphasis in the original; see Subchapter 4.3). The 'original' modernity is replaced with the parallel, counterfeit one. At times, local actors show understandings of this replacement that are reminiscent of the anti-Neoliberalism of the counter-hegemonic globalization 'from below': 'after the "brands" destroyed our economy and robbed us of our jobs, it was La Salada that enabled us "darkies" to crawl out from the bottom of the trash bin' (Forment 2015: S121–S122). 'Do we affect the United States and the European Union? No, because whoever buys in La Salada cannot buy what they want to sell them.' In fact, 'there is a social right that the person who does not have money can use Messi's sportshoes.' Interestingly, this latter statement was not made by an anonymous 'ant trader.' It is part of an interview given by the then administrator of Punta Mogote, Jorge Castillo (Peregil 2015). 'Ant traders' concur, and show an understanding of the role played by La Salada that goes far beyond their immediate mercantile interests: 'although "brands" portray us as a center for the sale of counterfeits, the market is a *social institution*' (Forment 2015: S121; emphasis added). Such statements show that common people genuinely appreciate the positive impact of the transnational informal economy on their livelihoods and explicitly acknowledge the legitimacy of this *sui generis* 'social institution.' By taxing counterfeiting – through the *'marca'* (brand) tax mentioned in the previous section – instead of repressing it, the state implicitly supports their views. This is indeed the picture of an alternative modernity that has little to do with the 'original' one.

At this point, it is critical to address the inferiority apparently associated with a modernity that, by definition, is a 'from below' one. Describing it as 'fake' and 'counterfeit' implicitly suggests a lower position with respect to the Western 'from above' 'original' modernity. In this view, La Salada becomes the low-end, inferior universe of those unable to access the 'real thing.' However, a different perspective exists, which perceives the Argentinean market as the locus of a set of emancipatory processes that 'provid[e] a sense of personal dignity, social justice, and a new "skill set" based on self-help productivism' (Forment 2015: S119). At La Salada, 'a series of innovative economic institutions (of savings, exchange, loans, and consumption) spread, combining survival strategies with new forms of popular entrepreneurship.' Individually and collectively, there is advancement. 'Those who migrate find the possibility of changing jobs, professions, aspirations. From there arises the strength of progress as the possibility of a transition, a change' (Gago 2014/2017: 6, 69). There have even been cases of trademarks that evolved from informality to formality. From minor brands in La Salada, 'Prestige,' 'Scombro,' or 'Puntot 1' became key providers for retailers all over the country (Savini 2011: 32). On a much larger scale, the role and position of migrants and women have improved as an effect of the development of the illegal textile industry, which led to the significant transformation of the informal economy. The clandestine textile workshop uses the migrant-inhabited *villas* (neighborhoods) as 'a space of community resources, protection, and favors, as well as the source of a workforce.' In this new socio-economic context, the traditional centrality of the father or breadwinner was challenged and eliminated by 'feminized figures (the unemployed, women, youth, and migrants) who go out to explore and occupy the street as a space of survival and, in that search, reveal the emergence of other vital logics.' Women, migrants, and the poor 'challenge the city and often struggle to produce situations of urban justice, conquering the city and defining a new "right to the city".' The migrant economy has allowed immigrants involved in the non-hegemonic globalization 'from below' 'to obtain resources to settle, invest, and produce and that functioned as a material resource and social guarantee for a popular productive rationality.' Eventually, the state, banks, and microfinance institutions 'recognize[d] and reinterpret[ed] this migrant economy'; their support critically included new sources of financing (Gago 2014/2017: 7, 8, 16, 32). The emancipatory dimension is not limited to socio-economic advancement; it includes episodes of actual social activism. Asamblea La Alameda, a neighborhood organization, was the first to initiate a public campaign against the sweatshops' 'slavery.' It established a cooperative, shops, and the 'No-Chains' brand. Second-generation young Bolivians created Simbiosis, an NGO that provides information about workers' rights and designs intervention and mobilization strategies (Sassen 2011). Progressively, these developments have 'allowed LS [La Salada] to build itself as a separate economic, political and cultural entity' (Savini 2011: 33). To describe this new reality, Carlos Forment has employed the term 'plebeian democracy.' This is the result of the engagement in 'noninstitutional politics, socioeconomic informality, and a-legality' of 'the "structural poor" and the recently impoverished middle class.' Created as 'a radical alternative to traditional populism,' it represents an effort 'to break with "ideological" and "party-centered" notions of politics' and adopt a 'pragmatic, issue-centered, and postideological conception of politics rooted in daily life and needs.' Actual initiatives included protests intended to protect workshops from abusive police raids, as well as the ambitious – and ultimately failed – attempt to secede from the Lomas de Zamora district. During their disputes with various representatives of the local government, La Salada-related impoverished middle class, urban poor, and undocumented immigrants 'developed their own ethicopolitical understanding of the rule of law, property rights, and the common good.' Importantly, they also 'develop[ed] their own conception of moral economy and reject[ed] those who sought to portray them as part of the informal sector' (Forment 2015: S116, S122, S124). This is a remarkable example of a movement that originated in the non-hegemonic globalization 'from below' of an informal market but expanded and upgraded its agenda up to the point where the movement became part of the counter-hegemonic globalization 'from below,' whose ideological discourse it explicitly adopted.

However, the emancipatory dimension should not be allowed to hide the darker side of La Salada. Not all is beautiful and harmonious there. Most of its day-to-day interactions are illustrative of an 'ambivalent reality': a strange and at times shocking combination of 'new forms of popular entrepreneurship and brutal forms of exploitation' (Gago 2014/2017: 6). Indeed, the market brings together 'the expansion of popular consumption and the promotion of a diverse employment reserve' and a 'form of production that is not entirely legal and is sustained by conditions of extreme exploitation.' Labor situations include small businesses, self-employment, as well as domestic and community labor that are tied to convoluted dependencies. The process of desalarization due to the 2001 crisis has not been reversed. On the contrary, it stabilized. Verónica Gago coined the term 'proletarian microeconomies' to describe this 'new landscape of the proletarian beyond its Fordist definition' that is characterized by 'a new composition of labor power – informal, illegal, precarious, innovative, and entrepreneurial.' Labor situations are fluid: they include periods of informality, persistent aspirations of finding formal employment, receiving subsidies from the state, taking advantage of community networks, and exploiting relationships that range from family to political ones. The ambiguous communitarian capital of the numerous Bolivian migrants mixes 'self-management, mobilization, and insubordination' with 'servitude, submission, and exploitation.' This puzzling situation 'call[s] into question the very limits of what is called work' (*Ibid.*, 16, 32–35). The 'proletarian microeconomies' of La Salada complement social innovation with new regimes of submission. They represent 'a nontraditional – and nonindustrial – economy,' a 'mode of production of heterogeneity' that combines high levels of expansion and extreme precarity; communitarian manifestations and brutal exploitation. Microentrepreneurs, workers, migrants, and community organizers enact informal economic processes that pertain to the non-hegemonic globalization 'from below' but also get involved in deals with major local brands and participate in transnational value chains (*Ibid.*, 17, 33–34). Major – and, at times, paradoxical – differences exist between the self-understandings of various actors. As already mentioned, many undocumented Bolivian immigrants who work in illegal sweatshops 'are held in semi-slavery, often confined' (Sassen 2011). The sweatshop owners may also be Bolivian: 'immigrants are both exploiters and exploited' (Savini 2011: 31). Activists from organizations such as Asamblea La Alameda conduct an active public campaign against this 'slavery' (Sassen 2011). In 2006, when a fire in a textile sweatshop killed six immigrants, La Alameda initiated a series of public forums, street marches, and other forms of protest against La Salada practices of 'engaging in slave labor, maintaining ties to sweatshops, undermining the rights of workers, and contributing to the spread of the informal economy' (Forment 2015: S123). In response, the police raided 365 sweatshops; 138 were found to use 'slave' labor. However, the 'victims' disagreed. The main organization of the Bolivian immigrants is the Asociación Civil Federativa Boliviana, which tries to protect them from police abuses that include 'raids against their home-based workshops.' This association vocally accused La Alameda and other human rights groups of 'perpetuating racism under the guise of defending human rights.' The head of Alameda 'is a liar and a cheat. We are not slaves, we are workers, and if we work as hard as we do it is because we want to earn more money.' Human rights activists 'treat Bolivians as if we were idiots. They think we are incapable of knowing whether we are being exploited or not.' Such understandings of self-exploitation and moral economy (*Ibid.*, S124) are illustrative of the aforementioned 'new regimes of submission' specific to La Salada's 'proletarian microeconomies.' Overall, the contradictory processes that coexist within the market reflect 'a fundamental ambivalence,' an 'oscillation [that] does not arrive at a synthesis' (Gago 2014/2017: 17, 34).

Nacho Girón, who wrote the first book offering a journalistic account of La Salada, subtitled it 'The Radiography of the Most Controversial Fair in Latin America.' The book was an editorial success: published by Ediciones B in 2011, it was reprinted in 2013 by Lanormal, and republished as an expanded edition by Editorial Planeta in 2017 (Girón 2017a). Girón placed his analysis of the market in a national context: 'the good and the bad of Argentina are embodied by La Salada.' Its complex and contradictory features represent 'at once a display of Argentine creativity, intelligence, resilience and grit, and an exhibit of Argentine cunning and corruption' (*The Economist*, January 25, 2014). Verónica Gago's more scholarly analysis (Gago 2012, 2014/2017) uses a conceptual framework closer to the non-hegemonic globalization 'from below' scrutinized in this chapter. She depicts 'the tense mix of calculation and freedom, obedience and resistance, individualism and community, and legality and illegality' visible in La Salada as a globalized characteristic of 'the increasingly powerful popular economies of the global South's large cities.' An important aspect she emphasizes is that, ultimately, these economies 'resist neoliberalism while simultaneously succumbing to its models of exploitative labor and production' (Duke University Press 2017; Gago 2014/2017). Julián d'Angiolillo, the director of *Hacerme feriante* (IMDB 2021; YouTube 2021), similarly noted that, while sabotaging and 'opening it to a distinct time and space,' La Salada *duplicates* the neoliberal city (d'Angiolillo 2015). To explain the paradoxical mixture of contradictory processes discussed in the previous paragraphs, Gago even coined the term 'neoliberalism from below,' which defines a situation characterized by the following chain of consequences: the state fails to enforce the conditions of Neoliberal competition. Calculation replaces them as a vital condition for economic survival; it creates a 'vitalist pragmatic' in sectors associated with the informal economy. More specifically, calculation provides a 'primordial subjective frame' and becomes 'the motor of a powerful popular economy.' This new economy 'combines community skills of self-management and intimate know-how as a technology of mass self-entrepreneurship in the crisis.' It 'organizes a certain idea of freedom, which, in its own way, challenges some of the most traditional forms of obedience.' But, at the same time, calculation-based popular entrepreneurship 'assumes a certain monstrosity' that includes new regimes of submission. To summarize, 'the neoliberal dynamic is problematically and effectively combined with [the] persistent vitalism that always attaches to the expansion of freedoms, pleasures, and affects' (Gago 2014/2017: 6). Not everybody will agree with the use of 'Neoliberalism' in a 'from below' context. But terminology is less important than Gago's apt depiction of a puzzling socioeconomic situation that is in no way limited to La Salada; entirely or in part, its features are reproduced in many other places in Latin America and the Global South. Ultimately, the Argentinean market is most effective in showing the power of the transnational informal economy to create what the same scholar has aptly called 'baroque economies': strange hybrids that can exist only within the 'counterfeit' modernity of the non-hegemonic globalization 'from below.'

4.8 Normative Clashes, Ambiguities, and Agency

Because it is based on the outlawed practices of the transnational informal economy, the non-hegemonic globalization 'from below' began as a marginal and discreet phenomenon. Today, its various forms of manifestation 'oscillate between hypervisibility and invisibility.' However, the previous subchapters show that the overall phenomenon 'can no longer be considered marginal from any point of view' (Gago 2014/2017: 17, 37). Especially, but not exclusively, in the Global South, its magnitude has reached a level that makes it comparable with – and, in many cases, superior to – the Western-centered globalization 'from above.' The supposedly marginal non-hegemonic globalization 'from below' has developed, spontaneously and successfully, in the numerous and at times vast economic niches and interstices neglected by the Neoliberal globalization. The obvious question is 'why.' At least at first view, the equally obvious answer is that 'ant trade' is one of the very few strategies of economic survival available to all those who face 'the dispossessive effects of neoliberalism' (Gago 2014/2017: 68; 2012: 77; Yükseker 2003: 134, 136; Sasunkevich 2015: 4–6). Ultimately, it is not without reason that the 'anthropological literature typically depicts neoliberalism as a profound evil' (Mathews 2011: 241). Yet, such a response is incomplete. People on the brink of starvation are far from representing the majority of the actors and beneficiaries of the non-hegemonic globalization 'from below.' Most of the latter are animated by a different reason: the 'hunger for modernity,' understood as the mainly psychological need of poor citizens in peripheral regions to feel connected with the rest of the globalized world (Peralva 2003: 191; Tarrius 2002), even if this connection is limited to a *'globalización popular'* (people's globalization) (Ribeiro 2012b). This is 'the only globalization' – and modernity – 'that many inhabitants of the extreme periphery may ever experience' (Mathews 2011: 236). They are satisfied as long as they get an acceptable *copy* of the original, Western-centered globalization 'from above.' This brings the discussion to the issue of counterfeiting and its social consequences. A superficial observer may think that piracy is just one of the many dimensions of the transnational informal economy that hardly influences the society beyond the futile realm of fashion. This is precisely why I presented the case study of La Salada. It clearly shows that, in the view of those excluded from participating in and benefiting from the Neoliberal globalization 'from above' – which is a strong form of 'social exclusion' (Khlif and Pousset 2014: 39) – 'there is a social right that the person who does not have money can use Messi's sportshoes' (Peregil 2015). This is not about fashion; this is about constructing a different self-understanding compatible with an otherwise inaccessible modern and globalized lifestyle. La Salada 'is a social institution' (*Ibid.*) that reconstructs identities and integrates the individual in the forbidden globalized world. To quote once more the African trader in Guangzhou and the street peddler in Mexico City, 'what I do is good for Africa'; it 'is not a problem, it is a solution. The problem was created elsewhere; we are solving it' (Yang 2011a: 115; Mathews and Alba Vega 2012: 2). Through the life-changing actions of the 'ant traders,' the non-hegemonic globalization 'from below' restores to the poor their 'capacity for initiative' (Peralva 2003: 192; Tarrius 2002). The result, however, is hardly ideal. The 'counterfeit' modernity triumphantly challenges the rule – and the rules – of the 'original,' Neoliberal modernity. It also has an important emancipatory dimension well captured by the concept of 'plebeian democracy' (Forment 2015). But it is based on the 'ambivalent reality' of 'proletarian microeconomies' that combine 'new forms of popular entrepreneurship and brutal forms of exploitation'; at times, its 'new regimes of submission' can be characterized by 'a certain monstrosity' (Gago 2014/2017; 2012). This is not limited to the Argentinean market. Various scholars have warned against the 'celebration of mobility' associated with the non-hegemonic globalization 'from below': 'caution (...) should be kept because the boundary between the empowering and exploitative aspects of geographical mobility in the case of shuttle trade may remain very ambiguous' (Sasunkevich 2015: 5). The literature 'tends to conceptualize mobility with a positive bias.' Sometimes there is indeed 'liberation, progress and change' (Verne 2017: 125); but flows and interconnections are always characterized by a 'power geometry.' 'Some people are more in charge of it than others; some initiate flows and movement, others don't; some are more on the receiving end of it than others; some are effectively imprisoned by it' (Massey 1994: 149; Verne 2017: 125). This is to say that, for the good and the bad, the non-hegemonic globalization 'from below' actually changes social relations. In fact, it can dramatically modify the very structure of the society, as shown by the post-Soviet example discussed in Subchapter 4.1 and reflected even in monumental art. Accordingly, it is hardly exaggerated to argue that this is a powerful globalization that significantly impacts the Global South in economic, social, political, and cultural terms.

Its 'greatest power,' however, is normative power. It is impressive that, by 1996, a tenth of Kyrgyzstan's population engaged in informal trade (Spector 2017: 27; 29–30); or that, in 2009, the value of goods sold at La Salada was two times higher than that of all shopping malls in Argentina (Gago 2014/ 2017: 34; 2012: 66). But such results of the transnational informal economy are negligible in comparison to its ability to resist the formidable pressure of the multilateral institutions, multinational corporations, and Neoliberal states that use their tremendous power in a global war meant to destroy the non-hegemonic globalization 'from below.' This successful resistance is the result of a projection of normative power that shapes understandings of 'normal': societies perceive the 'ant traders' and their commerce as legitimate; states tolerate them. In most of the Global South, the efforts of the Western-centered globalization 'from above' to repress its 'from below' rival and turn it into Neoliberal globalization through the use of banking, formalization, and fiscalization (Mathews and Alba Vega 2012: 10) have systematically failed. However, besides the Western-centered globalization, there are normative power interactions between the non-hegemonic globalization 'from below' and no less than four other entities: states that may not be Neoliberal; the Chinese-centered globalization 'from below'; the counter-hegemonic globalization 'from below'; and its own actors. In all five cases, a surprising amount of ambiguity is present.

Even the normative power clash between the non-hegemonic globalization 'from below' and the Western-centered globalization 'from above' is complicated by such ambiguity. The former globalization is an effective form of resistance to the latter, which, in turn, tries to destroy it. Yet, the 'ant trade' has reached impressive dimensions only because the Neoliberal globalization brought global interconnectedness and mutual awareness, diffused certain social values globally, and developed 'a conscience of transnationally-shared elements' (Fonseca and Malheiros 2004: 132). It created the specific historical, economic, and social context (Sasunkevich 2015: 4) without which the 'from below' globalization could have not emerged. Moreover, 'ant traders' do not seek to destroy capitalism and the Neoliberal globalization whose rules they infringe on a daily basis. Somewhat paradoxically, their success is measured in terms of being able to become fully fledged members of this 'from above' globalization. The most frequently mentioned triumph of La Salada is represented by minor local trademarks such as 'Prestige,' 'Scombro,' or 'Puntot 1' that evolved from informality to formality, transforming themselves into recognized brands of the Western-centered globalization 'from above' (Savini 2011: 32). The counter-hegemonic globalization 'from below' fights the Neoliberal one in the hope of fundamentally reshaping it. The non-hegemonic one also fights it; but the ideal of its actors is simply to join it. The 'counterfeit' modernity may be emancipatory, but it represents only a *faute de mieux*[1] solution for those unable to reach the enviable 'original' modernity and its equally 'original' Western-centered globalization 'from above.'

In large measure, the Neoliberal war against the non-hegemonic globalization 'from below' is fought through state policies. Consequently, success or failure is often understood as related to the strength or weakness of states expected to enforce the Neoliberal agenda. Political willingness is also taken into consideration, but in general, its absence is associated with various state weaknesses such as reliance on informal currency inflows, the inability to supply critical goods to the population through formal channels, and so on (see Subchapter 4.2). Ultimately, the governments of weaker states in the Global South represent the target of two competing projections of normative power: that of the Western-centered globalization 'from above,' which in practical terms takes the form of pressure and conditionalities imposed by the Bretton Woods institutions, Neoliberal states in the North, and various supranational, national, and subnational donors; and that of the non-hegemonic globalization 'from below,' which is more diffuse but frequently has the upper hand. This situation, however, concerns only actual or potential Neoliberal states. Those analyzed in the two case studies of this chapter pertain to a different category, which is rather small but analytically interesting. Both neo-communist China and Peronist Argentina adopted political ideologies and economic models that reject Neoliberalism and dramatically reduce their vulnerability to pressure intended to impose it. Yet, they are very different in one respect that has much to do with the situation of Neoliberal states: China inherited a strong state from its relatively recent totalitarian past. President Xi's concentration of power further reinforced the state (and party) control of numerous political, social, economic, and cultural fields. Accordingly, few scholars may question its ability to seriously damage the transnational informal economy; there is only the issue of political will. Argentina, on the contrary, has a weak state that, even before the Peronists came to power in 2003, was unable to limit the development of the non-hegemonic globalization 'from below.' La Salada's 'well-established informal taxation system' regulated by 'a robust institutional framework' (Dewey 2014: iii) that prominently includes the *'marca'* (brand) tax (see the previous subchapter) was set up before President Kirchner took power. The anti-IMF leftist governments in Buenos Aires simply provided a certain degree of official recognition of and support for La Salada's informal economic model and, implicitly, for a situation where political actors and the 'informal state' (Savini 2011: 33) feel legitimate to disrespect the law and extract profits from illegal activities. Unsurprisingly, ideologically motivated anti-Neoliberalism aligned itself with the non-hegemonic globalization 'from below' in a common normative struggle against the enemy represented by the Western-centered globalization 'from above.' Returning to the case of China, a puzzling picture emerges. The strong Chinese state initially encouraged the African 'ant traders' in Guangzhou, which resulted in the development of an impressive 'Chocolate City,' but has increasingly repressed them since 2008, while at the same time creating conditions for their relocation to Yiwu (see Subchapter 4.5). It is clear that the repression of the non-hegemonic globalization 'from below' in Guangzhou has nothing to do with Neoliberalism; the long arm of the Bretton Woods institutions cannot reach that far, even if China is a member of both the IMF and the World Bank. Another potential suspect is Beijing's support for the Chinese-centered globalization 'from below' mentioned in the next paragraph and discussed in the next chapter. But again, why repress in Guangzhou and show a smiling face in Yiwu? The (relative) 'fall of Chocolate City' was not caused mainly by another globalization. Rather, it represents one of the few cases where the naked logic of state actions can be examined in relative independence from external influences. Indeed, the attitude of the Chinese state toward the 'ant trade' has been dictated by the balance between economic benefits and perceived negative social effects. These effects were assessed by the leadership in Beijing based on a heavily authoritarian view shaped by an obsession with social stability that allows for effective society control; and a rejection of diversity and cosmopolitanism rooted in an immigration-free recent past. It is at this point that the definition of the non-hegemonic globalization 'from below' as a mainly 'migrant economy' becomes relevant. In a country constructed through immigration such as Argentina – 'Mexicans descended from the Aztecs; Peruvians descended from the Incas; the Argentines descended from the boats' (Warren 2009) – few will find shocking that 60 percent of La Salada's vendors are undocumented Bolivians (Forment 2015: S118). In former Canton, on the contrary, the communist authorities expelled all foreigners in 1950–1951 (Mathews 2017: 8). Under the wise leadership of Chairman Mao, connections with the outside world could easily put one in the *laogai* (the Chinese Gulag). Accordingly, the rapid development of a foreign 'middleman minority' after 2001 could not fail to raise racial tensions and official mistrust. Ultimately, the resulting post-2008 course of events in Guangzhou shows that a strong state does not need to be Neoliberal in order to effectively repress the non-hegemonic globalization 'from below': domestic policy considerations related to anti-migrant attitudes can provide equally strong reasons. More generally, the often scrutinized opposition between this globalization and the Western-centered 'from above' one has the demerit of hiding the very serious obstacles met by 'ant traders' due to the migrant dimension. At times, these obstacles can be more important than Neoliberalism.

176 The Non-Hegemonic Globalization 'from Below'

The confrontation between the non-hegemonic and the Chinese-centered globalizations 'from below' cannot be analyzed before discussing the latter. This is why the analysis is placed in Subchapter 5.4. The remaining two cases of normative power clashes are rather surprising. Both the non-hegemonic and counter-hegemonic globalizations 'from below' have emerged in reaction to and represent forms of resistance against the Neoliberal globalization 'from above.' However, as shown by the example of the Eastern Market in Washington discussed in Subchapter 4.2, strange alliances can develop between actors of the counter-hegemonic globalization 'from below' and the Western-centered globalization 'from above.' Their discourse of localism and authenticity rejects the 'cheap' and 'foreign' that represent the defining features of the non-hegemonic globalization 'from below.' One would be tempted to note that the normative power of the 'movement of movements' is used against the wrong target. Still, such situations are limited to affluent parts of the Global North where alter-globalization activists represent 'an urban, highly cosmopolitan and privileged group of elites' strongly marked by class and status differences (Shepherd 2012: 187, 200). Similar limitations are absent in the case of the last type of normative power clash, which is a surprising confrontation between actors of the same non-hegemonic globalization 'from below.' The La Salada case study has shown the puzzling conflict between human rights groups such as La Alameda and the main organization of the Bolivian immigrants, the Asociación Civil Federativa Boliviana. The former are the representatives *par excellence* of the emancipatory dimension of the non-hegemonic globalization 'from below' and the 'counterfeit' modernity it has created. The latter represents the actual individuals whose labor constructs the same globalization and modernity; in the process, they are willing to accept harsh exploitation and demeaning conditions as a price for future social advancement. By helping to shape understandings of 'normal,' both groups contribute to the production of normative power of the non-hegemonic globalization 'from below.' However, two diverging forms of normative power are involved, which are based on two equally diverging understandings of what social advancement should mean. To human rights activists, this is about putting an end to the excesses of what Verónica Gago calls the 'Neoliberalism from below': the 'monstrous' exploitative dimension of the non-hegemonic globalization 'from below' that, within 'proletarian microeconomies' such as those of La Salada, is no better than that of the Neoliberal globalization 'from above.' Ultimately, the struggle of La Alameda mirrors, in a different context, the logic of the counter-hegemonic globalization 'from below.' This activistic view is alien to the Bolivian migrants who follow the classical logic of 'ant traders': similar to the suitcase traders represented in post-Soviet monumental art, they accept present hardship with optimism and confidence in the future. If these two groups pertaining to the non-hegemonic globalization 'from below' are to be ranked in terms of 'which one is more genuine,' one key aspect has to be mentioned: La Alameda has been fighting practices of 'engaging in slave labor, maintaining ties to sweatshops, undermining the rights of workers, and *contributing to the spread of the informal economy*' (Forment 2015: S123; emphasis added). The latter aspect is reminiscent of Washington's Eastern Market alliance between alter-globalization activists and actors of the Neoliberal globalization. In the Argentinean case, human rights defenders want to 'save' the undocumented migrants by putting an end to the very transnational informal economy on which they rely for economic survival. The success of such efforts would paradoxically lead to the end of the non-hegemonic globalization 'from below' and to the integration of its actors into the Western-centered globalization 'from above.' This is to say that, paradoxically, the emancipatory dimension of the 'plebeian democracy' – which represents the bright side of the 'ambiguous reality' of the non-hegemonic globalization 'from below' – is not fully compatible with the survival of this globalization. There is no such contradiction when the darker, exploitative side is scrutinized. It can be concluded that this is a harsh globalization where hardship is the price for socio-economic advancement while the protection of human rights may have highly counterproductive consequences.

Despite their clashing views, La Alameda and the Asociación Civil Federativa Boliviana are illustrative of an important aspect discussed in Subchapter 4.2: the 'ant traders" agency. In that subchapter, I rejected the use of the World System Theory precisely because, as a structural International Relations approach, it emphasizes systemic constraints while denying the agency of actors. La Salada's activists and undocumented migrants show that, on the contrary, processes associated with the non-hegemonic globalization 'from below' can develop independently of structural factors and may not even result from rational choice calculations. The latter do motivate the reaction of Bolivian migrants who simply want to protect their source of revenue; but the activists' campaign for the protection of human rights has little to do with both structural constraints and calculation. They act based on cognitive factors represented by libertarian norms, principles, and values that World System Theory cannot take into consideration. Constructivism does, and is therefore able to explain the agency of various 'from below' actors mentioned in this chapter. Critically, the non-hegemonic globalization 'from below' restores the 'capacity for initiative' of victims of Neoliberalism (Peralva 2003: 192; Tarrius 2002). The agency of these small and weak actors is influenced by individual aspirations of upward social mobility, subjective personal plans and ambitions, and even adventurous entrepreneurial decisions. They are 'powerful actors who develop strategies and mobilise resources to overcome geographical, political or cultural boundaries.' This may include inventive solutions such as 'informal visa procurements or the strategy to remain a student while conducting trade activities' (Gilles 2015: 19). In Guangzhou, African traders 'are not voiceless and passive but proactive in questioning [hostile] views and practices, and in seeking to expand and deepen economic and broader social ties' (Liang and Le Billon 2020:

602). Facing discrimination, they 'are not just wallowing in passivity. They take matters into their own hands, and show a great amount of effort, of agency in ensuring their well-being in China.' This includes 'a substantial amount of African community agency' based on 'leadership provided by community and family heads,' underground medical services, counseling provided by religious leaders, and 'verbal, music, and dance therapies provided by leading cultural icons' (Bodomo 2020: 533). Furthermore, in July 2009 and June 2012, hundreds of Nigerians organized public protests in Guangzhou against police brutality and discriminatory treatment (Liang and Le Billon 2020: 612). Unlike the Western-centered globalization 'from above,' the non-hegemonic 'from below' one is based on individual actors and relies decisively on their aspirations, ideas, and actions.

The overall picture of the non-hegemonic globalization 'from below' is that of a complex, complicated, and often ambiguous and paradoxical economic, social, political, and cultural process that proposes an alternative, 'counterfeit' modernity to the numerous losers of the Western-centered globalization 'from above.' As long as Neoliberalism is dominant, this supposedly marginal and discreet globalization 'from below' will continue to develop quantitatively and qualitatively. Given its diversity and dynamism, the decades to come may well witness new geographies of nodes and flows, new forms of 'ant trade,' as well as new types of 'proletarian microeconomies' and 'plebeian democracies.' The non-hegemonic globalization 'from below' is not likely to solve the problems that led to its dramatic expansion; but it will continue to represent a fascinating object of study.

Note

1 For lack of something better (French).

References

Abazov, Rafis, (2003) 'The Parliamentary Elections in Kyrgyzstan, February 2000,' *Electoral Studies*, 22(3), pp. 545–552.

Akipress.com, December 6, 2018, 'Shuttle Traders' Monument Was Installed at the Entrance of Kyrgyzstan's Biggest Bazaar - Dordoi,' https://akipress.com/news:614043?from=mportal&place=project

Alff, Henryk (2016) 'Flowing Goods, Hardening Borders? China's Commercial Expansion into Kyrgyzstan Re-Examined,' *Eurasian Geography and Economics*, 57(3), pp. 433–456.

Amoah, Padmore Adusei, Obert Hodzi, Roberto Castillo (2020) 'Africans in China and Chinese in Africa: Inequalities, Social Identities, and Wellbeing,' *Asian Ethnicity*, 21(4), pp. 457–463.

Ben-Rafael, Eliezer, and Yitzhak Sternberg (2009) 'Introduction: Debating Transnationalism,' in Eliezer Ben-Rafael and Yitzhak Sternberg with Judit Bokser Liwerant and Yosef Gorny (eds.) *Transnationalism: Diasporas and the Advent of a New (Dis)Order*, Leiden; Boston: Brill, pp. 1–25.

Bertoncello, Brigitte and Sylvie Bredeloup (2007) 'The Emergence of New African "Trading Posts" in Hong Kong and Guangzhou,' *China Perspectives*, 1(94), pp. 94–105.
Blalock, Hubert M., Jr. (1967) *Toward a Theory of Minority Group Relations*, New York: John Wiley.
Bodomo, Adams (2010) 'The African Trading Community in Guangzhou: An Emerging Bridge for Africa-China Relations,' *The China Quarterly*, 203, pp. 693–707.
Bodomo, Adams (2015) 'African Traders in Guangzhou: A Bridge Community for Africa-China Relations,' in Carla P. Freeman (ed.) *Handbook on China and Developing Countries*, Cheltenham; Northampton, MA: Edward Elgar Publishing, pp. 133–165.
Bodomo, Adams (2018) 'The Bridge Is Not Burning Down: Transformation and Resilience within China's African Diaspora Communities,' *African Studies Quarterly*, 17(4), pp. 63–83.
Bodomo, Adams (2020) 'Historical and Contemporary Perspectives on Inequalities and Well-Being of Africans in China,' *Asian Ethnicity*, 21(4), pp. 526–541.
Bodomo, Adams B., and Grace Ma (2010) 'From Guangzhou to Yiwu: Emerging Facets of the African Diaspora in China,' *International Journal of African Renaissance Studies - Multi-, Inter- and Transdisciplinarity*, 5(2), 283–289.
Bonacich, Edna (1973) 'Theory of Middleman Minorities,' *American Sociological Review*, 38(5), pp. 583-594.
Bredeloup, Sylvie (2012) 'African Trading Post in Guangzhou: Emergent or Recurrent Commercial Form?,' *African Diaspora*, 5(1), pp. 27–50.
Bruneau, Michel (2010) 'Diasporas, Transnational Spaces and Communities,' in Rainer Bauböck and Thomas Faist (eds.) *Diaspora and Transnationalism: Concepts, Theories and Methods*, Amsterdam: Amsterdam University Press, pp. 35–49.
Campbell, Andy (2013) 'Ferrets Sold as Toy Poodles: Argentina Pet Dealers Reportedly Selling Weasels on Steroids,' *Huffpost*, April 8, updated April 13, https://www.huffpost.com/entry/ferrets-rodents-sold-as-toy-poodles-argentina_n_3037094
Casson, Mark (2010) 'Networks in Economic and Business History: A Theoretical Perspective,' in Paloma Fernández Pérez and Mary B. Rose (eds.) *Innovation and Entrepreneurial Networks in Europe*, Abingdon, Oxon: Routledge, pp. 14–40.
Castells, Manuel (1996/2009) *The Rise of the Network Society, The Information Age: Economy, Society and Culture*, Vol. I, Malden, MA; Oxford: Blackwell.
Castillo, Roberto (2014) 'Feeling at Home in the "Chocolate City": An Exploration of Placemaking Practices and Structures of Belonging amongst Africans in Guangzhou,' *Inter-Asia Cultural Studies*, 15(2), pp. 235–257.
Castillo, Roberto, and Padmore Adusei Amoah (2020) 'Africans in post-COVID-19 Pandemic China: Is There a Future for China's "New Minority"?,' *Asian Ethnicity*, 21(4), pp. 560–565.
Cherkasova, Veronika (2006) 'Эта страна напротив' (Eta strana naprotiv/ The Country in Front of Your Eyes), October 16, https://gazetaby.com/post/eta-strana-naprotiv/3071/
Cichocki, Bartosz, Andrzej Wilk, and Katarzyna Pełczyńska-Nałęcz (2001) 'The Kaliningrad Oblast in the Context of EU Enlargement,' *CES Studies*, July 15, Warsaw: Centre for Eastern Studies (OSW), pp. 53–64, https://core.ac.uk/download/pdf/11869765.pdf
Comaroff, Jean, and John L. Comaroff (2009) *Violencia y ley en la poscolonia: una reflexión sobre las complicidades Norte-Sur,* Buenos Aires: Katz.

Cox, Robert (1981/1986) 'Social Forces, States and World Order' in Robert Keohane (ed.) *Neorealism and Its Critics*, New York: Columbia University Press, pp. 204–254.
d'Angiolillo, Julian (2015) 'Become a Stallholder: Duplicating La Salada,' *Othermarkets.org*, http://www.othermarkets.org/index.php?tdid=19&txt=1
Dana, Leo-Paul, Markku Virtanen, and Wilhelm Barner-Rasmussen (2019) 'Shaking the Minority Box: Conceptualizing the Impact of Context and Social Capital on the Entrepreneurial Activity of Minorities,' in Maria Elo and Indianna Minto-Coy (eds.) *Diaspora Networks in International Business: Perspectives for Understanding and Managing Diaspora Business and Resources*, Cham, Switzerland: Springer, pp. 205–228.
Desai, Manisha (2009) 'Women Cross-Border Traders: Rethinking Global Trade,' *Development*, 52(3), pp. 377–386.
Dewey, Matías (2014) 'Taxing the Shadow: The Political Economy of Sweatshops in La Salada, Argentina,' *MPIfG Discussion Paper*, No. 14/18, Max Planck Institute for the Study of Societies, Cologne, https://www.econstor.eu/handle/10419/104712
Dewey, Matías, Katherine Walker, and Sarah Pabst (2017) 'Hope in the Sweatshops of Buenos Aires,' *Contexts. Sociology for the Public*, December 5, https://contexts.org/articles/hope-in-the-sweatshops-of-buenos-aires/
Dreamstime.com, October 05, 2015, 'Monument Celnoki aka Shuttle trading. Belgorod. Russia,' https://www.dreamstime.com/editorial-image-monument-celnoki-aka-shuttle-trading-belgorod-russia-october-chelnoki-chelnok-trader-buying-consumer-goods-small-bulk-lower-image64962165
Duke University Press (2017) 'Neoliberalism from Below: Popular Pragmatics and Baroque Economies,' https://www.dukeupress.edu/neoliberalism-from-below
Elo, Maria, and Indianna Minto-Coy (2019) 'The Concept of Diaspora from the Perspective of International Business and Economy: An Introduction to the Book,' in Maria Elo and Indianna Minto-Coy (eds.) *Diaspora Networks in International Business: Perspectives for Understanding and Managing Diaspora Business and Resources*, Cham, Switzerland: Springer, pp. 1–14.
Elochukwu, Anas (2016) 'Guangzhou's African Migrants: Implications for China's Social Stability and China–Africa Relations,' *Contemporary Chinese Political Economy and Strategic Relations*, 2(3), pp. 1195–1213.
Elochukwu, Anas (2019) 'A Survey of the African Diaspora in Guangzhou,' *International Journal of China Studies*, 10(2), pp. 181–197.
EME Outlook (2021) 'Dubai: A Global Hub,' https://www.emeoutlookmag.com/industry-insights/article/449-dubai-a-global-hub
Faist, Thomas (2010) 'Diaspora and Transnationalism: What Kind of Dance Partners?,' in Rainer Bauböck and Thomas Faist (eds.) *Diaspora and Transnationalism: Concepts, Theories and Methods*, Amsterdam: Amsterdam University Press, pp. 9–34.
Fonseca, Lucinda, and Jorge Malheiros (2004) 'Immigration and Globalisation from Below: The Case of Ethnic Restaurants in Lisbon,' *Finisterra*, 39(77), pp. 129–156.
Forment, Carlos A. (2015) 'Ordinary Ethics and the Emergence of Plebeian Democracy across the Global South: Buenos Aires's La Salada Market,' *Current Anthropology*, 56(S11), pp. S116–S125.
Gago, Verónica (2012) 'La Salada: ¿un caso de globalización «desde abajo»? Territorio de una nueva economía política transnacional,' *Nueva Sociedad*, Sep/Oct, 241, pp.63–78, https://nuso.org/articulo/la-salada-un-caso-de-globalizacion-desde-abajo-territorio-de-una-nueva-economia-politica-transnacional/

Gago, Verónica (2014/2017) *Neoliberalism from Below: Popular Pragmatics and Baroque Economies*, Durham: Duke University Press, revized edition of *La razón neoliberal: economías barrocas y pragmática popular*, Buenos Aires: Tinta Limón, 2014.

Gauthier, Mélissa (2012) 'Mexican "Ant Traders" in the El Paso/Ciudad Juárez Border Region: Tensions between Globalization, Securitization and New Mobility Regimes,' in Gordon Mathews, Gustavo Lins Ribeiro, and Carlos Alba Vega (eds.) (2012) *Globalization from Below: The World's Other Economy*, London and New York: Roudledge, pp. 138–153.

Gilles, Angelo (2015) 'The Social Construction of Guangzhou as a Translocal Trading Place,' *Journal of Current Chinese Affairs*, 44(4), pp. 17–47.

Girón, Nacho (2017a) *La Salada. Radiografía de la feria más polémica de Latinoamérica*, expanded edition, Buenos Aires: Editorial Planeta.

Girón, Nacho (2017b) 'Libro "La Salada",' http://www.nachogiron.com.ar/p/libro-la-salada.html

Gobe, Éric (2004) 'La Méditerranée des réseaux. Marchands entrepreneurs et migrants entre l'Europe et le Maghreb by Jocelyne Cesari; La fin des norias. Réseaux migrants dans les économies marchandes en Méditerranée by Michel Peraldi; La mondialisation par le bas. Les nouveaux nomades de l'économie souterraine by Alain Tarrius,' Book review, *Sociologie du Travail*, 46(3), pp. 420–423.

Haugen, Heidi Østbo (2018) 'From Pioneers to Professionals: African Brokers in a Maturing Chinese Marketplace,' *African Studies Quarterly*, 17(4), pp. 45–62.

Huynh, T. Tu (2016) 'A "Wild West" of Trade? African Women and Men and the Gendering of Globalisation from Below in Guangzhou,' *Identities-Global Studies in Culture and Power*, 23(5), pp. 501–518.

IMDB (2021) 'Hacerme feriante,' https://www.imdb.com/title/tt1636784/

Karrar, Hasan H. (2017) 'Kyrgyzstan's Dordoi and Kara-Suu Bazaars: Mobility, Globalization and Survival in Two Central Asian Markets,' *Globalizations*, 14(4), pp. 643–657.

Keyder, Çağlar (1999) 'A Tale of Two Neighborhoods,' in Çağlar Keyder (ed.) *Istanbul: Between the Global and the Local*, Lanham, MD: Rowman & Littlefield, pp. 173–186.

Khlif, Wafa, and Joanna Pousset (2014) 'It Takes (More than) Two to Tango: Informal Tango Market Dynamics in Barcelona,' *Society and Business Review*, 9(1), pp. 36–50.

Klipphan, Andrés (2021) 'El "Rey de La Salada" perdió su trono: José Castillo fue apartado de la feria popular más grande del país,' *Infobae*, February 14, https://www.infobae.com/politica/2021/02/14/el-rey-de-la-salada-perdio-su-trono-jose-castillo-fue-apartado-de-la-feria-popular-mas-grande-del-pais/

Koh, Minkyung, and Edward J. Malecki (2016) 'The Emergence of Ethnic Entrepreneurs in Seoul, South Korea: Globalisation from Below,' *Geographical Journal*, 182(1), pp. 59–69.

Kucera, Joshua (2009) 'Don't Call Them Twin Cities,' *Slate*, December 28, https://slate.com/news-and-politics/2009/12/don-t-call-them-twin-cities.html

La Nación, December 21, 2020, 'Coronavirus en la Argentina: preocupantes imágenes en la feria La Salada,' https://www.lanacion.com.ar/sociedad/coronavirus-preocupantes-imagenes-feria-la-salada-nid2547450/

Lee, Benjamin, and Edward LiPuma (2002) 'Cultures of Circulation: The Imaginations of Modernity,' *Public Culture* 14(1), pp. 191–213.

Lee, Margaret C. (2014) *Africa's World Trade: Informal Economies and Globalization from Below*, London: Zed Books, in association with Uppsala, Sweden: Nordic Africa Institute.

Li, Zhigang, Michal Lyons, and Alison Brown (2012) 'China's "Chocolate City": An Ethnic Enclave in a Changing Landscape,' *African Diaspora*, 5(1), pp. 51–72.

Liang, Kelly, and Philippe Le Billon (2020) 'African Migrants in China: Space, Race and Embodied Encounters in Guangzhou, China,' *Social & Cultural Geography*, 21(5), pp. 602–628.

Liang, Lawrence (2011) 'Beyond Representation: The Figure of the Pirate,' in Mario Biagioli, Peter Jaszi, and Martha Woodmansee (eds.) *Making and Unmaking Intellectual Property: Creative Production in Legal and Cultural Perspective*, Chicago: University of Chicago Press, pp. 167–180.

Liu, Hong, and Els van Dongen (2016) 'China's Diaspora Policies as a New Mode of Transnational Governance,' *Journal of Contemporary China*, 25(102), pp. 805–821.

Lyons, Michal, Alison Brown, and Li Zhigang (2012) 'In the Dragon's Den: African Traders in Guangzhou,' *Journal of Ethnic and Migration Studies*, 38(5), pp. 869–888.

Marfaing, Laurence, and Alena Thiel (2015) 'Networks, Spheres of Influence and the Mediation of Opportunity: The Case of West African Trade Agents in China,' *The Journal of Pan African Studies*, 7(10), pp. 65–84.

Marsden, Magnus (2018) 'Beyond Bukhara: Trade, Identity and Interregional Exchange across Asia,' *History and Anthropology*, 29(S1), pp. S84–S100.

Marsden, Magnus, and Vera Skvirskaja (2018) 'Merchant Identities, Trading Nodes, and Globalization: Introduction to the Special Issue,' *History and Anthropology*, 29(S1), pp. S1–S13.

Massey, Doreen (1994) *Space, Place, and Gender*. Minneapolis: University of Minnesota Press.

Mathews, Gordon (2011) *Ghetto at the Center of the World: Chungking Mansions, Hong Kong*, Chicago; London: The University of Chicago Press, epub edition.

Mathews, Gordon (2015) 'African Logistics Agents and Middlemen as Cultural Brokers in Guangzhou,' *Journal of Current Chinese Affairs*, 44(4), pp. 117–144.

Mathews, Gordon, and Carlos Alba Vega (2012) 'Introduction. What Is Globalization from Below?,' in Gordon Mathews, Gustavo Lins Ribeiro, and Carlos Alba Vega (eds.) *Globalization from Below: The World's Other Economy*, London and New York: Roudledge, pp. 1–15.

Mathews, Gordon, and Yang Yang (2012) 'How Africans Pursue Low-End Globalization in Hong Kong and Mainland China,' *Journal of Current Chinese Affairs*, 41(2), pp. 95–120.

Mathews, Gordon, with Linessa Dan Lin and Yang Yang (2017) *The World in Guangzhou: Africans and Other Foreigners in South China's Global Marketplace*, Chicago and London: The University of Chicago Press.

Moya, José C. (2018) 'Preface: The Syrian-Lebanese Diaspora in a Global Perspective,' in Oswaldo Truzzi (ed.) *Syrian and Lebanese Patrícios in São Paulo: From the Levant to Brazil*, Urbana, Chicago, and Springfield: University of Illinois Press, pp. xiii–xx.

Niu, Dong (2017) '"Unequal Sino-African Relations": A Perspective from Africans in Guangzhou,' in Young-Chan Kim (ed.) *China and Africa: A New Paradigm of Global Business*, Cham, Switzerland: Palgrave Macmillan, pp. 243–261.

Novos.mk.ru, September 3, 2015, 'В Бердске появился памятник "челнокам" / In Berdsk, a Monument to the "Shuttle Traders",' https://novos.mk.ru/articles/2015/09/03/v-berdske-poyavilsya-pamyatnik-chelnokam.html

Nyíri, Pál (2002) 'Globalising Chinese Migration: New Spaces, New Meanings,' *Migracijske i Etničke Teme*, 18(1), pp. 23–39.

Nyíri, Pál (2011) 'Chinese Entrepreneurs in Poor Countries: A Transnational "Middleman Minority" and Its Futures,' *Inter-Asia Cultural Studies*, 12(1), pp. 145–153.

OECD (2004) 'Shuttle Trade,' Glossary of Statistical Terms, *Organization for Economic Cooperation and Development*, https://stats.oecd.org/glossary/detail.asp?ID=2459

OECD and EUIPO (2016) 'Trade in Counterfeit and Pirated Goods: Mapping the Economic Impact,' April 18, *Illicit Trade*, Paris: OECD Publishing and European Union Intellectual Property Office, http://www.oecd.org/corruption-integrity/reports/trade-in-counterfeit-and-pirated-goods-9789264252653-en.html

OECD and EUIPO (2017) 'Mapping the Real Routes of Trade in Fake Goods,' June 23, *Illicit Trade*, Paris: OECD Publishing and European Union Intellectual Property Office, http://www.oecd.org/corruption-integrity/reports/mapping-the-real-routes-of-trade-in-fake-goods-9789264278349-en.html

OECD and EUIPO (2018) 'Why Do Countries Export Fakes? The Role of Governance Frameworks, Enforcement and Socio-Economic Factors,' June 26, *Illicit Trade*, Paris: OECD Publishing and European Union Intellectual Property Office, https://www.oecd.org/gov/risk/why-do-countries-export-fakes-brochure.pdf

OECD and EUIPO (2019) 'Trends in Trade in Counterfeit and Pirated Goods,' March 18, *Illicit Trade*, Paris: OECD Publishing and European Union Intellectual Property Office, http://www.oecd.org/corruption-integrity/reports/trends-in-trade-in-counterfeit-and-pirated-goods-g2g9f533-en.html

Office of the USTR (2020) '2019 Review of Notorious Markets for Counterfeiting and Piracy,' Office of the United States Trade Representative, Executive Office of the President, https://ustr.gov/sites/default/files/2019_Review_of_Notorious_Markets_for_Counterfeiting_and_Piracy.pdf

Online Etymology Dictionary (2021) 'Counterfeit,' https://www.etymonline.com/word/counterfeit

Peralva, Angelina (2003) 'Alain Tarrius, La mondialisation par le bas. Les nouveaux nomades de l'économie souterraine, Paris, Balland, 2002,' Book review, *Cahiers Internationaux de Sociologie*, Nouvelle série, 114, pp. 191–193.

Peregil, Francisco (2015) 'La Salada, el gran mercado negro de Latinoamérica,' *El País*, March 14, https://elpais.com/internacional/2015/03/13/actualidad/1426276499_218087.html

Polsergmich, September 8, 2016, 'Скульптурные композиции (9). Памятники торговцам-челнокам' (Sculptural Compositions (9). Monuments to Shuttle Traders), http://polsergmich.blogspot.com/2012/12/9-7.html

Quayson, Ato, and Girish Daswani (2013) 'Introduction - Diaspora and Transnationalism: Scapes, Scales, and Scopes,' in Ato Quayson and Girish Daswani (eds.) *A Companion to Diaspora and Transnationalism*, Chichester, West Sussex: Blackwell Publishing, pp. 1–26.

Rai, Rajesh, and Peter Reeves (2009) 'Introduction,' in Rajesh Rai and Peter Reeves (eds.) *The South Asian Diaspora: Transnational Networks and Changing Identities*, Abingdon, Oxon: Routledge, pp. 1–12.

Rauch, James E. (2001) 'Business and Social Networks in International Trade,' *Journal of Economic Literature*, 39(4), pp. 1177–1203.

Reynolds, Jana (2014) 'Inside Russia's Clandestine Showrooms,' *The Business of Fashion*, November 27, https://www.businessoffashion.com/articles/global-markets/inside-russias-clandestine-showrooms

Ribeiro, Gustavo Lins (2006) 'Economic Globalization from Below,' *Etnográfica*, X(2), pp. 233–249.

Ribeiro, Gustavo Lins (2012a) 'Conclusion: Globalization from Below and the Non-Hegemonic World-System,' in Gordon Mathews, Gustavo Lins Ribeiro, and Carlos Alba Vega (eds.) *Globalization from Below: The World's Other Economy*, London and New York: Roudledge, pp. 221–235.

Ribeiro, Gustavo Lins (2012b) 'La globalización popular y el sistema mundial no hegemónico,' *Nueva Sociedad* (Buenos Aires), No. 241, September-October, https://nuso.org/articulo/la-globalizacion-popular-y-el-sistema-mundial-no-hegemonico/

Ribeiro, Gustavo Lins (2013) 'What's in a Copy?,' *Vibrant - Virtual Brazilian Anthropology*, 10(1), pp. 20–39.

Richards, Joel (2017) 'Argentina Launches Effort to Formalize Black Market,' CGTN America, July 10, https://america.cgtn.com/2017/07/10/argentina-launches-effort-to-formalize-black-market

Roxburgh, Helen (2017) 'Welcome to Yiwu: China's Testing Ground for a Multicultural City,' *The Guardian*, March 23, https://www.theguardian.com/cities/2017/mar/23/welcome-yiwu-china-testing-ground-multicultural-city

Rudaz, Philippe (2020) 'Trading in Dordoi and Lilo Bazaars: Frontiers of Formality, Entrepreneurship and Globalization,' *Central Asian Survey*, 39(1), pp. 11–32.

Rui, Huaichuan (2018) 'Yiwu: Historical Transformation and Contributing Factors,' *History and Anthropology*, 29(S1), pp. S14–S30.

Russia-IC, July 21, 2009, 'Monument to Shuttle Traders Set Up in Yekaterinburg,' http://www.russia-ic.com/news/show/8628/

Sadovskaya, Yelena Y. (2016) *China's Rise in Kazakhstan and Its Impact on Migration*, Research Paper, Almaty-Moscow: MIRPAL, Regional Migration Program by the World Bank, IOM, UN Women, DFID.

Sassen, Saskia (2011) 'La Salada: The Largest Informal Market in South America,' *Forbes*, March 28, https://www.forbes.com/sites/megacities/2011/03/28/la-salada-the-largest-informal-market-in-south-america/?sh=7d4590ce7d46

Sasunkevich, Olga (2015) *Informal Trade, Gender and the Border Experience: From Political Borders to Social Boundaries*, Farnham, Surrey; Burlington, VT: Ashgate.

Savini, Romina (2011) *Enduring Informality: The Case of 'La Salada' Market and the Informal State in Argentina*, M.Sc. dissertation, London School of Economics and Political Science.

Schiavo, Ester, Paula Vera, and Camilla Dos Santos Nogueira (2016) 'La Salada: imaginarios y representaciones de la informalidad y las desigualdades territoriales en la prensa escrita,' *Question*, 1(50), pp. 387–404.

Schweidler, Christine, and Sasha Costanza-Chock (2009) 'Common Cause: Global Resistance to Intellectual Property Rights,' in Dorothy Kidd, Clemencia Rodriguez, and Laura Stein (eds.) *Making Our Media: Mapping Global Initiatives Toward a Democratic Public Sphere*, Volume II, Cresskill, NJ: Hampton Press, http://web.mit.edu/schock/www/docs/cs_scc_common_cause.pdf

Shepherd, Robert (2012) 'Localism Meets Globalization at an American Street Market,' in Gordon Mathews, Gustavo Lins Ribeiro, and Carlos Alba Vega (eds.) (2012) *Globalization from Below: The World's Other Economy*, London and New York: Roudledge, pp. 186–202.

Skvirskaja, Vera (2018) '"Russian Merchant" Legacies in Post-Soviet Trade with China: Moral Economy, Economic Success and Business Innovation in Yiwu,' *History and Anthropology*, 29(S1), pp. S48–S66.

Spector, Regine A. (2017) *Order at the Bazaar: Power and Trade in Central Asia*, Ithaca and London: Cornell University Press.

Tarrius, Alain (2001) 'Au-delà des États-nations: des sociétés de migrants,' *Revue européenne des migrations internationales*, 17(2), pp. 37–61.

Tarrius, Alain (2002) *La mondialisation par le bas. Les nouveaux nomades de l'économie souterraine*, Paris: Balland.

The Economist, January 25, 2014, 'Stall Stories,' https://www.economist.com/the-americas/2014/01/25/stall-stories

Tudoroiu, Theodor (2022) *China's Globalization from Below: Chinese Entrepreneurial Migrants and the Belt and Road Initiative*, Abingdon, Oxon: Routledge.

Verne, Julia (2017) 'Re-Enlivening the Indian Ocean through Contemporary Trade: East African Traders Searching for New Markets in Jakarta,' *Singapore Journal of Tropical Geography*, 38(1), pp. 123–138.

Vertovec, Steven (2009) *Transnationalism*, Abingdon, Oxon: Routledge.

Wallerstein, Immanuel (1974) *The Modern World-System, Vol. I: Capitalist Agriculture and the Origins of the European World-Economy in the Sixteenth Century*, New York; London: Academic Press.

Wallerstein, Immanuel (1980) *The Modern World-System, Vol. II: Mercantilism and the Consolidation of the European World-Economy, 1600–1750*, New York: Academic Press.

Warren, Sarah D. (2009) 'How Will We Recognize Each Other as Mapuche? Gender and Ethnic Identity Performances in Argentina,' *Gender and Society*, 23(6), pp. 768–789.

Wilkis, Ariel, and Sebastián Hacher (2012) 'La China Invisible,' *Anfibia*, Buenos Aires, UNSAM, May 14, http://revistaanfibia.com/cronica/la-china-invisible/

Xiang, Biao (2003) 'Emigration from China: A Sending Country Perspective,' *International Migration*, 41(3), pp. 21–48.

Yang, Fan (2016) *Faked in China: Nation Branding, Counterfeit Culture, and Globalization*, Bloomington and Indianapolis: Indiana University Press.

Yang, Yang (2011a) *African Traders in Guangzhou: Why They Come, What They Do, and How They Live*, M.Phil. thesis, The Chinese University of Hong Kong, https://core.ac.uk/download/pdf/48537913.pdf

Yang, Yang (2011b) 'A New Silk Road: African Traders in South China,' *The China Monitor*, April, The Centre for Chinese Studies, Stellenbosch University, pp. 4–7.

Yang, Yang (2012) 'African Traders in Guangzhou: Routes, Reasons, Profits, Dreams,' in Gordon Mathews, Gustavo Lins Ribeiro, and Carlos Alba Vega (eds.) *Globalization from Below: The World's Other Economy*, London and New York: Roudledge, pp. 154–170.

YouTube (2021) 'HACERME FERIANTE film completo,' https://www.youtube.com/watch?v=u73RhZ4Cdnk

Yükseker, Hatice Deniz (2003) 'The Informal Economy as a Transnational Category,' in Wilma A. Dunaway (ed.) *Emerging Issues in the 21st Century World-System*, Westport, CT: Praeger, pp. 128–140.

Zack, Tanya (2015) '"Jeppe" - Where Low-End Globalisation, Ethnic Entrepreneurialism and the Arrival City Meet,' *Urban Forum*, 26(2), pp.131–150.

Zhang, Yu (2016) 'As Guangzhou African Community Shrinks, Other Chinese Cities See Growing Numbers,' *Global Times*, August 9, https://www.globaltimes.cn/content/999376.shtml

Zhou, Min, Tao Xu, and Shabnam Shenasi (2016) 'Entrepreneurship and Interracial Dynamics: A Case Study of Self-Employed Africans and Chinese in Guangzhou, China,' *Ethnic and Racial Studies*, 39(9), pp. 1566–1586.

5 The Chinese-Centered Globalization 'from Below'

This chapter discusses the Chinese-centered globalization 'from below.' This socio-economic phenomenon is completely different from the non-hegemonic globalization 'from below' because it is stimulated, influenced, partly controlled, and instrumentalized by the Chinese state. Subchapter 5.1 starts by analyzing the Chinese entrepreneurial migrants that enact it. The transformation of the modest flows of Chinese 'suitcase traders' over the Amur River of the late 1980s into a vast system of global mobility is then depicted. This is followed by the discussion of the migrants' reliance on relationality-based transnational business and social ethnic Chinese networks, as well as their transformation into a transnational middleman minority centered on less developed states with poor governance. The dependence on China in terms of labor, goods, and capital is analyzed as comparative advantage and a constraint that places the entrepreneurial migrants in an inescapable situation of dependency on the Chinese state. Subchapter 5.2 analyzes the multifaceted influence of this state on the Chinese entrepreneurial migrants. The presentation of the historical evolution of China's outmigration-related policies is followed by the discussion of factors that have led to the present massive emigration process, Beijing's 'state transnationalism' and its use of a 'de-territorialised ideology of nationalism,' the huge bureaucratic apparatus known as the overseas Chinese state, and the overseas Chinese work and united front work that target both 'old' and 'new' migrants. Subchapter 5.3 presents the case study of China's presence in Ghana. It first discusses the development of the Sino-Ghanaian partnership and the Chinese socialization of Ghana's political elites in power that relies heavily on the use of prestige infrastructure projects. Then, it analyzes the arrival and economic activities of numerous Chinese entrepreneurial migrants in this country, as well as tensions between them and local socio-economic groups that led to negative African social agency at 'low end' society level. The overseas Chinese work of the overseas Chinese state is then scrutinized, showing its success in keeping the migrants under Beijing's influence. Finally, the galamsey episode is presented that illustrates China's transformation of its social norm into a strong form of conditionality intended to legitimize its influence on the Chinese entrepreneurial migrants

DOI: 10.4324/9781003314714-5

and to protect the Chinese-centered globalization 'from below.' Subchapter 5.4 provides a definition of the Chinese-centered globalization 'from below' and analyzes it as a Constructivist international regime, which successfully associates China's 'from above' hegemony with the 'from below' actorness of its entrepreneurial migrants. The discussion of the significant economic and political benefits brought by this globalization to the Chinese state is followed by the presentation of the antagonistic relationships between the Chinese-centered globalization 'from below,' on the one hand, and the Western-centered globalization 'from above' and the non-hegemonic globalization 'from below,' on the other hand. The subchapter also scrutinizes the characteristics of the projection of normative power on which China's globalization 'from below' relies. Finally, the frequent tensions and conflicts between the Chinese entrepreneurial migrants and socio-economic groups in their countries of residence are explained as consequences of the exclusionary character of the relationality promoted by China and its migrants.

5.1 From 'Ant Traders' to Entrepreneurial Migrants

Unlike the totally independent two globalizations 'from below' analyzed in Chapters 3 and 4, the Chinese-centered one shows how such a process can be stimulated, influenced, partly controlled, and instrumentalized by a rising global power as part of its efforts to construct a new international order. The resulting hybrid can be studied as a hijacked non-hegemonic globalization 'from below.' It is based on a transnational informal economy. In a certain measure, China's 'ant traders' reason and act in ways similar to those specific to their Lebanese or East Indian counterparts; but they are also encouraged, assisted, protected, as well as influenced and constrained, by the overseas Chinese state. With respect to terminology, 'entrepreneurial migrants' is generally used in the literature to designate Chinese 'ant traders' because, even if many start as small merchants, they eventually diversify their activities and upgrade their socio-economic status. Moreover, the use of 'entrepreneurial migrants' has the merit of contrasting their recent transnational entrepreneurship with the situation of the Maoist era. As shown in Subchapter 5.2, those were dark times for people suspected of intending to leave the country. For four decades, many Chinese migrants came from places such as Taiwan, Hong Kong, or Southeast Asia. Deng Xiaoping's reforms, however, had an effect similar to that of Mikhail Gorbachev's Perestroika. Borders were progressively opened. 'Service passports' could be obtained by the employees of the Chinese state when the Law on Exit and Entry Management was adopted in 1986. One year later, a simplified procedure made private passports available to citizens. In 1992, a treaty between China and Russia waved visa requirements for tourists traveling as a group to the border provinces of the neighboring country. It should be reminded that this was a time when massive numbers of Russian 'shuttle traders' traveled to China. Chinese nationals also seized the opportunity and began to conduct suitcase trade with Soviet and then Russian regions in the Soviet Far East and Siberia. *'Bianmao'* (border trade) became a popular occupation: in 1992, it took one million Chinese nationals over the Soviet border; in 1993, the number increased to 2.5 million (Nyíri 2002: 24; 2011: 145). In Heilongjiang and Inner Mongolia, cross-border trade became the dominant economic activity of towns such as Heihe, Suifenhe, and Manzhouli (Xiang 2003: 25). The latter has the only shuttle traders' monument located outside the former Soviet Union. Blagoveshchensk, where a similar Russian statue was erected, faces Heihe on the Chinese bank of the Amur River (see Subchapter 4.1). But border towns or Vladivostok represented only a small fraction of the vast post-communist market where a vacuum was created by the decline of state-controlled retail networks. This was particularly the case with cheap clothing and shoes. The Chinese petty traders soon took advantage of this opportunity. They traveled by train to European Russia and Eastern Europe. In 1988, Hungary stopped requiring visas for Chinese tourists. With Russia, it became the basis for the expansion of Chinese 'ant trade' in the eastern part of the European continent. No less than 14,200 Chinese citizens visited Romania in 1991 alone (Nyíri 2002: 24); few, if any, were genuine tourists. In addition to the unavailability of cheap consumer goods, their activity was encouraged by poorly regulated free markets, permissive immigration policies, and cheap train tickets. In the first half of the 1990s, this triggered an 'Eastern Europe fever' among large numbers of Chinese entrepreneurial migrants (Nyíri 2011: 145). Their features were different from those of their less numerous counterparts who chose western or Third World destinations. They were better educated and used to have skilled jobs. In fact, most had worked for the Chinese state; some had been small-scale private entrepreneurs. In geographical terms, the initial overrepresentation of provinces close to the Russian border was followed by the progressive increase in numbers of rural migrants from provinces with a migratory tradition such as Zhejiang and Fujian (*Ibid.*, 146). In the post-communist countries, at first, they sold goods on streets or in markets and shuttled to China to restock. Eventually, a network of Chinese markets of various sizes emerged that became clearinghouses at local, regional, and national levels for goods such as clothing, shoes, electrical appliances, toys, and hardware. Only some Chinese traders continued to shuttle to China. They imported goods that they sold to Chinese distributors and shopkeepers, to local small merchants, and directly to the local population. A Chinese economy developed based on markets and shops that represented the main supplier of consumer goods in villages and among the low-income urban population (Nyíri 2002: 25). Especially in the countryside, people grew dependent on Chinese shops. By 2001, in Hungary, it was in Chinese markets that 39 percent of total clothing sales took place, to which goods sold in the many Chinese shops outside markets need to be added (Nyíri 2011: 146). Yet, the mid-1990s brought significant economic changes to both Eastern Europe and China. In the former region, real incomes declined, competition increased, exchange rates became less advantageous to foreigners, and there were bureaucratic hurdles. In China, on the contrary, economic opportunities developed significantly. Consequently, the inflow of Chinese nationals was limited to those coming through chain migration centered on already present entrepreneurial migrants (Nyíri 2011: 145).

During the first half of the 1990s, China's traders also took advantage of conditions similar to those in the post-communist region associated with Global South transitions from closed dictatorships to open economies. Examples include Cambodia, Burma, Laos, Kazakhstan, Mongolia, Vietnam, and some South and Central American countries. Yet, these markets were less lucrative and consequently attracted smaller numbers of Chinese entrepreneurial migrants (Nyíri 2002: 25; 2011: 146). In the second half of the 1990s, such migrants that unfavorable local conditions pushed out of Eastern Europe needed new destinations. Interestingly, most of them relocated to Africa, and more specifically to South Africa, Zimbabwe, and Nigeria. By 2010, the majority of Chinese nationals in Africa were small merchants with an East European experience (Song 2011: 122). During the 2000s, China's drive for raw materials and energy made more information available to potential Chinese migrants about Global South countries. Consequently, from 'the mid-2000s, the Eastern European pattern appeared to be replicated around the globe' (Nyíri 2011: 149). Chinese networks of shopkeepers and importers developed from the Marshall Islands to Senegal. They prospered especially in countries with massive low-income populations that had recently adopted economic reforms. Financial crises and violent conflicts that had put local merchants out of business were equally attractive. In such places, the Chinese entrepreneurial migrants found the familiar 'combination of opportunity and need for the same kind of products and strategies that had already been successful in Eastern Europe' (*Ibid.*, 148). Their expansion was based on the same range of goods, mode of insertion into the local economy, and business model (*Ibid.*). More generally, even today their features do not differ from those identified by scholars such as Pál Nyíri more than two decades ago in Easter Europe. Migrants can come from regions in China without a tradition of relocating abroad. Emigration may represent the continuation of a process of internal migration to more developed provinces. The Chinese migrants are upwardly mobile and do not consider migration as representing a survival strategy. Their choice of destination countries is determined in large measure by the effort to avoid intra-Chinese competition. If too many migrants arrive in a given country or region, some of them re-migrate. Because, similar to the non-hegemonic globalization 'from below,' the Chinese-centered one is closely associated with the transnational informal economy, distinctions between legal and illegal migration are often blurred. So are those between various categories of migrants – traders, laborers, and students – which frequently overlap and shift. Finally, the Chinese migrants are not likely to adapt their economic and cultural mechanisms to the country of settlement (Nyíri 1999: 118–128;

Tjon Sie Fat 2009: 102; Tudoroiu 2022: 73). Most Chinese migrants arrive as either shuttle traders or workers on Chinese infrastructure projects who decide to overstay their contract and engage in small trade. Chain migration follows: members of the extended family and friends are brought as labor. Trade and financial networks are used to initiate various economic activities involving both relatives and acquaintances back home and in the host country. An ecosystem emerges that includes offering services to Chinese workers, producing foodstuff, setting up restaurants, selling Chinese necessities, opening Chinese clinics (including acupuncture ones), Chinese schools, massage parlors, and even brothels (French 2014: 169; Röschenthaler and Socpa 2017: 168; Cardenal and Araújo 2013: 47). It is this diversity that explains why terms such as 'ant trader' are rather inappropriate in the Chinese case and have been replaced with 'entrepreneurial migrant.' Today, their massive flow represents an important 'segment of globalized migration' (Tjon Sie Fat 2009: 102).

A Highly Mobile Middleman Minority

Perhaps the most visible feature of this migration besides its magnitude is represented by its actors' extreme mobility. In the long term, most Chinese entrepreneurial migrants intend to either return to their country of origin or settle in the West. This is why the identity of short- and medium-term host countries is rather irrelevant; such places only need to provide sufficient material incentives (Sullivan and Cheng 2018: 1176). This leads to 'surprisingly zigzagged trajectories' (Tudoroiu 2022: 74). Pál Nyíri documented numerous Chinese journeys starting in the 1990s in Hungary, continuing in Romania or the Czech Republic (while the Hungarian business continued to be active), and including semi-legal or illegal stays in Italy or Germany. There, the Chinese stopped acting as entrepreneurial migrants; they became workers in restaurants or workshops for as many as five years, accumulated capital, and reinvested it in Hungary or Romania. Individual trajectories encompassed Hungary, Romania, and Morocco; France, Hungary, Cameroon, and Uganda; or Hungary and South America (Nyíri 2002: 27–28; 2011: 149). Migrants who went bankrupt in Senegal returned to China and eventually re-migrated to other destinations (French 2014: 79).

Countries of settlement can be divided into three categories. The first is represented by developed states in the West. Chinese skilled workers are often the largest immigrant group in countries that have adopted a point-based immigration system such as Canada, Australia, or New Zealand. They are also numerous in the United States, Britain, and other West European states. However, it is important to note that this is not a migratory process associated with the Chinese-centered globalization 'from below.' It is part of the Western-centered globalization 'from above,' to which it provides much-needed labor. The Chinese in the previous paragraph who moved from Romania or the Czech Republic to Italy or Germany lost their status of entrepreneurial migrants. They became simple workers very similar to those coming from Africa or the Middle East. Equally important, while the government in Beijing tries to influence and in part control its migrants in the developed world, its ability to assist them is considerably limited by the fact that, different from the Global South, Western political elites have not been socialized by China (see Subchapter 2.3). Only the Chinese migrants who settle, be it temporarily, in the other two categories of countries are part of the Chinese-centered globalization 'from below.' States in both these categories are located in the Global South and, differently from Western ones, have little interest in integrating immigrants into their labor markets, formal social structures, and political systems. But the two categories differ with respect to the conditions they offer to the Chinese entrepreneurial migrants. As shown in the next paragraph, these migrants constitute a middleman minority whose modalities of social insertion are based on a clientelistic strategy (Nyíri 2011: 150). Some Global South states – which, during the 1990s, included East European ones such as Hungary – have adopted or are in the process of adopting Western-inspired norms of governance. This makes them reject the rent-seeking culture of the Chinese entrepreneurial migrants. The polity is based on the undifferentiated individual political participation of all nationals but excludes non-citizens. After 15 years spent in Hungary, Chinese migrants seldom had Hungarian friends, were not interested in Hungarian politics, did not speak Hungarian, and could not pass the language test needed to acquire Hungarian citizenship. Overall, they were not integrated into the local society. Consequently, they tended to perceive the host country as a temporary stopover. The situation is very different in the third category of countries, where 'rent-seeking is an entrenched and institutionalized element of the political economy.' In states such as Cambodia, 'rent-seeking corporatism is a more or less openly accepted principle of the way society operates' (*Ibid.*, 149–150). The Chinese entrepreneurial migrants can easily become citizens and develop large networks of personal connections that include members of power structures and, often, the elites. This brings webs of social embeddedness, as well as various forms of recognition, which result in significant economic benefits. Accordingly, long-term settlement is more likely than in countries pertaining to the previous category (*Ibid.*).

The previous chapter showed that many actors of the non-hegemonic globalization 'from below' become middleman minorities in the host countries. In the case of the Chinese-centered globalization 'from below,' the scale of this phenomenon is particularly large. Scholars have even noted that the Chinese entrepreneurial migrants have created a transnational middleman minority that is centered on less developed and transitional economies (Green and Liu 2017: 11). Such countries lack attractive jobs; moreover, their population tends to be hostile to immigrants. Consequently, traditional patterns of upward social mobility are not available to the Chinese. Acting as a middleman minority, on the contrary, is both possible and profitable. The

Chinese entrepreneurial migrants frequently take this path, following the historical example of Chinese merchants who adopted the same strategy in a number of imperial and colonial economies. As a result, they have all the advantages and encounter all the problems specific to this status (see Subchapter 4.4). Indeed, it is due to their activity as a middleman minority benefitting from transnational business and social ethnic Chinese networks (see below) that China's entrepreneurial migrants have been so successful economically. But this is also the reason for their negative perception by the local population and explains the 'partial transformation of the Chinese into "essential outsiders".' This adds to the non-citizen status – which exposes them to expulsion – to prevent 'long-term financial or emotional investment' in the country of settlement (Nyíri 2007: 138–139; 2011: 146–147).

The question remains, why do Chinese migrants prefer difficult Global South countries where they cannot integrate. The answer has two parts. On the one hand, middleman minorities in general and the Chinese one in particular are attracted by economies of scarcity. It is there that available market niches exist for cheap manufactured goods, which are produced in China (Nyíri 2007: 139). Furthermore, competition is far less intense than back home (French 2014: 12). Small enterprises – including one-man businesses – that could not survive in China are often prosperous in such environments (Song 2011: 118). Overall, the 'big fish in a small pond' strategy enhances the socioeconomic status of the Chinese entrepreneurial migrants who move to less developed economies and makes their success 'more assured' (Wang and Zhan 2019: 17; Lin 2014). On the other hand, the Chinese entrepreneurial migrants tend to choose states with poor governance, which in many cases overlap with those in the previous category. It should be reminded that these migrants are part of a transnational informal economy. In weak and corrupt states, it is easier for them to obtain entry visas and take advantage of poorly enforced laws in order to pay less or, at times, no taxes. The President of one of China's two policies banks, China ExIm Bank, made a corruption-related comment in Washington that included a traditional Chinese quote: 'if the water is too clear, you will never catch a fish' (Cardenal and Araújo 2013: 45–47, 126, 134–135). In fact, similar to its entrepreneurial migrants, the Chinese state itself 'does show a predilection for engaging with countries with already weak governance structures' (Oosterveld et al. 2018: 79). This trend is visible in the expansion of the Belt and Road Initiative (BRI). China's 'periphery policy' has to be added (see Subchapter 2.3) that turns Global South states into key targets of the Chinese-centered globalization 'from above.' The coincidence of state's and migrants' interest in the same type of countries – motivated by the intention to exploit the same weaknesses – has a major consequence: it significantly contributes to the mutual reinforcement of China's two globalizations and enhances the virtuous circle they form (see Subchapter 5.4).

When presenting the Chinese migrants' activity as a middleman minority, I mentioned their use of transnational business and social ethnic Chinese networks. Observers frequently associate the economic success of these migrants with 'the network of connections created by the "great Chinese lodge"' (Cardenal and Araújo 2013: 58). This highly dynamic and innovative networking system is based on connectivity, reciprocity, transnationality, and flexibility (Liu and van Dongen 2016: 808). It originates in the strong relationality-based links of solidarity that exist in China at family and regional levels and are reinforced by migration (Cardenal and Araújo 2013: 41). In fact, '"Chinese capitalism" is "guanxi capitalism"' (Nyíri 2005: 170). It developed in an economic environment where legal and financial institutions were deficient and antagonistic. Consequently, it created alternative informal mechanisms of coordination, enforcement, and dispute settlement. They foster confidence and create favorable conditions for business partnerships, community mutual aid, informal loans, and foreign investment. This is useful in China, but even more so in Global South countries where institutional guarantees are weak, contracts and property rights are insecure, legal regulations are lax or ambiguous, and there is widespread distrust of the system. Unlike Western businessmen, the Chinese entrepreneurial migrants are well equipped to 'raise capital, form partnerships, seek suppliers, gather information, and conduct relatively secure transactions' despite unfavorable local conditions (Hearn 2016: 15–16). *Guanxi* is visible even in the chain migration mentioned at the end of the previous section: trust is stronger within the first circle represented by the extended family and friends (French 2014: 11; Sullivan and Cheng 2018: 1179). When this is not sufficient, a second circle represented by the region of origin intervenes. Interactions are much more intense between Chinese migrants coming from the same village, town, or region or pertaining to the same ethnic, linguistic, or dialectal group. Such links develop social capital by creating a strong sense of trust. Cheating is exposed back home, which triggers an unacceptable loss of prestige (Cardenal and Araújo 2013: 44).

Relationality-based networks and aforementioned strategies have led to Chinese entrepreneurial success in the Global South, which has, in turn, further stimulated the migratory flow. Its exact magnitude, however, remains unknown. Various estimates place the total of ethnic Chinese outside China, Taiwan, Hong Kong, and Macao anywhere between 30 and 60 million (Wei 2016: 3; Liu and van Dongen 2016: 806; Kurlantzick 2008: 201; Chee-Beng 2012: 3). Children of mixed parentage and ethnic Chinese who do not speak Chinese further complicate the assessment (Wei 2016: 3). Fifty million might represent a reasonable, if arbitrary, compromise. Yet, only approximately ten million migrants have left the country since Deng Xiaoping's reforms. The largest part of the Chinese diaspora is older. Outmigration started in antiquity but became a mass phenomenon during the 19th century. Due to domestic instability, large numbers of people from Guangdong and Fujian, in the south, left to work as laborers, traders, and farmers in Southeast Asia. A second period started with the communist takeover in 1949. Outmigration from China and especially Hong Kong, Taiwan, and

Southeast Asia mainly targeted North America, Europe, and Oceania. It was only during the early 1990s that the present wave of entrepreneurial migrants became visible (Yang 2011a: 107). Consequently, there are 'old' and 'new' Chinese migrants. Since Deng Xiaoping, the former are known as *huaren*, which stands for foreign citizens of Chinese descent. The 'new' migrants, *huaqiao*, are officially considered Chinese citizens temporarily residing abroad. Accordingly, the term also refers to contract workers used by Chinese firms in their construction projects all over the Global South (Suryadinata 2017b: 101, 2017a: 6; Yang 2011a: 107). Importantly, this is in no way a 'natural' distinction based on the date of departure from China. It is a political distinction that reflects the official policy of the Chinese state toward ethnic Chinese abroad. This critical issue is discussed in the next subchapter. Here, I will only mention the fact that the leadership in Beijing tries to also associate the 'old' Chinese with the Chinese-centered globalization 'from below' and its construction of a new international order. Leaving this aspect aside, a frequently noted difference between 'old' and 'new' migrants is the latter's high transnational mobility and resulting lack of integration in the local society. This is very different from the situation of the *huaren* after their emigration. Furthermore, families that have been in a country for generations certainly are more integrated than newcomers. Another difference concerns the geographical origin of the two groups: the older migrants came mainly from China's southern provinces; today, outmigration is a nationwide trend (Suryadinata 2017a: 10, 12). There is also the idea that, unlike their mainly poor and uneducated predecessors, the new migrants possess capital and are better educated. Their 'quality' is superior (Suryadinata 2017a: 10; Yang 2011a: 107). But again, this assessment is in fact the result of a policy of the Chinese state, which uses it to manipulate and instrumentalize the diaspora (see the next subchapter).

Finally, there is a truly important difference that the leadership in Beijing has successfully used to influence and partly control the 'new' migrants. Many 'old' ones opportunistically try to take advantage of China's rise in order to promote their business interests; if and when this happens, it results in a revival of their links with the country their ancestors may have left one or two centuries ago. But for the 'new' migrants, maintaining good relations with the fatherland is not optional: in terms of labor, goods, and capital they are 'dependent on China in ways their predecessors were not' (Nyíri 2011; 147; Green and Liu 2017: 9). Indeed, the Chinese entrepreneurial migrants rely on extended family and friends back home for cheap labor. They also outcompete local, East Indian, or Lebanese 'ant traders' due to better access to manufacturers in their country of origin. Chinese state banks provide loans that most petty traders in the Global South can only dream of (Nyíri 2011: 147). Consequently, 'the very survival of the new merchants depends on their economic ties to China, through which they continue to be *transnationally reproduced* or sustained' (Green and Liu 2017: 10; emphasis in the original). Even Chinese entrepreneurial migrants who settle in countries that recognize Taiwan find themselves in this situation (Green 2012–2014: 24–25). The fact that China is at the center of the supply system and transnational entrepreneurial networks of the 'new' migrants gives them a considerable comparative advantage that explains much of their success in the Global South; but it also 'place[s] them in an inescapable situation of dependency on the Chinese state' (Tudoroiu 2022: 81).

Overall, the modest flows of Chinese 'suitcase traders' over the Amur River of the late 1980s have expanded into a vast system of global mobility. Migration spaces that cover the entire planet have been opened by China's entrepreneurial migrants. They move easily and frequently between their place of origin and various destination countries. There is also an important interchange between various categories of migrants: contract workers, illegal workers, and even students often become entrepreneurial migrants. The migratory 'phenomenon is global in scope, with significant similarities across the group of migrants involved' (Nyíri 2011: 152; 2002: 23, 28). A Chinese global entreprenariat has emerged, whose members may be socially marginal in the host countries but participate actively in transnational business networks. They control massive flows of goods, capital, and information. In combination with the migrants' high mobility, these flows have created a 'very intense kind of transnationalism'; as an effect, the Chinese entrepreneurial migrants 'became conduits of China's globalization' (Nyíri 2011: 148; Wang and Zhan 2019: 18).

This vast phenomenon has an undeniable 'from below' dimension and is strongly marked by informal practices that bring together – and often blur the differences between – legal, semi-legal, and illegal activities. Bribing customs officials and market inspectors to pay less or no taxes is as popular among the Chinese entrepreneurial migrants as among the 'ant traders' of the non-hegemonic globalization 'from below.' This is why many scholars make no difference between the two categories and analyze the Chinese migrants as pertaining to the non-hegemonic globalization. This is mistaken because their globalization 'from below' has a very clear hegemon: manipulative political and economic strategies have been adopted by the authorities in Beijing that create opportunities and constraints totally absent in the case of the non-Chinese 'ant traders.' Consequently, a Chinese-centered globalization 'from below' has developed that is separate and very different from the non-hegemonic globalization 'from below.' Critically, it combines with the Chinese-centered globalization 'from above' in contributing to the construction of a new, Chinese-led international order. The highly sophisticated mechanisms created by the Chinese leadership to serve this purpose are analyzed in the next subchapter.

5.2 The Influence of the Chinese State

The historical evolution of China's outmigration-related policies is most interesting. The Song and Yuan dynasties (960–1279 and 1206–1368, respectively) repressed it harshly. This changed under the Ming dynasty (1368–1644), but the Qing one (1644–1911) – fearing Ming loyalists abroad – reintroduced the ban and went as far as to relocate coastal populations inland. In 1603 and 1740, many Chinese were massacred in the Philippines by the Spaniards and in the East Indies by the Dutch. The Chinese Empire did not protest because, having migrated illegally, the victims were traitors (Nyíri 2005: 148). A 'clandestine' Chinese diaspora did emerge, but it was only during the 19th century that domestic instability led to massive migration to Southeast Asia, North America, and the southern and eastern parts of the African continent. The scale of this phenomenon compelled the Chinese government to abolish related punishments in 1893. Furthermore, in 'its belated and half-hearted modernization program,' it tried to take advantage of the considerable financial resources accumulated by the diaspora (Nyíri 2005: 148). The 1909 nationality law introduced the *jus sanguinis* principle: indifferent of their birthplace, all males of Chinese ancestry became citizens of China. Ancestry and race replaced the traditional emphasis on civilization. The 'wanderers, fugitives, traitors and conspirators' of the past were turned into *huaqiao*, or legitimate overseas Chinese (Nyíri 2005: 148; Yen 1985; Waltner 1987: 1256). To protect them, consulates were established and treaties were concluded. The Chinese 'merchants without empire' in Southeast Asia responded 'positively and with enthusiasm,' even if in practical terms China's weakness allowed for little international actorness (Peterson 2012: 15; Waltner 1987: 1255). The Republicans led by Sun Yatsen similarly cultivated the 'overseas orphans,' whose active support soon turned them into the 'mother of the Revolution.' An important redefinition of the national identity resulted in the inclusion of the diaspora into the nation, 'inflecting Chinese nationalism with a racial overtone which declared that all Chinese everywhere were to be regarded as sons of the Yellow Emperor' (Peterson 2012: 16). After 1911, six of the 274 senators of the newly proclaimed republic were designated by the Chinese Chambers of Commerce abroad. In 1931, the Nationalist Overseas Chinese Affairs Commission was established as part of the nationalist government in Nanjing. But it was during the Japanese invasion that massive material and human support from the diaspora represented 'the apogee of Huaqiao patriotism' (*Ibid.*, 17; Nyíri 2005: 149). The Communists won the civil war in 1949 and tried to take advantage of the flow of remittances; consequently, they initially behave courteously toward overseas countrymen. This, however, created tensions with Southeast Asian states that, sometimes appropriately, perceived their Chinese minorities as a communist fifth column (Nyíri 2005: 149). Financial inflows from the diaspora nevertheless diminished dramatically. In 1955, the leadership in Beijing decided to prioritize foreign policy objectives. At the Bandung Conference, China signed an agreement with Indonesia that replaced the *jus sanguinis* principle and dual nationality with the principles of territoriality and sovereignty. In 1958, the members of the Chinese diaspora stopped being part of China's People's United Front (Barabantseva 2011: 58–59).

They were encouraged to become loyal citizens of their host countries. Their enterprises on Chinese soil were nationalized while the 1957 Anti-Rightist Campaign turned most of them into 'bourgeois' and 'reactionary elements.' Chinese citizens with overseas contacts became agents of imperialism and class enemies, which made them targets of mass terror. The climax was reached during the Cultural Revolution, which defined outmigration as treason (Nyíri 2005: 147, 149–150; Barabantseva 2011: 61). Unsurprisingly, many diasporic Chinese adopted the nationality of their country of settlement. This led to 'acculturation, and shifting the locus of overseas Chinese politics away from the home country' (Nyíri 2005: 149–150).

This historical introduction was needed in order to emphasize the magnitude of the Deng Xiaoping era change that resulted in the present Chinese-centered globalization 'from below.' At first, everything was about attracting money. Nothing changed with respect to rejecting dual citizenship and encouraging loyalty toward the host country. But overseas Chinese began to be perceived as a key source of investments and donations. The government in Beijing made considerable efforts to stimulate their nationalism and involvement in China's domestic politics (Nyíri 2005: 150). Migrant-friendly institutional structures – such as the State Council's Overseas Chinese Affairs Office and the All-China Federation of Returned Overseas Chinese – were restored or created. At discourse level, the former 'traitors' became 'heroes who were crucial for China's future' (Thunø 2018: 185; Chee-Beng 2012: 4). This policy was highly successful: over 60 percent of the foreign direct investment received by China between 1979 and 2003 – whose total amount reached no less than US $501.47 billion – came from ethnic Chinese abroad (Guotu 2012: 39). More relevant for the emergence of China's globalization 'from below,' the official change in attitude toward the 'old' diaspora led to a more general reconsideration of all migration-related policies. In fact, during the 1990s, the focus of the Chinese state shifted from attracting investments from the 'old' overseas Chinese to an active policy centered on the 'new' migrants (Liu and van Dongen 2016: 815). Already in 1986, the Law on Exit and Entry Management represented the first step toward border exit liberalization, which was a key precondition for the eventual development of massive migratory outflows (see Subchapter 5.1). Two decades later, five business days were sufficient to get a passport. In 2007, a Passport Law was adopted that even defined this document as citizens' entitlement (Xiang 2012: 48). The so-called international labor cooperation system – which was, of course, managed by the state – began to be deregulated during the 1980s. It was only in 2002 that the state monopoly on the export of labor was completely dismantled. But from that moment on, private agencies started to play a formidable role in stimulating the migratory phenomenon: they 'constitute the central part of the booming migration industry' (Xiang 2015: 285). By 2005, there were more than 3,000 such agencies, both private and state-owned, as well as many unlicensed agents. Many of them cheat; their services and the migration process itself have become more expensive, more complicated, and less reliable (Xiang 2012: 48–49). However, nobody can deny their major contribution to the massive increase in the outmigration flow. Even remote villages are targeted by flyers, mass and social media adverts, house to house visits, loudspeakers messages, and square meetings advertising the benefits of moving abroad (Cardenal and Araújo 2013: 206–210). Less predictably, local governments have played a similar role. This started in the southern Guangdong and Fujian provinces that, during the Maoist era, received fewer resources for development but also less administrative interference from Beijing. Due to the proximity to Hong Kong and Taiwan, it was here that Deng Xiaoping created four Special Economic Zones in 1979 and, five years later, opened 14 coastal cities to foreign investment. Economic success convinced local authorities that strict communist policies do not represent the best option. At times, they regarded smuggling and irregular emigration as local development strategies because profits and remittances increased local GDP. Soon after traders from northern China started to shuttle over the Soviet border, emigration in the southern provinces took off. Local authorities assisted in various ways. For example, those of Fujian offered professional training to people intending to move to Japan. As an effect, two million Fujianese emigrated in 20 years. The model was followed by the authorities of regions without a tradition of emigration such as Shandong, Yunnan, and the Northeast. The active support of migrants became part of the official development and modernization strategies of these provinces (Smith 2013a: 331–332, 338; Xiang 2003: 23–24).

It is clear that policy changes made massive migratory flows possible and actors such as private agencies and local authorities enhanced them. But these were only responses to a situation created by the negative socio-economic consequences of Deng Xiaoping's reforms. On the one hand, the economic liberalization of 1980–2000 led to large-scale unemployment. On the other, privatization generated socio-economic stratification that forced many people to look for alternative occupations. Between 1982 and 1986, lifetime tenure jobs were replaced with contractual employment (Xiang 2015: 284). Toward the end of that decade, state companies facing overproduction and inflation offered continuing housing, pensions, and health insurance to employees willing to start their own businesses. The recession of 1989–1992 made many people look for opportunities abroad, which helps explain the massive shuttle trade to the Soviet Union (Nyíri 2011: 145). Finally, during the late 1990s, the privatization or shutting down of many state companies led to high levels of unemployment. In approximately one decade, 30 to 40 million people became jobless. The resulting socio-economic stratification was exacerbated by the decline of small household businesses that had emerged and prospered during the 1980s. The official encouragement of and support for emigration represented a response to growing unemployment and social tensions (Cardenal and Araújo 2013: 45–46; Xiang 2015: 284, 288). However, it should be noted that this was in no way the only possible option. Mao would have never chosen it. But for Deng and his successors, opening China to the outer world was a key priority. In this context, the idea of solving domestic problems through an expansion of the recent policies targeting the diaspora came naturally. Ultimately, the Chinese-centered globalization 'from below' does not originate in China's unemployment and social tensions of the 1980s and 1990s. Rather, it is the result of the new thinking adopted by the leadership in Beijing that established a strong connection between domestic and external actions. From that point on, exploiting international opportunities to solve domestic issues became the norm. It is this cognitive change that represents the root cause of China's two globalizations.

Returning to the unemployment of the late 1990s, it eventually diminished; but many people continue to feel 'anxiety about being left behind by China's competitive economy.' Interviews with Chinese entrepreneurial migrants all over the world show that they are obsessed with finding 'opportunit[ies] to carve out a niche that doesn't exist in uber-competitive China' (Sullivan and Cheng 2018: 1176, 1178; Smith 2013b: 7; French 2014: 77). Many candidates to emigration even reach a 'particular psychological state in which "waiting to go abroad" dominates their present existence' (Sullivan and Cheng 2018: 1179). It is the combination of objective and subjective factors – all of which are direct or indirect consequences of official policies – that has created the conditions for numerous Chinese nationals to get involved in a globalization 'from below.' Normally, this should have been the non-hegemonic one. But the leadership in Beijing seized the opportunity to construct a different globalization 'from below' that could serve its own interests. Consequently, its goal has been to encourage and support the entrepreneurial migrants' departure and economic activities abroad, but also to ensure their unquestioned loyalty to the Chinese state as explained in the next section.

'Upgrading' – and Instrumentalizing – the Migrant

During Mao's Cultural Revolution, migrants were, politically and legally, traitors. Since Deng, they have become 'an extension of the Chinese nation united with the goal of first "saving," then "serving," and now "rejuvenating the nation"' (Barabantseva 2012: 82). Domestically, they help China to develop. Internationally, they project its soft power and support its national interest as defined by the Communist Party. Officially, there is 'a collective portrayal of the overseas Chinese as promoters and model participants in the PRC's national modernisation project' (Barabantseva 2011: 100–101, 104–105). They are presented as mobile, successful, pragmatic, and motherland-loving individuals who show strong group solidarity due to their unquestioned patriotism and love for China (*Ibid.*, 105–106). Overall, the official discourse has brought 'a shift in what the social and cultural meaning of migration is to the migrant, to non-migrants, and to elites': it has 'upgrad[ed] the migrant' (Nyíri 2002: 23). The concept of transnationalism was presented in Subchapter 2.6 and discussed in Subchapter 4.4 in the context of the non-hegemonic globalization 'from below,' to which it is most relevant. In the case of the Chinese-centered globalization 'from below,' a related concept is useful for the analysis of the relationship between the Chinese state and 'its' migrants. Ku Sup Chin and David Smith have discussed 'state transnationalism,' which refers to state-initiated or sponsored transnational activities. In this case, it is the nation-state that 'initiates, promotes or sustains cross-border movements and connections of people, commodities, information, capital, institutions and culture' (Chin and Smith 2015: 83). All these actions are based on the state's perception – or, rather, definition – of what is beneficial to the migrants. State transnationalism has been noted in two situations that are also characteristic of China's globalization 'from below': when states pursue their national interests by implementing or contesting global processes; and when they try to valorize and control their migrants through diaspora engagement policies (*Ibid.*). The government in Beijing is in the process of constructing a new international order; and has set up well-designed policies that have turned the Chinese entrepreneurial migrants into 'a privileged partner – the most privileged – in serving the interests of China' (Ma Mung 2008: 105; Yang 2011a: 110). Another aspect of state transnationalism is very important with respect to the issue of the autonomy of the Chinese entrepreneurial migrants, which I discuss in Subchapter 5.4: states act proactively based on their interests; but also reactively in response to the grassroots transnationalism instigated by the diaspora (Liu and van Dongen 2016: 807). In the former case, to achieve their objectives, state institutions 'are the primary causal agents of transnational connections in that they incubate, trigger and manage transnational movements and processes' (Chin and Smith 2015: 84). This concerns state policies – such as the Chinese ones discussed in the previous section – that play a key role in the preparation and shaping of cross-border flows. The resulting social or trading networks facilitate and channel 'a latent potential among immigrants for massive transnational monetary or demographic flows "from below"' (*Ibid.*). Reactive state transnationalism seldom has the same magnitude and effects. Yet, non-state actors do start transnational activities that are responded to and sustained by the states. The extension of the repertoire of Chinese diaspora-related policies was in part due to the needs of and challenges faced by migrants. For example, Chinese entrepreneurial migrants in various parts of the Global South have asked for and have received Beijing's diplomatic support against harassment by the local population or even the police. When they were threatened by civil war or natural disasters, rescue missions were organized by the Chinese state. The leaders in Beijing understand the importance of such legitimating actions in ensuring the migrants' genuine support. Ultimately, in the case of China, the reactive state transnationalism can be understood as an instrument used to enhance the active one. Consequently, 'the Chinese overseas are actors who also influence policy structures' (Liu and van Dongen 2016: 807); but this influence is much weaker than that of the state on the migrants. Furthermore, 'the Chinese state tries to shape the way the diaspora constructs grassroots transnationalism, and responds to it on its own terms' (Tudoroiu 2022: 97). As explained below, the overseas Chinese state interacts closely with migrant associations and manipulates them in order to align the message they send to Beijing with China's own discourse and interests.

The Chinese state is heavily involved in a variety of emigration-related issues: different from the situation in most other countries, its citizens' very 'decisions to migrate, destination choices, and relations with local host societies are intimately entangled with Chinese state policies and processes' (Huynh *et al.* 2010: 290; Green 2012–2014: 26). President Jiang Zemin overtly invited jobless Chinese nationals to emigrate and become global actors in 1995. At the same time, instruments were created to preserve their loyalty (Röschenthaler and Socpa 2017: 167). As many as 360 laws were adopted from 1978 to 2000 alone that concern various outmigration-related aspects, as well as the migrants' duty to take part in China's development (Pokam 2015: 51, 53; Röschenthaler and Socpa 2017: 180). They have to 'serve the country from abroad'; this includes networking among themselves and with China (Green 2012–2014: 26; Ma Mung 2008). Policies 'designed to keep migrants loyal to the modernization project of the PRC' (Tjon Sie Fat 2009: 137; Green and Liu 2017: 10) are wide-ranging, complex, and highly coherent. Their ambitious goals include the construction of a new culture of the Chinese migrants; shaping the latter's transnational community; manipulating their imaginaries of the homeland and the province of origin; and influencing the very construction of their identity (Nyíri 2001: 635). The Chinese state is hardly the first to make use of a 'transnational national society' discourse as an instrument of symbolic nation-building (Gamlen 2006: 5–7). But it is one of the most successful in constructing a deterritorial Chinese identity in the diaspora based on a particular use of nationalism (Wang and Zhan 2019: 8) as a type of cultural control that takes the place of the administrative control used domestically (Nyíri 2010). This is not a new enterprise: 'since the 1980s, the Chinese government actively engages overseas Chinese to maintain a sense of Chinese identity'; the goal is to use their contribution in national projects that prominently include China's modernization (Wang and Zhan 2019: 12). It is through the use of a 'de-territorialised ideology of nationalism' (Duara 2003: 14) that migrants' collective memories are to be turned into 'a sense of belonging to the motherland, a symbolic and de-territorialized Chinese nation' (Wang and Zhan 2019: 12). This ambitious strategy intends to redefine the Chinese identity as based on flexibility, mobility, and deterritorialization that blurs differences between China and the overseas Chinese communities (*Ibid.*). In part, this is a return to the pre-1957 situation where all ethnic Chinese were Chinese citizens. Dual nationality and the *jus sanguinis* principle have not been reintroduced, but there is 'a fuzzily applied form of cultural-ethnic convergence' (Barabantseva 2011: 118) that serves the same purpose of increasing China's global influence.

At least among the 'new' migrants, the use of deterritorialized nationalism has been highly successful. As shown in the next subchapter, most of them unexpectedly develop Chinese nationalism in the host country instead of a cosmopolitan perspective that would seem more likely to an external observer. Migrants disembedded from the society of origin but not embedded in the recipient one find in cultural nationalism a 'mechanism for reembedding themselves into an imagined de-territorialized "Chinese" community' (Wang and Zhan 2019: 21–22). An explanatory framework is created that strongly influences their living experience and day-to-day practices. Chinese social and mass media contribute considerably to this process: they preserve emotional ties with the homeland, reproduce 'Chineseness' in daily life, and ultimately facilitate the construction of an essentialist Chinese collective identity. Beijing-controlled networks, associations, unions, media, and schools established in the diaspora enhance this process. Ultimately, the use of deterritorialized nationalism has helped the Chinese state to impose itself as the central axis of its migrants' public and private life, 'especially [the] newly established ones in the Global South by expanding its influence in both concrete and symbolic ways' (Wang and Zhan 2019: 23).

The Overseas Chinese State

The 'concrete' ways have much to do with the huge bureaucratic structure created to this effect. Making use of its numerous components, 'the Chinese state travels outside its national space using contemporary global processes to preserve its power over the identity of Chinese transnationals, and to legitimise and reinforce itself outside its territory'; the result is 'the transnationalisation of the Chinese nation-state' (Barabantseva 2011: 108, 109). Cecilia Green and Yan Liu were the first to write about the 'overseas Chinese state,' which consists of units and agents of the Chinese state – such as embassies, aid missions, and state-owned enterprises – that directly influence the migrants in ways conducive to their internalization of Beijing's deterritorialized nationalism (Green and Liu 2017: 25–27; Wang and Zhan 2019: 13). In a previous work, I argued that this narrow definition cannot provide a comprehensive picture of Beijing's vast enterprise (Tudoroiu 2022: 99). All units and agents of the Chinese state and Communist Party involved in the huge institutional effort targeting the Chinese diaspora have to be included. It makes no sense to exclude the Overseas Chinese Affairs Office, for example, only because it is physically located in China. In functional terms, its influence on the Chinese entrepreneurial migrants may be higher than that of China's state-owned enterprises active in their countries of residence. It should not be forgotten that the 'overseas Chinese state' is a global network that manages a fully fledged globalization. Understanding it in terms of territorially defined criteria makes little sense. This bureaucratic structure is so large and complex that its detailed analysis would uselessly overload this subchapter. I will therefore make only a brief presentation of its components, which is sufficient to understand what Alan Gamlen called the 'technologies – systems and institutions – [used] to "govern" diaspora populations' (Gamlen 2006: 8) (for a more detailed analysis of these components see Tudoroiu 2022: 99–105). I start from the idea that readers are aware of China's '*xitong*' bureaucratic architecture that relies on 'vertical systems' such as the party, the government, and the military. An equally original mechanism of coordination between these systems exists that is composed of 26 party and 57 State Council leading small groups (as of 2017) that 'help coordinate and build consensus on issues across different arms of governance' (Duggan 2020: 48–49, 70). The overseas Chinese state is served by the 'five overseas Chinese structures,' two small groups, and many ministries, departments, and commissions belonging to the state, party, and military. The most influential of the 'five structures' is the Overseas Chinese Affairs Office ('*Qiaoban*'). Established, under a different name, in 1949 and dismantled during the Cultural Revolution, it coordinates policy-making and monitors policy implementation in the field known as overseas Chinese work (see the next section). It is active in various political, economic, and cultural fields. It administers the China News Agency, the electronic-only Voice of China Newspaper Office (that, in 2005, became part of China News), and three universities. It has an Overseas Expert Advisory Committee made of prominent members of the diaspora. It sends consuls to countries with an important Chinese presence who report to both their ambassador and the Office (Liu and van Dongen 2016: 809–811). Domestically, it has branches in all provinces, autonomous regions, and municipalities except Tibet (Barabantseva 2011: 112). It also has an affiliated structure, the China Overseas Exchange Association, which connects diaspora and national organizations (Liu and van Dongen 2016: 814). The activity of the Office is based on a people-to-people 'systematic approach of persuasion, influence, and manipulation' that has been effective in 'guiding and directing' overseas Chinese groups – and especially the 'new' migrants – 'to be supportive of Beijing; and where it cannot do so, to at least seek to change their perceptions so that they are favourable towards the PRC' (To 2014: 4). The second of the 'five structures' has a somewhat misleading name: the All-China Federation of Returned Overseas Chinese ('*Qiaolian*') actually targets both returnees and the Chinese abroad. Established in 1956 and dismantled during the Cultural Revolution, it had 15,000 branches in 2009 at province, autonomous region, municipality, and even village level (Barabantseva 2011: 113; Liu and van Dongen 2016: 813). Its goal is to turn the returnees and the diaspora into 'a channel for gaining manpower, intellectual, financial and other resources from abroad for socialist modernization' (Barabantseva 2011: 113). The Federation liaises with these two groups, contributes to policy formulation, and supervises policy implementation (Liu and van Dongen 2016: 813). It controls a publishing company, a magazine, an academic research institute, a museum, and a Cultural Exchange Department that practices a form of public diplomacy targeting both officials and popular audiences abroad. Cultural exchanges include organizing 'overseas Chinese education camps' and sending arts troupes and delegations that meet ethnic Chinese organizations. Priorities include bringing together 'old' and 'new' Chinese migrants, as well as co-opting entrepreneurs and young members of the diaspora (Liu and van Dongen 2016: 813–814). The third structure was established in 1983 by the National People's Congress. The Overseas Chinese Affairs Committee is in fact a permanent parliamentary committee. Accordingly, it drafts law proposals and examines all official decisions and documents relevant to the diaspora. Similar Overseas Committees exist in counties and cities where outmigration is important (*Ibid.*, 812). The fourth structure is a consultative organ of the Chinese People's Political Consultative Conference. Its National Committee has a special committee, the Hong Kong, Macau, and Taiwan Compatriots and Overseas Chinese Affairs Committee, which brings together representatives of the Communist Party of China, the eight irrelevant 'democratic parties' that, unknown to many, continue to exist in the People's Republic, and 25 other groups. Its activities consist of political consultation, something called 'democratic' supervision, and involvement in the administration of state affairs (*Ibid.*). The last of the 'five structures' is quite unexpected. This is the China Zhigong Party, founded in San Francisco back in 1925, reorganized in Hong Kong in 1947, and eventually turned into a member of the United Front led by the Communist Party. The two political parties obviously have 'intimate relationships' (Barabantseva 2011: 113; Liu and van Dongen 2016: 811). Zhigong membership mainly consists of returnees and their families. The objective of the party is to promote multi-party cooperation and political consultation through visits to and exchanges with ethnic Chinese organizations in 40 countries. Their members are to be persuaded to either return to China or serve it from abroad (Liu and van Dongen 2016: 811). The five structures act as the 'five bridges' of the government in Beijing in its efforts to influence the diaspora. The impressive degree of bureaucratization of this activity 'shows the urgency and importance of the overseas Chinese element in China's formulation of policies conducive to modernisation' (Barabantseva 2011: 113) and to its global rise, which includes the development of the Chinese-centered globalization 'from below.' Furthermore, the continuous improvement of the resources, institutional capacity, coherence, political stature, and mandate of this apparatus has represented one of President Xi's priorities. Under his guidance, the National People's Congress approved a massive reorganization of the state bureaucracy in March 2017 (Gill and Schreer 2018: 159) that resulted in the adoption of the Masterplan of Deepening Institutional Reform of the Party and the Government in 2018. To increase coordination, all 'five structures' except the Overseas Chinese Affairs Committee were placed under the control of the United Front Work Department of the Central Committee of the Communist Party of China (Suzuki 2019: 89–90), which is in charge of political influence activities abroad (see the next section). This Department complements the 'five bridges' by targeting overseas Chinese social, professional, and student associations, Chinese-language media, and ethnic Chinese business elites (Hamilton 2018: 37). Wealthy and influential members of the diaspora are given special attention: they receive economic incentives to promote Chinese interests in their host country. They are expected to befriend local agents of influence and use material incentives to turn them into Beijing's supporters (Fitzgerald 2018: 64). The United Front Work Department also takes part in the formation and implementation of policies related to the overseas Chinese (Liu and van Dongen 2016: 814). Following the aforementioned reorganization, in May 2018, it incorporated the State Administration of Religious Affairs, the State Ethnic Affairs Commission, and the Overseas Chinese Affairs Office of the State Council. The All-China Federation of Returned Overseas Chinese, the Hong Kong, Macau, and Taiwan Compatriots and Overseas Chinese Affairs Committee of the Chinese People's Political Consultative Conference, and the China Zhigong Party are also under its control to a certain degree. In all, this brought no less than 40,000 new cadres to the Department. At the same time, its use of soft power as a foreign policy instrument has also been enhanced (Duggan 2020: 87; Suzuki 2019: 89; Gill and Schreer 2018: 158–159). Already in September 2015, a Central United Front Work Leading Group had been established. Illustrative of the importance of this new coordinating entity, its first meeting was chaired by President Xi (Shiu-Hing Lo *et al.* 2019: 3; Gill and Schreer 2018: 160). These changes 'have led to a situation where (...) it has become very difficult to make a clear-cut difference between overseas Chinese work and united front work' (Tudoroiu 2022: 103).

Another component of the bureaucratic apparatus targeting the overseas Chinese consists of the media and propaganda system, which was also reorganized after 2017. 'The ultimate arbiter of official Chinese media outputs' is the Propaganda Department of the Communist Party (Gill and Schreer 2018: 159). Its online, broadcast, and print presence abroad had already expanded dramatically before the reorganization. But the latter brought sweeping structural changes accompanied by the addition of well-resourced new international media platforms. Critically, the Department is now in control of Voice of China, a new media conglomerate that consists of China Central Television (including China Global Television Network), China National Radio, and China Radio International. Social media platforms created by Chinese companies have also been turned into 'increasingly important conduits of news and information for Chinese language-users around the world' (*Ibid.*). A large number of other institutional actors are involved in the management of various diaspora-related aspects. They include ministries that range from Foreign Affairs to State Security; the International Liaison Department of the Central Committee of the Communist Party; the Central Military Commission of the Communist Party and its Political Work Department; the Office of Foreign Propaganda (the State Council Information Office); and the Leading Small Group for Propaganda and

Ideology (Duggan 2020: 76–86). In key areas of outmigration, a similarly large number of local actors exist that may even include trade unions, as well as youth and women's federations (Nyíri 2005: 150–151). Finally, there is the foreign-based component of the overseas Chinese state that corresponds to the latter's narrow definition proposed by Cecilia Green and Yan Liu. It prominently includes the embassies, which have a specific consular department dedicated to the overseas Chinese in all countries where their number is relevant. Major efforts are made to have close and frequent interactions with Chinese associations, trade unions, and influential individuals. The embassy co-sponsors a large variety of cultural, social, recreational, and business events (Liu and van Dongen 2016: 809–811); it influences the local Chinese language media; and promotes the Chinese culture and language among the ethnic Chinese. One of the missions of the Confucius Institutes involved in these latter activities is to '"re-sinicise" people of Chinese descent abroad' (Kokko 2017: 367; Suryadinata 2017a). The final – and a bit surprising – actor is represented by the Chinese state-owned enterprises. They are very successful in generating pro-Beijing feelings among local Chinese businesses and networks by using them as subcontractors and providing other economic advantages.

One does not need to be an expert on diaspora-related policies to realize that the gigantic dimensions and impressive complexity of the bureaucratic apparatus targeting the overseas Chinese are unparalleled in today's world. They show beyond a shadow of a doubt that the leadership in Beijing perceives these small and weak actors as instrumental to its global projects. The actual working of these institutional mechanisms that has resulted in the development of the Chinese-centered globalization 'from below' is presented in the following section.

'Working' the Overseas Chinese

The activities of the vast bureaucracy that, for reasons of space, I have only briefly and rather superficially presented in the previous section are divided into two main categories: 'overseas Chinese work' and 'united front work.' The former, known in Mandarin as *qiaowu* – which, in fact, translates as 'overseas Chinese affairs' (Hamilton 2018: 33) and is also called 'diaspora management' (To 2014: 47) – takes advantage of the modernity that, 'with its inexhaustible cyber terrain and improved conditions for human mobility,' facilitates '"closeness" to home, or the PRC's poignant presence among the Chinese migrants abroad' (Barabantseva 2011: 121) to diffuse Beijing's 'de-territorialised ideology of nationalism' (Duara 2003: 14) and instrumentalizes its effects. James Jiann Hua To has defined overseas Chinese work as a massive operation based on the 'incorporation and cooptation' of overseas Chinese at every level of society. Their behavior and perceptions are to be managed using 'incentives or disincentives to suit the situation and structural circumstances that the CCP desires' (To 2014: 47). While intensive behavioral control and manipulation are involved, the entire process 'appears benign, benevolent and helpful' (Hamilton 2018: 38). The only acknowledged goal is to protect, maintain, and enhance the interests and rights of the overseas Chinese. This vast and costly effort is entirely disinterested; everything is about helping the migrants reach development, as well as a better lifestyle. The actual objectives are to (1) legitimize and protect the Communist Party's hold on power; (2) uphold Beijing's international image; and (3) control key channels of access to economic, social, and political resources through the management of overseas Chinese communities (To 2014: 46). Practical goals include (1) strengthening 'Chineseness' and ethnic affinity in the diaspora; (2) strengthening propaganda, cultural exchanges, and activities related to overseas Chinese work; (3) continually strengthening economic relations within and outside China; (4) acquiring the support of overseas Chinese against Taipei; (5) protecting returnees' rights and interests; and (6) protecting the overseas Chinese's rights and interests in their host countries and helping them to integrate into the local society. The overseas Chinese work is based on emotional exchange and integration: the choices and loyalties of the targets are influenced through social and psychological tools. Overt indoctrination would not be effective; instead, means of attraction and guidance are employed that are economic, ethnic, cultural, or political in nature (*Ibid.*, 47, 48). Moreover, Beijing's effort 'has been pragmatic and changing in its focus, in tandem with China's changing priorities in national development' (Liu and van Dongen 2016: 820). Overall, 'no other government initiative can match *qiaowu*'s scale of operation or sophistication' (To 2014: 4).

United front work is a term that refers to political influence activities directed toward both foreign states and their ethnic Chinese residents. The latter are to be co-opted and used to influence local political elites. Unlike the overseas Chinese work, the united front one is by definition secretive and therefore more difficult to scrutinize. Moreover, most of the cases revealed by media or judicial inquiries – mainly in Hong Kong, Taiwan, Australia, New Zealand, and the Pacific Islands (Fitzgerald 2018: 64; Garnaut 2018) – concentrate on interactions with local political elites. There is considerably less literature on the same type of activity targeting the overseas Chinese despite its much larger scale. In addition, the incorporation into the United Front Work Department of most of the overseas Chinese work structures discussed in the previous section is illustrative of the current intertwining of the two types of work; separating them is often impossible. As a concept, united front work 'can be summarised as a strategy of uniting with a lesser enemy in an attempt to defeat a greater common threat' (Barabantseva 2011: 41). Lenin conceived it as a tactic of strategic alliances that exploits 'every, even the smallest, "rift" among the enemies' to gain an ally no matter how 'temporary, vacillating, unstable, unreliable and conditional' such an ally may be (Brady 2017: 2). After a long history as an instrument of the Communist Party of China, united front work was oriented in 1992 to supporting economic growth (Liu and van Dongen 2016: 814) and, at present, represents 'a coordinated effort for all levels of class, society, government, party, and organizations both inside and outside of China,' which 'aims to win over non-CCP community leaders, neutralize Party critics, build temporary alliances of convenience, and systematically shut down adversaries' (To 2014: 48). Scholars labeled it 'penetrative politics' (Shiu-Hing Lo et al. 2019) while President Xi defined it in 2014 as one of the Communist Party's 'magic weapons' (Garnaut 2018). The following year, he held a united front work conference and created the Leading Small Group on United Front Work (Brady 2017: 7); in 2018, he put overseas Chinese work structures under the control of the United Front Work Department (see the previous section). Currently, there are four categories of united front work activities: (1) increased efforts to control the overseas Chinese communities; (2) a focus on people-to-people, party-to-party, and enterprise-to-enterprise relations in view of having foreigners promote the goals of the Communist Party of China; (3) a global, multiplatform communications strategy; and (4) the 'formation of a China-centered bloc through the Belt and Road Initiative' (Brady 2018: 69; 2017: 7). It is clear that the control of China's 'new' and 'old' migrants represents the critical first step of this vast enterprise. Practical activities include the establishment of Confucius Institutes; monitoring the Chinese students abroad; expanding the global impact of the Chinese state media; increasing the resources and expanding the mandate of involved bureaucratic structures; intimidating and apprehending individuals who promote anti-Chinese positions abroad; and using financial and other inducements to cultivate political elites and opinion-shapers abroad (Gill and Schreer 2018: 158).

A key target of both overseas Chinese work and united front work is represented by the tens of thousands of diasporic Chinese organizations. In addition to kinship- or locality-based traditional ones, newer types have emerged such as those established by professionals or alumni. Most are increasingly open and interested in business networking (Liu and van Dongen 2016: 817). Beijing's efforts have succeeded to 'rebuil[d] relations with ethnic Chinese organizations around the globe, from cultural associations to clan organizations to business chambers' (Kurlantzick 2008: 201). It is important to mention that the overseas Chinese state has directly contributed to or has endorsed the establishment and development of many of them. Consequently, approval of and support for closer relations with Beijing have constantly increased among these organizations (Barabantseva 2011: 125). A massive network of diasporic associations and unions now exists that is involved in cultural and economic interactions with China (Wang and Zhan 2019: 12–13). Moreover, overseas Chinese work and united front work have been successful in institutionalizing and centralizing the migrants' associations. Regional ones were unified; their activities have been coordinated and systematized using regional gatherings (Barabantseva 2011: 126). Much of this is the result of persuasive actions targeting the organizations' leaders

(*Ibid*.; Xiang 2003: 28). Various platforms are used to arrange frequent visits to China and meetings with Chinese counterparts and officials for them and other prominent members (Liu and van Dongen 2016: 817). An interesting case is that of older social organizations that have rejected the calls of the overseas Chinese state. On at least one occasion, to discredit and marginalize them, Beijing's propaganda apparatus launched a campaign against the 'old' migrants presented as the 'Three Knives' – that is, poorly educated migrants working in restaurants, market gardens, or the garment industry. The 'new' migrants were positively described as the 'Six Masters' (lawyers, doctors, engineers, accountants, professors, and scientists). Unlike their predecessors, they and their pro-Beijing organizations 'spread China's new vitality' (Hamilton 2018: 37). More generally, the idea that the 'new' migrants 'are no longer the poor people from a poor country' – as they are educated and possess capital (Suryadinata 2017a: 10; Yang 2011a: 107) – is used by the diasporic media controlled by Beijing to construct 'a transnational discourse of the new migrant' that is depicted as 'fascinated with the West, concerned with the techniques of migration, sensitive to discrimination, and preoccupied with "national power"' (Nyíri 2005: 162). The 'new' migrant is modern due to a clear association with the dominant culture of Northern China. The 'old' diaspora, on the contrary, 'has never fully shed its stain of boorishness inherent in its rural Southern origins and is not seen as sufficiently authentically Chinese, modern, global, or mobile' (*Ibid*.). This good vs. bad comparison has a direct effect on the official Chinese attitude toward 'old' migrants' associations. Their numerous and well-established charities, organizations, and social events simply tend to be ignored. The irony is that, in many places, the 'old' migrants that organize them pertain to the local economic elite, which Beijing's ambassadors and state-owned firms in need of local connections assiduously cultivate; while many of the 'educated and rich' 'new' migrants are in fact unskilled, poor, and illegal (Nyíri 2005: 162). However, members of the 'old' diaspora do establish positive relationships with the overseas Chinese state that rely on nostalgic feelings toward China or the ancestors' region of origin. Ensuing interactions are used by China to enhance the Chinese cultural identity of these 'old' migrants and, in the process, to make them favorable to Beijing's policies. To avoid a 'fifth column' symptom in the host country, contacts with both 'old' and 'new' migrants are often presented as people-to-people cooperation. The United Front Work Department has even created domestic non-governmental organizations in China that present themselves as independent actors spontaneously involved in this cooperation (Suzuki 2019: 92). However, 'given the nature of the Chinese regime and the penetration of the society by the party-state apparatus, this particular type of "people-to-people" cooperation should to a large extent be rather considered "government-to-people"' (Bachulska *et al*. 2020: 57).

Media is another field central to Beijing's efforts. Diasporic mass media such as magazines, newspapers, radio and TV stations, and websites have emerged and developed that play an important role in establishing a global Chinese identity based on shared values, elevating the migrants' level of cultural Chineseness, and generating new forms of transnational modernity among them (Ding 2015: 236). Official Chinese policies in this regard are twofold. On the one hand, digital, broadcast, and print platforms have expanded the reach of China's state-owned media among the members of the diaspora (Gill and Schreer 2018: 158). Their impact was further enhanced by the consequences of the 2017 institutional reorganization discussed in the previous section. Furthermore, President Xi launched a strategy of 'indigenizing' Chinese international broadcasting: audiences abroad, including ethnic Chinese ones, are now directly targeted by state-owned media instruments (Ding 2015: 236). On the other hand, the overseas Chinese state has been able to influence or take full control of a very large part of the overseas Chinese media. This has led to an 'upsurge in the overseas Chinese media' (Barabantseva 2011: 127), which 'use cultural elements in Chinese tradition and collective memory to shape the identity of overseas Chinese communities' (Wang and Zhan 2019: 12).

Overseas Chinese work and united front work also include various activities – mainly but not exclusively cultural and educational in nature – that target young members of the diaspora. This has become imperative when the United Front Work Department started to receive numerous reports indicating that its activity was seriously challenged by the new generation of overseas Chinese who have a very negative perception of Beijing's authoritarian policies in Hong Kong and elsewhere in China. The reaction took the form of a 'considerable effort to revive and preserve the sense of Chineseness among young people of Chinese descent abroad' (Barabantseva 2011: 129) in order to instrumentalize it politically. The United Front Work Department launched a policy of 'winning the youth back' that concentrates on young diasporic entrepreneurs, scholars, and leaders of interest groups and associations. A larger audience is similarly targeted by cultural activities and language education through Chinese media, language schools, and Confucius Institutes (Suzuki 2019: 91–93). The latter – which, in the Global South, have escaped the harsh criticism encountered in developed countries – have one mission that is part of the overseas Chinese work: to '"re-sinicise" people of Chinese descent abroad' (Kokko 2017: 367; Suryadinata 2017a). The Confucius Institutes are managed by the Office of Chinese Language Council International, the administrative organ of the Leading Group of Chinese Language Council International. This leading group has the Overseas Chinese Affairs Office as a partner unit. When, in 2018, the Overseas Chinese Affairs Office was put under the control of the United Front Work Department, the influence of this department on the Confucius Institutes increased significantly. Within China, a similar role is played by the Academy of Chinese Culture and its more than 400 schools. They organize exchange programs targeting members of the diaspora. The Chinese cultural and ethnic identity of these visitors is reinforced through courses on Chinese culture, as well as – less predictably – socialism (Suzuki 2019: 90, 93). Finally, there is a massive effort to preserve the loyalty of the Chinese students abroad; after graduation, many of them settle in the host country and become part of the diaspora. This is a very interesting topic, but most of these students prefer Western countries that are not concerned by the Chinese-centered globalization 'from below.' Exceptions such as New Zealand or Singapore do exist; yet, they cannot justify the large space required by their analysis in this chapter. I will therefore simply suggest to interested readers one of my previous works where this issue is addressed (Tudoroiu 2022: 112–114, 271–275).

To summarize, the overseas Chinese work and united front work represent an impressive effort that has been highly effective in expanding Beijing's impact on the diaspora. In turn, this has allowed the Chinese state to influence and, in part, control the actors of the Chinese-centered globalization 'from below.' Ultimately, the two 'works' represent a successful projection of normative power toward the ethnic Chinese abroad who have internalized China's deterritorialized nationalism. This process, however, would have not been possible without the material incentives presented in the next section.

Incentives

Many successful Chinese entrepreneurial migrants are proud to link their socio-economic advancement to 'the narratives of "great rejuvenation of the Chinese nation" and consider themselves an organic part of the enterprise' (Wang and Zhan 2019: 18). At first view, such patriotic sentiments may seem to be the exclusive result of Beijing's persuasive efforts. In fact, very pragmatic factors also are at work. Scholars have noted that displaying patriotism is often a self-serving action: 'photos with high Chinese officials and newspaper articles commending someone for patriotism are assets of considerable importance when doing business or dealing with officials back in China' (Nyíri 2005: 168). While this may sound a bit grotesque to readers unfamiliar with the topic, many associations of the overseas Chinese have been created only because their self-appointed leaders hope to take one day photos of themselves with the Chinese Prime Minister that can be exploited economically. Chinese patriotism can be used as an instrument of '"flexible accumulation" and legitimization of power by the migrant elites' (*Ibid.*, 169). Advantages exist in the host country, too. The Chinese entrepreneurial migrants are the preferred subcontractors of Chinese state-owned enterprises involved in the construction of numerous large infrastructure projects. They also benefit from the social networks that develop around these enterprises (Wang and Zhan 2019: 19–20). Migrant entrepreneurs – especially the 'old' ones, who are well established in the local business environment – can obtain significant benefits working as intermediaries for newly arrived Chinese firms with poor knowledge of the market and without access to local decision-makers (Ellis 2012: 33). For their part, the 'new' Chinese entrepreneurial migrants often profit from the favorable conditions negotiated by China with Global South states – especially in the framework of the BRI – 'for opening up new territories and creating enterprises' (Röschenthaler and Socpa 2017: 180). This is a direct consequence of Beijing's economic normative set that, as shown in Subchapter 2.3, is accepted by the Chinese-socialized BRI political elites in power. The social norm is even more important, as it was specifically conceived to protect the migrants and their economic activities. The next subchapter analyzes its working in the case of Ghana, but there are many other examples. In Jamaica and Cameroon, China intervened at the request of its entrepreneurial migrants to stop their harassment by police, fiscal, and customs officers. In Madagascar, Chinese pressure put an end to a wave of attacks on Chinese traders. In Suriname and Venezuela, Beijing's ambassadors reacted vocally to anti-Chinese riots (Ellis 2014: 184; Röschenthaler and Socpa 2017: 168; French 2014: 224). In fact, it is in this field that – as noted earlier in this subchapter – the Chinese reactive state transnationalism has been most visible. As the number of Chinese 'new' migrants increased, situations emerged where their security was seriously threatened by armed violence or natural disasters. In response, Beijing replaced its previous non-interventionist approach with active engagement, even if this complicated its foreign policy. It was in 2004 that President Hu Jintao first spoke of the protection of Chinese nationals abroad ensuing from the 'growing need to secure [China's] global economic activities' (Thunø 2018: 191–192). He offered assistance after 14 Chinese workers were killed in Afghanistan and Pakistan. The government in Beijing set up consular protection centers and coordination structures (*Ibid.*, 192). In 2006, the first air evacuation of Chinese migrants took place during riots in the Solomon Islands (Yang 2011a: 123). Until 2010, no less than 6,000 Chinese nationals were evacuated from eight countries. In 2011, the Arab Spring increased their number to 48,000 (Thunø 2018: 192). Progressively, China forged a set of diplomatic tools that include mediation, diversification of interlocutors, and power projection (Fulton 2016: 1288). They allow it to protect its threatened citizens without overt intervention. As shown in the previous subchapter, the Chinese-centered globalization 'from below' mainly targets less developed countries in the Global South characterized by poor governance. Such countries tend to be unstable and experience frequent security issues, which is extremely detrimental to entrepreneurs in general and migrant ones in particular. The fact that China is able and willing to protect or evacuate threatened Chinese migrants represents a considerable advantage, which can convince them that close relations with the government in Beijing are genuinely beneficial. In conjunction with the material benefits discussed in the first part of this section, this protection incentivizes the Chinese migrants' adoption of a pro-Beijing attitude, acceptance of China's deterritorialized nationalism, and support for its policies and actions.

Co-Opting the 'Old' Migrants

An interesting aspect concerns the extension of this type of protection beyond the circle of Chinese citizens. As briefly mentioned in the previous subchapter, the distinction between *huaren* and *huaqiao* – 'old' and 'new' Chinese migrants – is in fact political in nature. Official terms employed with respect to the overseas Chinese are 'subject to the situations and contexts to which they refer' (Yow 2016: 838). *Huaren* and *huaqiao* became central to this domain after the adoption of the Citizenship Law of 1980. Because it recognized single citizenship, the two terms are citizenship-based. Other terms are used that ignore this dimension: *huayi* simply designates Chinese descendants; *huazu* means ethnic Chinese; *hai'ou* is about 'seagulls,' or migrants that commute between their host country and China; *xin yimin* refers to post-1978 Chinese migrants; and *qiaobao* means Chinese compatriots overseas (Yow 2016: 838; Liu and van Dongen 2016: 816; Suryadinata 2017a: 5–6; Chee-Beng 2012: 2–3). During the last two decades, Chinese official documents have mainly used *xin yimin* and *qiaobao* while *huaqiao huaren* are put together. The goal is to eliminate the traditional separation between the latter two terms in order to 'blur their nationality distinction' (Suryadinata 2017a: 6; Nyíri 2001: 636). In the previous subchapter, I showed that the overseas Chinese state often pictures the 'new' migrants much more favorably than the 'old' ones. However, there is an official 'purposeful erosion of differences among ethnic Chinese abroad' intended 'to harness their energies in the service of the PRC and its growing overseas interests' (Chong 2018: 153; Suryadinata 2017a). Prominent members of the 'old' diaspora are cultivated by China's embassies, targeted by overseas Chinese work and united front work, and offered material incentives by Chinese state-owned firms. But all 'old' migrants are concerned by the ongoing trend to extend China's protection of its nationals to all ethnic Chinese abroad. In 1998, Beijing did not react to anti-ethnic Chinese riots in Indonesia because the victims were not Chinese citizens. Eventually, China began to provide consular assistance to endangered non-nationals of Chinese origin in the framework of its discourse on humanitarian aid (Thunø 2018: 193). In 2014, in a speech given at the Conference of World Federation of Huaqiao Huaren Associations, President Xi Jinping identified all overseas Chinese as members of the 'Zhonghua big family,' implicitly erasing citizenship differences (Suryadinata 2017b: 102–103). One year later, the undiplomatic intervention of the Chinese ambassador in Malaysia prevented the ignition of riots similar to the Indonesian ones. Known as the 'ambassador's walk,' the 2015 episode was triggered by a provocative Malay nationalist demonstration planned to take place on Petaling Street, in Kuala Lumpur's Chinatown. Importantly, the huge majority of the ethnic Chinese there are not China's citizens. One day earlier, the Chinese ambassador nevertheless took a 'politically highly symbolic walk down Petaling Street,' which he used to inform reporters that China would 'not sit by idly' if riots ignite (Chow-Bing and Chee-Beng 2018:

4–5, 108–110). This triggered serious disputes within the Malaysian government between nationalists asking for the ambassador to be expelled and those afraid of harming relations with Beijing. But the main organizer of the anti-Chinese demonstration was arrested and riots were avoided (*Ibid.*, 109). The willingness of the Chinese leadership to protect the entire Chinese diaspora illustrated by this event 'represent[s] a partial return to the pre-1957 policy of treating all overseas Chinese as Chinese nationals' (Barabantseva 2011: 118; Thunø 2018: 193). This is only a selective and limited policy; its practical consequences are ultimately less important than the reason that triggered its adoption. Beijing's 'increasingly blurring lines in its treatment of PRC citizens and non-PRC citizen ethnic Chinese overseas' are motivated by 'efforts to mobilize ethnic Chinese communities abroad to serve its national interests' (Chong 2018: 151; Suryadinata 2017a). The overseas Chinese state has been successful in convincing the 'new' migrants to accept its deterritorialized nationalism, which has shaped their identity and modified their interests in ways beneficial to Beijing's global plans. Critically, this has allowed for the development of the Chinese-centered globalization 'from below.' Erasing the differences between nationals and non-nationals of Chinese descent is part of a strategy intended to make the 'old' diaspora join the same globalization.

Before analyzing the features of this globalization and its instrumentalization by the Chinese leadership, I will present a case study that is useful for the understanding of the complex relationship between Chinese entrepreneurial migrants, the Chinese state, and Global South countries directly concerned by the Chinese-centered globalization 'from below.'

5.3 The Chinese Entrepreneurial Migrants in Ghana

While 'structural and government management volatilities' still exist (Hess and Aidoo 2015: 41), since 1992, Ghana has been one of Africa's most democratic and stable states. It has 'a vibrant media, strong public dialogue and scores high on measures of civil liberty, political rights and political stability' (Hardus 2014: 589). 'The maturity of its democratic culture' has also led to 'sound and persistent' economic growth (Hess and Aidoo 2015: 41; Hess and Aidoo 2014: 138). After independence, President Kwame Nkrumah turned the West African state into 'a spearhead for the liberation of the rest of Africa from colonial rule and the establishment of a socialist African unity under his leadership' (Fage and Maier 2020). He notably forged a special partnership with Maoist China. There were numerous mutual visits, cooperation agreements, support in international fora, as well as Chinese technical assistance, loans, and even training in Ghana of leftist guerrillas from other African states (Chau 2014: 80–81, 89–91; Embassy of the People's Republic of China in the Republic of Ghana 2020; Boateng 2020; Amoah 2016: 242; Odoom 2017: 600; Sarpong 2015: 1438; Power *et al.* 2012: 39). These close interactions led to the beginning of a process of Chinese socialization of the Ghanaian political elites around President Nkrumah. The latter developed a very strong personal relationship with Chinese leaders and especially Premier Zhou Enlai. However, he was overthrown by a military coup precisely during a stopover in Beijing. The new regime immediately expelled 430 Chinese citizens involved in various cooperation projects. There were no Sino-Ghanaian diplomatic relations from 1966 to 1972 (Chau 2014: 87, 95–96, 98–99; Power *et al.* 2012: 44; Amoah 2016: 242). In fact, the only significant episode of cooperation in three decades and a half was occasioned by Accra's opposition to the Western condemnation of the 1989 Tiananmen Square massacre, which helped prevent sanctions from international organizations (Freeman 2015: 2, 6). Jerry Rawlings, Ghana's dictator of the time, was rewarded with the Chinese-financed and built Ghana National Theater Complex (Odoom 2017: 600; Sarpong 2015: 1438). The situation changed only after the launching in 1999 of President Jiang Zemin's 'Go out' strategy. China's need for natural resources led to its 're-entry into Africa' (Stahl 2018: 8–9; Hess and Aidoo 2015: 16; Shen 2015: 113) and Ghana represented one of the main targets. Consequently, 'the Kufuor era (2001–2009) ushered in a golden age of Ghana-China relations' (Amoah 2016: 242). Indeed, President John Kufuor 'embraced China as a diplomatic and business partner' (Hess and Aidoo 2014: 141). Trade developed spectacularly: from US $93 million in 2000, it increased to US $1.5 billion in 2008, reached US $6.7 billion in 2017, and US $7.46 billion in 2019, turning China into Ghana's main commercial partner (Hess and Aidoo 2015: 47; Hess and Aidoo 2016: 310; Pilling 2018; Boateng 2020). The expansion of Chinese investment was much more modest. The largest number of foreign projects in Ghana are Chinese, but their total amount makes China only the sixth foreign investor. Importantly for this chapter, however, most of this investment was made by medium and especially small trade enterprises; the latter belong to Chinese entrepreneurial migrants and are part of the Chinese-centered globalization 'from below.' China is nevertheless present in many branches of Ghana's economy and is heavily involved in the loan-financing and construction of large infrastructure projects. It also provides valuable development assistance in education, agriculture, and health. Beijing-financed projects range from two Confucius Institutes and scholarship programs that have turned the Ghanaians into the largest group of African students in China (Pilling 2018) to the funding of 100 vehicles for the Ghana Police Service (Smith 2019). Critically, close and frequent interactions between the two countries' political elites that have included numerous high-level meetings – always accompanied by Chinese loans presented as 'gifts' – have resulted in the Chinese socialization of the successive governments led by Presidents John Kufuor of the New Patriotic Party (2001–2009), John Evans Atta Mills (2009–2012), and John Dramani Mahama (2012–2017) of the National Democratic Congress, as well as Nana Addo Dankwa Akufo-Addo (since 2017) of the New Patriotic Party. As usual, the main incentive that enhanced the

Chinese socialization process is represented by the aforementioned infrastructure projects. Their long list includes the large Bui hydroelectric dam, the Afefi Irrigation Project, the Dangme and Teshie Hospitals, the Complex of Ministry of Foreign Affairs and Regional Integration, the Office Block of Ministry of Defense, police and military barracks, the Sports Complex in Cape Coast, the Kumasi Youth Centre, the New Century Career training Institute Expansion Project in Accra, the campus of the University of Health and Allied Sciences in Ho, the Ofankor-Nsawam stretch of the Accra-Kumasi Road, and several rural schools (Smith 2019; Kailemia 2017: 2089; Verma 2017: 203). The Chinese packages have often been impressive. In 2010, President John Evans Atta Mills received a US $3 billion facility for the development of gas and oil infrastructure. He decided to miss a high-level United Nations meeting in New York in order to take part in the signing of the framework agreement in Beijing (Odoom 2017: 601). In 2012, Vice-President Mahama, who would become President later that year, signed agreements worth US $13 billion – one-third of the country's GDP – with China Development Bank and China ExIm Bank that covered, among others, road, railway, and dam projects amounting to US $9 billion (Sarpong 2015: 1439; French 2014: 185). In 2018, President Akufo-Addo signed a memorandum of understanding that turned Ghana into a BRI partner. On that occasion, he also signed a US $2 billion Sinohydro Master Project Support Agreement on infrastructure and a US $350 million agreement for a liquefied natural gas terminal in the Ghanaian port of Tema (Communications Bureau 2018; Gokoluk 2018; *Business News of Sunday*, September 2, 2018). Officials in Accra have constantly argued that 'the Chinese are serving genuine infrastructure needs' (Chipaike and Bischoff 2018: 1010). It is undeniable that, as elsewhere in the developing world, the emergence of Beijing as a new donor has increased the recipient's negotiation power with traditional donors: 'the availability of Chinese aid in addition to traditional aid gave Ghana more freedom to define its policy priorities' (*Ibid.*, 1011). Yet, the infrastructure projects are hardly the gifts Ghanaian and Chinese politicians speak about. They are financed by Chinese loans, not grants, and the conditions of these loans do not qualify them as development assistance if the criteria established by the Development Assistance Committee (DAC) of the Organization for Economic Cooperation and Development are used. Moreover, 'many high-profile ventures have become headaches for Accra' (Pilling 2018). The financing of the US $622 million Bui dam included a China ExIm Bank concessional loan of $263.5 million and a buyers' credit of $298.5 million. The latter was secured through net revenue from a Power Purchase Agreement, as well as receivables from the sale of Ghanaian cocoa beans to China (Odoom 2017: 608; Chipaike and Bischoff 2018: 1009). Typical for Chinese contracts, details were not made public (French 2014: 192). However, in 2017, the Parliament in Accra had to approve a US $1.3 billion loan for the Ghana Cocoa Board, which encountered serious financial problems 'partly because of difficulties in servicing its Bui dam loans' (Pilling

2018). The 2010 Master Facility Agreement that made President Atta Mills go to Beijing instead of attending a UN meeting, as well as the 2012 final agreement on the US $3 billion loan, compelled Ghana to pay a large commitment fee and to supply a collateral of 13,000 barrels per day of crude oil for fifteen and a half years (Hess and Aidoo 2015: 49; Hess and Aidoo 2016: 313; Hardus 2014: 601). Both were heavily criticized domestically. Furthermore, the oil price reached US $100 per barrel in 2014 but China Development Bank kept the price to pay back the loan at US $85. It also forced the Ghanaian side to transfer 49 percent of the price of the shipment into the debt service account. Commitment fees for the first US $600 million of the loan amounted to no less than US $54 million. Facing massive domestic pressure, the government in Accra decided in July 2014 not to draw the remaining US $1.5 billion tranche and required instead a US $1 billion loan from the IMF (Hardus 2014: 601; Hess and Aidoo 2016: 313; Aidoo 2016: 67). These Chinese actions helped critics to 'garner more ammunition to condemn Beijing's insatiable quest for African resources as well as corrupt motives that drive this appetite' (Hess and Aidoo 2016: 313). But such

> criticism misses a key dimension of the infrastructure projects financed by Beijing through its massive loans. Except at rhetorical level, these are not intended to benefit the entire country. They are conceived as socialization instruments targeting the political elites in power.
> (Tudoroiu 2022: 138)

Indeed, through their use, China has strongly incentivized the Ghanaian political elites to accept its socialization advances. As all over the BRI (see Tudoroiu 2021), Beijing has loan-financed and constructed in Ghana *prestige* infrastructure projects intended to increase the political legitimacy and electoral support of political elites in power. Projects are calculated to be completed shortly before elections when the President proudly inaugurates them as proof of his ability to bring Chinese-scented prosperity to the country. Unexpected delays occurred before the December 2008 presidential election in the completion of a key stage of the construction of the Bui hydroelectric dam. In similar situations, 'representatives of the Chinese SOEs [state-owned enterprises] often say that they are pressured to complete a project, or a significant phase of a project, before a political event takes place' (Lam 2017: 55). Indeed, the Kufuor administration put strong pressure on Sinohydro. The Chinese side fully understood the seriousness of the situation. Workers were made to take shifts and the stage was finally completed in time (*Ibid.*). The final agreement on the US $3 billion loan was signed only in April 2012 despite the fact that it was based on a framework agreement concluded back in 2010. The delay was due to the fact that it was in 2012 that elections were held; predictably, the incumbent National Democratic Congress won (Sarpong 2015: 1439; French 2014: 185). However, two years later, the excessively exploitative conditions imposed by China

Development Bank led to strong domestic pressure that compelled President Mahama to cancel the agreement before receiving the last US $1.5 billion tranche. One would have expected this conflictive situation to impact negatively the Sino-Ghanaian partnership. This was not the case: the Chinese-socialized President hurried to meet his Chinese counterpart, explained the situation, and was forgiven. 'This is exactly how socialized elites are expected to act' (Tudoroiu 2022: 138).

Common citizens tend to have a good general opinion of China. In 2009, this was the case of 62 to 75 percent of the Ghanaians. In 2013, 63 percent saw the Asian partner as influencing favorably Ghana's economy (the United States was similarly assessed by 60 percent of respondents). It is interesting to note that local experts often criticize the Chinese infrastructure projects for their poor quality and the use of contractors, labor, and materials from China (French 2014: 199). Most citizens, on the contrary, perceive the projects as positive (Mohan *et al.* 2014: 124), which suggests that they accept Ghanaian politicians' rhetoric on this matter. In part, this is explained by the existence of pro-Chinese interest and propaganda groups such as the Ghana-China Friendship Union and the Ghana-China Business Chamber of Commerce. They shape the popular discourse and influence debates related to the activities of Chinese firms (Hess and Aidoo 2015: 54). Ghanaian nationals are nevertheless very hostile to China on four important issues: the collapse of the Ghanaian textile industry and trade as an effect of Chinese competition back in the 1990s, when 25,000 factory workers and petty traders, mostly women, lost their jobs; the aforementioned US $3 billion loan, which the huge majority of the Ghanaians see as a Chinese predatory plan; illegal activities of the Chinese migrants that include trafficking and prostitution; and the galamsey episode discussed below (Aidoo 2016: 65; French 2014: 200; Hess and Aidoo 2015: 50). The last two aspects are directly related to the Chinese entrepreneurial migrants. Consequently, despite the genuine admiration for China's impressive economic development, there has been 'a gradual upwelling of anti-Chinese sentiments in Ghana' (Aidoo 2016: 63–64, 65) with 'significant episodes of anti-Chinese resentment' (Hess and Aidoo 2014: 131). As Kwasi Prempeh, the executive director of the Ghana Center for Democratic Development, stated, 'Ghanaian elites have responded enthusiastically to China's growing influence,' but this 'doesn't resonate well with the average African. I don't think there's a lot of love lost at the popular level' (Pilling 2018). This is to say that a typical Global South elites-society gap has developed in Ghana with respect to important aspects of the Chinese presence. But this gap has never prevented the socialization of the political elites in power. The Ghanaian ones have fully accepted China's norms. Due to the political subset, they support the 'One China' principle and have 'agreed to explore means of greater cooperation in the United Nations, World Trade Organisation and other international and regional organisations' (Tsikata *et al.* 2008: 5). Due to the economic one, they have joined the Chinese-centered globalization 'from above.' Finally, their respect for Beijing's social norm has brought Ghana within the Chinese-centered globalization 'from below.' In this case, however, the elites-society gap has created unexpected difficulties for China's entrepreneurial migrants.

The Chinese 'Ant Traders' in Ghana

'There is an enormous cloud of uncertainty about the absolute numbers of Chinese in Ghana' (Dankwah and Amoah 2019: 70). Extreme opinions place the figure at 700,000 in 2009 (Sarpong 2015: 1438). More credible assessments mention 4,000 to 7,000 Chinese entrepreneurial migrants before 2008, 70,000 to 90,000 at the height of the galamsey episode in 2013, and 25,000 to 35,000 in 2018 (Wang and Zhan 2019: 15; Cook et al. 2016: 62). With the exception of gold miners, most of them live in the capital and the neighboring port of Tema, while a smaller number inhabit the ancient royal city of Kumasi (Lam 2015: 17). The migratory process started, on a very small scale, at the end of the 19th century with indentured laborers who worked in the gold mines. By the mid-1950s, shortly before independence, industrialists from Hong Kong set up mainly textile factories. During the 1980s, Taiwanese businessmen arrived who were involved in manufacturing and trade. Some of the Chinese workers brought for the construction of projects such as the National Theater Complex overstayed their contracts. By the mid-1990s, representatives of Chinese state-owned enterprises came to promote exports in Ghana and, at times, opened their own private businesses. In all, these ethnic Chinese amounted to no more than 2,000 individuals. They are seen by more recent migrants as 'established and more successful' (Lam 2015: 15–16; Wang and Zhan 2019: 14; Botchwey et al. 2019: 313; Cook et al. 2016: 62). Two much larger waves of Chinese 'new' migrants arrived around 2001 and 2008, respectively. The first group consisted of small traders importing all sorts of daily-use and industrial goods. The second group covered a much larger range of formal and informal activities that included agriculture, garment production, telecommunications, electricity production and distribution, oil processing, and, in Tema, even prostitution (Wang and Zhan 2019: 14–15). The galamsey 'gold rush' brought 18,300 Chinese miners in 2012 and 20,300 in 2013, in addition to those who entered Ghana illegally from Togo (where China's nationals can get visas at their arrival) (Botchwey et al. 2019: 313); but most of them left in June–July 2013 (see below). The 2008 wave included more than 2,000 Chinese petty traders who joined Accra's largest commodity market, Makola. The 'clearly visible concentration of Chinese traders' (Giese 2013: 136) 'had big impacts on local trading spaces.' The newcomers 'account for a large share of the trading community, not only in numbers but in volume of trade and investments' (Dankwah and Valenta 2019: 1–2). It should be added that, as shown in Subchapter 4.6, many Ghanaians traders also import and sell Chinese goods. To this effect, 22,000 of them visited China in 2019 as compared to

10,500 Chinese arrivals in Ghana. Unsurprisingly, over 60 percent of the Ghanaians who settled in China have chosen the Guangdong Province, which produces the cheap goods sold in Ghana (Boateng 2020). Returning to the Chinese entrepreneurial migrants, they are also active in Ghana's real estate, health services, advertisement printing, manufacturing, hotels and restaurants, farming, intermediary services, and gold mining (Lam 2015: 16). This large Chinese presence is due to good Sino-Ghanaian relations; the country's stability, which is often contrasted with violence and political instability elsewhere in the region; and the 'big fish in a small pond' logic discussed in Subchapter 5.1: in Ghana, 'the market is less glutted and entrepreneurial success, regardless of business experience and even skill, more assured' (Wang and Zhan 2019: 17; Mohan *et al.* 2014: 54, 67).

The numerous Chinese petty traders interact with their local counterparts in both cooperative and conflictive ways. Some Ghanaians are unable to travel to China; they prefer to buy and re-sell goods imported by the Chinese. Hawkers, most of whom are women, are indirectly employed by Chinese merchants and appreciate their economic presence (Dankwah and Valenta 2019: 4–5, 16). So do local young aspiring traders, who traditionally were excluded from economic, social, and religious networks that control access to start-up capital, affordable goods, and selling space. To the dissatisfaction of established traders, this has changed as the arrival of the Chinese and their cheap goods has increased the number of markets and selling spaces, lowered the capital entry barrier, and created new ways to acquire such capital by working for the Chinese merchants (Marfaing and Thiel 2013: 647, 655). Yet, most of the 'employment relations in the trading sector [are] dysfunctional and conflict-prone.' The recruitment process, interpersonal relationships, the existence of very different concepts of authority, and the use of sanctions and incentives by the Chinese traders often lead to tensions and conflict with their Ghanaian employees (Giese 2013: 134). For their part, local small merchants that compete directly with the Chinese ones are overtly hostile. They criticize harshly their rivals' low-quality merchandise, which is also exposed in the media; the copies of Ghanaian goods they sell at a lower price; the repatriation of profit to China, which hinders Ghana's economic development; unfair macroeconomic advantages such as favorable exchange rate, access to cheap credits from Chinese banks, and better sourcing of Guangzhou-made products (Dankwah and Valenta 2019: 14, 18, 19; Dankwah and Amoah 2019: 78; Mohan and Lampert 2013: 107); and the migrants' lack of social integration: they only 'maintain loose social bonds' with the locals. The root cause of this hostility is the remarkable competitiveness of the Chinese merchants, which has resulted in a strong sense of unfairness and deep-seated tensions (Dankwah and Amoah 2019: 78, 79–80). Consequently, in 2005, the Ghana Union of Traders Association (GUTA) started an anti-Chinese crusade. It tried to put pressure on the government to enforce the 1994 Ghana Investment Promotion Centre Act, which forbids non-Ghanaians' retailing activities in public markets. Moreover, foreign-owned trading enterprises have to invest at least US $300,000 and hire at least ten local staff. However, the Chinese-socialized political elites in power were unwilling to infringe Beijing's social norm. GUTA's unsuccessful struggle against successive governments in Accra lasted for many years. The legislation was revised, but there was no visible change. In late 2007, shops were closed for one day and GUTA organized a march and a mass rally. In response, a multi-agency task force was created by the government that expelled the Chinese traders from a large retail complex in Accra known as China Town; but they simply moved to nearby streets. By 2011, they also occupied side roads and smaller complexes in the same area. GUTA again pointed to illegal practices that included the under-reporting of sales by the Chinese to reduce taxes, not paying social security, and using cheap loans from banks in China to inflate shop rents that put locals out of business. It argued that local officials did not enforce the law because they were bribed by the Chinese migrants, and that the government protected the latter through its inaction (Mohan *et al.* 2014: 112; Dankwah and Amoah 2019: 74). Despite GUTA's sustained efforts, nothing of this changed. It is interesting to note the attitude of the general population, which needs the cheap goods sold by the Chinese traders but also perceives the concerns of local merchants as legitimate. No less than 40.4 percent of Ghana's nationals 'see Chinese small businesses as helpful to local economic development and also a source of problems for local people' (Hess and Aidoo 2014: 141). GUTA's vocal years-long campaign, however, succeeded in progressively shifting the balance in favor of the local traders. As an effect, an atmosphere of hostility against the Chinese developed among the Ghanaian society that became highly visible during the galamsey crisis of 2013 and, more generally, contributed to the sentiment of vulnerability shared by the Chinese entrepreneurial migrants in Ghana.

Vulnerability

As elsewhere in the Global South, China's 'new' migrants are poorly integrated into the local society (Dankwah and Amoah 2019: 78). But they also experience fierce in-group competition, important divisions, and no solidarity. This is due to the fact that too many entrepreneurial migrants compete within the same economic sectors using strategies that lead to disturbances and conflicts. They defraud each other and are obsessed with fears of 'commercial espionage'; some go as far as putting 'Chinese don't enter' signs on their shops. Under these conditions, as much as half of the Chinese businesses in Ghana go bankrupt. Somewhat strangely, the migrants tend to keep Ghanaian people and institutions responsible for their problems. The 'old' Chinese do not share this opinion. They are mainly well-established Hong Kong industrialists known for their conviviality. In their view, the fault lies entirely with the bad behavior and 'poor quality' of the newcomers. They do not speak English, are poorly educated, and, more importantly, do not understand local rules. They rely on bribery to solve any problem and are not interested in anything else than short-term profit. They bring goods of poor quality, do not have proper documentation, are regular clients of casinos, and even bring Chinese women to work as prostitutes. Older migrants perceive such disreputable activities as affecting their own respectability. Because of the poor image created by the newly arrived entrepreneurial migrants, all ethnic Chinese are now harassed by Ghanaian officials (*Ibid.*, 71; Lam 2015: 9–10, 12, 22, 29, 30, 36; Mohan *et al.* 2014: 90–91, 92–93). Such criticism is most likely correct, but the split between 'old' and 'new' migrants further increases divisions. In particular, newly arrived Chinese cannot access the social networks of the 'old' ones. Lack of social capital makes their adaptation and economic success difficult as they cannot obtain the political and administrative protection provided by such networks. The number of Chinese migrants in Ghana is impressive, but this 'does not necessarily improve the social status of Chinese entrepreneurs or create a stronger, more unified Chinese community' (Lam 2015: 9, 36).

The negative internal dynamic of this community is one of the causes that have led to an unexpected situation. The 'widely publicized image of a "powerful China in Africa"' (*Ibid.*, 10) is seldom questioned. Yet, the 'new' Chinese entrepreneurial migrants in Ghana see themselves as vulnerable. The most important cause is the systematic harassment and extortion by corrupt Ghanaian officials. They compel the migrants to pay bribes regularly. Bribery is also the only way to avoid unjustified long bureaucratic delays. Immigration, revenue, and municipal services organize frequent inspections exclusively intended 'to extract unofficial and often unjustified payments' from the Chinese (Mohan *et al.* 2014: 109). Taxes have to be negotiated; what the Chinese traders actually pay depends more on the deal they are able to conclude with local officials than on the volume of their trade. Fines for tax evasion follow the same pattern. Visas can be obtained or renewed by paying Ghanaian or Chinese intermediaries (Lam 2015: 18–19). Newcomers are 'surprised by the levels of corruption relating to everyday micro-administrative procedures,' which are much higher even than those of China (Lam 2015: 17). Widespread corruption in Ghana and opportunistic calculation of self-interested officials certainly contribute to this situation. But scholars claim that, fundamentally, the corruption-based harassment of the Chinese migrants 'is reflective of negative African social agency at lower non-state levels of people-to-people interaction' (Chipaike and Bischoff 2018: 1012). This is to say that its root cause is the negative perception of and attitude toward these entrepreneurial migrants that have developed among the Ghanaian society. In addition to extortion by officials, the feeling of vulnerability is enhanced by the competition with Ghanaian traders and tensions with local employees. The Chinese have better connections in Guangdong, where goods are produced, and benefit from the macroeconomic advantages presented earlier in this section. Local merchants, however, understand better the local market as they are embedded in Ghana's cultural context (Chipaike and Bischoff 2018: 1013). Aforementioned conflicts with local employees are even more damaging; sometimes, they become 'the over-riding issue' (Mohan *et al.* 2014: 114) because they are mainly triggered by cultural incompatibilities. The Chinese employers often show racialized negative stereotyping of Ghanaians. The latter are lazy, lack initiative, have to be closely supervised, and are 'unfaithful' and 'untrustworthy.' In turn, local workers point to the poor pay and working conditions. They accuse the Chinese of being strict, hard, and patronizing. They fire arbitrarily, do not show any respect or compassion, use a master–slave logic, and 'are very bad people' (Mohan *et al.* 2014: 114–115, 116–117; Lam 2015: 25–26; Wang and Zhan 2019: 21). It is not difficult to understand the tensions that emerge in this context and the fact that they enhance the migrants' perceived vulnerability. This situation is hardly limited to Ghana. Importantly, it shows that the effectiveness of the protection offered by the Chinese government to its entrepreneurial migrants is rather limited at 'low end' society level. When large-scale violence against Chinese migrants ignites, Beijing can easily put pressure on the socialized elites in power to intervene. But the Chinese state and these elites are completely impotent against local bureaucrats who take bribes, merchants with a better understanding of the market, or employees that dislike their Chinese employers. Many of the day-to-day interactions of entrepreneurial migrants pertain to a universe that is completely different from the state-centered one. At state level, Ghana – as well as, more generally, Africa and the Global South – is weak while China is strong. At society level, Beijing's migrants are directly affected by 'the existence of the reverse dynamic: weak Chinese and strong Africans.' As a result, Ghanaians are able to advance their interests and aspirations despite the affiliation of the Chinese entrepreneurial migrants with a global power and their ensuing privileged status (Lam 2015: 11). In part, this is the consequence of the fact that the Chinese-centered globalization 'from below' produces much less normative power than the non-hegemonic globalization 'from below.' Instead, it relies mainly on China's normative power and therefore depends on conditions that allow for its projection. At the 'low end,' this projection is very weak because of the elites–society gap associated with the process of Chinese socialization, which only concerns the political elites in power and provides no benefits to or affects negatively large socio-economic groups. As further discussed in the next subchapter, this is an inbuilt problem of the Chinese-centered globalization 'from below.' The vulnerability of the Chinese entrepreneurial migrants is indicative of the fact that they are not mere agents of the government in Beijing. They are autonomous actors facing specific problems. Many of these problems can be solved only through specific forms of agency that are inaccessible to a state no matter its resources and will to intervene. The systematic use of bribes is one of them, even if it ends up creating a vicious circle and actually aggravating the problem. Precisely because they see no long-term solution, the Chinese entrepreneurial migrants continue to feel vulnerable;

this results in insecurity and creates a psychological need for a protector. In turn, this need is exploited by the overseas Chinese state to diffuse its deterritorialized nationalism and enhance its influence on the Chinese migrants.

Beijing's Influence

The government in Beijing is unable to solve most 'low end' problems, but – in Ghana as elsewhere in the Global South – does everything in its power to show that it protects the Chinese entrepreneurial migrants (a good example is the galamsey crisis discussed in the next section). This is a way to legitimize the overseas Chinese work and united front work of institutions, policies, and mechanisms discussed in the previous subchapter. The most visible actor involved in these activities is China's embassy in Ghana, which interacts closely with local Chinese business unions and finances a large number of business, social, and recreational activities. These activities are always marked by Beijing's official rhetoric. There is plenty of socialist core values, 'contributions to the great rejuvenation of Chinese nation from overseas,' 'the socialist road with Chinese characteristics,' and so on (Wang and Zhan 2019: 19). This, however, does not prevent the three business associations of the Chinese entrepreneurial migrants – that many accuse of serving personal interests instead of community ones – to struggle for official recognition. The embassy puts pressure on the Chinese-language media in Ghana to 'bridg[e] the Chinese communities in West Africa to the motherland and construct a positive image of China' (*Ibid.*). Somewhat surprisingly, its assistance to Chinese nationals has certain limits. There were cases of illegal Chinese immigrants complaining about a lack of official support. In 2009, a dozen small merchants arrested for overstaying their visas were visited at the police station by an embassy official only to be explained their legal rights; they had to bribe the police to be released. A strike of Chinese merchants against 'unfair treatment' was canceled under pressure from the embassy (Lam 2015: 18). However, it is widely believed that the Sino-Ghanaian close partnership does impact favorably the treatment of Chinese nationals by local authorities: 'imperceptibly, there is a kind of influence' (Cook *et al.* 2016: 67). Most likely, the embassy official did not intervene to free the illegal immigrants because he knew that their bribes would get the same result. But serious actions against the migrants such as those related to the galamsey crisis have triggered very aggressive Chinese official responses. This crisis also reveals the support received by entrepreneurial migrants from subnational entities in China, which, at times, may be more important than that of the embassy. The government of Shanglin County in Guangxi Province actively supported gold miners from that region who settled in Ghana. It closed its eyes to the illegal nature of their activities and financing, provided travel documents, made arrangements for the export of heavy equipment, sent special envoys to Ghana to deter anti-miners actions and to protect them from violence, arranged their repatriation, and made efforts to recover their lost property (Hess and Aidoo 2016: 315, 321–322). China's state-owned enterprises are also part of the overseas Chinese state. As shown at the beginning of this subchapter, they have constructed numerous infrastructure projects on Ghanaian soil. When contracts come to an end, most of them continue to be active in the local construction market. Chinese entrepreneurial migrants typically become their subcontractors and exploit in various ways the social networks created by these firms. There are migrants who systematically avoid the overseas Chinese state because it is 'unnecessary for business,' as well as 'over-bureaucratic and often low-efficient.' But even they are willing to do business with state-owned enterprises if invited (Wang and Zhan 2019: 19–20).

Such interactions are complemented by those taking place within formal and informal Chinese networks that provide information and business opportunities. TV programs and online forums from China, as well as diasporic social media, represent another instrument that keeps the migrants in Beijing's orbit. Against a backdrop of lack of integration in the local society and vulnerability-related insecurity, all these interactions create the conditions for the migrants to feel connected with China's 'great rejuvenation' process and to accept its deterritorialized nationalism. Indeed, fieldwork done among Chinese 'new' migrants in Ghana has never shown signs of an emerging cosmopolitan identity. Instead, they are proud of their Chinese cultural identity and make a clear connection between their economic success and the benefits of being Chinese. Nationalism has become 'an effective mechanism for reembedding themselves into an imagined de-territorialized "Chinese" community.' A process is at work that 'retains [migrants'] emotional ties with China and reproduces "Chineseness" in their everyday life' (*Ibid.*, 17, 18, 21–22). China's state transnationalism has been successful in making the 'new' Chinese entrepreneurial migrants in Ghana adopt a deterritorial Chinese identity. Accordingly, they perceive the 'party-state' of their country of origin as the central axis of their life both publicly and privately (*Ibid.*, 8, 22–23). These migrants live in a remote country and a 'low-end' social reality that the government in Beijing often cannot influence. They have their private interests and autonomous decision-making processes. Both result in specific adaptation strategies that have little to do with the Chinese state. And yet, they remain under Beijing's influence. In turn, 'this contributes to the coherence of the Chinese-centered globalization "from below" and, implicitly, to its alignment with the global objectives set by China's leaders' (Tudoroiu 2022: 153).

Galamsey and Social Conditionality

Most of the time, the Chinese entrepreneurial migrants act autonomously; but the general framework of their actions is controlled by the government in Beijing. They are actors of a globalization intended to bring about a Chinese international order. As such, any impactful action that prevents them from performing the role of a key pillar of China's globalization 'from below' is unacceptable to the Asian global power. Ghana provides an excellent example as domestic factors compelled its Chinese-socialized government to infringe China's social norm. Police officers in the Makola Market may arrest a handful of illegal Chinese migrants for some hours to extract bribes; nobody in Beijing will care. But the galamsey episode shows that, when the political elites in power of a BRI partner adopt *legitimate* large-scale measures targeting Chinese entrepreneurial migrants, swift and harsh retaliation ensues. This suggests that the respect of Beijing's social norm represents in fact a strong form of conditionality imposed on partner states in the Global South.

Historically, a part of Ghana was called the Gold Coast simply because it produced gold. This still is the case. A specific term exists, galamsey (which comes from 'gather them and sell') that designates the mainly unregistered and illegal activity of 50,000 to 200,000 people who practice small-scale artisanal – or 'subsistence' – gold mining. They may use explosives or highly toxic substances such as cyanide and mercury, which pollute the water and destroy soil layers and the forest (Hess and Aidoo 2016: 301). In 1989 and 2006, laws were adopted that introduced a lengthy and very expensive process of registration and licensing. Because this activity is poverty-driven, less than 30 percent of miners chose to register. Illegal ones are tolerated by the state because they use rudimentary methods; mechanization is very limited. In addition to locals, immigrants from Burkina Faso and Togo also practice galamsey (Crawford and Botchwey 2017: 447–449). Massive change came with the Chinese. More specifically, it was a group of ethnic Zhuang people from Shanglin County in Guangxi Province that, during the 1980s, developed alluvial mining machinery fit for galamsey conditions. This was hardly artisanal: equipment with exotic names such as *changfa* or crushing machine, the wash plant or trommel machine, water platforms, and more common pumps and suction equipment turned gold extraction into a highly effective industrial process. Shanglin miners used it in various parts of China and eventually all over the Global South (Botchwey *et al.* 2019: 313–314). In 2006, they reached Ghana. A trommel machine needs eight operators. Teams of eight miners were formed back home. Each of them took a US $25,000 bank loan and borrowed money from friends, relatives, and sometimes loan sharks. With the assistance of the government of Shanglin County, they bought and shipped to Ghana the necessary equipment that included excavators and bulldozers (Hess and Aidoo 2016: 314; Crawford and Botchwey 2017: 450). Then, they entered the African country as tourists, by bribing immigration officers, or illegally via Togo. Foreigners are not allowed to mine or purchase surfaces of less than 25 acres in Ghana, but the miners took advantage of large-scale corruption to bribe public officials, politicians, as well as tribal chiefs. Gold extraction was so profitable that they returned to China as US dollar millionaires, impressing neighbors with luxury cars and expensive houses. They 'spread the word that there were fortunes to be made mining in the faraway West African nation,' which triggered a gold rush (Hess and Aidoo 2016: 314–315; Crawford and Botchwey 2017: 449–450). By 2013, 50,000 Chinese nationals – two-thirds of whom came from Shanglin – had set up no less than 2,000 mining operations in Ghana and were 'dominat[ing] the supply chain of illegal small-scale mining with their financial, technical, managerial acumen, the sale and transfer of gold proceeds, and political patronage' (Antwi-Boateng and Akudugu 2020: 135; Botchwey *et al.* 2019: 313–314). In 2011, they were responsible for 40 percent of the country's gold production (Hess and Aidoo 2016: 315).

This is an interesting example of an activity pertaining to the informal transnational economy that enriched the repertoire of the Chinese-centered globalization 'from below.' In part, nobody among Ghana's political elites in power intended to antagonize the government in Beijing by taking action against its nationals. This cautious behavior is a consequence of Chinese socialization and, therefore, an effect of China's normative power. At the same time, the miners shaped understandings of 'normal' by bribing central and local elites and bureaucrats. These groups accepted the informal – in fact, fully illegal – activities of the Chinese migrants as legitimate. Such results would have been difficult to achieve in, say, a Scandinavian country. This is why the Chinese entrepreneurial migrants choose countries with poor governance. Ghana is one of them: there, 'the informality and corruption characteristic of neopatrimonialism remains predominant over legal-rational structures'; public office is an instrument of private enrichment (Crawford and Botchwey 2017: 444). The fact that informal activities are perceived as legitimate – even if this is done through corruption and is limited to elites and bureaucrats – is similar to the situation of the non-hegemonic globalization 'from below' where normative power is produced and projected by the migrants. The combination of China's and migrants' normative power was so effective that a 'culture of impunity' emerged, with the miners fully protected by Ghanaians in authority (Crawford and Botchwey 2017: 444). They even illegally purchased arms from the police for self-protection and hunting (Botchwey *et al.* 2019: 316). It goes without saying that they hardly cared to protect the environment. Two thousand mining operations that made use of toxic chemicals and heavy machinery had a dramatic impact on the local ecosystem. The Chinese migrants also put locals out of business. The latter's artisanal methods could not compete with the former's technology. As an effect, rural poverty increased. The newcomers started to be perceived as 'usurping critical resources that [we]re meant for locals in these low-income village communities' (Aidoo 2016: 64; Hess and Aidoo 2016: 316; Crawford and Botchwey 2017: 445); violence ensued. Armed Ghanaians began to rob the miners, who armed themselves and fought back. Violent and occasionally deadly clashes became common after mid-2012 (Hess and Aidoo 2016: 317; Crawford and Botchwey 2017: 450). The Ghanaian authorities were not bothered, but the media started to present extensively both the violent incidents and the increasingly frequent 'protests from local youths, farmers, mining activists and environmental groups' (Crawford and Botchwey 2017: 452–453). The Ghanaian society soon became very hostile to the Chinese miners and the government in Accra that allowed them to systematically infringe the law. When, in May 2013, the country was outraged by the killing of two Ghanaians at the hands of Chinese miners, President Mahama understood that his legitimacy was at stake. To restore confidence in his government, he promised to bring 'sanity' to gold mining by arresting and deporting illegal foreigners. In response to calls from alarmed Chinese migrants, the local governments of both Shanglin County and Guangxi Province sent 14 officials to Ghana to negotiate a compromise (Hess and Aidoo 2016: 317–319). Public pressure, however, compelled the government in Accra to ignore them. In June 2013, an army and police operation led to the deportation of 4,592 Chinese miners. In the process, mining equipment and facilities were set on fire. Armed locals took the opportunity to beat, rob, and at times kill the panicked Chinese. Protest demonstrations in Shanglin County led to the dispatch of a new Chinese delegation to Accra where it obtained the release of arrested Chinese and paid for their airfare to China. Many other Chinese miners also fled Ghana (*Ibid.*, 319–320; Crawford and Botchwey 2017: 453; Botchwey *et al.* 2019: 316).

This harsh move restored the legitimacy of the Ghanaian government domestically but did not represent the end of the crisis. The leadership in Beijing did not accept the claim that nobody in Accra is anti-Chinese and that all foreign illegal miners had been expelled (much smaller numbers of gold miners from Niger, Togo, and Russia had indeed shared the fate of the Chinese ones). China's social norm – which prevents BRI partners from regulating the inflow or economic activities of Chinese entrepreneurial migrants – had clearly been infringed. The fact that China's miners were illegal migrants performing illegal activities on Ghanaian soil was irrelevant. The Chinese government took 'irresponsive and downright retaliatory' actions that observers identified as a form of coercive diplomacy (Hess and Aidoo 2016: 313, 323). At that time, the US $3 billion Chinese loan was still presented by both sides as a historical contribution to Ghana's socio-economic development. It was used to finance a total of 12 projects ranging from railways and fishing harbors to oil and gas infrastructure. The government in Beijing immediately stalled payments and announced that it would change the loan's terms. It also made it more difficult for Ghanaian nationals to obtain Chinese visas. This created a serious problem for over 20,000 small traders that need to travel to Guangzhou to buy the goods they resell in Ghana. Worldwide, journalists and politicians hostile to China spoke of Chinese neocolonialism, questioned its win-win, South-South cooperation discourse, argued that its actions did not respect the non-interference principle and were 'threatening Chinese foreign policy priorities in Ghana' and 'soiling China's image' (Hess and Aidoo 2016: 323; Hess and Aidoo 2015: 52). But the leaders in Beijing were not impressed. They taught a lesson 'to Ghanaian and, more generally, BRI partners: he who hurts on a significant scale the interests of Chinese entrepreneurial migrants will be punished, even if their presence and activities are illegal and outrageous' (Tudoroiu 2022: 158). The Sino-Ghanaian partnership was soon restored, but successive governments in Accra fully understood the danger of infringing China's social norm. 'This is why there have been so few post-2013 official actions against Chinese nationals in Belt and Road countries' (*Ibid*.), which, in turn, enhanced the expansion of the Chinese-centered globalization 'from below.'

To summarize, the Ghanaian example is representative of China's pattern of action in a large part of the Global South. A strong partnership has developed that relies heavily on the interest of local political elites in large Chinese loan-financed and constructed prestige infrastructure projects, which increase their political legitimacy and electoral support. The use of these projects as material incentives combined with close and frequent interactions ensure the Chinese socialization of Ghana's political elites in power. Accordingly, successive governments in Accra have accepted Beijing's norms. The economic normative subset led to Ghana's joining of the Chinese-centered globalization 'from above.' The social norm had the same effect with respect to the Chinese-centered globalization 'from below.' Some of the consequences of the resulting increased Chinese presence, however, were perceived as very negative by Ghanaian society. Unlike the political elites, its members were not socialized. They had no reason to ignore China's predatory policies illustrated by the US $3 billion loan, the invasion of Chinese petty traders vocally condemned by GUTA, or the illegal galamsey activities of Chinese miners. Much of this discontent was related to Chinese entrepreneurial migrants and reflects a 'from below' rejection of China's 'from below' globalization. The resulting elites–society gap was so important that the very legitimacy of the pro-Chinese government in Accra came to be questioned. President Mahama took the difficult decision to repress the illegal activities of Chinese nationals whose presence on Ghanaian soil was also illegal. China retaliated harshly, showing that its social norm – which prevents the regulation of the inflow and economic activities of its entrepreneurial migrants – represents in fact a strong form of conditionality. After the galamsey episode, governments in Ghana and the rest of the BRI partner states fully understood the cost of acting against the Chinese migrants, which, in turn, reinforced the Chinese-centered globalization 'from below.' Beijing's protective actions, however, are effective only as long as the state level is concerned. The Ghanaian example is important because it shows how anti-Chinese feelings can translate into 'low end' migrant-hostile agency that China and the Chinese-socialized local elites cannot control. But even in this case, the vulnerability of the Chinese entrepreneurial migrants leads to insecurity, which makes them accept the deterritorialized nationalism that the overseas Chinese state tries to impose through overseas Chinese work and united front work. Ultimately, the 'weak Chinese and strong Africans' situation visible in Ghana (Lam 2015: 11) helps increase

China's influence on its migrants, which enhances the coherence of the Chinese-centered globalization 'from below.'

5.4 Defining a Complex Globalization

The Chinese-centered globalization 'from below' presented in this chapter can be defined as

> the massive transnational flow of people and goods that is enacted by Chinese entrepreneurial migrants, targets mainly Belt and Road Initiative partner states, relies on business and social ethnic networks, and is based in part on informal transactions. Critically, this process is in large measure entangled with China's policies and projection of normative power intended to construct a Chinese-centered international order.
>
> (Tudoroiu 2022: 2)

Nobody will question the 'from below' nature of this phenomenon enacted by small and weak entrepreneurial migrants. Its informal character is equally undeniable, as migrants' economic activities bring together – and often blur the differences between – legal, semi-legal, and illegal dimensions. What many scholars still do not fully acknowledge is the importance of the role played by the Chinese state, which turns the China-centered transnational flows into a globalization 'from below' different from the non-hegemonic one. Anthropologists, in particular, concentrate on the individual level and tend to come to the conclusion that the Chinese entrepreneurial migrants 'have come to Africa with little or no connection to or support from large firms or the national government' (Hess and Aidoo 2016: 321). They enact 'a spontaneous movement of people'; 'our research has found no evidence of any formal linkage with the Chinese government' (Botchwey et al. 2019: 314). 'Far from being a "silent army" promoting China's interests in Africa,' these migrants 'are mostly independent actors with little or no support from or even contact with the Chinese government': 'this is not a state-driven phenomenon, but rather a story of individuals' (Cook et al. 2016: 61). They may 'enjoy tangible benefits from the expanding presence of overseas Chinese state,' but this is nothing more than 'an unintended consequence' (Wang and Zhan 2019: 8). Moreover, 'independent' migrants such as the galamsey miners in Ghana

> present Beijing with a classic principal-agent dilemma, since in the implementation of its foreign policy in Africa, the national leadership relies on highly autonomous agents with narrow interests that often diverge from its own. (...) As a consequence, the policies advocated by national officials can become heavily distorted.
>
> (Hess and Aidoo 2016: 310)

This is indeed a 'story of individuals' who, at times, create undesired and embarrassing complications for the government in Beijing. I am far from denying their autonomy. The agency of the Chinese entrepreneurial migrants is influenced by the same kind of individual aspirations of upward social mobility, subjective personal plans and ambitions, and even adventurous entrepreneurial decisions as those of the 'ant traders' involved in the non-hegemonic globalization 'from below.' They may also face situations – such as that leading to their perceived vulnerability in Ghana – where they have to rely on specific forms of agency, which are inaccessible to a state no matter its resources and will to intervene. But the undeniable existence of private interests and autonomous decision-making processes resulting in specific adaptation strategies coexists with the equally undeniable influence of the Chinese state. The domestic socio-economic conditions, discourse, and policy frameworks that 'spontaneously' took migrants to the Global South were created by China's government. It is the highly effective overseas Chinese work and united front work of the huge bureaucratic apparatus of the overseas Chinese state that, through the use of state transnationalism, have constructed the deterritorial Chinese identity of the entrepreneurial migrants. They may be autonomous, but their very identity keeps them in Beijing's orbit and compels them to respect hundreds of Chinese laws that regulate their duties. At the same time, much of their economic success is due to the acceptance by the political elites of the BRI partner states of China's social norm that, as shown by the galamsey crisis, often represents a strong form of conditionality. Lebanese, East Indian, or Nigerian traders lack this type of protection, which explains in large part their inability to compete with the 'new' Chinese entrepreneurial migrants. Beijing's manipulative political and economic strategies create opportunities and constraints for its migrants that clearly place them outside the non-hegemonic globalization 'from below,' which is by definition independent from – and hostile to – state control. The Chinese-centered globalization 'from below' is, therefore, a separate globalization. Moreover, it represents a hegemonic construct. Indeed, the Chinese state is a hegemon with respect to both its entrepreneurial migrants – who are autonomous but in no way independent – and the Belt and Road Initiative states, which accept these migrants due to the Chinese socialization of their political elites in power. Accordingly, the Chinese-centered globalization 'from below' can be conceived of as a Constructivist international regime comprising the BRI partner states that, under Beijing's hegemony, cooperate in view of ensuring the free inflow of Chinese entrepreneurial migrants and their unrestricted economic activities. Stephen Krasner's classical definition of an international regime correctly describes the set of principles, norms, rules, and decision-making procedures around which the expectations of China and its partners converge with respect to the Chinese entrepreneurial migrants. The Constructivist version of the theory is preferable to Kindleberger's or Keohane's Realist and Neoliberal ones because it emphasizes the existence of fundamental rules that shape the cognition and interests of member states while providing legitimacy and embeddedness to the regime; China's normative set, which includes the social norm, plays exactly this role. The Constructivist approach also emphasizes the internalization of regime-related cooperation, which impacts cognition and interests (see Hasenclever *et al.* 1997: 156); this is done through the process of Chinese socialization of the BRI political elites. Such a regime may take decades to reach full maturity. Visibly, this is not yet the case: the galamsey episode shows that the process of internalization has not advanced enough to make the use of punishments unnecessary. Moreover, the fact that only the limited and reversible Type I socialization is involved (see Subchapter 2.3) makes this process vulnerable to internal crises and exogenous shocks; these may combine if the United States launches a coherent anti-Chinese offensive in the Global South (for possible scenarios see Tudoroiu 2022: 314–317). Yet, for the time being, the Constructivist international regime has led to the development of a Chinese-centered globalization 'from below' that is successful in associating the 'from above' hegemony of a global power with the 'from below' actorness of its entrepreneurial migrants.

Hegemony has never been disinterested and the Chinese one is hardly an exception. In fact, Beijing's critics go as far as claiming that 'in foreign policy, as in all things, China is the distilled essence of self-interest' (*The Economist*, October 4, 2018). In the case of the non-hegemonic globalization 'from below,' the list of beneficiaries is limited to 'ant traders' and their clients. The Chinese-centered globalization 'from below' is similarly profitable to the Chinese entrepreneurial migrants and their clients, but also – and perhaps on a larger scale – to its Chinese hegemon. The latter falls into the category of states that use their diaspora 'as a resource' (Röschenthaler and Socpa 2017: 180; Kokko 2017: 368; Suryadinata 2017a). The government in Beijing is 'extracting obligations' (Gamlen 2006: 13) from its migrants that are both economic and political. Economically, China's benefits start with diminishing unemployment and alleviating related social tensions domestically as the excess of labor is sent abroad (Cardenal and Araújo 2013: 45–46). Revenue is also generated (Nyíri 2005: 156). Chinese entrepreneurial migrants send most of their profit back home; consequently, China has become one of the largest recipients of migrant remittances (Röschenthaler and Socpa 2017: 180). When Deng's reforms took off, overseas Chinese were at the origin of 60 percent of the US $501.47 billion invested in China between 1979 and 2003 (Guotu 2012: 39). More recently, they have been instrumental in providing knowledge resources such as high technology and facilitating the expansion of Chinese firms on international markets (Xiang 2003: 27; Thunø 2018: 187). Politically, the 'from below' globalization reinforces China's transformation into a truly global power while spreading its civilization (Yang 2011a: 109–110). The massive presence of Chinese nationals generates a microcosm of interactions in the host society. When problems emerge, the embassy intervenes in various ways. Basically, due to its migrants, China becomes an actor in the domestic affairs of recipient Global South countries. The Chinese leadership also has a purely political objective: it 'pays considerable attention to spreading propaganda with the help of the overseas Chinese communities' (Barabantseva 2011: 132). The members of these communities that are most responsive to overseas Chinese work and united front work are required to play 'a cautious political role': they should present to local audiences the positions and actions of the government in Beijing 'in order to improve the political climate for China' (Thunø 2018: 187). Since 2005, Chinese migrants are officially expected to become Beijing's 'public diplomats.' In 2011, the 2011–2015 five-year Plan for the Development of National Overseas Chinese Work provided details of this activity (*Ibid.*, 194). The overseas Chinese state makes considerable efforts to use the overseas Chinese in fighting the Western 'misrepresentation' of China's behavior toward Tibet, Xinjiang, Taiwan (Barabantseva 2011: 105; Thunø 2018: 194, 196–198) and, more recently, Hong Kong. Chinese migrants are also mobilized to fight protests abroad directed against China's human rights abuses. Even in remote Fiji, the Chinese community took action in 2004 against several newly arrived Falun Gong members who were expelled under its pressure (Yang 2011a: 117). This is illustrative of Beijing's efforts to 'engage in transnational politics' prominent migrants, both 'new' and 'old,' who are expected to – and, often, do – act as political liaisons between their countries of origin and residence (Wang and Zhan 2019: 13). This mainly takes the form of lobbying. All over the BRI, it is through Chinese migrant middlemen that China often initiates and conducts much of its interactions with the local political and economic elites. These middlemen match China's capital and development assistance with local political patronage. This is part of a clientelistic strategy that often takes the form of 'predatory clientelism' (Nyíri 2011: 147–148, 150): the concerned migrants construct a complex web of obscure political and economic relationships that brings them considerable material advantages but also represents a decisive contribution to the Chinese socialization of local political elites. They

> may help agents of the Chinese state to identify the most appropriate material incentives – ranging from bribes to trade concessions or prestige infrastructure projects – to be used in a specific context; may open the doors of key local recipients for Chinese diplomats or heads of state-owned companies delivering those incentives; and, more generally, may clear the way for – or even participate in – secret diplomacy meetings that (…) help create appropriate conditions for socialization.
> (Tudoroiu 2022: 122–123)

Such migrants also become key vectors of the united front work that allows for the transformation of members of the local political elites into advocates of China's interests. In turn, these local politicians help to socialize their peers. Successful socialization leads to the respect of the Chinese social norm, which enhances the Chinese-centered globalization 'from below.' But Beijing's other norms are also accepted by local political elites, which is beneficial to the Chinese-centered globalization 'from above.' This brings the discussion to the important aspect of the virtuous circle formed by these two globalizations and, more generally, to the relationships between China's globalization 'from below' and the other globalizations.

Interacting Globalizations and Normative Power

In fact, the intertwining of the two Chinese globalizations needs little further comment. Both this chapter and Subchapter 2.3 have repeatedly mentioned their common reliance on the Chinese socialization of political elites in power in the BRI partner states. This process is, in principle, part of the 'from above' globalization. But its success also leads to the acceptance of the social norm, which enhances China's 'from below' globalization. Its actors include prominent Chinese entrepreneurial migrants who, as shown in the previous paragraph, help to further socialize the local political elites. The (virtuous) circle is closed: the 'from below' globalization enhances the 'from above' one that helped it to take off. This, of course, is not an accident. The two Chinese globalizations are part of Beijing's wider strategy to construct a new international order. Their coordination is a fundamental precondition for the success of this ambitious plan. The highly coherent activities of China's huge bureaucratic apparatus in support of the intertwined globalizations suggest that this coordination is one of its main priorities.

The Chinese-centered globalization 'from below' challenges the American-led international order indirectly – by enhancing China's globalization 'from above' – but also directly: similar to the non-hegemonic globalization 'from below,' it represents a form of resistance against the Western-centered globalization 'from above' that supports and is supported by the present international order. Indeed, the informal transnational economy of the Chinese entrepreneurial migrants is similar to that of the non-Chinese 'ant traders' presented in the previous chapter. It represents an identical 'response from below to the dispossessive effects of neoliberalism' (Gago 2014/2017: 68; 2012: 77). The Chinese traders sell the same Guangdong-made cheap goods to the same poor clientele as the street peddler from Mexico City who argued that the transnational trade he was involved in 'is not a problem, it is a solution. The problem was created elsewhere; we are solving it' (Mathews and Alba Vega 2012: 2). They take to the Global South the same merchandise as the African petty merchant who stated that 'what I do is good for Africa' (Yang 2011b: 115). They offer to large marginalized social groups unable to access the Western globalization 'from above' a poorer but nevertheless acceptable alternative: a globalization 'from below' that proposes the same counterfeit modernity as La Salada's 'ant traders' (see Subchapters 4.3 and 4.7). In the process, the Chinese entrepreneurial traders infringe laws and rules, bribe officials, sell pirated goods, and *de facto* fight Neoliberalism as much as their counterparts from the non-hegemonic globalization 'from below.' Given their numbers and the scale of their trade, this is a challenge that the Western-centered globalization 'from above' cannot easily ignore.

Having the same 'enemy,' however, does not turn the Chinese-centered and non-hegemonic globalizations 'from below' into allies. On the contrary: they compete for the same markets and are therefore engaged in a merciless struggle for economic survival. The Chinese entrepreneurial migrants have two key advantages over their non-Chinese counterparts. On the one hand, the Chinese socialization of the political elites of BRI partner states leads to the respect of Beijing's social norm. As an effect, China's migrants and their globalization are not concerned by at least a part of the restrictive policies and measures that limit the inflow of traders and their informal activities in the case of the non-hegemonic globalization 'from below.' On the other hand, comparative advantages result from easier access to production centers in Guandong and elsewhere in China, credits from Chinese banks, and other supportive measures taken by the Chinese state. Due to all these factors, the Chinese entrepreneurial migrants are able to aggressively outcompete their rivals. This is why, in Ghana, they have succeeded in taking much of the market from Nigerian, Lebanese, and Indian traders (Dankwah and Amoah 2019: 67) that are typical actors of the non-hegemonic globalization 'from below.' It should be added that the leadership in Beijing is obviously aware of the competition between its traders and foreign ones. Because it uses the Chinese-centered globalization 'from below' as an important instrument in its efforts to construct a new international order, the Chinese state cannot afford to be neutral with respect to this competition. It does its best to support the Chinese entrepreneurial migrants; and, as shown by the example of African traders in Guangzhou discussed in Subchapter 4.6, it has even started to repress their competitors. Of course, this has to be done cautiously in order to preserve China's position as the world's workshop. In Chocolate City, where the issue of society-related tensions is given priority, the solution has been to allow short-term visits by African petty merchants who come to buy goods, but to replace resident African middlemen with Chinese ones. In this way, a very profitable segment of the trade chain was taken away from the non-hegemonic globalization 'from below.' More generally, it can be argued that 'the leaders in Beijing perceive the interaction between their globalization "from below" and the non-hegemonic one as a zero-sum game: "it's our migrants or theirs"' (Tudoroiu 2022: 301). One might be tempted to speculate that, within a hypothetical future Chinese-led international order, the economic survival of the 'ant traders' of the non-hegemonic globalization 'from below' could be much more difficult than under the present Western-led order. Today, they are repressed by Neoliberal states and international agencies that also fight the Chinese informal transnational economy. Tomorrow, they could be repressed by pro-Chinese states and international agencies that would overtly support the Chinese entrepreneurial migrants. This is just a scenario; but the present progress of the Chinese-centered globalization 'from below' already exposes the 'ant traders' to the harsh competition of Chinese rivals. While the lack of quantitative data makes the magnitude of this process uncertain, the non-hegemonic globalization 'from below' is clearly shrinking under the pressure of the Chinese-centered one.

All globalizations are the result of projections of normative power. In the case of the Western- and Chinese-centered globalizations 'from above,' the normative power is produced by their respective hegemons. The counter-hegemonic and non-hegemonic globalizations 'from below' rely on the normative power of their small and weak actors. The Chinese-centered globalization 'from below' is more interesting: it combines the normative power produced by China with that of the Chinese entrepreneurial migrants. The former targets the political elites and leads to the acceptance of the social norm and the protection of the migrants. The latter comes from the legitimacy acquired by the Chinese migrants themselves as they respond to the needs of their clientele; their informal activities are accepted by the host society, a process that shapes understandings of 'normal' and therefore produces normative power similar to the case of the non-hegemonic globalization 'from below.' The problem is that this double projection of Chinese normative power is accompanied by tensions. The Chinese socialized elites redefine the national interest in ways beneficial to China but detrimental to certain domestic socio-economic groups, which often results in serious elites-society gaps. The Chinese entrepreneurial migrants similarly frustrate local groups, starting with the traders they outcompete. The Ghanaian case study shows that 40.4 percent of Ghana's nationals 'see Chinese small businesses as helpful to local economic development and also a source of problems for local people' (Hess and Aidoo 2014: 141). Moreover, the galamsey episode is an example of how migrants can effectively project normative power toward narrow socio-economic groups such as that of political elites, bureaucrats, and tribal leaders relevant to their economic activities. This was very beneficial in the short term but led to widespread frustration in the society. Out of the total projection of normative power in Ghana associated with the Chinese-centered globalization 'from below,' the part coming from the legitimacy acquired by the Chinese entrepreneurial migrants is quite limited. Even this part creates tensions, which the 'ant traders' of the non-hegemonic globalization 'from below' also face. But in the Chinese case, tensions related to the elites-society gap have to be added, as well as – in certain cases – galamsey-type ones. To summarize, this globalization 'from below' relies significantly on the 'from above' normative power of the Chinese state and is plagued by serious tensions. The latter may lead to outright violence such as that targeting the Chinese galamsey miners during the July 2013 crackdown; or to the more subtle but permanent perception of vulnerability experienced by all Chinese entrepreneurial migrants in Ghana. The paradox is that nothing of this should happen: the normative power associated with the two Chinese-centered globalizations is based on *guanxi*, the relationality centered on the 'harmonious respect for the other' (Kavalski 2018: 94) that commits all actors involved in social interactions to appropriately respond to social demands and expectations (Kavalski 2017: 151; see Subchapter 2.3). Yet, serious tensions and conflicts do exist due to the exclusionary character of the relationality promoted by China and its entrepreneurial migrants. *Guanxi* 'implies both a propensity and a capacity for living *with* and *in* ambiguity' (Kavalski 2018: 95). It replaces the respect for formal rules with a predilection for non-transparent deals that often involve morally questionable practices. From bribing customs officers to offering prestige infrastructure projects to ruling politicians, relationality-based methods are very effective for the economic success of China's entrepreneurial migrants. But they damage good governance and frustrate large socio-economic groups. From the point of view of host societies, the Chinese-centered globalization 'from below' 'does not represent a friendly and harmonious people-to-people cooperative process that is beneficial to all parties involved' (Tudoroiu 2022: 311). The situation is much better on the Chinese side. Globalizations in general and globalizations 'from below' in particular are very complex processes that are in no way easy to control. Still, despite the autonomy of the Chinese entrepreneurial migrants and the extreme diversity of conditions in their countries of residence, the leadership in Beijing has been most successful in steering and shaping the Chinese-centered globalization 'from below' and using it in its ambitious plan to construct a Chinese-led international order.

References

Aidoo, Richard (2016) 'The Political Economy of Galamsey and Anti-Chinese Sentiment in Ghana,' *African Studies Quarterly*, 16(3–4), pp. 55–72.

Amoah, Lloyd G. Adu (2016) 'China, Architecture and Ghana's Spaces: Concrete Signs of a Soft Chinese Imperium?,' *Journal of Asian and African Studies*, 51(2), pp. 238–255.

Antwi-Boateng, Osman, and Mamudu Abunga Akudugu (2020) 'Golden Migrants: The Rise and Impact of Illegal Chinese Small-Scale Mining in Ghana,' *Politics & Policy*, 48(1), pp. 135–167.

Bachulska, Alicja, Una Aleksandra Bērziņa-Čerenkova, and Nina Pejić (2020) 'We the People? The Challenges of Societal Relations with China,' in Ivana Karásková (ed.) *Empty Shell No More: China's Growing Footprint in Central and Eastern Europe*, Policy Paper, Prague: China Observers in Central and Eastern Europe (CHOICE), pp. 57–72.

Barabantseva, Elena (2011) *Overseas Chinese, Ethnic Minorities and Nationalism. De-Centering China*, London and New York: Routledge.

Barabantseva, Elena (2012) 'Who Are "Overseas Chinese Ethnic Minorities"? China's Search for Transnational Ethnic Unity,' *Modern China*, 38(1), pp. 78–109.

Boateng, Edward (2020) '60 Years of Ghana-China Diplomatic Relations: A Journey Worth Celebrating,' *China Global Television Network*, July 5, https://news.

cgtn.com/news/2020-07-05/Ghana-China-diplomatic-relations-A-journey-worth-celebrating-RStwASQigo/index.html

Botchwey, Gabriel, Gordon Crawford, Nicholas Loubere, and Jixia Lu (2019) 'South-South Irregular Migration: The Impacts of China's Informal Gold Rush in Ghana,' *International Migration*, 57(4), pp. 310–328.

Brady, Anne-Marie (2017) 'Magic Weapons: China's Political Influence Activities under Xi Jinping,' paper presented at the conference on *The Corrosion of Democracy under China's Global Influence*, Arlington, Virginia, USA, September 16–17, https://www.wilsoncenter.org/article/magic-weapons-chinas-political-influence-activities-under-xi-jinping

Brady, Anne-Marie (2018) 'China in Xi's "New Era": New Zealand and the CCP'S "Magic Weapons",' *Journal of Democracy*, 29(2), pp. 68–75.

Business News of Sunday, September 2, 2018, 'Ghana, China sign 8 Co-operation Agreements, MoUs,' https://www.ghanaweb.com/GhanaHomePage/business/Ghana-China-sign-8-Co-operation-Agreements-MoUs-681569

Cardenal, Juan Pablo, and Heriberto Araújo (2013) *China's Silent Army: The Pioneers, Traders, Fixers and Workers Who are Remaking the World in Beijing's Image*, New York: Crown Publishers, epub edition (translation of *La silenciosa conquista china*, Barcelona: Editorial Crítica, 2011).

Chau, Donovan C. (2014) *Exploiting Africa: The Influence of Maoist China in Algeria, Ghana, and Tanzania*, Annapolis, Maryland: Naval Institute Press.

Chee-Beng, Tan (2012) 'Introduction,' in Tan Chee-Beng (ed.) *Routledge Handbook of the Chinese Diaspora*, London and New York: Routledge, pp. 1–12.

Chin, Ku Sup, and David Smith (2015) 'A Reconceptualization of State Transnationalism: South Korea as an Illustrative Case,' *Global Networks. A Journal of Transnational Affairs*, 15(1), pp. 78–98.

Chipaike, Ronald, and Paul Henri Bischoff (2018) 'A Challenge to Conventional Wisdom: Locating Agency in Angola's and Ghana's Economic Engagements with China,' *Journal of Asian and African Studies*, 53(7), pp. 1002–1017.

Chong, Ja Ian (2018) 'The Rise of China and the Overseas Chinese by Leo Suryadinata,' *Journal of the Malaysian Branch of the Royal Asiatic Society*, 91(1), pp. 151–154.

Chow-Bing, Ngeow, and Tan Chee-Beng (2018) 'Cultural Ties and States' Interests: Malaysian Chinese and China's Rise,' in Bernard P. Wong and Tan Chee-Beng (eds.) *China's Rise and the Chinese Overseas*, London and New York: Routledge, pp. 96–116.

Communications Bureau (2018) 'Ghana Aiming to Replicate China's Success Story" - President Akufo-Addo,' *The Presidency - Republic of Ghana*, September 4, http://presidency.gov.gh/index.php/briefing-room/news-style-2/809-ghana-aiming-to-replicate-china-s-success-story-president-akufo-addo

Cook, Seth, Jixia Lu, Henry Tugendhat, and Dawit Alemu (2016) 'Chinese Migrants in Africa: Facts and Fictions from the Agri-Food Sector in Ethiopia and Ghana,' *World Development*, 81, pp. 61–70.

Crawford, Gordon, and Gabriel Botchwey (2017) 'Conflict, Collusion and Corruption in Small-Scale Gold Mining: Chinese Miners and the State in Ghana,' *Commonwealth & Comparative Politics*, 55(4), pp. 444–470.

Dankwah, Kwaku Opoku, and Marko Valenta (2019) 'Chinese Entrepreneurial Migrants in Ghana: Socioeconomic Impacts and Ghanaian Trader Attitudes,' *The Journal of Modern African Studies*, 57(1), pp. 1–29.

Dankwah, Kwaku Opoku, and Padmore Adusei Amoah (2019) 'Gauging the Dispositions between Indigenes, Chinese and Other Immigrant Traders in Ghana: towards a More Inclusive Society,' *Asian Ethnicity*, 20(1), pp. 67–84.

Ding, Sheng (2015) 'Engaging Diaspora via Charm Offensive and Indigenised Communication: An Analysis of China's Diaspora Engagement Policies in the Xi Era,' *Politics*, 35(3–4), pp. 230–244.

Duara, Prasenjit (2003) 'Nationalism and Transnationalism in the Globalisation of China,' *China Report*, 39(1), pp. 1–19.

Duggan, Niall (2020) *Competition and Compromise among Chinese Actors in Africa: A Bureaucratic Politics Study of Chinese Foreign Policy Actors*, Singapore: Palgrave Macmillan.

Ellis, R. Evan (2012) 'Learning the Ropes,' *Americas Quarterly*, 6(4), pp. 28–33.

Ellis, R. Evan (2014) *China on the Ground in Latin America. Challenges for the Chinese and Impacts on the Region*, New York: Palgrave Macmillan.

Embassy of the People's Republic of China in the Republic of Ghana (2020) 'Introduction of China-Ghana Relations,' http://gh.china-embassy.org/eng/zjgx/zzwl/t177920.htm

Fage, John D., and Donna J. Maier (2020) 'Ghana: History,' *Britannica*, https://www.britannica.com/place/Ghana/Contact-with-Europe-and-its-effects

Fitzgerald, John (2018) 'China in Xi's "New Era": Overstepping Down Under,' *Journal of Democracy*, 29(2), pp. 59–67.

Freeman, Carla P. (ed.) (2015) *Handbook on China and Developing Countries*, Cheltenham; Northampton, MA: Edward Elgar Publishing.

French, Howard W. (2014) *China's Second Continent. How a Million Migrants Are Building a New Empire in Africa*, New York: Alfred A. Knopf.

Fulton, Jonathan (2016) 'China's Strong Arm: Protecting Citizens and Assets Abroad. By Jonas Parello-Plesner and Mathieu Duchâtel,' Book review, *International Affairs*, 92(5), pp. 1287–1288.

Gago, Verónica (2012) 'La Salada: ¿un caso de globalización «desde abajo»? Territorio de una nueva economía política transnacional,' *Nueva Sociedad*, Sep/Oct, 241, pp. 63–78, https://nuso.org/articulo/la-salada-un-caso-de-globalizacion-desde-abajo-territorio-de-una-nueva-economia-politica-transnacional/

Gago, Verónica (2014/2017) *Neoliberalism from Below: Popular Pragmatics and Baroque Economies*, Durham: Duke University Press, revized edition of *La razón neoliberal: economías barrocas y pragmática popular*, Buenos Aires: Tinta Limón, 2014.

Gamlen, Alan (2006) *Diaspora Engagement Policies: What Are They, and What Kinds of States Use Them?*, Working Paper No. 32, COMPAS-Centre on Migration, Policy and Society, University of Oxford, https://www.compas.ox.ac.uk/2006/wp-2006-032-gamlen_diaspora_engagement_policies/

Garnaut, John (2018) 'Australia's China Reset,' *The Monthly* (Australia), August, https://www.themonthly.com.au/issue/2018/august/1533045600/john-garnaut/australia-s-china-reset

Giese, Karsten (2013) 'Same-Same But Different: Chinese Traders' Perspectives on African Labor,' *The China Journal*, 69, pp. 134–153.

Gill, Bates, and Benjamin Schreer (2018) 'Countering China's "United Front",' *The Washington Quarterly*, 41(2), pp. 155–170.

Gokoluk, Selcuk (2018) 'Ghana Agreeing China Deals With "Eyes Open," Says President,' *Bloomberg*, October 8, https://www.bloomberg.com/news/articles/2018-10-08/ghana-agreeing-china-deals-with-eyes-open-says-president

Green, Cecilia A. (2012–2014) 'Outbound China and the Global South. New Entrepreneurial Immigrants in the Eastern Caribbean,' *Ideaz*, 10–12, pp. 24–44.

Green, Cecilia A., and Yan Liu (2017) 'A "Transnational Middleman Minority" in the Eastern Caribbean? Constructing a Historical and Contemporary Framework of Analysis,' *Social and Economic Studies*, 66(3–4), pp. 1–31.

Guotu, Zhuang (2012) 'China's Policies on Chinese Overseas. Past and Present,' in Tan Chee-Beng (ed.) *Routledge Handbook of the Chinese Diaspora*, London and New York: Routledge, pp. 31–41.

Hamilton, Clive (2018) *Silent Invasion: China's Influence in Australia*, Richmond, Australia: Hardie Grant Books, epub edition.

Hardus, Sarah (2014) 'Chinese National Oil Companies in Ghana: The Cases of CNOOC and Sinopec,' *Perspectives on Global Development and Technology*, 13(5–6), pp. 588–612.

Hasenclever, Andreas, Peter Mayer, and Volker Rittberger (1997) *Theories of International Regimes*, Cambridge: Cambridge University Press.

Hearn, Adrian H. (2016) *Diaspora and Trust: Cuba, Mexico, and the Rise of China*, Durham and London: Duke University Press.

Hess, Steve, and Richard Aidoo (2014) 'Charting the Roots of Anti-Chinese Populism in Africa: A Comparison of Zambia and Ghana,' *Journal of Asian and African Studies*, 49(2), pp. 129–147.

Hess, Steve, and Richard Aidoo (2015) *Charting the Roots of Anti-Chinese Populism in Africa*, Cham; Heidelberg; New York; Dordrecht; London: Springer.

Hess, Steve, and Richard Aidoo (2016) 'Charting the Impact of Subnational Actors in China's Foreign Relations: The 2013 Galamsey Crisis in Ghana,' *Asian Survey*, 56(2), pp. 301–324.

Huynh, Tu T., Yoon Jung Park, and Anna Ying Chen (2010) 'Faces of China: New Chinese Migrants in South Africa, 1980s to Present,' *African and Asian Studies*, 9(3), pp. 286–306.

Kailemia, Mwenda (2017) 'Enter the Dragon: the Ecological Disorganisation of Chinese Capital in Africa,' *Third World Quarterly*, 38(9), pp. 2082–2096.

Kavalski, Emilian (2017) 'Normative Power Europe and Normative Power China Compared: Towards a Relational Knowledge-Production in International Relations,' *Korean Political Science Review*, 51(6), 147–170.

Kavalski, Emilian (2018) 'Chinese Concepts and Relational International Politics,' *All Azimuth*, 7(1), pp. 87–102, pp. 155–156.

Kokko, Ari (2017) 'The Rise of China and the Chinese Overseas: A Study of Beijing's Changing Policy in Southeast Asia and Beyond,' Book review, *Bulletin of Indonesian Economic Studies*, 53(3), pp. 367–370.

Kurlantzick, Joshua (2008) 'China's Growing Influence in Southeast Asia,' in Riordan Roett and Guadalupe Paz (eds.) *China's Expansion into the Western Hemisphere: Implications for Latin America and the United States*, Washington, DC: Brookings Institution Press, pp. 193–212.

Lam, Katy N. (2015) 'Chinese Adaptations: African Agency, Fragmented Community and Social Capital Creation in Ghana,' *Journal of Current Chinese Affairs. China Aktuell*, 44(1), pp. 9–41.

Lam, Katy N. (2017) *Chinese State-Owned Enterprises in West Africa: Triple-Embedded Globalization*, London and New York: Routledge.

Lin, Edwin (2014) '"Big Fish in a Small Pond": Chinese Migrant Shopkeepers in South Africa,' *International Migration Review*, 48(1), pp. 181–215.

Liu, Hong, and Els van Dongen (2016) 'China's Diaspora Policies as a New Mode of Transnational Governance,' *Journal of Contemporary China*, 25(102), pp. 805–821.

Ma Mung, Emmanuel (2008) 'Chinese Migration and China's Foreign Policy in Africa,' *Journal of Chinese Overseas*, 4(1), pp. 91–109.

Marfaing, Laurence, and Alena Thiel (2013) 'The Impact of Chinese Business on Market Entry in Ghana and Senegal,' *Africa*, 83(4), pp. 646–669.

Mathews, Gordon, and Carlos Alba Vega (2012) 'Introduction. What is Globalization from Below?,' in Gordon Mathews, Gustavo Lins Ribeiro, and Carlos Alba Vega (eds.) (2012) *Globalization from Below: The World's Other Economy*, London and New York: Roudledge, pp. 1–15.

Mohan, Giles, and Ben Lampert (2013) 'Negotiating China: Reinserting African Agency into China-Africa Relations,' *African Affairs*, 112(446), pp. 92–110.

Mohan, Giles, Ben Lampert, May Tan-Mullins, and Daphne Chang (2014) *Chinese Migrants and Africa's Development. New Imperialists or Agents of Change?*, London: Zed Books.

Nyíri, Pál (1999) *New Chinese Migrants in Europe: The Case of the Chinese Community in Hungary*, Aldershot, Hants, England; Brookfield, VT: Ashgate.

Nyíri, Pál (2001) 'Expatriating is Patriotic? The Discourse on "New Migrants" in the People's Republic of China and Identity Construction among Recent Migrants from the PRC,' *Journal of Ethnic and Migration Studies*, 27(4), pp. 635–653.

Nyíri, Pál (2002) 'Globalising Chinese Migration: New Spaces, New Meanings,' *Migracijske i Etničke Teme*, 18(1), pp. 23–39.

Nyíri, Pál (2005) 'The "New Migrant": State and Market Constructions of Modernity and Patriotism,' in Pál Nyíri and Joana Breidenbach (eds.) *China Inside Out: Contemporary Chinese Nationalism and Transnationalism*, Budapest; New York: Central European University Press, pp. 141–175.

Nyíri, Pál (2007) *Chinese in Eastern Europe and Russia: A Middleman Minority in a Transnational Era*, London and New York: Routledge.

Nyíri, Pál (2010) *Mobility and Cultural Authority in Contemporary China*, Seattle and London: University of Washington Press.

Nyíri, Pál (2011) 'Chinese Entrepreneurs in Poor Countries: A Transnational "Middleman Minority" and Its Futures,' *Inter-Asia Cultural Studies*, 12(1), pp. 145–153.

Odoom, Isaac (2017) 'Dam In, Cocoa Out; Pipes In, Oil Out: China's Engagement in Ghana's Energy Sector,' *Journal of Asian and African Studies*, 52(5), pp. 598–620.

Oosterveld, Willem, Eric Wilms, and Katarina Kertysova (2018) 'The Belt and Road Initiative Looks East. Political Implications of China's Economic Forays in the Caribbean and the South Pacific,' *The Hague Centre for Strategic Studies*, https://hcss.nl/report/belt-and-road-initiative-looks-east

Peterson, Glen (2012) *Overseas Chinese in the People's Republic of China*, London and New York: Routledge.

Pilling, David (2018) 'Ghana Relations with China Raise the Emotional Heat,' *Financial Times*, October 7, https://www.ft.com/content/bdb7c066-c1ad-11e8-84cd-9e601db069b8

Pokam, Hilaire de Prince (2015) *Migration chinoise et développement au Cameroun*. Paris: L'Harmattan.

Power, Marcus, Giles Mohan, and May Tan-Mullins (2012) *China's Resource Diplomacy in Africa. Powering Development?*, Basingstoke, Hampshire: Palgrave Macmillan.

Röschenthaler, Ute, and Antoine Socpa (2017) 'The China Challenge: Cameroonians between Discontent and Popular Admiration,' in Young-Chan Kim (ed.) *China and Africa. A New Paradigm of Global Business*, Cham, Switzerland: Palgrave Macmillan, pp. 155–188.

Sarpong, Linda Addie (2015) 'Ghana-China Bilateral Relations, (Figures of Controversy),' *Advances in Economics and Business Management*, New Delhi, 2(14), pp. 1438–1442.

Shen, Simon (2015) 'Another Angle on a New Intimacy: Chinese Perceptions of Africa and Latin America,' in Carla P. Freeman (ed.) *Handbook on China and Developing Countries*, Cheltenham; Northampton, MA: Edward Elgar Publishing, pp. 109–132.

Shiu-Hing Lo, Sonny, Steven Chung-Fun Hung, and Jeff Hai-Chi Loo (2019) *China's New United Front Work in Hong Kong. Penetrative Politics and Its Implications*, Singapore: Palgrave Macmillan.

Smith, Graeme (2013a) 'Beijing's Orphans? New Chinese Investors in Papua New Guinea,' *Pacific Affairs*, 86(2), pp. 327–349.

Smith, Graeme (2013b) 'Beyond the Reach of the Whip: Chinese Investment in Papua New Guinea,' *African East-Asian Affairs*, 73, pp. 4–10.

Smith, Helena (2019) 'Xi Jinping Comes to Greeks Bearings Gifts,' *The Guardian*, November 12, https://www.theguardian.com/world/2019/nov/12/xi-jinping-comes-to-greeks-bearings-gifts

Song, Hong (2011) 'Chinese Private Direct Investment and Overseas Chinese Network in Africa,' *China & World Economy*, 19(4), pp. 109–126.

Stahl, Anna Katharina (2018) *EU-China-Africa Trilateral Relations in a Multipolar World: Hic Sunt Dracones*, London: Palgrave Macmillan.

Sullivan, Jonathan, and Jing Cheng (2018) 'Contextualising Chinese Migration to Africa,' *Journal of Asian and African Studies*, 53(8), pp. 1173–1187.

Suryadinata, Leo (2017a) *The Rise of China and the Chinese Overseas: A Study of Beijing's Changing Policy in Southeast Asia and Beyond*, Singapore: ISEAS Publishing.

Suryadinata, Leo (2017b) 'Blurring the Distinction between *Huaqiao* and *Huaren*: China's Changing Policy towards the Chinese Overseas,' in Daljit Singh and Malcolm Cook (eds.) *Southeast Asian Affairs*, Singapore: ISEAS–Yusof Ishak Institute, pp. 101–113.

Suzuki, Takashi (2019) 'China's United Front Work in the Xi Jinping Era - Institutional Developments and Activities,' *Journal of Contemporary East Asia Studies*, 8(1), pp. 83–98.

The Economist, October 4, 2018, 'Chinese Investment, and Influence, in Europe is Growing,' https://www.economist.com/briefing/2018/10/04/chinese-investment-and-influence-in-europe-is-growing

Thunø, Mette (2018) 'China's New Global Position. Changing Policies toward the Chinese Diaspora in the Twenty-First Century,' in Bernard P. Wong and Tan Chee-Beng (eds.) *China's Rise and the Chinese Overseas*, Abingdon, Oxon: Routledge, pp. 184–208.

Tjon Sie Fat, Paul B. (2009) *Chinese New Migrants in Suriname: The Inevitability of Ethnic Performing*, Amsterdam: Vossiuspers UvA - Amsterdam University Press.

To, James Jiann Hua (2014) *Qiaowu: Extra-Territorial Policies for the Overseas Chinese*, Leiden: Koninklijke Brill.

Tsikata, Dela, Ama Pokuaa Fenny, and Ernest Aryeetey (2008) 'China-Africa Relations: A Case Study of Ghana,' Working Paper, *AERC Scoping Studies on*

China-Africa Economic Relations, African Economic Research Consortium (AERC), Nairobi, https://www.econstor.eu/bitstream/10419/93154/1/587548835.pdf

Tudoroiu, Theodor, with Amanda R. Ramlogan (2021) *China's International Socialization of Political Elites in the Belt and Road Initiative,* Abingdon, Oxon: Routledge.

Tudoroiu, Theodor (2022) *China's Globalization from Below: Chinese Entrepreneurial Migrants and the Belt and Road Initiative,* Abingdon, Oxon: Routledge.

Verma, Raj (2017) *India and China in Africa: A Comparative Perspective of the Oil Industry,* London and New York: Routledge.

Waltner, Ann (1987) 'Coolies and Mandarins: China's Protection of Overseas Chinese during the Late Ch'ing Period (1851–1911) by Yen Ching-Hwang, Review,' *The American Historical Review,* 92(5), pp. 1255–1256.

Wang, Jinpu, and Ning Zhan (2019) 'Nationalism, Overseas Chinese State and the Construction of "Chineseness" among Chinese Migrant Entrepreneurs in Ghana,' *Asian Ethnicity,* 20(1), pp. 8–29.

Wei, Li (2016) 'Transnational Connections and Multilingual Realities: The Chinese Diasporic Experience in a Global Context,' in Li Wei (ed.) *Multilingualism in the Chinese Diaspora Worldwide. Transnational Connections and Local Social Realities,* New York and London: Routledge, pp. 1–12.

Xiang, Biao (2003) 'Emigration from China: A Sending Country Perspective,' *International Migration,* 41(3), pp. 21–48.

Xiang, Biao (2012) 'Predatory Princes and Princely Peddlers: The State and International Labour Migration Intermediaries in China,' *Pacific Affairs,* 85(1), pp. 47–68.

Xiang, Biao (2015) 'The Rise of China, Changing Patterns of Out-Migration and Identity Implications,' in Robyn R. Iredale and Fei Guo (eds.) *Handbook of Chinese Migration: Identity and Wellbeing,* Cheltenham; Northampton, USA: Edward Elgar Publishing, pp. 278–296.

Yang, Jian (2011a) *The Pacific Islands in China's Grand Strategy: Small States, Big Games,* New York: Palgrave Macmillan.

Yang, Yang (2011b) *African Traders in Guangzhou: Why They Come, What They Do, and How They Live,* M.Phil. thesis, The Chinese University of Hong Kong, https://core.ac.uk/download/pdf/48537913.pdf

Yen, Ching-Hwang (1985) *Coolies and Mandarins: China's Protection of Overseas Chinese during the Late Ch'ing Period (1851–1911),* Singapore: Singapore University Press.

Yow, Cheun Hoe (2016) 'The Chinese Diaspora in China-Malaysia Relations: Dynamics of and Changes in Multiple Transnational "Scapes",' *Journal of Contemporary China,* 25(102), pp. 836–850.

6 The First Wave Globalization 'from Below'

This chapter analyzes the largely unexplored first wave globalization 'from below' that accompanied – and outlived – the 1870–1914 globalization 'from above.' Subchapter 6.1 discusses the concepts of semi-colonialism, extraterritoriality, and cosmopolitanism that defined the framework of this 'from below' process. Semi-colonialism is compared with neocolonialism, as it replaces formal domination with diffused ideological and cultural influence. Through extraterritoriality, great powers used their migrants as pawns to weaken extra-European states. But these migrants formed large and influential cosmopolitan minorities that took advantage of the relative balance between the weakness of local authorities and the incomplete Western control. This balance allowed for 'from below' agency, which resulted in processes and flows that no great power had planned or expected. These flows were significantly enhanced by the openness implicitly associated with the cosmopolitanism of their actors, which turned them into a fully fledged globalization 'from below.' Subchapter 6.2 presents the case study of semi-colonial cosmopolitan Alexandria. It starts by discussing the rise of the European influence in Egypt that resulted in the spectacular development of this port city and the massive expansion of its foreign minorities. Due to a semi-colonial balance of power, there were 'many authorities but no hegemon.' As an effect, an autonomous Alexandria municipality was established that 'let non-Egyptians run the city.' The involvement of the English, French, Italian, and Greek communities in the first wave globalization 'from below' is then examined, pointing to the fact that the main actors of this globalization were 'subaltern cosmopolitans' such as the Maltese, Algerian, and Tunisian colonial subjects of Britain and France, as well as unaffluent Italian and Greek petty traders. The example of the Italian language 'dissident literature' of Enrico Pea and Fausta Cialente is used to illustrate the discreet but nevertheless important cognitive and ideological dimension of the first wave globalization 'from below.' Progressive activists tried to project normative power based on Alexandria's cosmopolitan values to oppose the rise of (ultra)nationalism in Europe. On a more negative note, the transformation of 'Levantine' into a derogatory label applied to the 'subaltern cosmopolitans' might explain their contemporaries' refuse to perceive the flows they enacted as representing a fully fledged globalization. Subchapter 6.3 first discusses the development and features of the foreign concessions established as extraterritorial enclaves in China's treaty ports. It then presents Shanghai as a city run by the non-Chinese: the Shanghai Municipal Council in control of the International Settlement was 'a semi-independent governing structure' that showed 'substantial independence' from Chinese but also consular authorities. The political and administrative features of the Council are analyzed to show that, while the influence of the British minority was important, the International Settlement was governed by non-state actors outside the control of any power. This created the conditions for local agency conducive to the development of the first wave globalization 'from below.' The role played by Shanghai's main foreign minorities in this globalization is then examined, with an emphasis on the challenges represented by the connections between the German and Japanese minorities and their respective governments during the two World Wars. In addition to the migratory and commercial dimensions of the 'from below' globalization in Shanghai, the ideational one is analyzed with reference to the early initiative to establish the International Settlement as a cosmopolitan independent republic. Rejected by the great powers whose interests it threatened, this 'from below' plan was *de facto* turned into reality as a result of the normative power of small and weak actors. Subchapter 6.4 provides a definition of the first wave globalization 'from below' and analyzes its features. It then discusses the relationship between the parallel 'from above' and 'from below' globalizations in terms of normative power. Finally, the destructive effect of nationalism is discussed in relation to the alternative model of modernity proposed by the first wave globalization 'from below.'

6.1 Cosmopolitanism and Extraterritoriality in Semi-Colonial Port Cities

As shown in Subchapter 2.4, the 1870–1914 first wave globalization 'from above' overlapped with and significantly contributed to the development of the Western-centered modern world based on capitalism, imperialism, colonialism, and – somewhat incongruously in a globalizing context – nationalism. While some of its key features were very different from those of the present Neoliberal globalization 'from above,' the flows of people, goods, and ideas were ultimately similar. In particular, the migratory phenomenon was 'most impressively globalized, even compared with today' (Daudin *et al.* 2010: 15). Much of it was directly related to the need for labor that was manifest in the Americas but also in Western Europe (see Subchapter 2.4). Still, while millions of poor laborers flocked to New York, London, or Paris, the 'big fish in a small pond' strategy of the present Chinese entrepreneurial migrants (see Subchapter 5.1) was at the origin of less visible but nevertheless important opposite migratory flows. Merchants, entrepreneurs, and skilled workers from developed countries moved to peripheral ones where their capital and know-how represented considerable comparative advantages. This was hardly a new trend. The centuries-old port city economy that developed in various regions of the world (see Driessen 2005; Fuhrmann 2020; Gekas 2009; Marsden and Skvirskaja 2018) relied precisely on this type of interaction. Colonialism had reinforced it. Through the 'technology-induced compression of time and space' (Gekas 2009: 101) and the opening up of previously inaccessible economies such as those of China or Japan, the first wave globalization created the conditions for the massive expansion of these North to South flows. As a result, an already existing social phenomenon developed on an unprecedented scale: a significant degree of cosmopolitanism became the key characteristic of major port cities that represented the trading nodes of the new global economy. Some of them – such as Odessa, Trieste, or New Orleans – were located on the territory of powerful states that were directly and actively involved in the first wave globalization from above.' Some other – such as Singapore or Saigon (all these examples are discussed in Reimer 1977/2019: 6) – pertained to the colonial empires of these states. In both cases, cosmopolitanism developed but migrants could not play an autonomous role. They simply participated in the economic circuits of the globalization 'from above' as their contemporaries in Chicago, Liverpool, or Lyon did. The linguistic, cultural, social, and economic features of their cities of residence were often transformed by the foreign presence. But the political and legal ones were not, and states preserved their full power to control, regulate, and steer the migrants' economic activities in ways compatible with their officially proclaimed national interests. This dramatically limited 'from below' agency. Still, there was a third category of port cities where cosmopolitanism developed in an environment characterized by much weaker 'from above' constraints. This was specific to semi-colonial situations where Western powers imposed a high degree of control on declining non-European empires but, for various reasons, were unable or unwilling to turn them into genuine colonies. This category includes places such as Constantinople's Galata and Pera, as well as Salonica, Smyrna, Beirut, and – to a lesser extent – Jaffa, Latakia, and Alexandretta, in the late Ottoman Empire; the prominent example of Alexandria in Khedival Egypt; the very numerous foreign concessions in late imperial and republican China, with Shanghai as a model (see Subchapter 6.3); and cities in Persia and Siam (Reimer 1977/2019: 3, 5). In such places, the many consequences of the Western powers' control typically included, on the one hand, a special legal status for their nationals, which was based on the concept of extraterritoriality; and, on the other hand, political support for the same nationals in their interactions with the authorities of their nominally sovereign state of residence. This helped Western migrants to acquire privileged economic, social, and political positions. The prospect of social advancement further stimulated the North-South migratory flows. They were supplemented by equally large South-South flows of opportunistic migrants that, in various ways, tried to take advantage of the same opportunities.

New merchants, entrepreneurs, skilled workers, and adventurers arrived. Members of local ethnic or religious minorities joined them – for example, by actually buying Western citizenships – in order to upgrade their socio-economic status. This led to the development of numerically important cosmopolitan minorities, which were closely connected, economically and culturally, to the West. They were expected to – and effectively did – serve as vectors of colonial penetration for the great powers that protected them. However, a balance developed mainly due to the rivalry between competing Western powers, which prevented the concerned non-European countries from being turned into fully fledged colonies. Complicated relationships emerged between the weak authorities of these countries and the external powers divided by in-group competition. This situation allowed the cosmopolitan minorities to escape the strict constraints imposed by any single state. They acquired a degree of autonomy unknown to their counterparts in New Orleans or Saigon and exploited it to their own advantage. They created 'from below' economic processes and flows that were not planned or controlled by any specific state. Massive social change ensued, often mirrored by the migrant-inspired and financed transformation of the local urban landscape. At times, the fragile cosmopolitans went as far as politically challenging the very powers that protected them: as shown in Subchapter 6.3, the locally elected Shanghai Municipal Council – which controlled that city's International Settlement – 'secured for itself a degree of autonomy that proved highly frustrating' for the Western powers that created the Settlement. For its own reasons, the Council chose to antagonize Chinese anti-imperialism. This policy damaged those powers' relations with China; but they were unable to bring it to an end (Jackson 2016: 44). Importantly for this book, the agency of cosmopolitan minorities in semi-colonial port cities led to the development of a globalization 'from below' that, in certain respects, is comparable with the present Chinese-centered one. It was based mainly on the normative power projected by the hegemonic great powers whose nationals or *protégés* enacted it. It was supported by the first wave globalization 'from above' and by the Western-centered multipolar international order of the pre-WWI period. It nevertheless represented a separate, 'from below' globalization whose small and weak actors exploited the niche created by the aforementioned balance specific to semi-colonial situations. This is why, before scrutinizing cosmopolitanism as the defining feature of these actors, the next section analyzes the disputed concept of semi-colonialism.

Semi-Colonialism

There is little doubt that, in the Eastern Mediterranean, 'cosmopolitanism in the interstitial port towns was largely the result of the confrontation of Western European capitalism, colonialism and imperialism' with the declining Ottoman Empire (Driessen 2005: 138–139). Scholars tend to emphasize two factors: 'the colonial or quasi-colonial nature of the *rapport de forces*' and the 'weakness of a [local] political structure identifiable with the nation-state' (Eldem 2013: 221). In Egypt, Alexandria has been depicted as a 'colonial bridgehead,' the 'primary venue of colonizing activity' (Reimer 1977/2019: 9). Authors such as Hala Halim even insist on the fact that 'there is a failure to recognize the degree to which Alexandrian cosmopolitanism is complicit with colonialism' in the scholarly literature (Halim 2013: 3). Despite a number of 'anomalies' and 'internationalism' (Daly 1998: 240), these authors perceive the period of the 'Veiled Protectorate' (1882–1914) that overlaps with much of the first wave globalizations as little more than British colonial 'rule from behind a façade of Egyptian ministers who had little authority, and were rubber stamps for their British manipulators' (Al-Sayyid Marsot 2007: 89; for more details see Subchapter 6.2). They argue that Alexandria's institutions, including the Municipal Council – which shares many features with the similar structure in Shanghai – 'demonstrate the intimate connection between cosmopolitanism and colonialism,' as well as the city's 'colonial situation' (Halim 2013: 40–41). However, the 'colonial' camp has come under the, at times, virulent attack of a different group of scholars. Michael Haag went as far as condemning Hala Halim's trend or, indeed, agenda to 'reduce everything to the author's parochial and reactionary point of view' (Haag 2014: 451). Various authors have given a very different interpretation to the 'unique administrative structure [that] characterized Alexandria and reflected its cosmopolitanism, contributing to make it a very particular kind of colony' (Re 2003: 172). 'It was a city with many authorities but no hegemon' (Hanley 2017: 17). 'The diverse and powerful business interests that controlled the city' – which prominently included the cosmopolitan minorities – ensured 'a certain degree of autonomy within the colonial state' (Takla 2016: 17). The autonomous multinational municipality was so successful that 'Cairo began to demand its own municipality on the model of Alexandria – a privilege it did not obtain until 1949' (Mansel 2011: 131). Powerful community leaders participated in both municipal and local governance (Takla 2016: 26). Overall, Alexandria was 'far from becoming – like so many other African cities – a mere colonial bridgehead for the exploitation of an enslaved country.' The 'usual essentialist markers traditionally associated with coloniality' were absent. Accordingly, 'the word "colony" needs to be redefined in Alexandria's case' (Re 2003: 172–173).

This is equally true for the other cosmopolitan cities in the Eastern Mediterranean Basin. But it is with respect to – and, partly, in – China that such a redefinition began to be discussed at the very time of the first wave globalizations. As explained in Subchapter 6.3, during that period, there was 'a consortium of great powers collectively exercising informal domination' (Scully 2001: 5) over the declining Middle Kingdom on a scale comparable with the cases of Egypt or the Ottoman Empire. The only important difference was related to the way extraterritoriality was enforced: in China, this 'distinctive form of colonialism' led to the creation of foreign concessions (Crawford 2018: 970; see Subchapter 6.3). These concessions 'could not be regarded as genuine colonies' (Vandamme 2018: 41) but rather as a 'hybrid form of colonial urban governance' that was 'both colonial in its structures and subject to colonial influence (...), yet autonomous in its activities and transnational in its personnel' (Jackson 2018). Scholars have identified four specific features that prevent the concessions in China from being included in the category of fully fledged colonies. First, there is the rivalry, balance, and cooperation among no less than 18 foreign powers, which 'resulted in specific forms of colonial relationships,' as well as a 'multiple and multilayered domination.' In particular, the concept of colonialism is 'inadequa[te] in reflecting the relations of cooperation among the foreign powers' (Shih 2001: 32) that, between the two World Wars, allowed for the Shanghai 'International Settlement [to be] dubbed "a miniature League of Nations"' (Jackson 2018: 7). Second, the foreign 'multilayered domination' (Shih 2001: 32) prominently included 'effectively colonial governance by non-state actors' (Jackson 2018: 8). Surprisingly, 'imperial metropoles were comparatively insignificant in the exercise of colonial power' in the International Settlement. The latter was governed through the 'cooperation between non-state representatives of such powers' in the autonomous Shanghai Municipal Council. 'The British consul-general, diplomats and home government were regularly frustrated that they could not exercise control over the SMC,' a situation frequently criticized by MPs in London. But they were repeatedly reminded that the 'Council is an independent international body, over which His Majesty's Government have no control' (*Ibid.*, 8, 10). Third, despite its dramatic decline, the Chinese state – be it under the form of the late Qing empire or the new republic – preserved its sovereignty, as the Ottoman Empire did. Under such circumstances, the actual degree of sovereignty is both critical in determining the real status of indigenous governments and difficult to assess. 'The workings of an impaired yet active Chinese sovereignty' were 'dismissed as merely symbolic' by some scholars. Others, however, 'interpreted [them] as a capacity for resistance' (Reinhardt 2018: 7–9). In any case, there were clear situations where foreign powers could not impose their interests due to the opposition of the Chinese government. One example is the intention to deport German nationals from Shanghai when China joined the Entente in World War I. This measure 'had to be endorsed by the Chinese authorities, whose approval only came after the war' (Vandamme 2018: 59). Finally, there is the more subtle but equally important dimension of cultural frameworks and outcomes studied by authors such as Shu-mei Shih, Bryna Goodman, and Anne Reinhardt (Shih 2001; Goodman 2000; Reinhardt 2018). They point to the fact that the particular features of the colonial penetration of China produced a specific cultural result different from that of 'normal' colonies. More precisely, the 'Chinese did not view foreigners and their interactions with them "in terms of anything resembling colonized subjectivities"' (Reinhardt 2018: 5; Goodman 2000: 14).

The overall picture is clearly not that of typical colonialism. Certain scholars compared it with a situation of indirect or informal imperialism where 'outside powers, collectively unable or unwilling to rule China directly, had to reach a *modus vivendi* with indigenous authorities' (Scully 2001: 9). They analyzed the foreign domination as relying on the 'voluntary or enforced cooperation' of these elites, which facilitated 'imperialism on the cheap.' Eileen Scully explained the 'imperialist-collaborator alliance' (*Ibid.*, 10) using Johan Galtung's Structural Imperialism: elites in the South become a transmission belt in the process that allows the elites of the North to exploit the population of the South. A harmonious relationship develops between the two groups of elites as they both benefit from this process (Galtung 1971). Indeed, 'a dynamic that crosscut nationality' emerged in China: through their passive or active support of foreign penetration, 'indigenous elites became, paradoxically, a constituency capable of commanding the solicitous, albeit self-serving, attention of imperialists seeking to harness them' (Scully 2001: 10). In her study of the relationship between shipping, sovereignty, and nation-building in China, Anne Reinhardt identified four characteristics of associated collaborative mechanisms. First, the terms of collaboration were set by the foreign powers. Second, due to the greater experience and better access to resources and information of the external actors, their positions improved in time, which 'forwarded the imperialist/expansionist project.' Third, often, the participation of local elites was not the result of opportunism; rather, it was intended to ensure the survival of existing structures and institutions. Fourth, while collaboration favored the foreign powers, it also supported, in a certain measure, the exercise of indigenous sovereignty and agency (Reinhardt 2018: 10–11). This arrangement worked very well from 1860 to 1911. External powers avoided the costs of conquest, rule, and disputes among themselves, while local elites ensured the survival of the Chinese Empire. 'Therefore, at the same time the treaty system diminished Qing sovereignty, its remaining margin was indispensable to the functioning of the system' (*Ibid.*, 11). This system remained in place when the republic was proclaimed in 1911, but the absence of a central government during the 1916–1927 Warlord Era led to the collapse of the collaborative mechanism. China's political elites – now represented by the leaders of competing militarist regimes – had little interest in suppressing anti-foreign resistance (*Ibid.*, 11–12). This led to the unconstrained rise of nationalism and the rejection of the foreign presence in China by both Nationalists and Communists. A similar situation existed in Egypt. As shown in Subchapter 6.2, at the beginning of the first wave globalizations, the local elites consisted of the Turko-Circassian elite and the native Egyptian notables. By 1882, a triangular confrontation developed that involved them and the Europeans. This resulted in the British occupation and the beginning of the 'veiled protectorate.' *De jure*, until 1914, Egypt remained an Ottoman province governed by Mohammed Ali's dynasty. *De facto*, it was under British domination and European influence. 'But force would not have been effective in the long term.' Foreign control was possible only due to 'the active cooperation of the khedive' and the 'tacit collaboration' of parts of the two elites (Reimer 1977/2019: 9). This was a situation very similar to the Chinese one. Its end came when the 1952 Revolution brought to power a completely different elite, which vocally rejected collaboration with Western powers. The massive expulsion of foreigners that, four years later, put an end to the first wave globalization 'from below' in Egypt was the logical consequence of this change.

Returning to the analysis of the Chinese case, Isabella Jackson argued that 'colonialism in Shanghai was not a lighter-touch form of imperial control.' It consisted of 'locally directed autonomous governance by foreigners' that resulted in 'the development of a polity more akin to an independent city-state under foreign colonial control' (Jackson 2018: 16). This important aspect was noted by contemporaries, who were the first to associate it with the concept of semi-colonialism. The latter was defined by Lenin as 'a somewhat deficient colonialism' that represents only 'a transitional form on the way towards outright colonial takeover' (Osterhammel 1986: 296). It was John A. Hobson, Lenin's contemporary and, in many regards, inspirer, who understood semi-colonialism as 'an enduring state of affairs.' Writing specifically about China at the turn of the 20th century, he 'prophetically envisaged the possibility of a co-operative *mise en valeur* of [its] resources under conditions of formal sovereignty.' In the 1930s, the Chinese Marxists paired 'semi-colonial' with 'semi-feudal' to 'describe the socioeconomic formation that inhibited China's transition to full capitalism' (*Ibid.*). They argued that colonialism penetrated but failed to supersede the feudal system; this created a hybrid formation that classical Marxism had not anticipated. Semi-colonialism and semi-feudalism continue to be employed by the present communist authorities in their depiction of China at the time of the Western domination (Reinhardt 2018: 3–4, Osterhammel 1986: 296; Shih 2001: 31). However, even semi-colonialism has had its detractors. The first was the very founder of republican China, Sun Yat-sen, who chose instead the term 'hypo-colony' to emphasize the lower status associated with China's colonization by many nations (Jackson 2018: 16): 'the Chinese were not just the "slaves of one country, but of all"' (Shih 2001: 32). Closer to our times, Ruth Rogaski employed the opposing term 'hypercolony' to depict 'Tianjin's distinctive juxtaposition of many concessions within a single urban space' that was 'divided among multiple imperialisms' (Rogaski 2004: 11; Marinelli 2009: 402; Jackson 2018: 16). Jeffrey Wasserstrom preferred to write about 'quasi-colonialism' (Wasserstrom 2003: 56). Isabella Jackson, a prominent student of the topic, explicitly rejected semi-colonialism because 'the residents of the Settlement experienced a form of colonialism that was far greater in reach than the prefix "semi" implies.' Instead, she proposed 'transnational colonialism' to define Shanghai's 'hybrid form of colonial urban governance.' Moreover, she explicitly noted the validity of this concept in the case of both Egypt and Siam (Jackson 2018: 6, 8–9, 16). Still, other authors chose to build on Jürgen Osterhammel's view of semi-colonialism (Osterhammel 1986: 296; Yang 2019: 2) while 'keeping both sides of the hyphen under active consideration,' to quote Anne Reinhardt (Reinhardt 2018: 4). Ultimately, the term itself is less relevant than the evolving meanings assigned to it. If appropriately defined, semi-colonialism can correctly 'encompass the particularity of China's experience, its comparability with colonial contexts, and its enmeshment within the process of the global ascent of European empires' (*Ibid.*). Such a *démarche* was proposed by Shu-mei Shih, who started by making clear that 'the "semi-" here is not to denote "half" of something, but rather the fractured, informal, and indirect character of colonialism, as well as its multilayeredness.' She used semi-colonialism as a term mirroring 'the multiple, layered, intensified, as well as incomplete and fragmentary nature of China's colonial structure' that, different from genuinely colonial cases, lacked 'a central colonial government implementing extensive colonial institutions and structures' (Shih 2001: 35). Shih identified four implications of this understanding of the concept. First, there was no outright external domination or transfer of formal sovereignty. Foreign powers exercised their domination 'through less formal, although no less destructive or transformative, channels.' Second and most importantly, in terms of economic penetration, race relationships, and jurisdiction, semi-colonialism was closer to neocolonialism than to classical colonialism. Third, each of the numerous foreign powers 'potentially occupied a different place within the Chinese cultural imaginary.' Fourth, multiple colonial presences prevented 'a tight-fitting, unified colonial management and containment of native spheres of activity.' In turn, this allowed for a variety of political, ideological, and cultural attitudes among local actors that were very different from 'the ordinary Manichean division of nationalists and collaborators' in formal colonies. To summarize, semi-colonialism 'operated like neocolonialism, through diffused ideological and cultural interpellation rather than institutionalized, formal domination' (*Ibid.*, 35, 37). Far from being restricted to China, this pattern was reproduced in the cosmopolitan port cities of Egypt, the Ottoman Empire, Persia, and Siam. The comparison with neocolonialism is critical to the understanding of the conditions that led to the development of the first wave globalization 'from below.' The mainly ideological and cultural nature of the foreign domination allowed for considerably more local agency than the formal structures and institutions of classical colonialism would have allowed. This 'local' agency concerned the indigenous actors but even more so the cosmopolitan minorities. Between the weakened authority of their states of residence and the informal domination of foreign powers, these minorities found a niche free from the constraints of states and their globalization 'from above.' Their efforts toward economic, social, cultural, and political advancement ultimately resulted in the construction of a fully fledged globalization 'from below.'

Extraterritoriality

Before scrutinizing the cosmopolitan dimension of this process, an important component of semi-colonialism at the time of first wave globalizations needs to be examined: extraterritoriality. It was used – and abused – by Western powers as an instrument that greatly extended their influence. Extraterritoriality was based on a 'from above' rationale that simply used Western migrants as pawns to weaken and control target states. However, by creating a privileged status for foreign nationals, it caused a massive inflow of merchants, entrepreneurs, and skilled workers; turned these 'from below' actors into an essential element of the semi-colonial port cities where they formed large and influential cosmopolitan communities; and ultimately allowed them to create a globalization 'from below' that no Western power had planned or expected. In the Ottoman Empire (including Egypt), extraterritoriality was introduced in 1536, when the Capitulations system was first created by a treaty with France. In exchange for alliances, as part of commercial treaties, or due to military defeats, the Sultan granted a number of advantages to foreign merchants. Between 1718 and 1782, the declining Ottoman Empire made such concessions to England, the Habsburg Empire, Sweden, Tuscany, Denmark, Russia, and Spain. The 1740 treaty with France, which extended the capitulary privileges, became a model followed by other European states (Shlala 2018: 3; Rosenthal 1980/2005: 129). On the one hand, their merchants were granted freedom of trade and an exemption from certain forms of taxation that included lowered custom duties. On the other hand and more importantly in the long term, European consuls were admitted in the Ottoman Empire who had almost complete control over their nationals. The latter were not subject to Ottoman judicial or administrative authority. They could be tried – by their consuls – only for the infringement of their own national law (Halim 2013: 40; Al-Sayyid Marsot 2007: 84; Shlala 2018: 3, 5; Rosenthal 1980/2005: 129). To this effect, consular courts were established. In Egypt, they 'grew so powerful in the 1860s and 1870s that the period was deemed the Consular Era due to the consulates' influence directly interfering in Egyptian national affairs' (Shlala 2009: 7; see below). In 1876, the Mixed Courts were added, which were also independent of the Egyptian government's control. European and Egyptian judges administered justice in civil matters where Egyptians and non-Egyptians were involved. These courts – whose proceedings were held in French – used a combination of the Napoleonic Code, English common law, Islamic law, and local laws. They were created on an Egyptian proposal intended to reach a reforming compromise on the consular courts, which continued to try foreigners for criminal offenses. Khedive Isma'il presented the change as a triumph, but in fact 'the mixed courts provided yet another instrument by which Europeans were tightening their grip on Isma'il and Egypt' (Reid 1998: 219; Hunter 1998: 194; Halim 2013: 39–40; Jackson 2018: 8). It was only in 1937 that the Montreux Convention abolished the

Capitulations in Egypt. It also phased out the Mixed Courts over a 13-year period; they were completely dismantled only in 1949 (Goldschmidt 2004: 79; Botman 1998: 295).

Extraterritoriality basically created an *'imperium in imperio'* (Vatikiotis 1980: 86; Halim 2013: 39). Nobody noted it in the 16th century because privileges concerned only a few diplomats and merchants; a parallel could be drawn with the present immunities and privileges granted to members of the diplomatic corps. But this changed considerably in the 19th century when the 'skewed balance of power' allowed Western power to quickly expand the Capitulations' legal system (Shlala 2018: 3; Rosenthal 1980/2005: 129). This was hardly specific to Egypt or the Ottoman Empire. It was in the context of China that Eileen Scully wrote about the 'Midas touch' of extraterritoriality, which allowed foreigners to 'extend their privileges and immunities to employees, protégés, institutions, businesses and land' (Scully 2001: 5; Cassel 2016: 23; see below). On Ottoman soil, European consulates extended their jurisdiction to numerous non-Muslims who were actually allowed to buy foreign citizenships. The protection of religious minorities was a convenient way to place many Armenians, Greeks, and Jews on the protected lists. These new 'foreigners' escaped the jurisdiction of the Turkish courts and dramatically diminished the taxes they paid (Rosenthal 1980/2005: 129; Shlala 2018: 3). Moreover, 'with the complicity of their consuls, Europeans in the empire could commit any crime with impunity.' When punishment consisted of deportation, 'they could return on the next ship and local authorities could do nothing about it' (Al-Sayyid Marsot 2007: 84). Greeks and Italians 'were the most numerous abusers of the Capitulations, but every Western country exploited them' (Goldschmidt 2004: 33). The system encouraged illegal activities such as smuggling; but it was through the support for dubious or fraudulent claims for indemnification that, in Egypt, 'the consuls facilitated abuse by foreigners of the concessions granted them by the viceroys, bringing huge losses to the Egyptian treasury' (Hunter 1998: 187–188). 'Savvy Mediterranean cosmopolitans were able to manipulate the system in order to increase their wealth and power.' Taking advantage of the competing legal codes, they 'were able to exert enormous influence over the political system' using various foreign consular courts to launch contentious property lawsuits against the Egyptian government. By abusing extraterritoriality, these migrants 'negotiated the legal landscape to their advantage, but to the ultimate disadvantage of the Egyptian state' (Shlala 2009: 5, 7). To summarize, in the 19th century, the old capitulatory system was instrumentalized by Western powers to weaken semi-colonial states. It was most effective in this regard. But, in the process, the migrant pawns considerably upgraded their status, as well as the potential for self-interested agency.

This was very visible in the case of Alexandria where, by 1907, no less than 14 non-Muslim communities benefitted from numerous legal and social privileges conferred by their respective consulates. As a result, the prominent members of the cosmopolitan minorities 'effectively regulate[d] the life of the city' (Ostle 2002: 315; see Subchapter 6.2). More modest foreign nationals found 'creative ways' to elude the law. 'Alexandria became a space of immunity for many' (Re 2003: 173). Foreign citizenships were particularly easy to obtain. For example, many Levantine Jews took advantage of the fact that the register of births of Leghorn (Livorno) had burned. They claimed that their families originated in that Tuscan free port and had their Italian citizenship 'restored' (*Ibid.*). Moreover, in order to exploit differences between various national laws, members of the same family often acquired different nationalities. They became 'legal chameleons' (Fahmy 2013) that 'manipulated the flux and fluidity of identities (...) by giving preference to the national, gender, or class identity most advantageous in a given situation' (Shlala 2009: 7). This obviously has nothing to do with the expansionist intentions of the Western powers. Rather, it is illustrative of the considerable autonomy of their nationals – be they 'genuine' or not – settled in Alexandria and similar port cities in the Eastern Mediterranean Basin. Ultimately, it is due to ambiguous national allegiances, the exploitation of associated legal and economic privileges, and ensuing socio-economic and political advancement that the supposedly small and weak members of the cosmopolitan minorities could create a fully fledged globalization 'from below' in this region.

As mentioned earlier in this section, the 'Midas touch' of extraterritoriality was first discussed by Eileen Scully with respect to semi-colonial China. Except for the existence of clearly delimitated foreign concessions (see Subchapter 6.3), this country's situation was identical to that of Egypt and the Ottoman Empire. Extraterritoriality was brought to the Middle Kingdom by the British as a consequence of their victory in the First Opium War. The 1842 Treaty of Nanking granted British nationals privileges similar to those of the Capitulations. The example was soon followed by other powers. By the 1860s, 'most foreigners resident in China enjoyed virtual immunity from native law, and were instead under the extraterritorial authority of their own home governments' (Scully 2001: 5). The familiar pattern of extending initial privileges and immunities was followed, too. Its main effect was the transformation of the early 'makeshift self-governance among a hundred or so foreigners in a few coastal enclaves' into a situation of semi-colonial domination where 'burgeoning cosmopolitan Sino-foreign populations were shielded from indigenous fiscal and political control' (*Ibid.*). Progressively, the extraterritorial legal order intruded into almost any aspect of everyday life in treaty port China and anything a foreigner touched could obtain an extraterritorial aspect' (Cassel 2016: 23). No less than 18 states acquired extraterritorial privileges for their citizens and, in the case of the United Kingdom, France, and the United States, for subjects from their colonies and protectorates (Scully 2001: 6), which was also the case in Egypt. Unsurprisingly, a court system developed that 'enforced the law of any foreign nationals implicated in a case' (Jackson 2018: 6). There were 'a myriad of treaty port consular courts (including American, British, French,

German, and Japanese)'; the British Supreme Court for China established in 1865 in Shanghai; and 'the various permanent "mixed courts" set up in Shanghai, Amoy and Hankow to handle Sino-foreign cases' (Scully 2001: 6; Nield 2015: 202). The first of the Mixed Courts was created in 1863 in Shanghai. They were active until 1928. In such courts, a Chinese magistrate heard cases involving Chinese nationals. When one of the parties was foreign, the Chinese judge was joined by an assessor who was a foreign consular official of the relevant country. Cases between foreigners, both civil and criminal, were tried by consular courts (Nield 2015: 15, 202, 206).

Extraterritoriality, in China and elsewhere, 'was portable, transferable, almost irrevocable, and buttressed (...) by gunboats and coercive treaties' (Scully 2001: 5). There can be little doubt about its destructive effects on the target states. However, scholars such as Eileen Scully rejected the idea that it represented 'a blunt instrument imposed on a passive, victimized indigenous society by single-minded imperialists.' Instead, it was a 'complex balancing act' based on the competition between 'metropolitan governments, colonial sojourners, indigenous elites, and opportunists of all nationalities' that should be assessed against the backdrop of the imperialist-collaborator alliance (*Ibid.*, 9, 10). The first goal of extraterritoriality was to weaken the semi-colonial states, which was done by supporting the 'colonial sojourners.' But its 'more sophisticated and subtle tasks' included the protection of collaborating local elites. The predatory behavior of foreigners – which included genuinely criminal acts – stimulated nationalist feelings that threatened the political survival of these elites and their commitment to collaborate with foreign powers. The extraterritoriality-related judicial apparatus helped control criminal foreign elements and, more generally, stabilize a society that foreign powers had brought to the brink of implosion (*Ibid.*, 9).

Most foreigners, however, did not migrate to Shanghai or Alexandria to commit murder and rape and expose themselves to legal retribution. On the contrary, they shrewdly exploited extraterritoriality-related legal privileges and ambiguities to upgrade their economic, social, and political status. They were remarkably successful, and the sum of their individual enterprises gave birth to a globalization 'from below.' It can be concluded that the migrants' success and globalization are in large measure a consequence of extraterritoriality, which, in turn, was a normative imposition of Western powers. In other words, the first wave globalization 'from below' was the unintended result of the projection of normative power used by Western states to expand their imperialist influence – a process that was part of the first wave globalization 'from above.'

Cosmopolitanism

The first wave globalization 'from below' can be compared with the present Chinese one: both are the result of normative power projected by actual or aspiring hegemons. However, there are two important differences.

One concerns intentionality. Beijing is the architect and coordinator of the Chinese-centered globalization 'from below.' For its part, the first wave globalization 'from below' was the *unintended* product of Western powers' actions, which were interested only in the construction of a globalization 'from above.' The other difference concerns the values shared by actors involved in the two processes. As shown in the previous chapter, the Chinese entrepreneurial migrants have developed a specific form of deterritorialized nationalism. The first wave globalization 'from below,' on the contrary, was created by cosmopolitans. This is not an accident. The inter-communal fluidity and integration – the 'social porosity' – that define cosmopolitanism (Eldem 2013: 217–218) represent the root cause of actor openness and mobility on which the flows of this globalization were based. It is in this context that the present and following sections analyze the concept of cosmopolitanism and the 'actually existing' forms it took in Levantine and Chinese port cities.

There is a 'standard narration of the historical development of cosmopolitanism' (Inglis 2012: 12) that necessarily starts with Greek Cynicism and Stoicism, noting the contributions of Diogenes – 'I am a citizen of the world'– and Zeno, which were eventually adapted by Roman Stoics such as Marcus Aurelius and Cicero. It was only under the influence of the French Revolution that a new stage was reached when Immanuel Kant studied cosmopolitanism in his *Idea for a Universal History with a Cosmopolitan Purpose* and *Toward Perpetual Peace: A Philosophical Sketch* (Skrbiš and Woodward 2013: 41). The rise of nationalism in the 19th century led to a marked decline in interest. However, the 'rejuvenation of cosmopolitical concerns after World War II' and the key contribution of Martha Nussbaum have led to the 'remarkable flourishing and diversification of the cosmopolitan intellectual field in recent times' (Inglis 2012: 12; Skrbiš and Woodward 2013: 42–43). This is a fascinating topic; unfortunately, its presentation falls outside the scope of this chapter. I will only remind that, in classical Greece, 'cosmopolitanism' – formed from universe ('cosmos') and citizen ('politēs') – designated a type of personal attitude associated with 'global citizenship.' It was during the Enlightenment that it became popular as a political theory (Gusejnova 2018: 3). Today, the concept is associated with 'curiosity about boundary crossing underpinned by a universal ethical project'; it is conducive to an attitude that is 'transgressive, open-minded, even utopian' (Hanley 2012: 92; Hanley 2017: 32). Anthropologists define it as referring 'both to the ethos and practice of individuals and groups that are open to cultural difference and strive towards intercultural respect and coexistence.' Cosmopolitans are familiar with 'different social and cultural arenas, master several languages and draw on various cultural repertoires and life styles' (Driessen 2005: 137). Steven Vertovec and Robin Cohen proposed six 'characterizations' of cosmopolitanism that apply to all social sciences. They understand cosmopolitanism as (1) a socio-cultural condition; (2) a kind of philosophy or worldview; (3) a political project toward building transnational institutions; (4) a political project for recognizing multiple identities; (5) an attitudinal or dispositional orientation; and (6) a mode of practice or competence (Vertovec and Cohen 2002: 21; Rovisco and Nowicka 2011: 1). Zlatko Skrbiš and Ian Woodward analyzed four dimensions of cosmopolitanism. The first is cultural and represents a disposition of openness to the surrounding world. The second is political and refers to the commitment – which is also present at institutional and global levels in terms of regimes of global governance or even supra-national state-building – 'to appreciate and recognise difference, embed our politics in universal principles and commit ourselves to the dethronement of one's unique cultural identity' (Skrbiš and Woodward 2013: 3). The third dimension is ethical and relies on 'an inclusive ethical core that emphasises worldliness, hospitality and communitarianism.' Finally, there is the methodological dimension: a new type of social analysis is needed to 'open up to the relational processes which bind local and global, universal and particular, familiar and other' (*Ibid.*, 4). In their analysis of cosmopolitanism as a 'robust but somewhat confused adolescent,' the same scholars noted that 'cosmopolitanism is not a state of nirvana; it is not an endpoint of societal affairs.' It should be understood as a project, an 'ongoing effort of incorporation of cosmopolitan ambition through all its dimensions' (*Ibid.*). Historically, there have been periods where such efforts encountered favorable conditions; after 1870 and closer to our times, this contributed to the rise of globalizations. At other times, however, the cosmopolitan project faced 'reversals, twists of fate and counter-reactions that inhibit[ed] its full flowering'; the term itself became 'largely pejorative, suggestive of moral and ethnic inferiority' (*Ibid.*, 7, 11). The end of the first wave globalizations 'from above' and 'from below' is such an example. The contemporary progress of populist nationalist politicians and parties is a reminder of the fact that such reversals still are – and may always be – possible.

Returning to more theoretical aspects, scholars have debated 'whether the cosmopolitan is simply an "ideal type"' (Rai and Reeves 2009: 5). The theorists involved in the study of cosmopolitanism may tend to 'specialize in abstraction' (Malcomson 1998: 238) and ignore the fact that, even in the present globalized world, 'the negotiation of "homeland" socio-cultural, political and economic identities remain important components' of 'migrant lives and their "imaginaries"' (Rai and Reeves 2009: 5). As a result of this debate, a distinction is made at present 'between cosmopolitanism as an abstract moral ideal and cosmopolitan practices, or "actually existing cosmopolitanism"' (Lewis 2016: 7). Furthermore, Scott Malcomson – who was the first to write about this 'actually existing' process (Malcomson 1998) – and many other scholars have noted that, while there could be only one 'old ideal of the cosmopolitan,' 'cosmopolitanisms are now plural and particular.' They shape and are shaped by specific collectivities; are geographically and socially situated; and are 'both limited and empowered.' Cosmopolitanisms can be 'weak and underdeveloped as well as strong and privileged';

European, as well as non-European (Robbins 1998: 2). A good example is represented by the difference between the Western understanding of cosmopolitanism and that specific to the Ottoman Empire at the time of the first wave globalization (Eldem 2013: 217). Accordingly, Malte Fuhrmann insisted on the need to study cosmopolitanism by integrating 'four common definitions': publicly visible diversity; the ability of individual or collective agents to navigate between differently coded spheres; an active practice of sociabilities that cross-community borders; and a belief and a policy of enhancing cohesion without a monolithic base (Fuhrmann 2007: 12; Gekas 2009: 102). While all are important, 'the notion of cosmopolitanism as a practice, and more specifically a process,' is critical. This is true in general and even more so in the particular case of port cities such as Alexandria or Shanghai: it allows the analysis to shift 'from the stark, anachronistic boundaries of nations' to more relevant 'cross-border flows, hybrid identities, and modes of affiliation that cross-cut communal divides' (Lewis 2016: 7). Levantine cosmopolitanism – as the form of cosmopolitanism specific to the Eastern Mediterranean Basin is known in the literature – 'was first and foremost a social praxis,' as shown by the complex social interactions in the port cities of the late Ottoman Empire (see Eldem 2013: 223). A 'process of negotiation between diverse communities participating in a dynamic and shared public sphere' led to the 'appropriation, integration, and hybridisation of various cultural influences,' which, in turn, 'produce[d] new visions of modernity' (Lewis 2016: 10). The cosmopolitan identity is always the product of 'encounters with difference' that are based on 'an attitude of openness within spaces of cultural flows' (Skrbiš and Woodward 2013: 10–11). Students of Levantine cosmopolitanism have further insisted on the already mentioned inter-communal fluidity and integration that define cosmopolitanism in Eastern Mediterranean ports as a social and cultural praxis resulting from diversity. A 'certain consciousness' – or even a 'political intent' – was associated with this particular sort of social porosity. Critically, it overlapped with the existence of an environment conducive to a culture that is not the simple overlapping of distinct cultures that remain separate. This social environment 'is shaped by the diversity of its constituents, while they, in turn, are also transformed by the [resulting] cosmopolitan cultural milieu' (Eldem 2013: 217–218).

It is important to note that cosmopolitanism is different from and better adapted to the analysis of the first wave globalization 'from below' than the transnationalism discussed in Subchapter 4.4. On the one hand, transnationalism is implicitly associated with 'transcending the borders and limits of the nation-state'; the latter type of polity, however, did not exist in the semi-colonial context under scrutiny. On the other hand and more importantly, the migratory flows of the first wave globalization 'from below' were different from those of the present non-hegemonic or Chinese-centered globalizations. They did not consist of highly mobile individuals or groups whose trade-related activities include the frequent crossing of borders. Most of their actors tended to be settlers: they became stable long-term or permanent inhabitants of the semi-colonial port cities, which changed the very 'nature of the mixed social, cultural, ethnic, and religious fabric of the [local] population' (*Ibid.*, 214). This successful transformative integration into the local society brings the discussion to the critical point of the relationship between cosmopolitanism and the nationalism that, at the time of the first wave globalizations, was conquering the migrants' countries of origin and residence. As discussed in Subchapter 2.4, we tend to identify a clear antinomy between globalization and cosmopolitanism, on the one side, and nationalism, on the other. We have good reasons for such a stand: the first wave globalizations, as well as the cosmopolitanism that supported the 'from below' one, were brought to an end precisely by the rise of nationalism. They were followed by historical periods where the cosmopolitan – 'a rootless, "passportless wanderer"' – was despitefully depicted by Hitlers and Brezhnevs as 'a polluter of the purity of national identity,' 'a threat to patriotism and national identity' that 'confronts the interests of national citizens' (Skrbiš and Woodward 2013: 13). However, for almost half a century, globalizations, semi-colonial cosmopolitanism, and nationalism developed simultaneously. This shows that cosmopolitanism has to be conceived as 'a process working alongside nationalism, sometimes as complementary and sometimes as competitor' (*Ibid.*, 7). Indeed, cosmopolitanism is not necessarily opposed to nationalism if it is seen as a social praxis instead of an ideology. During the first wave globalization 'from below,' the 'fluctuating equilibrium' between declining extra-European empires, powerful but remote Western states, and 'the still diffuse but powerful surge of nationalist currents' created the conditions for enough pragmatic flexibility on all sides to avoid destructive confrontations (Eldem 2013: 223–224). 'Blockages, resistances and immobilities' did exist. More than one century ago as today, the development of cosmopolitanism was 'marked by anomalies, inconsistencies and inequalities' (Skrbiš and Woodward 2013: 11). Ultimately, antagonism erupted and nationalism had the upper hand. In fact, historians and anthropologists insist on 'the fragile nature of cosmopolitanism in places where people deal with heterogeneity as a matter of fact' (Marsden and Skvirskaja 2018: S6). However, for many decades, this did not prevent cosmopolitanism from shaping semi-colonial port cities and giving birth to a globalization 'from below.'

It should be added that the historical ups and downs of 'actually existing cosmopolitanism' have been paralleled by waves of criticism targeting various features of cosmopolitanism as a theoretical concept: since Kant, 'cosmopolitanism as a project of global conviviality in the modern/colonial world' has been Eurocentered and imperial; this is unacceptable and needs to be corrected, possibly through the establishment of a dialogue among civilizations that may include exotic participants such as Iranian Islamists, Spanish Socialists, and Turkish followers of Recep Tayyip Erdoğan (Mignolo 2012: 85, 90–91). Levantine cosmopolitanism may well be only 'nostalgic celebrations by elites of a lost world that never really existed' (Driessen 2005: 135–136; Eldem 2013: 215), with Lawrence Durrell's splendid and much-criticized *Alexandria Quartet* immediately coming to mind. Moreover, its discussion pays no attention to the Western theoretical literature on cosmopolitanism. Cosmopolitanism at the time of first wave globalizations masks colonial or quasi-colonial domination; and, instead of being centered on inclusiveness and fluidity, it excludes the majority of the population and only refers to the elites (Eldem 2013: 215). Much if not all this criticism was valid at the time of its formulation. Yet, I believe that at least the part of such criticism that could have interfered with the analysis of this chapter has already been correctly addressed. In particular, the semi-colonial framework discussed earlier in this subchapter makes no secret of the exploitative context of the cosmopolitanism-based first wave globalization 'from below.' The emphasis on elites is today much less prominent due precisely to the contribution of its critics to the construction of the 'subaltern cosmopolitanism' presented in the following section. Overall, Zlatko Skrbiš and Ian Woodward's 'somewhat confused adolescent' (Skrbiš and Woodward 2013: 4) is 'robust' enough to provide a solid basis to the analysis proposed in this chapter. Accordingly, the next two sections discuss the specific aspects of cosmopolitanism in the semi-colonial port cities of the Eastern Mediterranean and China.

Levantine Cosmopolitanism

I do not make separate presentations of these two cases because they illustrate different types of cosmopolitanism. On the contrary, geographical, cultural, and political diversity did not translate into significant differences when the features and consequences of Levantine and Chinese cosmopolitanism are scrutinized. The separation simply comes from the existence of two different groups of scholars that have studied them independently. While their key findings are similar, they have followed different research paths that I cannot ignore.

To oversimplify, the story of Levantine cosmopolitanism overlaps with the historical 'trajectory of merchants in Eastern Mediterranean ports, from a commercial bourgeoisie to cosmopolitan citizens' (Gekas 2009: 95). The term 'Levantine cosmopolitanism' was coined by Edhem Eldem who wrote about its cultural and, 'to a certain extent, ideological' nature (Eldem 2013: 214). Indeed, much of the criticism discussed in the previous paragraph was formulated in an Eastern Mediterranean context; at times, disputes among concerned scholars have been unusually harsh. These scholars pertain to the fields of Social History, Cultural History, Diaspora Studies, History of Entrepreneurship, and Diaspora Business Studies (for an analysis of successive turns in scholarship see Gekas 2009: 95–97). The recent – but by no means generalized – trend is to assess Levantine cosmopolitanism as 'first and foremost a social praxis, which surfaced in those environments where it was of use or even of necessity' (Eldem 2013: 223). This praxis was 'limited, superficial, socially skewed, and fraught with colonial undertones,' but it was nevertheless relatively successful in 'handling a very complex social and cultural structure' (*Ibid.*, 226). A variety of 'peoples and races' shared a 'particular kind of sociability' (Ilbert 1996: 102) that, as shown in the section about semi-colonialism, led to the emergence of a society lacking 'the usual essentialist markers traditionally associated with coloniality' even in British-occupied Alexandria (Re 2003: 173). In the Ottoman Empire, cosmopolitanism developed in a socio-political context strongly marked by the *millet* system, which was based on a significant degree of autonomy of non-Muslim religious communities. Some scholars view it as an early form of cosmopolitanism (Driessen 2005: 138). Others argue that this 'premodern imperial multiculturalism' was 'hardly more than a basic level of coexistence and *convivenza*.' The creation of Levantine cosmopolitanism 'was characterized by rupture rather than continuity' (Eldem 2013: 220). Critically, the new hybrid culture did not rely mainly on preexisting local cultural elements. The shock between rising Western powers and the declining Ottoman Empire led to a 'new kind of Western-dominated fluidity' accompanied by the 'sudden shift in the center of gravity (...) from Istanbul and Ottoman power to Paris and Western civilization' (*Ibid.*, 221). All dimensions of social life, from fashion to business praxis, were modified to fit French, English, German, or Italian models. French was adopted as a *lingua franca*. Names were changed from Ioannis to Jean and from Stephanos to Étienne. In Istanbul's Pera and Galata, street signs were first in French while urbanism and architecture were clearly European. Levantine cosmopolitanism was strongly marked by a 'globalizing ambition, if not character.' It intended to replace the local dimension with an external one whose key reference was Paris, the center of the civilized world (*Ibid.*, 220, 222–223). This trend was enhanced by the various exchanges and influences associated with the first wave globalization 'from above' and contributed considerably to the development of the parallel 'from below' globalization.

At first view, this depiction of Levantine cosmopolitanism would be difficult to reject. However, it is not free from criticism in one important regard: it relies almost exclusively on elites. The Levantine cosmopolitan is depicted in a way reminiscent of Walter Benjamin's well-to-do *flâneur* (Gusejnova 2018: 17). But the typical multi-lingual merchants operating on international markets and adopting a European lifestyle (Gekas 2009: 104) hardly represented more than a tiny minority that 'was bound to remain extremely marginal with respect to the bulk of the population' (Eldem 2013: 224). Even in Alexandria, there were only a 'few thousand Europeans who spoke French, supported by a thin layer of servants with whom they communicated in pidgin French and Arabic' (Hanley 2017: 166). Most European urban infrastructure was also constructed in the wealthiest neighborhoods. If Levantine cosmopolitanism was limited to small rich elites that may have dismissed locals as 'inferior and repugnant' (Gekas 2009: 106), critics could be right in their attacks against the 'elitist, grieving, nostalgic' vision that 'amplifies the experience of a tiny group of elites and broadcasts it across the whole of a heterogeneous social past' (Hanley 2017: 31). Such cosmopolitanism would have been rather irrelevant and certainly unable to support a fully fledged globalization 'from below'; its affluent actors were typical participants in the first wave globalization 'from above.' In particular, 'the applicability of the concept of cosmopolitanism to (...) Alexandria has been the subject of a longstanding debate among scholars of modern Egypt' (Takla 2016: 11). But this was a fruitful debate as it resulted in a development of the concept of cosmopolitanism that makes it fully compatible with the social landscape of the first wave globalization 'from below.' Levantine cosmopolitanism was not exclusively associated with the elites. Rather, it was concentrated 'at both extremes of the social ladder.' There were the elites that, in addition to successful migrant merchants and entrepreneurs, prominently included the highly cosmopolitan Ottoman and Khedival courts. But there was also the bottom of the society, 'the lowlife of harbors and arsenals, brothels and taverns' with its 'caste of wandering marginals' made of 'scores of sailors and other proletarians roaming the Mediterranean basin' (Eldem 2013: 219). In fact, many in the latter group were not that 'marginal.' Immigrants included various Mediterranean petty-bourgeois (Reimer 1977/2019: 11). Because 'a job around the Eastern Mediterranean was an opportunity for upward mobility for skilled workers' (Fuhrmann 2020: 314), the flows of the first wave globalization 'from below' included many such migrants (Gekas 2009: 104). They settled in cosmopolitan port cities and, as shown in the next subchapter, at times succeeded in significantly improving their socio-economic status. Not all came from developed countries. Their places of origin may have been Greece, various Italian regions, or Slovenia. A large category that is difficult to ignore is that of subjects from the French and British colonial empires. The numerous Algerians, Tunisians, and Maltese who settled in Alexandria were treated as 'second-class foreigners.' Yet, despite their lower status, they represented cosmopolitan minorities. Overall, 'subaltern foreigners (...) overwhelmed the foreign elite.' Between the wealthy Europeans and the poor Arabic-speaking population, the middle of Alexandria's social hierarchy 'was a murky mix of overlapping characters and statuses' that benefited from capitulatory privileges and were undeniably cosmopolitan in nature (Hanley 2017: 13, 175–177). By taking into consideration these important social strata, scholars such as Khaled Fahmy, Will Hanley, and Nefertiti Takla shifted the focus of Levantine cosmopolitanism to non-elites (Takla 2016: 2–3) and turned it into a cosmopolitanism of the unprivileged (Robbins 1998: 1). Will Hanley proposed the concept of 'vulgar cosmopolitanism,' which he defined as 'not obscene but low, unrefined, plain, common, ordinary cosmopolitanism' (Hanley 2017: 31). Its actors include the 'alcohol drinker, café goer, curser and accursed, walker and driver, public official, newcomer and native, foreign and local.' Settings are expanded to Alexandria's obscure streets with their grog shops, fighting drunken seamen, and police interventions. This 'spatial as well as conceptual relocation of analysis' 'pushes the concept of cosmopolitanism beyond its traditionally elite and Eurocentric framework' (Takla 2016: 12; Gekas 2009: 102; Hanley 2017: 33). 'Subaltern,' rather than 'vulgar,' cosmopolitanism is perhaps a more appropriate term, which is also used in the case of the counter-hegemonic globalization 'from below' (see Subchapter 3.1); but the point is that this upgrade of the analytical framework neutralized an important part of the criticism questioning Levantine cosmopolitanism as a concept. Moreover, by including large subaltern cosmopolitan socio-economic groups, it reveals the diversity of actors involved in the first wave globalization 'from below' and illuminates its class-related dimension. While ethnic and religious divisions were visible, cosmopolitan Eastern Mediterranean port cities lacked rigid caste-like stratification (Reimer 1977/2019: 11). Class, however, 'is still a valuable analytical tool, and is compatible with the notion of cosmopolitanism.' In particular, it can help explain inter-communal conflicts (Gekas 2009: 95). In Alexandria, the most pronounced social tensions were those between the poor Arabic-speaking population and the relatively poor South European immigrants. Economic competition between the two groups was 'skewed by the international connections, exemptions from taxation, and diplomatic protection' enjoyed by foreigners. Unsurprisingly, the 1882 riots that ultimately resulted in the British occupation were sparked by a conflict between a Maltese and a local Arab (Reimer 1977/2019: 11).

Despite such tensions and occasional conflicts, numerous scholars insist on the fact that – as repeatedly mentioned in the previous pages – Levantine cosmopolitanism represented a particular kind of sociability associated with fluidity and porosity in communal and individual boundaries, as well as integration, that was structurally induced by the 'frequent demographic flux' of Eastern Mediterranean port cities (Takla 2016: 3, 13; Ilbert 1996: 102; Re 2003: 172; Eldem 2013: 217–218). This 'demographic flux' consisted mainly of migratory flows that, while considerably more modest than transatlantic ones, were nevertheless important. During the first wave globalization 'from below,' Mediterranean 'migration took place on a scale that had not been seen since the time of the Reconquista' (Fuhrmann 2020: 31). The region became 'a maritime space of colonial interactions and entanglements that transcended continental and national boundaries' (Borutta and Gekas quoted in Fuhrmann 2020: 31–32). The inhabitants of port cities in the Eastern Mediterranean Basin 'felt more affinity with each other than they did with the inhabitants of non-port cities' in their vicinity. These cities became a 'major breeding ground of globalization' (Driessen 2005: 129, 131), a 'complex field of negotiation between local, overseas, and in-between agents' (Shlala 2018: 16) that represented the actors of the first wave globalization 'from below.'

The most representative of these cities, Alexandria, is analyzed in the next subchapter. However, it may be useful to remind the existence of other similar cosmopolitan places located in the Ottoman Empire. At the beginning of the 20th century, its very capital, Constantinople, was inhabited by no less than 130,000 foreign residents that represented 15 percent of the total population. Furthermore, they were concentrated in the contiguous neighborhoods of Galata and Pera, whose urban landscape was strongly 'European.' Pera was a residential area, but Galata became the epicenter of globalized economic activities (Eldem 2013: 220–221, 223). During the Byzantine Empire, it had been the site of the Genoese commercial colony. Later, European embassies were established. Already in 1858, more than 100,000 of its 237,000 inhabitants were 'Europeans'; most of them were in fact Ottoman Christians who had acquired Western citizenship. Out of the Ottoman nationals, 32,000 were Greek, 28,000 Armenian, and 25,000 Jewish. Muslims numbered only 40,000. Administratively, the municipality of Galata was eventually created with a council whose members were, as in Shanghai's International Settlement, local property owners (Rosenthal 1980/2005: 129, 131). Accordingly, it is hardly surprising that, as mentioned earlier in this section, the preferred language of advertisements, as well as street signs, was French. The architecture and urbanism were European. 'Major economic, political, and cultural institutions of integration with the West' also existed (Eldem 2013: 223). Elsewhere in the Ottoman Empire, until the 'destruction of its social fabric' in 1922, Smyrna was inhabited by a Greek majority but had a complex demographic composition that contributed to its cosmopolitan character, as did the efforts of city merchants to 'promot[e] a European culture including socialization in clubs and literary societies, and reading habits' (Gekas 2009: 102, 105, 107). In Beirut, foreign consuls, bankers, and merchants were highly influential but not numerous. It was the indigenous Christian Arab commercial bourgeoisie that acquired the protection of Western consuls and used fiscal and judicial exemptions to considerably upgrade its socio-economic status (Reimer 1977/2019: 190). This merchant elite relied on business networks to export mainly silk and attracted West European capitals. Its 'strong sense of urban identity' allowed it to resist both Ottoman centralizing efforts and the control by the elite of notables in Damascus. A lower-middle class also made up of Christian Arabs developed and got involved in transnational economic activities, too (Gekas 2009: 106). Other examples include Salonica – inhabited mainly by Sephardic Jews – and, to a lesser extent, Jaffa, Latakia, and Alexandretta (Reimer 1977/2019: 5). In all these Levantine ports, cosmopolitanism combined with semi-colonialism to launch and maintain the first wave globalization 'from below.' At the other end of Asia, a similar development characterized China's treaty ports.

Treaty Port Cosmopolitanism in China

The so-called treaty ports are – or rather, were – China's 92 ports opened to the foreign presence by the series of 'unequal' treaties that followed the first Opium War. Fourteen foreign powers took advantage of the dramatic decline of the Chinese state to create extraterritorial concessions and settlements (Jackson 2018: 3; see Subchapter 6.3), which led to the development of cosmopolitanism on a scale comparable with the Levantine one. The topic has been thoroughly studied and, different from Alexandria's case, scholarly disputes have been polite. The only challenge comes from the fact that much of the research has concentrated on the truly fascinating cosmopolitan turn taken by the *Chinese* culture in Shanghai. This is a very beautiful topic indeed; but what I study here is the first wave globalization 'from below,' whose main actors were the cosmopolitan *foreign* residents of the concessions. Accordingly, I do not explore the various kinds of cosmopolitanism that China has experienced during different historical periods or the details of the radical transformation triggered by its encounters with the West (Rofel 2012: 443). Moreover, I painfully try to limit my analysis of Shanghai, 'the Paris of the Orient' (Wakeman 1995: 19; Wu 2004: 164), to those cosmopolitan aspects that are relevant to this chapter.

While cosmopolitanism developed in all treaty ports, it was Shanghai that, due to the existence of the International Settlement and the French Concession, 'became the epitome of the European-oriented cosmopolitanism that was prevalent on China's eastern coast.' As shown in more detail in Subchapter 6.3, extraterritorial privileges brought important European, American, and Japanese minorities that progressively turned Shanghai into a semi-colonial 'cosmopolitan city par excellence.' 'This cosmopolitan world was built out of the transformations in the world economy fueled by industrial capitalism' (Rofel 2012: 445). The first wave globalization 'from above' created the conditions for multifaceted interactions that went far beyond the early trade activities. Textile factories were established whose output was exported to Europe and America. Western ideas arrived and shaped everything from culture to politics. The architecture of the Bund still 'features Romanesque, Gothic, renaissance, baroque, neo-classical, beaux arts and art deco buildings that were once European banks and trading houses, as well as hotels and clubs' (*Ibid.*, 445–446; see Subchapter 6.3). Western dress and habits were adopted by locals. Major Chinese stores hired European sales assistants to attend to customers from the foreign elite (Nield 2015: 207). Fashion and cuisine got Westernized. Ballrooms and movie theaters were opened. Missionary zeal was invested in the spread of modernist literature, feminism, and Christianity. Elites and non-elites were equally concerned (Rofel 2012: 446). 'This electric and lurid city more exciting than any other in the world' (J. G. Ballard quoted in Abbas 2002: 214) 'experienced the rise of modern industrial entertainment': the old 'pre-electric city of pleasure' was replaced with 'a garishly illuminated metropolis of night-life vice in cabarets, dance halls, and bordellos.' It developed a department-store culture based on 'merchandised performances' in 'multi-storied amusement centers.' And, most importantly, it moved 'from Sino-foreign segregation to intermixed social intercourse' (Wakeman 1995: 19). A sophisticated urban culture developed that 'involved the growth of both socioeconomic institutions and new forms of cultural activities in modern literature, print media, cinema, and theater' (Wu 2004: 159). The foreign presence led to the emergence of new types of public and social spaces that were unknown in China. Their initial beneficiaries were the migrants, but soon they were 'appropriated by the Chinese themselves and used to construct a Chinese version of modern cosmopolitan culture' (Abbas 2002: 214), as beautifully shown in Leo Ou-fan Lee's *Shanghai Modern* (Lee 1999). In parenthesis being said, this is a book that I recommend as much as Durrell's *Quartet*. While fundamentally different in nature, both are essential to the understanding of semi-colonial cosmopolitanism as a concept and a mythology. In more practical terms, cosmopolitanism was enhanced in Shanghai by a specific feature uncharacteristic to other, more conservative parts of China: 'a local tradition of easy acceptance to outsiders, which formed as the city opened its door to foreigners,' as well as migrants from other Chinese provinces (Wu 2004: 159). The latter came to represent over 70 percent of the population; but 'the city seemed most receptive to those who spoke a Western language.' The modernity they brought generated 'a pattern of shock, wonder, admiration, and imitation' (*Ibid.*, 164). As a result, in 1928, Francis Pott depicted Shanghai as 'a meeting ground for people from all countries, a great and a unique city, one of the most remarkable in the world' (quoted in Wu 2004: 159). Christine Cornet labeled it 'the most cosmopolitan city of China and of the world' (quoted in Vandamme 2018: 37).

On the migrants' side – which is relevant to the first wave globalization 'from below' – cosmopolitanism was the result of 'the symbiosis of the different imperial diasporas, sharing a similar raison d'être.' Intercultural bonds emerged that were the product of social practices of conviviality showing a 'willingness to share a single social space and to create an international community, albeit totally excluding Chinese society' (Vandamme 2018: 38; Fuhrmann 2007: 15–16). In the 'polycentric, decentered city controlled by many different hands' (see Subchapter 6.3) that was 'subject to constant negotiations,' a 'cosmopolitanism of extraterritoriality' developed (Abbas 2002: 214). The extraterritoriality-related privileges were indeed an important factor, as were the common challenges faced by the migrants and their feeling of cultural superiority over the Chinese. Similar to the case of Alexandria, this was an 'everyday cosmopolitanism': foreigners went to the same bars, attended the same park concerts, participated in the management of local institutions, and became business partners. German and British merchants frequently created common companies, whose nationality became blurred. Before 1914, nationalisms were considerably softened by mutual respect (Vandamme 2018: 48–49). In fact, class differences were more important among foreigners than nationality-based ones. British, French, or German clubs, bars, and tennis courts were frequented by all elites. The municipal orchestra sponsored by the International Settlement and the French Concession had a German conductor, as well as musicians from Germany and Austria-Hungary. Apparent national schools and churches had in fact an international clientele. The French Jesuits did the sermon in both French and English and invited Germans to attend. National holidays of Western powers were celebrated in common, with the final night torchlight procession bringing together the municipal band and foreigners of all nationalities (*Ibid.*, 46–48). Far from being limited to the upper classes, Shanghai's cosmopolitanism had a strong subaltern component. There was an inflow of 'such illegitimate social players as fugitives from justice, former bandits, and prostitutes.' There were 'wanted criminals [and] business[men] that had fled lawsuits in their homelands.' Prostitutes and 'urban vice figures' were constantly accused of having imported 'amoral practices' in Shanghai's entertainment milieu. The Civil War in Russia brought large numbers of impoverished White Russians. Many Jews persecuted in Russia and, later, Germany also arrived. Political dissidents and radicals took refuge in the city, where they continued to promote anti-capitalist and anti-imperialist ideas (Yue 2006: xxiii). At the same time, similar to Alexandria and the port cities of the Ottoman Empire, immigrants brought with them the cultural luggage specific to their places of origin. Western culture, lifestyle, and urbanism visibly influenced all inhabitants of the International Settlement and the French Concession, including non-Western ones. The only important difference between Shanghai and Alexandria was linguistic: instead of French, English was the lingua franca. Still, the important British and American influence did not prevent French culture from being highly influential. These diverse flows of people and ideas added to the important economic exchanges conducted by Shanghai's cosmopolitan small merchants and entrepreneurs to create and expand the first wave globalization 'from below.'

However, it was noted that 'there was always something very fragile about Shanghai cosmopolitanism.' The city certainly was the 'most open' in China, but its 'linkage to the world went together with a delinkage' from the rest of the country (Abbas 2002: 215–216). The 'exclusionary nature of Settlement cosmopolitanism' was obvious to any observer. The municipal motto was *omnia juncta in uno* (all joined into one); but the municipal coat of arms included only the flags of countries that had a consul in Shanghai, thus excluding China (Goodman 2000: 896). The huge 1893 celebration of Queen Victoria's Jubilee was conceived as representative of the unity of Shanghai's 'truly cosmopolitan community.' It was nevertheless 'almost entirely Western in terms of conception and participation' (*Ibid.*). The Chinese were treated as equals only when they were useful, which reversed the pre-1842 attitude of the Chinese authorities toward foreigners (Tomášek 2021: 70). An example of clearly established social hierarchy is provided by differences between the staff of the police of the French Concession. A small number of French nationals were at the top. The second layer was represented, after the Bolshevik revolution, by White Russians that were treated as cheap white labor. Most policemen were Vietnamese and Chinese, but they had the lowest and poorest paid positions (Xiaoming 2020: 66). Anti-Chinese discrimination was harsher in the International Settlement. An extreme example is that of public parks: while financed with public money that included taxes paid by the Chinese, they were literally closed to the latter (Hudson 1927: 83). Already in the 1850s, a Russian writer had noted that, in Shanghai, the English 'get rich on account of the Chinese, poison them [with opium], and then despise their victims' (Ivan Goncharov quoted in Crawford 2018: 974). Alexandria's poor Arabs were not in a better position, but at least discrimination against them was not formal. Of course, in the long run, such differences did not matter: in both cities, resentment against foreigners led to nationalist reactions (Veeser 2013: 1141) that ultimately put an end to cosmopolitanism and the first wave globalization 'from below.' It is interesting, however, to note a detail of the early emancipatory movement in Shanghai. At the turn of the 20th century, in their rejection of Western imperialism, local Chinese intellectuals tended to replace the translation of American, British, French, and German literature with that of works written in places such as Greece, Scotland, or Poland (Yue 2006: xxiv; Karl 2002). In other words, the means they initially chose to fight imperialist cosmopolitanism was a differently flavored cosmopolitanism. Until the communist takeover in 1949, Shanghai remained deeply cosmopolitan in almost all of its dimensions; and this contributed considerably to its transformation into one of the key nodes of the first wave globalization 'from below.'

To summarize, previous sections show the importance of semi-colonialism, extraterritoriality, and cosmopolitanism for the development of the first wave globalization 'from below.' Western powers used extraterritoriality to turn their migrants into pawns that weakened semi-colonial states. These pawns, however, took advantage of the interstices created by the relative balance between the weakness of local authorities and the incomplete, neocolonial-type Western control. Lack of state-imposed constraints allowed for 'from below' agency, which resulted in economic processes and flows that were not planned or expected by great powers. This agency was greatly enhanced by the cosmopolitan nature of migrant communities. Cosmopolitanism led to openness locally and globally, which stimulated the flows of people, goods, and ideas up to the point of turning them into a fully fledged globalization 'from below.' The following case studies analyze the details of this process using the examples of the most representative nodes of this globalization: Alexandria and Shanghai.

6.2 The First Wave Globalization 'from Below' in Alexandria

As discussed in the previous subchapter, a considerable amount of criticism targeted Alexandria's Eurocentric, imperialist, colonial, exploitative, anti-Egyptian, anti-Arab, racist, discriminatory, elitist, nostalgic, or even inexistent cosmopolitanism. In fact, such criticism concerned specific scholarly understandings and literary depictions of this social phenomenon. Recent conceptual progress – which prominently includes the introduction of subaltern cosmopolitanism – makes possible a more consensual assessment of its features, historical trajectory, and impact. However, even prior to this theoretical development, only radical Egyptian nationalists went as far as denying that, between the 1860s and 1956, Alexandria developed into 'one of the most sophisticated cities in the Mediterranean' (Mansel 2004). Ismail Serageldin, the Egyptian founding director of the Bibliotheca Alexandrina, described it as 'a great city by any standard' (Haag 2014: 449). This 'greatness' may have been irrelevant to the lower Arabic-speaking classes, but it completely dissipated after the massive expulsion of the 'Levantines' as the city 'was sidelined by history and overshadowed by Cairo' (Naguib Mahfouz quoted in Haag 2014: 449). More importantly for this chapter, the death of Alexandrian cosmopolitanism in 1956 marked the end of its almost nine-decade-old globalization 'from below.' To understand this remarkably long globalization, a brief incursion in Egypt's history is needed.

Khedives and Great Powers

Egypt became part of the Ottoman Empire in 1516, but the viceroys sent from Constantinople relied on the Mamluks – mainly Turco-Circassian slave-soldiers who had ruled the country since 1250 – to impose their authority. The brief 1798–1801 Napoleonic occupation was, 'more than anything else, (...) an effort to rewrite a cultural order' (Maghraoui 2006: 2–3, 37). It failed, but one of its unintended consequences changed Egypt's historical trajectory. Muhammad Ali, an Albanian volunteer officer whose family house can still be visited in Kavalla, then located in Ottoman Thrace, arrived in 1801 to fight the French, whom he would eventually greatly admire. Four years later, he became governor of Egypt. He stayed in power until 1848 and founded a dynasty overthrown only in 1952 (Al-Sayyid Marsot 2007: 64; Mansel 2011: 56; Maghraoui 2006: 3). Most importantly, he turned the Ottoman province into a powerful *de facto* state; and initiated a Meiji era of European-inspired modernization. His policies were followed by his successors, even if they did not have 'half his energy or imagination, to say nothing of his political skill' (Al-Sayyid Marsot 2007: 78). During the first decade of the first wave globalizations, Egypt was ruled by Ali's grandson Ismail (1863–1879). He was formally recognized by the Sultan as Khedive (ruler) and famously inaugurated the Suez Canal in 1869. Less propitiously, he borrowed far beyond Egypt's means while the cotton boom due to the American Civil War came to an end in 1866. That was a huge political mistake. In 1876, creditor Western powers imposed the so-called Dual Control system. The Egyptian debt was managed by the *Caisse de la Dette Publique* made up of four commissioners designated by England, France, Austria, and Italy. Two controllers, one English and one French, supervised state revenue and expenditure. From August 1878, the Minister of Finance was English and that of Public Works French. Tensions developed. The Khedive was deposed in 1879. His son and successor, Tawfiq (1879–1892), negotiated in 1880 the Law of Liquidation: a large part of the national revenue would be used to repay the foreign debt. This 'law effected a stranglehold on Egypt, which from that moment on was unable to move without European permission' (*Ibid.*, 80–84; Hunter 1998: 188–189, 194–197; Reid 1998: 219). In 1876, the foreign control over Egyptian finances had created 'a state within a state.' By 1879, 'Europe had taken over the state itself': 'Egypt's relative political independence (...) existed no more' (Hunter 1998: 181, 197). However, a certain balance of power between interested great powers prevented the country from becoming a colony. Among these powers, it was France that brought the largest contribution to the modernization of Egypt under both Muhammad Ali and Ismail. But Britain perceived Egypt as essential to its communications with India (Goldschmidt 2004: 38) and legitimated its claims to predominant influence by invoking its larger economic presence (Hunter 1998: 195). Indeed, by 1880, Britain represented the destination of 80 percent of Egyptian exports, the source of 44 percent of imports, and owned much of the foreign debt. Its ships made up 80 percent of those using the French-constructed Suez Canal, whose control it acquired in 1875 by buying Ismail's shares. It was in 1882 that London finally succeeded in upgrading its control of Egyptian affairs. The 1881–1882 'Urabi Revolt – or Revolution – 'tried to roll back Anglo-French financial and political predominance, the Turco-Circassian monopoly on high military posts, and the authority of Khedive Tawfiq' (Reid 1998: 217, 219). The crisis escalated from an anti-European riot in Alexandria to the bombarding of the city by the British fleet and the occupation of the country by Britain's military. The resulting 'veiled protectorate' lasted until 1914. It was based on the Granville Doctrine: all key ministries were monitored by British advisers. Egyptian ministers who did not obey British directives had to resign their office. 'The Khedive fully acquiesced in the system and, since he was utterly pusillanimous, was content to obey [the British] in all matters' (Al-Sayyid Marsot 2007: 87–90; Reid 1998: 217–219). But even during this period, Egypt did not become a fully fledged colony. The historiography makes constant reference to a number of important 'anomalies.' *De jure*, Egypt continued to be an Ottoman province occupied by a friendly power against the Sultan's will. The British simply 'advised' the local government, which was responsible only to the Khedive; but their advice was compulsory. The British representative that ruled the country was only an 'agent and consul-general.' Moreover, to limit French hostility, the 'internationalism' of the previous period was in part preserved. The Dual Control was abolished, but the Capitulations, the *Caisse de la Dette Publique*, and the mixed courts introduced in 1876 were preserved (Daly 1998: 240). Economically, Egypt's exploitation was more neo-colonial in nature, with an emphasis on the production of raw materials. The industry declined while Egyptian agriculture was transformed 'into a monoculture, cotton, to feed the mills of Lancashire' (Al-Sayyid Marsot 2007: 93). Overall, the semi-colonial situation created by the European powers in the 1870s continued to exist under British rule. When the Ottoman Empire entered World War I in 1914, London finally proclaimed Egypt a protectorate. Ironically, the title of the new Khedive, Husayn Kamil, was upgraded to Sultan (Daly 1998: 246). A new nationalist revolution ignited and was suppressed in 1919. In response, Britain abolished the protectorate and declared unilaterally Egypt's independence in 1922. Predictably, four 'Reserved Points' severely limited it. Interestingly, one of them explicitly mentioned the protection of foreign minorities in Egypt (Goldschmidt 2004: 72; Daly 1998: 250; Al-Sayyid Marsot 2007: 96–98). It was the Anglo-Egyptian Treaty of 1936 that was perceived as the final step toward political independence. With British support, Egypt joined the League of Nations. In 1937, the Montreux Convention abolished the Capitulations. The Mixed Courts were phased out over a 13-year period, which ended in 1949 (Botman 1998: 295; Goldschmidt 2004: 79). Foreign residents started to leave Egypt, even if the scale of this phenomenon was still limited (Al-Sayyid Marsot 2007: 116). In January 1952, guerrilla attacks in the Canal Zone and an anti-British riot in Cairo led to the burning of a large part of that city. Against this backdrop, the Free Officers' July 1952 coup d'état marked the end of liberal democracy in Egypt (Botman 1998: 307) and the accession to power of a resolutely nationalist political force. President Nasser took advantage of the 1956 Suez War to expel and expropriate the assets of large numbers of foreign nationals and permanently resident Greeks, Italians, Jews, Armenians, and Syrian Christians (Beinin 1998: 310; Al-Sayyid Marsot 2007: 137; Goldschmidt 2004: 126). This dramatic event put an end to semi-colonialism, cosmopolitanism, and the first wave globalization 'from below' in Egypt.

Alexandria and Its Foreigners

In 1798, when Napoleon arrived in Alexandria, Egypt lacked even roads for wheeled vehicles (Goldschmidt 2004: 36). In 1806, Chateaubriand described the 6,000-inhabitant port as 'the saddest and most deserted place in the world.' By 1849, however, 'Alexandria was a city of over 100,000: at once a port, a cosmopolis, and the key to the future of Egypt' (Mansel 2011: 56). By 1878, it had wide streets, railroad stations, restaurants, hotels, and department stores that made it resemble Western cities. In 1881, telephones began to be installed. While Arabic-speaking lower classes continued to live in abject poverty, 'the elite culture was Egypt's cutting edge' (Goldschmidt 2004: 36–37). This remarkable development was export-driven and followed the opening and modernization of Egypt under Muhammad Ali. Alexandria was the main port for the export of food crops and raw materials such as cotton. Due to its economic role, by 1850, it became 'the bridgehead and bastion of the European presence in Egypt' (Reimer 1977/2019: 5, 194). During the first half of the 1860s, the American Civil War dramatically affected British imports of cotton. In conjunction with the completion of the Cairo-Alexandria railway, this triggered a cotton boom that brought spectacular growth in various economic sectors (Shlala 2009: 49). The first wave globalization 'from above' further stimulated economic expansion in Alexandria as 'Egypt was more closely integrated into the world economy in a dependent status' (Toledano 1998: 284). Large banks and companies were established such as the Bank of Alexandria, the Bank of Egypt, and the Alexandria General Produce Association. 'The "palpitating heart" of the city was the bourse on the Place Muhammad Ali' (Mansel 2011: 133). The city had the second largest Cotton Exchange in the world (Awad and Hamouda 2006/2012: 24) and was the third Mediterranean port in volume of traffic. This made Egypt's government locate here, and not in Cairo, the headquarters of the customs and postal services, as well as those of the ports and quarantine system (Mansel 2011: 132). Alexandria played an important role in the advancement of European semi-colonialism in Egypt, which in many regards was similar to more recent neocolonialism (see the previous subchapter): through its economic activities, the city accelerated the country's dependence on agricultural exports; it provided key services – including financial and legal – to European businesses penetrating Egypt; and, importantly for this chapter, it 'host[ed] the country's largest and most assertive colony of foreigners, which possessed unassailable extraterritorial rights' (Reimer 1977/2019: 187). The presence of these foreigners was the direct consequence of the port's need for 'services to lubricate the wheels of commerce, such as merchant banking, money lending, currency exchange, commodities brokerage, maritime insurance, warehousing, post offices, telegraph services, and so forth' (*Ibid.*, 9). Certain scholars went as far as stating that 'Alexandria's cosmopolitanism was the result of Egypt's incorporation into the world market' (Re 2003: 172). While, as shown in Subchapter 6.1, more is needed for the emergence of cosmopolitanism than the mere presence of ethnic minorities, it is clear that this process could have not developed in Alexandria without economy-related massive immigration.

Mohammed Ali was the first to attract French, British, Italians, and Greeks into the port he turned into his summer capital (Mansel 2004). This trend visibly intensified under the rule of his Paris-educated son, Sa'id (1854–1863), who encouraged foreigners to settle in both Alexandria and Cairo (Goldschmidt 2004: 33). This policy was very successful due to the cotton boom. But immigration rates remained high even after its end in 1866. The effect on Alexandria was 'dramatic' (Shlala 2009: 42, 49). The foreign communities contributed significantly to the process of modernization (Polyzoides 2014: 118). They were in large measure responsible for the 'rapid development in industry, construction, infrastructure, and cultivation,' as well as the spatial and economic expansion of the city (Shlala 2009: 42). Many engineers, entrepreneurs, and educators 'performed great services.' But they were accompanied by 'a demimonde of stock speculators, swindlers, and vice peddlers' who exploited capitulatory privileges in any possible way (Goldschmidt 2004: 33). The Capitulations previously granted by the Ottoman Sultans were valid in Egypt and allowed foreigners to benefit from all the advantages of extraterritoriality discussed in the relevant section of the previous subchapter. As shown there, they benefitted from important legal and economic privileges. On the fiscal side, Egypt was different from the rest of the Ottoman Empire in one key aspect: taxes could be imposed on foreigners only when sanctioned by a specific international convention (Rosenthal 1980/2005: 128). This was a strong incentive for numerous non-Muslim natives to buy a passport and become 'foreigners.' However, both the possibility and the temptation existed to buy *more than one* passport: the aforementioned 'legal chameleon' (Fahmy 2013) could choose the national law that best fit each situation, thus taking full advantage of the consular and, from 1876, Mixed Courts. Consequently, in Alexandria 'one could (...) have several nationalities and use them like credit cards' (Ilbert quoted in Minkin 2009: 24). At the same time, facilitating employment and commercial transactions with various countries made members of the same family choose different nationalities (Giuliani Caponetto 2008: 145; Re 2003: 173). Such situations may seem highly exotic even to an observer familiar with the present globalized world. It should nevertheless be reminded that it was only in 1926 that Egyptian citizenship became effective. From 1866, any Ottoman subject living in Egypt since 1848 was considered Egyptian. But 'the difference between native and non-native, between indigenous and foreigner (...) were rather fluid and ambiguous in Alexandria' (Re 2003: 173). Due to advantages associated with this ambiguity, to the city's foreign inhabitants, 'the desire *not* to be affiliated with any specific country was as important as any feeling of belonging to their respective homelands' (Giuliani Caponetto 2008: 145; emphasis in the original). Accordingly, to designate them, historians have employed terms such as '*gens de passage*, local notables, cultural intermediaries, "cultural creoles," "trans-imperial subjects," [and] "communitarian cosmopolitans"' (Shlala 2018: 4). These terms are perhaps more useful than 'legal chameleons' as they emphasize an important dimension of Alexandria's cosmopolitanism: it was based on 'a certain fluidity of identity in a city that saw itself as neither totally of Egypt nor determined by a European sense of nationality' (Minkin 2009: 24). Moreover, the immigrants were in no way passive targets of a process beyond their control. On the contrary, it was their agency that 'manipulated the flux and fluidity of identities' in ways 'most advantageous in a given situation' (Shlala 2009: 7). An example is that of the Consular Era when, as mentioned in the previous subchapter, such 'savvy Mediterranean cosmopolitans' (*Ibid.*) brought huge losses to the Egyptian treasury through dubious or fraudulent claims for indemnification that were supported by consuls (Hunter 1998: 187–188). This example is also illustrative of the complex relationship between the normative power of the Western powers and the role of pawn these powers ascribed to their migrants. Western consular offices in Egypt acquired political power by protecting their nationals who abused capitulatory privileges. This was a means of domination as important as the instrumentalization of the Egyptian public debt presented in the previous section (*Ibid.*). (It should be noted that both are semi-colonial in nature and are much closer to neocolonialism than to a genuinely colonial situation). But no European power intended to share its loyal pawns in Alexandria with rivals; nor did it expect – or like – their daily shifting between possibly many citizenships to better exploit economic, legal, and perhaps political circumstances. This was most visible in the case of Fascist Italy, which 'was unable and unwilling to deal with the fluid and indeterminate nature of the [Italian] Alexandrian community' and abhorred 'its ambiguous national and religious identity games' (Re 2003: 189). Mussolini launched a campaign of 'italianization' intended to restore patriotic values and a 'more appropriate lifestyle,' but his initiatives encountered considerable resistance. Even after two decades of efforts, 'the Italian community remained anchored to its feelings of non-affiliation and non-belonging' (Giuliani Caponetto 2008: 147, 148). The Alexandrian 'pawns' did take advantage of Western powers' projection of normative power when it was beneficial to their own interests; but resisted it when it became counterproductive. Blind subordination was out of the question. Immigrants' self-interested agency was centered on one clear goal: to benefit from the legal and fiscal privileges of extraterritoriality that gave them a huge comparative advantage with respect to indigenous rivals. It was 'nearly impossible for Egyptians to compete in large-scale commerce, finance, and construction' (Reid 1998: 220). Sacrificing the cosmopolitan ambiguity that enhanced this advantage for the sake of a remote fatherland was not an option. It is this inbuilt opportunism that explains the success of the first wave globalization 'from below' in Alexandria.

Unsurprisingly, the Egyptian port became a pole of attraction for immigrants from all over the Mediterranean and beyond. The number of foreigners in Egypt increased from 6,000 in 1840 to about 68,000 in 1870, 85,822 in 1882, 103,512 in 1897, 140,847 in 1907, and about 200,000 in 1922. By 1907, they owned most of Egypt's manufacturing and trading companies, as well as about 15 percent of the land (Toledano 1998: 254, 274; Shlala 2009: 205; Goldschmidt 2004: 72). They were also overrepresented in the upper echelons of the state bureaucracy. In 1882, only 2 percent of all officials were foreigners; but they drew 16 percent of the payroll (Reid 1998: 220). When Egypt's independence was unilaterally proclaimed by Britain in 1922, 'the country remained almost wholly dependent on foreigners.' Most of the higher military positions were staffed by the British. The majority of government officials were British, European, Syrian, and Armenian. Foreigners continued to own and manage 'nearly all public utilities, manufacturing firms, transportation companies, hotels, banks, and insurance companies' (Goldschmidt 2004: 72). Turning to Alexandria, its overall population reached 232,636 in 1882 and 444,617 in 1917; 20 to 25 percent of them were foreigners (Mansel 2011: 132–133; Reid 1998: 231). The percentage eventually increased. In 1927, the city's first statistical survey showed that there were 230,000 Egyptians and 110,000 foreigners in the city. The largest groups were the Greeks (36,000), Italians (22,000), Jews (20,000), British (15,000), and French (9,000). By 1950, the numbers of Egyptians and foreigners had increased to half a million and 195,000, respectively. There were 100,000 Greeks, 30,000 Italians, 30,000 Jews, and 10,000 British. All this came to an end in 1956. Only 1,500 foreigners lived in the city in 1993 and less than 800 in 2012 (Polyzoides 2014: 117–118, 123). Before the Suez War, however, the massive foreign presence and the influential economic, social, and political positions occupied by its elites had a very strong impact on Alexandria's development as a cosmopolitan semi-colonial city.

A City Run by Non-Egyptians

Internationalized economic activities and the presence of foreigners in Alexandria 'almost inevitably called forth a more sophisticated sort of civic administration than had traditionally existed.' Immigrant merchants and entrepreneurs pressed for improved transportation and communication, efficient mechanisms to settle commercial disputes, and 'a more orderly, sanitary, and esthetically satisfying urban environment' (Reimer 1977/2019: 10). In principle, all these should have fallen under the responsibility of Egyptian authorities. But, during the Consular Era, consulates acquired a high degree of formal and informal influence over urban policy and administration, which they used to introduce beneficial reforms but also to preserve the *status quo* that privileged their nationals (*Ibid.*). Other factors have to be added: 'dozens of formal legal institutions drew on international' – rather than Egyptian – 'law to ask and answer questions about the categories of affiliation of individuals' (Hanley 2017: 17). In large measure, the city was informally controlled by 'diverse and powerful business interests' often connected with immigrant elites (Takla 2016: 17). By exploiting capitulatory privileges and the informal influence of foreign consulates, the notables of the 14 non-Muslim communities 'effectively (…) regulate[d] the life of the city' (Ostle 2002: 315). Consequently, Alexandria 'was a city with many authorities but no hegemon' (Hanley 2017: 17). As a result, different from fully fledged colonies, it lacked a unified administration (Reimer 1977/2019: 10; Re 2003: 172); and, until World War I, it maintained a certain degree of autonomy (Takla 2016: 17). Alexandria's administrative structure included the Khedival administration and a separate 'complex system of intersecting offices' such as the *Intendence Sanitaire* in charge of health issues or the *Commissione dell'Ornato* responsible for urban planning. Most of these offices were jointly managed by Khedival administrators and the foreign consulates (Re 2003: 172–173). Most importantly, in 1890, the autonomous Alexandria municipality was established that 'let non-Egyptians run the city' (Mansel 2011: 131). Out of its 28 members, eight were appointed by Egypt's government while the rest were elected by property owners (eight), inhabitants who paid a new municipal tax (six), exporters (three), and importers (three). Public municipal documents were in French and Arabic, but internal ones were always in French. The staff was multinational. The first director-general, Joseph Chakour, was a locally born Lebanese Maronite educated in France who had a German wife. The first council included, in addition to the eight Egyptians nominated by the government in Cairo, six Greeks and four Englishmen. Some did not speak Arabic. In 1912, out of the 2,713 general voters who elected 20 of the council's 28 members, only 357 were Egyptians (Mansel 2011: 131). The situation was further complicated by 'the emergence of powerful community leaders at the level of both municipal and local governance' (Takla 2016: 26). For example, rather than directly financing social services, the municipality partly funded the benevolent societies established by ethnic communities (*Ibid.*). Each such community, as well as subdivisions of them such as those of Cypriots and Cretans, managed a variety of welfare organizations whose activities ranged from assisting the poor to providing a home to retired governesses (Mansel 2011: 132). Another type of organizations was, on the contrary, inter-ethnic. Alexandria's commercial associations, chambers of commerce, and merchant societies represented the common interests of merchants of all nationalities. They had formal membership, elected representatives, and headquarters where 'cosmopolitan merchants met, socialized, conducted business, [and] read newspapers (local and international) in their numerous languages.' Besides representing an 'area of sociability [and] business practice,' these associations provided a 'space of negotiation with central authorities': they acted as powerful pressure groups that promoted the economic interests of the foreign economic elite (Gekas 2009: 104).

The multidimensional influence of the immigrants over Alexandria's urban policy and administration led to major changes in the urban landscape. In addition to the old 'Turkish town,' the European quarter developed where consulates, commercial offices, banks, churches, and 'rows of long rectangular apartment blocks fronting on geometrically aligned streets' were constructed (Reimer 1977/2019: 11). In addition to this area 'designed, built and inhabited by the foreign population' that became Alexandria's 'commercial and financial heart,' numerous elitist mansions and garden villas were built in Ramleh, east of the city (Awad and Hamouda 2006/2012: 12). But there was also a new peripheral area, close to the canal and the railway, where 'the warehouse with its retinue of ramshackle outbuildings' and the workers' shanties were located (Reimer 1977/2019: 11). In more prosperous neighborhoods, European architects constructed the remarkable Passage Menasce, the Nouzha Gardens, the Corniche, and the elegant villas of prominent business dynasties (Mansel 2011: 133). The latter contributed to the Europeanization of Alexandria's culture by funding the municipal library, schools, and a museum that emphasized the city's Greco-Roman past. In 1892, *Al-Fatat*, the first Egyptian feminist paper, was launched. The Frères Lumière came in 1897 to open the first cinema in Egypt with the short documentary *Place des Consuls à Alexandrie*. The cultural life of the elites and much of the middleclass was resolutely modern and cosmopolitan, as illustrated by the activity of the *Association des Amis de l'Art* or the *Atelier d'Alexandrie*

(Association d'Artistes et d'Ecrivains). Many cosmopolitan clubs were established, which were centered on sailing, swimming, or tennis but also including the Desert Exploration Society and the Archaeological Society (Mansel 2011: 132, 134–135, 243). There were many French, English, and Italian schools and colleges open to all nationalities (Polyzoides 2014: 118–121). By 1912, out of the 28,000 children who went to school in Alexandria, 7,000 were educated in French-language schools and 9,000 in other foreign schools. Government schools had only 12,000 pupils (Mansel 2011: 145).

Multilingualism is a typical feature of cosmopolitans in general and Alexandrian cosmopolitans in particular. They usually spoke three to four languages that included French, English, Italian, Greek, Ladino (Sephardic Spanish), and – not always – Arabic. They needed, however, a common language. Until the 1860s, this was Italian or, at times, the Levantine lingua franca, which added to an Italian base a 'colorful mix' of Greek, Catalan, Arabic, and Turkish words and expressions (Eldem 2013: 219; Mansel 2011: 145). By the time of the first wave globalizations, however, French had imposed itself in Alexandria as in the rest of the region. Against a backdrop of 'galloping gallomania,' the language of Voltaire 'became as characteristic of the Levant as foreign schools, or the sea' (Mansel 2011: 147; Ostle 2002: 315). 'French was a language of the streets, as well as the salons' (Mansel 2004). In Alexandria, street signs, as well as official documents, were in Arabic and French; shop signs tended to keep only the French, which most shop assistants understood. Moreover, 'a French education was considered a sign of modernity' (Mansel 2011: 147). British advisers and employees of the Egyptian administration had to use French to speak with their colleagues and subordinates (Boulad-Ayoub 2004: 7). When, in 1911, Lord Kitchener presented his credentials as British consul general to Khedive Abbas Hilmi at the palace of Ras el-Tin in Alexandria, instead of the diplomatic uniform he wore his field marshal's uniform that made a clear reference to his role in the occupation of the city back in 1882. However, he had to speak French: 'if he had used English, he would not have been understood' (Mansel 2011: 147). As French was 'sovereignly established as the language of Alexandria' (*Ibid.*, 245), French cultural influence was, in the words of a contemporary British lady, 'enormous' (Awad and Hamouda 2006/2012: 43). 'French standards of taste in clothing, furniture, and art were adopted by the European and Europeanized population' (Reimer 1977/2019: 192). Paris came to be regarded as the region's 'second capital,' after Constantinople (Mansel 2011: 147). This was ironic as the French in Alexandria were less numerous than the British. Importantly, their overwhelming cultural influence provided a certain balance to the latter's military and economic domination: 'Britain ruled the waves; France ruled hearts and minds' (*Ibid.*). In a subtle way, this balance enhanced the differences between Alexandria's semi-colonial status and that of Britain's fully fledged colonies. In response, a frustrated Lord Cromer – Egypt's *de facto* ruler from 1883 to 1907 in his capacity as British 'agent and consul-general' – harshly criticized the 'Gallicised Egyptian, who is too often lured to his moral destruction' by the 'flimsy tinsel and moral obliquity' of the 'civilisation of the Paris Boulevards' (Cromer 1916: 335–336).

There can be little doubt that Alexandria's cosmopolitanism – which relied on Western powers' penetrative policies and immigrants' self-interested agency – exposed the city to powerful external influences while keeping it in a semi-colonial state that provided a certain degree of autonomy from the governments of Egypt, Britain, and other interested powers. It was this special situation that allowed the members of the foreign communities to create the first wave globalization 'from below' as discussed in the next section.

Alexandria's Ethnic Minorities and the Globalization 'from Below'

Day-to-day life in Alexandria was a permanent encounter with ethnic and linguistic diversity. In his *Out of Egypt: A Memoir*, André Aciman described his childhood in a Sephardic Jewish family that he believed, to the surprise of his father, to have French nationality (their passports were in fact Italian). His mother came from Constantinople. He spoke French at home but received an English education. In an episode of his memoirs, he was accompanied, on a Sunday morning, by his governess, a Zoroastrian Persian girl who had studied dance in Spain and was living with a British journalist; and his tutor and professor of Greek, who was an Italian and an atheist. The story turns around their meeting with a street vendor who was a Christian Copt (Aciman 1995: 210–211, 223). As a small child in Alexandria, Jacqueline Kahanoff found it natural that people speaking different languages and wearing different names – 'Greek, Moslem, Syrian, Jewish, Christian, Arab, Italian, Tunisian, Armenian' – understood each other. Arabs were poorer and more numerous; however, 'rich Arabs were pashas, but then many of them were Turks, and the Turkish ladies were princesses' (Starr and Somekh 2011: 1). For his part, Will Hanley analyzed the dossier of a criminal trial in Alexandria that he labeled a 'cosmopolitan dream.' It contained testimonies in four languages; all witnesses were recorded in languages different from their own. Evidence coming from Maltese people was in Italian. Percy Bagwell, lieutenant in the Second Essex Regiment, recorded the testimony of four Englishmen in French. One Guglielmo Farrugia signed 'William.' The testimony of a barmaid, an illiterate 24-year old Austrian, was written in Arabic and contained the usual Islamic oath formulas (Hanley 2017: 27).

To present observers, all this may look rather puzzling. But it is even more surprising that this 'crucible of races and nationalities' and the undeniable interdependence among Alexandria's various communities (Re 2003: 171, 172) failed to 'develop one overriding identity which (...) cancelled prior loyalties' even after two or three generations (Mansel 2011: 246). The city remained community-centered. Its inhabitants preserved their 'attach[ment] to their original national and religious community.' They even fought in their respective country's wars (*Ibid.*, 246–247). This can be explained as a consequence of Alexandria's semi-colonial status. Socio-economic success relied on extraterritoriality; this was associated with the protection of a foreign power, which, in turn, discouraged assimilation. This is the cause of the vitality of cosmopolitanism in places such as Alexandria or Shanghai and its progressive decline in port cities such as New York, New Orleans, or Buenos Aires. These latter metropolises received much larger inflows of international migrants. Still, three generations later, only cultural and sentimental links with the countries of origin survived. In Alexandria, the connection was also legal and political. Its benefits preserved the integrity of ethnic communities. Most importantly, it also ensured the continuity of flows of people, ideas, and goods between these communities and their countries of origin, which led to the first wave globalization 'from below.'

As Egypt was under British occupation after 1882, one would expect the British community to have been the most important. This was the case in terms of political and economic influence, but Britons were surprisingly few and, socially, somewhat isolated. In 1882, they were less numerous than the Greeks, the Italians, the French, and even the Austrian-Hungarians. From 7.1 percent of all foreigners in Egypt at that time, their weight increased to 18.9 percent in 1897 but then diminished to 14.7 in 1907. In 1927, the 15,000 British in Alexandria represented 13.6 of the city's foreigners. During the entire period, they were significantly outnumbered by Greeks and Italians (Shlala 2009: 205; Polyzoides 2014: 117). Socially, they were 'insular' (Mansel 2004) as they 'remained aloof from other nationalities.' 'Protective barriers' preventing them from 'going native' included the use of governesses from England, attendance of English schools, spending summers in England, and the military service in the British army (Mansel 2011: 251). In addition, like the French and the Germans, most of the British 'regard[ed] Egypt as a foreign country in which, by force of circumstances, they [we]re destined to spend a part of their lives.' Many did not perceive themselves as part of a colony of settlers (Shlala 2009: 45). Of course, there were prominent British families – such as the Finney, Barker, Carver, Moss, and Peel ones – that, for generations, were highly successful in economic terms and used their considerable fortunes to subsidize various cultural and social activities (Polyzoides 2014: 114). Rich British entrepreneurs and merchants, however, were not involved in the first wave globalization 'from below' for a very simple reason: they were key actors of the parallel 'from above' globalization. Such elites represented the transmission belts that allowed industrial Britain to extract raw materials from Egypt as part of the wider economic flows of the globalized world. Furthermore, many middle-class Britons in Alexandria were military officers or held public office positions, which also isolated them from the 'from below' globalization. Petty merchants did join it, but their number was hardly impressive. Ironically, the 'British' who massively participated in this globalization have much to do with the subaltern cosmopolitanism discussed in the previous subchapter. They were formally known as 'Maltese British subjects.' The Maltese 'were systematically excluded from the category "European'" and represented a sort of 'second-class foreigners' who lacked many of the Europeans' informal privileges. But they were nevertheless viewed as 'more than native'; the British consulate 'grudgingly assumed the burden of protection.' As imperial subjects, they were offered 'equivalence – if not equality – with Europeans' in terms of legal and taxation extraterritorial rights. By 1900, when there were 20.000 'British' in all of Egypt, about 5,000 of those living in Alexandria were in fact Maltese (Hanley 2017: 175–176, 179). Out of the 6,500 people who migrated from Malta to the Eastern Mediterranean between 1814 and 1825, a part settled in Egypt. There were 2,000 Maltese in the entire country in 1842, 5,000 in 1865, and 7,000 in 1885 (Chircop 2015: 6). Some sources place their number at 20,000 in 1927 (Farrugia 2004). In addition to traders, many skilled and unskilled laborers, artisans, clerks, and merchants left four Maltese towns – Vittoriosa, Senglea, Cospicua, and La Valletta – to work for the Suez Canal Company. When the canal was completed in 1869, a part of them adopted the strategy of many present Chinese workers active in Chinese infrastructure projects in the Belt and Road Initiative countries: they overstayed their contracts, turning to trade and other economic activities. During the 1882 anti-European riots, the Royal Navy repatriated no less than 8,000 Maltese from Egypt (Chircop 2015: 6). While Catholic and clearly distinct from Alexandria's natives, the Maltese spoke an Arabic dialect that allowed them 'the possibility of community with the majority of the city's population.' They were very often mentioned in descriptions of the day-to-day life in Alexandria's less affluent neighborhoods; Will Hanley even argued that 'Maltese, not French, may have been Alexandria's "European voice" par excellence' (Hanley 2017: 166). These Maltese were as far from the first wave globalization 'from above' as La Salada's Bolivians are today from the Western-centered globalization 'from above.' But their very migration to Alexandria – which was accompanied by a significant return movement – represented a flow of the first wave globalization 'from below,' as did their many transnational trade activities associated with Maltese diasporic networks, which had expanded all over the Mediterranean and in various parts of the British colonial empire (for details see Chircop 2015).

Fewer and less influential than the British in political and economic terms, the French nevertheless represented an important part of Alexandria's cultural, educational, missionary, administrative, and economic landscape. In all Egypt, they were 15,716 in 1882 (18.3 percent of all foreigners), 14,172 (13.7 percent) in 1897, and 14,591 (10.4 percent) in 1907 (Shlala 2009: 205). In Alexandria, their number decreased from 8,215 in 1882 to 5,221 in 1897 and 4,304 in 1907 but increased to 8,556 in 1917. However, there were only 3,350 fully fledged French citizens in the city in 1882, 3,713 in 1897, and 3,555 in 1917. The rest were French subjects: mainly Algerians and Tunisians – certain sources place the size of each group at 5,000 people in 1900 – but also Jews and Syrians (Hanley 2017: 176, 178–179). Indeed, 'most foreigners in Alexandria were not European' (*Ibid.*, 175). Out of the less than 4,000 French citizens, only a limited number were petty traders that enacted the 'from below' globalization. The French-protected Algerians and Tunisians, on the contrary, played the same role as the 'Maltese British subjects': they were subaltern cosmopolitans that, despite a lower socio-economic position, benefitted from capitulatory privileges and consular protection to outcompete natives while joining the migratory and trade flows of the first wave globalization 'from below.'

As already mentioned, the 'genuine' British and French, as well as the less numerous Germans, Austrians, or Scandinavians, tended to perceive themselves as temporary sojourners in Alexandria even if 'temporary' meant decades and only concerned a part of them. Southern European groups – mainly Greeks and Italians – were much larger, came in general from poorer backgrounds, and were seen as settlers. Their integration into the local society was more pronounced (Shlala 2009: 45). While there were very prosperous Greek and Italian elites, the large number of less affluent immigrants of these nationalities involved in 'low-end' economic activities predisposed them to join the first wave globalization 'from below' on a scale comparable with that of the Maltese, Algerians, and Tunisians. There were 18,665 Italians in Egypt in 1882, 24,454 in 1897, and 34,926 in 1907, which represented 21.7, 23.6, and 24.8 percent of all foreigners, respectively (Shlala 2009: 205). Some of them, however, were only 'passport Italians.' This category prominently included the aforementioned Levantine Jews who claimed that their families originated in Leghorn (Livorno), where the register of births had burned (see the previous subchapter). They had no past or present link with Italy, were not native speakers of Italian, and did not participate in local Italian community life. However, they headed most of the administration councils of Alexandria's Italian businesses (Lazarev 1992: 97; Giuliani Caponetto 2008: 145) and were deeply involved in the first wave globalization 'from above.' This was also the case of rich 'genuine' Italian families that, from the time of Mohammed Ali, contributed to Egypt's and Alexandria's development. The Vaccarini, Avoscani, and Demarchi families were active in naval shipbuilding. The Dovretti, Colucci, and Mochi families helped set up medical services, which included the establishment of Alexandria hospital. The Meratti and Muzzi families contributed to the creation of the postal service. The De Rossetti family served Egypt as diplomats (Shlala 2018: 6). The 1936 census found that no less than 9.1 percent of the Italians in Alexandria were industrialists, businessmen, and bankers (Viscomi 2019: 344). They had established two banks, *Banca di Roma* and *Banca Commerciale Italiana* (Shlala 2009: 48). Many of the city's most impressive buildings were designed by Alessandro Loria, an architect born in Mansoura in a family of Tuscan immigrants (Polyzoides 2014: 117). Construction was also a sector that attracted very many Italian workers (Takla 2016: 19) as skilled builders and technicians (Polyzoides 2014: 117; Shlala 2009: 46). In 1897, Italians represented a third of the foreigners engaged in lumber and construction. However, they were also active in commerce. That same year, 34.7 percent of the foreign males active in the trade of textiles, cotton, wire, wool, and silk were Italian. It should be noted that Italian males represented only 18.77 percent of the foreign male population (Shlala 2009: 46). Moreover, it was noted that 'most Italian "businessmen" were small agents and shopkeepers living from hand to mouth, who are too poor to do more than support their large families' (Elizabeth Monroe quoted by Viscomi 2019: 372). When their low-end commerce had an international dimension – which was frequent, as many of them had trade partners in Italy – they adopted the informal approach of the 'ant traders' involved in the present non-hegemonic globalization 'from below.' More specifically, they had 'not a piastre to spare for the hungryman of the Italian treasury' (*Ibid.*), i.e., used bribery to avoid paying customs duties. This is why Italian small merchants were important actors of the first wave globalization 'from below' in Alexandria. Interestingly, there was another Italian component of this globalization. The Italian community was culturally active. There were four Italian newspapers and magazines founded in 1845, 1876, 1892, and 1930, and a cultural center, Dante Alighieri (Shlala 2009: 48). The first cinemas in Alexandria were opened in 1897 by Italians (Polyzoides 2014: 117). There were four Italian elementary schools (in addition to Catholic Salesian and Franciscan ones), middle schools, and two high schools, one scientific and one centered on the liberal arts (Shlala 2018: 5). Four important Italian writers were connected to this larger cultural context. Filippo Tommaso Marinetti, the famous creator of Italian Futurism, was born in 1876 in Alexandria, where he studied at the French Jesuit St. François-Xavier College. He continued his studies in Paris and then moved to Italy, which he wanted to rescue from 'its rotten cancerous tumor of professors, archaeologists, cicerones, and antique dealers' (Rodenbeck 2001–2002: 553). We can debate the results of this ambitious enterprise. Giuseppe Ungaretti, a major modernist Italian poet, was similarly born in Alexandria in 1888 and studied, in French, at the *École Suisse* (Swiss School) *Jacot*. He left Alexandria in 1912 to study law in Paris. The views and works of both Marinetti and Ungaretti were strongly influenced by their Alexandrian background (see Re 2003: 168) but two less-known Italian writers are more relevant for this chapter. Enrico Pea (1881–1958) was an atypical self-taught, working-class Italian modernist writer who arrived in Alexandria as a teenager in 1896. Until his return to Italy in 1914, he worked as a house servant, a laborer in a foundry, a mechanic in a naval shipyard, and a railroad worker. As a mechanic, he was seriously injured in two accidents, which made him start a small commerce in marble, wood, and wine that was indirectly involved in import operations. Pea consequently joined the first wave globalization 'from below' as an 'ant trader,' but his much more visible contribution to this globalization pertains to the realm of ideas. He turned '*La Baracca Rossa*' (the Red Cabin), the shack he used as a warehouse for his enterprise, into an anarchist club, which became a mythic place for Alexandrians that included Ungaretti. In addition to the anti-system ideas imported from Europe, they discussed issues closely related to their cosmopolitan experiences. As Pea put it in one of his novels that were widely read in Italy, 'the international living together of this Egyptian Babel had convinced me of the uselessness and harmfulness of homelands' (Re 2003: 167, 174–175; Rodenbeck 2001–2002: 550). A similar export of Italian language 'dissident literature' (Giuliani Caponetto 2008: 133) that pertained to the flows of ideas associated with the first wave globalization 'from below' was that of Fausta Cialente (1898–1994), who lived in Alexandria between 1921 and 1956. One of the most important Italian women modernist writers between the two World Wars, she was the wife of the writer, painter, and composer Enrico Terni. Both found in Alexandria 'an "absolute liberty" which Italy no longer enjoyed' (Mansel 2011: 243) under the rule of Mussolini, whose ultranationalist ideas of 'regenerating' the Italian society they vocally condemned (Giuliani Caponetto 2008: 133). An outspoken antifascist and feminist (see Re 2003: 167), Cialente paralleled in many regards Pea's efforts to turn Alexandrian cosmopolitan experiences into universal societal models.

Pea and Cialente were by no means singular examples of libertarian activism among Alexandria's foreigners. As shown in the section about extraterritoriality of the previous subchapter, 'Alexandria became a space of immunity for many.' This had negative consequences, but also positive ones: it 'made Alexandria one of the few places where one could escape (...) the political and racial persecution of any number of European and Mediterranean countries' (Re 2003: 173). The city became a shelter for political refugees from the Russian and Ottoman empires, anarchists from various countries, White Russians (including Prince Nicolas Petrovitch), anti-colonial fighters such as Libya's Sayyid Idris al-Senussi, Italian antifascists, Jews fleeing Germany, and even the deposed royal families of Albania (which was occupied by fascist Italy), Greece (after the German invasion), Bulgaria (after the communist takeover), and Italy (after the instauration of the republic in 1946) (Mansel 2011: 243, 260; Polyzoides 2014: 114, 118–119). Not all these refugees were politically active or could be labeled 'progressive.' But many did, and those who spent enough time in the city had their political views influenced by the cosmopolitan environment. Their activism shows that the first wave globalization 'from below' included a discreet but nevertheless important cognitive – and ideological – dimension: small and weak actors in Alexandria tried to shape understandings of 'normal' worldwide. In other words, they were projecting normative power, which was based on cosmopolitan values and opposed the rise of (ultra)nationalism. Different from what a superficial observer might think, the first wave globalization 'from below' was a very complex multifaceted phenomenon.

The largest foreign community was the Greek one. It constantly represented 40 percent or more of all foreigners in Egypt and, in most regards, it was similar to the Italian one. The Greeks came from poorer backgrounds and tended to settle in Alexandria (Shlala 2009: 45, 205), where they numbered

36,000 in 1927 and no less than 100,000 in 1950. In the 19th century, Greek entrepreneurs developed the production and export of cotton, cigarettes, and other goods that made the Salvago, Benaki, Averoff, Tositsas, and Choremis families immensely rich (Polyzoides 2014: 115–116, 117–118, 123). They saw themselves as an aristocracy and more modern than mainland Greeks. Paradoxically, these Alexandrian cosmopolitans were also Greek nationalists (Mansel 2011: 138). George Averoff financed the Athens marble stadium where the first modern Olympics Games were held in 1896. He also donated to the Greek navy its first frigate (Polyzoides 2014: 115). Emmanuel Benaki moved to Athens in 1911 to become Minister of Finance and, eventually, mayor of Athens. In 1927, Anthony Benaki took to the same city the famous family collection; today, it can be seen in the Benaki Museum. Still, these families also used their financial resources to fund charitable organizations and schools for the Greek community in Alexandria. This community had two hospitals, two orphanages, nine primary and two secondary schools, a sports club, a chamber of commerce, and 24 associations ranging from the Ptolemy Hellenic Scientific Syllogos and the Hellenic Nautical Circle to the Corporation of Greek Grocers of Alexandria (*Ibid.*; Mansel 2011: 137, 139, 140). The majority of Alexandria's Greeks were hardly opulent. Many worked in the cigarette industry (Takla 2016: 19). Others were traders. During the 19th century, Greek merchants 'acted as the foremost agents of capitalist penetration into the villages of Egypt' (Reimer 1991: 142; Gekas 2009: 99). Moreover, they 'were often able to beat the northern Europeans at their own game' due to factors that included 'business skills and long-standing commercial traditions'; superior knowledge of local conditions, languages, and culture; 'links to well-placed compatriots in the interior and abroad,' i.e., in Greece and the Ottoman Empire; and, critically, 'their extensive and well-organized smuggling operations' (Reimer 1977/2019: 192) that clearly associated the Greek petty merchants with the informal trade flows of the first wave globalization 'from below.' The latter also included important flows of people. A perhaps unexpected example is that of Alexandria's greatest poet, Constantine Cavafy (1863–1933). His half-Phanariot family originated in Constantinople but became rich by exporting Egyptian cotton to Britain. After his father died, the family moved from Alexandria to England in 1872. Four years later they went bankrupt. Elder brothers stayed in Britain, but younger ones were taken by their mother back to Alexandria. For the rest of his life, Constantine would speak Greek with a slight English accent. In addition to joining at an early age the two-way migratory flows connecting Alexandria to the rest of the world and the associated globalization 'from below,' his eventual career is illustrative of another aspect of this globalization. In Alexandria, Cavafy became a clerk and an extraordinary poet. He was in no way a radical and his literary output had nothing to do with the activism of Enrico Pea and Fausta Cialente. But 'he was the most daring homosexual poet of the early twentieth century,' and this was clearly visible in his oeuvre. 'In all other cities except Paris, Cavafy's poems would have provoked horror or imprisonment.' Nothing of this happened in Alexandria because its cosmopolitanism was 'tolerant and progressive' (Mansel 2011: 142–143). It would be exaggerated to identify this tolerance as a key feature of the first wave globalization 'from below.' However, it did represent a direct consequence of this globalization's location in cosmopolitan semi-colonial environments where states were weak and anti-system ideas and lifestyles had more chances to pass unrepressed.

Space limitations prevent me from discussing other Alexandrian minorities such as the Sephardic Jewish, Syrian Christian, or Slovenian ones; the participation of their unaffluent members in the first wave globalization 'from below' follows the pattern of the larger minorities examined in the previous paragraphs. It is worth, however, to briefly analyze the issue of 'Levantines.' *Stricto sensu*, the term designates a highly heterogeneous group that included 'European and Eastern (mainly Uniate) Catholics, Orthodox, Apostolical Christian Armenians,' and – in a lesser measure – Jews (Schmitt 2007: 14). In fact, it evolved in time from identifying Latin Catholics who came from the Italian maritime city-states to also include protected non-Muslim residents of the Ottoman Empire (Shlala 2018: 4). Eventually, people of French, Maltese, Dalmatian, Italian, Austrian, and German origin who settled in the Eastern Mediterranean Basin were added (Fuhrmann 2020: 289–290). All these 'Levantines' tended to represent an urbanized commercial bourgeoisie characterized by Western or Westernized education and culture (Oppenheim 1996: 1099). However, deep divisions in terms of 'nationality, status, language, origins, and *ancienneté* of residence in the Levant' led to what Malte Fuhrmann called 'the relative obscurity of Levantine identity' (Fuhrmann 2020: 292), which remains an issue of academic debate. Still, it is the extended definition of Levantines that is of more interest to this chapter. By the mid-19th century, 'it had gradually moved in the direction of a derogatory label used to describe the hybrid identities of half-Westernized local non-Muslims and of Westerners who had "gone native"' (Eldem 2013: 222). By the 1900s, the term had clearly 'acquired a negative moral coloration' (Oppenheim 1996: 1099–1100). Lord Cromer depicted Levantines as 'semi-orientalised Europeans' that are 'recruited from the southern races of Europe.' Germans and Englishmen 'rarely become typical Levantines' while this is an easy transition for Italians who settle in Egypt. Critically, these individuals 'are tainted with a remarkable degree of moral obliquity' (Cromer 1916: 246–249). The trend continued. In the 1920s, the defeat of the Ottoman Empire in World War I was explained by the fact that Constantinople had 'become Levantiny.' By the 1940s, 'the spread of Levantinism was the characteristic malady of Islamic and Arab society.' Being a Levantine was associated by various observers with 'lostness, pretentiousness, cynicism and despair' (Oppenheim 1996: 1099–1100). In the Mediterranean context, 'European' and 'Levantine' became opposites. Only those in the first category were 'uncontaminated' by negative cultural influences (Fuhrmann 2020: 298). The Levantine was perceived as 'a borderline figure' that was 'inferior not only to Europe but also to Europe's imagined Other, the Orient' (Gil Hochberg quoted in Starr and Somekh 2011: xxiii). Levantinization was a corrupting force (Starr and Somekh 2011: xxiv). It is not difficult to note that the 'subaltern cosmopolitans' involved in Alexandria's first wave globalization 'from below' – Maltese, Algerian, and Tunisian colonial subjects of Britain and France, unaffluent Italian and Greek petty traders, and similar members of smaller communities – pertain precisely to the categories identified as most vulnerable to 'Levantinization.' This might explain why none of their contemporaries wanted to see the flows they enacted as representing a fully fledged globalization. They were despicable tiny actors contaminated by corrupting non-European influences. Their actions could in no way be compared to the triumphant first wave globalizations 'from above.'

It can be concluded that, in many respects, the case study of Alexandria is most relevant for the analysis of the 'from below' globalization that survived there until 1956. However, I will discuss its findings only after examining the situation of semi-colonial cosmopolitan Shanghai.

6.3 The First Wave Globalization 'from Below' in Shanghai

Concessions-based Semi-Colonialism

China's Treaty Port Era (1842–1943/1946[1]) began with the Treaty of Nanjing that concluded, to Britain's advantage, the 1840–1842 First Opium War. The treaty opened five Chinese ports to trade and introduced the principle of extraterritoriality (Keller *et al.* 2016: 5). Britain became the dominant foreign power in China, but other great powers soon joined it in extracting similar concessions from the imperial government (Nield 2015: 6). External pressure that occasionally included open warfare triggered internal crises, which invited further external interference. A vicious circle developed that dramatically weakened the Chinese state. By the turn of the century, Britain, France, Germany, Russia, Japan, and – to some extent – the United States were contemplating splitting China into spheres of influence or domination. It was the balance between these powers that saved the decaying Middle Kingdom from being turned into a mere set of colonies (*Ibid.*, 7). A compromise solution was found that led to the semi-colonial status discussed in Subchapter 6.1. As shown there, this status was characterized by rivalry, balance, and cooperation among the foreign powers; 'effectively colonial governance by non-state actors' in the concessions (Jackson 2018: 8); the preservation of the sovereignty of the Chinese state; and cultural frameworks and outcomes incompatible with 'colonized subjectivities' (Reinhardt 2018: 5; Goodman 2000: 14). Foreigners imposed their presence in many economic sectors. They also 'introduced steam ships to China, dredged harbors, ran the postal system,' and, critically, took control of the customs service (Keller *et al.* 2016: 2). Because many taxes were not paid during the

1850–1864 Taiping Rebellion, the Chinese government was forced to formally employ Western officials to run the Chinese Maritime Customs Service, which began to operate in 1859 in Shanghai (*Ibid.*, 5). In symbolic and practical terms, this development mirrored the creation of the Egyptian *Caisse de la Dette Publique* mentioned in the previous subchapter. Jeremy Taylor appropriately described the overall treaty port system as 'a social system of exclusion and exploitation.' He also presented it as 'unique in the imperialist movement of the western powers' of the concerned period (Taylor 2002: 125). This latter statement may seem to ignore the strong similarities with the situation of Egypt and the Ottoman Empire, but is absolutely valid in regard to one aspect specific to China alone: the existence and importance of foreign concessions.

Of course, such concessions were in no way limited to China. In fact, 'from the mid-1800s through the 1930s, concessions were an institutional foundation of modern capitalism' (Veeser 2013: 1136). The term was used to designate a variety of arrangements, but all concessions can be defined as 'contracts given by governments in less-developed states to foreign investors.' Their goal was to provide economically useful elements that included 'a congenial legal order and an attractive investment environment' (*Ibid.*, 1139). To develop infrastructure and commercial agriculture, all colonial powers granted such contracts in their African and Asian possessions. Independent states such as Mexico, Russia, or the Dominican Republic adopted the same policy. A special type of concession concerns enclaves that are protected by extraterritoriality. Such cases – which include the Chinese treaty ports, as well as the Suez and Panama canal concessions – 'resemble treaties between states more than they do contracts between a state and private investor' (*Ibid.*). In China, they included two different categories of areas where foreigners were allowed to settle and lease land. In concessions, a state leased the entire area and paid a rental to the Chinese Government for it. In turn, that state subleased parcels of land to private lessees. In settlements, the Chinese owners leased the parcels directly to foreigners. Both foreigners and Chinese could reside in a foreign settlement, where all the Treaty Powers had equal rights. In practice, however, the two terms were used interchangeably (Quigley 1928: 150; Johnstone 1937: 942). The French Concession in Shanghai, for example, was technically a settlement (Jackson 2016: 43). While Chinese sovereignty was preserved in both concessions and settlements, they were dominated politically and economically by 'a set of imperial diasporas' that 'were part of the expansionist logic of Western powers' (Vandamme 2018: 38). In the case of Britain, it was argued that the concessions in China not only served its interests but 'expressed the ideals' of its worldwide commercial expansion. Historians of British imperialism have in fact studied these concessions as part of the British 'informal empire' that, contrary to a formal territorial empire, minimized risk and expense in securing access to China's economy as part of a larger world system (Crawford 2018: 971, 972). While two different types of 'informal imperialism' were defined to explain differences between British involvement in China and Latin America, other historians questioned the validity of this approach in the case of the Chinese concessions. On the one hand, Britain was only one of the involved great powers. On the other, the degree of control exercised by the Shanghai Municipal Council – which was 'run by settlers and expatriates' (see below) – 'did not feel very informal to the millions of Chinese who lived under its governance, even if the legal underpinnings of its authority were insecure' (Jackson 2018: 16). No matter the theoretical model used to analyze them, the foreign concessions in China followed the model of Shanghai, where the British, American, and French created extraterritorial enclaves in the 1840s. In 1863, the merger of the British and American ones resulted in the creation of the International Settlement. After the 1856–1860 Second Opium War, Shanghai was presented explicitly as a 'model settlement' to be duplicated by new concessions in second-wave treaty ports. 'Developing concessions became a modular process of importing "versions of Shanghai precedents" for administration, regulation, and infrastructure' (Crawford 2018: 973). In terms of governance, the Chinese authorities initially granted to foreigners only the right to live and trade in designated areas. But Western immigrants took advantage of China's weakness to set up their own municipal institutions. As the authority of the Chinese Government was severely limited by the privilege of extraterritoriality, China ended up formally or tacitly recognizing such institutions (Vandamme 2018: 42–43; Quigley 1928: 150). Settlements were typically governed by an autonomous locally elected body, a municipal council. Its members were foreigners. It was only in 1928 that a minority of Chinese members was accepted by the Shanghai Municipal Council (Vandamme 2018: 43; Johnstone 1937: 942; see below). Concessions also had councils of three to ten members who were elected by the ratepayers. But it was only in British concessions that the council tended to take precedence over the consul. Elsewhere, the latter – who was also chairman of the municipal council – played a dominant role. In the Shanghai French Concession, for example, 'the French consul general, who received orders from Paris, increasingly tightened his grip on local politics' (Vandamme 2018: 43; Quigley 1928: 150–151; Johnstone 1937: 942).

In all, there were 18 Treaty Powers. They included Britain, France, the United States, Japan, and Russia; the latter renounced its rights after the Bolsheviks took power. There were also Germany and Austria-Hungary, which were eliminated after World War I; other European states such as Italy, Spain, Portugal, Norway, Sweden, Denmark, the Netherlands, Belgium (which 'was declared by China to have lost her rights' in 1927), and even Switzerland; as well as Latin American ones such as Peru and Mexico (Johnstone 1937: 942; Shih 2001: 32). At first view, the number of their concessions was impressive. By 1917, they had opened 92 treaty ports in China (Jackson 2018: 3). Settlements, concessions, consular, diplomatic, and customs stations, and hill stations and resorts with foreign non-missionary presence or jurisdiction, amounted to no less than 250 (Nield 2015: 9). In fact, a surprisingly large number of concessions reverted to Chinese ownership. In addition to those lost by Russia, Germany, Austria-Hungary, and Belgium, Britain gave up four. The same power, as well as the United States and Japan, gained rights to exclusive concessions but did not use them where trade was insufficient. By 1937, there were only four powers that controlled ten concessions: Britain (2), Japan (3), France (4), and Italy (1). Thirteen had reverted to China (Johnstone 1937: 944; Quigley 1928: 150). In addition, there were only two international settlements: the one in Shanghai and the much smaller one created in 1902 on the Kulangsu/Gulangyu Island, off Amoy (Nield 2015: 8; Jackson 2016: 56). There were also three informal settlements in Chefoo, Foochow, and Ningpo where foreigners 'set up a quasi-municipal organization' with the 'tacit but not explicit consent of the Chinese government.' More land was expropriated by the same government and set aside for foreign residence in Yochow, Wuhu, Soochow, Hangchow, Foochow, Nanning, and Nanking. But China retained full jurisdiction over all these areas, and the informal settlements were progressively absorbed into the Chinese city (Johnstone 1937: 943). Many of the foreign concessions were small. Some of them, however, were impressive examples of intense economic, social, and political interactions. With its nine concessions, Tianjin was such a case. As mentioned in Subchapter 6.1, Ruth Rogaski coined the term 'hypercolony' to depict its 'distinctive juxtaposition of many concessions within a single urban space' that was 'divided among multiple imperialisms' (Rogaski 2004: 11; Marinelli 2009: 402; Jackson 2018: 16). 'A complex, hybrid space (in)between East and West' emerged in Tianjin that was 'defined by social practices, symbolic representations, and legal categories, which does not coincide simply with the area defined by the entity as a state, nation, or city' (Nuzzo 2018: 569). However, an even more complex situation was created by the foreign presence in Shanghai.

A City Run by the Non-Chinese

Shanghai was the sixth-largest port in the world both in 1863 and 1926. Its spectacular growth had the same origin as that of Alexandria: the international demand for cotton during the American Civil War. This added to the constant rise of trade that followed the city's opening by foreign powers. The latter's merchants arrived in large numbers to exchange opium, as well as cotton and woolen goods, for tea, silk, and porcelain (Nield 2015: 4, 202, 206). Economic development, the decline of Beijing, and the fact that in 1927 the more modest city of Nanjing became the new capital turned Shanghai into the most important city of Republican China in demographic, economic, cultural, and political terms (Jackson 2018: 2). Its population increased to one million in 1880, 1.29 million in 1910, 3.5 million in 1930 – when it became the fifth-largest city in the world – and 4.98 million in 1950 (Wu 2004: 161; Jackson 2018: 6). The economic activity was centered on the International Settlement and the French Concession, which also increased considerably from a demographic point of view. The Settlement had 100,000 inhabitants in 1880, half a million in 1910, and over 1 million in 1930. The numbers for the smaller French Concession were 85,000 in 1905, 145,000 in 1915, and 170,000 in 1920, respectively (Jackson 2018: 6; Vandamme 2018: 43). However, the huge majority of the people in both enclaves were Chinese. This had not initially been the case. When the concessions were established in Shanghai, only foreigners and their Chinese employees could live there. Yet, in 1860, the Taiping Rebellion made thousands of Chinese take refuge in the concessions. Eventually, their number increased considerably (Goodman 2000: 890). Different from Alexandria where, at times, foreigners reached almost a third of the population, their total number in the International Settlement amounted to only 3,821 in 1890, 11,497 in 1905, 13,536 in 1910, 18,519 in 1915, and 23,307 in 1920. The number of Chinese increased from 452,716 in 1905 to 759,839 in the Settlement alone. Accordingly, its Chinese to foreigners ratio was 40 in 1890, 36 in 1910, and 32.6 in 1920. In the French Concession, it reached no less than 90 in 1890, 102 in 1905, and 46.8 in 1920 (Vandamme 2018: 43; Goodman 2000: 893–894). Furthermore, these proportionally few foreigners had no control over the Chinese part of the city, which by 1930 was inhabited by almost 2.5 million people. Shanghai was nevertheless 'the concession city par excellence' (O. A. Westad quoted in Crawford 2018: 971). The foreigners' control of the International Settlement and the French Concession turned them into the main economic, social, and political actors of the city.

However, the latter's semi-colonial status prevented any monopoly on power. The rivalry between foreign powers created a situation where the 'internal control of the city always had to be negotiated.' Shanghai was 'a polycentric, decentered city controlled by many different hands' that, at times, included the local 'triad underworld' (Abbas 2002: 214). The parallel with Alexandria seen as 'a city with many authorities but no hegemon' (Hanley 2017: 17) is obvious. Similar to the case of its Egyptian counterpart, 'the space of Shanghai was subject to constant negotiations, and every initiative was observed from multiple perspectives.' This is a key factor that contributed to the development of a 'special brand of cosmopolitan urban culture: what we might call a cosmopolitanism of extraterritoriality' (Abbas 2002: 214; see the appropriate section of Subchapter 6.1). The parallel with Alexandria is visible in administrative terms, too. The Shanghai Municipal Council 'evolved into a semi-independent governing structure' that showed 'substantial independence' from both Chinese and consular authorities (Goodman 2000: 893). In fact, the very merger of the British and American settlements in 1863 that led to the creation of the International Settlement was the consequence of an effort undertaken by influential foreigners in Shanghai: 'business interests combined to assert its independence from any country's formal control' (Crawford 2018: 973). It is relevant that, under the influence of its own prominent members, the French Concession also joined the new International Settlement in 1863. It was the government in Paris that did not ratify the decision and imposed the preservation of the French Concession as a separate entity. In Shanghai, the general feeling among foreigners of all nationalities was that weak state control is good for business. Eventually, this enhanced the first wave globalization 'from below.'

The Shanghai Municipal Council was 'the single most important institution that governed the International Settlement' (Yang 2019: 3). Initially, it was expected to simply administer – under the authority of the consuls – the policies set up by the ratepayers. In time, however, it became the ruling body of the Settlement. It made and implemented policies 'with occasional advice from the consuls, that were rubber-stamped by the ratepayers' (Jackson 2018: 5). Contemporaries compared its powers with those of an independent state; foreign powers tacitly accepted them. In 'its distance from imperial oversight, the SMC epitomises the peculiarity' of the foreign control in China that, as a semi-colonial construct, was significantly different from colonial situations (*Ibid.*). The numerous functions of the Council included the management of police, fire, and health services. It had a paramilitary force (Yang 2019: 3–4; see below). Residents 'were keenly aware of the authority of the SMC to police their lives, tax their property, and regulate their living environment.' The Council's control extended to the roads it built outside the International Settlement and 'those who lived on and used them' (Jackson 2016: 44). By 'exerting extensive governmental authority (...) independent of imperial oversight,' it deeply 'shaped the development of Shanghai' (Jackson 2018: 2). The members of the Council were elected annually by the ratepayers. Consequently, it was to them that the Shanghai Municipal Council was responsible in practice despite the fact that its powers derived from the consuls, who represented the foreign powers (Jackson 2016: 44). Because only ratepayers voted, it was argued that the Council operated 'like a company board of directors' (Jackson 2018: 5; Yang 2019: 4). To vote, one had to be a foreigner and to own property in the Settlement or to pay high rents indicating control over land. It was frequent for ratepayers to have multiple votes as they represented property-owning firms in addition to having their own property (Jackson 2016: 44–45). In 1925, there were 2,742 ratepayers. They were mainly British (1,157), Japanese (552), and American (328) (Hudson 1927: 80). But there were periods when the British had more than half of the votes. The pool of candidates for the position of Council member was limited to affluent landowners or renters who amounted to only 3 percent of the foreigners living in the International Settlement. Unsurprisingly, all elected members represented the major foreign trading houses, which therefore had a strong influence on the Council (Jackson 2016: 44–45). While no such formal provision existed, seats were unofficially reserved for some nationalities. From 1873 to 1914, there was a stable composition of seven Britons, one American, and one German. Changes began with World War I. In 1914, the German member was replaced by a Russian and, in 1915, a Japanese replaced one of the British members. In 1918, the Russian was replaced by a second American while in 1927 a second Japanese replaced another

British member. Up to this time, only foreigners were part of the Council. After much debate, three Chinese members were admitted in 1928 and two more in 1930. The final composition of the Council included five Britons, two Americans, five Chinese, and two Japanese. While elections were to be held annually, in 16 years from 1900 to 1940 the number of candidates was inferior or equal to that of seats and they were co-opted without an election (Jackson 2016: 45, 47, 49; Jackson 2018: 5–6; Hudson 1927: 80). The staff employed by the Municipal Council numbered almost 10,000 people recruited among 25 nationalities. Seventy-four percent were Chinese, but the British clearly dominated senior positions (Jackson 2018: 6). By 1927, the commissioner-general and the highest officials of the fire brigade, police, and paramilitary forces, the Secretariat, and the departments of health, public works, electricity, sewage disposal, and finance were all Britons. As a contemporary American noted ironically, only the director of the municipal band was Italian. Out of the 1,076 municipal employees listed in a Shanghai directory at that time, 965 were British. Only four Americans were shown as holding positions of responsibility. An American became chairman of the Council only because his strongly pro-British views brought him the support of British members. In principle, a member of the Council had 'no strictly representative capacity with reference either to his government or to his conationals among the rate-payers' (Hudson 1927: 80, 81). But one would hardly expect British or Japanese members to act against the interests of their respective national minority; and, given the predominance of Britons among Council members and high-ranking staff, the Municipal Council could have tacitly adopted and implemented a British agenda. Yet, Shanghai's – and the Settlement's – semi-colonial status prevented such a development: 'no national group could act alone.' Moreover, diversity 'was celebrated by [the] Council as evidence of the desirably cosmopolitan community they claimed for themselves' (Jackson 2018: 7). Both members of the Council and staff were perfectly aware of their national identities; but this did not prevent them from fully cooperating at an institutional, professional, and personal level. As already mentioned, the International Settlement was even described as 'a miniature League of Nations' (*Ibid.*). It is relevant that, after the Japanese occupation of the Settlement that followed Pearl Harbor, the Allied members of the Council resigned in January 1942. But, for several months, they continued to serve on the Council's committees. The staff also continued their activities. The relations between British and Japanese employees remained good, reflecting the cooperative pattern that had developed in previous decades (Jackson 2016: 47).

A large part of the municipal staff was employed by the Shanghai Municipal Police, whose composition was also multinational. The largest branch was the Chinese one, which in 1919 had 1,400 members. The Sikh branch was created in 1884 and 'became a great source of prestige for the British community.' It had 370 members in 1919 (*Ibid.*, 53–54) and 792 by 1927 (Hudson 1927: 81; see Yin 2017; Jackson 2012). In 1916, when it became difficult to recruit personnel due to the war, a Japanese branch was established. Given its discipline, acceptance of lower salaries, and lower cost of the passage from the home country, this branch – which had only 30 members in 1919 – was expanded and its officers promoted. Still, the most important branch was the 'foreign' one, which was predictably dominated by the British. In 1919, it was only 146 strong, but it supervised all other branches (Jackson 2016: 53–54). The International Settlement's paramilitary force was even more ethnically diverse. During crises, British forces were normally sent to protect the Settlement; but the latter had to be ready to defend itself (Goodman 2000: 893). In 1853, a Chinese uprising led to the creation of the Shanghai Volunteer Corps and the *Compagnie Française des Volontaires* in the British and French Concessions, respectively. Both were eventually kept in service as 'foreign Shanghai feared an invasion of intruders more than imperialist rivalries' (Vandamme 2018: 45–46). The Volunteer Corps was, from the very beginning, a voluntary international militia set up by countries that included Britain, Russia, Japan, and the United States. It was mobilized to protect their trade missions during riots, serve as a strategic reserve for regular foreign garrisons in Shanghai, and be part of expeditionary forces (Sugarman 2007: 183). In 1940, when Britain withdrew its forces from Shanghai, the Volunteer Corps was put in control of the International Settlement until the Japanese occupation in early 1942. The Corps was funded by the Municipal Council. However, its members were not paid except for the professional White Russian Company (*Ibid.*), which was established in 1927, 'essentially providing the Council with a standing army' (Jackson 2016: 55). But it was only one of the many national companies. Volunteers from more than 20 countries joined the Shanghai Volunteer Corps as part of its units that, in the late 1930s, amounted to 23 for a total of 2,300 men. There were Light Horse, Artillery, and Air Defense units, as well as national ones (Sugarman 2007: 183) that, at different times, included British, Eurasian, Italian, Portuguese, German, American, Scottish, Jewish (from 1932), Filipino (under American command), Chinese, and the aforementioned White Russian companies (*Ibid.*; Vandamme 2018: 46; Jackson 2016: 55; Goodman 2000: 897). They had specific uniforms, but drilled together and were under the same command. As in the rest of the International Settlement's administrative apparatus, the British influence was very visible. The commander of the Shanghai Volunteer Corps was a British Army senior officer on secondment. The arms were provided by the British Army and ammunition came from the British colony of Hong Kong (Jackson 2016: 55). But this did not turn the Corps into a British-controlled force. Similar to the rest of the Settlement, it was subordinated to the Municipal Council and therefore found itself outside the authority of any foreign power.

The only participation of such powers in the governance of the International Settlement was represented by the actions of the Shanghai Consular Body, which consisted of the consuls of all Treaty Powers except, after World War I, those of Germany, Austria, Finland, and the Soviet Union.

The participation of the French consul general was formal given the existence of the French Concession (Hudson 1927: 81). However, the Consular Body had authority on a very limited number of issues. Perhaps the most important was that of the courts discussed in the section about extraterritoriality of Subchapter 6.1. As shown there, foreigners in Shanghai were able to take advantage of consular courts, as well as the first Mixed Court established in China in 1863 and dismantled in 1928. The British Supreme Court for China was also created in 1865 in Shanghai (Scully 2001: 6; Nield 2015: 15, 202, 206; Jackson 2018: 6). Similar to the case of Alexandria, access to these courts represented a major privilege of foreigners in Shanghai with respect to Chinese nationals. At the same time, it was a reminder of the fact that each of these foreigners remained subject to the consul of their nationality and could not completely escape the control of their remote governments (Jackson 2016: 44). Accordingly, there was a balance between the power exercised by the foreign powers on their respective nationals and the International Settlement's governance by non-state actors (i.e., the Municipal Council) (Jackson 2018: 8). This hybrid situation was specific to Shanghai's – and Alexandria's – semi-colonial status discussed in Subchapter 6.1. The associated complex and multilayered exercise of power (Jackson 2016: 44) led to a high degree of autonomy of local actors; one of the forms of manifestation of their resulting agency was the enhancement of the first wave globalization 'from below.'

However, it should be mentioned that the hybrid power structure at the origin of this agency was hardly positive in all its manifestations. In particular, its working mirrored the 'exclusionary nature of Settlement cosmopolitanism' (Goodman 2000: 896) discussed at the end of Subchapter 6.1. Cosmopolitan semi-colonial environments were highly beneficial to foreigners due to legal and economic privileges that were inaccessible to the locals. Unless they could get a foreign passport – which was not an option in Shanghai – the latter, and especially the indigenous lower social strata, often found themselves on the looser side. This typically resulted in rising nationalism and occasional outbursts of violence. In the International Settlement, the number of Chinese inhabitants was 30 to 40 times higher than that of foreigners (Vandamme 2018: 43; Goodman 2000: 893–894). The Chinese paid 60 percent of the taxes against the foreigners' 40 percent. Yet, for a long time, no Chinese was involved in the Settlement's governance. Moreover, the interests of the Chinese were seldom taken into consideration. There were many discriminatory policies. The most outrageous was that of closing the parks – where the municipal band played – to all Chinese, despite the fact that their taxes were used to fund both the parks and the band. This was still the case in 1927 when 'old residents sa[id] that the prohibition formerly read "Chinese and dogs".' Observers noted that 'the Settlement doubtless has the best municipal government to be found on Chinese territory. But it is governed in the interests of a small minority of its inhabitants' (Hudson 1927: 82–84). Predictably, this stimulated the rise of nationalism among the Chinese. The Municipal Council 'encountered frequent opposition and challenges from the local population.' Especially after the turn of the century, the Chinese demanded representation in the Council, launched organized campaigns against paying taxes, and were frequently in conflict with the municipal police (Yang 2019: 4). In the 1920s, the Treaty Powers tried to put an end to policies in the International Settlement that antagonized Chinese anti-imperialism because their own foreign relations with China were negatively affected. Accordingly, they put pressure on the Shanghai Municipal Council to accommodate at least some of the Chinese demands (Jackson 2016: 44). But the Council used the opportunity to show the high degree of autonomy it had acquired and, for a long time, rejected any change. As shown in Subchapter 6.1, 'the British consul-general, diplomats and home government were regularly frustrated that they could not exercise control over the SMC,' but there was little they could do because the 'Council is an independent international body, over which His Majesty's Government have no control' (Jackson 2018: 8, 10). This resistance was remarkable in terms of non-state actorness (see the section on semi-colonialism in Subchapter 6.1), but very detrimental with respect to local and international politics. Finally, three Chinese members joined the Municipal Council in 1928 and two more in 1930. Furthermore, the same ratepayers meeting that decided the 1928 change agreed to return the Mixed Court in Shanghai to Chinese jurisdiction (Nield 2015: 206). But it was too little, too late. By then, the rise of Chinese nationalism had become unstoppable.

The situation was somewhat different in the French Concession. The latter was much less populated than the International Settlement: in 1920, it had 3,562 foreign and 166,667 Chinese inhabitants against the Settlement's 23,307 and 759,839. Many 'preferred its quiet residential areas,' but economic activities were concentrated in the International Settlement (Vandamme 2018: 43). Surprisingly, French nationals were a minority even among the foreigners living in the French Concession: in 1925, the latter had 2,312 British, 1,403 Russians, 1,151 Americans, and only 892 Frenchmen (Hudson 1927: 84). The *Conseil municipal* had 14 members that, after 1914, included two and eventually three prominent Chinese businessmen (Nield 2015: 206). The foreign ratepayers elected four French members and four members belonging to three other nationalities. The remaining three French and three Chinese members were appointed by the consul-general. However, the powers of the Municipal Council were limited. Its decisions on the public order and administration of the Concession needed to be promulgated by the French consul general, who could – and sometimes did – suspend the Council for up to three months. In fact, 'the French administration rest[ed] very largely with the Consul-General and his associates' (Hudson 1927: 85). In comparison to the International Settlement, the administration of the Concession was in some respects less efficient; but it promoted much more accommodating policies toward the Chinese who, 'under some restrictions,' were admitted to the public park (*Ibid.*, 84–85). The Chinese presence in the Municipal

Council was in fact largely symbolic due to the subordinate position of the Council (Jackson 2016: 46–47); but it contributed to the 'marked difference in the attitude of the local Chinese population' toward the administrations of the French Concession and International Settlement (Hudson 1927: 85). Counterintuitively, there was less hostility toward the French Concession ruled directly by a foreign power through its consul general than to the semi-independent, self-administered International Settlement.

Despite these differences, in the second half of the 1930s, both the International Settlement and the French Concessions found it increasingly difficult to 'negotiate the tricky waters of growing Chinese nationalism and accelerating Sino-Japanese tensions' (Jackson 2016: 49). When the Chinese part of Shanghai was conquered by Japan in 1937, 'the foreign settlements became an island in a Japanese sea' (Nield 2015: 208). In early 1942, shortly after the beginning of the Pacific War, the Japanese occupied the International Settlement. Interestingly, they did not dismantle it. On the contrary, they claimed that they were promoting 'a genuine internationalism' different from the previous British domination (Jackson 2016: 56). The then Provisional Council was asked to 'cooperate with Imperial forces and carry on as usual' (Nield 2015: 209). Technically, the end of the International Settlement came from London and Washington. While they had no control of the area, on May 20, 1943, Britain and the United States ratified the treaties they had signed on January 11 with the Chinese government of Chiang Kai-shek (then located in Chongqing) for the Relinquishment of Extraterritorial Rights in China. This friendly act toward the allied nationalist government formally put an end to British and American participation in the extraterritorial system. Other Treaty Powers were not concerned, and the Japanese kept the Shanghai Municipal Council working until August 1943. But the *de jure* withdrawal of British and American members completely delegitimized it. It is nevertheless interesting to note that, in October 1945, the pre-1942 members of the Municipal Council met the British and American consuls general and asked to be involved in the implementation of the Relinquishment treaties: in the words of the American consul general, the 'Council considers itself still in being.' To the city's foreigners, 'Shanghai without foreign governance was unimaginable' (Jackson 2018: 240). The end of the French Concession was even more tortuous. Because it pertained to Vichy France, the Japanese did not occupy it in early 1942. However, under their pressure, on May 18, 1943, the government in Vichy signed an agreement with the Japanese-controlled Chinese government of Wang Jingwei that relinquished French extraterritorial rights. The French Concession was taken over by the government in Nanking on July 18. Still, the French forces in the Concession were disarmed and interned by the Japanese only on March 10, 1945, one day after Tokyo took full control of French Indochina. Some months later, when the war came to an end, both the French government in Vichy and the Chinese government in Nanking had disappeared. Consequently, the French extraterritorial rights were relinquished once more by a treaty between France and China signed at Chongqing on February 28, 1946 (Bergère 1997: 26, 28, 33, 39). This date marked the formal end of China's Treaty Port Era and semi-colonialism, even if English language sources associate it with the 1943 British and American treaties. Shanghai ceased to be ruled by the non-Chinese. Culturally and demographically, its cosmopolitanism did not instantly disappear; but it was swiftly and thoroughly eliminated after the communist takeover of the city in 1949 (Abbas 2002: 216). The dismantlement between 1942 and 1949 of the political, legal, and economic conditions that had ensured the prosperity of foreigners, as well as their ensuing physical departure, brought the end of Shanghai's globalization 'from below.' Its features and actors are analyzed in the next section.

Shanghai's National Minorities and the Globalization 'from Below'

In 1925, the foreigners in the International Settlement and the French Concession included British (8,191), Americans (3,093), Portuguese (1,506), French (1,174), Indians (1,154), Germans (1,040), Danes (327), Italians (280), and 'lesser numbers of more than thirty other nationalities' (Hudson 1927: 76). Their daily interactions were characterized by the 'cosmopolitanism of extraterritoriality' (Abbas 2002: 214) discussed in the last section of Subchapter 6.1. This 'symbiosis of the different imperial diasporas' was an 'everyday cosmopolitanism' (Vandamme 2018: 38) identical to the Alexandrian one. Bars, clubs, schools, churches, municipal institutions, and businesses convivially brought together foreigners of all nationalities, while totally excluding the Chinese (*Ibid.*, 48–49; see Subchapter 6.1). Carroll Alcott, an American radio broadcaster, published in 1943 a book about his experience in the International Settlement during the very last years before the Japanese occupation. The title – *My War with Japan* – is relevant: Alcott witnessed, unsympathetically, the Japanese conquest of the Chinese part of the city, as well as Tokyo's efforts to infiltrate and intimidate the inhabitants and authorities of the International Settlement. Yet, despite this disturbing situation and the uncertainties triggered by the war in Europe, his book depicts an urban landscape that Alexandrian contemporaries would have found familiar. Alcott worked in the International Settlement but lived in the French Concession. He had American, British, Russian, Greek, Portuguese, and Swiss neighbors, as well as 'a Nazi and Fascist colony [that] populated the eighth and ninth floors.' On the seventh, 'there was a small Syrian community' (Alcott 1943: 14). He had a Japanese tailor, listened to Russian and Filipino jazz bands, and noted the 'Germans, French, Italians, Portuguese, Dutch and others' who, in addition to British and Americans, were contributing to the Settlement's building and industrial expansion. While he would have very much preferred to avoid this kind of cosmopolitan encounter, the incisive anti-Axis broadcaster survived assassination attempts organized by members of the Japanese and Italian minorities (Alcott 1943).

It can be argued that, as a cosmopolitan immigrant pioneering in Shanghai the new and still small-scale business of commercial radio broadcasting, Carroll Alcott was a genuine actor of the first wave globalization 'from below.' So were many of the members of the British and American communities that were not associated with the large local or foreign trading companies or banks. As repeatedly shown earlier in this chapter, the Britons were the most influential and, until the 1910s, the largest foreign group in Shanghai. Their number in the International Settlement increased from 3,713 in 1905 to 4,465 in 1910, 5,341 in 1920, and 8,191 in 1925. They were the largest foreign minority even in the French Concession, where they amounted to 1,044 people in 1920, twice the number of French nationals (530). Their significant presence and influence in the Shanghai Municipal Council came from numbers, but also the economic weight of British businesses. For their part, until the arrival of the White Russians, the Americans represented the third minority after the British and the Japanese. They were less than one thousand in 1905 and 1910, 1,307 in 1915, 2,264 in 1920, and 3,093 in 1925 (Vandamme 2018: 43; Hudson 1927: 76). But they were very active economically, and joined the British in forming a group that 'shaped the social relations and gave rhythm to daily life inside the foreign community.' Accordingly, English became the *lingua franca* of all foreigners (Vandamme 2018: 44). The British and the Americans even introduced a neologism, Shanghailanders, to identify themselves. Certain observers perceived it as nothing less than a claim to Shanghai. The local Chinese were called Shanghainese: their 'own birthright was thereby implicitly challenged' (Goodman 2000: 893). The explanation of this imperialist claim was obvious. Shanghai had become the fifth-largest city and the sixth-largest port in the world due to the spectacular economic development associated with the foreign presence (Veeser 2013: 1153); British and American nationals were responsible for much of the city's economic activities. By 1929, no less than 77 percent of the British and 65 percent of the American investment in China went into Shanghai, which essentially meant the International Settlement (Jackson 2018: 6). From the very beginning and differently from Japan in the 1930s and 1940s, both powers were 'more interested in territory than trade' (Nield 2015: 6). From the 1840s, the opening of the treaty ports in general and Shanghai, in particular, triggered a major influx of foreign merchants who, as already mentioned earlier in this chapter, sold opium, as well as cotton and woolen products, while buying tea, silk, and porcelain. Major China Coast firms such as Jardine, Dent, and Russell were prominent in this trade (*Ibid.*, 4). The largest one, Jardine, Matheson, and Company, was Scottish and became a long-term actor of Chinese foreign trade (Jackson 2016: 47–48). After 1870, such large companies turned Shanghai into a major Asian node of the first globalization 'from above.' Physically, the still visible Bund represents an impressive illustration of this prosperous period. More than one hundred banks and trading houses, as well as many hotels and clubs, had their headquarters on the embankment of Huangpu River. These neoclassical and Art Deco buildings that mixed older British styles and New York-inspired skyscrapers (Wu 2004: 164–165; Rofel 2012: 445) became the public face of Shanghai and all treaty ports in China. They were presented – and perceived – worldwide as 'symbolic of the Western space created and maintained among Chinese chaos' (Crawford 2018: 986–987). 'The bund was created by, and represented, a system of Victorian mercantile imperialism' (Taylor 2002: 141). However, the triumph of the first wave globalization 'from above' in Shanghai illustrated by the Bund did not prevent a similar but more discreet 'from below' phenomenon. From the very opening of Shanghai to foreign trade, the large firms were accompanied by independent traders involved in the same type of commerce (Nield 2015: 4). When, in 1863, business interests led to the creation of the International Settlement as an entity that 'assert[ed] its independence from any country's formal control' (Crawford 2018: 973), British and American small merchants supportive of *laissez-faire* capitalism strongly encouraged a move that improved their business prospects. For the next seven decades, they fully benefitted from extraterritorial rights to conduct their trade with the rest of the world. It should be added that, similar to the traders in Alexandria but different from the entrepreneurial migrants of the current Chinese-centered globalization 'from below,' Shanghai's British and American small merchants – as well as those of other nationalities – were not suitcase traders. They did not shuttle between China and their countries of origin or other destinations. Instead, they were long-term residents of the International Settlement who sent and received goods through their transnational networks. Shanghai's foreigners tended to be settlers and the city's flows of people related to the first wave globalization 'from below' were mainly migratory in nature.

This was also the case for the French. They were not numerous and were distributed among the French Concession and the International Settlement. In fact, in 1905, more lived in the latter than in the former (393 vs. 274). The ratio changed eventually (330 vs. 436 in 1910 and 316 vs. 530 in 1920), but not in a radical manner. In 1925, there were only 1,174 French in all of Shanghai as compared to 8,191 Britons (Vandamme 2018: 43; Hudson 1927: 76). Moreover, their economic activities were much more modest than those of the British and Americans. The French were mainly a small 'group of missionaries, shopkeepers, and municipal officials' who were nevertheless strongly attached to 'the national character of their small "colony"' (Vandamme 2018: 44). They were very active in the fields of religion, intellectual life, and entertainment. Accordingly, the French Concession was strongly marked by the presence of the Catholic Church and by activities related to theater, cinema, and books (*Ibid.*). Shanghai's French minority may have not played an important economic role in the first wave globalization 'from below,' but certainly represented one of the main actors of its flows of ideas. The Germans, who lived mainly in the International Settlement, were slightly more numerous than the French except after their expulsion at the end of World War I: 832 in 1905, 959 in 1910, 1,425 in 1915, only 289 in 1920, but 1,040 in

1925 (Vandamme 2018: 43; Hudson 1927: 76). They were very active economically; in fact, most of them were merchants. Some represented large trading companies in Germany, but many had small businesses that traded with counterparts back home or elsewhere in the German colonial empire, thus joining the 'from below' globalization. Economic power allowed the German inhabitants of the International Settlement to participate in local politics. Until 1914, they had one Council member. But – different from the other minorities except for the Japanese one – they perceived themselves 'as part of a network of outposts of the German Reich.' They even established a branch of the German Naval League, a strongly nationalist structure created in 1898 to promote the construction of a powerful German Navy. In this context, the relationship between Shanghai's German and Entente nationals is most relevant for the evolution of cosmopolitanism and nationalism during the first wave globalizations. Before 1914, the 'shared feeling of cosmopolitan solidarity superseded the nationalist reflexes of the Westerners' in Shanghai (Vandamme 2018: 41, 44–45). The same Germans who supported the idea of a dominant Reich lived in the International Settlement and the French Concession, established common businesses with Britons, went to French churches, and – like everybody else among Shanghai's foreigners – celebrated with equal enthusiasm 'the birthday of the emperor Wilhelm II or Bastille Day' (*Ibid.*, 48). Different from the situation in Europe, the beginning of World War I did not bring immediate interethnic hostility to Shanghai. Such hostility nevertheless developed as a consequence of the military conflict. Concerned minorities revalued their national identity in a way that put an end to the decades-long cosmopolitan solidarity with nationals of the other camp. The nationalist trend that was dominant in Europe (and brought the first wave globalization 'from above' to an end in 1914) ceased to be a remote threat. While there were no violent clashes in Shanghai and political actions against Germans and Austrian-Hungarians had to be delayed until China declared war on Germany in 1917, nationalist tensions challenged cosmopolitan solidarity and questioned fundamental features of the foreign presence (*Ibid.*, 42, 48, 49, 63–64). Still, cosmopolitanism survived. The split was between the huge majority of foreigners and two relatively small minorities. Solidarity within the anti-German camp, the common threat of rising Chinese nationalism, and the economic boom of the 1920s turned the World War I nationalist tensions into a soon forgotten episode. A few years later, German merchants returned to the International Settlement. Nationalism would ultimately kill Shanghai's cosmopolitanism and the associated globalization 'from below.' But it would not be the nationalism of foreigners.

One World War later, it was the turn of the Japanese minority to find itself in a peculiar situation. From only 736 individuals in 1900, this group increased to 2,157 in 1905, 3,361 in 1910, 7,169 in 1915, 10, 215 in 1920, and 13,804 in 1925. In the first half of the 1910s, it became the most numerous among the foreigners in Shanghai (Vandamme 2018: 43; Hudson 1927: 76). Atypically for Shanghai, the Japanese did not have much contact with other foreigners. Most of them lived in their own neighborhood in the International Settlement (Vandamme 2018: 43) and were well organized communally in the framework of the Japanese Residents' Association (Jackson 2016: 49). Some worked for a few large Japanese corporations. The majority established small businesses: Carroll Alcott's tailor was Japanese. Small merchants traded with the homeland, thus contributing to the commercial flows of the first wave globalization 'from below.' Another contribution was the important migratory flow connecting Japan to Shanghai. Locally, the resulting increase in the demographic and economic weight of the Japanese minority led to changes in the composition of the Shanghai Municipal Council. Two Japanese members joined it in 1915 and 1927, respectively (Jackson 2016: 45, 47, 49; Jackson 2018: 5–6; Hudson 1927: 80). In 1927, they were invited to also join the Council's committees, which debated specific policy decisions; finally, the Japanese could exercise more power within the International Settlement (Jackson 2016: 49). But they were far from balancing the influence of the British minority in the Council and the International Settlement as a whole (Nield 2015: 207). Accordingly, the change was not perceived as sufficient by the Japanese minority and especially by the government in Tokyo. As Japan's leaders became 'more interested in territory than trade' in China (*Ibid.*, 6), they used the Japanese minority in Shanghai as a fifth column. Alcott discovered that his tailor had been recruited by the Japanese intelligence and participated in a propaganda campaign. When the Chinese part of Shanghai was occupied, the tailor became a low-rank officer of a local Japanese militia and was directly involved in military actions in the city (Alcott 1943). The situation was much more serious than the World War I tensions and should have been perceived as a major challenge to Shanghai's cosmopolitanism. Surprisingly, this was not the case. On the one hand, different from the German case, the Japanese were only marginally involved in the city's cosmopolitan interactions. Racial and cultural differences and prejudice had limited their acceptance by the Western minorities; cosmopolitan solidarity did not fully apply to Japanese, Vietnamese, Indian, and other Asian groups. On the other hand, it would have been unrealistic to expect the Japanese nationals in the International Settlement to resist the aggressive Japanese government that stationed its military a few hundred yards away. This is why Carroll Alcott's criticism targeted Tokyo's intelligence services that instrumentalized the Japanese minority rather than the minority itself. It was from the Japanese occupation of the International Settlement in early 1942 to the dismantlement of the Provisional Municipal Council in the summer of 1943 that this instrumentalization reached its climax. As shown in the previous section, Japan imposed militarily a short-lived political fiction. Its only genuine supporters were the Tokyo-controlled members of the Japanese minority in Shanghai. However, Japan claimed that, freed from the British domination, the International Settlement finally incarnated 'a genuine internationalism' (Jackson 2016: 56). During the entire period of the first wave globalization 'from below,' this may well have been the most extreme rhetorical and political use of cosmopolitanism as a mask for imperialist domination.

All the minorities examined in the previous paragraphs included social layers ranging from affluent merchants and entrepreneurs fully involved in the first wave globalization 'from above' to more modest individuals that were part of the migratory and, at times, trade flows of the globalization 'from below.' But the Civil War in Russia led to the massive expansion of a group almost entirely associated with subaltern cosmopolitanism. Until the Bolshevik Revolution, Russia was an important Treaty Power whose nationals were present in both Russian and other countries' concessions. Five hundred of them lived in Shanghai by 1905. Military defeat in the Civil War dramatically increased this presence while breaking the link between White Russian refugees and the communist state. The 1925 census found 2,766 Russians in the International Concession, but many more went unregistered or had settled in the French Concession. In 1927, the number of recent arrivals was estimated at 10,000. In the late 1930s, they could have been as many as 35,000 (Hudson 1927: 76; Alcott 1943: 305). Just a few were wealthy. The rest struggled to establish restaurants, stores, and various businesses, but often 'worked for wages on a scale not much better than that paid the Chinese' (Alcott 1943: 305). In most cases, they lacked a trade or entrepreneurial background, which was a serious handicap in an environment dominated by highly skilled entrepreneurs from all over the world. They also lacked the protection of a consul, which made them unable to benefit fully from the advantages of extraterritoriality. Overall, the social and economic status of the White Russians was superior to that of most of the Chinese, but not comparable to that of Western or Japanese immigrants. They could be compared with Alexandria's Maltese, Algerians, or Tunisians. This was visible in structures such as the police force, where they shared subaltern positions with the Sikhs or Vietnamese brought by the British or the French. Few White Russian petty merchants were active in international trade because, unlike other foreigners, they were cut from counterparts in the homeland. As a result, their main involvement in the first wave globalization 'from below' was represented by their massive migratory inflow. A somewhat better but not completely different situation was that of another massive group of refugees, the Jews. In fact, some of them had arrived as traders, not refugees, after the opening of the treaty ports. The Sassoon, Hardoon, Kadoorie, and other families of Sephardic Jews from Baghdad and Bombay – which acquired British citizenship – set up major businesses in 19th century Shanghai. Much larger numbers of Jews arrived from Russia after the Bolshevik Revolution and especially from Germany and other parts of Europe when they faced Nazi persecutions. In 1939, estimates of the total number of Jews in Shanghai varied between 30,000 and 50,000. They were communally well organized but, as refugees, were hardly prosperous (Sugarman 2007: 184) and joined the other groups of subaltern cosmopolitans. Many arrived shortly before or even after the beginning of World War

II when conditions were hardly favorable to setting up 'from below' international economic exchanges. However, as in the case of the White Russians, the Jews significantly contributed to the migratory flows of the first wave globalization 'from below' in Shanghai. It is interesting to note that these flows intensified during the 1920s and 1930s, giving a new life to the 'from below' globalization at a time when the 'from above' one had already come to an end.

Other national minorities in Shanghai that were similarly involved in its globalization 'from below' included the Portuguese, the Indians, the Danes, the Italians, the Spaniards, the Austro-Hungarians, the Ottomans, the Belgians, and other smaller groups (Hudson 1927: 76; Vandamme 2018: 44). Still, as their features were not significantly different from those of larger minorities, it is more useful to move to the analysis of a different dimension of that globalization. The first wave globalization 'from above' significantly contributed to the diffusion of many Western values, ideas, and practices. Remote cultures started to be Europeanized. Politically, new understandings of 'sovereignty, development, progress and political governance' became known worldwide 'along with changing politico-cultural beliefs that embraced nationalism and bourgeois democracy as well as anti-imperialism' (Rofel 2012: 446). The 'from below' globalization also had an important cognitive dimension, which added to the migratory and commercial ones. On the cultural side, the bookshops and theaters of the French Concession were instrumental in connecting Shanghai's intellectual life to radical trends in Paris. Political anti-establishment activism was even more popular. Chinese but also foreign political refugees, dissidents, and radicals that were 'not only opponents of the Chinese government but also enemies of capitalism and imperialism abroad' (Yue 2006: xxiii) took refuge in the International Settlement and the French Concession. Chinese communism was born in Shanghai (Abbas 2002: 216) due to the activity of transnational 'from below' networks. But the most interesting – and important – ideological construct of the city's foreigners had much to do with the very creation of the International Settlement. When the first concessions were established in the mid-19th century, Britain and France championed liberal values that 'accompanied visions of a peaceful, progressive, commercial "Commonwealth of Europe".' They perceived themselves as European and Christian – and, eventually, civilized and white – powers bringing progress to 'backward, "Asiatic" China' (Crawford 2018: 973). It was against this ideational background rooted in Enlightenment values and principles that the British and American settlements were merged in 1863 under the pressure of business interests looking for independence from all states. The *Omnia juncta in uno* (All joined in one) motto on the municipal seal introduced in 1869 reflected the International Settlement's 'image of itself as a pan-European "cosmopolitan republic" that transcended national attachments in the pursuit of commerce and progress' (*Ibid.*, 973, 975). In 1893, foreign Shanghai 'celebrat[ed] its fiftieth year "as a foreign city," and as "the only republic on Asiatic soil," "a unique instance of a republic dropped down on an alien empire'" where various minorities were 'unitedly living in harmonious intercourse' (Goodman 2000: 893). Of course, the International Settlement was not independent and was not a republic. But it did try to become both. In 1862, the leaders of the foreign minorities launched an initiative to actually declare the future International Settlement a free city with its own elected government that would be placed under the protectorate of the four great Powers in coordination with China. The initiative was rejected by the foreign consuls as impractical. However, by the 1880s, the Municipal Council *de facto* reached a semi-independent status that was comparable with that planned two decades earlier (*Ibid.*). As repeatedly shown in this chapter, the International Settlement was governed by local non-state actors (Jackson 2018: 8) that, at times, acted overtly against the interest of the Treaty Powers. Accordingly, it was 'a polity more akin to an independent city-state under foreign colonial control' (*Ibid.*, 16; Yang 2019: 11). At first view, the association of this political construct with a 'from below' effort could be questioned. After all, the initial proposal was prepared by the leaders of national minorities, who also participated in its eventual *de facto* implementation. These were important businessmen deeply involved, after 1870, in the first wave globalization 'from above.' Without their contribution, the similarly self-interested efforts of the petty traders of the globalization 'from below' would have never succeeded in reaching such a spectacular result. But in this case the affluent foreign merchants in Shanghai joined the 'from below' camp. They shared the interests of the small traders and followed a 'from below' strategy that clashed with the policies of the 'from above' Treaty Powers. When the latter's consuls opposed the 1862 plan, they did it for a very good reason: a semi-independent International Settlement would have escaped state control and become able to dictate its own rules. This actually happened, and the arrival of the first wave globalization 'from above' found in Shanghai a political, legal, economic, and social situation where no foreign power could control 'from below' initiatives and activities. Autonomous small actors were able to launch their own globalization 'from below,' which was impossible on the metropolitan territory or in the colonial empires of the same Treaty Powers. As Shanghai was a 'model settlement' duplicated, to different degrees, by all new concessions in second-wave treaty ports (Crawford 2018: 973), its atypical political-institutional structure became one of the key causes of the expansion of the first wave globalization 'from below' in China. Ultimately, the small and weak actors of this globalization were at the origin of a projection of normative power that shaped the very nature of the foreign presence in this country in ways unintended by – or even contrary to the interests of – the great powers that had made it possible.

Overall, the study of semi-colonial cosmopolitan Shanghai reveals many similarities and a few differences with respect to the case of Alexandria. The next subchapter uses them in order to identify the main features of the first wave globalization 'from below.'

6.4 Of Globalizations and Modernities

Based on the findings of this chapter, I define the first wave globalization 'from below' as the flows of migrants, goods, and ideas associated with semi-colonial cosmopolitan port cities, made possible by the changes brought by the 1870–1914 first wave globalization 'from above,' and enacted by subaltern cosmopolitans that imperialist great powers used to weaken non-European states. By exploiting extraterritoriality and the semi-colonial balance of power, these small and apparently weak actors became highly autonomous from all states. Their agency led to 'from below' globalized processes that no great power had planned, expected, or could control. The independent nature of these processes allowed the first wave globalization 'from below' to significantly outlive the 'from above' one.

It is obvious that the former globalization could have not emerged in the absence of the latter. First, the globalization 'from above' created the infrastructure and cultural prerequisites essential to massive transnational flows. Second, it represented a projection of normative power of the hegemonic Western great powers that, in line with their imperialist and colonial policies, opened previously closed non-European economies. Third, its large 'from above' flows significantly contributed to the development of cosmopolitanism in its trading nodes, which included semi-colonial port cities. In addition to the first wave globalization 'from above,' semi-colonialism represented another critical precondition. Full state control meant 'from above' constraints that inhibited 'from below' agency. This could not be avoided on metropolitan soil or in the colonies. But in the Ottoman Empire, Egypt, China, Persia, and Siam, the authority of the surviving indigenous states was dramatically weakened. For their part, external great powers balanced each other. Because semi-colonialism 'operated like neocolonialism, through diffused ideological and cultural interpellation rather than institutionalized, formal domination' (Shih 2001: 35, 37), actors 'from below' had a much higher margin of maneuver. Alexandria 'was a city with many authorities but no hegemon' (Hanley 2017: 17). Shanghai became a 'polycentric, decentered city controlled by many different hands' (Abbas 2002: 214). The increasingly large cosmopolitan minorities in such port cities found a niche free from the constraints of states and their globalization 'from above.' Critically, they were able to create autonomous administrative structures at the local level. In 1890, the autonomous Alexandria municipality was established that 'let non-Egyptians run the city' (Mansel 2011: 131). The Shanghai Municipal Council 'evolved into a semi-independent governing structure' that showed 'substantial independence' from both Chinese and consular authorities (Goodman 2000: 893). Governance by local non-state actors (Jackson 2018: 8) resulted in policies and regulatory frameworks that were tailored to fit the interests of cosmopolitan immigrants, not of the great powers that protected them. At times, these powers explicitly expressed their frustration. Immigrants achieved such results due to the 'Midas touch' of extraterritoriality, which allowed them to dramatically extend their privileges and immunities (Scully 2001: 5; Cassel 2016: 23). Extraterritoriality was an expression of the normative power that Western great powers projected in the target states to serve their own interests. The pawns of those powers, however, opportunistically exploited the associated legal and economic privileges to their own benefit. They even became 'legal chameleons' (Fahmy 2013) that gave 'preference to the national (...) identity most advantageous in a given situation' (Shlala 2009: 7). Such overtly disloyal behavior made few consuls happy; but the migrant pawns considerably upgraded their status, as well as the potential for self-interested agency. The ability of this 'from below' agency to create a fully fledged globalization was greatly enhanced by the cosmopolitanism of its actors. A social praxis emerged (Eldem 2013: 223) in the port cities based on 'cross-border flows, hybrid identities, and modes of affiliation that cross-cut communal divides' (Lewis 2016: 7). This everyday cosmopolitanism that made a variety of 'peoples and races' share a 'particular kind of sociability' (Ilbert 1996: 102) had two direct consequences, which stimulated the first wave globalization 'from below.' On the one hand, the inter-communal 'social porosity' (Eldem 2013: 217–218) and conviviality (Gekas 2009: 105) were the root cause of actor openness locally and globally. On the other hand, they produced a 'certain consciousness' (*Ibid.*) that led to strong cosmopolitan solidarity. Intercultural bonds developed that showed a 'willingness to share a single social space and to create an international community' (Vandamme 2018: 38; Fuhrmann 2007: 15–16) among the cosmopolitan immigrants. It is this community that made possible the construction of autonomous administrative structures that protected the immigrants' interests and stimulated their agency. Immigrants included affluent businessmen actively involved in the first wave globalization 'from above.' But the much more numerous group of 'subaltern cosmopolitans' composed of Maltese, Algerian, and Tunisian colonial subjects, Italian and Greek petty traders, as well as White Russian and Jewish refugees, had no access to that globalization. Instead, they enacted the more discreet globalization 'from below.' Most of them were settlers, not shuttle traders. Accordingly, the flows of people of the first wave globalization 'from below' were dominated by the migratory component. There were large numbers of entrepreneurs, traders, skilled workers, and adventurers attracted by the opportunities of socio-economic advancement created by extraterritoriality in semi-colonial port cities. As they adopted the 'big fish in a small pond' strategy, migration in the Mediterranean Basin 'took place on a scale that had not been seen since the time of the Reconquista' (Fuhrmann 2020: 31). There were also political refugees ranging from European anarchists and Libyan anti-colonial fighters to tenths of thousands of fleeing White Russians and persecuted Jews, which became Shanghai's largest foreign minorities. Flows of goods were also important. Migrant petty traders of all nationalities took advantage of two elements: their networks in the country of origin and its diaspora and extraterritoriality-related tax exemptions in the country of residence. Often, they conducted informal commercial activities. Italian small merchants in Alexandria who traded with partners in Italy had 'not a piastre to spare for the hungryman of the Italian treasury' (Elizabeth Monroe quoted by Viscomi 2019: 372). The Greek ones set up 'extensive and well-organized smuggling operations' (Reimer 1977/2019: 192). The third type of flow concerned ideas. Immigrants brought with them the highly diversified cultural luggage specific to their places of origin. Equally important, they imported Western understandings of 'sovereignty, development, progress and political governance' and 'politico-cultural beliefs that embraced nationalism and bourgeois democracy as well as anti-imperialism' (Rofel 2012: 446). In Alexandria, progressive immigrant activists engaged in disputes with nationalists and fascists in Europe in an effort to counter their ascension by promoting the city's cosmopolitan values. In Shanghai, a proposal was made in the early 1860s to turn the new International Settlement into an independent pan-European cosmopolitan republic, a free city with its own elected government. Far from representing a utopia, this plan had *de facto* been implemented by the 1880s. The semi-colonial cosmopolitan port cities connected by these flows of migrants, goods, and ideas became a 'complex field of negotiation between local, overseas, and in-between agents' (Shlala 2018: 16) and a 'major breeding ground of globalization' (Driessen 2005: 129, 131). They were the nodes of the first wave globalization 'from below' that, indeed, no great power had planned, expected, or was able to control.

In terms of normative power, a paradoxical situation developed after 1870. The 'from below' globalization was constructed by the agency of small actors whose economic success relied heavily on extraterritoriality. The latter was introduced earlier, but its use considerably expanded when all types of interactions between the Western hegemonic powers and semi-colonial states intensified during the first wave globalization 'from above.' The normative power of the hegemonic powers was projected toward these weaker states to impose both the extension of the extraterritoriality-related privileges of their migrants and those states' opening to the globalization 'from above.' This is to say that, similar to the case of the present Chinese-centered globalizations, the first wave globalizations 'from below' and 'from above' were the result of the same projection of normative power. However, for their part, the cosmopolitan immigrants fully accepted that normative power only as long as its use against their states of residence gave them a huge comparative advantage with respect to indigenous economic rivals. When the immigrants themselves were the target of the same 'from above' normative power, they resisted it. They even proposed and actually constructed autonomous administrative frameworks that protected the 'from below' flows and processes contrary to the interests of the hegemonic great powers and their globalization 'from above.' The first wave globalization 'from below' emerged as the junior normative companion of the 'from above' one; but it was an uninvited and highly rebellious companion. The senior partner responded in kind: consuls of great powers opposed the plan to establish the International Settlement in Shanghai as a free city. 'Genuine' Europeans turned 'Levantine' into a derogatory label intended to marginalize the 'subaltern cosmopolitan' actors of the globalization 'from below' in Egypt and the Ottoman Empire. Despite the intimate relationship between the two first wave globalizations, there was considerable uneasiness in their normative interactions.

They were, nevertheless, similarly targeted by the same lethal enemy. For almost half a century, nationalism and the two globalizations developed in parallel. But 'the violent explosion of national rivalries that constituted World War I' (Stearns 2010: 117–118) put an end to the first wave globalization 'from above' and, in places such as Shanghai, seriously challenged the cosmopolitan solidarity that sustained the 'from below' one. The paradox is that it is the latter that survived. Despite its heavy reliance on cosmopolitanism, the first wave globalization 'from below' was more resilient than its apparently unstoppable 'from above' counterpart. As a social praxis (Eldem 2013: 223), semi-colonial cosmopolitanism itself was in fact 'a process working alongside nationalism, sometimes as complementary and sometimes as competitor' (Skrbiš and Woodward 2013: 7). The tensions between German and Entente nationals in the International Settlement during World War I were part of the 'blockages, resistances and immobilities' that characterized the dynamic of the interactions between cosmopolitanism and nationalism (*Ibid.*). The situation worsened when such tensions were stimulated and instrumentalized politically. Mussolini's sustained efforts to 'italianize' the Italian community in Alexandria (see Giuliani Caponetto 2008: 147) and Tokyo's instrumentalization of the Japanese minority in Shanghai were based on the radical rejection of cosmopolitanism by regimes that had adopted ultranationalism as one of their fundamental features. The objective was to take full control of the migrant minority, 'cleaning' it of foreign leanings and completely eliminating its agency. If successful, such actions would have brought both cosmopolitanism and the associated globalization 'from below' to an end. Yet, during the first wave globalization, migrant minorities succeeded to preserve much of their cosmopolitan features as long as military occupation and aggressive nationalist policies were not used to physically dislocate or assimilate them. Both Mussolini and the Japanese failed in their enterprise. But, a few years later, Nasser and Mao – two leftist dictators that half of the world continues to hail today as champions of freedom and emancipation – expelled foreigners, confiscated their assets, and killed the globalization 'from below' in Alexandria and Shanghai in a matter of months. In fact, these were two episodes of a larger series. The first cosmopolitan port city of the first wave globalization 'from below' that indigenous nationalists killed – and this is not a metaphor – was Salonica. Occupied by Greece during the First Balkan War in 1912, it burned in 1917 and was replaced with the Greek Thessaloniki. In 1922, it was Smyrna that was put to fire after its occupation by the Turkish military. Its place was taken by Turkish Izmir. Greeks representing as much as 30 percent of the city's population, as well as many other foreigners, had to leave Constantinople in 1923. Pera and Galata disappeared from the map of cosmopolitanism. Shanghai and the other port cities in China were taken over by the Chinese communists in 1949, Alexandria's cosmopolitans were expelled after the 1956 war, and finally Beirut was turned into a battlefield in 1975. Each time, the departure of foreign minorities from a major node of the globalization 'from below' further diminished the latter's reach. The socio-economic phenomenon that once embraced significant parts of what we call today the Global South became less and less relevant. At times, it mainly relied on flows of political refugees as 'from below' trade declined dramatically due to international tensions, warfare, military occupation, or restrictive national policies. Ultimately, the nationalist agendas of various regimes had the upper hand and completely eliminated the last surviving elements of a globalizing phenomenon that had started back in 1870. The first wave globalization 'from below' was much more resilient than the 'from above' one; but it was hardly immortal.

Besides the relationship between these two globalizations discussed, in terms of normative power, in the previous paragraphs, the 'from below' one shared a number of common features with and showed certain differences from the present similar globalizations scrutinized in the previous chapters of this book. I believe that it is more appropriate to examine them in the next chapter. Here, I will only briefly mention one aspect that is often ignored. The idea is widely accepted that, by opening the entire world to Western influences, the first wave globalization 'from above' also diffused the Western model of modernity. In places such as China, this generated 'a pattern of shock, wonder, admiration, and imitation' (Wu 2004: 164). Yet, in many regions, this attractive model was as difficult to reach as that proposed by the Western-centered globalization 'from above' is today to the poor masses of the Global South. The first wave globalization 'from below' was inspired by the same Western values as the 'from above' one: in Shanghai, the independent 'free city' it wanted to construct was explicitly based on the Liberal philosophy of the Enlightenment. But it considerably expanded the importance of cosmopolitanism, which progressive activists such as Enrico Pea and Fausta Cialente explicitly and systematically opposed to the rising nationalism in the West. Critically, at societal level, the 'social praxis' of 'everyday cosmopolitanism' led to the 'appropriation, integration, and hybridisation of various cultural influences,' which, in turn, 'produce[d] new visions of modernity' (Lewis 2016: 10). Similar to the present situation in Argentina's La Salada (see Subchapter 4.7), the first wave globalization 'from below' proposed an alternative modernity inspired by but somewhat different from that of the contemporary globalization 'from above.' Maltese and White Russian 'subaltern cosmopolitans' in Alexandria and Shanghai played one century ago the same unexpected role as Bolivian undocumented workers in today's Buenos Aires: they were constructing a modernity that everybody could afford. By expelling the cosmopolitans and, whenever possible, burning their cities, nationalists and communists destroyed more than a globalization 'from below.' They eliminated a modernity that had taken root in their own countries and whose main features were openness, 'social porosity,' and conviviality. This was the only way to impose their own authoritarian or totalitarian models of modernity, which have dominated the Global South during much of the 20th century.

Note

1 See the end of the next section.

References

Abbas, Ackbar (2002) 'Cosmopolitan De-scriptions: Shanghai and Hong Kong,' in Carol A. Breckenridge, Sheldon Pollock, Homi K. Bhabha, and Dipesh Chakrabarty (eds.) *Cosmopolitanism*, Durham and London: Duke University Press, pp. 209–228.
Aciman, André (1995) *Out of Egypt: A Memoir*, epub edition, New York: Farrar, Straus and Giroux.
Alcott, Carroll (1943) *My War with Japan*, New York: Henry Holt and Company.
Al-Sayyid Marsot, Afaf Lutfi (2007) *A History of Egypt. From the Arab Conquest to the Present*, Second edition, Cambridge; New York: Cambridge University Press.
Awad, Mohamed, and Sahar Hamouda (eds.) (2006/2012) *Voices from Cosmopolitan Alexandria*, Alexandria: Bibliotheca Alexandrina.
Beinin, Joel (1998) 'Egypt: Society and Economy,' in Martin W. Daly (ed.) *The Cambridge History of Egypt, Volume 2, Modern Egypt, from 1517 to the End of the Twentieth Century*, Cambridge; New York, pp. 309–333.
Bergère, Marie-Claire (1997) 'L'épuration à Shanghai (1945–1946). L'affaire Sarly et la fin de la concession française,' *Vingtième Siècle, revue d'histoire*, 53, January-March, pp. 25–41.
Botman, Selma (1998) 'The Liberal Age, 1923–1952,' in Martin W. Daly (ed.) *The Cambridge History of Egypt, Volume 2, Modern Egypt, from 1517 to the End of the Twentieth Century*, Cambridge; New York, pp. 285–308.
Boulad-Ayoub, Josiane (2004) 'Le Français comme langue de travail au Moyen-Orient,' paper presented at the Colloqium *Alexandrianism in the 21st Century. Evoking the Spirit. Recreating the City*, Bibliotheca Alexandrina, Alexandria, April 28–30.
Cassel, Pär (2016) 'Extraterritoriality in China: What We Know and What We Don't Know,' in Robert Bickers and Isabella Jackson (eds.) *Treaty Ports in Modern China*, London: Routledge, pp. 23–42.
Chircop, Nicholas D. (2015) *A Transient Colony in the Valley of the Nile. The History of the Maltese Colony in Egypt throughout the 19th and 20th Century*, Melbourne: Published by the author.
Crawford, Alan (2018) 'Imagining the Russian Concession in Hankou,' *The Historical Journal*, 61(4), pp. 969–989.
Cromer, The Earl of (1916) *Modern Egypt*, Volume II, New York: Macmillan.
Daly, Martin W. (1998) 'The British Occupation, 1882–1922,' in Martin W. Daly (ed.) *The Cambridge History of Egypt, Volume 2, Modern Egypt, from 1517 to the End of the Twentieth Century*, Cambridge; New York, pp. 239–251.

Daudin, Guillaume, Matthias Morys, and Kevin H. O'Rourke (2010) 'Globalization, 1870–1914,' in Stephen Broadberry and Kevin H. O'Rourke (eds.) *The Cambridge Economic History of Modern Europe Volume 2. 1870 to the Present*, Cambridge: Cambridge University Press, pp. 5–29.

Driessen, Henk (2005) 'Mediterranean Port Cities: Cosmopolitanism Reconsidered,' *History and Anthropology*, 16(1), pp. 129–141.

Eldem, Edhem (2013) 'Istanbul as a Cosmopolitan City: Myths and Realities,' in Ato Quayson and Girish Daswani (eds.) *A Companion to Diaspora and Transnationalism*, Chichester, West Sussex: Blackwell Publishing, pp. 212–230.

Fahmy, Ziad (2013) 'Jurisdictional Borderlands: Extraterritoriality and "Legal Chameleons" in Precolonial Alexandria, 1840–1870,' *Comparative Studies in Society and History*, 55(2), pp. 305–329.

Farrugia, Massimo (2004) 'Maltese Left Their Mark in Countries of Adoption,' *Times of Malta*, December 9, https://timesofmalta.com/articles/view/maltese-left-their-mark-in-countries-of-adoption.104820

Fuhrmann, Malte (2007) 'Meeresanrainer - Weltenbürger? Zum Verhältnis von hafenstädtischer Gesellschaft und Kosmopolitismus' (The Seaside Resident - A Citizen of the World? On Port City Societies and Cosmopolitanism), *Comparativ* 17(2), pp. 12–26.

Fuhrmann, Malte (2020) *Port Cities of the Eastern Mediterranean: Urban Culture in the Late Ottoman Empire*, Cambridge: Cambridge University Press.

Galtung, Johan (1971) 'A Structural Theory of Imperialism,' *Journal of Peace Research*, 8(2), pp. 81–117.

Gekas, Athanasios (Sakis) (2009) 'Class and Cosmopolitanism: The Historiographical Fortunes of Merchants in Eastern Mediterranean Ports,' *Mediterranean Historical Review*, 24(2), pp. 95–114.

Giuliani Caponetto, Rosetta (2008) *'Going Out of Stock:' Mulattoes and Levantines in Italian Literature and Cinema of the Fascist Period*, Ph.D. thesis, University of Connecticut.

Goldschmidt Jr., Arthur (2004) *Modern Egypt: The Formation of a Nation-State*, Second edition, Boulder, Colorado; Cumnor Hill, Oxford: Westview Press.

Goodman, Bryna (2000) 'Improvisations on a Semicolonial Theme, or, How to Read a Celebration of Transnational Urban Community,' *The Journal of Asian Studies*, 59(4), pp. 889–926.

Gusejnova, Dina (ed.) (2018) *Cosmopolitanism in Conflict: Imperial Encounters from the Seven Years' War to the Cold War*, London: Palgrave Macmillan.

Haag, Michael (2014) 'Alexandrian Cosmopolitanism: An Archive by Hala Halim,' Book review, *Journal of Modern Greek Studies*, 32(2), 449–452.

Halim, Hala (2013) *Alexandrian Cosmopolitanism: An Archive*, New York: Fordham University Press.

Hanley, Will (2012) 'Cosmopolitan Cursing in Late Nineteenth Century Alexandria,' in, Sikeena Karmali Ahmed and Derryl MacLean (eds.) *Cosmopolitanisms in Muslim Contexts: Perspectives from the Past*, Edinburgh: University Press, Edinburgh, pp. 92–104.

Hanley, Will (2017) *Identifying with Nationality: Europeans, Ottomans, and Egyptians in Alexandria*, New York: Columbia University Press.

Hudson, Manley O. (1927) 'International Problems at Shanghai,' *Foreign Affairs*, 6(1), pp. 75–88.

Hunter, F. Robert (1998) 'Egypt under the Successors of Muhammad 'Ali,' in Martin W. Daly (ed.) *The Cambridge History of Egypt, Volume 2, Modern Egypt, from 1517 to the End of the Twentieth Century*, Cambridge; New York, pp. 180–197.

Ilbert, Robert (1996) *Alexandrie 1830–1930: Histoire d'une communauté citadine*, 2 volumes, Cairo: Institut d'Archéologie Orientale.

Inglis, David (2012) 'Alternative Histories of Cosmopolitanism: Reconfiguring Classical Legacies,' in Gerard Delanty (ed.) *Routledge Handbook of Cosmopolitanism Studies*, Abingdon, Oxon; New York: Routledge, pp. 11–24.

Jackson, Isabella (2012) 'The Raj on Nanjing Road: Sikh Policemen in Treaty-Port Shanghai,' *Modern Asian Studies*, 46(6), pp. 1672–1704.

Jackson, Isabella (2016) 'Who Ran the Treaty Ports? A Study of the Shanghai Municipal Council,' in Robert Bickers and Isabella Jackson (eds.) *Treaty Ports in Modern China*, London: Routledge, pp. 43–60.

Jackson, Isabella (2018) *Shaping Modern Shanghai: Colonialism in China's Global City*, Cambridge: Cambridge University Press.

Johnstone, William C. (1937) 'The Status of Foreign Concessions and Settlements in the Treaty Ports of China,' *The American Political Science Review*, 31(5), pp. 942–948.

Karl, Rebecca (2002) *Staging the World: Chinese Nationalism at the Turn of the Twentieth Century*, Durham, NC: Duke University Press.

Keller, Wolfgang, Javier Andres Santiago, and Carol H. Shiue (2016) *Foreigners Knocking on the Door: Trade in China during the Treaty Port Era*, Working Paper 21886, January, Cambridge, MA: National Bureau of Economic Research, http://www.nber.org/papers/w21886

Lazarev, Anouchka (1992) 'Italiens, italianité et fascisme,' in Robert Ilbert and Ilios Yannakakis (eds.) *Alexandrie, 1860–1960. Un modèle éphémère de convivialité : Communautés et identité cosmopolite*, Paris: Autrement, pp. 92–109.

Lee, Leo Ou-fan (1999) *Shanghai Modern: The Flowering of a New Urban Culture in China, 1930–1945*, Cambridge, MA: Harvard University Press.

Lewis, Su Lin (2016) *Cities in Motion: Urban Life and Cosmopolitanism in Southeast Asia, 1920–1940*, Cambridge: Cambridge University Press.

Maghraoui, Abdeslam M. (2006) *Liberalism without Democracy: Nationhood and Citizenship in Egypt, 1922–1936*, Durham and London: Duke University Press.

Malcomson, Scott L. (1998) 'The Varieties of Cosmopolitan Experience,' in Pheng Cheah and Bruce Robbins (eds.) *Cosmopolitcs: Thinking and Feeling beyond the Nation*, Minneapolis: University of Minnesota Press, pp. 233–245.

Mansel, Philip (2004) 'Alexandria Leaving,' Review of Alexandria: City of Memory by Michael Haag, *The Guardian*, November 13, https://www.theguardian.com/books/2004/nov/13/featuresreviews.guardianreview10

Mansel, Philip (2011) *Levant: Splendour and Catastrophe on the Mediterranean*, New Heaven, CT and London: Yale University Press.

Marinelli, Maurizio (2009) 'Making Concessions in Tianjin: Heterotopia and Italian Colonialism in Mainland China,' *Urban History*, 36(3), pp. 399–425.

Marsden, Magnus, and Vera Skvirskaja (2018) 'Merchant Identities, Trading Nodes, and Globalization: Introduction to the Special Issue,' *History and Anthropology*, 29(S1), pp. S1–S13.

Mignolo, Walter D. (2012) 'De-Colonial Cosmopolitanism and Dialogues among Civilizations,' in Gerard Delanty (ed.) *Routledge Handbook of Cosmopolitanism Studies*, Abingdon, Oxon; New York: Routledge, pp. 85–100.

Minkin, Shane Elizabeth (2009) *In Life as in Death: The Port, Foreign Charities, Hospitals and Cemeteries in Alexandria, Egypt, 1865–1914*, Ph.D. thesis, New York University.

Nield, Robert (2015) *China's Foreign Places: The Foreign Presence in China in the Treaty Port Era, 1840–1943*, Hong Kong: Hong Kong University Press.

Nuzzo, Luigi (2018) 'The Birth of an Imperial Location: Comparative Perspectives on Western Colonialism in China,' *Leiden Journal of International Law*, 31(3), pp. 569–596.

Oppenheim, Jean-Marc R. (1996) 'Levantine,' in Reeva Simon, Richard W. Bulliet, and Philip Mattar (eds.) *Encyclopedia of the Modern Middle East*, Volume 3, New York: Macmillan, pp. 1098–1100.

Osterhammel, Jürgen (1986) 'Semi-Colonialism and Informal Empire in Twentieth-Century China: Towards a Framework of Analysis,' in Wolfgang J. Mommsen and Jürgen Osterhammel (eds.) *Imperialism and After: Continuities and Discontinuities*, London: Allen & Unwin, pp. 290–314.

Ostle, Robin (2002) 'Alexandria: A Mediterranean Cosmopolitan Center of Cultural Production,' in Leila Tarazi Fawaz and C. A. Bayly (eds.) with the Collaboration of Robert Ilbert, *Modernity and Culture from Mediterranean to Indian Ocean 1890–1920*, New York: Columbia University Press, pp. 314–329.

Polyzoides, Apostolos J. (2014) *Alexandria: City of Gifts and Sorrows: From Hellenistic Civilization to Multiethnic Metropolis,* Eastbourne: Sussex Academic Press.

Quigley, Harold S. (1928) 'Foreign Concessions in Chinese Hands,' *Foreign Affairs*, 7(1), pp. 150–155.

Rai, Rajesh, and Peter Reeves (2009) 'Introduction,' in Rajesh Rai and Peter Reeves (eds.) *The South Asian Diaspora: Transnational Networks and Changing Identities*, Abingdon, Oxon: Routledge, pp. 1–12.

Re, Lucia (2003) 'Alexandria Revisited: Colonialism and the Egyptian Works of Enrico Pea and Giuseppe Ungaretti,' in Patrizia Palumbo (ed.) *A Place in the Sun: Africa in Italian Culture from Post-Unification to the Present*, Berkeley and Los Angeles: University of California Press, pp. 163–196.

Reid, Donald Malcolm (1998) 'The 'Urabi Revolution and the British Conquest, 1879–1882,' in Martin W. Daly (ed.) *The Cambridge History of Egypt, Volume 2, Modern Egypt, from 1517 to the End of the Twentieth Century*, Cambridge; New York, pp. 217–238.

Reimer, Michael J. (1977/2019) *Colonial Bridgehead: Government and Society in Alexandria, 1807–1882*, New York; Abingdon, Oxon: Routledge.

Reimer, Michael J. (1991) 'Ottoman-Arab Seaports in the Nineteenth Century: Social Change in Alexandria, Beirut, and Tunis,' in Resat Kasaba (ed.) *Cities in the World System*, New York: Greenwood, pp. 135–156.

Reinhardt, Anne (2018) *Navigating Semi-Colonialism: Shipping, Sovereignty, and Nation-Building in China, 1860–1937*, Cambridge, MA and London: Harvard University Asia Center, distributed by Harvard University Press.

Robbins, Bruce (1998) 'Introduction Part I: Actually Existing Cosmopolitanism,' in Pheng Cheah and Bruce Robbins (eds.) *Cosmopolitcs: Thinking and Feeling beyond the Nation*, Minneapolis: University of Minnesota Press, pp. 1–19.

Rodenbeck, John (2001–2002) 'Literary Alexandria,' *Massachusetts Review*, 42(4), pp. 524–572.

Rofel, Lisa (2012) 'Between *Tianxia* and Postsocialism: Contemporary Chinese Cosmopolitanism,' in Gerard Delanty (ed.) *Routledge Handbook of Cosmopolitanism Studies*, Abingdon, Oxon; New York: Routledge, pp. 443–451.

Rogaski, Ruth (2004) *Hygienic Modernity: Meanings of Health and Disease in Treaty-Port China*, Berkeley: University of California Press.

Rosenthal, Steven (1980/2005) 'Urban Elites and the Foundation of Municipalities in Alexandria and Istanbul,' in Elie Kedourie and Sylvia G. Haim (eds.) *Modern Egypt: Studies in Politics and Society*, London: Frank Cass, pp. 128–136.

Rovisco, Maria, and Magdalena Nowicka (eds.) (2011) *The Ashgate Research Companion to Cosmopolitanism*, Farnham, Surrey, England; Burlington, VT: Ashgate.

Schmitt, Oliver Jens (2007) *Les Levantins: cadres de vie et identités d'un groupe ethno-confessionnel de l'empire ottoman au "long" 19e siècle*, Istanbul: Isis.

Scully, Eileen P. (2001) *Bargaining with the State from Afar: American Citizenship in Treaty Port China, 1844–1942*, New York: Columbia University Press.

Shih, Shu-mei (2001) *The Lure of the Modern: Writing Modernism in Semicolonial China, 1917–1937*, Berkeley; Los Angeles; London: University of California Press.

Shlala, Elizabeth H. (2009) *Mediterranean Migration, Cosmopolitanism, and the Law: A History of the Italian Community of Nineteenth-Century Alexandria, Egypt*, Ph.D. thesis, Georgetown University.

Shlala, Elizabeth H. (2018) *The Late Ottoman Empire and Egypt: Hybridity, Law and Gender*, Abingdon, Oxon; New York, NY: Routledge.

Skrbiš, Zlatko, and Ian Woodward (2013) *Cosmopolitanism: Uses of the Idea*, Los Angeles; London; New Delhi; Sigapore; Washington, DC: Sage.

Starr, Deborah A., and Sasson Somekh (eds.) (2011) *Mongrels or Marvels. The Levantine Writings of Jacqueline Shohet Kahanoff*, Stanford, CA: Stanford University Press.

Stearns, Peter N. (2010) *Globalization in World History*, Abingdon, Oxon: Routledge.

Sugarman, Martin (2007) 'Hagedud Ha-Sini: The Jewish Company of the Shanghai Volunteer Corps, 1932–42,' *Jewish Historical Studies*, 41, pp. 183–208.

Takla, Nefertiti Mary (2016) *Murder in Alexandria: The Gender, Sexual and Class Politics of Criminality in Egypt, 1914–1921*, Ph.D. thesis, University of California Los Angeles.

Taylor, Jeremy E. (2002) 'The Bund: Littoral Space of Empire in the Treaty Ports of East Asia,' *Social History*, 27(2), pp. 125–142.

Toledano, Ehud R. (1998) 'Social and Economic Change in the "Long Nineteenth Century",' in Martin W. Daly (ed.) *The Cambridge History of Egypt, Volume 2, Modern Egypt, from 1517 to the End of the Twentieth Century*, Cambridge; New York, pp. 252–284.

Tomášek, Michal (2021) 'Origins of the Legal Regulation of Foreigners in China,' *The Lawyer Quarterly*, 11(1), pp. 70–82.

Vandamme, Tobit (2018) 'The Rise of Nationalism in a Cosmopolitan Port City: The Foreign Communities of Shanghai during the First World War,' *Journal of World History*, 29(1), pp. 37–64.

Vatikiotis, Panayiotis J. (1980) *The History of Egypt: From Muhammad Ali to Sadat*, London: Weidenfeld and Nicolson.

Veeser, Cyrus (2013) 'A Forgotten Instrument of Global Capitalism? International Concessions, 1870–1930,' *The International History Review*, 35(5), pp. 1136–1155.

Vertovec, Steven, and Robin Cohen (eds.) (2002) *Conceiving Cosmopolitanism: Theory, Context and Practice*, Oxford: Oxford University Press.

Viscomi, Joseph John (2019) 'Mediterranean Futures: Historical Time and the Departure of Italians from Egypt, 1919–1937,' *The Journal of Modern History*, 91, pp. 341–379.

Wakeman, Jr., Frederic (1995) 'Licensing Leisure: The Chinese Nationalists' Attempt to Regulate Shanghai, 1927–49,' *The Journal of Asian Studies*, 54(1), pp. 19–42.

Wasserstrom, Jeffrey N. (2003) 'The Second Coming of Global Shanghai,' *World Policy Journal*, 20(2), pp. 51–60.

Wu, Weiping (2004) 'Cultural Strategies in Shanghai: Regenerating Cosmopolitanism in an Era of Globalization,' *Progress in Planning*, 61(3), pp. 159–180.

Xiaoming, Zhu (2020) 'Social Hierarchy of the Policemen in the French Concession of Shanghai, 1911–37,' *Frontiers of History in China*, 15(1), pp. 66–104.

Yang, Taoyu (2019) 'Redefining Semi-Colonialism: A Historiographical Essay on British Colonial Presence in China,' *Journal of Colonialism & Colonial History*, 20(3), pp. 1–16.

Yin, Cao (2017) 'Policing the British Empire on the Bund: The Origin of the Sikh Police Unit in Shanghai,' *Britain and the World*, 10(1), pp. 53–73.

Yue, Meng (2006) *Shanghai and the Edges of Empires*, Minneapolis, MN; London: University of Minnesota Press.

7 A Constructivist Theory of Globalizations 'from Below'

This chapter uses the findings of Chapters 3–6 to continue, complement, and complete the theoretical discussion in Chapter 2. More specifically, it sets up an International Relations Constructivist analytical framework centered on normative power and uses it to define globalizations 'from below' as a new concept in Social Sciences. Subchapter 7.1 explains why theories pertaining to fields other than International Relations are ill-equipped to place the four globalizations 'from below' under a common analytical roof. It then examines how normative power is projected by the hegemon toward other states and the 'from below' actors, and by these small actors toward the hegemon and various sectors of the local society. It also emphasizes the importance of small actors' agency. Then, it shows why international regimes cannot be employed as a central concept in the analysis of globalizations 'from below.' It also reminds the major flaws that plague the combination of World System Theory and Gramscian understanding of hegemony, which is the only International Relations approach ever used to study a globalization 'from below.' Finally, the subchapter proposes a Constructivist theoretical framework that takes into consideration both structural factors and agency, emphasizes cognitive factors, and is centered on the concept of normative power. Subchapter 7.2 uses this approach to analyze the features of globalizations 'from below' in order to establish a definition of this concept. It begins by presenting the three main enemies of these globalizations: the Neoliberal globalization 'from above'; nationalism, racism, and xenophobia in the local society; and authoritarian regimes that try to avoid the destabilization triggered by nationalist or racial tensions, which can endanger their control of the society. The sometimes surprising clashes between various globalizations 'from below' are also examined. This is followed by a detailed analysis of their shared characteristics that include common forms of manifestation, the 'from below' nature of actors, the importance of informal activities, the exploitation of interstices and niches ignored by the globalizations 'from above,' the mobility of actors, transnationalism that may evolve into cosmopolitanism, an impact in terms of social emancipation and progress, the proposition of alternative modernities, and the trend toward heterogeneity, contradictions, and tensions. Finally, the definition of globalizations 'from

DOI: 10.4324/9781003314714-7

below' is provided, which is followed by a discussion of their impact on the scholars involved in their study. Subchapter 7.3 scrutinizes the future evolution of the three current globalizations 'from below.' By giving preference to power transition theorists in their rejection of the lock-in thesis, it relies on John Mearsheimer's view that a hybrid between the Cold War and the pre-1914 bloc rivalry will develop. This will result in the emergence of two antagonistic thick bounded orders led by the United States and China, respectively. Most likely, the non-hegemonic globalization 'from below' will eliminate the Chinese-centered one in Washington-friendly countries. The opposite will happen in states associated with Beijing. Guangzhou will probably cease to represent the world's workshop, and the geography of production centers, flows, and nodes of both globalizations will change considerably. For its part, the counter-hegemonic globalization 'from below' may be weakened significantly by the Sino-American conflict.

7.1 Theoretical Considerations

Previous chapters have shown the significant differences that exist between the four globalizations 'from below' examined in this book. Accordingly, the academic fields that scrutinize them seldom overlap. The counter-hegemonic globalization 'from below' is analyzed by specialists of transnational social movements. The non-hegemonic and Chinese-centered ones have been explored by scholars from Anthropology, Sociology, Development Studies, Entrepreneurship, Diaspora Studies, and Diaspora Business Studies. Only the last two fields also cover the first wave globalization 'from below,' which interests mainly researchers in Social History, Cultural History, and History of Entrepreneurship. Accordingly, it is hardly surprising that, until now, no work has addressed the general concept of globalization 'from below.' In turn, this has contributed to the low profile of the research targeting various aspects of this topic, which is dwarfed by the interest in the Western-centered globalization 'from above' and largely unknown to the general public. Progress is possible only by placing the four globalization 'from below' within the same theoretical framework. While other approaches may be contemplated, I believe that the theory of International Relations provides the best instruments to capture the various aspects of such global phenomena. Theories of transnational social movements, Anthropology, Sociology, History, and other social sciences may be very useful in exploring some of these aspects but are ill-equipped to understand the triangular relationship discussed in Chapter 2 between an actual or emerging hegemonic international order, a globalization 'from above' that both supports and is reinforced by this order, and one or more globalizations 'from below' that either join this virtuous circle or challenge it. In particular, they will encounter serious difficulties in proposing a unifying element comparable to the normative power of the hegemon, which I identify as the cement that binds together the triangle's components. Indeed, it is not easy for small and weak actors to construct 'from below' globalizations. Empirical evidence suggests that they may succeed only when they either take advantage of or act in reaction to the hegemon's projection of normative power at the origin of the current or emerging international order and associated globalization 'from above.' In the first case, they simply rely on the 'conceptions of normal' imposed by the hegemon, which represents a tremendous advantage. In the second case, they have to project their own normative power, which leads to a normative clash with the hegemon and repression organized by its numerous agents and associates. Yet, the actions of the 'from below' actors are legitimized by the inbuilt injustices and detrimental effects of the globalization 'from above' they challenge. They also benefit from the comparative advantage of occupying interstices and niches neglected by that globalization. There, the latter's powerful actors – typically, large multinational corporations – are absent or poorly represented; the resulting vacuum can easily be filled by 'low-end' actors. Consequently, despite the hegemon's hostility, such small and weak actors often succeed in having their own, rebellious understandings of 'normal' accepted by society and – especially in the Global South – tolerated by states. Counter-intuitively, both the globalizations 'from below' supported by the hegemon and those it tries to suppress are powerful and resilient processes. They cannot emerge without a globalization 'from above,' which creates opportunities and challenges that 'from below' actors exploit; but, once created, globalizations 'from below' may significantly outlive 'from above' ones (see Subchapter 7.3).

Normative Power, Agency, and Constructivism

Given the centrality of normative power, the way it is exercised requires closer scrutiny. Within a globalization 'from below,' both the hegemon and the small actors project this type of power. The former uses it in relation to other states and the 'from below' actors; the latter, toward the hegemon and various sectors of the local society. To begin with, the hegemon shapes the understandings of 'normal' of states that are part of its international order and participate in its globalization 'from above.' These states – or, rather, their political elites – are made to consider as fully legitimate both fighting 'hostile' globalizations 'from below' and opening their doors to the actors of 'friendly' ones. For example, the United States and, under its leadership, multilateral institutions, the European Union, and Western states in general have succeeded in convincing all governments that the transnational informal economy of the non-hegemonic globalization 'from below' is immoral, illegal, and has to be suppressed. The effectiveness of actual repressive measures varies greatly, but no state overtly argues that counterfeiting, smuggling, or tax evasion are legitimate and should be encouraged. For their part, the hegemonic powers of the first wave globalization 'from below' turned extraterritoriality into something 'normal' for semi-colonial states, which consequently opened their borders and economies to the cosmopolitan immigrants. Similarly, today's China ensures that the inflow and economic activities of its entrepreneurial migrants are perceived as 'normal' and are not restricted in the Belt and Road Initiative countries by socializing the relevant local elites, which internalize Beijing's social norm. At this point, it is useful to remind that I understand hegemony in Gramscian terms. On the one hand, this is a direct consequence of my Constructivist orientation. On the other, only a Gramscian view allows hegemony to be compatible with normative power (Diez 2013: 195, 200; Hyde-Price 2006; Diez and Manners 2007: 174; see Subchapter 2.2). However, the rejection of a Realist understanding of hegemony does not prevent me from acknowledging the fact that hegemons such as the United States, first wave great powers, and China have often used a combination of pure normative power and other instruments, which are not ideational or based on normative justification. As discussed in Subchapter 2.2, 'in its ideal or purest form,' normative power should be completely alien to the use of physical force or material incentives (Manners 2009: 2). In practical terms, however, it can go alongside other forms of power. Economic incentives and military capabilities may – and frequently do – underpin it (Diez 2005: 616; Diez and Manners 2007: 176). Unlike civilian power, normative power is not incompatible with the use of military force to back up the spread of normative values (Diez and Manners 2007: 180). Accordingly, the economic conditionality of the Bretton Woods institutions has been used by the American hegemon to fight the non-hegemonic globalization 'from below' in Global South countries. Financial support from the IMF and the World Bank depends decisively on the adoption by concerned states of measures against the transnational informal economy. The first wave globalization 'from below' was greatly enhanced by the actual military intervention of the hegemonic great powers in both Egypt and China, which were turned into semi-colonial states. Even the present use by China of its relationality-based normative power has been accompanied by harsh retaliatory measures such as those adopted against Ghana in response to the galamsey crisis. These instruments complement and reinforce the hegemon's normative power projection in ways that make it highly effective. Consequently, states tend to comply, which greatly enhances the globalizations 'from below' supported by the hegemon and seriously threatens those opposing it. The very survival of this second category depends on the ability of small actors to exploit state weaknesses, which explains why it is in the Global South that the non-hegemonic globalization 'from below' is much more successful. States' compliance with the repressive use of the hegemon's normative power against 'hostile' globalizations 'from below' is due to these states' inclusion in the current international order and associated globalization 'from above,' both of which can be conceived of as sets of international regimes. There is hardly any need to explain that, for example, the IMF and the World Bank are US-led regimes, which fight the transnational informal economy by virtue of their Neoliberal principles, norms, and values. While these 'from above' international regimes ensure states' participation in the repression of 'hostile' globalizations 'from below,' specific regimes can be constructed by the hegemon to protect the actors of 'friendly' ones. As shown in Subchapter 5.4, the Chinese-centered globalization 'from below' represents an international regime comprising the Belt and Road Initiative partner states that, under Beijing's hegemony, cooperate in view of ensuring the free inflow of Chinese entrepreneurial migrants and their unrestricted economic activities. This is best understood as a Constructivist regime, which emphasizes the existence of fundamental rules that shape the cognition and interests of member states while providing legitimacy and embeddedness to the regime; China's normative set, which includes the social norm, plays exactly this role. The Constructivist dimension also emphasizes the internalization of regime-related cooperation, which impacts cognition and interests (see Hasenclever *et al.* 1997: 156); this is done through the process of Chinese socialization of the BRI political elites. However, not all globalizations of this type are associated with an international regime. The first wave globalization 'from below' was not: the hegemonic great powers intervened separately and differentially in each semi-colonial state. The general pattern was the same, but differences did exist. Foreign concessions were established in China but not in the Eastern Mediterranean Basin. Out of the hegemonic powers, the United States was a key actor in Shanghai but had a negligible influence in Alexandria. The conclusion is that international regimes can help understand the working of certain globalizations 'from below' but are not necessarily associated with this type of phenomena. This is why they cannot be employed as a central concept in the theoretical analysis of 'from below' globalizations.

In all such globalizations, the normative power of the hegemon targets states. But in the case of 'friendly' globalizations 'from below,' the same power is also projected toward their small actors. The rationale is obvious: these actors serve a purpose and have to be guided. First wave hegemonic powers and present China have used cosmopolitan migrants and Chinese entrepreneurial migrants, respectively, as their pawns expected to contribute to larger enterprises: the weakening of semi-colonial states in the first case and the construction of a new international order in the second. It was important to align the migrants' actions with the hegemon's objectives, which was done through the use of normative power. The Chinese-centered globalization 'from below' represents the best example. Its migrants' very 'decisions to migrate, destination choices, and relations with local host societies are intimately entangled with Chinese state policies and processes' (Huynh *et al.* 2010: 290; Green 2012–2014: 26). As many as 360 laws were adopted from 1978 to 2000 alone that concern various outmigration-related aspects, as well as the migrants' duty to take part in China's development (Pokam 2015: 51, 53; Röschenthaler and Socpa 2017: 180). Through overseas Chinese work and united front work, the huge bureaucracy of the overseas Chinese state has been successful in convincing the 'new' migrants to accept its deterritorialized nationalism, which has shaped their identity and modified their interests in ways beneficial to Beijing's global plans. This shows that a globalization 'from below' whose actors rely on the normative power of the hegemon – which encourages, assists, and protects them – can be stimulated, influenced, partly controlled, and instrumentalized through the projection of the same normative power. Yet, such efforts are not always successful. The hegemonic powers of the first wave also encouraged, assisted, and protected their cosmopolitan migrants, who accomplished the task of weakening semi-colonial states. They fully accepted their subordinate role as long as this was beneficial to their own interests. Yet, when they saw the opportunity of getting higher benefits by acting autonomously, the pawns began to resist the normative power of their masters. Some of them became 'legal chameleons' (Fahmy 2013) that gave 'preference to the national (...) identity most advantageous in a given situation' (Shlala 2009: 7). Others proposed and actually constructed autonomous administrative frameworks, which protected the 'from below' flows and processes that clashed with the interests of the hegemonic great powers and their globalization 'from above.' Despite the intimate relationship between the two first wave globalizations, there was considerable uneasiness in the normative interactions between them, as well as between the hegemonic powers and the 'from below' actors: consuls of great powers opposed the plan to establish the International Settlement in Shanghai as a free city; 'genuine' Europeans tried to marginalize the 'Levantines' by turning their very name into a derogatory label. As discussed in Subchapter 2.4, this important difference between the Chinese-centered and first wave globalizations 'from below' has much to do with the quality of the normative power exercised by their respective hegemons. On the one hand, present China's projection of normative power targeting its entrepreneurial migrants is based on a clear, coherent, and highly effective strategy, benefits from good leadership, and is implemented by the huge and well-structured bureaucratic apparatus of the overseas Chinese state. This is complemented by a key material factor: the migrants' total reliance on goods, labor, and capital from China. Accordingly, nobody should be surprised by the successful diffusion of Beijing's deterritorialized nationalism among the Chinese entrepreneurial migrants, which changed their understandings of 'normal' in ways that have allowed China to shape and steer its globalization 'from below.' On the other hand, the first wave globalization 'from below' was based on the hegemony exercised collectively by an evolving group of rival Western powers. Except for Britain, they shared liberal values only during the first decade of that globalization; and were unable or unwilling to set up a formal institutional framework. Unsurprisingly, the lack of unity, coherence, and effectiveness detrimentally affected their projection of normative power. This weakness was exploited by the cosmopolitan migrants, who constructed a globalization 'from below' that the hegemonic powers did not even expect (see Subchapter 2.4). A further aspect is worth mentioning. The normative power projection of the first wave globalization 'from below' was multinational and targeted port cities already marked by a cosmopolitan foreign presence. It, therefore, promoted cosmopolitanism, which is characterized by diversity, openness, and a dangerous leaning toward free-thinking and independence: in Shanghai and Alexandria, instead of following 'orders from above,' the cosmopolitan migrants created autonomous municipalities and spoke of free republics. Heavily authoritarian present China fully understood this danger. The normative power it projects toward its entrepreneurial migrants replaces cosmopolitanism with a deterritorialized nationalism that excludes the slightest temptation of rebellious behavior: they always follow 'orders from above.' This is to say that, besides the features of the hegemon, the quality and effectiveness of the normative power it projects toward the small actors of a 'friendly' globalization 'from below' is also influenced by the values on which it is based.

While the normative power of the hegemon is used, positively or negatively, to influence the small actors of all globalizations 'from below,' these actors also project the same type of power toward two very different targets: the hegemon itself and various sectors of the local society. In the first case, an important variance exists from one globalization to another. The Chinese-centered one is the most limited in this regard. The Chinese entrepreneurial migrants are able to influence their hegemon only through the reactive state transnationalism discussed in Subchapter 5.2. As shown there, states such as China mainly act toward their diasporas proactively based on their interests; but also reactively in response to the grassroots transnationalism instigated by the diaspora (Liu and van Dongen 2016: 807). Indeed, the extension of the repertoire of Beijing's policies toward the Chinese entrepreneurial migrants has in part been due to their needs and the challenges they face. This includes diplomatic support against harassment by the local population or even the police, as well as rescue missions in response to civil war or natural disasters. 'The Chinese overseas are actors who also influence policy structures' (*Ibid.*): despite the complications, this creates for China's foreign policy, the small actors that enact its globalization 'from below' have succeeded in influencing Beijing's understandings of 'normal' with respect to their situation. The reach of this change, however, is modest. It seldom goes beyond the protection of entrepreneurial migrants from local threats. Their normative power is unable to affect more important features of the Chinese-centered globalization 'from below' because 'the Chinese state tries to shape the way the diaspora constructs grassroots transnationalism, and responds to it on its own terms' (Tudoroiu 2022: 97). More specifically, the overseas Chinese state interacts closely with migrant associations and manipulates them in order to align the message they send to Beijing with China's own discourse and interests. The migrants' projection of normative power is therefore very limited. The situation of the first wave globalization 'from below' was very different. Its undisciplined small actors acted vigorously in support of their own interests and, despite the, at times, hostile attitude of the hegemonic great powers, were able to turn their views into generally acknowledged normalcy. In 1862, the consuls rejected the cosmopolitan migrants' idea of a 'free city' in Shanghai. Two decades later, the International Settlement had reached exactly that status. Nobody could deny the effectiveness of the projection of normative power that allowed the migrants to reach such results. But even this is little in comparison to the non- and counter-hegemonic globalizations 'from below': they rely entirely on the normative power of their small actors who are permanently involved in a normative struggle with the hostile hegemon of the Western-centered globalization 'from above.' In the case of the non-hegemonic globalization, the transnational informal economy on which it is based represents a day-to-day resistance to Neoliberalism that challenges – very effectively, at least in the Global South – the understandings of 'normal' imposed by the American hegemon, its international order, and the dominant globalization 'from above.' The only limitation concerns the intentionality of the 'ant traders.' Their very economic survival depends on the success of the permanent struggle to be accepted by society and tolerated by states despite the norms imposed by the hegemon. But their ultimate goal is not to continue this struggle *ad infinitum*. What they dream of is to 'take off' and join the rival globalization 'from above.' At La Salada, everybody envies 'Prestige,' 'Scombro,' or 'Puntot 1' that, from minor brands, became key providers for retailers all over the country (Savini 2011: 32). Yet, such situations are exceptional; to the average 'ant trader,' they represent only an unattainable dream that cannot influence the daily struggle against the normative obstacles set up by the global Neoliberal establishment. In the case of the counter-hegemonic globalization 'from below,' this ambiguity is absent. The activists of the alter-globalization transnational social movements wage overtly a normative crusade against Neoliberalism that leaves no place for compromise or hopes of reconciliation. This is a projection of normative power intended to result in 'benevolent forms of world order' (Falk 1997: 19). As the present one and the associated globalization 'from above' hardly pertain to this category, it is the confrontation with the actors of the counter-hegemonic globalization 'from below' that represents the most radical normative challenge faced by the American hegemon.

The small actors of all globalizations 'from below' project normative power toward the hegemon, but also the local society. Once more, important differences exist between various globalizations that mainly concern the social sectors they target. The counter-hegemonic globalization 'from below' is the only one that tries to project its normative power toward everybody on Earth. But even its actors are fully aware of the fact that their message is completely ineffective in the case of Neoliberal elites. The other globalizations 'from below' either concentrate on specific sectors or treat them differentially. The first wave one was hardly interested in the lower strata of the Alexandrian or Shanghainese societies that, at best, were used as a source of cheap labor. They only took into consideration local elites; as shown in Subchapter 6.1, semi-colonialism itself relied on the 'voluntary or enforced cooperation' of indigenous elites, which resulted in an 'imperialist-collaborator alliance' (Scully 2001: 9) that also benefitted 'from below' foreign actors. The non-hegemonic globalization 'from below,' on the contrary, relies fundamentally on its ability to project normative power toward the unaffluent members of the local society that represent, by far, the main clientele of the transnational informal economy. The 'ant traders' can survive economically only if their activities are perceived as legitimate by this large part of Global South societies, which compels local authorities to tolerate informal, semi-legal, and illegal processes and transactions that they formally forbid. It is the Chinese-centered globalization 'from below' that provides the most interesting case study. On the one hand, it pertains to the transnational informal economy and its entrepreneurial migrants need the same type of legitimacy as the 'ant traders' of the non-hegemonic globalization. But their projection of normative power toward the local society is weaker because their relationality-based business approach and the support of the Chinese state make them able to use normative power in their interactions with local elites, which is simpler and much more effective. The galamsey episode is an extreme example showing how China's migrants limited their projection of normative power to the narrow social groups represented by political elites, bureaucrats, and tribal leaders relevant to their economic activities; the rest of the society was completely ignored and deeply resented the Chinese presence. Also in Ghana, the government's lack of reaction to the years-long protests of the Ghana Union of Traders Association against the illegal activities of Chinese petty traders shows the effectiveness of the normative power projected by the Chinese state in support of its migrants toward the Ghanaian political elites in power, which were socialized and accepted China's social norm (see Subchapter 5.3). This use of small actors' projection of normative power combined with that of the protecting hegemon may seem to represent the ideal recipe for a highly successful globalization 'from below.' Yet, this combination has the inbuilt disadvantage of making the entrepreneurial migrants vulnerable to the effects of the elites-society gap created by the Chinese overall presence in the Belt and Road Initiative partner states. This can have dramatic consequences such as the beating, robbing, and even killing of the Chinese miners at the hands of frustrated locals during the galamsey crisis. It can be concluded that small actor reliance on the normative power of a hegemon certainly brings considerable benefits, but is in no way free of major risks. A final consideration can be made with respect to the compared production of normative power of the various globalizations 'from below.' All small actors project such power. But that of the Chinese entrepreneurial migrants is very limited with respect to both their hegemon and the local society. The cosmopolitan migrants of the first wave globalization 'from below' were more effective in regard to their collective hegemon, yet similarly weak in their interactions with the locals. The non-hegemonic 'ant traders' are at the origin of a strong projection of normative power toward both the hostile hegemon and the lower strata of the local society, but they harbor petty-bourgeois dreams of joining the enemy camp. It is within the counter-hegemonic globalization 'from below' that small actors fully and radically project normative power toward both hegemon and society. The somewhat predictable conclusion is that the normative power of the small actors is proportional to their degree of independence from the hegemon. The latter's support may be profitable in material terms but, to a certain degree, infantilizes the 'from below' actors and subordinates their globalization to 'from above' interests.

This discussion of normative power cannot be dissociated from the analysis of the agency that is a key feature of the small actors of all globalizations 'from below.' At first view, the simple ability to produce and project normative power could be taken as proof of agency. In fact, such a line of reasoning is debatable. Non-autonomous actors exist that shape local understandings of 'normal' on behalf of a great power. This is the role ascribed by the Japanese state to the Japanese migrants in Shanghai's International Settlement after its military occupation. The fiction of autonomy was preserved, but the Japanese minority was compelled to redefine 'normal' in accordance with orders received from Tokyo. Their (modest) projection of normative power was in no way illustrative of small actor agency. The case of the genuine actors of the first wave globalization 'from below' was fundamentally different. Their success in constructing a *de facto* 'free city' in Shanghai or their occasional transformation in 'legal chameleons' in Alexandria remove any possible doubt related to the existence and importance of their self-interested agency. Far from being passive targets of processes beyond their control, the cosmopolitan migrants exploited extraterritoriality to their own advantage, considerably upgraded their economic, social, and political status, and constructed a globalization 'from below' that relied exclusively on their agency. The situation is more ambiguous in the case of the Chinese entrepreneurial migrants, whose globalization could have not taken off or survived without the active involvement of the leadership in Beijing. The domestic socio-economic conditions, discourse, and policy frameworks that took them to the Global South were created by China's government. It is the highly effective overseas Chinese work and united front work of the huge bureaucratic apparatus of the overseas Chinese state that, through the use of state transnationalism, have constructed the deterritorial Chinese identity of the entrepreneurial migrants, which keeps them in Beijing's orbit and compels them to respect hundreds of Chinese laws that regulate their duties. However, the undeniable influence of the Chinese state coexists with the migrants' private interests and autonomous decision-making processes that result in specific adaptation strategies. They show the same kind of individual aspirations of upward social mobility, subjective personal plans and ambitions, and even adventurous entrepreneurial decisions as the 'ant traders' of the non-hegemonic globalization 'from below.' Moreover, the 'low-end' social reality of their daily life in countries such as Ghana places them in situations of vulnerability that the government in Beijing often cannot influence. Accordingly, they have to rely on specific forms of agency – such as the systematic use of corruption in interactions with the lower echelons of public administration – that are inaccessible to the Chinese state no matter its resources and will to intervene (see Subchapter 5.3). Out of the four globalizations 'from below,' the Chinese-centered one may be characterized by the lowest levels of actor agency; yet, these levels are far from being negligible. For its part, the non-hegemonic globalization 'from below' restores to victims of Neoliberalism their 'capacity for initiative' (Peralva 2003: 192; Tarrius 2002). This globalization is, in large part, the result of the agency of 'ant traders' who use informal trade as 'a resistance to the nation-states and to the logic of capital' that 'serves the purpose of economic survival' (Yükseker 2003: 136). The Western-centered globalization 'from above' did create the structural conditions that led to the emergence of the rival, 'from below' one. But the latter's shuttle traders and street vendors are 'powerful actors who develop strategies and mobilise resources to overcome geographical, political or cultural boundaries' (Gilles 2015: 19). The Guangzhou case study shows that the African petty merchants of 'Chocolate City' 'are not voiceless and passive but proactive in questioning [hostile] views and practices, and in seeking to expand and deepen economic and broader social ties' (Liang and Le Billon 2020: 602). Facing discrimination, they 'are not just wallowing in passivity. They take matters into their own hands, and show a great amount of effort, of agency in ensuring their well-being in China.' This includes 'a substantial amount of African community agency' based on elements as diverse as 'leadership provided by community and family heads,' underground medical services, counseling provided by religious leaders, and 'verbal, music, and dance therapies provided by leading cultural icons' (Bodomo 2020: 533). Nigerian traders have even organized public protests in Guangzhou against police brutality and discriminatory treatment (Liang and Le Billon 2020: 612). Therefore, the non-hegemonic globalization 'from below' is based on the agency of individual actors, which relies decisively on their aspirations, ideas, and actions. This is also the case of the counter-hegemonic globalization 'from below,' whose actors are highly voluntaristic social activists that explicitly try to change the world based on their libertarian ideas. It goes without saying that agency is fundamental to their socio-political enterprise.

The important role played by actors' agency within all globalizations 'from above' is most relevant for the construction of the theoretical framework employed to analyze them. The very use of the non-hegemonic and counter-hegemonic labels is due to the introduction by the prominent anthropologist, Gustavo Lins Ribeiro, of the term 'non-hegemonic world-system' to designate 'the markets, flows, and trade networks that are part of globalization from below' (Ribeiro 2012a: 221). As explained in the section 'Structure, Agency, and International Relations Theories' of Subchapter 4.2, this is the only effort to place the non-hegemonic globalization 'from below' in the framework of International Relations theories. Ribeiro called this globalization non-hegemonic 'simply because it is not the dominant form of globalization seeking to mold us in its image, but rather an alternative to this, following different pattern and rules' (*Ibid.*). The resulting theoretical construct combines Immanuel Wallerstein's World System Theory with a Gramscian understanding of hegemony, which represents 'the naturalized and silent exercise of power, the naturalization by different social groups and classes of the sanctioned modes of the reproduction of social life' (*Ibid.*, 233). I will not repeat here the details of Gustavo Ribeiro and Gordon Mathews' apt criticism of Wallerstein's approach, which appropriately rejects its emphasis on states (Mathews 2011: 235; see Subchapter 4.2). But I will repeat – and extend to all globalizations 'from below' – my critique of the use of the World System Theory, as well as the reasons that make Constructivism a more appropriate theoretical framework. On the one hand, Wallerstein constructed a positivist structural theory that explains all international interactions as direct and inevitable consequences of the way the international system is structured (Wallerstein 1974; Wallerstein 1980). In his view, any political or economic international development is due to the basic fact that the core dominates and exploits the periphery. Such structural (or systemic) theories leave no place for the agency of actors; the transnational social activists, 'ant traders,' Chinese entrepreneurial migrants, and cosmopolitan migrants are all prisoners of higher forces and act as mere puppets of systemic factors they cannot challenge. Implicitly, the globalizations 'from below' have to be understood as expressions of impersonal, overwhelming factors very similar to those taken into consideration by the globalist view of the Western-centered globalization 'from above': they lead to an unstoppable process that human decisions and actions cannot influence or control. Such a view clashes with both the actual importance of agency analyzed in the previous paragraph and Gustavo Ribeiro's stated intention to 'seriously tak[e] into account one of anthropology's most powerful assets: the consideration of the agent's points-of-view' (Ribeiro 2006: 234). His work, as well as that of Mathews, clearly shows the agency of 'ant traders.' This is simply incompatible with the use of Wallerstein's theory. Constructivism, on the contrary, developed as an International Relations theory centered on the structure–agency debate. This allows it to fully take into consideration both structural factors and actors' agency. On the other hand, the heavy positivism of the World System Theory translates into a strong form of determinism. Wallerstein combined two neo-Marxist theories – Dependency Theory and Johan Galtung's Structural Imperialism – with Fernand Braudel's *long durée* approach to explain the present hierarchical core-periphery structure of the international system as the direct consequence of historical developments initiated in the early modern era, which critically included the industrialization and ensuing international supremacy of West European states. There seems to be no escape from this purely materialist chain of causality, which is uncomfortably close to Marx's iron law of history. More sophisticated forms of post-positivist neo-Marxism exist, which are inspired by the Frankfurt School and Antonio Gramsci. In particular, Robert Cox's Critical Theory adds to material (i.e., economic) factors the power of ideas and institutions. Being post-positivist, this approach denies the existence of 'objective,' inescapable laws of history: ideas can and do change the course of historical events. Importantly, Critical Theory is explicitly based on a Gramscian understanding of hegemony similar to that mentioned by Ribeiro (Cox 1981/1986). Such an understanding, however, is incompatible with the determinism of Wallerstein's view, where ideas have no place: the core dominates the periphery due to a historical process based on the early transition to capitalism that led to economic, political, and military superiority; legitimacy is, at best, a mere side effect. Gustavo Ribeiro's aforementioned combination of World System Theory and legitimacy-based, Gramscian hegemony is therefore inherently flawed (see Subchapter 4.2).

The Constructivist theoretical framework I propose acknowledges the importance of both structural factors and agency. With respect to structure, all globalizations 'from below' are consequences of or responses to a globalization 'from above.' In part, as shown in Subchapter 4.2 for the 'ant traders' of the non-hegemonic globalization 'from below,' the activities of small actors are simple rational choice reactions to the constraints and opportunities created by the 'from above' globalization. But they are not entirely due to these structural causes. Ideas of a different nature also are at work. Agency is the result of factors that include individual aspirations of upward social mobility, subjective personal plans and ambitions, adventurous entrepreneurial decisions, anti-Neoliberal ideological convictions, cosmopolitan anti-nationalist and anti-fascist ideas, and self-interested political agendas seeking the establishment of a 'free republic.' This agency can transform entire societies up to the point of creating semi-independent polities and being reflected in monumental art. All this can be understood using Constructivism, which gives a prominent role to the intersubjective dimension and acknowledges the importance of agency. As shown earlier in this chapter, the Constructivist Theory of International Regimes can be applied to the case of the Chinese-centered globalization 'from below.' This is not possible for the other three globalizations 'from below,' but all such globalizations perfectly fit the general analytical framework of Constructivism. This starts with the unit of analysis used by Constructivist scholars such as Alexander Wendt in their study of international relations. The state is replaced with the more versatile concept of state-society complex, first introduced by Robert Cox. The Canadian critical theorist argued that the separation between the spheres of activity of the state and the society has become vague and imprecise (Cox 1981/1986: 205), which imposes their merger into one concept. Wendt further noted that 'not only is the state constituted by its relationship to society, but so is society constituted by the state' (Wendt 1999/2003: 210). Despite their close connection, however, the state and the society – as well as various groups within the latter – may be simultaneously but differently involved in and affected by the external interactions of the complex.

This helps explain why states, various groups of migrants, host societies, and local elites play independent roles within globalizations 'from below.' Moreover, as it is 'centrally concerned with the role of ideas in constructing social life' (Carlsnaes *et al.* 2002: 57–58), Constructivism places considerable emphasis on cognitive factors such as norms, values, and ideas. Through international interactions, actors are involved in transformative processes that modify their interests and identity; in turn, this leads to changes in the international environment that can even result in the construction of a different 'culture of anarchy' (Wendt 1999/2003). Norms play a major role in both the transformation of individual actors and the overall evolution of the international system. Within the state–society complex, there can even be a 'bifurcation of causal dynamics in relation to different norms' (Flockhart 2006: 99), as shown by the successful Chinese socialization of the elites in power – but not of the society – in the Belt and Road Initiative partner states. While Constructivism was created before the introduction of the concept of normative power, one does not need to be a specialist of this field in order to understand that, as mentioned in Subchapter 2.2, the 'normative power argument has a distinctly social constructivist ring to it' (Diez 2005: 616). In particular, normative power has 'palpable constitutive effects' as it alters perceptions, attitudes, and identities through the internalization of norms promoted by normative powers (Kavalski 2014: 305), which is a typical Constructivist process. Consequently, I argue that globalizations 'from below' are best studied by an International Relations Constructivist approach centered on the concept of normative power, which eliminates the weaknesses of the World System Theory and is highly effective in dealing with the actorness of hegemons, states, societies, elites, anti-Neoliberal social activists, 'ant traders,' and various types of migrants. While I look forward to any effort to construct alternative analytical frameworks addressing these issues, I believe that it is only within the field of International Relations, and more specifically within the group of post-positivist theories, that the concept of globalization 'from below' can appropriately be studied.

7.2 Globalizations 'from Below' – Characteristics and Definition

Enemies and In-Group Clashes

Turning to less abstract aspects, the analyses of previous chapters suggest that the globalizations 'from below' have three key enemies: the Neoliberal globalization 'from above'; nationalism, racism, and xenophobia in the local society; and authoritarian regimes that try to avoid the destabilization triggered by nationalist or racial tensions, which can endanger their control of the society. There is little need to insist on the hostility of the Western-centered globalization 'from above.' The counter- and non-hegemonic globalizations 'from below' are its enemies *par excellence*. The Chinese-centered one adds to the reliance on the anti-Neoliberal transnational informal economy the anti-American dimension of Beijing's effort to construct a new international order. It is only the first wave globalization 'from below' that had no interaction with the Neoliberal process initiated many decades after its end. Nationalism, racism, and xenophobia manifest themselves – in a deeply negative way – in two different circumstances. On the one hand, the first wave globalization 'from below' provides the sinister examples of cosmopolitan port cities such as Salonica and Smyrna, which were actually burned by the nationalist forces that had militarily occupied them. The cosmopolitan migrants in Pera and Galata, Shanghai, and Alexandria equally experienced ethnic cleansing; the same nationalist political agenda was implemented that constructed authoritarian or totalitarian nation-states, which had no understanding and no place for cosmopolitans and their globalization. A similar, if weaker, threat came from nationalist forces that took control of the migrants' countries of origin and wanted to restore 'patriotism' among the diasporas, which involved the repudiation of cosmopolitanism and migrants' transformation into a fifth column at the service of a purely colonial project. Italy under Mussolini and Japan during the invasion of China tried to place their nationals in Alexandria and Shanghai in this uncomfortable position. On the other hand, in very many cases, the actors of globalizations 'from below' are targeted because they form middleman minorities. This obviously does not apply to the counter-hegemonic globalization 'from below' but is very visible in the case of the non-hegemonic and Chinese-centered ones. As discussed in Subchapters 4.4, 4.6, and 5.1, hostility due to different cultural, religious, or racial features, as well as legal vulnerability to expulsion, often pushes migrants toward marginal middleman roles, which are often perceived as deviant. In turn, the local society begins to identify the group with a specific type of business and sees it as an economic and moral threat. While middleman merchants may be recognized as useful, they are always perceived as alien. Further reasons for hostility come from conflicts of interests with the local clientele, businesses, and labor; the perceived solidarity of the middleman community, which is accused of being disloyal to the host country; and 'predatory clientelism.' As a result, 'middleman groups are seen as parasites'; the 'country is being "taken over" by an alien group' (Bonacich 1973: 584, 590–592; Nyíri 2011: 147–148; see Subchapter 4.4). Ironically, this concerns both the Chinese entrepreneurial migrants in African countries such as Ghana and the African middlemen in Guangzhou. In the latter case, short-term African shuttle traders still are accepted because the prosperity of the city as a node of the non-hegemonic globalization 'from below' depends on their trade. But the well-established African middlemen became targets of a well-organized offensive intended to supplant them: 'Chinese should sell to Africans in Guangzhou. Africans shouldn't sell to Africans in Guangzhou' (Mathews 2015: 142, 216–217). The Chinese example is also illustrative of the way tensions due to nationalism, racism, and xenophobia make certain authoritarian regimes act against globalizations 'from below' in order to preserve domestic stability and their control of the society. This has nothing to do with Neoliberal policies, even if the suppression of the informal economy – which, in the Chinese case, is depicted as including 'drug trafficking, Internet fraud and prostitution' (Elochukwu 2016: 1204) – is often invoked to justify repressive measures. Two factors are at work. One is objective: in order for such policies to be set up, a certain level of social tensions needs to actually develop. The other is subjective: authoritarian leaders arbitrarily decide if and when this level is reached based on their own perceptions of the social reality and paranoid overreactions to anything that may even remotely threaten their power. Preconceived ideas about the harmful effects of cosmopolitanism and the opening of the society to foreign influences further reinforce the repressive trend. To all external observers, nationalist and racial tensions in Guangzhou have never reached alarming levels that could actually destabilize the local society; but the leadership in Beijing thought otherwise and this is why, since 2008, we have been witnessing the 'fall of the "Chocolate City"' (Li et al. 2012: 62). Adams Bodomo's beautiful 'bridge' between Africa and China – 'it is not far-fetched to foresee that in 100 years' time an African-Chinese Minority Ethnic Group could be demanding self-identity and full citizenship rights in the heart of Guangzhou' (Bodomo 2010: 693) – was downgraded to ethnic enclave and then trading post (see Subchapter 4.6). Of course, when speaking of paranoid reactions, there is worse: totalitarian North Korea represents the perfect example of a country completely kept outside the circuits of all 'from below' globalizations. Some small traders do exist: before the total closing of the borders due to the Covid crisis, Chinese ones were involved in the border trade that represents one of the ways to smuggle goods affected by United Nations sanctions (Wertz 2020). But the idea of genuine shuttle traders commuting between North Korea and the not so remote markets of Yiwu or Guangzhou pertains to the realm of fiction. It is easier for globalizations 'from below' to face the enormous normative power of the hegemon and its globalization 'from above' than the harsh domestic policies of nationalist or communist dictators.

In addition to these aggressive adversaries, 'from below' globalizations have to face a number of, at times, unexpected in-group clashes. A predictable one is that between the non-hegemonic and Chinese-centered globalizations. The (partial) fall of 'Chocolate City' mentioned in the previous paragraph is mainly due to policies adopted by the leadership in Beijing. The replacement of African intermediaries with Chinese ones is a typical example of rejection of a middleman minority that involves nationalist and racial aspects. But the competition between Chinese and African intermediaries, as well as official measures targeting African settlers, are also associated with the rivalry between the two globalizations 'from below.' Both are based on informal economic processes enacted by small traders that often sell the same Chinese goods to the same Global South clientele. Accordingly, competition is inevitable; and, unlike their Lebanese or East Indian rivals, the Chinese entrepreneurial migrants benefit from the important support of their country of origin, where most of the goods are produced. As explained in Subchapter 5.4, the lack of quantitative data makes the magnitude of this process uncertain. However, the non-hegemonic globalization 'from below' is clearly shrinking under the pressure of the Chinese-centered one. A much less predictable clash is that between the non-hegemonic globalization 'from below' and the *alliance contre nature*[1] between the Neoliberal globalization 'from above' and the counter-hegemonic globalization 'from below' exemplified by Washington's Eastern Market as discussed in Subchapter 4.2. A coalition of anti-globalization critics, local vendors, organic and natural food proponents, community leaders, urban planners, and city officials (Shepherd 2012: 187) – that is, a strange mixture of counter-hegemonic 'from below' actors and Neoliberal ones – sought to restrict the activities of immigrant traders on the basis of a discourse of localism and authenticity that rejects the 'cheap' and 'foreign,' i.e., the defining features of the non-hegemonic globalization 'from below.' This puzzling situation is mainly due to the class status of many alter-globalization activists who pertain to 'an urban, highly cosmopolitan and privileged group of elites.' There is an underlying tension between these 'privileged people located at the center of the global trade system' and the 'ant traders' of the non-hegemonic globalization 'from below' who are poor and come from more marginal areas. While situations of this kind are not frequent, they show how factors such as class can negatively impact the convergence of interests and actions that one would expect to connect the counter- and non-hegemonic globalizations 'from below.' In Argentina, La Salada provides another example of a clash between these two globalizations that is even more puzzling. As discussed in Subchapter 4.8, the emancipatory dimension of the 'plebeian democracy' that developed as a consequence of the non-hegemonic globalization led to the creation of human rights associations such as La Alameda: a neighborhood organization that initiated a public campaign against the exploitation of Bolivian immigrants kept in sweatshop 'slavery.' It tried to put an end to the 'monstrous' exploitative dimension of the market's 'proletarian microeconomies,' which is no better than that of the Neoliberal globalization 'from above' (Gago 2014/2017). This struggle mirrors, in a different context, the logic of the counter-hegemonic globalization 'from below.' But – to the despair of the Bolivian 'victims,' who voluntarily accept harsh work conditions to accumulate capital for their own businesses – it ultimately led La Alameda to fight all practices 'contributing to the spread of the informal economy' (Forment 2015: S123). In other words, a libertarian movement produced by the non-hegemonic globalization 'from below' evolved into an entity closer to the counter-hegemonic one and started to act against the globalization that created it. To conclude, globalizations 'from below' have to face powerful enemies at global and state level; but they also hamper each other in ways that reveal various and often unexpected features and factors that influence their development.

Features

The globalizations 'from below' share features that include common forms of manifestation, the 'from below' nature of actors, the importance of informal activities, the exploitation of interstices and niches ignored by the globalizations 'from above,' the mobility of actors, transnationalism that may evolve into cosmopolitanism, an impact in terms of social emancipation and progress, the proposition of alternative modernities, and the trend toward heterogeneity, contradictions, and tensions. To begin with, these globalizations' forms of manifestation largely – even if not entirely – overlap. In this regard, informal economic activities are the most prominent; they are absent only in the case of the counter-hegemonic globalization 'from below.' It is by providing accessible goods to the poor masses of the Global South that 'ant traders' and, in part, Chinese entrepreneurial migrants legitimize their presence; these goods are accessible because, unlike the multinational corporations of the Western-centered globalization 'from above,' small merchants lower prices through the use of informal, semi-legal, or illegal methods. The Greek and Italian petty traders of the first wave globalization 'from below' were similarly involved in large-scale smuggling operations. In extreme situations such as that of La Salada, even the state is overtly co-opted: in the case of counterfeiting, the illegal 'economic activity is not abolished but taxed' (Dewey 2014: 13, 14, 16). Peronist governments provided state credit lines to the market's small entrepreneurs and took their representatives in visits abroad in official recognition of and support for La Salada's informal economic model (Schiavo *et al.* 2016: 401; Dewey 2014: 13; Peregil 2015). Another form of manifestation is that promoted by the activists of the counter-hegemonic globalization 'from below': political struggle. While it has included impressive mass protests such as those held in Seattle (1999), Washington (2000), Quebec City (2001), and Genoa (2001), 'the battle against neoliberalism plays out primarily in the realm of ideas'; sustainable social transformation is to be reached through ideological change (Pleyers 2019: 747). The World Social Forum mainly represents an arena where ideas on global issues are exchanged (see Subchapter 3.2). A strong similarity, therefore, exists with the 'dissident literature' (Giuliani Caponetto 2008: 133) of the first wave globalization 'from below' illustrated by Alexandrian writers such as Enrico Pea and Fausta Cialente (see Subchapter 6.2) and with proposals to establish the International Settlement in Shanghai as a 'free city' (see Subchapter 6.3). In both cases, progressive cosmopolitan migrants launched an ideological struggle against 'from above' ideas and practices. For its part, the direct protest dimension of the counter-hegemonic globalization 'from below' is mirrored within the non-hegemonic globalization by the public protests organized by Nigerian traders in Guangzhou against police brutality and discriminatory treatment (Liang and Le Billon 2020: 612; see Subchapter 4.6) and by La Alameda's public campaign against the exploitation of Bolivian immigrants in La Salada's sweatshop (see Subchapter 4.7). Finally, there is the legal struggle of the 'movement of movements' against the Neoliberal international legal regimes and, in particular, the bottom-up challenge of the intellectual property international regime, which the counter-hegemonic globalization 'from below' rejects as it perpetuates structural inequalities between the Global North and Global South. This is complemented by the 'culture of the copy' associated with the massive counterfeiting on which a large part of the non-hegemonic and Chinese-centered globalizations 'from below' rely. While the approaches are not identical, there can be no doubt about their convergence. Overall, the forms of manifestation of globalizations 'from below' enacted by social activists, 'ant traders,' Chinese entrepreneurial migrants, and cosmopolitan migrants have much more in common than theorists of transnational social movements or anthropologists may think based on the separate analysis of their respective fields.

More obvious common features of all such globalizations include the 'from below' nature of their actors, which is well captured by the 'subaltern' dimension analyzed by scholars of the first wave globalization 'from below' (Hanley 2017: 13, 175–177; see Subchapter 6.1), as well as those who explore the 'subaltern cosmopolitan' politics and legality of the counter-hegemonic globalization 'from below' (Santos 2005: 29; see Subchapter 3.1). Gustavo Ribeiro's analysis of the non-hegemonic globalization 'from below' as a *'globalización popular'* (people's globalization) (Ribeiro 2012b) is relevant for the same aspect in the case of the latter globalization, as is the actorness of petty traders and galamsey miners for the Chinese-centered one. All globalizations 'from below' are exclusively enacted by small and weak actors that range from the social activists of Seattle to the White Russian immigrants in Shanghai. This, however, does not prevent them from being powerful global phenomena able to face the huge power of globalizations 'from above.' The mainly informal nature of their activities is another general feature of the globalizations 'from below.' The flows of people, goods, and ideas, as well as the business, social, and activistic transnational networks that make them possible, have a pronounced tendency to take advantage of the lower costs, lack of constraints, and flexibility associated with informality. At the same time, they cannot completely elude the rules imposed by globalizations 'from above' and states. Hence the frequent mix of formal, informal, semi-legal, and illegal features specific to all globalizations 'from below.' The same need to adapt to the constraints imposed by globalizations 'from above' is the root cause of another feature of 'from below' ones. They infiltrate and exploit all interstices and niches ignored by the actors of globalizations 'from above.' These range from poor markets in underdeveloped countries where global supermarket chains go bankrupt but petty traders still make a profit to socio-political arenas where 'from above' actors fail to repair the damages caused by Neoliberal policies. Another important characteristic is the high mobility of the actors of the globalizations 'from below.' A relative exception is represented by the alter-globalization activists, but even they travel to attend protest movements and social forums. The World

Social Forum brought 100,000 people to Porto Alegre in 2003, 120,000 to Mumbai in 2004, and 170,000 in 2005, again to Porto Alegre. No less than 25,000 participants from 147 countries attended the People Summit against Global Warming in 2010 in Bolivia's remote Cochabamba (Pleyers 2019: 745–746, 747). There is little need for any explanation in the case of the non-hegemonic and Chinese-centered globalizations 'from below,' whose shuttle traders often commute between Guangzhou, Yiwu, Dubai, or Istanbul and various Global South locations. Shuttle trade was not frequent during the first wave globalization 'from below,' whose actors were mainly settlers. But their migratory flows to semi-colonial port cities were large and continuous, which compensates for the absence of commuting. This mobility has important socio-economic consequences that define another feature of the globalizations 'from below': their transnationalism that may evolve into cosmopolitanism. The 'movement of movements' is transnational by definition; its actors often have cosmopolitan profiles and worldviews. 'Ant traders' act based on a logic of deterritorialization: they are 'actors between worlds with the ability to be here and there at the same time.' Making use of ethnic business and social networks, they define 'circulatory territories' (Khlif and Pousset 2014: 39) and construct transnational communities (Bruneau 2010: 44). Places such as La Salada or Guangzhou's 'Chocolate City' become 'migrant territories' (Gago 2014/2017: 30) and parts of a 'migrant economy.' Moreover, due to encounters between mobile groups, 'new forms of identities then occur, founded on the capacity of multiple belonging.' Migrant societies emerge that generate 'new cosmopolitanisms' (Bruneau 2010: 45–46; Tarrius 2001; Tarrius 2002). A relative exception to this trend is represented by the Chinese entrepreneurial migrants. Their worldwide expansion is undeniably associated with transnationalism. However, through overseas Chinese work and united front work, the huge bureaucracy of the overseas Chinese state has been successful in making them discard cosmopolitan temptations and adopt instead Beijing's deterritorialized nationalism. Furthermore, following a similar logic, the repressive measures of the Chinese leadership have put an end to the development of Sino-African cosmopolitanism in Guangzhou. It can be concluded that globalizing processes influenced or controlled by China are systematically prevented from taking the cosmopolitan turn. The first wave globalization 'from below,' on the contrary, was more advanced in this regard than the present non-hegemonic one. It fully adopted cosmopolitanism as a social and cultural praxis, which led to the openness of its actors locally and globally, as well as their strong cosmopolitan solidarity (see Subchapter 6.1). One might wonder if, in time, the aforementioned 'new cosmopolitanisms' of the non-hegemonic globalization 'from below' may follow the first wave trajectory and lead to the emergence of consolidated, fully fledged cosmopolitan communities. The response is probably negative as the effects of the non-hegemonic globalization 'from below' on its actors are characterized by contradictions that prevent the development of a strong cosmopolitan solidarity.

This aspect is related to another critical feature of the globalizations 'from below': their impact on their own actors, on the one hand, and the host society, on the other, understood in terms of social emancipation and progress. To assess the case of the counter-hegemonic globalization 'from below' and its actors, it is useful to remind that the World Social Forum has been described as 'a radical experiment in participatory democracy,' which accordingly developed links with similar movements such as Occupy, the Arab Spring, and global feminism (Ritzer and Dean 2019: 498). Instead of being hampered by the extreme diversity of its actors, this globalization turned it into one of its central values. Common anti-Neoliberal interests and mutuality have led to a solidarity that 'increasingly forms the basis for the relationships among different parts of the movement' (Brecher *et al.* 2000: 16). Intense processes of frame bridging have led to the development of tolerant identities (della Porta *et al.* 2006: 235; see Subchapters 3.1 and 3.2). Diversity, solidarity, and tolerance also characterized the first wave globalization 'from below.' As illustrated by the case of Cavafy discussed in Subchapter 6.2, cosmopolitan Alexandria was 'tolerant and progressive' (Mansel 2011: 142–143). Enrico Pea turned the shack he used as a warehouse, '*La Baracca Rossa*,' into an anarchist club attended by Alexandrians that included Giuseppe Ungaretti. Fausta Cialente and Enrico Terni, her famous husband, took advantage of the fact that 'Alexandria became a space of immunity for many,' 'one of the few places where one could escape (…) political and racial persecution' (Re 2003: 173) to wage an ideological crusade against Fascism. In Shanghai, the International Settlement was imagined and, eventually, *de facto* constructed by the cosmopolitan migrants as a 'free city' strongly marked by the solidarity of its various foreign groups. The Chinese-centered globalization 'from below,' however, is rather different. The overseas Chinese state has imposed a discourse that replaces the very real ethnic, linguistic, and regional diversity of its entrepreneurial migrants with the homogenous model of the mobile, successful, pragmatic, and motherland-loving individuals who show strong group solidarity due to their unquestioned patriotism and love for China (Barabantseva 2011: 105–106; see Subchapter 5.2). The Ghanaian case study discussed in Subchapter 5.3 shows, on the contrary, a situation where China's 'new' migrants experience fierce in-group competition, important divisions, and no solidarity. Because too many entrepreneurial migrants compete within the same economic sectors, they tend to use strategies that lead to disturbances and conflicts. They often defraud each other and are obsessed with fears of 'commercial espionage'; some go as far as putting 'Chinese don't enter' signs on their shops (Dankwah and Amoah 2019: 71; Mohan *et al.* 2014: 90–91, 92–93; Lam 2015: 9–10, 12, 22, 29, 30, 36). At first view, harsh economic competition prevents the development of solidarity. However, it may be argued that in-group solidarity would have prevented the rise of tensions by eliminating cheating and establishing a mutually beneficial cooperative environment. The root cause of the present situation may well be the lack of interest in community-based social capital of the 'new' Chinese entrepreneurial migrants in Ghana due to their reliance on the normative power of the Chinese state. This suggests the existence of a direct link between the small actors' uncritical subordination to a hegemon – which, in exchange, is expected to protect them – and their inability to develop genuine bonds of solidarity and mutual tolerance. In practical terms, their absence may be compensated, in a certain measure, by the 'patriotic' discipline imposed by the overseas Chinese state through its overseas Chinese work and united front work. But the point is that the Chinese-centered globalization 'from below' itself is not conducive to the development of the positive values seen in the previous two cases. The most interesting situation, however, is that of the non-hegemonic globalization 'from below.' On the one hand, the example of La Salada shows that huge markets of this kind can lead to the development of emancipatory processes that 'provid[e] a sense of personal dignity, social justice, and a new "skill set" based on self-help productivism' (Forment 2015: S119). At La Salada, 'a series of innovative economic institutions (of savings, exchange, loans, and consumption) spread, combining survival strategies with new forms of popular entrepreneurship.' Individually and collectively, there is advancement. 'Those who migrate find the possibility of changing jobs, professions, aspirations. From there arises the strength of progress as the possibility of a transition, a change' (Gago 2014/2017: 6, 69). This has 'allowed LS [La Salada] to build itself as a separate economic, political and cultural entity' (Savini 2011: 33) where 'the "structural poor" and the recently impoverished middle class' engaged in 'noninstitutional politics, socioeconomic informality, and a-legality' and constructed nothing less than a 'plebeian democracy' (Forment 2015: S116, S122, S124). Moreover, human rights associations such as La Alameda were established that have evolved into entities closer to the counter-hegemonic globalization 'from below' as they fully share both its values and activism (see Subchapter 4.7). However, not all is beautiful and harmonious in this globalization. In Guangzhou's 'Chocolate City,' 'there exists a tremendous sense of loyalty (...) among fellow countrymen and women' (Lee 2014: 57). National, ethnic, and hometown associations have been established that 'function as social capital platforms for members' (Elochukwu 2019: 189). But this is just a reaction to the major cleavages that exist between the various groups of African traders: 'business secrets, ethnic backgrounds, and national reputation have shaped a culture with a high degree of mistrust within the community' (Niu 2017: 252). There is antipathy between Arabs and Africans, as well as Indians and Africans, respectively (Mathews 2017: 12). Among the Africans, language, ethnic, and religious clusters have developed. There is no 'Pan-Africanist camaraderie.' English speakers, especially those from Nigeria, deride French speakers. The importance of nationalism and ethnicity is illustrated by the absence of any common African association. There is even inter-church rivalry, with churches defined by their national origins. Tensions have resulted in the instigation to expel members of rival churches from China (Elochukwu 2019:

189; see Subchapter 4.6). Returning to the case of La Salada, its market is, in fact, illustrative of an 'ambivalent reality': a strange and at times shocking combination of 'new forms of popular entrepreneurship and brutal forms of exploitation.' The market's 'proletarian microeconomies' are 'sustained by conditions of extreme exploitation' that rely on 'new regimes of submission' (Gago 2014/2017: 6, 17, 33–34; see Subchapter 4.7). This leads to the conclusion that the 'baroque economies' of the non-hegemonic globalization 'from below' are in fact strange hybrids whose small actors are simultaneously exposed to contradictory processes of emancipation and submission, progress and exploitation. Among other negative consequences, this is unlikely to allow for the development of closely knit cosmopolitan communities similar to those of the first wave globalization 'from below.'

Moreover, similar ambiguity can be identified when the impact in terms of social emancipation and progress is scrutinized with respect to the other type of relationships, which connect globalizations 'from below' to the host society. The exception is the counter-hegemonic globalization 'from below': in its case, it is too early for an assessment. Transnational social activists argue that 'a better world is possible' and their agenda allows for high hopes in this regard. The problem is that actual effects on the society at large are too modest to allow for an assessment. The 'movement of movements' has contributed to the emergence of a global public sphere and global civil society, but for the time being they only remotely and slightly impact our day-to-day lives. Furthermore, it should be reminded that, historically, many promising libertarian movements have ultimately led to the establishment of repressive political regimes. There is a long list of 'failed' and 'betrayed' revolutions. To correctly assess the counter-hegemonic globalization 'from below,' practical results are needed; and these are not likely to materialize in the predictable future. For its part, the first wave globalization 'from below' was marked by the harmonious development of solidarity and mutual tolerance among its actors; but this globalization was hardly benevolent with regard to host states and societies. In fact, it was characterized by a strong exploitative dimension. The cosmopolitan migrants played well their role of pawns of the hegemonic great powers: they used extraterritoriality to considerably weaken their host countries and place them under semi-colonial domination. At the same time, they took advantage of extraterritorial fiscal and legal privileges to outcompete and bankrupt local traders and entrepreneurs. The local population was marginalized economically, socially, and even politically and was in no way concerned by cosmopolitan expressions of solidarity and tolerance; hence its frustration that eventually resulted in nationalism and the end of the first wave globalization 'from below.' The non-hegemonic globalization 'from below' could not have developed and survived without the support of the local society. The transnational informal economy on which it relies depends, by definition, on the legitimacy acquired among its clientele, i.e., the vast majority of the Global South people. Indeed, as repeatedly shown in Chapter 4, this globalization replaces the inaccessible Western-centered globalization 'from above' as 'the only globalization that many inhabitants of the extreme periphery may ever experience' (Mathews 2011: 236). Without the foreign goods brought by 'ant traders,' these people 'would be excluded from globalisation' (Zack 2015: 135). What the African trader in Guangzhou does 'is good for Africa' (Yang 2011: 115). The transnational trade enacted by the street peddler from Mexico City 'is not a problem, it is a solution. The problem was created elsewhere; we are solving it' (Mathews and Alba Vega 2012: 2). And yet, 'ant trader' legitimacy and ensuing societal acceptance have their limits. Successful migrant merchants are perceived as forming 'middleman minorities.' Conflicts of interest with the local clientele, competing businesses, and labor emerge. They are perceived as clannish and inassimilable while considering themselves superior to the locals. They are accused of being disloyal to the host country and draining it of its resources: they send money back home, do not engage in productive activities, and import necessities from their country of origin instead of contributing to local industries. 'In a word, middleman groups are seen as parasites' (Bonacich 1973: 584, 590–592; Nyíri 2011: 147). When they protect themselves from xenophobic attacks and possible legal discrimination through the patronage of local political elites, this is seen as 'predatory clientelism' that is synonymous with high-level corruption (Nyíri 2011: 147–148). The ensuing acute hostility can lead to riots, pogroms, exclusion movements, and large-scale expulsion. Overall, the relationship of the non-hegemonic globalization 'from below' with the local society is not less ambiguous than that with its own small actors discussed in the previous paragraph. Finally, the Chinese-centered globalization 'from below' adds to the same combination of acceptance and rejection the highly negative effects of the exclusionary character of the relationality adopted by both China and its entrepreneurial migrants. As discussed in Subchapter 5.4, *guanxi* 'implies both a propensity and a capacity for living *with* and *in* ambiguity' (Kavalski 2018: 95). It replaces the respect for formal rules with a predilection for non-transparent deals that often involve morally questionable practices. Chinese migrants bribe customs officers and low-level bureaucrats. China similarly offers prestige infrastructure projects to ruling politicians. Such relationality-based methods are very effective in terms of economic success, but damage good governance and frustrate large socio-economic groups. A typical elites-society gap emerges; from the point of view of host societies, the Chinese-centered globalization 'from below' 'does not represent a friendly and harmonious people-to-people cooperative process that is beneficial to all parties involved' (Tudoroiu 2022: 311; see Subchapter 5.4). To summarize, the effects of the globalizations 'from below' on the social emancipation and progress of both their actors and local societies are highly ambiguous. They range from solidarity and tolerance to outright exploitation, from 'plebeian democracies' to 'regimes of submission,' and from the struggle against the injustices of Neoliberalism to the imposition of semi-colonial domination.

It is clear that they all significantly impact social reality. But, in most cases, they do it in a very contradictory way.

While closely connected to their impact in terms of social emancipation and progress, one of the key features of the globalizations 'from below' stands out as the least discussed in the literature. Unknown to many, these globalizations propose alternative modernities. Of course, modernity itself is a disputable concept. *Britannica* understands it as 'the self-definition of a generation about its own technological innovation, governance, and socioeconomics' (Snyder 2016), a definition perhaps more appropriate – in the context of this book – than those of, say, Cassiodorus or Baudelaire. The same encyclopedia further anchors the concept in our times by emphasizing its association 'with individual subjectivity, scientific explanation and rationalization, a decline in emphasis on religious worldviews, the emergence of bureaucracy, rapid urbanization, the rise of nation-states, and accelerated financial exchange and communication' (*Ibid.*). It is easy to note that both the first wave and the Western-centered globalizations 'from above' have directly contributed to the development of these social phenomena. The situation of the globalizations 'from below,' however, is more complicated. The first wave one was inspired by the same values of the Enlightenment and positivist belief in progress as its 'from above' counterpart. It was compatible with and supportive of all the phenomena in *Britannica*'s depiction, with one key exception: the rise of nation-states. Its migrants were cosmopolitan, and so was the modernity they tried to construct. They turned cosmopolitism into a social and cultural praxis, used it as the basis of their autonomous municipalities, and even tried to impose it in an ideological crusade fought against the rising nationalism and fascism of their countries of origin. Had they been able (and willing) to expand this model to the then semi-colonial countries, at least a part of the Global South would be living today in a cosmopolitan modernity free from endless ethnic and religious conflicts. It is not exaggerated to argue that, when nationalists and communists burned cosmopolitan cities or submitted them to ethnic cleansing, humankind lost the chance of a kinder modernity. There is worse: we may be repeating this experience. The counter-hegemonic globalization 'from below' similarly proposes a 'better world' that would most likely lead to a new, non-Neoliberal modernity. Yet, after a quarter of a century, it can show little actual progress and, after 2005, it even entered a phase of decline. The latter is not irreversible: 'even if its current expression were to fail, the movement would rise again, because it is rooted in a deep social reality: the need to control the forces of global capital' (Brecher *et al.* 2000: 17). But continued struggle is not a guarantee of success and, for the time being, it would be highly unrealistic to forecast the fall of the Neoliberal modernity at the hands of transnational social activists. The case of an alternative modernity associated with the Chinese-centered globalization 'from below' is even more obscure. China's two globalizations are intended to contribute to the construction of a new, Chinese international order; this aspect is analyzed in the next subchapter. But it is not clear if and to what degree the values shared by a new Chinese hegemon would be imposed worldwide. China's relationality may tone down the temptation to remake the world in its image. Accordingly, a different modernity may emerge; but discussing its possible features would be pure speculation. The situation of the non-hegemonic globalization 'from below' is, on the contrary, very clear. As shown in Subchapter 4.8, this globalization responds to a 'hunger for modernity' – which is understood as the mainly psychological need of poor citizens in peripheral regions to feel connected with the rest of the globalized world (Peralva 2003: 191; Tarrius 2002) – even if the connection it provides is limited to a *'globalización popular'* (people's globalization) (Ribeiro 2012b). This is 'the only globalization' – and modernity – 'that many inhabitants of the extreme periphery may ever experience' (Mathews 2011: 236). They are satisfied as long as the 'counterfeit' modernity offered by the 'ant traders' of the non-hegemonic globalization 'from below' provides an acceptable copy of the original, Western-centered globalization 'from above.' In fact, this simply adds another layer to the pre-existing Global South 'illegal city,' where 40 percent of the population lives in illegal conditions, 70 to 95 percent of all new housing is built illegally, and stealing electricity and water is a common practice (Liang 2011: 171–172). A way of life based on informality is constructed that diverges from that prescribed by the Neoliberal view of modernity (see Subchapter 4.3). Importantly, this 'from below' alternative modernity is not a proposal that may materialize in an uncertain future. It already exists, and its redefinition of 'normal' is so powerful that, at times, political actors and the state itself overtly accept it: as shown by La Salada's example, they may feel legitimate to disrespect the law and extract profits from illegal activities through methods that include their formal taxation (see Subchapter 4.7). This is to say that, in much of the Global South, the 'counterfeit' modernity of the non-hegemonic globalization 'from below' triumphantly challenges the rule – and the rules – of the 'original,' Neoliberal modernity. However, different from the modernities proposed by the first wave and counter-hegemonic globalizations 'from below,' this is hardly a harmonious phenomenon. It is characterized by the aforementioned combination of emancipation and submission, as well as progress and exploitation, specific to the non-hegemonic globalization 'from below.' Overall, the alternative modernities reviewed in this paragraph may significantly diverge; but they show that each globalization 'from below' tends to construct its own modernity, which is likely to mirror its qualities and problems. These 'from below' modernities are always different from and often radically opposed to the established modernity 'from above.' Their advocates may propose idealistic agendas and there is the implicit expectation that they will correct that modernity's flaws. However, the example of La Salada suggests that 'from below' modernities do not necessarily bring about a 'better world' free of social injustice and exploitation.

The features of the four globalizations 'from below' scrutinized in this section lead to the conclusion that all such global processes are characterized by the key trait first identified by Richard Falk in his study of the counter-hegemonic globalization 'from below': unlike the globalizations 'from above,' which are conducive to homogeneity and unity, 'from below' ones 'tend towards heterogeneity and diversity, even tension and contradiction' (Falk 1997: 24). This difference is mainly due to the fact that all globalizations 'from above' have a hegemon that, even in the case of collective hegemony, imposes a high degree of coherence on the easy-to-control large actors represented by states, multilateral institutions, and multinational corporations. Globalizations 'from below' may not have a hegemon; and even when they do, there is enough actor agency to limit and hamper its control. In turn, this leads to the autonomous actions of perhaps millions of small actors, which necessarily leads to diversity, contradictions, and tensions. The fact that globalizations 'from below' have to infiltrate and exploit all interstices and niches ignored by the actors of globalizations 'from above' also needs to be taken into consideration. These are typically difficult economic, social, and political environments where scarce resources, competing interests, and poor or missing governance inevitably lead to antagonism and conflict. Accordingly, globalizations 'from below' are always heterogeneous and contradictory processes.

Definition

Based on the previous section's analysis of the features of globalizations 'from below,' a definition of this phenomenon can be proposed. I acknowledge the fact that it incorporates an aspect mentioned by T. Tu Huynh in her study of the gendering of the non-hegemonic globalization 'from below' in Guangzhou. Emphasizing the anti-hegemonic dimension of this globalization, the American scholar described it 'also [as] a social phenomenon, involving peoples who transgress, contest and redefine various cultural norms and boundaries' (Huynh 2016: 504). I define globalizations 'from below' as heterogeneous and often contradictory socio-economic or socio-political processes that involve large transnational flows of people, goods, and/or ideas characterized, at least in part, by informality. They are enacted by entrepreneurial or activistic individuals who either take advantage of the normative power of the hegemon of an international order and an associated globalization 'from above,' or – explicitly or implicitly – oppose it by transgressing, contesting, and trying to redefine dominant economic, legal, political, and socio-cultural norms in ways that challenge the existing international order and globalization 'from above.' In all cases, they exploit the interstices and niches unoccupied by the globalizations 'from above'; and propose nothing less than alternative versions of modernity.

The elements of this definition have been discussed earlier in this chapter and need no further comment. There is, nevertheless, a related aspect that has to be addressed. The previous section has explored the impact of the globalizations 'from below' on their own actors and the host society.

A Constructivist Theory of Globalizations 'from Below' 345

From an analytical point of view, another impact may be more important: that on the academics who scrutinize these processes. Social Sciences scholars usually do not reveal their subjective attitude toward the object of their research. Some go as far as making strange claims of objectivity. As an International Relations Constructivist, I obviously share post-positivist convictions. However, despite my skepticism toward illusions of absolute truth and objective knowledge, I find a bit surprising the large number of works dealing with globalizations 'from below' that, overtly or not, are positively biased. Their authors may even note that there is something 'fascinating' or 'beautiful' about these phenomena; the Preface of this book, which provides such an example, is in no way exceptional. The explanation is only seldom esthetical in nature. Contemporary globalizations 'from below' represent, entirely or in part, responses to the dispossessive effects of Neoliberalism. Many students of these, at times, dramatic effects end up by scrapping analytical neutrality. To give a relevant example, the 'anthropological literature typically depicts neoliberalism as a profound evil' (Mathews 2011: 241; see Subchapter 4.8). It is due to their humane and libertarian dimension that much of the literature tends to conceptualize globalizations 'from below' 'with a positive bias.' Sometimes, they bring indeed 'liberation, progress and change' (Verne 2017: 125). But flows and interconnections are always characterized by a 'power geometry.' 'Some people are more in charge of it than others; some initiate flows and movement, others don't; some are more on the receiving-end of it than others; some are effectively imprisoned by it' (Massey 1994: 149; Verne 2017: 125). Accordingly, as discussed in Subchapter 4.8, various scholars have warned against the 'celebration of mobility' associated with globalizations 'from below': caution 'should be kept because the boundary between the empowering and exploitative aspects (...) may remain very ambiguous' (Sasunkevich 2015: 5). Sometimes, the 'brutal forms of exploitation' and the establishment of 'new regimes of submission' even reveal, as reminded in the previous section, 'a certain monstrosity' specific to these globalizations (Gago 2014/2017; 2012). Perhaps to our disappointment, they are not necessarily benevolent. Globalizations 'from below' simply represent powerful phenomena that change social relations globally and locally through various projections of normative power. Effects on actors and society may be – or, rather, may be perceived as being – beneficial or detrimental due to multiple factors that ultimately rely on the interplay between structural constraints and actor agency. It is on the basis of the same interplay that the probable future evolution of the present globalizations 'from below' is scrutinized in the next subchapter.

7.3 The Future of the Globalizations 'from Below'

At least in the field of International Relations, the discussion of future developments is expected to avoid speculative long-term scenarios. This is why I will not analyze here the possibility of the emergence of new globalizations 'from below.' This can happen, and not necessarily in a remote future. To mention just one of the many possible hypotheses, the expansion of the knowledge economy – of which we are only witnessing a very early stage – may well turn some of today's 'digital nomads' into tomorrow's 'from below' actors. But this is a topic for a different book. The goal of this subchapter is much more limited: it simply tries to extrapolate the evolution of the present three globalizations 'from below' based on predictable developments. The counter-hegemonic and non-hegemonic globalizations 'from below' are direct responses to the Neoliberal features of the dominant Western-centered globalization 'from above.' In part, this is also true for the Chinese globalization 'from below': independent from Beijing's geopolitical and geoeconomic plans, China's entrepreneurial migrants take advantage of the same Global South 'hunger' for an acceptable copy of the inaccessible globalization 'from above' as the 'ant traders' they try to outcompete. Therefore, at first view, the best way to approach the future evolution of all globalizations 'from below' should be centered on their relationship with the Western-centered globalization 'from above' and the latter's trajectory. This is correct but not sufficient. The entire triangle has to be taken into consideration that consists of globalizations 'from below,' the globalization 'from above,' and the hegemonic international order on which the latter relies. At present, this order is particularly important because of the challenges brought by China's rise. If the international order dimension is ignored, changes in the Western globalization 'from above' and its Neoliberal character may still occur due to various structural factors. *The Economist*, for example, keeps pointing to post-Covid scenarios that diverge with respect to various trade, finance, infrastructure, and firm aspects. For their part, President Trump's protectionist ideas and, in a lesser measure, policies showed the power of unexpected agency associated with the populist wave (even if populism itself has globalization-related structural causes). But such changes are unlikely to affect the Neoliberal globalization 'from above' in ways that may significantly transform the globalizations 'from below.' A Chinese-triggered change in the international order, on the contrary, could have dramatic consequences. I will not repeat here the analysis of Subchapter 2.3, which I first developed – in more detail – in a different work (see Tudoroiu 2022: 314–317). I will only remind that it gives preference to power transition theorists in their rejection of the lock-in thesis: as mentioned in the literature, Beijing 'is playing a double game.' It operates both in the framework of the current international order and outside of it, 'sponsoring a new China-centric international system which will exist alongside the present system and probably slowly begin to usurp it' (Jacques 2009: 362; Layne 2018: 109). While they continue to 'follow a path of progressive engagement with the liberal international order, Beijing's leaders are also leading a formidable assault on this order' (Halper 2010: 2; Layne 2018: 109). Since about 2018, President Xi has made terms such as 'probably' and 'slowly' irrelevant. China and the United States are now on a collision course. In Washington, bipartisan agreement on the need for resolute anti-Chinese action is legitimized by the typical argument of any hegemon: the self-interested preservation of the status quo. In Beijing, the traits of President Xi's psychological profile prevent him from stepping back. We are simply waiting for the word 'containment' to be officially pronounced. When this happens, many scenarios can be envisaged but the most probable one is that proposed by John Mearsheimer (see Subchapter 2.3). A hybrid between the Cold War and the pre-1914 bloc rivalry will develop. Intense security and economic competition 'will be the central feature of international politics over the course of the twenty-first century' (Mearsheimer 2019: 44). This will result in the transformation of the present liberal international order into a thin realist one able to ensure only a minimum of global cooperation. Under this weak common roof, two antagonistic thick bounded orders will emerge led by the United States and China, respectively (*Ibid.*). Being a Neorealist and writing during President Trump's tenure, Mearsheimer argued that both these regional orders would be realist. The previous Cold War experience, however, suggests that the American one is likely to preserve its present liberal – and, more specific, Neoliberal – nature. China's reliance on relationality is similarly indicative of a non-, or not entirely, realist construct. Under such conditions, it is logical to expect the coexistence of two geographically separate globalizations 'from above,' each of them overlapping with one of the bounded orders (Tudoroiu 2022: 316–317). The present Western-centered globalization 'from above' will shrink but preserve most of its features within the American-led part of the world, as it did during the Cold War. The present Chinese-centered globalization 'from above' will come to maturity within a geographically smaller but institutionally stronger and sectorally more comprehensive Belt and Road Initiative.

This new configuration will obviously impact the present globalizations 'from below.' However, it is important to note that the factors at the origin of the non-hegemonic and Chinese-centered ones are not going to disappear. Within the Western-centered globalization 'from above,' some of the features of Neoliberalism may change and certain protectionist trends could develop. The Chinese-centered one will preserve and possibly further develop specific characteristics related to authoritarianism, the economic role of the state, the emphasis on infrastructure, and the relationality-based normative power of its hegemon. But it is certain that the socio-economic situation of the poor masses in Global South countries pertaining to the two globalizations 'from above' will not rapidly improve. They will still envy and need inaccessible goods that 'ant traders' and Chinese entrepreneurial migrants can replace with cheaper but acceptable copies. Accordingly, the non-hegemonic and Chinese-centered globalizations 'from below' will certainly not vanish. This, however, does not mean that they will not change. The Chinese one will seriously be affected. China's entrepreneurial migrants will try to continue their economic activities in 'various Global South states, but their presence there will be only as secure as the host country's preference for Beijing' (*Ibid.*, 317). On the one hand, China's unchallenged normative power and dominating position within the shrunk BRI will further enhance their status. All partner governments will find it wise, useful, and especially 'normal' to respect the Chinese social norm; the galamsey episode will not be repeated. The local political elites' increased support will allow the Chinese entrepreneurial migrants to outcompete the 'ant traders' of the non-hegemonic globalization 'from below.' Moreover, as mentioned in Subchapter 5.4, it is even possible that the government in Beijing expands the policies already used against African traders in Guangzhou's 'Chocolate City.' The pretext in that case was the fight against the damaging transnational informal economy, which of course ignored its numerous Chinese actors and beneficiaries. A similarly selective large-scale campaign could be launched internationally by setting up repressive international agencies and compelling friendly states to curb the transnational informal, semi-legal, and illegal activities of non-Chinese actors 'from below.' Such a strategy would simply replicate the structures and practices of the present Western-centered globalization 'from above'; they would only need to be fine-tuned in order to keep the Chinese entrepreneurial migrants below the radar. With or without such a campaign, the Lebanese or East Indian small merchants will not completely disappear; but the balance between the two 'from below' globalizations will resolutely change in favor of the Chinese-centered one. On the other hand, a contrary development is likely to occur within the American bounded order. Under Washington's pressure, incentives, and normative power, the political elites of its member states will sever political links with Beijing. Numerous beautifully sounding comprehensive strategic partnerships, all-weather strategic cooperative partnerships, all-round partnerships of friendship and cooperation, mutually beneficial strategic partnerships, and innovative strategic partnerships concluded by China with its present partners (Li and Ye 2019: 68) will fall into oblivion. As the Chinese socialization of political elites will be brought to an end, Beijing's social norm will become irrelevant; in these countries, official responsiveness to anti-Chinese societal protests will increase dramatically. If historical examples can provide a reference, radical populist leaders may go as far as occasionally expelling all Chinese nationals from their territory. More generally, the inflow and economic activities of the Chinese entrepreneurial migrants will decline dramatically in Washington-friendly states, and 'ant traders' of various nationalities will happily fill the vacuum. The non-hegemonic globalization 'from below' will expand while the very survival of the Chinese-centered one will be endangered.

If the non-hegemonic globalization 'from below' is scrutinized beyond this contradictory geographical evolution, its present negative relationship with the Western-centered globalization 'from above' and the American-led international order will paradoxically be complemented by a positive one. The former globalization emerged as a resistance to the latter; they are engaged in a formidable normative power clash that cannot fade out. Yet, after the predictable splitting of the present international order, they will follow the same trajectory: both will prosper within the US bounded order and decay within the Chinese one. Inside the shrunk Belt and Road Initiative, the 'ant traders' will fall victim to the normative power of the Chinese hegemon that favors their Chinese competitors. Within the American-led international order, the hegemon's normative power will target the Chinese entrepreneurial migrants and involuntarily put the 'ant traders' at an advantage. Their globalization will nevertheless experience an important transformation. In addition to severely declining in the BRI states, it will most likely lose China as its source of merchandise. As shown by the galamsey case, when the political elites of a Global South country adopt anti-Chinese policies, their shuttle traders have serious difficulties in getting Chinese visas. It is hard to believe that nationals of pro-American former BRI states will be allowed to travel freely to Guangzhou or Yiwu. At first, Dubai and other nodes of the non-hegemonic globalization 'from below' will be used to buy Chinese goods, at a higher price, from Chinese intermediaries. In time, however, it is certain that other countries with abundant cheap labor will replace Guangzhou as the world's workshop. In ten years' time, the geography of the non-hegemonic globalization 'from below' may be very different from the present one. Furthermore, as mentioned in Subchapter 4.8, given the diversity and dynamism of this globalization, new forms of 'ant trade' may emerge, as well as new types of 'proletarian microeconomies,' 'plebeian democracies,' and 'regimes of submission.' Anthropologists and sociologists are likely to be offered a stimulating renewed field of research.

Finally, the counter-hegemonic globalization 'from below' will face dramatically changed conditions that might considerably weaken it. Once more, this is not because the causes that led to the emergence of this globalization will disappear. None of the future international orders will soon turn into the 'better world' promised by the transnational social activists, thus making their efforts unneeded. It is the sudden and important shift in political priorities that will distract their audiences. This has already happened: between 1999 and 2001, the series of Seattle-type massive mobilizations seemed unstoppable. Yet, the 9/11 attacks and the ensuing anti-terrorist discourse of the Bush administration had a strong and lasting negative impact on mass participation in the Global North. Accordingly, the 'movement of movements' had to significantly change its approach (see Subchapter 3.2). The Sino-American confrontation will also create an obstacle of a different nature. After 9/11, nobody credibly accused the alter-globalization activists of being an Islamist fifth column. But during the previous Cold War, exposing the association between anti-system militants in the West and the Kremlin was a convenient way to discredit the former. This instrument will certainly be used once more. China hardly proposes a socio-economic model able to respond to the emancipatory agenda of the 'movement of movements.' At first view, there can be no connection between such diverse international actors. But, as shown in Subchapter 3.1, radical leftist regimes such as those of Presidents Hugo Chávez in Venezuela and Evo Morales in Bolivia supported and tried to use the global justice movement in their wider effort to construct a coalition directed against American imperialism and Neoliberalism that critically included China (Martell 2017: 326; Pleyers 2019: 751). In the coming conflict, similar regimes will certainly join the Chinese bounded order and continue to support anti-Neoliberal – i.e., anti-US – forces. World Social Forums and similarly minded initiatives will be enthusiastically promoted in these countries; but within the American-led order, the association with a hostile camp will not be beneficial to their perception as a disinterested emancipatory and libertarian movement. It will be interesting to see how the counter-hegemonic globalization 'from below' will adapt to these new geopolitical conditions. Furthermore, an expansion of its scope may occur. Exclusively concentrating on the fight against Neoliberalism makes sense within a dominant American-led international order closely associated with the Neoliberal globalization 'from above.' China's 'savage capitalism' may not be more humane, but only concerns one state. However, the situation is different when this state becomes the hegemon of an important part of the international system, where it imposes its own bounded order and globalization 'from above.' Refusing to acknowledge, criticize, and fight the dispossessive effects of Chinese capitalism while crusading against the American one is ethically untenable. This issue is likely to generate considerable debate and dispute within the alter-globalization movement. In the past, serious conflicts developed between and within anti-system groups in the West due to diverging attitudes toward the heavily repressive regime of the Soviet Union. Some presented it as an ally against Western capitalism and even a model to follow; others rejected it as a brutal form of totalitarianism. China may well become the source of similar tensions and splits within the global justice movement. Overall, the Sino-American confrontation will bring serious challenges that may significantly weaken the counter-hegemonic globalization 'from below.'

Yet, despite the considerable problems created by such a major reordering of the international system, none of the 'from below' globalizations will come to an end. The example of the first wave globalization 'from below' shows that these are resilient social phenomena. To emerge and develop, they depend on structural conditions that include a hegemonic international order and a globalization 'from above.' But the agency of their small actors – which are much more flexible and can adapt easier to changed conditions than the large 'from above' ones – is equally important: it may even allow globalizations 'from below' to outlive the associated 'from above' one. If the normative power dimension is taken into consideration, such a situation is reminiscent of Keohane's *After Hegemony*. As discussed in Subchapter 7.1, small actors begin their globalized journey only when there is a hegemonic projection of normative power, which they exploit or fight. However, they project their own normative power toward the host society. This projection may vary in intensity but always contributes to the perception of the globalizations 'from below' as 'normal' among the society. Such perceptions tend to persist even if the hegemon fades away. To eliminate them, conditions would need to change fundamentally. Humane economic relations should be established and the Global South should escape the trap of underdevelopment. With or without a Chinese-led international order, nobody can realistically expect such developments in the predictable future. In their absence, there will always be room for 'ant traders' and social activists. The geography, features, and intensity of globalizations 'from below' may change; but they will most likely adapt and survive.

To conclude, this book argues that the Social Sciences concept of globalizations 'from below' it proposes is most relevant to the way we understand the international system, its actors, and their interactions. Small and weak actors have reshaped international trade flows and constructed alternative modernities. They fight the hegemon and project their own normative power. Still, the huge majority of social scientists have hardly heard of their globalizations. The time has come for the study of these massive and impactful 'from below' processes to take a qualitative leap that will emancipate it from the counterproductive parochialism of recent decades and put an end to its almost confidential nature. These globalizations are 'from below,' but they deserve more than our 'low-end' attention. While proposing an International Relations approach, this book opens a new field of interdisciplinary research that has the potential to eliminate fragmentation and disconnectedness in the analysis of huge social phenomena that are important for the Global North and critical for the Global South. In terms of social emancipation and progress, the impact of the globalizations 'from below' is rather ambiguous. But a change of scholarly 'conceptions of normal' conducive to their better understanding will certainly contribute to the advancement of Social Sciences.

Note

1 Unholy alliance (French).

References

Barabantseva, Elena (2011) *Overseas Chinese, Ethnic Minorities and Nationalism. De-Centering China*, London and New York: Routledge.
Bodomo, Adams (2010) 'The African Trading Community in Guangzhou: An Emerging Bridge for Africa-China Relations,' *The China Quarterly*, 203, pp. 693–707.
Bodomo, Adams (2020) 'Historical and Contemporary Perspectives on Inequalities and Well-Being of Africans in China,' *Asian Ethnicity*, 21(4), pp. 526–541.
Bonacich, Edna (1973) 'Theory of Middleman Minorities,' *American Sociological Review*, 38(5), pp. 583-594.
Brecher, Jeremy, Tim Costello, and Brendan Smith (2000) *Globalization from Below: The Power of Solidarity*, Cambridge, MA: South End Press.

Bruneau, Michel (2010) 'Diasporas, Transnational Spaces and Communities,' in Rainer Bauböck and Thomas Faist (eds.) *Diaspora and Transnationalism: Concepts, Theories and Methods*, Amsterdam: Amsterdam University Press, pp. 35–49.

Carlsnaes, Walter, Thomas Risse, and Beth A. Simmons (eds.) (2002) *Handbook of International Relations*, Second Edition, London: SAGE Publications.

Cox, Robert (1981/1986) 'Social Forces, States and World Order,' in Robert Keohane (ed.) *Neorealism and Its Critics*, New York: Columbia University Press, pp. 204–254.

Dankwah, Kwaku Opoku, and Padmore Adusei Amoah (2019) 'Gauging the Dispositions between Indigenes, Chinese and Other Immigrant Traders in Ghana: Towards a More Inclusive Society,' *Asian Ethnicity*, 20(1), pp. 67–84.

della Porta, Donatella, Massimiliano Andretta, Lorenzo Mosca, and Herbert Reiter (2006) *Globalization from Below. Transnational Activists and Protest Networks*, Minneapolis; London: University of Minnesota Press.

Dewey, Matías (2014) 'Taxing the Shadow: The Political Economy of Sweatshops in La Salada, Argentina,' *MPIfG Discussion Paper*, No. 14/18, Max Planck Institute for the Study of Societies, Cologne, https://www.econstor.eu/handle/10419/104712

Diez, Thomas (2005) 'Constructing the Self and Changing Others: Reconsidering "Normative Power Europe",' *Millennium: Journal of International Studies*, 33(3), pp. 613–636.

Diez, Thomas (2013) 'Normative Power as Hegemony,' *Cooperation and Conflict*, 48(2), pp. 194–210.

Diez, Thomas and Ian Manners (2007) 'Reflecting on Normative Power Europe,' in Felix Berenskoetter and Michael J. Williams (eds.) *Power in World Politics*, New York: Routledge, pp. 173–188.

Elochukwu, Anas (2016) 'Guangzhou's African Migrants: Implications for China's Social Stability and China–Africa Relations,' *Contemporary Chinese Political Economy and Strategic Relations*, 2(3), pp. 1195–1213.

Elochukwu, Anas (2019) 'A Survey of the African Diaspora in Guangzhou,' *International Journal of China Studies*, 10(2), pp. 181–197.

Fahmy, Ziad (2013) 'Jurisdictional Borderlands: Extraterritoriality and "Legal Chameleons" in Precolonial Alexandria, 1840–1870,' *Comparative Studies in Society and History*, 55(2), pp. 305–329.

Falk, Richard (1997) 'Resisting "Globalisation-from-Above" through "Globalisation-from-Below",' *New Political Economy*, 2(1), pp. 17–24.

Flockhart, Trine (2006) '"Complex Socialization": A Framework for the Study of State Socialization,' *European Journal of International Relations*, 12(1), pp. 89–118.

Forment, Carlos A. (2015) 'Ordinary Ethics and the Emergence of Plebeian Democracy across the Global South: Buenos Aires's La Salada Market,' *Current Anthropology*, 56(S11), pp. S116–S125.

Gago, Verónica (2012) 'La Salada: ¿un caso de globalización «desde abajo»? Territorio de una nueva economía política transnacional,' *Nueva Sociedad*, Sep/Oct, 241, pp. 63–78, https://nuso.org/articulo/la-salada-un-caso-de-globalizacion-desde-abajo-territorio-de-una-nueva-economia-politica-transnacional/

Gago, Verónica (2014/2017) *Neoliberalism from Below: Popular Pragmatics and Baroque Economies*, Durham: Duke University Press, revized edition of *La razón neoliberal: economías barrocas y pragmática popular*, Buenos Aires: Tinta Limón, 2014.

Gilles, Angelo (2015) 'The Social Construction of Guangzhou as a Translocal Trading Place,' *Journal of Current Chinese Affairs*, 44(4), pp. 17–47.

Giuliani Caponetto, Rosetta (2008) *'Going Out of Stock:' Mulattoes and Levantines in Italian Literature and Cinema of the Fascist Period*, Ph.D. thesis, University of Connecticut.

Green, Cecilia A. (2012–2014) 'Outbound China and the Global South. New Entrepreneurial Immigrants in the Eastern Caribbean,' *Ideaz*, 10–12, pp. 24–44.

Halper, Stefan (2010) *The Beijing Consensus: How China's Authoritarian Model Will Dominate the Twenty-First Century*, New York: Basic Books.

Hanley, Will (2017) *Identifying with Nationality: Europeans, Ottomans, and Egyptians in Alexandria*, New York: Columbia University Press.

Hasenclever, Andreas, Peter Mayer, and Volker Rittberger (1997) *Theories of International Regimes*, Cambridge: Cambridge University Press.

Huynh, T. Tu (2016) 'A "Wild West" of Trade? African Women and Men and the Gendering of Globalisation from Below in Guangzhou,' *Identities-Global Studies in Culture and Power*, 23(5), pp. 501–518.

Huynh, Tu T., Yoon Jung Park, and Anna Ying Chen (2010) 'Faces of China: New Chinese Migrants in South Africa, 1980s to Present,' *African and Asian Studies*, 9(3), pp. 286–306.

Hyde-Price, Adrian (2006) '"Normative" Power Europe: A Realist Critique,' *Journal of European Public Policy*, 13(2), pp. 217–234.

Jacques, Martin (2009) *When China Rules the World: The Rise of the Middle Kingdom and the End of the Western World*, London: Allen Lane.

Kavalski, Emilian (2014) 'The Shadows of Normative Power in Asia: Framing the International Agency of China, India, and Japan,' *Pacific Focus*, 29(3), pp. 303–328.

Kavalski, Emilian (2018) 'Chinese Concepts and Relational International Politics,' *All Azimuth*, 7(1), pp. 87–102, 155–156.

Khlif, Wafa, and Joanna Pousset (2014) 'It Takes (More than) Two to Tango: Informal Tango Market Dynamics in Barcelona,' *Society and Business Review*, 9(1), pp. 36–50.

Lam, Katy N. (2015) 'Chinese Adaptations: African Agency, Fragmented Community and Social Capital Creation in Ghana,' *Journal of Current Chinese Affairs. China Aktuell*, 44(1), pp. 9–41.

Layne, Christopher (2018) 'The US-Chinese Power Shift and the End of the Pax Americana,' *International Affairs*, 94(1), pp. 89–111.

Lee, Margaret C. (2014) *Africa's World Trade: Informal Economies and Globalization from Below*, London: Zed Books, in association with Uppsala, Sweden: Nordic Africa Institute.

Li, Quan, and Min Ye (2019) 'China's Emerging Partnership Network: What, Who, Where, When and Why,' *International Trade, Politics and Development*, 3(2), pp. 66–81.

Li, Zhigang, Michal Lyons, and Alison Brown (2012) 'China's "Chocolate City": An Ethnic Enclave in a Changing Landscape,' *African Diaspora*, 5(1), pp. 51–72.

Liang, Kelly, and Philippe Le Billon (2020) 'African Migrants in China: Space, Race and Embodied Encounters in Guangzhou, China,' *Social & Cultural Geography*, 21(5), pp. 602–628.

Liang, Lawrence (2011) 'Beyond Representation: The Figure of the Pirate,' in Mario Biagioli, Peter Jaszi, and Martha Woodmansee (eds.) *Making and Unmaking Intellectual Property: Creative Production in Legal and Cultural Perspective*, Chicago: University of Chicago Press, pp. 167–180.

Liu, Hong, and Els van Dongen (2016) 'China's Diaspora Policies as a New Mode of Transnational Governance,' *Journal of Contemporary China*, 25(102), pp. 805–821.
Manners, Ian (2009) 'The Concept of Normative Power in World Politics," *DIIS BRIEF*, May, Danish Institute for International Studies, https://pure.diis.dk/ws/files/68745/B09_maj_Concept_Normative_Power_World_Politics.pdf
Mansel, Philip (2011) *Levant: Splendour and Catastrophe on the Mediterranean*, New Heaven and London: Yale University Press.
Martell, Luke (2017) *The Sociology of Globalization*, Second Edition, Cambridge, UK; Malden, MA: Polity Press, epub edition.
Massey, Doreen (1994) *Space, Place, and Gender*. Minneapolis: University of Minnesota Press.
Mathews, Gordon (2011) *Ghetto at the Center of the World: Chungking Mansions, Hong Kong*, Chicago; London: The University of Chicago Press, epub edition.
Mathews, Gordon (2015) 'African Logistics Agents and Middlemen as Cultural Brokers in Guangzhou,' *Journal of Current Chinese Affairs*, 44(4), pp. 117–144.
Mathews, Gordon, and Carlos Alba Vega (2012) 'Introduction. What Is Globalization from Below?,' in Gordon Mathews, Gustavo Lins Ribeiro, and Carlos Alba Vega (eds.) *Globalization from Below: The World's Other Economy*, London and New York: Roudledge, pp. 1–15.
Mathews, Gordon, with Linessa Dan Lin and Yang Yang (2017) *The World in Guangzhou: Africans and Other Foreigners in South China's Global Marketplace*, Chicago and London: The University of Chicago Press.
Mearsheimer, John (2019) 'Bound to Fail: The Rise and Fall of the Liberal International Order,' *International Security*, 43(4), pp. 7–50.
Mohan, Giles, Ben Lampert, May Tan-Mullins, and Daphne Chang (2014) *Chinese Migrants and Africa's Development. New Imperialists or Agents of Change?*, London: Zed Books.
Niu, Dong (2017) '"Unequal Sino-African Relations": A Perspective from Africans in Guangzhou,' in Young-Chan Kim (ed.) *China and Africa: A New Paradigm of Global Business*, Cham: Palgrave Macmillan, pp. 243–261.
Nyíri, Pál (2011) 'Chinese Entrepreneurs in Poor Countries: A Transnational "Middleman Minority" and Its Futures,' *Inter-Asia Cultural Studies*, 12(1), pp. 145–153.
Peralva, Angelina (2003) 'Alain Tarrius, La mondialisation par le bas. Les nouveaux nomades de l'économie souterraine, Paris, Balland, 2002,' Book review, *Cahiers Internationaux de Sociologie*, Nouvelle série, 114, pp. 191–193.
Peregil, Francisco (2015) 'La Salada, el gran mercado negro de Latinoamérica,' *El País*, March 14, https://elpais.com/internacional/2015/03/13/actualidad/1426276499_218087.html
Pleyers, Geoffrey (2019) 'The Global Justice Movement,' in Frank J. Lechner and John Boli (eds.) *The Globalization Reader*, Sixth Edition, Hoboken, NJ; Chichester, West Sussex: John Wiley & Sons, epub edition, pp. 745–752.
Pokam, Hilaire de Prince (2015) *Migration chinoise et développement au Cameroun*. Paris: L'Harmattan.
Re, Lucia (2003) 'Alexandria Revisited: Colonialism and the Egyptian Works of Enrico Pea and Giuseppe Ungaretti,' in Patrizia Palumbo (ed.) *A Place in the Sun: Africa in Italian Culture from Post-Unification to the Present*, Berkeley and Los Angeles: University of California Press, pp. 163–196.

Ribeiro, Gustavo Lins (2006) 'Economic Globalization from Below,' *Etnográfica*, X(2), pp. 233–249.

Ribeiro, Gustavo Lins (2012a) 'Conclusion: Globalization from Below and the Non-Hegemonic World-System,' in Gordon Mathews, Gustavo Lins Ribeiro, and Carlos Alba Vega (eds.) (2012) *Globalization from Below: The World's Other Economy*, London and New York: Roudledge, pp. 221–235.

Ribeiro, Gustavo Lins (2012b) 'La globalización popular y el sistema mundial no hegemónico,' *Nueva Sociedad* (Buenos Aires), No. 241, September-October, https://nuso.org/articulo/la-globalizacion-popular-y-el-sistema-mundial-no-hegemonico/

Ritzer, George, and Paul Dean (2019) *Globalization: The Essentials*, Second Edition, Hoboken, NJ; Chichester, West Sussex: John Wiley & Sons.

Röschenthaler, Ute, and Antoine Socpa (2017) 'The China Challenge: Cameroonians between Discontent and Popular Admiration,' in Young-Chan Kim (ed.) *China and Africa. A New Paradigm of Global Business*, Cham, Switzerland: Palgrave Macmillan, pp. 155–188.

Santos, Boaventura de Sousa (2005) 'Beyond Neoliberal Governance: The World Social Forum as Subaltern Cosmopolitan Politics and Legality,' in Boaventura de Sousa Santos and César A. Rodríguez-Garavito (eds.) *Law and Globalization from Below. Towards a Cosmopolitan Legality*, New York: Cambridge University Press, pp. 29–63.

Sasunkevich, Olga (2015) *Informal Trade, Gender and the Border Experience: From Political Borders to Social Boundaries*, Farnham, Surrey, England; Burlington, VT: Ashgate.

Savini, Romina (2011) *Enduring Informality: The Case of 'La Salada' Market and the Informal State in Argentina*, M.Sc. dissertation, London School of Economics and Political Science.

Schiavo, Ester, Paula Vera, and Camilla Dos Santos Nogueira (2016) 'La Salada: imaginarios y representaciones de la informalidad y las desigualdades territoriales en la prensa escrita,' *Question*, 1(50), pp. 387–404.

Scully, Eileen P. (2001) *Bargaining with the State from Afar: American Citizenship in Treaty Port China, 1844–1942*, New York: Columbia University Press.

Shepherd, Robert (2012) 'Localism Meets Globalization at an American Street Market,' in Gordon Mathews, Gustavo Lins Ribeiro, and Carlos Alba Vega (eds.) *Globalization from Below: The World's Other Economy*, London and New York: Roudledge, pp. 186–202.

Shlala, Elizabeth H. (2009) *Mediterranean Migration, Cosmopolitanism, and the Law: A History of the Italian Community of Nineteenth-Century Alexandria, Egypt*, Ph.D. thesis, Georgetown University.

Snyder, Sharon L. (2016) 'Modernity,' *Encyclopædia Britannica*, https://www.britannica.com/topic/modernity

Tarrius, Alain (2001) 'Au-delà des États-nations: des sociétés de migrants,' *Revue européenne des migrations internationales*, 17(2), pp. 37–61.

Tarrius, Alain (2002) *La mondialisation par le bas. Les nouveaux nomades de l'économie souterraine*, Paris: Balland.

Tudoroiu, Theodor (2022) *China's Globalization from Below: Chinese Entrepreneurial Migrants and the Belt and Road Initiative*, Abingdon, Oxon: Routledge.

Verne, Julia (2017) 'Re-Enlivening the Indian Ocean through Contemporary Trade: East African Traders Searching for New Markets in Jakarta,' *Singapore Journal of Tropical Geography*, 38(1), pp. 123–138.

Wallerstein, Immanuel (1974) *The Modern World-System, Vol. I: Capitalist Agriculture and the Origins of the European World-Economy in the Sixteenth Century*, New York; London: Academic Press.

Wallerstein, Immanuel (1980) *The Modern World-System, Vol. II: Mercantilism and the Consolidation of the European World-Economy, 1600–1750*, New York: Academic Press.

Wendt, Alexander (1999/2003) *Social Theory of International Politics*, New York: Cambridge University Press.

Wertz, Daniel (2020) 'China-North Korea Trade: Parsing the Data,' February 25, *38north*, https://www.38north.org/2020/02/dwertz022520/

Yang, Jian (2011) *The Pacific Islands in China's Grand Strategy: Small States, Big Games*, New York: Palgrave Macmillan.

Yükseker, Hatice Deniz (2003) 'The Informal Economy as a Transnational Category,' in Wilma A. Dunaway (ed.) *Emerging Issues in the 21st Century World-System*, Westport, CT: Praeger, pp. 128–140.

Zack, Tanya (2015) '"Jeppe" - Where Low-End Globalisation, Ethnic Entrepreneurialism and the Arrival City Meet,' *Urban Forum*, 26(2), pp. 131–150.

Index

Academy of Chinese Culture 211
Accra 216–22, 229, 230
advocacy networks 55, 57, 59
Africa 3, 4, 17, 23, 24, 31, 33, 41, 42, 44, 47, 94, 100, 107, 109, 111, 113, 116, 123, 127, 130, 134, 136, 138, 139–58, 172, 175, 177, 178, 187, 190, 192, 197, 215–31, 235, 236, 249, 289, 328, 332, 333, 337, 339, 341, 348
African-Chinese minority ethnic group 155, 333
Alexandria municipality 245, 277, 307
Alexandria Quartet 262, 268
Algerian 5, 245, 264, 282, 283, 288, 304, 308
alien 107, 137, 158, 306, 332
All-China Federation of Returned Overseas Chinese 198, 204, 206
alter-globalization 76, 77, 78, 81, 95, 125, 126, 176, 177, 325, 334, 336, 349, 260
alternative law 99
Amur River 115, 187, 189, 196
anthropology 3, 8, 28, 55, 67, 117, 120, 134, 180, 182, 184, 185, 313, 314, 319, 352
anti-globalization 76, 78, 79, 84, 96, 334
antipiracy 101
Argentina 44, 109, 130, 159–62, 165, 170, 173, 174, 179–81, 184, 185, 334, 352, 355
Armenian 41, 266, 276, 280
Assyro-Chaldeans 134
ATTAC (Association for a Tobin Tax to Aid Citizens) 78, 80, 92
Australia 17, 44, 45, 100, 104, 105, 138, 191, 208, 240, 241
Austrian-Hungarians 281, 302

Bagrationovsk 114
Bangkok 90, 106, 130, 140, 142, 143, 153
banks 32, 33, 38, 86, 147, 152, 168, 193, 195, 221, 222, 236, 267, 274, 276, 278, 283, 300
Baracca Rossa 284, 338
Barbados 111
Battle of Seattle 2, 71, 80, 89–92, 107, 335, 336
bazaar 115, 130, 136, 159
Beirut 247, 266, 311
Belgorod 114, 115
Benaki 286
Berdsk 115
bias 15, 27, 40, 107, 172, 345
big fish in a small pond strategy 193, 221, 246, 308
biopiracy 101, 102
Blagoveshchensk 115, 189
Bolivian 80, 159, 161, 163, 166, 169, 170, 176, 177, 311, 334, 335
Bové, José 78
brand 123, 127, 128, 131, 164, 166–68, 292
Braudel, Fernand 40, 42, 43
Brazil 17, 26, 79–81, 89, 91, 92, 94, 129, 130
Brazilian rat 166
Brecher, Jeremy 72, 86, 87, 89, 95, 97
bribe 108, 110, 225, 227, 235, 341
BRICS 23, 24, 32
bridge 107, 155–58, 333
British Supreme Court for China 257, 296
Buenos Aires 158, 160, 161, 163–66, 174, 281, 311
Bund (in Shanghai) 267, 300, 301

Caisse de la Dette Publique 271, 272, 289
calculator communication 150
Cameroon 191, 213

Index

Canada 17, 45, 138, 191
capacity for initiative 117, 120, 172, 177, 328
Capitulations 254–56, 272–74
Caribbean 24, 27, 35, 111, 138, 353
Cavafy, Constantine 286, 338
chain migration 135, 190, 191, 194
chelnoki (shuttle traders) 110
Cherkasova, Veronika 114
China Development Bank 32, 217, 218
China Zhigong Party 205, 206
Chinese socialization 33, 39, 187, 216, 217, 224, 228, 230, 232–36, 322, 331, 348
Chinese state-owned enterprises 37, 38, 207, 212, 220
Chineseness 208, 211
Chocolate City 146, 149, 152, 175, 236, 328, 333, 337, 339, 348
Cialente, Fausta 245, 285, 286, 311, 335, 338
circuits 162, 166, 247, 333
Ciudad del Este 130
clientelistic strategy 192, 234
Cold War 13, 14, 26, 55, 83, 111, 319, 347, 349
comercio hormiga (ant trade) 110
Commissione dell'Ornato 277
Commonwealth of Independent States 106, 110, 112–16, 141
communism 55, 110–12, 115, 305
Compagnie Française des Volontaires 295
concessions 234, 246, 247, 250, 252, 254–56, 267, 288–92, 295, 298, 304–6, 322
Confucian 27, 38
Confucius Institutes 207, 209, 211, 216
connectivity 44, 133, 194
Constantinople 266, 271, 279, 280, 286, 287, 311
Constructivist 4, 7, 9, 15, 16, 57, 120, 188, 232, 233, 318, 322, 330, 331, 345
Consular Era 277
consuls 204, 254, 255, 266, 275, 278, 293, 295, 298, 306, 308, 309, 323, 325
corruption 36, 112, 121, 123, 125, 128, 137, 140, 162, 170, 223, 227, 228, 328, 341
counterfeit modernity 4, 107, 132, 171, 172, 174, 176, 178, 235, 343
counterfeiting 106, 116, 127–31, 139, 159, 162, 163, 172, 320, 335, 336
Cox, Robert 13, 15, 59, 119, 330

Creative Commons 101
criminal activities 108, 122
cross-border trade 109, 110, 148, 189
Cultural History 5, 8, 262, 319

debt-trap 28
Deira 141
Deng 23, 188, 194, 195, 198–200
desalarization 169
deterritorial Chinese identity 4, 202, 232, 327
de-territorialised ideology of nationalism 207
Development Studies 3, 8, 108, 117, 319
diaspora 133–36, 138, 157, 194, 195, 197, 198, 200–6, 208, 210–12, 214, 215, 233, 308, 324
Diaspora Business Studies 3, 5, 8, 117, 262, 319
Diaspora Studies 3, 5, 8, 117, 262, 319
diffuse reciprocity 28
dispossessive effects 22, 107, 123, 160, 171, 235, 345, 350
dissident literature 245, 285, 319, 335
domination 15, 27, 38, 50, 72, 75, 245, 249–53, 256, 262, 275, 279, 288, 298, 303, 304, 307, 340, 341
Dordoi 113–15, 130, 159
Dubai 106, 114, 121, 129, 140, 141, 143, 149–51, 153, 337, 349
Duchêne, François 16
Durrell, Lawrence 262, 268

East Asia 25
East Indian 134, 188, 195, 232, 333, 348
Eastern Market (in Washington) 125, 176, 177, 334
Eastleigh (in Kenya) 140, 142
economics of shortage 112
El Paso-Ciudad Juarez 110
emancipatory 4, 107, 167–69, 172, 174, 177, 270, 334, 339, 349, 350
enclave 107, 155–58, 333
entrepreneurship 3, 5, 8, 117, 118, 120, 138, 168, 169, 171, 172, 188, 262, 319, 339, 340
Epistemic communities 55, 57, 59
ethic 93, 101, 127
ethnic businesses 133
ethnic Chinese networks 187, 193
European Union 16–19, 26, 27, 29, 34, 37, 110, 114, 127, 129, 130, 135, 142, 166, 167, 320

exploitation 5, 28, 36, 75, 161, 164, 169, 172, 176, 249, 256, 272, 289, 318, 334, 335, 340, 341, 343, 345
extraterritoriality 5, 245–47, 249, 254–57, 268, 270, 275, 276, 281, 285, 288–90, 292, 296, 299, 304, 307–9, 320, 327, 340

fair use 100
Falk, Richard 22, 82, 84, 86, 87, 89, 95, 97, 344
family 28, 54, 58, 107, 113, 135–38, 148, 150, 161, 162, 169, 178, 191, 194, 195, 214, 256, 271, 275, 280, 283, 286, 328
filesharing 100
Five Principles 29, 53
flexibility 2, 6, 102, 133, 139, 194, 202, 261, 336
fluidity 5, 256, 258, 260, 262, 263, 265, 275
France 5, 41, 42, 45, 47, 110, 191, 245, 254, 256, 271, 272, 278, 279, 288, 290, 291, 298, 299, 305
Franco-German axis 23, 29, 37
free city 5, 306, 309–11, 323, 325, 327, 335, 338
French Concession (in Shanghai) 267–69, 289–93, 295–305
French language 47, 279
Fujian 189, 194, 199

galamsey 6, 187, 219, 220, 222, 225–27, 230–33, 237, 238, 321, 326, 336, 348, 349
Galata 247, 263, 266, 311, 332
Galtung, Johan 251
generic drugs 101
genetic use restriction technologies (GURTs) 101, 103
Geneva 49, 90
Ghana Union of Traders Association (GUTA) 221, 222, 230, 326
global capital 22, 73, 74, 78, 83, 103, 342
global civil society 77, 84, 93, 340
global justice movement 2, 58, 74, 76, 77, 81, 89–92, 97, 98, 102, 350
Global North 21, 77, 80, 85, 89, 90, 91, 98, 101, 109, 118, 122, 123, 125, 126, 127, 130, 176, 336, 349, 351
globalización popular (people's globalization) 3, 6, 117, 131, 172, 336, 343

governance 17, 23, 25, 28, 30, 38, 56, 74, 77, 78, 84, 85, 128, 135, 187, 192, 193, 204, 213, 228, 238, 249, 250, 252, 259, 278, 288, 290, 295, 296, 298, 305, 307, 309, 341, 342, 344
Gramsci, Antonio 13, 59, 119, 330
Gramscian 15, 19, 20, 118, 119, 318, 321, 329, 330
Grand Bazaar (in Istanbul) 130
Greek 5, 156, 245, 258, 266, 279, 280, 283, 285, 286, 288, 299, 308–10, 335
Greeks 134, 136, 255, 273, 274, 276–78, 281, 283, 285, 286, 310
Green, Cecilia 203, 207
Greenpeace 78
Guangdong 139, 143, 150, 152, 199, 221, 223
guanxi 27–29, 33, 194, 238, 341

Haag, Michael 249
Hacerme feriante (documentary) 158, 167, 170
hegemony 4, 13–15, 19, 20, 23, 46–48, 50, 52, 75, 97, 117–19, 188, 232, 233, 318, 321–23, 329, 330, 344, 350
Heihe 115, 189
higglers (in Jamaica) 111
History of Entrepreneurship 5, 8, 262, 319
huaqiao 195, 197, 214
huaren 195, 214
Hungary 112, 189, 191, 192
hunger for modernity 172, 343
hybridisation 5, 136, 311
hypercolony 291

Igbo 148, 151, 152
Ikenberry, G. John 26, 34
illegal 3, 4, 6, 21, 60, 101, 107–9, 112, 116, 122, 123, 131, 144, 151, 152, 157–59, 161–66, 168, 169, 175, 190, 191, 196, 210, 219, 222, 225, 227–31, 238, 255, 320, 326, 335, 336, 343, 348
illegal city 131, 343
illegal workshops 158, 162, 166
indebtedness engineering 28
Indo-Pacific 31, 37
informal economy 3, 106–12, 116, 120–22, 139, 151, 152, 157, 158, 160, 162–64, 166–68, 170–74, 177, 188, 190, 193, 320, 321, 325, 326, 332–34, 340, 348
informal notaries 3, 106, 136, 144

360 Index

informal state 163, 165, 175
intellectual property 2, 71, 98–102, 126–28, 131, 336
intergovernmental organization 55–58
intermediaries 39, 107, 136, 137, 140, 144–46, 151, 155, 157, 158, 212, 223, 275, 333, 349
International Monetary Fund (IMF) 12, 38, 73, 89, 90, 111, 174, 175, 218, 321
International Settlement (in Shanghai) 5, 246, 248, 250, 266–70, 290–303, 305, 306, 309, 310, 323, 325, 327, 335, 338
Istanbul 106, 116, 130, 142, 263, 337
Italian 5, 47, 245, 256, 263, 264, 276, 279, 280, 283–85, 287, 288, 294, 295, 299, 308–10, 335
Italians 45, 255, 273, 274, 276, 277, 281, 283, 284, 287, 299, 305

Jamaica 30, 213
Japan 13, 26, 100, 146, 199, 247, 288, 290, 291, 295, 298–300, 303, 332
Jews 134, 136, 255, 256, 266, 269, 273, 276, 277, 282, 283, 285, 304, 305, 308
jus sanguinis 197, 202

Kaliningrad 110, 114
Karasuu 113, 114
Keohane, Robert O. 39, 54, 56, 57
Khedive 252, 254, 271–73, 279
Kindleberger, Charles 13
Kufuor, John 216, 218
Kula exchange 28
Kyrgyzstan 113, 159

La Alameda 168, 170, 176, 177, 334, 335, 339
Latin America 4, 31, 49, 81, 85, 94, 99, 107, 111, 146, 158, 162, 170, 171, 290
Le Monde 95
Le Monde Diplomatique 78, 92
Lebanese 134, 136, 138, 188, 195, 232, 236, 278, 333, 348
legal chameleon 275
legal regime 2, 71, 98–102, 126, 127, 336
legal resistance 98, 126
Levantine 245, 256, 258, 260–67, 279, 283, 287, 310
Levantine cosmopolitanism 260–65
liberalization 36, 90, 161, 198, 199
Lilliput Strategy 87
limited change 25, 26, 100
lingua franca 147, 263, 269, 279, 300
Lithuania 110

Louis Vuitton 127
low-end globalization 141

mafia 110, 121, 162
Maghreb 94, 110, 136, 144
Makola Market 220, 227
Malaysia 129, 139, 143, 214
Malinowski, Bronislaw 28
Maltese 5, 245, 264, 265, 280–83, 287, 304, 308, 311
Manners, Ian 6, 16–19
Manzhouli 115, 189
market mysticism 72, 83
marketplace diversity 125
Mathews, Gordon 118, 119, 154
Mauss, Marcel 28
Mearsheimer, John 26, 347
Media Studies 134
Mediterranean 40, 41, 135, 136, 144, 248, 249, 255, 256, 260, 262, 264, 265, 271, 274–76, 282, 285, 287, 308, 322
Midas touch 256
middleman minorities 106, 136, 137, 157, 158, 192, 193, 332, 341
migrant economy 151, 168, 175, 337
migrant networks 57, 58, 60, 139
migrant societies 110, 135, 337
Migration Studies 56, 57, 133, 134
migratory flow 194, 199, 246, 247, 260, 265, 286, 303, 305, 337
millet system 263
Mixed Courts 254, 255, 257, 272, 273, 275
mobile societies 135
Mohammed Ali 251, 274, 283
monotributistas 164
Montreux Convention 254, 273
monument 114, 115, 189
movement of movements 2, 3, 22, 74, 79, 82, 85, 89, 94, 101–3, 176, 336, 337, 340, 349
multilateral institutions 6, 13, 19, 21, 23, 24, 30, 33, 37, 38, 48, 50, 52, 53, 59, 85, 91, 96, 103, 116, 173, 320, 344
Mumbai 80, 92, 337
Mussolini 276, 285, 310, 332

nationalism 49–51, 54, 76, 135, 149, 187, 197, 198, 202, 203, 207, 212, 213, 215, 225, 226, 230, 245, 246, 251, 258, 261, 285, 296–98, 302, 305, 309–11, 318, 322–24, 331, 332, 337, 339, 340, 342
neoliberalism from below 166, 176
New Zealand 17, 44, 191, 208, 212

Nigeria 149, 156, 190, 339
nodes 3, 106, 132, 133, 139–43, 159, 162, 178, 247, 270, 307, 309, 319, 349
nomadic 136
normative actors 7, 18, 20–22, 26, 27
normative basis 17
Nyíri, Pál 136, 157, 191

Occupy 93, 94, 338
open-source software 101
organized crime 55, 108, 122, 130, 162
Ottoman Empire 5, 47, 247–50, 253–56, 260, 263, 265, 266, 269, 271, 273, 275, 286, 287, 289, 307, 310
Overseas Chinese Affairs Committee 205–6
Overseas Chinese Affairs Office 198, 203–4, 206, 211
overseas Chinese state 4, 51, 57, 187, 188, 202–4, 207, 209–11, 214, 215, 225, 226, 230–32, 234, 322–24, 327, 337–39
overseas Chinese work 4, 187, 204, 206–9, 211, 212, 214, 225, 230, 232, 234, 322, 327, 337, 339

Pacific 17, 27, 28, 31, 44, 208, 298
Paris 48, 246, 263, 267, 279, 280, 284, 286, 290, 292, 305
Patpong Market (in Bangkok) 130
Pax Americana 23, 25–6
Pea, Enrico 245, 284, 286, 311, 335, 338
peddler 3, 117, 172, 235, 341
pendular movements 133, 140
Pera 247, 263, 266, 311, 332
Perestroika 112, 188
periphery 3, 17, 23, 31, 116, 118–20, 142, 158, 172, 193, 329, 330, 341, 343
periphery policy 23, 193
Persia 5, 41, 44, 247, 253, 307
Petaling Street (in Kuala Lumpur) 214
petty merchants 110, 236, 281, 286, 304, 328
pharmaceutical 127, 129
piracy 99, 101, 123, 127–32, 139, 166, 167, 172
plebeian democracy 107, 166, 168, 172, 177, 334, 339
Poland 110, 112, 114, 270
political culture 71, 79
political elites 4, 11, 18, 20, 27, 28, 33–36, 39, 83, 85, 121, 137, 187, 192, 208, 209, 213, 216, 218, 219, 222, 224, 227, 228, 230, 232–37, 251, 322, 326, 341, 348, 349
political resistance 89
Political Science 56, 134
porosity 5, 258, 260, 265, 308, 312
port cities 5, 51, 246–48, 253, 254, 256, 258, 260–62, 264, 265, 269, 281, 307–9, 311, 324, 332, 337
Porto Alegre 80, 81, 91–93, 108, 337
Postcolonialism 134
power geometry 172, 345
power transition 26, 319, 346
Pratunam (in Bangkok) 142
predatory 82, 93, 137, 219, 230, 234, 257
predatory clientelism 137, 234
privatization 83, 199
production centers 3, 106, 139, 236, 319
progressive 5, 25, 77, 78, 81, 94, 152, 189, 245, 281, 285, 287, 305, 309, 311, 335, 338, 346
projection of normative power 4, 7, 20–22, 30, 37, 38, 50–52, 59, 73, 75, 84, 85, 89, 97, 99, 107, 123, 164, 173, 188, 212, 231, 237, 257, 276, 306, 307, 309, 320, 323–27, 350
proletarian microeconomies 4, 161, 166, 169, 170, 172, 176, 340, 349
Propaganda Department 206
Psychology 28
public domain 100
pyramid 15, 121

Qin, Yaqing 17

race 38, 86, 87, 134, 197, 253
racialization 153
racism 154, 156, 170, 318, 331, 332
reciprocity 27, 28, 132, 133, 194
regimes of submission 4, 107, 169–72, 340, 341, 345, 349
relationality 27–30, 35, 53, 188, 238, 341, 343, 347
religion 76, 134, 147, 301
Relinquishment of Extraterritorial Rights in China 298
resistance 3, 19, 29, 38, 50, 72, 73, 75–77, 82, 87, 89–91, 93, 98, 100–2, 106, 120, 123, 124, 126, 131, 132, 170, 173, 176, 235, 250, 251, 276, 297, 325, 328, 348
Ribeiro, Gustavo Lins 118, 119, 121, 328–30
Romania 189, 191
Rua 25 de Março market (in São Paulo) 130

Saigon 247, 248
Salonica 247, 310, 332
Sanyuanli (in Guangzhou) 147–49, 156
self-help productivism 167, 339
semi-colonialism 245, 248, 253, 254, 263, 274, 288, 297, 299, 307
semi-feudal 252
semi-legal 3, 6, 21, 108, 116, 151, 157, 162, 196, 231, 326, 335, 348
Shanghai Cooperation Organization 24
Shanghai Municipal Council 5, 246, 248, 250, 290, 292, 293, 297, 298, 300, 303, 307
Shanghai Volunteer Corps 295
Shanglin County (in Guangxi Province) 225, 227–29
Shenzhen 32, 143
shuttle traders 3, 108, 110, 116, 120, 143, 144, 189, 191, 308, 328, 332, 333, 337, 349
Siam 5, 247, 253, 307
Sinohydro 217, 218
Sino-Russian treaty (1992) 113
Six Masters 210
slave labor 170, 177
Slavyansk 114, 115
small traders 98, 107, 111, 141, 220, 229, 306, 333
smuggling 110, 111, 116, 127, 139, 145, 151, 162, 199, 255, 286, 309, 320, 335
Smyrna 247, 266, 310, 332
sociability 263, 265, 278, 308
social capital 3, 106, 132, 133, 138, 149, 150, 194, 223, 339
social exchange 28
Social History 5, 8, 262, 319
social ills 152
social praxis 5, 260–62, 308, 310, 311
Social Sciences 1, 52, 55, 56, 134, 258, 318, 319, 345, 351
Sociology 3, 8, 28, 55, 117, 319
software 99, 101, 127, 152
South Africa 17, 100, 190
Southeast Asia 136, 138, 188, 194, 195, 197
Soviet Far East 189
Soviet Union 48, 111–13, 115, 189, 199, 295, 350
state transnationalism 4, 57, 201, 213, 226, 324, 327
statue 114, 189
structural power 11, 14–16, 72
subaltern cosmopolitan 6, 75, 98, 102, 265, 336

subaltern cosmopolitanism 75, 281, 304
subaltern cosmopolitans 5, 283, 304, 307, 308, 311
suitcase traders 176, 196, 301
Sun Yat-sen 252
superlogos 128
Suriname 213
sweatshops 73, 79, 107, 159, 161, 168–70, 177
Syrian 273, 276, 280, 287, 299

Tagansky Ryad 115
Taiwan 29, 30, 38, 139, 188, 194, 196, 199, 205, 206, 208, 234
Tea Party 71, 89, 94–97
territories of movement 136
Third World 13, 37, 78, 83, 108, 111, 112, 153, 189
Three Knives 210
Tianjin 291
Tianxia Approach 24
Toynbee, Arnold 40, 43
Trade-Related Aspects of Intellectual Property Rights (TRIPS) 98–101, 126–27
trading post 107, 155, 156, 158, 333
transformationalist 12
transnational actors 12, 54–60, 91, 93
transnational informal economy 3, 106, 110, 139, 151, 152, 157, 160, 163, 164, 167, 171–74, 177, 188, 190, 193, 320, 321, 325, 326, 332, 340, 348
treaty ports 246, 266, 267, 289, 290, 300, 301, 304, 306
Treaty Powers 289, 290, 295, 297, 298, 306
triple illegal person 151
Tunisian 5, 245, 280, 288, 308
Turkey 26, 41, 49, 110, 113, 123, 129, 135, 136, 139, 142
Type I socialization 34–36, 233
Type II socialization 35

Ungaretti, Giuseppe 284, 338
united front work 4, 187, 205–12, 214, 225, 230, 232, 234, 322, 327, 337, 339
United Front Work Department 205, 206, 208–11
Universal Postal Union 48

valiz ticareti (suitcase trading) 110
Veiled Protectorate 251
Venezuela 81, 111, 165, 213, 350

visas 29, 144–46, 148, 152–54, 189, 193, 220, 223, 225, 229, 349
Vladivostok 189
vulgar cosmopolitanism 264, 265
vulnerability 137, 174, 222–24, 230, 232, 237, 327, 332

Wallerstein, Immanuel 41–43, 118, 119, 329
Western Europe 13, 42, 46, 50, 54, 79, 91, 94, 100, 129, 144, 150, 246
White Russians 5, 269, 285, 300, 304, 305, 308
World Intellectual Property Organization 99
World System Theory 41, 118–20, 177, 318, 329–31
World Trade Organization (WTO) 13, 73, 126, 143

World War I 50, 54, 250, 273, 277, 287, 290, 293, 295, 301–3, 310
World War II 13, 40, 45, 138, 258, 304
world-empire 41
world-system 41–43, 117, 133

xenophobia 318, 331, 332
Xi, Jinping 25, 27, 30, 32, 38, 206, 209, 211, 214, 346
Xiaobei (in Guangzhou) 146–49, 156
xitong 204

Yiwu 106, 130, 140–44, 153, 157, 175, 333, 337, 349

zabarama 149
Zapatista 80, 89, 92
Zhejiang 130, 141, 189
Zimbabwe 190
Zongo 156

Taylor & Francis eBooks

www.taylorfrancis.com

A single destination for eBooks from Taylor & Francis with increased functionality and an improved user experience to meet the needs of our customers.

90,000+ eBooks of award-winning academic content in Humanities, Social Science, Science, Technology, Engineering, and Medical written by a global network of editors and authors.

TAYLOR & FRANCIS EBOOKS OFFERS:

A streamlined experience for our library customers

A single point of discovery for all of our eBook content

Improved search and discovery of content at both book and chapter level

REQUEST A FREE TRIAL
support@taylorfrancis.com

Printed in the United States
by Baker & Taylor Publisher Services